CONTENTS

Chapter 8: Preventive Offences — 207

PART III

PREFACE TO THE SECOND EDITION

The criminal law of Scotland continues to be a rich and rewarding object of study. Since the publication of the first edition of this book, many changes have been made to it by the courts, as well as the legislatures. The former include more than 70 reported cases worthy of mention, including key cases such as *Elsherkisi*[1] and *Petto*,[2] in relation to the *mens rea* of murder, and *Harris*[3] with regard to breach of the peace. There is also the unreported case of *Anderson*, in relation to the defence of necessity. Statutory developments include the coming into force of many sections of the Sexual Offences (Scotland) Act 2009; and the enactment of the Criminal Justice and Licensing (Scotland) Act 2010; the Terrorism Prevention and Investigation Measures Act 2011; the Police and Fire Reform (Scotland) Act 2012; and the Offensive Behaviour at Football and Threatening Communications (Scotland) Act 2012. The interaction between statute and common law has also been of interest, especially in relation to crimes previously coming within the ambit of the common law offence of breach of the peace.

The law is stated as at 31 May 2014.

---

[1] *Elsherkisi v HM Advocate* 2012 SCL 181.
[2] *Petto v HM Advocate* 2012 JC 105.
[3] 2010 JC 245.

PREFACE TO THE FIRST EDITION

Twenty-five years ago when we were students, there were relatively few books in this field. There was Sir Gerald Gordon's magnificent *Criminal Law of Scotland*,[1] and the extremely useful and (crucially for students) less expensive *A Casebook on Scottish Criminal Law*[2] by Chris Gane and Charles Stoddart. There was also, of course, Baron David Hume's *Commentaries on the Law of Scotland, Respecting Crimes*,[3] and Sir John H A Macdonald's *A Practical Treatise on the Criminal Law of Scotland*,[4] both of which were oft quoted in lectures but rarely read by students. Now, however, there are several excellent books on the subject. Gerald Gordon's lament 30 years ago that criminal law "has long been neglected by Scots lawyers"[5] is no longer true. This, of course, generates the question: why yet another book? In explaining to the reader his reasons for writing the *Commentaries*, Hume made clear that he had no intention "of turning censor on our practice; and of suggesting changes and reformations, which might fit it to some standard of higher perfection than our forefathers had in view".[6] He viewed such a critique as "a very delicate task indeed" and suggested that this would be contemplated only by those whose "scholastic vanity and gross ignorance of the real business of life conceal its difficulty".[7] We harbour no illusions as to the difficulty of

---

[1] 2nd edn (1978). The 1st edition was published in 1967. A *Supplement* was published in 1984 and also in 1992. There is now a 3rd edition, edited by M G A Christie: *Criminal Law* (vol I (2000); vol II (2001)). A 3rd *Supplement* (also by M G A Christie) appeared in 2004.
[2] Published in 1980. See now C H W Gane, C N Stoddart and J Chalmers (3rd edn, 2001).
[3] 4th edn (1844) (edited by B R Bell).
[4] 5th edn (1948).
[5] Gordon (1978) at p 3.
[6] Hume, i, 14.
[7] *Ibid*.

the task, yet believe that a critical assessment of Scots criminal law, with proposals for "changes and reformations", is required.

Referring to the future development of Scots law, generally, Alan Rodger, former Lord President and Lord Justice-General, has stated:

> "... most people realise that Scots law is one among many systems of law wrestling with the problems thrown up sometimes by recent technological and social developments ... Whether we find the appropriate solutions to these problems in the classical Roman law of Julian, in the writings of Grotius, in the opinions of Lord Chancellor Brougham or in an article by some Australian academic seems to me to be, almost, a matter of indifference. We are, happily, citizens of a legal world which stretches not only backwards for more than two thousand years but outwards across the globe. Provided we abandon any notions of false superiority and go forward in that spirit, the future state of Scots law is likely to be happy".[8]

Countries with legal cultures similar to our own have to grapple with issues of criminal responsibility: whether or not to criminalise particular forms of undesirable behaviour, whether to allow certain circumstances peculiar to the offence or the offender to mitigate or exonerate. While mindful of the dangers of "cherry-picking" selected aspects of foreign legal systems, it does seem obvious that such jurisdictions may offer solutions which could be equally appropriate in Scotland, hence we draw comparisons throughout the text with other legal systems whose approach seems worthy of consideration. Lord Rodger's reference to "notions of false superiority" is an apt one; Scots law has often been portrayed, historically at least, as being better than other legal systems, particularly English law.[9] An attitude of superiority may, in large part, have been a protective mechanism, designed to act as a safeguard against the encroachment of English law by the Westminster Parliament. Now that devolution has occurred, and the future development and reform of criminal law are largely in the hands of the Scottish Parliament, it is time for a re-assessment to determine whether the law is indeed as good as it could, and should, be. Elish Angiolini, the current Lord Advocate, has suggested that "it is appropriate for us to look to what the 21st century's law should be. Much of our common law remains unchanged since Hume's time, when the status of women was different".[10] The context of the Lord Advocate's statement

---

[8] A Rodger in Preface to L Farmer and S Veitch (eds), *The State of Scots Law* (2001) at pp v–vi.

[9] For a criticism of the attitude of "moral superiority" in Scots law, see L Farmer, *Criminal Law, Tradition and Legal Order: Crime and the Genius of Scots Law 1747 to the Present* (1997).

[10] *Justice Committee Official Report*, 25 November 2008, col 1401.

was in relation to sexual offences,[11] but her remarks have a wider resonance. Indeed, one of the strands of this book is to consider whether Scots criminal law has recognised the criticisms feminist theorists have made about law's historic failure to address women's perspectives and concerns.

While feminist analyses offer one way of determining whether our law is fit for the 21st century, another criterion by which to assess the law relates to the issue of criminalisation; that is, to consider not only what is, but also *what ought to be*, its subject-matter. It has been suggested that "criminalization remains the single most widely neglected issue among contemporary criminal theorists".[12] Certainly, there has been no systematic attempt to answer this question in relation to Scots law. The law proscribes certain undesirable behaviours (such as fraud, stealing and assault) but not others (such as lying,[13] or adultery). This book asks whether (and how) such distinctions can be justified. Theories of criminalisation have formed the subject-matter of many scholarly books and articles, but these have tended to be written by philosophers rather than lawyers, and to take their examples from American or English law. Many of these theorists approach the issue of criminalisation from a liberal perspective, and indeed liberalism has been the dominant political and legal philosophy of the twentieth century. The liberal focus on the paramountcy of the individual and individual freedoms naturally leads to calls for *de*criminalisation, with theorists offering various lists of the behaviours which ought, in their view, to be free from the reaches of the criminal law. Other theorists have argued that liberalism has over-emphasised the importance of the individual and individual rights at the expense of the wider community. We consider the communitarian criticisms of liberalism, and the extent to which such considerations have influenced, and should influence, the development of Scots criminal law. Feminist scholars have criticised both liberalism and communitarianism, suggesting that each has reinforced gender stereotypes. We discuss the work of some of these theorists also, in considering what types of behaviour our criminal law ought to proscribe. While both of us are persuaded by many of the feminist arguments, the book does not purport to provide a

---

[11] *Ibid*. The Lord Advocate was giving evidence to the Justice Committee of the Scottish Parliament in its consideration of the Sexual Offences (Scotland) Bill 2008.

[12] D Husak, "Limitations on criminalization and the general part of criminal law" in S Shute and A P Simester (eds), *Criminal Law Theory: Doctrines of the General Part* (2002) 13 at p 20.

[13] Lying can be criminal in certain circumstances – if the speaker is on oath (perjury) or the lie is told with a view to achieving a particular result (fraud).

definitive answer to questions of criminalisation: our aim is rather to highlight some of the major theories in order to engender debate on the appropriate scope of the criminal sanction.

In summary, then, the book aims to promote a reflective approach to the study of Scots criminal law, and a consideration of some of the values, often unarticulated, behind its norms. To this end, we engage with the work of a range of leading legal theorists, British and international, in order to introduce law students to their arguments and to inspire them to read further. The book is also intended to stimulate and provoke readers, not only students but experienced practitioners, legal theorists and legislators, to continue the debate over the future development of Scots criminal law.

ACKNOWLEDGEMENTS

The issues arising in writing a book of this type have not changed in the period between the first and second editions. In the first edition, we noted that Virginia Woolf had famously asserted that, in order to write, a woman "must have money and a room of her own".[1] In 2014, as in 2009, we found that we required a good deal more than an office and an income; we needed the support of colleagues, friends and family. We reiterate our thanks to those who helped with the first edition: Alan Page and the Law School at Dundee University; Rachel Maxwell; Anne Lambie; Betty Bott; James Chalmers; Lindsay Farmer; Fiona Raitt; Thérèse O'Donnell; Lorraine Almond; Robin White; Jenifer Ross; and Euan Macdonald.

For this second edition, we are very grateful to Eamon Keane for his assistance in formatting the text. Our main thanks continue to go to our families. In writing the first edition, on more than one occasion we found ourselves wondering whether Joel Feinberg had found himself breaking off in the middle of writing a chapter of his *Moral Limits of the Criminal Law* in order to sew on some Cub Scout badges, or to glue a tiny mast onto a toothpick, in order to help his child make a ship-in-a-bottle. Did Herbert Packer or Lon Fuller ever pause in mid-thought, in order to escort their offspring to Brownies, swimming lessons or football practice, or to construct "Cat in the Hat"-style headgear, *à la* Dr Seuss? This time around, our now slightly older children have accommodated and encouraged the writing, fitting their own computer use around it. Involvement in their activities still creates welcome diversions. We continue to owe our husbands (Euan and John) and children (Fraser, Calum and Anna) a great debt for their love, encouragement, patience, numerous cups of

---

[1] V Woolf, *A Room of One's Own* (1928) at 4.

tea and some penetrating questions (including "Why on earth do academics want to write books?"), as we persevered with our endeavours.

PAMELA R FERGUSON and CLAIRE McDIARMID

1 June 2014

TABLE OF CASES

OTHER JURISDICTIONS
Australia

Canada

European Court of Human Rights

International Criminal Tribunal

Ireland

New Zealand

South Africa

United States of America

TABLE OF LEGISLATION

United Kingdom

Statutes

1995   Criminal Law (Consolidation) (Scotland) Act (*cont.*)
    s 49A 8.11.10, 8.13.1
       (4)(b) 8.11.10
    s 49C 8.11.10, 8.13.1
    s 50A 7.9.1, 22.9.1
       (2) 7.10.2
    s 52 .... 4.6.2, 5.14.1, 13.3.1, 15.2.2
       (1) 17.1.2
       (2) 13.3.1, 13.5.5
    Criminal Procedure (Scotland) Act (c 46) 2.3.3, 5.3.1, 5.7.1,
                5.13.1, 6.18.2, 7.9.1, 8.1.2, 8.6.8, 9.3.1, 9.18.3,
             9.21.2, 10.3.1, 12.11.1, 12.12.1, 12.14.1, 12.16.1,
             Part VII, 19.3.1, 19.4.1, 20.1.1, 20.1.2, 20.2.1,
             20.3.1, 20.4.1, 20.4.3, 20.4.4, 20.6.1, 20.7.2,
             20.8.1, 20.8.2, 20.8.3, 20.10.1, 20.10.3, 21.8.1
    s 1(1) 2.3.3
    s 7(8)(b)(ii) 12.11.1
    s 11A 5.7.1, 8.6.8
       (3A)(a) 8.6.8
       (b) 8.6.8
    ss 35–39 .... 5.5.1
    s 41 .... 6.18.2, 19.3.1, 19.4.1
    s 41A(1) 6.18.2, 19.3.1
       (2) 19.3.1
    s 51A 9.16.1, 20.1.1, 20.1.2, 20.7.2,
                20.7.4, 20.8.2, 20.9.1, 22.8.1
       (1) 20.7.3, 20.7.6
       (2) 20.7.5, 20.7.6, 20.11.4
       (3) 20.2.1
       (4) 20.3.1
    s 51B 9.16.2, 20.1.1, 20.1.2, 20.10.1, 20.10.2,
         20.10.3, 20.10.4, 20.10.5, 20.11.2 20.11.3, 20.11.4
       (1) 20.10.1, 20.11.2
       (2) 20.11.3
       (3) 20.11.5
       (4) 20.3.1, 20.10.2
    s 53F 20.1.1, 20.1.2, 20.4.1, 22.8.1
       (1) 20.3.1, 20.4.1, 20.6.2
       (2)(a) 20.6.2
       (3) 20.4.1
    ss 53F–56 .... 20.4.1
    s 54(1) 20.4.3
       (b) 20.4.3, 20.4.4
    s 55 .... 20.4.4, 20.8.2
       (1) 20.4.4
       (a) 20.5.1
       (5) 20.6.1
       (6) 20.5.1, 20.6.1

Statutory instruments

Bills

Draft Criminal Codes

European Community legislation

Legislation of other jurisdictions

Australia

COMMONLY USED ABBREVIATIONS

Alison   A Alison, *Principles of the Criminal Law of Scotland* (1832)

Hume, i   D Hume, *Commentaries on the Law of Scotland Respecting Crimes* (with supplement by B R Bell), vol I (4th edn, 1844)

Hume, ii   D Hume, *Commentaries on the Law of Scotland Respecting Crimes* (with supplement by B R Bell), vol II (4th edn, 1844)

Gordon (2000)   G H Gordon, *The Criminal Law of Scotland* (3rd edn, edited by M G A Christie, vol I: 2000)

Gordon (2001)   G H Gordon, *The Criminal Law of Scotland* (3rd edn, edited by M G A Christie, vol II: 2001)

Macdonald   J H A Macdonald, *A Practical Treatise on the Criminal Law of Scotland* (5th edn by J Walker and D J Stevenson, 1948)

Draft Criminal Code   E Clive, P R Ferguson, C H W Gane and R A A McCall Smith, *A Draft Criminal Code for Scotland with Commentary* (2003), published under the auspices of the Scottish Law Commission, Edinburgh. The *Code* is available at the SLC's website: http://www.scotlawcom.gov.uk

NOTE: Reversing the approach taken in the Interpretation Act 1978, our use of the pronoun "she" generally includes "he".

PART I

DETERMINING THE APPROPRIATE SCOPE
OF THE CRIMINAL LAW

"It is an appalling prospect that professors might teach and students might learn about both the general and special parts of criminal law without paying any attention to the crucial issue of what conduct should or should not be criminalized."[1]

The first part of this book explores the philosophical underpinnings of current Scots criminal law. This is a neglected area, yet a jurisdiction's criminal laws cannot properly be analysed, critically or otherwise, without first giving some consideration to what political and philosophical precepts these laws are to express. Criminal law can be defined as rules promulgated by the state which proscribe conduct, on penalty of punishment, but one's view of what the scope of these rules ought to be will differ, depending on which political theory of the state one favours. There are many competing accounts of how we should view the relationship between the state and its citizens. In Western societies, liberalism has been the predominant political philosophy for more than 200 years, though frequently challenged by communitarian ideas. In the last half-century, feminism has offered a critique of both, as well as its own substantive philosophy. Chapter 1 outlines some of the key ideas associated with each of these philosophies.

Chapters 2–4 consider principles of criminalisation. While much of the literature has tended to discuss *de*criminalisation (what forms of behaviour ought *not* to be criminalised) rather than criminalisation (how best to determine whether something ought to be proscribed by the criminal law) these are, of course, two sides of the same coin. This is considered in Chapter 2. Chapter 3 takes a closer look at one highly influential liberal argument, namely that the law ought to

---

[1] D Husak, "Limitations on criminalization and the general part" in S Shute and A P Simester, *Criminal Law Theory: Doctrines of the General Part* (2002), 13–47 at p 19.

1

interfere with a person's liberty of action only where this is necessary to prevent harm to other people. Theories which reject exclusive focus on this "harm principle", such as legal paternalism, are also considered. Chapter 4 highlights some key precepts, such as the requirements of the "rule of law" and of "fair labelling", which have also been suggested as being important in determining what sort of criminal law we ought to have.

CHAPTER 1

PHILOSOPHICAL UNDERPINNINGS

"Law may be said to represent order *simpliciter*. Good order is law that corresponds to the demands of justice, or morality, or [people's] notions of what *ought to be*."[1]

1.1 INTRODUCTION

In November 2007 Robert Stewart pled guilty at Ayr Sheriff Court   **1.1.1** to having committed "a sexually aggravated breach of the peace" by attempting to have sexual intercourse with a bicycle.[2] He was in a locked bedroom in a hostel at the time; cleaners had used a master key to unlock the door when he had failed to answer their knocks.[3] Many people might find Stewart's behaviour shocking, or even offensive, but is this the sort of behaviour that ought to be proscribed by the criminal law? And, if it is, was the fact that he was in a hostel (albeit with the door locked) rather than in the privacy of his own home a necessary condition for classifying his behaviour as criminal? To what extent should the criminal law treat differently behaviour committed "in private" from that committed "in public"?[4]

What of the behaviour of the so-called "Naked Rambler"? In   **1.1.2** June 2003 Stephen Gough attempted to walk naked (save for a sun hat and some hiking boots) from Land's End to John O'Groats, in the course of which he was repeatedly prosecuted (though not always successfully) for "breach of the peace" during the Scottish

---

[1] L L Fuller, "Positivism and fidelity to law – a reply to Professor Hart" (1957) 71 *Harv LR* 630 at 644 (second emphasis added).
[2] Reported at http://news.bbc.co.uk/1/hi/scotland/glasgow_and_west/7098116. stm.
[3] Mr Stewart was put on probation for 3 years and his name was added to the Sex Offenders' Register, by virtue of the Sexual Offences Act 2003, s 80.
[4] Feminist theorists have argued that the law frequently draws inappropriate distinctions between the "public" and the "private". This is discussed further below, at section 1.18.

part of his journey.[5] Gough also refused to wear clothes during court appearances and was found to be in contempt of court as a result.[6] This was not treated as a trivial issue, dealt with by way of admonition or a minor fine; by July 2012, he had spent more than 6 years in prison for various breaches of the peace, often in solitary confinement.[7] Nudity in public is a criminal offence under the Canadian Criminal Code.[8] Scotland has no criminal code,[9] nor is there any relevant statutory provision in Scotland, hence the prosecution's reliance on the common law crime of "breach of the peace".[10] Should Mr Gough's behaviour be regarded as meriting proscription by the criminal law? If so, should we enact legislation to make public nudity a specific statutory offence, as the Canadians have done? Given that neither the Westminster nor the Scottish Parliament has seen fit to do so, ought the crime of breach of the peace to be interpreted by the courts as including the behaviour of the "Naked Rambler"? Some people are likely to be offended by the sight of a naked man walking down the street, perhaps being seen by their children. They could also be frightened or upset, depending on the circumstances. How can we decide whether this type of behaviour ought to be criminalised, or tolerated?

1.1.3   The criminal law, at least in our society, purports to enforce rules about which there is general (if not always universal) agreement. If it is to stigmatise and punish individuals, the law must focus on behaviours that citizens accept as being worthy of such a response, otherwise it risks losing its moral force. But, clearly, some people believe that criminal law should focus on only the worst forms

---

[5] By April 2007 he had been convicted of breach of the peace on eight occasions: see http://news.bbc.co.uk/1/hi/scotland/edinburgh_and_east/6542329.stm. His convictions in England were for "public order" offences. See case comment: *Gough (Sephen Peter) v Director of Public Prosecutions* [2014] *Crim LR* 371.

[6] See *Robertson v HM Advocate*; *Gough v HM Advocate* 2008 JC 146, discussed further at section 14.11.3 below.

[7] In June 2013 he was jailed for 11 months by an English court for defying an anti-social behaviour order ("ASBO") requiring him to wear clothes in public. See "Naked rambler Stephen Gough jailed for breaching asbo", *The Guardian*, 19 June 2013, available at http://www.guardian.co.uk/society/2013/jun/19/naked–rambler–stephen–gough–jailed–asbo.

[8] The Canadian Criminal Code 1985, s 174(1), provides: "Every one who, without lawful excuse ... is nude in a public place ... is guilty of an offence." "Nudity" is defined as being "so clad as to offend against public decency or order" (s 174(2)).

[9] There is, however, an unofficial draft criminal code: see E Clive, P R Ferguson, C H W Gane and A McCall Smith, *A Draft Criminal Code for Scotland with Commentary* (2003), available at: http://www.scotlawcom.gov.uk/download_file/view/521.

[10] For a description of this crime, see Chapter 15 below.

of undesirable behaviour, while others take a more expansionist perspective. The stance one takes is dependent on the view one has of the individual's relationship to the state.[11] Many theorists have considered this relationship from a normative perspective – that is, they explore not just what that relationship is, but what it ought to be. As Antony Duff has suggested:

"if we are to make normative sense of the law, we must look beyond it to the political–moral values on which it depends: in explicating such values, we will also be laying the ground for a more external critique of the law and its principles".[12]

In a work of this nature we can touch on only a small number of the many competing philosophies, and offer only the barest outline of these. The aim here is to give an overview of their core arguments.

1.2 LIBERALISM

This is the dominant political philosophy in the modern Western world. It emphasises the importance of individuals, and their civil and political rights. Politically, modern liberalism champions the rule of law,[13] a market or mixed economy, and transparency in government. Many of the legal philosophers to whose works we will refer are within the liberal tradition, but it must be remembered that it encompasses many different approaches, and spans several centuries.[14] According to Will Kymlicka:

1.2.1

"The defining feature of Liberalism is that it ascribes certain fundamental freedoms to each individual. In particular, it grants people a very wide freedom of choice in terms of how they lead their lives. It allows people to choose a conception of the good life, and then allows them to reconsider their decision, and adopt a new and hopefully better plan of life."[15]

Elizabeth Frazer and Nicola Lacey have suggested that liberalism's post-war resurgence was in large part a reaction to the political climate of the 1930s and 1940s:

---

[11] N Peršak, *Criminalising Harmful Conduct: The Harm Principle, its Limits and Continental Counterparts* (2007), p 9.
[12] R A Duff, *Answering for Crime: Responsibility and Liability in the Criminal Law* (2007), p 7.
[13] That is, that laws conform to certain requirements such as being clear, accessible, non-retroactive and of general application. This is discussed further from section 4.2 below.
[14] For an introduction to the work of various liberal philosophers, see J Gray, *Liberalism* (1995).
[15] W Kymlicka, *Multicultural Citizenship: A Liberal Theory of Minority Rights* (1995), p 80.

"Immediately after the Second World War the apparent dangers of nationalism and collectivism were at the forefront of popular and academic consciousness. Hence, political theories ... which emphasise individual rights against the state and society were influential and set the agenda for political thought."[16]

While it may be true that there was a revival of liberalism in the 1950s as a reaction to fascism and communism, liberalism's roots go deeper. According to Alan Norrie, by the end of the 18th century there was growing recognition of the view that "at the heart of moral, political, social, economic – *and legal* – discourse there should be placed the idea of the free individual".[17]

1.2.2   One of liberalism's most famous advocates was the 19th-century philosopher John Stuart Mill, who argued that the state should recognise a "sphere of individual liberty" in which people should be allowed to choose how best to conduct their lives:

"neither one person, nor any number of persons, is warranted in saying to another human creature of ripe years, that he shall not do with his life for his own benefit what he chooses to do with it. He is the person most interested in his own well-being".[18]

Despite their differences, liberals share this belief in the paramountcy of individual liberty.[19] Historically, liberalism insisted that the role of the state should be a minimal one. It should not attempt to limit freedom of thought and speech, and should interfere with freedom of action only where absolutely necessary.[20] Liberalism regards the role of the state as an essentially neutral one: the state should protect

[16] E Frazer and N Lacey, *The Politics of Community: A Feminist Critique of the Liberal–Communitarian Debate* (1993), p 127.
[17] A Norrie, *Crime, Reason and History: A Critical Introduction to Criminal Law* (2001), p 17 (emphasis in original).
[18] J S Mill, "On Liberty" (1859) in J Gray (ed), *On Liberty and other Essays* (1991) at pp 84–85. The reference to the person being of "ripe years" is designed to exclude children; paternalism towards children is acceptable to the great majority of liberals. The same idea has been expressed rather more bluntly: "For the criminal law at least, man has an inalienable right to go to hell in his own fashion, provided he does not directly injure the person or property of another on the way" (N Morris and G Hawkins, *The Honest Politician's Guide to Crime Control* (1970), p 2).
[19] "Individualism is perhaps the most fundamental assumption underpinning liberal ideas": R Leach, *British Political Ideas* (1991), p 59, cited in C Bird, *The Myth of Liberal Individualism* (1999) at p 1. See also D Johnston, *The Idea of a Liberal Theory* (1994), p 191: "liberal individualism – the claim that only individuals count – is the substance and strength of the liberal tradition".
[20] More recently, liberals emphasise the role of the Welfare State, and those who believe in minimal state interference tend now to be called "conservatives". A useful description of the various facets of liberalism is provided in A M Jaggar, *Feminist Politics & Human Nature* (1983).

people's rights, but should not try to impose any particular vision of what it means to lead a good or worthwhile life. Many liberals regard individuals as inherently self-interested:

"[People] are naturally in competition for available resources, and the individual's program for fulfilment of desires is subject to constant interference from other individuals and their competing programs. The political question is therefore how to organize society best to protect opportunities for self-fulfilment and to resolve inevitable conflicts. In the classical liberal conception, people create governments because we can't get along in the 'state of nature.' The purposes of government are to provide defense from external threats, and domestically only to provide conditions conducive to peaceful coexistence and self-fulfilment of all of the individuals thus described. This 'night watchman' theory of the state defines political power by its limits. It is a given that the individual is primary and his self-determination must not be encroached upon unless absolutely necessary".[21]

However, this portrait – of individuals being in competition with one another, fighting to safeguard their territory, their freedoms, their rights, from the claims of others – has been challenged by some as failing to reflect reality.[22]

1.3   THE PUBLIC AND THE PRIVATE

According to Alison Jaggar: 1.3.1

"In trying to determine the limits of legitimate state intervention in the life of an individual, liberal theory distinguishes between what it calls the public and the private realms. The ubiquitous terms *public* and *private* are used by different political theorists to mark a variety of contrasts. In the context of liberalism, those aspects of life that may legitimately be regulated by the state constitute the public realm; the private realm is those aspects of life where the state has no legitimate authority to intervene. Just where the line between the two realms should be drawn has always been controversial for liberals; but they have never questioned that the line exists, and that there is some private area of human life which should be beyond the scope of legal government regulation."[23]

Similarly, Frazer and Lacey have emphasised that for the liberal:

"The state's activities are to be limited to a clearly demarcated public sphere, while human individuality and diversity is to be respected in the private sphere. This doctrine is expressed most famously in Mill's argument that the

---

[21] A Scales, *Legal Feminism: Activism, Lawyering and Legal Theory* (2006), pp 64–65.
[22] See the communitarian and feminist critique of liberalism, from sections 1.6 and 1.11 below, respectively.
[23] Jaggar (1983) at p 34.

only reason for which the state should use force to coerce a citizen's conduct is the prevention of harm to others."[24]

They are referring to the "harm principle", a principle that is associated closely with the philosophy of John Stuart Mill. That the law ought to interfere with a person's liberty of action only where this is necessary to prevent harm to other people is a key tenet of liberalism. This is discussed in greater detail in Chapter 3. In relation to the public/private divide, liberalism is concerned to delineate a private sphere in which the individual can behave as she chooses, immune from interference from the state.[25] This has led Steven Lukes to conclude that "Liberalism may be said largely to have been an argument about where the boundaries of [the] private sphere lie, according to what principles they are to be drawn, whence interference derives and how it is to be checked".[26] As we shall see, other theorists, particularly feminists, have questioned whether this private/public distinction is a valid one, and have drawn attention to the detrimental effects on women caused by the law's neglect of aspects of life delineated as "private".[27]

1.4 HUMAN RIGHTS

1.4.1 Liberals exalt freedom of conscience, of speech, and of association, each of which is now reflected in the European Convention on Human Rights (ECHR). This protects, *inter alia*, individuals' rights to: life;[28] liberty;[29] a fair trial;[30] respect for private and family life;[31] freedom of thought, conscience and religion;[32] freedom of expression;[33] freedom of assembly and association;[34] and freedom to marry and found a family.[35] States may limit some of these, but only if this is "necessary in a democratic society". There is also a right not to be discriminated against in relation to these

---

[24] Frazer and Lacey (1993) at p 47.
[25] Loren Lomasky refers to this as "a zone of protected activity" in *Persons, Rights and the Moral Community*, cited in Bird (1999) at p 34. See also J Reiman, *Justice and Modern Moral Philosophy* (1990), p 171; and S Lukes, *Individualism* (1973), p 59.
[26] Lukes (1973), p 62.
[27] This is discussed further in section 1.18 below.
[28] Art 2.
[29] Art 5.
[30] Art 6.
[31] Art 8.
[32] Art 9.
[33] Art 10.
[34] Art 11.
[35] For those of marriageable age: Art 12.

Convention rights on the grounds of sex; race; colour; language; religion; political or other opinion; national or social origin; association with a national minority; property; birth; or other status.[36] The Convention also prohibits torture or inhuman or degrading treatment or punishment;[37] slavery and forced labour;[38] and retrospective criminalisation of behaviour.[39] The ECHR was given further effect in Scots law by the Human Rights Act 1998. This means that the provisions of the 1998 Act can be relied upon in domestic courts.[40] The "public/private" distinction is apparent in that the ECHR generally applies to public/state actions, only.[41] This shows the Convention's liberal foundations, being conceived of as providing limitations on *state* power. In the human rights case of *Brüggemann and Scheuten* v *Germany*,[42] the European Commission stated:

> "The right to respect for private life [provided by Art 8 of the ECHR] is of such a scope as to secure to the individual a sphere within which he can freely pursue the development and fulfilment of his personality. ... In principle, therefore, whenever the State sets up rules for the behaviour of the individual within this sphere, it interferes with the respect for private life and such interference must be justified in the light of Article 8(2)."[43]

Article 8(2) provides that a state must show that any interference with these rights is prescribed by law, necessary in a democratic society and proportionate.

---

[36] Art 14.
[37] Art 3.
[38] Art 4.
[39] Art 7.
[40] Hitherto, claims that the state had infringed any of these rights had to be taken to the European Court of Human Rights, in Strasbourg.
[41] Even here, however, the line is not rigid. For example, in *A* v *United Kingdom* (1999) 27 EHRR 611, a 9-year-old child took a case to the European Court of Human Rights, claiming that beatings he had received from his stepfather with a garden cane violated his rights under Art 3 of the Convention. This prohibits torture and/or inhuman or degrading treatment or punishment. Despite the fact that the beatings had taken place at home – the epicentre of the private sphere – the European Court held that the boy's rights under Art 3 had been infringed, since the state did not have sufficiently robust domestic laws to protect him. See also Art 8(1) which provides a right to respect for one's private and family life.
[42] (1981) 3 EHRR 244 at 252, para 55.
[43] The case is discussed in C M Pelser, "Criminal legislation in the nineteenth century: The historic roots of criminal law and non-intervention in the Netherlands" in P Alldridge and C Brants (eds), *Personal Autonomy, the Private Sphere and Criminal Law: A Comparative Study* (2001), p 183.

1.4.2   The emphasis on the rights of the *individual* has led to accusations that liberalism fails to accord sufficient weight to the wider interests of the community, and has not given adequate credence to the fact that individuals have responsibilities to others. Mary Ann Glendon has bemoaned the way in which political debate in the USA has, in her view, degenerated into exchanges in which one side asserts that its "rights" ought to be decisive:

> "Discourse about rights has become the principal language that we use in public settings to discuss weighty questions of right and wrong, but time and again it proves inadequate, or leads to a standoff of one right against another. The problem is not, however, as some contend, with the very notion of rights, or with our strong rights tradition. It is with a new version of rights discourse that has achieved dominance over the past thirty years."[44]

Similar criticisms could be made about the UK. Glendon lists the distinctive elements of what she refers to as the "dialect" of rights:

> "its penchant for absolute, extravagant formulations, its near-aphasia concerning responsibility, its excessive homage to individual independence and self-sufficiency, its habitual concentration on the individual and the state at the expense of the intermediate groups of civil society, and its unapologetic insularity".[45]

1.5 LIBERALISM AND CRIMINAL LAW

1.5.1 In relation to the criminal law, liberalism manifests itself in the belief that individuals should have the greatest degree of freedom to pursue their own life choices without state interference. While all liberals extol the virtues of autonomy, some take a more profoundly individualistic approach than others. Robert Nozick, for example, rejects any form of paternalism.[46] He believes that individuals have absolute sovereignty over their own bodies, and are free to use them as they see fit. This extreme strand of liberalism, often referred to as "libertarianism", clearly has implications for the approach the criminal law should take to sado–masochistic activities, surrogate motherhood, the selling of human organs, pornography, prostitution and suicide, to give but a few examples.[47] The liberal public/private

---

[44] M A Glendon, *Rights Talk: The Impoverishment of Political Discourse* (1991), preface, at p x.

[45] *Ibid*, p 14.

[46] R Nozick, *Anarchy, State, and Utopia* (1974). For a critique, see S M Okin, *Justice, Gender, and the Family* (1989), pp 74–88.

[47] Interestingly, some of these activities are proscribed only when there is payment involved; organ donations and surrogacy arrangements are not otherwise criminal: see the Human Tissue (Scotland) Act 2006, s 20, and the Surrogacy Arrangements Act 1985, s 2. While prostitution is not criminal *per se*, it is the

divide is also reflected in the criminal law, in so far as there is a range of behaviour that the criminal law proscribes if committed in public, but not in private. Examples include the carrying of knives and other weapons; engaging in certain sexual behaviours, such as masturbation and sexual intercourse; and being "drunk and incapable".[48]

1.6 COMMUNITARIANISM

The liberal conception of the individual as autonomous and unencumbered by social bonds has been attacked by those who hold a more "communitarian" perspective. Communitarianism emphasises the connectedness of human beings. Theorists such as Alasdair MacIntyre, Michael Sandel and Charles Taylor argue that the liberal "atomistic" approach does not reflect reality, since it fails to appreciate that individuals are to a great extent products of their society, with roles and relationships as members of a family, an ethnic group, a community, a country.[49] Iris Marion Young sums up the position:

1.6.1

> "Critics of liberalism frequently invoke a conception of community as an alternative to the individualism and abstract formalism they attribute to liberalism.... They reject the image of persons as separate and self-contained atoms, each with the same formal rights, rights to keep others out, separate. ... [T]he ideal of community evokes the absence of the self-interested competitiveness of modern society. In this ideal, critics of liberalism find an alternative to the abstract, formal methodology of liberalism. Existing in communities with others entails more than merely respecting their rights; it entails attending to and sharing in the particularity of their needs and interests."[50]

---

fact that the prostitute receives payment for sex which makes it unacceptable to many people. This is discussed in more detail in P Alldridge, "The public, the private and the significance of payments" in Alldridge and Brants (2001) at pp 79–92.

[48] Being drunk and incapable in a public place is a contravention of the Civic Government (Scotland) Act 1982, s 50. As Peter Alldridge has pointed out, this list of behaviours does not include the consumption of narcotic drugs; unlike alcohol, mere possession of such drugs is an offence, whether in public or in private (Alldridge (2001) at p 83).

[49] A MacIntyre, *After Virtue: A Study in Moral Theory* (1981); M Sandel, *Liberalism and the Limits of Justice* (1982); C Taylor, *Sources of the Self: The Making of Modern Identity* (1989). These authors do not label themselves as communitarians, but have been classed as such by others. Indeed, Sandel states in the preface to the 2nd edition of his book (1998) that he wishes "to register some unease with the 'communitarian' label" that has been applied to his views (*ibid*, p ix).

[50] I M Young, *Justice and the Politics of Difference* (1990), pp 227–228.

One does not freely choose one's family relationships and social bonds, but rather is born into a pre-existing web of relationships.[51]

> "A vision of humans as primarily social beings conduces to putting the emphasis on values which express the mutually supportive aspects of human life. This in turn conduces to the promotion of cultural practices and institutions which recognise, reaffirm and develop the communal and mutually supportive aspects of human life to the top of the political agenda. Thus reciprocity, solidarity, fraternity and community itself take the place of the liberal priorities such as fulfilment of individual rights and respect for individual freedom in the sphere of political value."[52]

1.6.2 Communitarians do not deny the importance of individual rights, but caution that we should not lose sight of community values.[53] Of course, the liberal accepts that individuals have social roles and relationships, but tends to view this as something one is at liberty to choose – individuals are free to join organisations, take up employment etc, as they see fit. It is clear, however, that while some roles and relationships are a matter of choice, others are less so; the liberal must concede that some roles related to or derived from gender and ethnic origin are not chosen and cannot be abandoned easily, if at all.

1.7 THE INDIVIDUAL VERSUS THE COMMUNITY

1.7.1 Liberals such as Ronald Dworkin and John Rawls have focused on the interaction between the individual and the community and have argued that the rights of the former, in Dworkin's phrase, ought always to "trump" those of the latter. The rights of the individual should not be over-ridden or denied for the greater good of the community.[54] In contrast to this, Daniel Bell suggests that communitarians:

---

[51] See J Crittenden, *Beyond Individualism: Reconstituting the Liberal Self* (1992), p 13.

[52] Frazer and Lacey (1993) at pp 110–111.

[53] Mention must also be made of "cosmopolitanism". Based on the Greek word *kosmopolitês* ("citizen of the world"), its proponents urge liberals to promote global human rights, enforceable by individuals against nation states: see S Benhabib, *Another Cosmopolitanism* (2006).

[54] R Dworkin, *Taking Rights Seriously* (1977); J Rawls, *A Theory of Justice* (1971, reprinted 1999); J Rawls, *Political Liberalism* (1993, reprinted 2005). Rawls's first principle of justice is restated in *Political Liberalism* as: "Each person has an equal claim to a fully adequate scheme of equal basic rights and liberties, which scheme is compatible with a similar system for all" (at p 5). This is a refinement of the principle he originally formulated: "Each person is to have an equal *right* to the *most extensive total system* of equal *basic liberty* compatible with a similar system for all." (*A Theory of Justice* (1971), p 302 (emphases added)). *Political Liberalism* is Rawls's response to communitarian critiques of *A Theory of Justice*.

"are more inclined to argue that individuals have a vital interest in leading decent communal lives, with the political implication that there may be a need to sustain and promote the communal attachments crucial to our sense of well-being. This is not necessarily meant to challenge the liberal view that some of our communal attachments can be problematic and may need to be changed, and therefore that the state needs to protect our powers to shape, pursue, and revise our own life-plans. But our interest in community may occasionally conflict with our other vital interest in leading freely chosen lives, and the communitarian view is that *the latter does not automatically trump the former in cases of conflict*".[55]

Bell's conclusion is that the value of community may indeed exceed that of individual liberty:

"The need for freedom, arguably, is only instrumentally valuable – to the extent we need freedom, it is a means to achieve the things we really care about. Community – our ties to family, nation, religion, etc – are [*sic*] often the things we really care about, the ends crucial for human flourishing, not simply valuable as means for other things, and in that sense the need for community is more valuable than the need for freedom."[56]

1.8   WHICH COMMUNITY?

Communitarians have been accused of failing to give an adequate account of what they mean by "community";[57] communities can be based on nationality or ethnic origin, religion, political affiliations, geographical location of one's home or workplace, membership of a professional organisation, to name but a few. They have also been criticised for yearning for a bygone era when society was supposedly better. Duff cautions that we should treat invocations of "community" with a degree of scepticism, since too often these "amount to little more than rhetorical appeals to vague but currently resonant ideas or to romanticized images of a premodern golden age of small, stable communities".[58] We should remember that appeals to "community values" can be a mechanism for suppressing dissent. As Marilyn Friedman reminds us:

1.8.1

---

[55] D A Bell, "A communitarian critique of liberalism" (2005) *Analyse & Kritik* 215 at 227 (emphasis added).
[56] *Ibid* at 236, fn 36. See also D Bell, *Communitarianism and Its Critics* (1993).
[57] Frazer and Lacey (1993) at p 137.
[58] R A Duff, *Punishment, Communication, and Community* (2001), p 40. See also Frazer and Lacey (1993), who refer to the "politically conservative" aspects of communitarianism, which appeal "to a romantic and unrealistic vision of the past" but which provide "no critical basis for assessing or trying to modify the status quo" (at p 130).

"Many communities are characterised by practices of exclusion and suppression of non-group members, especially outsiders defined by ethnicity and sexual orientation."[59]

1.9 COMMUNITARIANISM AND CRIMINAL LAW

1.9.1 Communitarianism does not regard law, far less criminal law, as the solution to all social problems. In fact, Amitai Etzioni, one of its main proponents, has suggested that enhancing the role of community and its moral voice may be "[t]he best way to minimize the role of the state, especially its policing role".[60] This means that both communitarians and liberals may advocate the decriminalisation of certain behaviours, albeit that they approach the issue from very different perspectives. Such congruence is not inevitable; communitarians may favour criminalising the selling of pornographic literature, if pornography offends that community's values and way of life, but liberals are more likely to advocate tolerance for those who wish to purchase such material.[61]

1.9.2 It may be suggested that the use of juries in solemn proceedings;[62] lay judges in the justice of the peace courts;[63] and the lay involvement in the children's hearing system are examples of an attempt to give the community a voice in the criminal justice process.[64] References to the criminal law's function in upholding community standards or values appear in the work of Hume, who viewed the role of the criminal law as "exacting ... atonement"[65] from one who

"has infringed, in some respect, those duties *which he owes to the community*: He has set a dangerous example of violence, dishonesty, falsehood, indecency, irreligion; or he has trespassed with respect to some of those other articles of

---

[59] M Friedman, "Feminism and modern friendship: dislocating the community" in S Avineri and A de-Shalit (eds), *Communitarianism and Individualism* (1992) 101 at p 106.

[60] A Etzioni, *The Spirit of Community: Rights, Responsibilities and the Communitarian Agenda* (1995), p 44.

[61] The example is based on one used by Michael Sandel in "Morality and the liberal ideal" 1984 *The New Republic* 15 at 17, cited in A Gutman, "Communitarian critics of liberalism" (1985) 14 *Philosophy & Public Affairs* 308 at 318.

[62] That is, proceedings on indictment in the High Court or sheriff courts.

[63] Formerly the district courts – see Pt 4 of the Criminal Proceedings etc (Reform) (Scotland) Act 2007. For an assessment, see R M White, "Lay criminal courts in Scotland: the justification for, and origins of, the new JP court" (2012) 16 *Edin LR* 358.

[64] In relation to juries, see G C Harris, "The communitarian function of the criminal jury trial and the rights of the accused" (1995) 74 *Neb L Rev* 804 at 806–810.

[65] Hume, i, 21.

wholesome discipline, or wise economy, which affect the public welfare, and are matters of general concernment".[66]

In a similar vein, Sandra Marshall and Antony Duff define the appropriate scope of the criminal law as "those kinds of wrong which are matters of public concern, and which therefore require a collective response from the whole community".[67] According to Douglas Husak:

> "Because punishments are imposed in a public forum *in the name of the state*, criminal conduct must be regarded as a *public* wrong – not in the sense that it is a wrong done *to* the public, but rather that it is a wrong that is the *proper concern* of the public."[68]

1.10 THE PUBLIC INTEREST AND POLICY CONSIDERATIONS

While Scottish judges may seldom talk of "liberalism" or "liberal values", they do refer to "individuals' rights", particularly in the context of the ECHR. Although they do not explicitly espouse communitarian approaches, the judges frequently have resort to consideration of the "public interest".[69] Since such references are often employed where a novel point of law is under consideration – where, in other words, there is *no* pre-existing law – it is clear that the value attached to the position, views and interests of "the public" is high. In the absence of clear legal precedent, it can be a point of first resort. This is most commonly employed when determining whether some irregularity in procedure should be overlooked, and in

1.10.1

---

[66] Hume, i, 21 (emphasis added). The importance of citizens' obligations to their community is stressed also in the work of Henry M Hart, who argued that the role of the criminal law was to define and enforce "those minimum obligations of conduct which the conditions of community life impose upon every participating member if community life is to be maintained and to prosper" (H M Hart, "The aims of the criminal law" (1958) 23 *Law & Contemporary Problems* 401 at 413).
[67] S E Marshall and R A Duff, "Criminalization and sharing wrongs" (1998) 11 *Canadian J of L and Jurisprudence* 7. See also Duff (2007), and Duff (2001) at p 61.
[68] D Husak, *Overcriminalization: The Limits of the Criminal Law* (2008), p 135 (emphases in original). William Wilson has noted that: "The crimes of rape, assault and theft are examples of offences where the vindication of individual interests in autonomy are subsumed within the public interest. These are attacks on individuals which, as an attack on core values, are experienced as an attack on everyone both as individuals and collectively." (W Wilson, *Central Issues in Criminal Theory* (2002), p 25). See also G Lamond, "What is a crime?" (2007) 27 *OJLS* 609 at 621.
[69] Note also that "The public interest is at the heart of all [the Crown Office and Procurator Fiscal Service (COPFS)] do as independent prosecutors". See their website at: http://www.copfs.gov.uk/about–us/about–us.

sentencing, but it has also been invoked by the courts in delimiting the boundaries of crimes and of defences.

1.10.2   A clear example of this is *Brennan* v *HM Advocate*,[70] in which the appeal court held that the act of becoming extremely drunk was in itself so reckless as to supply the necessary "mental element"/ forbidden state of mind in a murder charge.[71] It did so on the basis that the "public interest" required the law to ensure that acutely intoxicated people could not evade criminal liability.[72] Similarly, in *Cochrane* v *HM Advocate*,[73] the court referred to "sound policy reasons" for employing an objective standard in the defence of coercion.[74] A further example is the case of *Lieser* v *HM Advocate*,[75] in which the appeal court had to determine whether an error as to the degree of force required in self-defence had to be a reasonable one. Rejecting the argument that a person who makes such an error lacks the *mens rea* of murder,[76] Lord Kingarth stated that the requirements for "self-defence" had been chosen by the law "for reasons *essentially of policy*".[77] He referred to the case of *Drury* v *HM Advocate*[78] in which Lord Rodger, then Lord Justice-General, had stressed that the court's approach to provocation was "a matter of policy".[79] Other judges have referred to the requirement that criminal laws "meet the needs of the community".[80] Of course, the term "policy reasons" is not always synonymous with "the public interest", and both terms are notoriously vague and are frequently left undefined by the courts. Nevertheless, judicial appeals to the "public interest" or "public policy" reflect a communitarian approach and a hesitancy to allow a truly individualistic stance to criminal law – even if few, if any, judges would articulate their approach in these terms.

1.10.3   Alan Norrie has suggested that, in England, references by the judges to the public interest are less about reflecting a genuine

---

[70] 1977 JC 38.

[71] This mental element, referred to as *"mens rea"*, is discussed further from section 6.9 below.

[72] See section 20.14 below.

[73] 2001 SCCR 655.

[74] *Ibid* at 666. See also the arguments of the Crown that the status quo in the defence of provocation ought to be retained for public policy reasons, in *Gillon* v *HM Advocate* 2007 JC 24, at para 12. These arguments were accepted by the court. This case is discussed further in section 21.10.15 below.

[75] 2008 SLT 866.

[76] The *mens rea* of murder is discussed in more detail from section 9.10.1 below.

[77] 2008 SLT 866, at 869, para 10 (emphasis added).

[78] 2001 SLT 1013, discussed in section 9.11.1 below.

[79] *Ibid* at 1020–1021.

[80] See *Lord Advocate's Reference (No 1 of 2001)* 2002 SCCR 435 at 461, per Lord Nimmo Smith.

communitarianism or concern for the public, and more about upholding the interests of the ruling, propertied classes.[81] He has emphasised the "conflict between a conception of law based upon a logic of universal individualism, and the need to protect a particular social order".[82] Lindsay Farmer contends that:

> "the criminal law, and Scots law in particular, is frequently enforced in the name of the community to buttress the authority of the common law. Judges labour to connect the operation of the law to community feelings or community interests, connecting the law to the present through the assumed presence of the community in the law."[83]

He concludes, however, that "the modern criminal law has lost any connection that it might once have had with community".[84] Elsewhere, Farmer has argued that references to the "reasonable man" in criminal law reflect a communitarian philosophy.[85] If communitarian ideas are reflected in judicial recourse to "the public interest", we must ask who it is that defines the public interest. If it is the judges, how then does this give those who have traditionally gone unheard – such as women and children – a voice? Critics have suggested that communitarianism needs to answer the question "but whose community?". Furthermore, it also raises the issue of whether judicial appeals to the public interest really do reflect communitarian concerns, or are more akin to "law and order" rhetoric, designed to preserve social order and the status quo.

1.11 FEMINISM(S)

Feminist theories embrace a range of doctrines, united by the desire to end the oppression and unequal treatment of women. We focus here mainly on feminist critiques of liberalism and communitarianism, but it should be borne in mind that feminism offers its own substantive political philosophy. In the words of Lucinda Finley: **1.11.1**

> "Feminist theory starts from the perspective of women, and examines and critiques existing doctrines, practices and structures in light of women's experiences and needs. By taking seriously the idea that women's perspectives differ from and call into question men's values and perceptions, feminist theory casts doubt on the possibility of a universal aperspectived objective

---

[81] Norrie (2001) at p 24. See also J Griffith, *The Politics of the Judiciary* (1985), p 234.

[82] *Ibid.*

[83] L Farmer, *Criminal Law, Tradition and Legal Order: Crime and the Genius of Scots Law 1747 to the Present* (1997), p 183.

[84] *Ibid.*

[85] L Farmer, "The obsession with definition: The nature of crime and critical legal theory" (1996) 5 *Social & Legal Studies* 57 at 66.

reality. The purpose and the practice of feminist theory is to name, expose, and eliminate the unequal position of women in society. While there is much debate among those who embrace the various strands of feminist theory about the appropriate vision of equality and the best ways to achieve it, all feminist theorists share the underlying goal of eradicating the socially and economically inferior position of women."[86]

Finley urged feminist legal theorists:

"to grapple with the nature of law itself, to understand the extent to which it is male defined, and the extent to which its language and its process of reasoning are built on male conceptions of problems and of harms – and on male, or epistemologically 'objective' and 'neutral', methods of analysis".[87]

Thus, a commitment to feminism requires us to question whether law's claim to be "neutral, impartial and therefore fair" reflects reality.[88]

1.11.2   Much of Scots criminal law is largely based on the common law, with the writings of Baron David Hume continuing to be recognised as an important source.[89] Hume wrote his first edition of the *Commentaries* more than 200 years ago, in a very different era from our own.[90] One key difference lies in the attitude taken by the law towards women. That law has tended to view the world through the eyes of men is well described by Leslie Bender:

"Men historically have enjoyed the privileges of constructing our cultures. They used themselves as the invisible norms, and their perspectives have been represented as point-of-viewlessness. Not all men were invited to create the components of our dominant ideology, but all who were invited (at least initially) were men. The political, social, and legal cultures they created are infused with their experiences, perspectives, understandings, and assumptions about human nature and human relationships."[91]

1.11.3   Like liberalism and communitarianism, feminism represents a broad church. As Jaggar has put it:

"Contemporary feminists are united in their opposition to women's oppression, but they differ not only in their views of how to combat that oppression, but even in their conception of what constitutes women's oppression in contemporary society. Liberal feminists ... believe that women are oppressed

---

[86] L M Finley, "The nature of domination and the nature of women: Reflections on feminism unmodified" (1988) 82 *Nw U L Rev* 352 at 352–353 (reference omitted).
[87] *Ibid* at 384.
[88] M Weait, "On being responsible" in V E Munro and C F Stychin (eds), *Sexuality and the Law: Feminist Engagements* (2007) at p 25.
[89] Sources of criminal law are discussed in more detail in Chapter 5.
[90] Hume's *Commentaries* were first published in 1797. The most recent edition dates from 1844.
[91] L Bender, "From gender difference to feminist solidarity: Using Carol Gilligan and an ethic of care in law" (1990–91) 15 *Vermont L Rev* 1 at 17 (fnn omitted).

insofar as they suffer unjust discrimination; traditional Marxists believe that women are oppressed in their exclusion from public production; radical feminists see women's oppression as consisting primarily in the universal male control of women's sexual and procreative capacities; while socialist feminists characterize women's oppression in terms of a revised version of the Marxist theory of alienation."[92]

1.12 LIBERAL FEMINISM

Liberal feminism has tended to dominate the legal landscape. **1.12.1** Siobhán Mullally summarises this approach:

"Building a just and equal society required the recognition and enforcement of equal rights for women. Early liberal feminists saw their task as being a relatively straightforward, if daunting one. Liberal political theory ascribed rights to human beings on the basis of their capacity for reason. The task for feminism was to show that women had the same capacity for rationality and moral action as did men and to claim for women the same rights as were ascribed to men."[93]

Accepting Aristotle's precept that like cases ought to be treated alike, and unalike cases treated differently,[94] the aim of the liberal feminist was to show that women were sufficiently similar to men to be afforded equality of treatment under the law:[95]

"Most obviously, this means that laws should not grant to women fewer rights than they allow to men. Liberal feminists have fought consistently against laws which do just this. In the 19th century, they fought for such basic liberties as women's right to own property and to vote. In the 20th century, liberal feminists ... opposed laws that ... [gave] husbands more rights than their wives within marriage. As well as opposing laws that establish different rights for women and for men, liberal feminists have also promoted legislation that actually prohibits various kinds of discrimination against women."[96]

This "gender neutrality" brings dangers, as it can backfire. This is well illustrated by the Canadian case of *Chase*,[97] in which it was held that touching a woman's breast could not be classed as a

---

[92] Jaggar (1983) at p 353. See also "radical–libertarian feminism", "radical–cultural feminism", "psychoanalytic feminism" and "gender feminism", discussed in R P Tong, *Feminist Thought* (2nd edn, 1998) at pp 130–172. Carol Smart lists "standpoint feminism", "feminist empiricism" and "post-modern feminism": C Smart, *Law, Crime and Sexuality: Essays in Feminism* (1995), p 3.

[93] S Mullally, *Gender, Culture and Human Rights: Reclaiming Universalism* (2006), p xxix.

[94] Aristotle, *Nicomachean Ethics* (Roger Crisp, ed) (2000).

[95] For a critique of Aristotle's approach, see section 4.4.2.

[96] Jaggar (1983) at p 35.

[97] (1984) 40 CR (3d) 282 (New Brunswick Court of Appeal). The case was reversed on appeal.

"sexual" assault, on the basis that allowing such secondary sexual characteristics to be included in the definition would mean that touching a man's beard would have to be categorised similarly. The fallacy in this argument is that breasts have been sexualised in social culture in ways in which beards never have been. Accordingly, breasts and beards cannot be equated in this way.[98]

1.13 FEMINISM VERSUS LIBERALISM

1.13.1 Liberalism has proved problematic for many feminists in other ways. As Finley puts it, for the liberal:

> "law is conceptualized as a rule-bound system for adjudicating the competing rights of self-interested, autonomous, essentially equal individuals capable of making unconstrained choices. Because of the law's individualistic focus, it sees one of the central problems that it must address to be enforcing the agreements made by free autonomous individuals, as well as enforcing a few social norms to keep the battle of human life from getting out of hand. It envisions another central task to be eliminating obvious constraints on individual choice and opportunity. The constraints are thought to emanate primarily from the state or from the bad motivations of other individuals. An individualistic focus on choice does not perceive constraints as coming from history, from the operation of power and domination, from socialization, or from class, race and gender. A final key task for individualistic liberal law is to keep the state from making irrational distinctions between people, because such distinctions can frustrate individual autonomy. It is not an appropriate task to alter structures and institutions, to help the disempowered overcome subordination, to eliminate fear and pain that may result from encounters masquerading as 'freely chosen', to value nurturing connections, or to promote care and compassion for other people".[99]

Feminists have been suspicious of liberalism's claims to champion the cause of the individual, arguing that the rights lauded by liberals in large part reflect the interests and concerns of "propertied white men", only.[100] They have also attacked the liberal emphasis on autonomy:

> "Respect for autonomy is basic to the liberal conceptions of freedom and equality and provides one of liberalism's main arguments for limiting the

---

[98] Compare the English law case of *R v Bassett* [2009] 1 Cr App R 7 in which the Court of Appeal overruled the trial judge and decided that for the purposes of s 68(1)(a) of the Sexual Offences Act 2003 (which involved the offence of voyeurism) the word "breasts" should be interpreted to mean "female breasts", and not the exposed male chest.
[99] L M Finley, "Breaking women's silence in law: The dilemma of the gendered nature of legal reasoning" (1989) 64 *Notre Dame L Rev* 886 at 896 (references omitted). See also Frazer and Lacey (1993) at p 127.
[100] N J Hirschmann, "Freedom, Flathman and feminism" in B Honig and D R Mapel (eds), *Skepticism, Individuality, and Freedom* (2002) at p 145.

power of the state. Central to this concept of autonomy is the idea of self-definition, a reliance on the authority of individual judgments. If individual desires and interests are socially constituted, however, the ultimate authority of individual judgment comes in to question. Perhaps people may be mistaken about truth, morality or even their own interests; perhaps they may be systematically self-deceived about these matters or misled by their society."[101]

Some feminists have argued for a conception of the "social self", recognising "the role of social relationship and human community in constituting both self-identity and the nature and meaning of the particulars of individual lives".[102]

1.14 A FEMINIST ETHIC OF CARE

In criticising the liberal (over)emphasis on the rights of the individual, feminist scholars have suggested that this neglects our responsibilities to care for others. Carol Gilligan suggests that focusing on "rights" and "justice" in resolving ethical dilemmas is a predominantly male approach. The "justice" view of morality which she attacks includes utilitarianism[103] and deontology,[104] both of which stress the importance of universal rules in moral reasoning. She argues that women tend generally to affirm an "ethic of care" which emphasises the interconnectedness of human beings, and the impact of a person's choices on family, friends and community.[105]   **1.14.1**

Gilligan, a feminist psychologist, criticised research done by other psychologists, such as Lawrence Kohlberg, on the moral development of children, which had concluded that boys tended to attain a higher level of moral development than that attained by most girls.[106] Kohlberg's focus was on why some people chose to break laws for a purpose they believed to be more important than the law. He interviewed children of various ages and asked them to   **1.14.2**

---

[101] Jaggar (1983) at p 44.

[102] Friedman (1992) at p 102.

[103] A person who adopts a utilitarian philosophy believes that one can determine the moral worth of an action solely by its consequences – in particular, whether the action produces a net gain in happiness or pleasure.

[104] A deontologist believes that the moral worth of an action is dependent on the rightness or wrongness of the action itself, as opposed to the consequences of that action. For example, if lying is an activity that is always wrongful, the fact that a particular lie might have had better consequences than telling the truth does not alter its wrongfulness.

[105] C Gilligan, *In A Different Voice: Psychological Theory and Women's Development* (1982). See also N Noddings, *Caring: A Feminine Approach to Ethics and Moral Education* (1984); and N Noddings, *Starting at Home: Caring and Social Policy* (2002).

[106] L Kohlberg, *The Philosophy of Moral Development: Moral Stages and the Idea of Justice (Essays on Moral Development)* (1981), vol 1.

discuss a problem known as "Heinz's dilemma". This was based on the following vignette:

> "[A] woman was near death from a very bad disease, a special kind of cancer. There was one drug that the doctors thought might save her. It was a form of radium for which a druggist was charging ten times what the drug cost him to make. The sick woman's husband, Heinz, went to everyone he knew to borrow the money, but he could only raise about half of what it cost. He told the druggist that his wife was dying, and asked him to sell the drug cheaper or let him pay later. But the druggist said, 'No, I discovered the drug and I'm going to make as much money as I can from it.' So Heinz broke into the man's store to steal the drug for his wife. Should Heinz have stolen the drug? Why? Why not?".[107]

Responding to the dilemma, Jake, one of Kohlberg's 11-year-old participants, concluded that stealing the drug was clearly "the solution" to the problem, since life was more important than money. Kohlberg viewed this response as one which demonstrated appropriate moral reasoning; Jake based his opinion on moral principles, and on a hierarchy within those principles. Amy, another of Kohlberg's 11-year-old subjects, did not reach the same conclusion as Jake. She felt that there might be other alternatives open to Heinz. According to Amy:

> "he really shouldn't steal the drug – but his wife shouldn't die either. … If he stole the drug, he might save his wife then, but if he did, he might have to go to jail, and then his wife might get sicker again, and he couldn't get more of the drug, and it might not be good. So, they should really just talk it out and find some other way to make the money".[108]

Kohlberg concluded that Amy's moral development was less advanced than Jake's, since she had failed to rank the moral principles involved in the dilemma.

1.14.3   Gilligan conducted similar studies on moral reasoning with women who were trying to decide whether or not to terminate an unwanted pregnancy. She found that the women tended to focus on the inter-relatedness of human beings, and the need to solve moral dilemmas in a way which recognises and respects the interests and concerns of others. Her female subjects reasoned in a similar way to Amy, with emphasis being given to the impact of their decisions on their personal relationships. Gilligan criticised Kohlberg's conclusions, arguing that (some) women have a different way of approaching moral problems, but that this is not an inferior one: Kohlberg's approach is based on the questionable assumption that moral reasoning based on "principle" and "rationality" is superior to moral reasoning which places more emphasis on the sustaining

---

[107] Quoted in Crittenden (1992) at p 52.
[108] J Rachels, *The Elements of Moral Philosophy* (3rd edn, 1999), pp 164–165.

of relationships, particularly among family and friends. Although her subjects were female, Gilligan's argument is not that all women adopt an "ethic of care" while all men base their moral reasoning on rules and principles, but that in general women are more likely to adopt a care-based approach. Selma Sevenhuijsen summarises the implications of Gilligan's thesis:

> "In contrast to an atomistic view of human nature, the ethics of care posits the image of a 'relational self'; a moral agent who is embedded in concrete relationships with other people and who acquires an individual moral identity through interactive patterns of behaviour, perceptions and interpretations. ... Individuals are no longer seen as atomistic units with a pre-determined identity, who meet each other in the public sphere to create social ties."[109]

There are echoes of the communitarian approach, here.

1.15 CRITIQUES OF THE ETHIC OF CARE

Gilligan's claim to have discovered a distinctive female way of reasoning about moral dilemmas is highly controversial. Other feminist theorists have been critical of her emphasis on difference and, in particular, on the belief that women generally are "naturally" more caring than men.[110] They point out that women's propensity to care – if indeed there is such a propensity – may have less to do with genetic predispositions than with the roles to which they have traditionally been assigned in a male-dominated society. It certainly appears that there are more women than men in the "caring professions" such as nannies, primary teachers and nurses, and women are still predominantly the primary child-rearers. It may be that they are more likely than men to work part-time to accommodate childcare or to have the primary role in caring for ill or elderly relatives. Is this because they are genetically more caring and place greater emphasis on relationships than do men,[111] or because these are the roles which society expects, and, historically, required, them to fulfil, and which social structures, including the law, maintain?[112] Critics have argued

1.15.1

---

[109] S Sevenhuijsen, *Citizenship and the Ethics of Care* (1998), p 55.

[110] See, for example, S L Bartky, *Femininity and Domination* (1990), pp 104–105; C A MacKinnon, *Feminism Unmodified* (1987), pp 38–39; B Puka, "The liberation of caring: A different voice for Gilligan's *Different Voice*" (1990) 5 *Hypatia* 58; J C Williams, "Deconstructing gender" (1988–89) 87 *Mich L Rev* 797.

[111] For the argument that there is a genetic basis for women's greater caring propensity, see R Dawkins, *The Selfish Gene* (1989), p 146.

[112] Parental leave is more generous for women (at least 26 weeks' paid maternity leave under the Employment Rights Act 1996, s 71) than for men (at least 2 weeks' paid paternity leave under s 80A(3) of that Act, as inserted by the the Employment Act 2002, s 1). Even now, it may also be more socially acceptable, hence easier, for a woman to take time out of work for childcare than for a man to do so.

that Gilligan's work reinforces unhelpful stereotypes; if women are best suited for the "caring professions" then perhaps they are ill suited for professions which require a strong focus on justice and rule-following (for example, as lawyers, or judges)?

1.15.2 Catharine MacKinnon is one of those who have voiced concern:

> "The work of Carol Gilligan on gender difference in moral reasoning ... achieves ... the affirmative rather than the negative valuation of that which has accurately distinguished women from men, by making it seem as though those attributes, with their consequences, really are somehow ours, rather than what male supremacy has attributed to us for its own use. For women to affirm difference, when difference means dominance, as it does with gender, means to affirm the qualities and characteristics of powerlessness.[113] ...
>
> I do not think that the way women reason morally is morality 'in a different voice'. I think it is morality in a higher register, in the feminine voice. Women value care because men have valued us according to the care we give them ... Women think in relational terms because our existence is defined in relation to men. ... the damage of sexism is real, and reifying that into difference is an insult to our possibilities."[114]

MacKinnon urges:

> "[G]ive women equal power in social life. Let what we say matter, then we will discourse on questions of morality. Take your foot off our necks, then we will know in what tongue women speak."[115]

1.15.3 In similar vein, Bill Puka has suggested that the traits identified by Gilligan's study do not represent a system of moral reasoning, equally as valid as the more hierarchical system commonly employed by men. Instead, he argued, they are coping mechanisms which (some) women have developed in order to deal with sexism.[116] In order to avoid hurt and rejection, women typically try to satisfy the expectations of others; they care because they cannot afford not to care. The concern that Gilligan's work may be interpreted as meaning that women are ill equipped to employ moral (and legal) principles in a detached fashion has led other feminists to attempt to reconcile the ethic of care with that of justice. Susan Moller Okin suggests that

> "the distinction between an ethic of justice and an ethic of care has been overdrawn. The best theorizing about justice ... has integral to it the notions of care and empathy, of thinking of the interests and well-being of others who may be very different from ourselves".[117]

---

[113] MacKinnon (1987) at pp 38–39.
[114] *Ibid* at p 39.
[115] *Ibid* at p 45.
[116] Puka (1990).
[117] Okin (1989) at p 15.

1.16   FEMINISM VERSUS COMMUNITARIANISM

It has been suggested that communitarianism is "a perilous ally for **1.16.1**
feminist theory":

> "Communitarians invoke a model of the community which is focused
> particularly on families, neighbourhoods, and nations. These sorts of
> communities have harboured social roles and structures which have been
> highly oppressive for women."[118]

Similarly, Frazer and Lacey accuse communitarianism of having
failed to recognise gender as an important issue, and of offering little
critique of existing community structures.[119] As they point out:

> "Given facts such as the history of women's exclusion from many spheres
> and the importance of male bonding in exclusive and powerful clubs and
> associations in many cultures, obvious doubts arise about the implications
> for women of a theory which takes 'our' membership of 'communities' as
> its starting point. Just what are these 'communities', and why should they
> be valued? Given that the notion of membership entails non-membership,
> exclusion from the private or impure public goods to which the club gives
> access is an explicit part of the meaning and indeed value of membership.
> This raises a fundamental question hardly addressed by communitarians,
> who, in the relevant context, are *we*?"[120]

Communitarianism has offered no satisfactory answer to this, so far
as many liberals and feminists are concerned.

1.17   FEMINISM AND CRIMINAL LAW

Feminism has much to say about certain aspects of substantive **1.17.1**
criminal law, such as rape and sexual offences, domestic violence and
abuse, abortion law, prostitution and soliciting, and the limitations of
the defences of provocation and self-defence for battered women who
kill their abusive partners. Its influence is, however, more pervasive
than this list suggests. Whether or not we believe that women are
naturally more caring, or that they tend to resolve moral dilemmas
in a more holistic fashion than traditional justice-based approaches,
it is clear that the feminist ethic of care chimes with communitarian
calls for less emphasis to be placed on the rights of the individual,
and more scope to be afforded to community values:

> "The major target of feminist criticism has been liberal individualism.
> By contrast, and in response, feminists emphasise the collective, or

---

[118] Friedman (1992) at p 103.
[119] Frazer and Lacey (1993) at p 139.
[120] *Ibid* at p 146 (emphasis in original).

communitarian nature of social life, of values, of the processes which disadvantage women and other groups in liberal societies. The elaborated feminist answer to liberalism emphasises the necessity of public goods, the forging of a public political culture. It emphasises the ways we are connected with each other … All these themes occur in the work of the communitarian critics of liberalism too."[121]

Legal paternalism is a philosophy which holds that the state may, on occasion, be justified in attempting to prevent individuals from harming themselves – an anathema to liberalism. One can see that those who favour an ethic of care may have much in common with paternalists, since both philosophies put greater store on our relationships with others than on individual liberties.[122]

1.17.2   As Andrew Ashworth and Jeremy Horder have pointed out, the notion of autonomy is central to the criminal law, emphasising as it does that "individuals in general have the capacity and sufficient free will to make meaningful choices".[123] The more holistic approach favoured by communitarians and feminists moves away from liberalism's obsession with the primacy of individual autonomy. This has implications for criminal justice. Views taken of the role of victims in the criminal process provide an example of the differing outcomes to which the two approaches might lead. Victims are increasingly portrayed as holders of rights which they seek punitively to exercise on an individual basis, as liberalism both permits and expects them to do. Thus the Criminal Justice (Scotland) Act 2003 gives victims of certain offences the right to make a statement to the court as to the way in which, and degree to which, the offence has affected them.[124] Victims also have the right to receive information about the release or escape of an offender, and in some cases to make representations to the parole board before it makes a decision about an offender's release.[125]

1.17.3   Kent Roach has postulated an alternative vision of a "circle" model of the criminal process, based around victims' needs.[126] This seeks, in the first instance, to prevent crime by bringing communities

---

[121] Frazer and Lacey (1993) at p 100.
[122] Legal paternalism is discussed further from section 3.5 below.
[123] A Ashworth and J Horder, *Principles of Criminal Law* (7th edn, 2013), p 23.
[124] Criminal Justice (Scotland) Act 2003, s 14(2). For an assessment, see J Chalmers, P Duff and F Leverick, "The pilot victim statement scheme in Scotland" 2007 SLT (News) 103; F Leverick, J Chalmers and P Duff, *An Evaluation of the Pilot Victim Statement Schemes in Scotland* (Scottish Executive, 2007); J Chalmers, P Duff and F Leverick, "Victim impact statements: Can work, do work (for those who bother to make them)" [2007] *Crim LR* 360.
[125] Criminal Justice (Scotland) Act 2003, ss 16 and 17.
[126] K Roach, "Four models of the criminal process" (1998–99) 89 *J Crim L and Criminol* 671 at 706–713.

together and, if some crime is committed, to "heal" the harm which this has caused through, for example, restorative justice techniques which bring victim and perpetrator together. Roach's model emphasises that both victims and offenders are embedded within a community which shares responsibility for crime and which could utilise other approaches – from better education, to better lighting in public places – in its prevention. It recognises that victims may not necessarily be focused on the punishment of someone who has committed an offence against them; rather, their response may be based more on "care" than on "justice". The current Lord Advocate, Frank Mulholland, has commended "strong models of restorative justice placing the victim or community at the heart of the process, focusing on repairing the harm caused by the offender to the victim and the wider community".[127] Of course, there are dangers if this approach is employed inappropriately. Domestic abuse is sometimes regarded as a suitable subject for mediation, rather than prosecution, but we must be wary lest this leaves victims in a yet more vulnerable position.

1.18 FEMINISM AND THE PUBLIC/PRIVATE DIVIDE

Liberalism's demand for an extensive private sphere which is not **1.18.1** within the control of the state sits uneasily with the knowledge that the historical emphasis on distinguishing "public" from "private" allowed many women to be harmed and exploited, and without recourse to the law.[128] Twenty-five years ago, men who forced their wives to have sexual intercourse with them did not breach Scots criminal law, largely because this was viewed as a "private" matter.[129] Verbal and physical abuse occurring between family members, particularly men assaulting wives and cohabitees, was rarely prosecuted 50 years ago, again at least in part because of the notion that this was "domestic" and thus a private matter which was not the concern of the criminal law.[130] As Vanessa Munro explains:

---

[127] *SACRO Annual Conference*, 18 March 2009, Edinburgh. Mr Mulholland was the Solicitor General for Scotland at that time.
[128] "[L]aw's operation within a perceived dichotomy of public/private, and its preference for the public as the proper area for its concern, leaves law largely ignorant of and unresponsive to what happens to women within the private realm": Finley (1989), p 899. See also C A MacKinnon, *Women's Lives, Men's Laws* (2007), p 262.
[129] The first case in which the indictment libelled a charge of rape by a man of his wife while she was cohabiting with him was *S v HM Advocate* 1989 SLT 469. The abolition of the marital rape exemption in England occurred in the case of *R* [1991] 4 All ER 481.
[130] "Domestic abuse" is considered further from section 10.4 below.

"The boundaries of public and private drawn and maintained in liberal theory emerge, under a feminist analysis, as deeply political and inherently constructed. Indeed, determinations of what counts as public and what counts as private are the result of a conscious process of decision making. The downside of this has been that those with power in society, typically men, have been able to relegate sexual and familial situations in which women are most vulnerable to the unregulated private sphere.

... the feminist slogan that 'the personal is political' is intended both to highlight the extent to which non-intervention by the state into the private sphere is itself a political choice and to campaign for greater state intrusion into hitherto unregulated areas where this is necessary to secure women's freedom."[131]

Of course, it is not correct to say that the law was neutral in family matters; in failing to criminalise behaviours such as marital "rape", the law in effect favoured the position of men. In the words of Nicola Lacey:

"law in fact keeps out only where it is satisfied to leave in place the social arrangements and power relations which characterise the unregulated situation. Where law has the power to intervene, the decision not to do so is itself a political decision: omission, feminists argue, calls for justification as much as does intervention, for it effectively legitimises the status quo".[132]

1.18.2 In the United States of America, the decriminalisation of abortion in the early stages of pregnancy was based on the right to "privacy". In *Thornburgh* v *American College of Obstetricians & Gynecologists*,[133] the court defended the right to abortion on the basis that few decisions are "more properly private, or more basic to individual dignity and autonomy, than a woman's decision ... whether to end her pregnancy".[134] This purports to uphold

---

[131] V E Munro, "Dev'l-in disguise? Harm, privacy and the Sexual Offences Act 2003" in Munro and Stychin (eds) (2007) at p 11. See also Frazer and Lacey (1993) at p 72: "feminists have argued that the public–private distinction is analytically flawed. At a material level, it turns out to be extremely difficult to identify where the line between public and private is to be drawn".

[132] N Lacey, *Unspeakable Subjects: Feminist Essays in Legal and Social Theory* (1998), p 29 (emphasis in original). See also Okin, who argues that the state "has not just 'kept out of' family life ... For hundreds of years, the common law deprived women of their legal personhood upon marriage. It enforced the rights of husbands to their wives' property and even to their wives' bodies" (Okin (1989), pp 129–130).

[133] 476 US 747 (1986). See also the landmark decision in *Roe* v *Wade* 410 US 113 (1973).

[134] *Thornburgh* 476 US 747 (1986) at 772. See also the approach taken by the European Commission of Human Rights in *Brüggemann and Scheuten* v *Germany* (1981) 3 EHRR 244 which held that not every restriction on the termination of an unwanted pregnancy constituted an interference with the right of respect for the private life of the mother.

liberal values of individual self-expression and autonomy but, as MacKinnon has pointed out, since abortion decisions are deemed to fall within the private realm, this means that the state has no obligation to provide assistance for pregnant women who want to exercise this option. As a result, while there may be a constitutionally recognised "right" to choose to terminate a pregnancy, it cannot effectively be exercised by women who lack sufficient money to pay for the operation.[135]

The feminist critique is not that there ought to be no distinction **1.18.3** between the public and the private, nor that the criminal law ought to be enforced irrespective of the locus of the behaviour. Rather, the argument is that whether or not to criminalise certain behaviour cannot be determined merely by labelling something as a "public" matter (and hence fit for criminalisation) or "private" (and thus free from proscription). The descriptors "public" and "private" should only be given after there has been a debate about the respective values which are at stake if the behaviour at issue is, or is not, criminalised.[136]

1.19 CONCLUSIONS

There is no doubt that many facets of liberalism have been highly **1.19.1** beneficial, and most critics would concede this.[137] The rights of the individual, exalted by liberalism, have been hard won, and we must not lose sight of their importance. As Frazer and Lacey remind us:

> "In a world of overt discrimination and exclusion, ideas of formal equality and the rule of law were powerful in arguing for women's access to education, to suffrage and citizenship, to the professions from which they had been excluded."[138]

---

[135] MacKinnon (1987).

[136] See Duff (2007) at pp 50–51. Nicola Lacey makes a similar point: "[A]rguments about public and private spheres are all too often hived off from their underlying liberal rationales and used as if we were simply *describing* spheres of activity, obscuring the normative premises of the argument" (Lacey (1998) at p 57 (emphasis in original)).

[137] "Any critic of liberal moral and political thought who aspires to be in the least fair minded must begin with a forthright acknowledgement of the genuine contributions of the liberal tradition to the identification and protection of valuable human liberties" (R P George, *Making Men Moral: Civil Liberties and Public Morality* (1993), p vii).

[138] Frazer and Lacey (1993), p 79. See also Michael Walzer: "The language of individual rights – voluntary association, pluralism, toleration, separation, privacy, free speech, the career open to talents, and so on – is simply inescapable. Who among us seriously attempts to escape?" (M Walzer, "The communitarian critique of liberalism" (1990) 18 *Political Theory* 6 at 14).

It is easy to take for granted key human rights embodied by internationally recognised prohibitions on slavery, genocide, arbitrary detention, and torture. As John Braithwaite contends: "Communitarianism without rights is dangerous. Rights without community are vacuous."[139] Both feminist and communitarian critiques remind us that there may be factors other than individual liberties to be considered in the criminalisation debate, and that an over-emphasis on the rights of "the individual" can be oppressive to others, some of whom – such as women and children – may have less of a voice in society. Feminist critiques remind us of the importance of our relationships with others. Whether the emphasis on care is inherent in women's nature (per Gilligan) or a social construct (per MacKinnon), it is nonetheless keenly felt by many. Indeed, it may be at least a partial explanation for the fact that women commit far fewer crimes than men.[140] Communitarianism, for all its faults, reminds us that individuals cannot be entirely separated from their societies, and that this may have implications for the extent to which we wish to allow one individual's rights to "trump" the greater good of society. It must also be borne in mind that there are commonalities within these philosophies. Etzioni recognises the claims of both communitarianism and liberalism:

> "The answer lies in imagining the course of a community as akin to that of a bicycle, forever teetering in one direction or another. That is, either towards the anarchy of extreme individualism and the denial of the common good *or* towards the collectivism that views itself as morally superior to its individual members. Hence communities constantly need to be pulled towards the centre course, where individual rights and social responsibilities are properly balanced."[141]

1.19.2 Liberalism has largely dictated the vocabulary of debates on criminalisation. We see this, for example, in the extent to which the debate on the regulation of pornography in the USA has become a clash between the right to freedom of speech (protected by the First Amendment of the American Constitution)[142] and the claims by feminists that the making and viewing of pornography infringes women's interests.[143] Feminists have engaged battle on liberalism's own terrain, believing that the proscription of pornography can be justified only if it can be shown to be a harm to others (that

---

[139] J Braithwaite, cited in D L Martin, "Retribution revisited: A reconsideration of feminist criminal law reform strategies" (1998) 36 *Osgoode Hall LJ* 151 at 183.

[140] See N Naffine, *Feminism and Criminology* (1997), pp 6–7.

[141] Etzioni (1995) at preface, p x (emphasis in original).

[142] This provides: "Congress shall make no law ... abridging the freedom of speech."

[143] Pornography is discussed further from section 11.15 below.

is, to those other than the viewers of pornography).[144] Hence they have attempted to show that it harms those (mainly women) who participate in its making[145] and that it impacts on women more generally in ways which the law recognises as harms, such as leading to increased violence, including rape.[146]

As we noted previously,[147] Glendon has argued that, too often, **1.19.3** important issues are expressed in terms of a clash of rights. When one side invokes their "rights" this seems to foreclose further debate, with those arguing against the "right" finding it difficult to articulate their concerns. Glendon illustrates her point by reference to the "flag-burning" disputes in the USA, an issue which

> "elicited passionate defenses of freedom of expression on the one hand, and equally fervent protests against desecration of the national symbol on the other. The arguments for the former position were easy to make, fitting into familiar First Amendment grooves. They carried the day. The rebuttals tended to have a sputtering quality; they sounded more in emotion than in reason. The problem for the flag defenders, in part, was that the flag-burning controversy pitted individual rights against community standards. Accustomed as we are to the notion that a person's liberty should not be curtailed in the absence of direct and immediate harm to specified others, we can barely find the words to speak of indirect harms, cumulative injury, or damages that appear only long after the acts that precipitated them".[148]

The flag-burning issue is hard for those of us who are not US citizens to understand fully; the deep emotions associated with a national flag are somewhat alien in the UK where we turn the Union Jack into paper handkerchiefs, napkins and shorts, and where a sizeable proportion of Scots, in particular, feel little allegiance to what lies behind the flag, let alone to the flag itself.[149] A more pertinent example for us could be the behaviour of the "Naked Rambler".[150] If the Rambler's behaviour is viewed from a liberal perspective, it is easier to assert that he has a right to freedom of expression (Art 10

---

[144] C W Daum, "Feminism and pornography in the twenty-first century: The Internet's impact on the feminist pornography debate" (2008–09) 30 *Women's Rights Law Reporter* 543.

[145] For example, Linda Marchiano, who was coerced into acting in the porn film *Deep Throat*: see MacKinnon (1987) at pp 10–15; and also C A MacKinnon, *Toward a Feminist Theory of the State* (1991), pp 195–215.

[146] For a critique of this approach, see Frazer and Lacey (1993) at pp 94ff and Daum (2008–09) who argues in favour of women utilising the internet in order to promote a female perspective on sexuality, by creating their own pornography.

[147] See section 1.4.2 above.

[148] Glendon (1991) at p 110.

[149] See, for example, R Ford, "Scots lead rebellion against oath of allegiance", *The Times*, 12 March 2008.

[150] See section 1.1.2 above.

of the ECHR) than it is for those who are upset by his behaviour to articulate a contrary claim. The Rambler may even have a right to privacy (Art 8 of the ECHR)[151] if this is interpreted as encompassing a "right to be one's own, uninhibited self".[152] On which, if any, "rights" are those who wish to curb the Rambler's behaviour able to rely? A "right" not to be offended? A "right" not to be upset or disgusted? These seem weak claims in the face of a recognised right to freedom of expression, yet the Rambler's behaviour *does* have the potential to impact adversely on others. The strongest argument against permitting him to roam free may be an assertion that his behaviour is harmful to others, yet such an argument is unlikely to be regarded as persuasive given the narrow approach the criminal law tends to take to the concept of harm.[153] As Munro explains:

> "Within the liberal tradition, the concept of harm is treated as denoting an injury, typically inflicted upon the body, which can be identified independently of both the context in which it takes place and the understanding of the experience from the point of view of the people involved. While this represents one of the ways in which what we experience as harmful can be identified, it is by no means the only way. In this light, then, this notion of harm, largely unquestioned in liberal thinking ... emerges as itself a construction, which is created as coherent and self-evident only through a process that deliberately renders other experiences of harm incomprehensible or irrelevant."[154]

Paradoxically, while we may struggle to articulate the "wrong" being committed by the "Naked Rambler", the Scottish courts have had little difficulty in repeatedly finding that his behaviour is a breach of the peace. In *Kara* v *United Kingdom*[155] the European Human Rights Commission held that constraints imposed on a person's mode of dress constitute an interference with private life under Art 8 of the ECHR.[156] Any interference with this could also be challenged as a breach of freedom of expression. An attempt by the Rambler to argue that he has a "right" to behave as he does is likely to founder by virtue of Art 8(2). This permits state interference with the right where this is necessary "for the prevention of disorder or crime". His

---

[151] See from section 1.4 above.

[152] See C Brants, "The state and the nation's bedrooms: The fundamental right of sexual autonomy" in Alldridge and Brants (2001) at p 118.

[153] This is discussed further in Chapter 3 below.

[154] Munro (2007) at pp 12–13.

[155] (1999) 27 EHRR CD 272.

[156] Prior to 1988, individuals who wished to claim that their rights under the European Convention on Human Rights had been breached had no direct access to the European Court of Human Rights. They had to apply to the Human Rights Commission, which would take to the Court cases which it held to be well founded. Direct access to the Court by individuals became permitted in 1989 because of the enactment of Protocol 11 to the ECHR, and the Commission was abolished.

repeated convictions for breach of the peace seem likely to continue. Nevertheless, it does raise the question whether Scots criminal law is employing moralistic principles, albeit couched in terms of "the public interest", behind a thin veneer of liberalism.[157]

This sketch of some normative approaches taken by legal **1.19.4** theorists and political philosophers to the position of the individual vis-à-vis society provides a context for the criminal law. There is clearly a tension between, on the one hand, liberalism's emphasis on individuals' rights and, on the other, the communitarian appeal to the public interest – the greater good of society. In subsequent chapters we will identify areas in which the criminal law is recognisably underlain by one or other or both of these philosophies. The evident conflict between them at the theoretical level may help to explain the fact that the law itself does not always appear internally consistent. We noted earlier that the "harm principle" – that the law ought to interfere with a person's liberty of action only where this is necessary to prevent harm to other people – is a key tenet of liberalism.[158] We look more closely at this principle, and at its limitations, in Chapter 3. Prior to this, however, we attempt to explain why it is important to place limits on the forms of behaviour that should be subject to the criminal law sanction.

---

[157] "Legal moralism" is considered further from section 2.6 below.
[158] At section 1.3.1 above.

CHAPTER 2

PRINCIPLES OF CRIMINALISATION

2.1 INTRODUCTION

At the beginning of his exploration of *The Limits of the Criminal*   **2.1.1**
Sanction, Herbert Packer asks the reader to:

> "hypothesize the existence of a rational law-maker – [someone] who stops,
> looks, and listens before he legislates. What kinds of questions should he ask
> before deciding that a certain kind of conduct (bank robbery, income tax
> evasion, marijuana use) ought to be subjected to the criminal sanction?"[1]

In this chapter, we examine the work of leading theorists on this
vexed issue of what behaviour should be criminalised and what
should remain free from the criminal sanction. In Packer's terms,
the sort of questions we might ask in order to determine whether
any particular criminal prohibition passes the test of being "right"
or justified is dependent on what we think the purposes of the
criminal law ought to be. At the outset, a distinction can be made
between the purposes of the law itself, and the purposes served
by punishing those who infringe such laws. This distinction is
not always made. For example, a United Nations policy paper on
the proposed criminalisation of HIV transmission states that the
"functions of criminal law" are:

> "to incapacitate the offender from harming anyone else during the term
> of their imprisonment ... to rehabilitate the offender, enabling him/her to
> change his/her future behaviour so as to avoid harming others ... to impose
> retribution for wrongdoing – to punish for the sake of punishing ... [and]
> to deter the individual offender and others from engaging in the prohibited
> conduct in the future".[2]

---

[1] Packer (1969) at p 3.
[2] UNAIDS, *Criminal Law, Public Health and HIV Transmission: A Policy Options Paper* (2002), p 6.

Although this confuses the functions of punishment with those of
the substantive law, it does at least suggest that one ultimate goal is
to prevent the offender from "harming anyone else", in the future,
albeit that its focus is on the situation *after* the person has been
found guilty of the offence. The prevention of harm to others is a key
theme in arguments about criminalisation and decriminalisation, as
we shall see below.[3]

2.1.2   Trevor Nyman has suggested that the criminal law's purpose is
to "define the behaviour which all society views with indignation,
apprehension or disapproval and to provide means of adjudication
and punishment".[4] This seems both too narrow and too broad. It
is surely too narrow in suggesting that "all society" must react in
the manner suggested; what of the paedophile who believes that the
age of consent to sexual intercourse ought to be reduced to 12, and
would not disapprove of sex with a 13 year old? What of the father
who sees nothing wrong in having a sexual relationship with his
adult daughter? Our counter-examples need not be so extreme. Many
people would favour the decriminalisation of possession or supply of
some types of narcotic drugs, such as cannabis and cannabis resin,
but if the majority are in favour of continued prohibition this may
be regarded by them as sufficient reason to maintain the status quo.
Does "all society" have to be read as "almost all of society", or "the
majority of society"? In a democracy, criminal sanctions which are
not supported by the majority of the community seem destined to
fail. Nyman's definition is at the same time too broad in suggesting
that "indignation, apprehension or disapproval" is a sufficient basis
for criminalising some activity. If A is falsely accused of being a flirt,
she may feel justifiably indignant. If B sees a rock climber dangling
from a cliff by one finger, she may experience apprehension. Upon
discovering that her neighbour is committing adultery, C may feel
disapproval. Even if most people would share these sentiments, this
surely does not provide an adequate justification for a criminal law
response. Many people disapprove of adultery, but few nowadays
would wish to see it criminalised.[5]

---

[3] See Chapter 3. Note that when we refer to "decriminalisation" we mean rendering
certain forms of conduct free from the reaches of the criminal law, rather than
employing some form of alternatives to prosecution, such as a "fiscal fine" or fixed
penalty, which results in punishment, albeit of a minor sort, without the due process
safeguards inherent in a prosecution. See section 5.3.1 below.

[4] T Nyman, "The dilution of crime" (1981) 55 *The Australian L J* 506 at 506.

[5] Adultery was a criminal offence in Hume's day. He referred to it as "this high
breach of moral and social duty ... which breaks in so deeply on the happiness of
private life, and the welfare of a family, as well as on the interests of decency and
public order" (Hume, i, 453). However, he later conceded that the laws against
adultery "may indeed be suspected not so much to have originated in any rational

An alternative offered by Norval Morris and Gordon Hawkins **2.1.3**
suggests that the purpose of the criminal law is "to protect the
citizen's person and property, and to prevent the exploitation ... of
the young and others in need of special care or protection".[6] This
identifies some of the most important interests which the criminal law
tries to safeguard. It also reflects the common practice of textbook
writers to divide crimes into those which are "against the interests
of the person" (by which is meant the physical person), and "against
property interests".[7] These categories are often further divided, such
that offences against the person include "sexual offences" and "non-
sexual offences", and offences against property can be subdivided
into those which involve misappropriation (theft, robbery, fraud,
embezzlement, reset etc) and those which involve property damage
(for example, vandalism, malicious mischief and fire-raising).
Citizens also have an interest in living in a well-ordered society, so
we may want to add "preservation of good order" to Morris and
Hawkins' list of protected interests.[8]

2.2 THE BREADTH OF THE CRIMINAL SANCTION

Infractions of the criminal law in Scotland are not rare events; one **2.2.1**
might go so far as to say that they are commonplace. Although
the most recent statistics from the Scottish Government note that
crime is currently at its lowest level for 39 years, nearly a quarter
of a million crimes were recorded by the police in 2012–13.[9] These
statistics generally use the term "crime" to describe "the more

---

consideration of the injury, or a temperate regard to the interest of morals, as in
that morose and austere temper, with which the people of Scotland were infected at
the Reformation, and which bred an extreme antipathy to all irregular or licentious
intercourse of the sexes" (*ibid*). See also n 102 below.

[6] N Morris and G Hawkins, *The Honest Politician's Guide to Crime Control*
(1970), p 4. Compare the conclusions of the Wolfenden Committee that the
function of the criminal law "is to preserve public order and decency, to protect
the citizen from what is offensive and injurious, and to provide sufficient safeguards
against exploitation and corruption of others, particularly those who are specially
vulnerable": *Report of the Committee on Homosexual Offences and Prostitution*
(Cmnd 247, 1957), para 13. Despite their predominantly liberal approach, each
recognises that legal paternalism can be justified in relation to particularly
vulnerable groups. Legal paternalism is discussed further from section 3.5 below.
[7] See, for example, A M Cubie, *Scots Criminal Law* (3rd edn, 2010); C McDiarmid,
Criminal Law Essentials (2nd edn, 2010); T H Jones and M G A Christie, *Criminal
Law* (5th edn, 2012).
[8] Lord Devlin argued that a society was justified in criminalising conduct in order
to ensure its "smooth functioning and ... the preservation of order" (P Devlin, *The
Enforcement of Morals* (1965), p 5). See further from section 2.6 below.
[9] *Recorded Crime in Scotland 2012–13*, para 4.1, available at: http://www.
scotland.gov.uk/Resource/0042/00425198.pdf.

serious criminal acts" (based on the maximum sentence which may be imposed), while less serious acts are termed "offences".[10] "Crimes" include non-sexual crimes of violence, sexual offences, crimes of dishonesty, fire-raising and vandalism.[11] In addition to the 273,053 recorded crimes,[12] the police also recorded 543,768 offences[13] in 2012–13. We will use the terms "crimes" and "offences" interchangeably, since there is no clear distinction between the two. Not all criminal acts are reported to the police; indeed, it has been estimated that only 39 per cent are reported.[14] To obtain a more accurate picture, the *Scottish Crime and Justice Survey* periodically interviews thousands of members of the public and asks them to recount details of any crimes they have experienced within a 1-year period. The most recent survey estimated that more than 815,000 crimes were committed against individuals or households in 2012–13,[15] with less than 17 per cent[16] of the 12,000 interviewees[17] having been the victim of at least one such crime within the previous year. This figure excludes a great many infractions, including most road traffic, revenue or social security offences, some public order offences, and crimes against businesses, such as shoplifting. Since the interviewees in the *Survey* must be aged 16 or older,[18] it does not record crimes against children.

2.2.2   As Peter Alldridge has pointed out, "criminal law (as a process) constructs criminality, criminals and crime"[19] and Herbert Packer rightly suggested that we "can have as much or as little crime as we please, depending upon what we choose to count as criminal".[20] Clearly, the number of offences a society has in its criminal calendar is, to a great extent, a reflection of its political philosophy. James Chalmers and Fiona Leverick compared the number of offences created by the Scottish Parliament to that created by the Westminster Parliament in a 12-month period between 2010 and 2011.[21] This

---

[10] *Recorded Crime in Scotland 2012–13*, para 3.2.
[11] *Ibid*, para 3.3.
[12] *Ibid*, para 4.1.
[13] *Ibid*, para 4.10.
[14] *Ibid*, para 3.6.
[15] *Scottish Crime and Justice Survey 2012/13*, para 2.1, available at: http://www.scotland.gov.uk/Publications/2014/03/9823.
[16] *Ibid*.
[17] *Ibid*, para 1.
[18] *Ibid*, para 1.2.
[19] P Alldridge, *Relocating Criminal Law* (2000), p 12. See also Morris and Hawkins (1970): "[Criminal law] is the formal cause of crime. If we had no criminal law we would have no crime" (at p 4).
[20] Packer (1969), p 364.
[21] J Chalmers and F Leverick, "Scotland: twice as much criminal law as England?" (2013) 17 *Edin LR* 376.

revealed that twice as many Scottish criminal offences were created compared to those applying to England.[22] The authors concluded that the Scottish Parliament "appears to have great difficulty regulating without criminalising" and that its "propensity to create criminal offences is a cause for concern".[23] A liberal might point out that one obvious way of reducing the number of crimes/offences committed each year would be to reduce the number of activities which we label as criminal, in the first place. This is not an entirely facetious proposal; many criminal law theorists believe that there is now an over-abundance of criminal prohibitions, and argue that some forms of behaviour which are currently regarded as criminal ought to be decriminalised.[24] Such an approach is not without its dangers; if the criminal law leaves many undesirable or unpleasant forms of behaviour unregulated, this can result in a reduced quality of life for those who have to put up with that behaviour. This could include noisy neighbours, littered pavements, parks soiled with dog excrement and the like.[25] We can readily see the liberal/communitarian tensions which underlie such debates.

Why ought we to care about the appropriate demarcations of the criminal law? What does it matter whether the range of criminal prohibitions is a narrow one, with relatively few types of behaviour within its purview, or is broadly defined, so that a great many types of behaviour breach the criminal law's provisions? This issue, rarely addressed in books about Scots criminal law, is a matter of much debate in other jurisdictions, most notably in the United States.[26] In practice, most of those who champion "decriminalisation" are less concerned with the sheer abundance of criminal prohibitions now

2.2.3

---

[22] Chalmers and Leverick (2013).

[23] *Ibid* at 380 and 381.

[24] For instance: D Husak, *Overcriminalization: The Limits of the Criminal Law* (2008); Packer (1969); S H Kadish, *Blame and Punishment: Essays in the Criminal Law* (1987), pp 21–35; S S Beale, "The many faces of overcriminalization: from morals and mattress tags to overfederalization" (2004–5) 54 *Am U L Rev* 747.

[25] Civil penalties could be employed to regulate such minor anti-social behaviours; this is advocated by Packer (1969) at pp 273–274, and by R A Duff and S E Marshall, "How offensive can you get?" in von Hirsch and Simester, *Incivilities: Regulating Offensive Behaviour* (2006) at 57. Civil penalties are not, however, unproblematic: see R M White, "'Decriminalisation': a pernicious hypocrisy?" (2009) 13 *Edin LR* 112.

[26] See, for example, J Feinberg, *The Moral Limits of the Criminal Law: Harm to Others* (1984); J Schonsheck, *On Criminalization: An Essay in the Philosophy of the Criminal Law* (1994); N Jareborg, "Criminalization as last resort (*ultima ratio*)" (2005) 2 *Ohio St J Crim L* 521 at 522. More recently, in relation to English law: S Uglow, *Criminal Justice* (2002) (at pp 23 *et seq*); von Hirsch and Simester (2006); A Ashworth, "Conceptions of overcriminalization" (2008) 5 *Ohio St J Crim L* 407.

on the statute book, and instead have in mind particular "victimless crimes" or "private offences", so called because they (arguably) do not involve harm to anyone other than the actor (and some do not involve harm to the actor, either).[27] Attempted suicide, abortion and male homosexuality were the favoured issues in the UK in the mid-20th century, leading Nigel Walker to observe that: "A bibliography of decriminalisation would give the impression that our civilisation was preoccupied by sex and death."[28] Other crimes falling into this category included those relating to the use and possession of narcotic drugs,[29] gambling[30] and public drunkenness.[31] Sex continues to be a dominant theme, with sexual sado–masochism[32] and incest[33] being potential targets for decriminalisation. Each theorist has his or her favourites.[34] It is often contended that the existence of such offences leads to a diminished respect for the law – a point made by James Fitzjames Stephen more than a century ago:

> "You cannot punish anything which public opinion, as expressed in the common practice of society, does not strenuously and unequivocally condemn. To try to do so is a sure way to produce gross hypocrisy and furious reaction."[35]

---

[27] Nyman refers to these as "offences which are the pathetic conduct of an individual who is harming nobody except perhaps himself" (Nyman (1981) at pp 507–508). Whether it is appropriate for the criminal law to attempt to prevent people from self-harming is a question to which we return in section 3.4 below.

[28] N Walker, *Punishment, Danger and Stigma: The Morality of Criminal Justice* (1980), p 2. Norval Morris and Gordon Hawkins advocated the decriminalisation of, *inter alia*, "bigamy, incest, sodomy, bestiality, homosexuality, prostitution, pornography, and obscenity": Morris and Hawkins (1970) at p 3.

[29] This was also listed by Morris and Hawkins (1970). See also "The case of heroin" in Uglow (2002) at p 23.

[30] See Morris and Hawkins (1970).

[31] *Ibid.* According to Packer: "Drunkenness is the paradigm case of an improvident use of the criminal sanction" ((1969) at p 345).

[32] In its report which led to the Sexual Offences (Scotland) Act 2009, the Scottish Law Commission recommended that consensual sado–masochism be decriminalised: see *Report on Rape and Other Sexual Offences* (SLC No 209, 2007), recommendation 57 – but this provision did not find favour with the Scottish Government.

[33] Incest between consenting adults is included in Stuart Green's list of crimes which are "anti-liberal" (S P Green, *Lying, Cheating, and Stealing: A Moral Theory of White-Collar Crime* (2006), pp 42–43). See also K McK Norrie, "Incest and the forbidden degrees of marriage in Scots law" (1992) 37 *JLSS* 216.

[34] See, for example, Morris and Hawkins (1970) at 3. They include public drunkenness, possession of narcotics, sexual behaviour involving consenting adults, abortion, vagrancy, disorderly conduct and gambling.

[35] J Fitzjames Stephen (1873) *Liberty, Equality, Fraternity, edited with an introduction and notes by R J White* (1967), p 159. See also Packer (1969) at p 359: "If we make criminal that which people regard as acceptable, either nullification occurs or, more subtly, people's attitude towards the meaning of criminality undergoes a change."

Of course, the fact that something is the subject of a criminal **2.2.4**
prohibition, or increased penalties are imposed for infractions,
may lead to a change in attitude by society. Steve Uglow has
remarked on the changing boundaries of acceptable behaviour in
respect of financial services: "two decades ago, insider dealing was
seen as clever use of the system by sharp manipulators whereas
today the same behaviour is morally reprehensible and severely
punished".[36] Thirty years ago, it was commonplace, and almost
socially acceptable, for people to drive their cars after consuming
quite a lot of alcohol. Nowadays it is recognised that drunk
drivers risk harm not only to themselves, but to other drivers and
pedestrians, and driving with excess alcohol in the bloodstream
attracts high penalties. Stephen was, however, right to caution
that there may be limits to the public's tolerance of the creation
of crimes which do not accord with commonly held views of
unacceptable behaviours.[37] Proponents of a narrowly defined
criminal law employ two key arguments, based on the "evil" of
punishment (and, to some extent, of the criminal process itself),
and the "good" of liberty.[38]

2.3 PUNISHMENT AND THE CRIMINAL PROCESS

The harms caused by conviction and punishment form a strong **2.3.1**
argument for curtailing the reaches of the criminal law. Conviction
entails condemnation and denunciation. Dennis Baker has argued
that there is a "right not to be criminalized":

> "The right is not only about having the freedom [to] do as one chooses so long
> as it does not wrong others, but also about not being subjected to the harmful
> consequences that flow from unfair criminalization (detention, penal fines,
> conviction, stigmatization, etc)."[39]

Jonathan Schonsheck refers to the "encumbrances of a criminal
conviction" as including not only the actual punishment but also the
long-term effects which a conviction may have on an individual's life,
including civil disabilities such as the right to sit on a jury, and the
ability to gain employment in many fields.[40] When the state punishes
one of its own citizens, this is, by definition, an evil, albeit a necessary

---

[36] Uglow (2002) at p 6. See also S P Green and M B Kugler, "When is it wrong to
trade stocks on the basis of non-public information? Public views of the morality of
insider trading" (2011) 39 *Fordham Urban L J* 445.
[37] Stephen (1873) at p 159.
[38] See from section 2.4 below.
[39] D J Baker, *The Right Not to Be Criminalized* (2011) at p 2.
[40] Schonsheck (1994) at pp 5–6.

one. Criminal penalties have been described by Stuart Green as "the most weighty kind of sanction we have in a civil society" and the "heavy artillery" of a legal system, "to be used only as a 'last resort', when other kinds of legal or non-legal sanctions prove inadequate".[41] It involves harsh treatment and therefore requires to be justified and only meted out when absolutely required. It is the very fact that the convicted person has breached the norms of the criminal law that justifies its infliction. Nils Jareborg has argued:

> "To the extent that we live in a social/liberal/conservative-democratic *Rechtsstaat*,[42] we are not any longer allowed to use criminal punishment just because we want it, or because a god is said to want it, or because we have always done it, or because it seems to be a natural or an effective means to some end. The basic reason for this is that punishment involves hard treatment, inflicting harm that is often serious. Given that a state organization is justified only if it is largely to the advantage of the citizens, a punishment system and its design and contents must be justified by reference to convincing, rational (moral) reasons, including reasons that refer to some notion of the common good."[43]

2.3.2   As well as the evil of punishment, the criminal process itself can be deeply unpleasant for accused persons,[44] particularly for those who are in fact innocent. As Schonsheck points out, the enforcement of the criminal law "is the most intrusive and coercive exercise of domestic power by a state".[45] He details the consequences to the individual when the police attempt to enforce the criminal law, referring to the "indignities of arrest" and the expense of defending oneself, including "psychic costs" as well as financial ones.[46]

2.3.3   The criminal process is distinct from the procedures used in the civil law in several ways – it involves different courts, separate mechanisms for determining factual matters including different

---

[41] Green (2006) at p 1 (footnote omitted). In similar vein, Paul Roberts states that "Criminal law is expensive to enforce and heavy-handed in its methods – a blunderbuss rather than a rapier, of moral discrimination": P Roberts, "Penal offence in question: some reference points for interdisciplinary conversation" in von Hirsch and Simester (2006) at p 14. See also R A Duff, *Punishment, Communication, and Community* (2001) at p 67.

[42] A *Rechtsstaat* is a state which conforms to the "rule of law", that is, the exercise of power by the Government is constrained by the law. For a more detailed discussion of the rule of law, see section 4.2 below.

[43] Jareborg (2005) at p 522. See also L Farmer, "Tony Martin and the nightbreakers: criminal law, victims and the power to punish" in S Armstrong and L McAra (eds), *Perspectives on Punishment: The Contours of Control* (2006) at pp 49–67, on the shift from private vengeance to state-sponsored punishment.

[44] See M M Feeley, *The Process is the Punishment: Handling Cases in a Lower Criminal Court* (1979).

[45] Schonsheck (1994) at p 1.

[46] *Ibid* at pp 2–4.

rules of evidence and standards of proof, as well as different outcomes.[47] Many of these variations reflect the fact that the stakes are different in a criminal trial, compared with civil litigation. This is not only the case if we compare a murder trial, with the potential for life imprisonment for the accused, with a small claims action, where damages of only a few pounds might be awarded. In an important sense, the stakes are different in, say, the prosecution of a petty theft than in a civil suit for a negligently performed medical procedure. While the latter has the potential to lead to an award of hundreds of thousands of pounds in compensation, and the reputation of the allegedly negligent doctor hangs in the balance, the opprobrium a person faces as a result of a criminal conviction is of an altogether different quality to that incurred by the unsuccessful defender of a civil suit.[48] As Packer states:

> "Being punished for a crime is different from being regulated in the public interest, or being forced to compensate another who has been injured by one's conduct ... The sanction is at once uniquely expensive. It should be reserved for what really matters."[49]

The enforcement of certain types of crimes, particularly those regarded by many as "victimless",[50] can cause more harm than good if it involves subterfuge by the police or intrusion into private lives.[51] Coupled with the unpleasantness of being subjected to the criminal process and the evil of punishment, these provide powerful arguments for limiting the reach of the criminal sanction.

---

[47] In some countries it is the same individuals who simultaneously hold office as judges in the civil law courts and in the criminal courts. This is the case in Scotland with sheriffs. Another example is that the posts of Lord President of the Court of Session and of Lord Justice-General of the High Court of Justiciary are held by the same person; see s 1(1) of the Criminal Procedure (Scotland) Act 1995 which provides: "The Lord President of the Court of Session shall be the Lord Justice General and shall perform his duties as the presiding judge of the High Court." The two roles are, however, kept separate, with the office bearer wearing different robes when acting in these different capacities.

[48] Subjectively, the person who is successfully sued for damages arising from negligence may feel the impact of the court's decision to be greater than had that same person been successfully prosecuted for, say, petty theft or assault. But objectively (that is, in the eyes of society) the moral opprobrium towards the thief or attacker is greater than that felt towards someone who has failed to be as careful as the "reasonable person".

[49] Packer (1969) at p 250.

[50] See section 2.2.3 above.

[51] For example, adultery remains a crime in some American states, albeit rarely enforced.

2.4   THE ARGUMENT FROM LIBERTY

2.4.1   As we saw in Chapter 1, liberalism has as its basis the belief that freedom from interference is a positive good, perhaps one of the ultimate goods, in society. Individuals, or at least those who are mentally competent adults, ought generally to be permitted to fashion their own lives, make their own decisions, and pursue their own interests and desires without interference from others, particularly from the state. Joel Feinberg refers to this as the "presumption in favour of liberty".[52] It requires that:

> "[W]henever a legislator is faced with a choice between imposing a legal duty on citizens or leaving them at liberty, other things being equal, he should leave individuals free to make their own choices. Liberty should be the norm; coercion always needs some special justification."[53]

As we noted in Chapter 1, John Stuart Mill argued that the state should recognise a "sphere of individual liberty" in which people should be allowed to choose how best to conduct their lives.[54] We shall consider the "harm principle" (which Mill proposed for determining whether any particular conduct ought to be within the individual's, or society's, sphere of influence) in Chapter 3. However, at this point it is important to note that, according to Mill, even where something falls within society's jurisdiction (that is, within the "public" sphere) this does not necessarily mean that the state is justified in employing the law, far less the criminal law, in an attempt to prevent its occurrence. This is an argument which has been made in relation to global attempts to eradicate female circumcision/female genital mutilation (FC/FGM):

> "Much of the current thrust from human rights discourses to eradicate FC/FGM is wary of advocating criminal law as a solution.... a less invasive, more gradual approach to the goal of eradication is adopted which suggests that criminal measures should only be used when appropriate, bearing in mind the particular social and cultural context."[55]

In relation to prostitution and pornography, it can be argued that criminalisation is not the best means of discouraging these

---

[52] Feinberg (1984) at p 9.

[53] *Ibid*. Compare this with the ECHR; any attempt to limit the rights it contains has to be specially justified. See section 1.4.1 above.

[54] J S Mill, "On Liberty" (1859) in J Gray (ed), *John Stuart Mill on Liberty and Other Essays* (1991), pp 84–85.

[55] L Bibbings, "Human rights and the criminalisation of tradition: the practices formerly known as 'female circumcision'" in P Alldridge and C Brants (eds), *Personal Autonomy, the Private Sphere and Criminal Law* (2001) at p 144.

activities.[56] It may be that society should try to discourage such conduct by extra-legal means, for instance by moral censure, or education. It may well be that "[t]he smooth functioning of society and the preservation of order require that a number of activities should be regulated",[57] but regulation of an activity need not be by way of criminalisation. This is an important, though sometimes neglected, point: the first question to be asked is whether a particular behaviour ought to be regulated by law at all and, if so, which branch of law is the most appropriate.[58]

As well as proscribing an activity by means of the criminal law, the state can promulgate laws governing the formation and enforcement of contracts, resolution of disputes by civil actions, redistribution of resources by taxation, etc. For instance, even if there is widespread agreement that cigarette smoking is an undesirable behaviour, an initial question is whether the state has any role in trying to prevent or limit this and, if so, whether this is best achieved by extra-legal means.[59] This could include educational campaigns highlighting the dangers of smoking, including the harm caused to others by passive smoking. If a legal response is judged to be appropriate, resort could be had to revenue law (increased taxation may deter smoking), or reforms in contract law, delict or consumer protection legislation (making it easier for smokers to sue retailers and/or tobacco manufacturers), rather than to the criminal law.[60] Likewise, a state could discourage the consumption of pornography by levying high taxes on media (for example, magazines and films) which contain this type of subject-matter. It could attempt to eradicate female circumcision/genital mutilation by requiring professional bodies which regulate doctors to treat such practices as a form of

2.4.2

---

[56] See N Lacey, *Unspeakable Subjects: Feminist Essays in Legal and Social Theory* (1998).

[57] Devlin (1965) at p 5.

[58] "[O]ne cannot have shown that the state is justified in criminalizing an action without investigating whether there are ways of successfully reducing the incidence of that action *without* engaging the machinery of the criminal justice system": Schonsheck (1994) at p 68 (emphasis in original). See also Packer (1969) at p 250: "The question of alternatives is really crucial. If there are readily available alternatives that avoid or minimize the formidable battery of objections and obstacles we have been considering, they must be carefully weighed."

[59] For a critique of the anti-smoking legislation, see P R Ferguson, "'Smoke gets in your eyes ...' : the criminalisation of smoking in enclosed public places, the harm principle and the limits of the criminal sanction" (2011) 31 *Legal Studies* 259.

[60] If it were easier for those injured by smoking to sue cigarette manufacturers, then the latter would have to produce a safer product, or risk going out of business. For the difficulties in suing tobacco manufacturers for negligence under the current law, see *McTear* v *Imperial Tobacco Ltd* 2005 2 SC 1.

professional misconduct, leading to those involved being struck off the medical register, or denied registration.[61]

2.4.3   It must, however, be borne in mind that invoking non-criminal laws is not without difficulty; the decision to respond to unwanted conduct by resort to mental health legislation, for example, can also involve serious restrictions on an individual's liberties, and the protections offered by the criminal process (such as the presumption of innocence and the requirement that the case be proved "beyond reasonable doubt") are lacking in such cases.[62] In some instances, society may have to tolerate certain behaviours, since attempts at prevention might be ineffective, or even produce greater harm. As Packer has put it: "There is always the alternative of doing nothing."[63]

2.5   THE PROLIFERATION OF STATUTORY OFFENCES

2.5.1   It seems almost trite to say that since liberty is highly prized, and punishment an evil, we should limit the ambit of criminal law prohibitions. Yet the proliferation of statutory offences suggests that legislators do not proceed from the premise that we should be cautious in employing the criminal law. In relation to England and Wales, it has been estimated that there are now more than 10,000 statutory offences, with 3,000 of them having been introduced within 11 years of the Labour Party having most recently come to power.[64] James Chalmers and Fiona Leverick have "attempted to establish a methodology for a systematic analysis of the number of criminal offences created during a particular time period".[65] They note that in the period 2010–11 (selected as the first year of Conservative/LibDem coalition for the UK) 1,223 offences applicable in Scotland were created.[66] Their work provides the only

---

[61] There are, however, dangers with this if it leads to a black market, or to an increased market elsewhere. An example of the latter is that many women seeking an abortion travel from Northern Ireland (where abortion is legal, but only in exceptional circumstances) to the mainland UK (where it is more easily available).

[62] A good example of this is the case of *Enhorn* v *Sweden* (2005) 41 EHRR 30, involving the lengthy detention under public health legislation of a man who was HIV positive. The European Court of Human Rights held that there had been a breach of his right to liberty, under Art 5(1) of the ECHR. Convention rights are described in section 1.4.1 above.

[63] Packer (1969) at p 258.

[64] N Morris, "Blair's 'frenzied law-making' has created a new offence for every day spent in office", *The Independent*, 16 August 2006 at p 2, cited in J Chalmers and F Leverick, "Fair labelling in criminal law" (2008) 71 *MLR* 217 at 217.

[65] "Tracking the creation of criminal offences" [2013] *Crim LR* 543 at 547.

[66] *Ibid* at 551 and Table 3.

comparison of Scottish and English figures in this area. It should also be noted that as well as offences enacted by the Westminster Parliament which apply north and south of the Border,[67] there has been no shortage of criminal law offences created by the Scottish Parliament.[68] A quick survey of legislation emanating from the latter suggests that there is a tendency to create specific statutory offences to proscribe behaviours which are already covered by the common law. For example, s 16 of the Building (Scotland) Act 2003 makes it an offence to make a false application for a building warrant, and s 20 to submit a false building completion certificate. Under s 52 of the Regulation of Care (Scotland) Act 2001 it is an offence for a person to pretend to be a social worker. The behaviours prohibited by each of these three sections are sufficiently covered by the common law crime of fraud. On the one hand, the elimination of needless duplication would be a step forward in limiting the number of offences in the criminal calendar, and a clearly worded definition of fraud in statutory form would obviate the need for multiple other offences, applying fraud to a range of different circumstances.[69] On the other, not all new offences can fit so readily within the definition of an existing crime, and there is also an argument that it can be useful to specify clearly what is, and what is not, acceptable in a particular area – in other words, that specific legislation for builders and social workers is merited by the requirements of "fair labelling".[70]

Another reason for the large number of new offences may be a tendency to view the creation of a criminal offence as some sort of panacea for unwanted behaviours. Western democracies are increasingly pluralistic, largely secular, societies, where there is growing reluctance to upbraid people for behaviour which is not proscribed by the criminal law, even where that behaviour may be regarded as dishonest, dishonourable or otherwise immoral. Condemnation of others' undesirable conduct may be seen as ineffectual, perhaps even inappropriate. For example, 50 years

2.5.2

---

[67] "Tracking the creation of criminal offences" [2013] *Crim LR* 543 at 550.

[68] Some examples include: providing an unregistered care service (Public Services Reform (Scotland) Act 2010, s 80); hunting a wild mammal with a dog (Protection of Wild Mammals (Scotland) Act 2002, s 1(1)); and keeping or breeding animals for slaughter for their fur (Fur Farming (Prohibition) (Scotland) Act 2002, s 1(1)). For a review of the Parliament's law making in this area, see P R Ferguson, "Criminal law and criminal justice: an exercise in ad hocery" in E E Sutherland, K E Goodall, G F M Little and F P Davidson (eds), *Law Making and the Scottish Parliament: The Early Years* (2011) at pp 208–224.

[69] See the *Draft Criminal Code*, s 86. For the background to the *Code*, see section 5.10.4 below. For a critique of overlapping offences, see Husak (2008) at pp 36–38, and Gerald Gordon's commentary to *Hamilton v Byrne* 1997 SCCR 547 at 551.

[70] Fair labelling is discussed further from section 4.6 below.

ago, our perception is that children's bad behaviour at the level of ringing doorbells and running away and the like was regarded merely as naughty. It was probably appropriate for such infractions to be dealt with unofficially, by the victims speaking to the child's parents, or the local police constable reprimanding the child. Now it is not always possible to do this, since the victim may believe that remonstrating with parents or child is unlikely to produce the desired result. Societies are less cohesive. People tend to live in larger cities. Even in smaller communities it may be that one is less likely to know one's neighbours. Such childish behaviour is more likely today to be labelled as "criminal",[71] or to be used as grounds for an anti-social behaviour order (ASBO).[72]

2.5.3   Of course, if we go back further, to Hume's era, children were imprisoned or transported for theft,[73] so we should be wary of imagining that there was a golden age in criminal procedure. Nevertheless, it seems that in earlier eras, the community may have had more of a shared religious and moral code, enforced strictly by the Church and/or society. If so, then the role of the criminal law may have been to act as a back-up, to provide an additional reason for compliance and to mete out punishment for serious infringements. Now that there is less homogeneity, it may be that the criminal law offers the only normative standards, common to all, or almost all, segments of society.[74] As Lord Devlin complained more than 40 years ago: "Statutory additions to the criminal law are too often made on the simple principle that 'there ought to be a law against it'."[75] Andrew Ashworth has noted:

> "Politicians, pressure groups, journalists and others often express themselves as if the creation of a new criminal offence is the natural, or the only appropriate, response to a particular event or series of events giving rise to social concern. ... There is little sense that the decision to introduce a new offence should only be made after certain conditions have been satisfied,

---

[71] L Adams, "Revealed: the under-eights who commit serious crime", *The Herald*, 14 November 2007, p 1.

[72] Breach of an ASBO in Scotland is a criminal offence, by virtue of the Antisocial Behaviour etc (Scotland) Act 2004, s 9. According to a Scottish Govern-ment report: "The tools provided by the 2004 Act have clearly made a difference to the lives of people across Scotland" but the media's focus on ASBOs has "fuelled the flames of the negative reporting and demonisation of young people that we seek to overcome" (*Promoting Positive Outcomes: Working Together to Prevent Anti-social Behaviour in Scotland* (2009) at paras 1.4 and 9.3 respectively).

[73] See Hume, i, 30–37; and C McDiarmid, *Childhood and Crime* (2007), Chapter 5.

[74] On this point, see R A Duff, "Law, language and community: some preconditions of criminal liability" (1998) 18 *OJLS* 189, where he discusses the moral authority of the criminal law in addressing certain communities.

[75] Devlin (1965) at p 1.

little sense that making conduct criminal is a step of considerable social significance."[76]

Unless proper consideration is given to the question of determining   2.5.4
which types of behaviour ought not to be subject to the criminal sanction, social problems will increasingly be "fixed" by resort to the criminal law.[77] Commenting on the Bill which became the Protection of Wild Mammals (Scotland) Act 2002, Lord Hope noted that the hunting of mammals with dogs was a highly controversial area, and that since 1980 the Westminster Parliament had failed to enact 17 Bills containing similar provisions to the Scottish legislation.[78] He concluded:

> "the fact that the Scottish Parliament has succeeded where Westminster has failed will be regarded either as testimony to the new institution's effectiveness in taking a moral stand and translating it into legislation, or evidence of a disquieting tendency of MSPs to adopt populist policies at the expense of the freedoms and liberties of a particular section of the community".[79]

Is it the case, then, that the only limit on criminalisation is a pragmatic one? Politicians rely on the votes of their constituents and would not criminalise behaviour without the backing of a significant proportion of the population. This leaves the development of the criminal law at the mercy of popular sentiment – the "tyranny of the prevailing opinion and feelings" against which Mill cautioned 150 years ago.[80]

2.6   LAW AND MORALS

Whether or not we are persuaded by the arguments of those who   2.6.1
favour decriminalisation of certain behaviours, or who favour a reduced criminal calendar, more generally, it would be useful to have some mechanism(s) by which to judge whether certain behaviour has been appropriately criminalised. It might be suggested that one purpose of the criminal law is to enforce a society's ideas of correct conduct by making clear what kinds of behaviour will not be tolerated and will render perpetrators liable to be stigmatised and punished by

---

[76] A Ashworth, "Is the criminal law a lost cause?" (2000) 116 *LQR* 225 at 225.
[77] The Canadian Law Commission has likewise cautioned against over-use of the criminal law to attempt to regulate unwanted behaviours, noting that "a reflex to criminal law has come to dominate": Law Commission of Canada, *What is a Crime? Challenges and Alternatives* (2003), p 5.
[78] Lord Hope of Craighead, "What a second chamber can do for legislative scrutiny" (2004) 25 *Stat LR* 3.
[79] *Ibid* at 9. The hunting of wild mammals with dogs is now also an offence in English law: see the Hunting Act 2004, s 1.
[80] See W Wilson, *Central Issues in Criminal Theory* (2002), p 19.

the state. In this way, the criminal law serves to give state backing
to a society's moral code.[81] The criminal law does indeed reflect a
community's sense of morality by proscribing the most egregious
immoralities. To kill, steal, deliberately injure, defraud, or infringe
someone's liberty – all of these are (at least *prima facie*) decried
as breaches of morality, as well as of the criminal law.[82] As Victor
Tadros has put it, "it is central to the criminal justice system that it
morally criticises defendants for their conduct".[83] Yet as well as these
core crimes, there are a great many others which do not, in and of
themselves, target behaviour which would generally be regarded as
immoral. Examples include the offences of failing to obey a traffic
sign[84] or wear a seat-belt;[85] or driving marginally over the speed
limit.[86] Behaving in these ways may be regarded as, in some sense,
"wrongful" because each involves "breaking a rule", but this of
course raises the question why we have such rules about speed limits
and seat-belts etc in the first place.

2.6.2   The relationship between law and morality has been the subject
of much debate among philosophers and lawyers, with some authors
arguing that we should only label as "criminal" conduct which is
also regarded as immoral:

> "To create a large number of offences which do not excite moral indignation
> may weaken general respect for the law and weaken the feeling, based in
> part on the coincidence of the basic crimes with moral prohibitions, that it is
> morally wrong to disobey the criminal law."[87]

As well as those who believe that *only* immoral behaviour ought
to be criminalised, there are those who would wish to criminalise
conduct purely on the basis that it is regarded as morally wrong.
Feinberg has defined "legal moralism" as the principle that: "It may
be morally legitimate to prohibit conduct on the ground that it is
inherently immoral, even though it caused neither harm nor offence
to the actor or to others".[88]

---

[81] For the view that "crimes should be a sub-set of all moral wrongs", see J Tasioulas,
"Crimes of offence" in von Hirsch and Simester (2006) at p 149.

[82] Some may be shown to be justified in light of further information: the killing may
be in self-defence, the deprivation of liberty may be a lawful arrest or result from a
court order, but the point remains that they are forms of behaviour which demand
an explanation if they are to avoid censure.

[83] V Tadros, *Criminal Responsibility* (2005) at p 2.

[84] See the Road Traffic Act 1988, s 36(1).

[85] Road Traffic Act 1988, s 14(3). See also the Motor Vehicles (Wearing of Seat
Belts) Regulations 1993 (SI 1993/176), reg 5.

[86] Road Traffic Regulation Act 1984, Pt VI, and in particular s 89.

[87] Gordon (2000) at para 1.14.

[88] J Feinberg, *The Moral Limits of the Criminal Law: Harmless Wrongdoing*
(1988), p xx.

Lord Devlin argued that: "Society cannot ignore the morality **2.6.3** of the individual any more than it can his loyalty; it flourishes on both and without either it dies."[89] He believed that society had not merely a right, but a duty, to punish any act which is "grossly immoral": "[T]he moral judgement of society must be something about which any twelve men or women drawn at random might after discussion be expected to be unanimous".[90] He concluded that: "No society can do without intolerance, indignation and disgust; they are the forces behind the moral law."[91] Devlin has been described as a communitarian, but his form of communitarianism is deeply conservative.[92] Robert George has pointed out that, in deciding whether or not to criminalise any particular behaviour:

> "a Devlinite legislator would not enquire of a putatively immoral act, 'Does it do moral harm to those who indulge in it?', but, rather, 'Does its legal toleration in the face of condemnation under society's dominant morality threaten social cohesion (and thereby work to cause serious social harms to the members of that society)?'. He would not ask of the alleged vice, 'Is it truly wicked?' but, rather, 'Is it widely considered to be truly wicked?'."[93]

As Ronald Dworkin notes, "what is shocking and wrong" about Devlin's arguments "is not his idea that the community's morality counts, but his idea of what counts as the community morality".[94] It should, however, be noted that Devlin's argument for enforcing a community's dominant morality was in fact in keeping with the *liberal* ideal that criminal prohibitions ought to be limited to behaviour which causes or risks harm to others; according to Devlin, failure to criminalise conduct which is widely condemned by morality risks a very serious harm indeed: that of social disintegration.[95] Reference has already been made to the fact that the European Convention on Human Rights reflects a liberal philosophy, but it must be borne in mind that several of the rights it protects are qualified, such that a state may criminalise conduct for the "protection of morals".[96] Peter Alldridge and Chrisje Brants conclude:

---

[89] Devlin (1965) at p 22.

[90] *Ibid* at p 15. The significance of there being 12 people in Devlin's argument is that this is the number of people who comprise a criminal jury in England and Wales. There are 15 people on a Scottish jury.

[91] Devlin (1965) at p 17.

[92] See E Frazer and N Lacey, *The Politics of Community: A Feminist Critique of the Liberal–Communitarian Debate* (1993), p 112.

[93] R P George, *Making Men Moral: Civil Liberties and Public Morality* (1993) at p 6.

[94] R Dworkin, "Lord Devlin and the enforcement of morals" (1966) 75 *Yale LJ* 986 at 1001.

[95] See George (1993), pp 5–6.

[96] See Arts 8(2), 9(2), 10(2) and 11(2).

> "Taken together with the other requirement, that however legitimate the aim *in abstracto*, intervention must also be necessary in a given democratic society, we must surmise that this has something to do with holding together the (moral) fabric of society, if necessary by criminalising autonomous individual behaviour that threatens it."[97]

Reference to the moral fabric of society is highly reminiscent of Devlin's approach.

2.7 THE SEPARATION OF LAW AND MORALS

2.7.1 Other theorists have stressed that the question of whether something is a legal wrong ought to be kept quite separate from whether it is morally wrong. According to H L A Hart:

> "[I]n every ... [criminal law system] there are necessarily many actions ... that if voluntarily done are criminally punishable, although our moral code may be either silent as to their moral quality, or divided. Very many offences are created by legislation ... the ... moral character of which may be genuinely in dispute. ... [W]hat is essential is that the offender, if he is to be *fairly* punished, must have acted 'voluntarily', and not that he must have committed some moral offence."[98]

Packer reached the same conclusion:

> "The dictates of individual culpability are satisfied if a person engages in forbidden conduct without having a valid excuse for it. He is culpable because he has behaved in a way that the law has told him is unacceptable. If he knows that the law forbids him to sell oleomargarine, he is culpable if he sells it, regardless of whether – the law apart – the sale of oleomargarine is considered to be morally good, bad or indifferent. He is culpable because he knowingly violated a legal prohibition. ... punishment is justifiable, quite apart from the moral quality of the forbidden act."[99]

2.7.2 The criminal law generally holds that people have legal liability for their actions, and the reasonably foreseeable consequences of these actions, so long as they are capable of understanding what they are doing, and could have chosen to do otherwise.[100] In practice, the criminal law proscribes certain immoral behaviours (for example, murder, rape, theft) but not others (for example, in

---

[97] Alldridge and Brants (2001) at p 14 (emphasis in original).

[98] H L A Hart, *Punishment and Responsibility* (1968), p 37 (emphasis in original).

[99] Packer (1969) at pp 261–262.

[100] This has implications for the sorts of defences that the criminal law recognises, as well as for the types of behaviour which it criminalises.

[101] Lying may be criminal in specific circumstances, for example if done under oath, or in an attempt to pervert the course of justice, or if the lie is told with a view to gaining some practical result (the basis of fraud).

Scots law, lying,[101] adultery[102] and promise-breaking[103]). The link between crime and immorality is necessarily a close one, if only because both are concerned with harms, but many would be wary of adopting Lord Devlin's approach and relying on the views of a group of randomly selected lay people to determine that something was morally wrong, and therefore that it ought to be proscribed by the criminal law.[104] In practice, it would not be the views of 12 or 15 lay people which would be decisive for Scots law, but those of a small number of senior judges, and the morality of the latter group may well differ from that of the former, given that the judiciary are unlikely to be representative of the population as a whole in respect of such characteristics as, for example, age, class, gender or ethnic origin.

A contrary stance to that of Devlin was also taken by the **2.7.3** Wolfenden Committee, which was appointed by the Government in 1957 to consider whether to amend the laws against homosexuality and prostitution in force at that time.[105] The Committee's approach was a quintessentially liberal one, stressing the separation of the "public" and "private" spheres and arguing for the criminal law to stay out of that which it labelled as "private". In a statement which has been often quoted, Wolfenden argued:

> "Unless a deliberate attempt is to be made by society, acting through the agency of the law, to equate the sphere of crime with that of sin, there must remain a realm of private morality and immorality which is, in brief and crude terms, not the law's business."[106]

The Committee recommended the decriminalisation of homosexual acts between consenting adult males, believing that the social stigma associated with such practices would mean that they would continue to be regarded as immoral by the majority of people, despite

---

[102] Adultery was a capital crime in Hume's time, though rarely prosecuted in practice. Hume contrasts the Scottish crime of adultery with the position in England, where adultery was regarded as "a mere civil trespass" which resulted in "the feeble censure of an award of damages" (Hume, i, 453). It remains a criminal offence in several states in the USA: see Beale (2004–05) at p 752. See also n 5 above.

[103] "It is generally considered immoral to break a promise simply because it has become inconvenient to keep it ... Yet we do not put promise-breakers in jail. What they do may be viewed as both immoral and harmful; but it does not result in the invocation of the criminal sanction": Packer (1969) at pp 264–265.

[104] As Packer notes: "The extent of disagreement about moral judgments is an obvious reason for hesitancy about an automatic enforcement of morals" (*ibid* at p 265).

[105] Wolfenden (1957).

[106] *Ibid* at para 61.

decriminalisation.[107] This recommendation was not implemented in Scotland until 1980,[108] but hindsight allows us to see that the Committee was quite wrong about the effect decriminalisation would have; social attitudes towards homosexuality have changed to the extent that we now live in an era where the state acknowledges gay marriages.[109] The impact of equality discourse must be considered here; when the criminalisation of a behaviour seems *prima facie* to discriminate on the basis of race, gender, religion or (in this case) sexuality, there is rightly a demand for some other, non-discriminatory justification to be provided.[110]

2.7.4   Chloe Kennedy has assessed the influence of Protestant theology on Scots criminal law in the 16th and 17th centuries, and concludes that there remain aspects of the contemporary law "which are, at least nominally, peculiarly moralistic", such as the continued references by the courts to "dole", "evil intent", "wicked intention" and "wicked recklessness" when describing *mens rea*.[111] She also instances the post-Reformation enactment of statutes criminalising "blasphemy, witchcraft, incest, adultery and fornication".[112] In a series of cases starting in 1934 and lasting for almost 70 years, a belief by some senior judges that immorality equated to criminality, at least so far as sexual matters were concerned, led to a range of behaviours being successfully prosecuted for "shameless indecency".[113] More recently, however, the appeal court has stressed the distinction between immoral and criminal behaviour. In *Paterson* v *Lees*[114] the appellant was convicted at first instance of shameless indecency by permitting children whom he was babysitting to view an indecent video. The children had switched on the video, but Paterson took no action once he realised its contents. Lord Rodger stated:

---

[107] According to Wolfenden, "moral conviction or instinctive feeling, however strong, is not a valid basis for over-riding the individual's privacy and for bringing within the ambit of the criminal law private sexual behaviour of this kind" (*ibid*, Chapter V, para 54).

[108] By the Criminal Justice (Scotland) Act 1980, s 80(1). This set the age of consent at 21. For an account of this delay, see R Davidson and G Davis, "'A field for private members': the Wolfenden committee and Scottish homosexual law reform, 1950–67" (2004) 15 *Twentieth Century British History* 174; R Davidson and G Davis, "Sexuality and the state: the campaign for Scottish homosexual law reform, 1967–80" (2006) 20 *Contemporary British History* 533.

[109] See the Marriage and Civil Partnership (Scotland) Act 2014.

[110] Issues of equality are considered further in Chapter 4.

[111] C Kennedy, "Criminal law and religion in post-Reformation Scotland" (2012) 16 *Edin LR* 178 at 179. Some of these terms are discussed further in section 9.11.5 below.

[112] *Ibid* at 180 (footnotes omitted).

[113] This is no longer a crime. The matter is discussed further at section 4.3.1 below.

[114] 1999 SCCR 231.

"The fact that the appellant sat back and allowed the children to watch an obscene and indecent film is deplorable and no right-thinking adult would have done what he did. Saying that does not, however, answer the question before the court since we have to consider, not whether the appellant behaved anti-socially or immorally, but whether he behaved criminally."[115]

The appeal court answered that question in the negative and quashed the conviction. It drew a clear line in this case between illegality and immorality, and refused to adopt the approach that all immoral conduct is *ipso facto* a breach of the criminal law. One can imagine that a less liberal, more communitarian approach would have resulted in a conviction for Paterson.

Both the Scottish and Westminster Parliaments have introduced 2.7.5 legislation which criminalises the possession of "extreme pornography".[116] While this is justified ostensibly on the basis of the harm which is caused to those (mainly women) who are involved in the creation of such extreme images, many commentators have argued that legal moralism is a more likely motivation. Referring to the English offences, Erika Rackley and Clare McGlynn have suggested that "by the time [these] measures were adopted ... the Government had lost sight of any original ambition to focus on the harm of pornography and reverted to the weakest possible justification for action: disgust".[117] This reminds us of the need to scrutinise carefully the true motivations behind criminalisation decisions.

2.8 WRONGFUL BEHAVIOUR AND BLAMEWORTHY INDIVIDUALS

While few believe that "criminality" is, or ought to be treated as, 2.8.1 synonymous with "immorality",[118] there is something to be said for the criminal law concerning itself with conduct that is in some sense "wrongful", as offending against the shared values of society. As Herbert Weschler stated, "it is the distinctive feature of the penal law that it condemns offenders as wrongdoers, marshalling the formal

---

[115] 1999 SCCR 231 at 233.
[116] See section 11.15.2 below.
[117] E Rackley and C McGlynn, "Prosecuting the possession of extreme pornography: a misunderstood and mis-used law" [2013] *Crim LR* 400 at 401. See also C McGlynn, "Marginalizing feminism?: debating extreme pornography laws in public and policy discourse" in K Boyle (ed), *Everyday Pornography* (2010) at p 190.
[118] Cf *R v Instan* [1893] 1 QB 450, in which Lord Coleridge CJ stated: "It would not be correct to say that every moral obligation involves a legal duty; but every legal duty is founded on a moral obligation" (at 453). The case is discussed further at section 6.7.4 below.

censure of conviction and coercive sanctions on this ground".[119] The corollary of this is that:

> "The law promotes the general security by building confidence that those whose conduct does not warrant condemnation will not be convicted of a crime. This is a value of enormous moment in a free society."[120]

Conduct may not be inherently wrong, but once made criminal it becomes appropriate to label it as "wrongful". For example, there is nothing intrinsically wrong about driving on a particular side of the road; some countries mandate driving on the "left" side, others on the "right" side. But once a legislature decrees that a country's road users are to drive on a particular side, any driver who ignores the law's requirements can be said to have behaved in a "wrongful" manner, not merely in the sense that the driver has done something contrary to a particular criminal law, but in the sense that in doing so, in the face of the danger such behaviour poses to others, the accused chose to behave in an unacceptable way. However, it is not the case that all infringements of the criminal law are "wrongful" in this sense. Until recently it was an offence to sell a sweater labelled "made in Scotland" when in fact, and *unknown to the seller*, the garment was made in Berwick-upon-Tweed, in England.[121] Few people would say that a shopkeeper who sold such a sweater had behaved in a really wrongful fashion, yet she could nonetheless have been prosecuted. Would we really say that her conduct was "wrongful"? And if it *was* wrongful, was it *sufficiently* wrongful to justify criminalisation? Hyman Gross has rightly suggested that a high level of moral wrongfulness ought to be required:

> "There is a common notion that having a particular law on the books making some conduct or other punishable is a good thing just because it tells everyone that the conduct in question is wrong. But merely the doing of something that is wrong is not enough to justify the violation of basic human rights that criminal punishment inevitably involves. ... [C]riminalisation requires proof beyond a reasonable doubt that it would be *intolerable to allow the conduct in question to pass with impunity*."[122]

---

[119] H Weschler, "The Model Penal Code and the codification of American criminal law" in R Hood (ed), *Crime, Criminology and Public Policy: Essays in Honour of Sir Leon Radzinowicz* (1974) at p 432. (Weschler was the principal drafter of the American Model Penal Code.)
[120] *Ibid* at p 433.
[121] This was under the Trade Descriptions Act 1968, s 1 which made it an offence to supply goods to which a false description had been applied. The supplier did not need to know that the description was false. This has now been repealed by the Consumer Protection from Unfair Trading Regulations 2008 (SI 2008/1277).
[122] H Gross, "Rape, moralism, and human rights" [2007] *Crim LR* 220 at 227 (emphasis added).

Closely allied to the idea that the behaviour of the accused must in **2.8.2**
some sense be "wrongful" is the idea that the accused must also be
"blameworthy". This is directed more at the voluntariness of the
accused's behaviour, rather than the wrongfulness of that behaviour,
per se. As Lon Fuller put it:

> "If a man is held accountable for a condition of affairs for which he was
> not to blame – either because he intentionally brought it about or because
> it occurred through some neglect on his part – then he has ascribed to him
> responsibility for an occurrence that lay beyond his powers."[123]

A criminal law system which took the criterion of blameworthiness
seriously would provide defences of insanity, non-age and self-defence
(as our system does). It would also have fewer offences involving strict
liability,[124] would acquit those whose actions were otherwise lacking
in voluntariness, and would allow coercion to operate as, at the least,
a mitigating factor. As we shall see, our system has a plethora of
strict liability offences, does not always acquit those whose conduct
is involuntary, and may not allow coercion to exonerate or mitigate
in cases of murder.

As we saw from our discussion on liberty in Chapter 1, Western **2.8.3**
democracies put great store on the idea of autonomy: that individuals
should generally be free to live their lives as they see fit. Liberalism
does, however, concede that there must be some limitations on
an individual's freedoms in the interests of others. One person's
freedoms, choices or desires may come into conflict with those
of another person; for example, A's decision to play her electric
guitar at 2 am may conflict with B's desire for sleep. One must have
her liberty curtailed, whether it is to play loud music whenever
she wishes, or to have a peaceful sleep during the early hours of
the morning. Most people would reason that the interest of the
person wishing to sleep ought to take precedence in this scenario.
However, if the sleeper is a person who works night-shifts, and
is trying to get to sleep at 2 pm, the argument for allowing the
guitar player to indulge in her hobby becomes stronger (though not
necessarily decisive). The issue is, of course, how much interference
in one's freedoms is acceptable in any situation, and what type of
interference ought to be employed. The role of the law is to set
limits on behaviour to avoid such clashes, but in the least restrictive
way possible. Mill claimed that:

> "There is, in fact, no recognized principle by which the propriety or
> impropriety of government interference is customarily tested. People decide

---

[123] L L Fuller, *The Morality of Law* (1964) at p 71.
[124] Not all strict liability offences involve conduct which is free from blame – for
example, driving while under the influence of alcohol.

according to their personal preferences. Some, whenever they see any good
to be done, or evil to be remedied, would willingly instigate the government
to undertake the business; while others prefer to bear almost any amount
of social evil, rather than add one to the departments of human interests
amenable to governmental control."[125]

Yet Mill himself proposed that there was "one very simple principle"
which ought to be employed in determining whether state interference
in a person's actions was justified. He proposed that the *only* types of
conduct which should be subject to such interference are those which
harm, or risk harm, *to other people*.[126] This principle is explored in
Chapter 3.

---

[125] Mill (1859) at p 13. Mill also stated: "The likings and dislikings of society, or of
some powerful portion of it, are ... the main thing which has practically determined
the rules laid down for general observance, under penalties of law" (*ibid* at p 11).
[126] Mill (1859) at pp 13–14.

CHAPTER 3

HARMING AND OFFENDING

3.1 INTRODUCTION

John Stuart Mill was a utilitarian, that is, one who judges actions **3.1.1** on whether or not they tend to promote greater happiness.[1] In his essay *On Liberty* he suggested that happiness requires a domain of non-interference in which the individual could freely choose what to do.[2] It should be noted that Mill's philosophy was not a theory of criminal law as such, since he was interested in the limits of social control, not just legal control, on individual behaviour.[3] His harm principle provides:

> "That the sole end for which mankind are warranted, individually or collectively, in interfering with the liberty of action of any of their number, is self-protection. That the only purpose for which power can be rightfully exercised over any member of a civilized community, against his will, is to prevent harm to others."[4]

Since the aim is the *prevention* of harm, the principle can be employed to justify the criminalisation of conduct which risks

---

[1] See nn 103 and 104 in section 1.14.1 above for definitions of "utilitarianism" and "deontology", respectively.

[2] J S Mill, 'On Liberty' (1859) in J Gray (ed), *On Liberty and other Essays* (1991) at p 16. For an early critique of Mill, see J Fitzjames Stephen, *Liberty, Equality, Fraternity* (1873) (ed with introduction and notes by R J White, 1967).

[3] Mill intended his philosophy to "govern absolutely the dealings of society with the individual in the way of compulsion and control, whether the means used be physical force in the form of legal penalties, or the moral coercion of public opinion" (*ibid*, p 14). He warned that individual liberty needed protection "against the tyranny of the prevailing opinion and feelings; against the tendency of society to impose, by other means than civil penalties, its own ideas and practices as rules of conduct on those who dissent from them; to fetter the development, and, if possible, prevent the formation of, any individuality not in harmony with its ways, and compel all characters to fashion themselves upon the model of its own" (*ibid*, p 9).

[4] *Ibid*, p 14.

harm, as well as that which actually causes harm.[5] Thus it may be used to justify the prohibition of conduct which is harmless in itself – such as having a knife in a public place – but which may make subsequent harm more likely.[6] The term "remote harm" is used to refer to behaviour which does not cause harm in itself, but which nonetheless creates an unacceptable risk of harm.[7] As Jeremy Horder has noted:

"One key justification for the criminal law is that, through the threat of punishment, it can deter conduct that either causes harm, in itself involves a risk of harm, or will lead to such a risk if it is left unpunishable. Clearly, this is only a starting point, because – to give just a few examples – many direct, victimising, harms do not warrant criminalisation, many risks of harm are too remote for the criminal law to be worth invoking in order to deter them, and even some vivid risks of harm are justifiably taken in everyday life."[8]

3.2   THE HARM PRINCIPLE APPLIED TO CRIMINAL LAW

3.2.1   The harm principle has been described as "the cornerstone of the liberal state's approach to criminalisation".[9] Mill did not, however, provide sufficient detail to make the principle a practical tool for the legislator; he did not describe the extent of the sphere of liberty, nor provide a clear definition of "harm".[10] Joel Feinberg has put some flesh on the principle's bones and his four-volume work, *The Moral Limits of the Criminal Law*,[11] comprises a detailed account of liberal political philosophy as applied to the criminal law. He proposed that:

"[I]t is legitimate for the state to prohibit conduct that causes serious private harm, or the unreasonable risk of such harm, or harm to important public institutions and practices. In short, state interference with a citizen's behavior

---

[5] See A P Simester and A von Hirsch, "Rethinking the offense principle" (2002) 8 *Legal Theory* 269.
[6] See the discussion of offensive weapons, from section 8.11.2 below.
[7] A von Hirsch, "Extending the harm principle: 'remote' harms and fair imputation", in A P Simester and A T H Smith (eds), *Harm and Culpability* (1996). For an excellent discussion of the issues raised by criminalising behaviours which do not cause harm, but merely the risk of harm, see Chapter 6 of R A Duff, *Answering for Crime: Responsibility and Liability in the Criminal Law* (2007).
[8] J Horder, "Bribery as a form of criminal wrongdoing" (2011) *LQR* 37 at 53–54.
[9] W Wilson, *Criminal Law: Doctrine and Theory* (4th edn, 2011) at p 37.
[10] As Gray has suggested: "If ... conceptions of harm, and in particular, judgements about the relative severity of harms, vary with different moral outlooks, then Mill's principle will be virtually useless as a guide to policy" (Gray (1991) at p xviii).
[11] J Feinberg, *The Moral Limits of the Criminal Law: Harm to Others* (1984); *The Moral Limits of the Criminal Law: Offense to Others* (1985); *The Moral Limits of the Criminal Law: Harm to Self* (1986); and *The Moral Limits of the Criminal Law: Harmless Wrongdoing* (1988).

tends to be morally justified when it is reasonably necessary (that is, when there are reasonable grounds for taking it to be necessary as well as effective) to prevent harm or the unreasonable risk of harm to parties other than the person interfered with".[12]

He defined "harm" as a serious setback to interests, the most important of which were "welfare interests",[13] defined as including good health; "at least minimal income and financial security"; and "a tolerable environment".[14] These interests were regarded by Feinberg as paramount, since their satisfaction was essential for individuals to lead their lives as they choose.[15] As well as being a setback to one's welfare interests, a harm must also be a "wrong", by which he meant a violation of a person's rights.[16] This is to ensure that legitimate setbacks to interest are not regarded as "harms" from the perspective of the criminal law. A person who is stabbed has suffered a setback to her interests, but if the wound was inflicted by someone who was acting in self-defence then the injured party has not been "wronged" (and so has not been "harmed" in a Feinbergian sense). In any competition, the losers may feel that they have sustained a setback to their interests but they have not been "wronged" so long as the competition was conducted fairly. A business may operate in such a way as to make its rivals unprofitable; a supermarket may sell some of its goods at a lower price than it paid for them to encourage consumers to shop there, and this may force its competitors out of business, but this is not generally regarded as the sort of "wrong" which ought to be proscribed by the criminal law. For Feinberg, criminal prohibitions are legitimate "only when they protect individual rights".[17] One has no "right" to win a competition, or for one's business ventures to thrive, hence no "wrong" (in Feinberg's terms) has occurred in such circumstances. This presupposes, of course, that society has made correct choices in decreeing some sorts of setbacks as legitimate and

---

[12] Feinberg (1984) at p 11. There are similarities here with the requirement under the ECHR that interference with Convention rights is permissible only where this is "necessary" and "proportionate".

[13] Feinberg (1984) at p 34.

[14] *Ibid*, p 37. See also pp 61–64.

[15] For a criticism of his approach, see A von Hirsch and N Jareborg, "Gauging criminal harm: a living-standard analysis" (1991) 11 *OJLS* 1.

[16] Feinberg (1984) at p 36. For a criticism of Feinberg for separating "setbacks to interest" from "wrongdoing", see R A Duff, "Harms and wrongs" (2001) 5 *Buff Crim LR* 13; and P Roberts, "Penal offence in question: some reference points for interdisciplinary conversation" in A von Hirsch and A P Simester, *Incivilities: Regulating Offensive Behaviour* (2006) 1 at 9. For the counter-argument (that Feinberg erred in not sufficiently separating the two), see H Stewart, "Harms, wrongs, and set-backs in Feinberg's *Moral Limits of the Criminal Law*" (2001) 5 *Buff Crim LR* 47.

[17] Feinberg (1984) at p 144.

others as illegitimate, and there is room for debate as to whether the criminal law has prioritised certain interests (for example, those of wealthy property owners) over the interests of others (the poorer sections of society).[18]

3.2.2   A legislature implementing Feinberg's thesis would require to consider both the magnitude of the harm and its probability: "the greater the probability of harm, the less grave the harm need be to justify [state] coercion; the greater the gravity of the envisioned harm, the less probable it need be".[19] Feinberg excludes from his definition of "harm" various unpleasant states of mind, such that one cannot complain of having being harmed merely because of being made to feel anxious or bored by another's behaviour.[20] Jean Hampton has offered a broader definition of "harm", namely as: "a disruption of or interference in a person's well-being, including damage to that person's body, psychological state, capacities to function, life plans, or resources over which we take this person to have an entitlement".[21] The reference to harm to a person's "psychological state" may allow offensive behaviours to be proscribed under Hampton's definition.[22] In similar vein, Victor Tadros has suggested that:

> "If harm is to be understood as a setback to one's interests or one's well-being, there is no good reason to exclude unpleasant feelings from the idea of harm. For unpleasant feelings erode well-being, and one has an interest in not experiencing them."[23]

3.2.3   For Feinberg, that certain behaviour posed a risk of harm and constituted a "wrong" were necessary but not sufficient criteria for proscribing it; other factors, such as the cost of enforcement, might cause a legislator to eschew the criminal sanction.[24] Nevertheless, the principle does not really serve as an adequate brake on the reach of the criminal law. It does not tell us how legislators ought to determine which "harms" are to be proscribed, and which tolerated. It tells us nothing about how likely, or

---

[18] See A Norrie, *Crime, Reason and History: A Critical Introduction to Criminal Law* (2001). See also P Hillyard, C Pantazis, S Tombs and D Gordon (eds), *Beyond Criminology: Taking Harm Seriously* (2004), in which it is argued that societies do not focus sufficiently on certain harms, such as environmental pollution, or workplace injuries and fatalities.

[19] Feinberg (1984) at p 191.

[20] *Ibid*, p 45.

[21] J Hampton, "Correcting harms versus righting wrongs: the goal of retribution" (1992) 39 *UCLA Law Review* 1659 at 1662. See also Feinberg (1985).

[22] The "offence principle" is discussed further from section 3.10 below.

[23] V Tadros, "Harm, sovereignty and prohibition" (2011) 17 *Legal Theory* 35 at 39.

[24] By this Feinberg meant the cost to the perpetrator, as well as to society.

how serious, the risk of harm requires to be before it should be the subject of a criminal sanction.[25] Feinberg recognised that before criminalising particular unwanted conduct, the legislator ought to be satisfied that the magnitude of harm and the likelihood of it occurring outweighed the social value of the conduct in question, and the extent of the interference with personal liberty that criminalisation would involve.[26] This formula is, however, easier to state than to apply. In practice, rather than being treated as a limitation on the criminal law ("behaviour should not be proscribed if it does not risk harm to others") the harm principle has become a component in arguments in favour of prohibitions ("any behaviour which offers a risk of harm to others is a suitable candidate for criminalisation"): quite the opposite of what Feinberg envisioned.[27] This makes it all the more important that a more sophisticated theory of criminalisation should be developed.

3.3 RELEVANT HARM

As Elizabeth Frazer and Nicola Lacey point out: 3.3.1

> "The harm principle is not, however, as determinate as it might appear at first sight. It is susceptible of various interpretations, depending on the conception of 'harm' adopted or, more fundamentally, on the relative weight attached to individual freedom and other deontological considerations on the one hand, and to utilitarian considerations on the other."[28]

What kinds of harms are in fact regarded as relevant by the criminal law? As espoused by Mill and Feinberg, the harm principle generally focuses exclusively on physical harms to one's person or property. Louis Schwartz has suggested that "citizens may legitimately demand of the state protection of their psychological as well as their physical integrity".[29] He claims that this would allow the criminal law to "ban loud noises, offensive odors, and tumultuous behavior disturbing the peace",[30] but psychological integrity is surely at risk only where the noise or odour was of an extreme intensity or lengthy

---

[25] See Wilson (2011) at pp 34–35.
[26] Feinberg (1984), Chapter 5.
[27] It has been suggested that the harm principle has been used in the USA to justify laws against prostitution, pornography, public drinking, drugs, loitering, and various homosexual and heterosexual behaviours: see B E Harcourt, "The collapse of the harm principle" (1999) 90 J Crim L and Criminol 109 at 139.
[28] E Frazer and N Lacey, The Politics of Community: A Feminist Critique of the Liberal–Communitarian Debate (1993) at p 47.
[29] L B Schwartz, "Morals offenses and the Model Penal Code" (1963) 63 Colum L Rev 669 at 671.
[30] Ibid.

duration, such that it causes physical harm, or at least a risk of such harm.[31] Schwartz concludes:

> "If, then, penal law frequently or typically protects us from psychic aggression, there is basis for the popular expectation that it will protect us also from blasphemy against a cherished religion, outrage to patriotic sentiments, blatant pornography, open lewdness affronting our sensibilities in the area of sexual mores, or stinging aspersions against race or nationality."[32]

Few liberals would advocate such a broad application of the harm principle, yet there are some items in Schwartz's list that people may favour criminalising, and indeed the law does currently proscribe some of these. For instance, "aspersions against race or nationality" can aggravate conduct which is itself a crime, independently of such disparaging remarks, and is a crime in its own right if it causes or is intended to cause alarm or distress – which takes us back to the harm principle.[33]

3.3.2	It could be suggested that the accused's behaviour ought to be a "social harm", that is, one that harms, or threatens to harm, society. This type of reasoning can be used to explain why breaking contracts, lying and adultery are not crimes. All do cause harm – some may cause serious harm – but they are regarded as not being harms *against society*. Of course, this is a somewhat circular argument. What we choose to label as a social harm becomes criminal, and what we label as a private harm does not, and we have already noted the potential injustice that can result from this public/private dichotomy.[34] Mill envisaged the relevant harms as being those affecting people, and even Schwartz's extended definition of "harm" fails to go beyond the protection of individuals. This has been criticised,[35] and we would suggest that harms to animals and to the environment ought to count here too, even when the harm caused to people might be minimal or non-existent. For example, if global warming results in the extinction of the polar bear, many people would consider this to be a "harm", even if the human race is not harmed as a result.

3.3.3	Laureen Snider has argued that the law focuses too much on harm by individuals, rather than by corporate entities:

> "crime and punishment have become a cultural obsession of modernity. But this obsession is one-sided. The harm that primarily powerless individuals do to themselves, their relatives and acquaintances, and occasionally to strangers

---

[31] Cf *R v Ireland*; *R v Burstow* [1998] AC 147, involving a prolonged campaign of silent telephone calls, leading to psychiatric illness.

[32] Schwartz (1963) at 672. The reference to "patriotic sentiments" may include the US flag-burning disputes. See section 1.19.3 above.

[33] Racially aggravated crimes are discussed further in section 7.9.1 below.

[34] See section 1.18 above.

[35] Duff (2007) at p 124.

is demonized, decried and exaggerated, while the harm that corporations do to their employees, communities, competitors and the environment is minimized, rationalized and denied".[36]

As we shall see when we look at corporate liability, the criminal law has tended to focus on individual, as opposed to corporate, wrongdoing.[37]

Iatrogenic injury – that is, illness caused by doctors, hospitals,   3.3.4 medical drugs or procedures – is but one example of the type of harm which is rarely recognised as being within the ambit of the criminal law. Many pharmaceutical products have been found to be extremely harmful, and some have become notorious because of the injuries they have caused.[38] In the 1960s, hundreds of babies whose mothers were given thalidomide, a drug designed to combat "morning sickness" during pregnancy, were born with incomplete limbs, or without limbs.[39] In the 1970s, diethylstilbestrol (DES) was prescribed for pregnant women to prevent miscarriages, but was ineffective at doing so. It caused a rare form of vaginal and cervical cancer in thousands of young women whose mothers had taken the drug decades earlier. Tranquillisers and oral contraceptives have been responsible for mass disasters. The Dalkon Shield intrauterine device was inserted in 4.5 million American women in the 1970s, 1 in 20 of whom became pregnant while using this form of contraceptive. The Shield caused pelvic inflammatory disease (an infection which damages women's reproductive capacity), spontaneous miscarriages and ectopic pregnancies.[40] Clearly, patients who consumed or used these products sustained great harm, yet the civil law of negligence is relied on to deal with such problems, rather than the criminal law.[41]

Of course, this is often because the harms caused were not the   3.3.5 result of any intention to injure on the part of the pharmaceutical

---

[36] L Snider, "Abusing corporate power: the death of a concept" in S C Boyd, D E Chunn and R Menzies, [Ab]using Power: The Canadian Experience (2001) at p 127, cited in Law Commission of Canada, What Is a Crime? Defining Criminal Conduct in Contemporary Society (2004) at p xi.

[37] See from section 18.5 below.

[38] See P R Ferguson, Drug Injuries and the Pursuit of Compensation (1996).

[39] For a detailed account, see H Teff and C R Munro, Thalidomide: the Legal Aftermath (1976).

[40] See M Mintz, At Any Cost: Corporate Greed, Women, and the Dalkon Shield (1985).

[41] Note that while Scots law does not recognise punitive or "exemplary" damages in delictual actions, these can be awarded in the United States. According to Lord Hope, "The function of the law of delict in Scotland is to ensure that if loss is caused by another person's wrongful act the loss will be compensated. ... It is not the function of the law of delict to exact anything more, and certainly not anything by way of punishment" (Watkins v Home Office and Others [2006] UKHL 17 at [31]).

manufacturers, nor even any reckless act on their part. The criminal law is rightly concerned with deliberate or, on occasion, recklessly caused harms, not merely negligent ones. Yet some pharmaceutical manufacturers have been grossly reckless, without attracting criminal liability. In the case of the Dalkon Shield, for example, the manufacturing company, A H Robins Co, learned at an early stage that its product was flawed and potentially dangerous. It could have fixed the problem at the cost of a few cents per device, but decided not to do so, since this would impact on its profit margins. Addressing the company's executives in a civil action against them, Chief Judge Miles Lord summarised the attitude of the company:

> "[N]one of you have [sic] faced [up to the fact that more than 9,000 women have made claims that they gave a part of their womanhood so that your company might prosper. ... If one poor young man were by some act of his, without authority or consent, to inflict such damage upon one woman, he would be jailed for a good portion of the rest [of] his life. And yet your company, without warning to women, invaded their bodies by the millions and caused them injuries by the thousands. And when the time came for these women to make their claims against your company, you attacked their characters, you inquired into their sexual practices and into the identity of their sex partners. You exposed these women and ruined families and reputations and careers in order to intimidate those who would raise their voices against you. You introduced issues that had no relationship whatsoever to the fact that you planted in the bodies of these women instruments of death, mutilation, and of disease."[42]

Thousands of women suffered serious harm, yet no criminal charges were brought against the company. It has been suggested that there is a gendered element to this; Lucinda Finley has noted that:

> "Too many of the most tragic and preventable instances of unsafe drugs and medical devices have been products used in women's bodies, often in connection with sexuality and reproduction."[43]

Robin West makes a more general point about the gendered nature of the law's approach to harms:

> "the harms, minimization of which is largely assumed to be in some way the 'point' of law, have for most of our history not included the harms suffered distinctively or disproportionately by women".[44]

---

[42] "The Dalkon Shield litigation: revised annotated reprimand by Chief Judge Miles W Lord" (1986) 9 *Hamline L Rev* 7 at 8–9.

[43] L M Finley, "The pharmaceutical industry and women's reproductive health: the perils of ignoring risk and blaming women" in E Szockyj and J G Fox (eds), *Corporate Victimization of Women* (1996) at p 59.

[44] R West, *Caring for Justice* (1999) at p 9.

3.4   SELF-HARM

As we have seen, the harm principle provides that only harm to **3.4.1**
others ought to be within the potential scope of the criminal law.
This precludes criminalisation of behaviours that harm only the actor
(the person engaging in the behaviour). Can this exclusion of self-
harm be justified? Douglas Husak offers a hypothetical example of
lawmaking in which a state decides to tackle the problem of obesity
by criminalising the consumption of doughnuts. In practice, it is more
likely that a state would criminalise the selling of doughnuts (harm
to others), rather than their consumption (self-harm), but Husak's
example postulates the latter. In either event, prohibiting the sale
of a product restricts the right of purchasers to buy that product.
According to Husak:

> "If we assume that the liberty to eat doughnuts is not especially valuable,
> the state should need only a minimal reason to dissuade persons from doing
> so. Clearly, the fact that doughnuts are unhealthy provides such a reason.
> This reason might justify *non*criminal means to discourage consumption –
> increased taxation, bans on advertising, educational programs, and the like.
> But the interests implicated by a *criminal* law against eating doughnuts are
> much more significant. Persons not only have an interest in eating doughnuts,
> but also have an interest in not being punished if and when they disregard the
> proscription. This latter interest is far more important than the former, and
> qualifies as a right. Even though the state may have a good enough reason to
> discourage the consumption of doughnuts, it may lack a good enough reason
> to subject those who persist in this conduct to the hard treatment and censure
> inherent in punishment." [45]

He concludes:

> "Thus the crucial question to be asked about my imaginary crime is not
> whether persons have a right to eat doughnuts. They do not. Instead, the
> crucial question is whether persons have a more complex right: a right not to
> be punished for eating doughnuts."[46]

To ask: "Does one have a right to eat doughnuts?" does sound
odd, even risible. But if we ask instead: "Assuming that it has been
acquired by legitimate means, does one have a right to choose which
food to consume?" then it becomes a more plausible question. We
suggest that people do have such a moral right, and indeed that they
have a legal right to do so.

If we think of a right as a legally protected choice, this means that **3.4.2**
A does no legal wrong by doing X, that no other person can acquire

[45] D Husak, *Overcriminalization: The Limits of the Criminal Law* (2008) at
p 102 (emphases in original).
[46] *Ibid.* See also D Husak, "The criminal law as last resort" (2004) 24 *OJLS* 207.

an interdict or injunction to prevent A from doing X,[47] and that there is no criminal sanction associated with the doing of X. Morally, it includes the proposition that no one ought to be able to prevent A from doing X, and that there ought not to be any criminal sanction associated with X. It would seem to follow from this (contrary to Husak's conclusion) that people do indeed have a right (morally and legally) to eat whatever food they please, including doughnuts. In Husak's example, however, a decision has been taken to label doughnuts as "unhealthy". Arguably, this is the case only if they are taken in an excessive amount, or if taken by someone who suffers from a contraindicated medical condition (for example, diabetes). Should the existence of such people prevent others from being able to eat a doughnut? Presumably the "unhealthiness" of doughnuts in Husak's example is intended to apply generally – in his hypothetical state, it has been decided that it is in no one's health interest to eat doughnuts, therefore their consumption ought to be proscribed. Husak's doughnut example makes clear that he, like Mill and Feinberg, would eschew use of the criminal sanction against those who risk harm only to themselves. In Mill's terms, a person

> "cannot rightfully be compelled to do or forebear because it will be better for him to do so, because it will make him happier, because, in the opinions of others, to do so would be wise or even right ... The only part of the conduct of anyone, for which he is amenable to society, is that which concerns others. In the part which merely concerns himself, his independence is, of right, absolute. Over himself, over his own body and mind, the individual is sovereign".[48]

3.4.3   This liberal stance means that the law ought not to criminalise the behaviours of mentally competent adults who choose to harm/risk harm to themselves, or who consent to others harming them.[49] As John Kleinig reminds us:

> "So far as the harm is concerned, there may not seem to be any significant difference whether it is inflicted upon another or upon oneself. And in one sense this is so. A broken leg is a broken leg. But the harm principle is not concerned with harm merely in the sense of damage. It is concerned with harm as an injury, a wrong. ... The person who endangers him- or herself does no wrong, violates no rights."[50]

---

[47] Interdicts (Scotland) and injunctions (England) are court orders, prohibiting a particular action.

[48] Mill (1859) at p 14.

[49] There may in fact be different considerations at stake in determining whether the criminal law has a legitimate role as between harming oneself, and consenting to the infliction of harm by another, and the two may need to be considered separately. This is a point which will be returned to later in the chapter – see from section 3.6 below.

[50] J Kleinig, *Paternalism* (1983), p 16.

It may, of course, be argued that doughnut eating *is* a harm to others, in so far as those others have to pay increased taxes, or find that their taxes are diverted from uses of which they approve to fund healthcare for diabetics and the obese. We return to this argument below.[51]

3.5   LEGAL PATERNALISM

In contrast to the liberal harm principle, "legal paternalism" is a   **3.5.1** philosophy which accepts that the state may sometimes be justified in protecting people from themselves, and that this may include using the criminal law to attempt to prevent conduct which harms no one other than the actor (that is, the person doing the act). Few people would doubt that there may be occasions on which paternalistic criminal laws are justified. Many criminal laws are designed to safeguard those who are vulnerable through ill health, mental deficiency or youth. Legislation which prevents children from purchasing alcohol is an example of this; the law is making the assumption that allowing children themselves to choose whether, when and/or how much alcohol to drink would be detrimental to them.[52] There is less enthusiasm for this type of legislation when it impacts on the choices of adults who are fully competent to determine their own best interests. As we previously noted,[53] those advocating the criminalisation of possession of "extreme pornography" attempted to justify this on the basis of the harm done to those who participate, not always consensually, in its making, as well as by trying to show that some of those who view such pornography are encouraged to emulate what they have seen, causing great harm to others.[54] At times, however, the arguments in favour of criminalisation seemed to focus on the moral harm such extreme images could cause to those who view the images – a paternalistic basis.[55]

For the advocate of liberalism, legal paternalism is an anathema;   **3.5.2** as Kleinig has put it: "Within liberal circles, paternalism is frequently considered a distasteful and insulting practice, without any redeeming features."[56] The very word "paternalism" has come

---

[51] See section 3.8.3 below.

[52] See the Licensing (Scotland) Act 2005 which provides a number of offences relating to the sale or consumption of alcohol by children (ss 102–109).

[53] See section 2.7.5 above.

[54] The offences relating to possession of extreme pornography are described in section 11.15.2 below.

[55] For a discussion of paternalism in relation to prohibitions on smoking, see P R Ferguson, "'Smoke gets in your eyes ...': the criminalisation of smoking in enclosed public places, the harm principle and the limits of the criminal sanction" (2011) 31 *Legal Studies* 259.

[56] Kleinig (1983) at p 4.

to be associated with negative connotations, since it implies that the state knows better what a person ought to do than the person him- or herself. Western democracies promote personal autonomy – the idea that individuals must decide for themselves how best to pursue their own interests. However, autonomy requires the individual to be in possession of relevant knowledge. Mill postulated the example of a person who is about to cross a bridge, unaware that the bridge is in poor condition and liable to collapse.[57] Is stopping such a person from using the bridge an act of paternalism, and therefore to be condemned? Mill's response is to point out that the pedestrian is unaware of the full facts and circumstances, thus the decision to cross the bridge was based on inadequate knowledge of the full ramifications of this. One who prevents the crossing, thereby infringing the pedestrian's right to cross the bridge, in order to tell the pedestrian about the condition of the bridge does not, therefore, act in an unjustifiably paternalistic manner; it enhances, rather than diminishes, people's autonomy to provide them with information about their future well-being which is relevant to their decision-making process. This type of interference is commonly called "soft" paternalism, though arguably it is not any kind of paternalism at all.[58] Crucially, of course, the person who is told about the poor condition of the bridge but who nonetheless decides to cross cannot, according to Mill, be restrained from doing so, since that *would* be an unwarranted interference with liberty. In contrast, advocates of "hard" paternalism believe that the state may be justified in criminalising particular behaviour solely on the grounds that it harms, or risks harm, to the actor herself; A is prohibited from doing X because the doing of X may harm A.

3.5.3   The harm principle seems at first blush to embody a strong anti-paternalistic stance, yet it may be suggested that there are in fact few forms of behaviour that are detrimental to the actor, alone. As Nigel Walker notes:

> "many of the types of behaviour which [John Stuart Mill] wished to protect against interference were not, in the long run, self-regarding after all. As our subsequent experience has emphasised, the drinker, the drug-user, the gambler are likely to cause suffering to their dependents, relatives, and friends and to become eventually a burden which society has to carry".[59]

If A drives without wearing a seat-belt, cycles without a helmet, or engages in dangerous mountain climbing, she risks her health (and possibly her life), and if this risk materialises she harms her family

---

[57] Mill (1859) at pp 106–107.
[58] See Feinberg (1986) at pp 12 *et seq.*
[59] N Walker, *Punishment, Danger and Stigma: The Morality of Criminal Justice* (1980) at p 9.

and also society, which has to expend resources on patching her up, rescuing her, or providing for her while she is unable to work. Were she to die, the state may have to bear the burden of looking after A's dependants.

Paternalistic legislation such as compulsory seat-belts in vehicles **3.5.4** and helmets for motor bike riders gives liberals cause for concern. Failure to wear a seat-belt or helmet is regarded as a relatively minor infraction of the law, and punishment is generally a small monetary fine. It should, however, be noted that not all paternalistic legislation results in a minor penalty. Possession of narcotic drugs is a contravention of the Misuse of Drugs Act 1971, the penalty for which can be high.[60] In respect of the seat-belt and helmet prohibitions, Feinberg accepted that the distress to third parties in witnessing accidents in which those flouting the law had been seriously injured could be regarded as a harm. So too could the cost to the state of healing injured passengers and cyclists, and the vicarious harm to their families. But where such costs are not sufficient to override the presumption in favour of liberty, then he concluded that criminal sanctions were not appropriate and that other options for reducing injury, such as education, licensing systems, or compulsory insurance for dangerous activities, ought to be preferred.[61]

3.6   CONSENSUAL HARM

For both the harm and offence principles, Feinberg emphasises that **3.6.1** no wrong is done to one who consents:

> "One can in fact be offended by conduct to which one has consented ... [A person] may quite voluntarily enter a pornographic cinema quite confident that the film he is about to see will disgust, embarrass, and annoy him, yet he will be willing to suffer that offense for the sake of curiosity, or for some other good reason of his own. The offended states induced by such voluntarily undertaken experiences are perfectly real, just as the broken bones incurred by the stunt motorcyclist are perfectly real harms, but in neither case can the victim complain of a grievance. In so far as they undertook the dangerous activity or the offensive experience voluntarily, they were not wronged by anyone."[62]

That the individual must have been wronged, and that no wrong is done to one who consents, is a key strand in Feinberg's argument:

---

[60] The maximum penalty for simple possession of a Class A drug when prosecuted on indictment is 7 years' imprisonment. See the Misuse of Drugs Act 1971, Sch 4. Drugs offences are described further from section 8.9 below.

[61] Feinberg (1986) at p 141.

[62] Feinberg (1985) at pp 32–33.

> "The harm principle will not justify the prohibition of consensual activities even when they are likely to harm the interests of the consenting parties; its aim is to prevent only those harms that are wrongs."[63]

Defining consensual harms as not being wrongs seems to beg the question; it is arguable that some forms of physical harms *are* wrongs, even where the harm has been done with the informed consent of the injured party. Ought the law to allow consent to operate in such a way that it prevents the behaviour being criminal? This would mean that the *actus reus* of assault ought to be defined as "causing or threatening injury to a person *without that person's consent*".[64] Alternatively, consent could operate as a defence, such that it is for the accused to raise this as an issue. Feinberg's analysis puts emphasis on the maxim *volenti non fit injuria* (no harm is done to one who consents to the injury or risk of injury). This maxim is frequently found in the civil law of delict. It does seem fair that if B has consented to A "interfering" with him (whether by touching, punching, stabbing him etc) then B ought not to be able to sue A for that very same behaviour. By the same token, it seems equally reasonable that a person who consents to running a risk of a particular injury cannot then seek compensation through the civil courts should that very injury become manifest. For example, if A is advised by the operator of an amusement park that 1 in 100 people who take part in bungee jumping suffer an injury to their backs, and A nonetheless decides to take part, her consent to do so does mean that she has no moral (nor ought she to have any legal) claim against the operator of the park should she suffer such an injury. The *volenti* defence allows people freedom of choice, while protecting others from being sued as a result of these choices.

3.6.2   The criminal law proscribes certain behaviour because of concerns that purported consent may not in fact be sufficiently informed to be treated as genuine, or that, even if informed, the alternatives open to the person consenting are so limited, or even non-existent, such that it would be unfair to treat their assent as freely given. A mother may well understand the risks involved in selling her kidney, but if her child is dying from hunger and this is the mother's sole option, the law might decide not to recognise the validity of any consent she gives to the surgery. As Belgian academic Koen Raes noted:

---

[63] Feinberg (1984) at pp 35–36.

[64] "*Actus reus*" means the prohibited behavioural element of a crime: see section 6.2.1 below. The prosecution would also have to establish the requisite *mens rea* or "mental element", ie that the accused intended to cause physical harm. See section 10.2.3 below.

"That informed consent is not always the final arbiter in defining 'personal boundaries' and 'harm to others' may nowadays be illustrated by the fact that sharp debates are going on about such issues as surrogate motherhood and organ donation on the one hand and about sado–masochism and midget-tossing 'between consenting adults' on the other. While in these former cases, the major reason for making reservations seems to be the presumption that inequalities in power may bias what is considered a 'fair' informed consent, the latter cases seem to presume some notion of 'human dignity'. Thus a Dutch court decided that whether midgets accepted their being tossed as objects in a game, was totally irrelevant: it is against human dignity to do this with human beings, in the same way as it is against human dignity to exploit or discriminate [against] them."[65]

Raes's point is that even where we are satisfied that consent is adequately informed *and* freely given, the criminal law may nevertheless be justified in refusing to recognise this consent as valid. While a liberal might respond, however, that "human dignity" is a notoriously illusive concept, which could easily become a front for paternalism,[66] dignity is an important concept; Karon Monaghan has argued that it prevents a "levelling down" – it rebuts the argument that there has been no discrimination if everyone is treated equally badly.[67]

The criminal law serves an altogether different function from the civil law. A criminal prosecution is not in the nature of a disagreement between two actors. Even if the injured party does not feel that she has been wronged by the person who caused the injury, this need not necessarily be determinative. If A deliberately stabs B in the arm, causing serious injury, but B says "Oh, I don't hold it against her. It doesn't matter to me", that may not necessarily be an end to the matter so far as the criminal law repercussions are concerned. The state may nevertheless decide that A has acted wrongfully, and deserves to be tried and punished for that wrong. This is particularly so in a system such as the Scottish one where it is for the prosecution to decide whether or not to pursue a criminal case, and the opinion of the victim is but one factor to be taken into account in determining whether or not the prosecution is justified as being "in the public interest".[68] Following Feinberg's example

3.6.3

---

[65] K Raes, "Legal moralism or paternalism? Tolerance or indifference? Egalitarian justice and the ethics of equal concern" in P Alldridge and C Brants (eds), *Personal Autonomy, the Private Sphere and Criminal Law* (2001) at p 32.

[66] Raes himself referred to notions of human dignity as "seriously flawed" which may "moralise and put under the control of the state lots of human activities" (*ibid*).

[67] K Monaghan, "Constitutionalising equality: new horizons" (2008) *EHRLR* 20 at 33. See also G Moon and R Allen, "Dignity discourse in discrimination law: a better route to equality?" (2006) *EHRLR* 610.

[68] The COPFS website states that "The public interest is at the heart of all we do as independent prosecutors". See: http://www.copfs.gov.uk/about-us/about-us, and section 1.10.1, n 69 above.

(above)[69] the stunt motorcyclist's broken bones are not something which the criminal law ought to try to prevent; Feinberg is correct in saying that no wrong *is done to someone*, either civilly or criminally, where that person is an adult of sound mind who undertakes a risky activity and is injured as a result. We might think stunt riders are foolish, and try to persuade them to refrain from trying to propel their motor bike over several double-decker buses, but they ought to be free to risk their own limbs, and indeed their lives, if they make free and informed choices to do so. The situation is arguably different where the risk B is taking involves the infliction of what would otherwise (were it not for B's consent) be regarded a wrongful behaviour *on the part of* A.[70]

3.7   CONSENSUAL HARMS AND THE COMMUNITY

3.7.1   Feinbergians would no doubt argue that what makes A's behaviour wrongful is that she breaches B's rights or, in Feinberg's terminology, "sets back" B's interests. Where B consents to this, and especially where B actively encourages A to do this, then there is no "wrong". A communitarian approach would view this as too narrow a description of what makes A's conduct "wrongful". To be sure, in the vast majority of cases, part at least of what makes us condemn/ wish to criminalise A's conduct is that she has set back B's interests. But it might also be suggested that A's behaviour is wrongful if it wrongs "us", the wider community. As previously noted, Sandra Marshall and Antony Duff have suggested that the criminal law should address the types of wrong which are "matters of public concern, and which therefore require a collective response from the whole community".[71] This idea of a crime being a wrong done to the community is explored by Marshall and Duff, using the crime of rape as an example:

> "Why should rape be a crime? We can agree that it should be socially proscribed and condemned. It is not a 'private' matter in which the community has no proper interest ... nor is the rape victim simply involved in a 'conflict' with her attacker, which they need to 'negotiate' and resolve: ... we should say that rape is a non-negotiable wrong which the community should declare to be so."[72]

---

[69] See section 3.6.1 above.

[70] In practice, Scots criminal law does not allow consent to be a defence to assault or murder, but it is an important aspect in the crime of rape, as will be discussed further below. See also from section 11.2.3 below.

[71] See section 1.9.2 above.

[72] S E Marshall and R A Duff, "Criminalization and sharing wrongs" (1998) 11 *Can J L & Jurisprudence* 7 at 18.

And later:

> "But why should rape be dealt with by a 'criminal' rather than by a 'civil' process? Why should rape not be defined simply as a civil wrong, so that it is for the victim to bring a case herself (if but only if she wishes) against her attacker? Part of the answer will be that the rapist should be punished, rather than being liable only to pay compensation to his victim – and we must ask why we should think that. But there is, we think, more to it than that; and that 'more' has to do with the *kind of interest the community as a whole should take in such wrongdoing* – with, we will argue, the sense in which the community should see the wrong done to her *as a wrong done to 'us'*."[73]

For present purposes, rape is a difficult crime to use, since it is at the **3.7.2** core of the wrong of rape that there is non-consensual intercourse, and we do not think of consensual intercourse as something which is intrinsically "wrongful".[74] We could think instead of the crime of assault: B is beaten up by A and sustains a broken arm and leg as a result. What if B reflected on the ordeal and decided that she had not been wronged? Perhaps she believes in a form of fatalism ("what will be will be"), or reasons that the experience was her own fault, because she looked at A the wrong way, or walked home using the "wrong" route. None of this is intended to suggest that in reality anyone would take this approach, far less that anyone *should* do so (though it is not in fact uncommon for battered women to rationalise their partners' conduct by blaming themselves for the beating, for having cooked a "poor meal" or failing to tidy the house "well enough"). But were a victim to feel that no wrong had been done to her (for whatever reason) does this mean that we, the community, should concur in this assessment? Would we not feel that the attacker nonetheless deserved to be prosecuted and punished, for having done wrong? Crimes, therefore, ought to involve public wrongs, but only in this limited sense – as wrongs which require a response from society, rather than being left to the individual to deal with as a private matter (by social conventions), or a private *law* matter (that is, a matter for the civil law).[75]

It is possible to agree with Feinberg's view that the criminal law **3.7.3** sanction ought to be applied to conduct that is (a) wrongful and (b) harmful, but to insist that what makes conduct wrongful is

---

[73] Marshall and Duff (1998) (emphases added). See also R A Duff and S E Marshall, "Public and private wrongs" in J Chalmers, F Leverick and L Farmer (eds), *Essays in Criminal Law in Honour of Sir Gerald Gordon* (2010) 70 at 71–72.

[74] See, however, M M Dempsey and J Herring, "Why sexual penetration requires justification" (2007) 27 *OJLS* 467. Andrea Dworkin and Catharine MacKinnon also view heterosexual intercourse as intrinsically diminishing of women, and disempowering – see, for example, A Dworkin, *Intercourse* (1987), pp 141–142, and C A MacKinnon, *Toward a Feminist Theory of the State* (1991), p 175.

[75] Marshall and Duff (1998) at p 11.

either that it sets back the interests of an identifiable individual or individuals, or that it sets back the interests of the community. It is not merely that the community has an interest in the well-being of each of its members, and is wronged when they are harmed in certain ways.[76] A communitarian approach suggests that society has an interest in upholding standards of appropriate behaviour. In relation to the notorious English law sado–masochism case of *R v Brown*[77] it might be argued that the criminal law's interest in this type of behaviour is not in the masochists, who are at liberty to self-injure if they wish to do so, but in the sadists, who wrong the community when they inflict injury on others, *even where these others have consented.*[78]

3.8   REHABILITATION OF LEGAL PATERNALISM

3.8.1   Liberalism portrays the legal paternalist as keen to seize any opportunity to enact new criminal prohibitions. As we have already noted, paternalism is the justification for road traffic legislation which requires motor-bikers to wear helmets and car drivers and passengers to wear seat-belts.[79] Having criticised such types of legislation, Jonathan Schonsheck states:

> "[The] arguments by Legal Paternalists … go something like this: 'Laws which mandate the use of motorcycle helmets and seat belts are justified. Furthermore, these laws are paternalistic laws. So some paternalistic laws are justified. A fortiori, Legal Paternalism is an acceptable 'liberty-limiting principle' … and pure Liberalism – defined as acceptance of the Harm Principle and the Offense Principle only – is untenable.' Any liberal of intelligence and good character, the argument continues, must countenance *some* paternalistic laws. And once some paternalistic laws are acknowledged as justified, why not some *others*: why not _____, and _____, and also _____? Once the dam against paternalism has been breached it becomes ever more difficult to staunch the flow of yet more paternalism."[80]

---

[76] See also G Lamond, "What is a crime?"(2007) 27 *OJLS* 609.

[77] [1994] 1 AC 212.

[78] This is in contrast to the position adopted by the Scottish Law Commission in its approach to sado–masochistic sexual offences: see *Report on Rape and Other Sexual Offences* (Scot Law Com No 209, 2007), recommendation 57. The characterisation of sado–masochistic practices as sexual rather than violent in nature is discussed in L Bibbings and P Alldridge, "Sexual expression, body alteration, and the defence of consent" (1993) 20 *J Law and Society* 356; and N Bamforth, "Sado–masochism and consent" [1994] *Crim LR* 661.

[79] The Automobile Association estimated in 2010 that seat-belts are worn by 95% of drivers and 88% of adult rear-seat passengers: *"Clunk Click": The AA Seat Belt Report*, pp 5–6, available at: http://www.theaa.com/public_affairs/reports/aa-seat-belt-report.pdf.

[80] J Schonsheck, *On Criminalization: An Essay in the Philosophy of the Criminal Law* (1994), p 107 (emphases in original).

Thus the legal paternalist is portrayed as an over-zealous legislator, champing at the bit, desperate for the opportunity to curb our freedoms.[81] As against this, it may be suggested that it is possible for someone to favour liberalism as a starting point, but nevertheless (and with some reluctance) to accept the pragmatic benefits of legal paternalism in some limited situations. Such a theorist might even insist that criminalisation should not be considered until it is demonstrated that there is no feasible alternative. The legal paternalist may be envisioned as a reluctant paternalist, rather than Schonsheck and Feinberg's "gung ho" caricature.[82]

Let us take Schonsheck's example of motor bike helmets and seat-belt laws.[83] The arguments he makes against criminalising the failure to wear either helmets or seat-belts are broadly similar and can be treated as one. Schonsheck, like Feinberg before him,[84] ultimately concludes that the liberal position should triumph in the seat-belt/helmet argument, and that such laws are not therefore justified. The liberal starting point is that competent adults ought to have the freedom to decide for themselves whether or not to wear a helmet or seat-belt,[85] and that interference with this freedom is permissible only if this can be justified by the harm principle. It must be remembered that, for liberalism, the harm principle permits criminalisation only where the conduct in question poses harm to *other people*. In fact, there is now good evidence that the failure by back-seat passengers to wear seat-belts increases the risks of injury and death to those travelling in the front seat.[86] Schonsheck does

3.8.2

---

[81] In similar vein, in discussing the legitimacy of seat-belt and motorbike helmet laws, Joel Feinberg stresses the importance of not conceding "the game" to the legal paternalist "thereby giving him encouragement to use his principle to justify criminal penalties for other forms of self-regarding risk-taking, from cigarette smoking to surfing" (Feinberg (1986) at p 136).

[82] Even Feinberg points out that paternalism "is a label that might have been invented by paternalism's enemies" (*ibid*, p 4).

[83] Schonsheck (1994) at pp 109 *et seq*.

[84] Feinberg (1986) at p 141.

[85] The arguments employed in the seat-belt legislation debate are similar to those involving the criminalisation of failing to wear a motorbike helmet. But note that Schonsheck suggests that, while there is clear evidence that the wearing of seat-belts saves lives and prevents more injuries than travelling without a seat-belt, he is less convinced that the wearing of a motorbike helmet is necessarily a better option for the biker, suggesting that while it leads to fewer fatalities and less serious injury in the event of a collision, the wearing of a helmet may in fact make a collision more likely: Schonsheck (1994) at pp 132–134.

[86] One study has estimated that front-seat passengers who wear their seat-belts have a five-fold risk of death when passengers in the back seats fail to wear seat-belts. See M Ichikawa, S Nakahara and S Wakai, "Mortality of front-seat occupants attributable to unbelted rear-seat passengers in car crashes" (2002) 359 *The Lancet* 43.

not mention this point, so we shall leave that aside and assume that the debate concerns the wearing of seat-belts by drivers or front-seat passengers. Clearly, the harm at issue here is primarily that caused to the person who fails to wear a seat-belt or helmet. One might suppose that this would be an end to the matter; such laws are paternalistic and therefore not justified. However, given the amount of attention paid to this topic in the literature, perhaps some liberals have, at the least, a gut sense that we ought to require the wearing of these protective devices. Or perhaps they are trying to find a justification for the fact that so many jurisdictions have these types of laws.

3.8.3   In searching for some rationale for criminalisation, liberals have argued that failing to wear a seat-belt can in fact result in harm to other people. Some critics, such as Mary Ann Glendon, believe that the seat-belt/motorcycle helmet issue results from an overemphasis on the "rights" of the individual, and a correspondingly under-appreciation of the community. Hence Glendon has argued that:

> "those who contest the legitimacy of mandatory automobile seat-belt or motorcycle-helmet laws frequently say: 'It's my body and I have the right to do as I please with it.' In this shibboleth, the old horse of property is harnessed to the service of an unlimited liberty. The implication is that no one else is affected by my exercise of the individual right in question. This way of thinking and speaking ignores the fact that it is a rare driver, passenger, or biker who does not have a child, or a spouse, or a parent. It glosses over the likelihood that if the rights-bearer comes to grief, the cost of his medical treatment, or rehabilitation, or long-term care will be spread among many others. The independent individualist, helmetless and free on the open road, becomes the most dependent of individuals in the spinal injury ward".[87]

Mill, it seems, would not have accepted that such harms to society could satisfy his harm principle:

> "But with regard to the merely contingent, or, as it may be called, constructive injury which a person causes to society, by conduct which neither violates any specific duty to the public, nor occasions perceptible hurt to any assignable individual except himself; the inconvenience is one which society can afford to bear, for the sake of the greater good of human freedom. If grown persons are to be punished for not taking proper care of themselves, I would rather it were for their own sake, than under pretence of preventing them from impairing their capacity of rendering to society benefits which society does not pretend it has a right to exact."[88]

It must, however, be borne in mind that Mill was writing in an era in which there was no National Health Service, nor much in the way

---

[87] M A Glendon, *Rights Talk: The Impoverishment of Political Discourse* (1991), pp 45–46. See also Schonsheck (1994) at p 111 and Feinberg (1986) at p 138.
[88] Mill (1859) at p 91.

of a social security system. The burden to society is arguably greater in the modern world. Modern liberals who want to argue in favour of such laws do so by interpreting the "harm (to others) principle" broadly, so that it includes wider social harms. This approach was adopted by the Federal District Court of Massachusetts in the case of *Siman v Sargeant*:[89]

> "While we agree with plaintiff that [the legislation's] only realistic purpose is the prevention of head injuries incurred in motorcycle mishaps, we cannot agree that the consequences of such injuries are limited to the individual who sustains the injury ... The public has an interest in minimizing the resources directly involved. From the moment of the injury, society picks the person up off the highway, delivers him to a municipal hospital and municipal doctors; provides him with unemployment compensation if, after recovery, he cannot replace his lost job, and, if the injury causes permanent disability, may assume the responsibility for his and his family's subsistence. We do not understand a state of mind that permits plaintiff to think that only he himself is concerned."[90]

As Schonsheck explains, since the point of the exercise for the liberal is to reduce the financial harm caused to society by the increased injuries and deaths of those who fail to wear their seat-belts, the problem can be solved without recourse to the criminal law, simply by the requirement that those who wish to travel without a seat-belt buy additional insurance. This "special" insurance scheme would provide financial compensation to those injured while travelling without a seat-belt – but the cost would be borne only by those who opted for this freedom, not by the rest of us who would "belt up" even without it being required by the criminal law. Such an arrangement "would enhance liberty while financially protecting others from the harmful consequences of the exercise of that liberty".[91] Schonsheck does have to deal with the person who cheats the system – the individual who does not buy the special insurance, but who nonetheless drives without a seat-belt or helmet and sustains injuries. He proposes that such people be given medical care, despite their lack of insurance, in the same way that uninsured drivers are compensated by everyone else's insurance, at present. Feinberg also wrestled with the problem of what to do about the injured biker who has failed to take out extra insurance,[92] and whether we would then need to make it a crime to fail to wear a helmet without having acquired such insurance. After all, Feinberg says, it is *"unthinkable* that we leave the reckless,

3.8.4

---

[89] 346 F Supp 277 at 279 (1972, Mass); affirmed 409 US 1020 (1972).
[90] Cited in Kleinig (1983) at pp 92–93.
[91] Schonsheck (1994) at p 115.
[92] Feinberg (1986) at pp 139–140.

bareheaded, young motorcyclist to die in his own pool of blood because he has not contributed to the costs of his own care".[93] Schonsheck too is anxious to stress that liberalism "is perfectly consistent with compassion":

> "The liberal is not compelled by consistency to abandon [uninsured, road traffic] victims in the street. The liberal can wholeheartedly support the care of victims; insurance programs can be implemented to indemnify other motorists, and the state."[94]

3.8.5 Superficially, this seems like a reasonable solution: liberalism wants to minimise harm to others; the compulsory insurance scheme provides this. However, the proposal is a satisfactory one only if we accept that the harm we are trying to prevent is indeed the financial cost to society. But surely this is not what lies behind our seat-belt and helmet laws. It seems almost obscene to suggest that the major problem with people failing to wear seat-belts/motor bike helmets is that when they sustain horrific injuries or are killed in a traffic accident we as a society have to fork out our hard-earned cash to the taxman to pay for medical costs, or support the bereaved families. The provision of a "special" insurance fund does not, of course, stop the horrific injuries and deaths from occurring; it merely shifts the cost of the injuries from the careful majority to the more reckless/freedom-loving minority. The liberal may not be accused of abandoning the dying or seriously injured biker in the street, but has arguably abandoned her at an earlier stage, at the stage of trying to prevent the injuries from occurring in the first place.

3.9   BEHIND THE VEIL OF IGNORANCE

3.9.1 John Rawls's *A Theory of Justice*[95] has been described as "the paradigm statement of contemporary liberal theory" because it

> "contains both of the two components which standardly go together as the liberal package: the commitment to the freedom of the individual embodied in the standard liberal support for civil liberties, and that belief in equality of opportunity and a more egalitarian distribution of resources than would result from the market alone which leads to support for a redistributive welfare state".[96]

---

[93] Feinberg (1986), p 140 (emphasis in original).
[94] Schonsheck (1994) at p 141.
[95] (1971). See also J Rawls, *Justice as Fairness: A Restatement* (2001).
[96] S Mulhall and A Swift, *Liberals and Communitarians* (1st edn, 1992), preface at p vii.

Rawls developed a thought experiment whereby citizens representing different social classes are placed behind a "veil of ignorance"[97] in order to facilitate the making of decisions that affect themselves and others in an impartial manner. Rawls invites us to imagine that such a person is unaware of

> "his place in society, his class position or social status, ... his fortune in the distribution of natural assets and abilities, his intelligence and strength, and the like ... his conception of the good, the particulars of his rational plan of life, or even the special features of his psychology".[98]

From behind this veil of ignorance, the self is able to choose principles which will shape society. Although Rawls did not attempt to apply his theory in order to predict what sorts of criminal law people would choose from behind the veil, he did conclude that they would agree that: "Each person is to have an equal right to the most extensive total system of equal basic liberties compatible with a similar system of liberty for all."[99] But is this necessarily so? Although ignorant of their own psychological make-up, including whether they are risk-takers or are risk averse, Rawlsian citizens do have information about human psychology, hence they must be supposed to be aware of the propensity for some people to put greater store on "looking cool" than on protecting their health and lives. Such people are likely to underestimate the risk of death associated with not wearing motor bike helmets, for instance. Behind a veil of ignorance, might people want to build in safeguards, to try to protect themselves from their own poor choices? Communitarians have criticised Rawls on the basis that his emphasis on individual liberties "reveals a mistaken prioritization of individuals over their communities".[100] Critics have pointed out that the person in the original position is not really a gender-neutral apolitical figure:

> "If in fact the notion of a completely disembodied, degendered, yet choosing subject is incoherent or vacuous, then the choices represented as being made by such subjects must in fact reflect the judgements of some other

---

[97] Rawls (1971) at pp 12 and 136. People behind the veil of ignorance are also referred to by Rawls as being in the "original position" (*ibid*, p 120) but it should be noted that he was not claiming that this position has ever existed, as a historical fact.

[98] *Ibid*, p 137. For a critique, see "Justice as fairness: for whom?" in S M Okin, *Justice, Gender, and the Family* (1989) at pp 89–109.

[99] Rawls (1971), p 302.

[100] Mulhall and Swift (1992) at p xi. See also A Finlayson, *Contemporary Political Thought: A Reader and Guide* (2003): "Communitarian philosophers wonder how the self can be said to exist prior to or outside social settings and communal attachments. Surely, it is the latter that create the possibility of a self which develops preferences and goals" (p 247).

kind of being – an embodied, gendered and otherwise socially situated being".[101]

3.9.2 Nonetheless, this concept of choosing from behind a veil of ignorance may assist us further in our assessment of legal paternalism. It might be suggested that what motivates the legal paternalist is not a desire to curb other people's freedom for its own sake, but rather is a concern for other human beings. At its basis, the clash between liberalism and paternalism is based on different visions of the sort of society we wish to live in. The liberal paints a picture of a society in which the "sphere of individual liberty", so beloved of Mill, is maximised. People have the freedom to choose the sort of lives they lead, the activities that give them most happiness, the paths they wish to follow, free from state interference, with the only limitation being that they must refrain from harming or offending others. What could be better than this utopia? But would this be utopian? The legal paternalist's vision is for a more compassionate, caring society. Concern for other human beings leads the paternalist to suggest that there is a fatal flaw in the liberal approach: the fundamental premise on which liberalism is based is that individuals are competent, rational beings, all equally capable of determining where their best interests lie.

3.9.3 Schonsheck puts forward some reasons why a biker, fully aware of the risks associated with not wearing a helmet, may nonetheless make an informed choice to decline to do so:

> "convenience, a sense of freedom, romantic symbolism, adventurous life style ... including ... image and self image. For any given individual, personal safety may or may not be the decisive consideration. For any given individual, appearance or pleasure may take precedence over safety".[102]

He concludes that the state is not justified "in compelling competent adults to exalt one value over all others, to exalt safety over the values of pleasure, image and self-image".[103] There seem to be two fallacies in this. Schonsheck points out in his introductory chapter that legal theorists frequently make an "assumption of compliance", that is, they assume (without empirical evidence) "that the reaction of citizens to new criminal legislation will be *compliance*".[104] As he rightly states, "the enactment of a criminal law does not, strictly speaking, 'prevent' people from electing [to do] the proscribed activity".[105] Yet he makes a similar error when he suggests that the

---

[101] Frazer and Lacey (1993) at p 55.
[102] Schonsheck (1994) at p 136. See also Feinberg (1986) at p 141.
[103] Schonsheck (1994) at p 136.
[104] *Ibid* at p 8 (emphasis in original).
[105] *Ibid* at p 9.

criminalisation of helmet-less biking "compels" anything. This is not merely a pedantic point; it should be borne in mind that the biker who is determined to exercise her freedom to ride without a helmet can continue to do so even after helmet legislation is enacted – she may periodically have to pay a fine as a result, but she cannot be *forced* to wear the helmet. At most, the criminalisation of helmet-less biking is an attempt by society to try to persuade bikers to exalt safety.

The second fallacy, it may be suggested, is the idea that it is a matter of chance whether "any given individual" will favour safety over freedom, romantic symbolism etc. For example, younger people may have less experience on which to base their assessment of risk.[106] Liberalism's benchmark is the competent adult, and the assumption is made is that all are equally competent: they may have different preferences, value some activities more than others, choose different lifestyles and follow different life plans, but, at base, they are all equally competent. This is clearly not the case. As Kleinig has stated:

3.9.4

> "Were the choices people make always their best choices, the product of settled preferences and cool reflection on alternatives, it would be difficult to justify the intrusions of others. But they are often stupid and ill-considered, the outcome of temporary concerns or a lackadaisical attitude. What is stubbornly insisted upon today is regretted tomorrow: 'If only I had listened.'"[107]

Furthermore,

> "Our lives do not always display the cohesion and maturity of purpose that exemplifies the liberal idea of individuality, but instead manifest a carelessness, unreflectiveness, short-sightedness, or foolishness that not only does us no credit but also represents a departure from some of our own more permanent and central commitments and dispositions. That is characteristic of the self-regarding vices, and most of us are prey to some. On many occasions, the consequences of such lapses and deviations will not be serious, and we must wear them as best we can. But sometimes because of our actions, consequences of a more catastrophic kind may become inevitable or considerably more probable, consequences that would be quite disproportionate to the conduct's value for us. This we may fail to appreciate, not because we are incapable of it, but because of our lack of discipline, our impulsiveness, or our tendency to rationalize the risks involved. It would not take much to act more prudently, yet we are inclined to negligence."[108]

---

[106] Kleinig quotes an ice hockey player: "It's foolish not to wear a helmet. But I don't – because the other group don't. I know that's silly, but most of the players feel the same way. If the league made us do it, though, we'd all wear them and nobody would mind" (Kleinig (1983) at p 85).

[107] *Ibid*, p 45.

[108] *Ibid*, pp 67–68.

Both the liberal and the legal paternalist would agree that the criminal law should be employed only when it seems that other mechanisms for dissuading citizens from engaging in the conduct have little chance of success. Where, however, the potential harm is great (such as a risk of death or serious bodily injury) and the liberty being sacrificed is by comparison a minor one (such as the inconvenience of wearing a seat-belt) then paternalists would argue that criminal laws may be justified.[109] Let us suppose that, instead of employing the criminal sanction, the state put resources into alerting people to the dangers of driving without seat-belts or helmets, and let us further suppose that this had the desired effect of reducing injury and death to an appropriate level[110] or to the same level as could be achieved by the criminal law prohibition. Neither the liberal nor the paternalist would opt for criminalisation, in these circumstances. Unfortunately, where education and persuasion fail to have the desired impact, criminal prohibition may be the only method left to the state.

3.10   OFFENCE TO OTHERS

3.10.1   However broadly "harm" is defined, it can be argued that the liberal focus on this as the sole justification for criminalising conduct is too narrow. According to Mill

> "there are many acts which, being directly injurious only to the agents themselves, ought not to be legally interdicted, but which, if done publicly, are a *violation of good manners* and, coming thus within the category of offences against others, may rightfully be prohibited".[111]

This seems to go against his general thesis that harm or the threat of harm ought to be the sole liberty-limiting principle. Feinberg also considered an "offence principle":

> "It is always a good reason in support of a proposed criminal prohibition that it would probably be an effective way of preventing serious offense (as opposed to injury or harm) to persons other than the actor, and that it is probably a necessary means to that end."[112]

---

[109] See B Barry, *Justice as Impartiality* (1995), p 87.

[110] Of course, no level of fatalities or injuries can really be described as "acceptable", but, realistically, neither an educational programme nor the criminal sanction is able to reduce the incidence of injuries to zero. What is at issue is which of the two methods produces fewer injuries.

[111] Mill (1859) at pp 108–109 (emphasis added).

[112] Feinberg (1985) at p 1. See also Packer's view that the criminal law should proscribe conduct that gives, or is likely to give, offence to innocent bystanders: H L Packer, *The Limits of the Criminal Sanction* (1969) at p 306.

He described offensive behaviour as that which gives rise to disliked mental states in on-lookers. As with the harm principle, his offence principle applies only to wrongful (that is, rights-violating) conduct.[113]

Feinberg offers a thought experiment in which the reader is invited   **3.10.2** to imagine that she is on a bus journey, during which a passenger engages in a series of behaviours which might be regarded as highly offensive.[114] That the reader is on a bus is important – it emphasises Feinberg's view that the criminal law can only ever be concerned with offensive behaviour which occurs in public, not with behaviour committed in private. This is also the view of John Tasioulas:

> "the space in which the offending behaviour is experienced must be public rather than private, that is, a domain in which the community as a whole has a substantial interest in regulating ... the nature of what might be experienced".[115]

We criticised the public/private distinction in Chapter 1.[116] What other people do in private *can*, of course, cause offence; the knowledge that someone is fornicating with an animal, engaging the services of a prostitute, or attempting to have sex with a bicycle[117] may all deeply offend a given individual, even though she does not directly experience any offence to her senses – she neither sees nor hears these activities. However, as H L A Hart argued, "bare knowledge" of offensive behaviour by others should not be regarded as an adequate basis on which to criminalise that behaviour:

> "[A] right to be protected from the distress which is inseparable from the bare knowledge that others are acting in ways you think wrong, cannot be acknowledged by anyone who recognises individual liberty as a value ... If distress incident to the belief that others are doing wrong is harm, so also is the distress incident to the belief that others are doing what you do not want them to do. To punish people for causing this form of distress would be tantamount to punishing them simply because others object to what they do; and the only liberty that could coexist with this extension of the utilitarian principle is liberty to do those things to which no one seriously objects."[118]

In contrast to offence deriving from bare knowledge, Feinberg's bus   **3.10.3** passenger is actually present when the offensive activities are taking place, and has not consented to witnessing them. She cannot readily remove herself from the scene, or at least not without an unreasonable degree of inconvenience. The types of behaviour witnessed on the bus journey are subdivided into "affronts to the senses" (seeing, hearing

---

[113] See section 3.2.1 above.
[114] Feinberg (1985) at pp 10 *et seq*.
[115] J Tasioulas, "Crimes of offence" in von Hirsch and Simester (2006) at p 151.
[116] See from section 1.18.1 above.
[117] See sections 1.1.1 above and 15.2.7 below.
[118] H L A Hart, *Law, Liberty and Morality* (1966), pp 46–47.

or smelling); "disgust and revulsion" (behaviour that literally sickens the rider); "shock to moral, religious or patriotic sensibilities"; "shame, embarrassment and anxiety" (mainly concerning nudity and fornication); and "fear, resentment, humiliation and anger". In determining what offensive behaviours ought to be criminalised, Feinberg suggests that consideration be given to factors such as the seriousness of the offence, which includes its magnitude (intensity, duration and extent) and how readily one could avoid being exposed to it.[119]

3.10.4   The legal principle of *volenti non fit injuria* – that no wrong is done to one who consents – is pressed into service here, such that no offence is caused to those who have consented to being exposed to the behaviour in question.[120] Once the seriousness of the offence has been determined, this must be balanced against the reasonableness of the behaviour which happens to have caused offence, and here consideration must be given to the social importance of the conduct; how important it is to the actor; the importance of allowing freedom of expression; the extent to which it could have been done elsewhere (for example, in private); the nature of the locality in which it occurs (the type of neighbourhood); and whether the behaviour was motivated by spite or malice.[121] The matter is not to be decided by the subjective reaction of any particular person, who may be abnormally susceptible to taking offence. For Feinberg, if the behaviour in question is offensive to almost everyone, that in itself is an adequate reason for proscribing it, despite the fact that people may be unable to articulate a rational basis for their sense of "offendedness":

> "Provided that very real and intense offense is taken predictably by virtually everyone, and the offending conduct has hardly any countervailing personal or social value of its own, prohibition seems reasonable even when the protected sensibilities are not."[122]

Feinberg's test for criminalising conduct on the grounds of offensiveness seems to correspond to liberal ideals – it targets only behaviours that almost everyone would find offensive, the conduct must be committed in public, and factors such as the importance of the conduct to the offender's way of life, and the opportunities for alternative behaviours, must all be considered. However, while this may have appeared liberal in the 1980s when Feinberg was writing, society in the 21st century is less tolerant of some forms of conduct. As Andrew von Hirsch suggests, relatively innocuous activities such

---

[119] Feinberg (1985) at pp 34–35.
[120] See the earlier discussion of the *volenti* principle in section 3.6.1 above.
[121] Feinberg (1985) at p 44.
[122] *Ibid* at p 36.

as begging, or being homeless and living on the street, may well cause general irritation, and Feinberg's theory offers little succour to those who would argue against their criminalisation.[123] Von Hirsch has proposed that "offensiveness" is too broad a criterion for criminalisation, and that we focus instead on behaviours which cause offence in specific ways, such as by amounting to "(1) affronts to privacy, (2) insult, and (3) unfair pre-emption of others' options concerning the use of shared public facilities and space".[124] This is a valuable contribution to the debate, drawing attention to the ulterior reasons for classifying certain behaviours as "offensive". We would, however, argue that the inclusion of behaviours which "insult" others is itself quite a broad criterion, and we are not persuaded that it is an appropriate basis for criminalisation. Circumstances where it might appear useful, such as, for example, in relation to offences aggravated by racial hatred, are sufficiently serious that they could be said to constitute "harm". The third of von Hirsch's suggestions does cover activities which the harm principle would not, or at least not unless "harm" is given a very broad interpretation indeed. There are many behaviours, such as playing loud music on a train or in the park, or the dropping of litter on the street, which cannot easily be described as harms, but which do impact adversely on others. We suggest that the offence principle, as refined by von Hirsch, does merit consideration as a criterion for criminalisation.

3.11 CONCLUSIONS

It would be convenient if there were just one principle against **3.11.1** which we could judge the criminal law, or any proposal to add to its prohibitions, but the idea that the harm principle ought to be the sole criterion to be employed seems to us to be untenable.[125] As we have seen, it is unattractive for those who reject the liberal exaltation of the atomistic individual:

> "Buried deep in our rights dialect is an unexpressed premise that we roam at large in a land of strangers, where we presumptively have no obligation towards others except to avoid the active infliction of harm."[126]

---

[123] A von Hirsch, "The offence principle in criminal law: affront to sensibility or wrongdoing?" (2000) 11 *KCLJ* 78 at 82. Paul Roberts cautions that it might actually be "socially beneficial and healthy for personal growth and well-being" to be offended, on occasion: see Roberts (2006) at p 19.

[124] Von Hirsch (2000) at p 88.

[125] For a critique of the "grand theory" of criminal law – the notion that there could be "a unitary, all-embracing, normative account of *the* function or purpose of a system ... of criminal law", see R A Duff, "Theorizing criminal law: a 25th anniversary essay" (2005) 25 *OJLS* 353 at 356 (emphasis in original).

[126] Glendon (1991) at p 77.

It may be suggested that the criminal law ought not to be confined
to preventing harm to others; there are other values and interests of
concern to society, and it may sometimes be appropriate to employ
the criminal sanction to safeguard these interests, even where no
"harm" in the Feinbergian sense has been caused or threatened to
others. Drawing together the discussions in Chapters 2 and 3, we
see that there is little consensus as to the proper subject-matter of
the criminal law: should we criminalise incest, bestiality, assisted
suicide, sado–masochistic behaviour, gambling, prostitution, the
sale or possession of narcotics or pornography ("extreme" or
otherwise)? Even if there were agreement that the criminal law
ought to target "wrongs" and/or "harms", there would remain
disagreement over what should count as a wrong or harm. Perhaps
the best we can come up with is a number of principles – some
of which may conflict in any given case. While the prevention of
harm to other people has a strong claim as a limiting principle, the
criminal law may, on occasion, take a paternalistic stance, whether
to prevent its citizens from self-harm, or from harming others, even
with their consent. Ofer Raban argues that liberalism ought to be
the dominant approach, but concedes that other considerations may
impose limits on this.[127] Thus "liberalism requires that any state
regulation of the private sphere be justified either as (1) creating a
free personal sphere where individuals pursue their personal well-
being free from coercion by others"[128] (thus justifying criminal
laws which protect persons and their property), "(2) correcting for
a cognitive malfunction that distorts individuals' ability to pursue
their own personal well-being"[129] (thus justifying prohibitions
on gambling and recreational drugs[130]) or "(3) advancing an
interest other than personal well-being – like economic efficiency
or national security"[131] (thus justifying mandatory seat-belt or
motorcycle helmet laws[132]).

3.11.2   A broader approach than that traditionally associated with the
harm principle could treat conduct as "harmful" if it violates, or poses
a serious risk of violating, the core interests of another person, *or of
the actor herself.* We may wish to define "core interests" differently,
depending on whether the harm is directed by A towards B, or by
A towards herself. Core interests recognised by the law as deserving
of protection *from others* could include life; bodily integrity; health;

---

[127] O Raban, "Capitalism, liberalism, and the right to privacy" (2011–12) 86 *Tul
L Rev* 1243.
[128] *Ibid* at 1251.
[129] *Ibid.*
[130] *Ibid* at 1249.
[131] *Ibid* at 1251.
[132] *Ibid* at 1249.

freedom of movement; enjoyment of one's home, public areas (such as parks and public transport) and the environment; and peaceful enjoyment of one's possessions. When the harm is being inflicted by an individual on herself, it is appropriate that core interests be defined more narrowly – conduct may be regarded as "harmful" if it impacts adversely (or poses a serious risk of such an impact) on the actor's *life, bodily integrity, or health*. Even then, not all such harms should be criminalised. Attempting to commit suicide is an activity which risks the most serious form of harm, yet other factors, such as compassion for the victim's plight, and the fact that such people can be protected by invoking civil law measures, may militate against a criminal law solution. Kleinig has pointed out that:

> "One of the virtues of extreme positions is consistency. They usually reflect the single-minded and undeviating application of one principle. If other principles are acknowledged, they must always bow to it. The middle ground is much messier, and consistency much more difficult to achieve."[133]

When it comes to devising principles of criminalisation, there may be no alternative to accepting this messier middle ground.

---

[133] Kleinig (1983) at p 116.

CHAPTER 4

FAIRNESS AND JUSTICE IN CRIMINALISATION

4.1   INTRODUCTION

As we saw in Chapters 2 and 3, there is a variety of criminalisation   **4.1.1**
principles, any one of which, or combination of which, a legislator
may choose to follow. These include the "harm principle", the
"offence principle", legal moralism and legal paternalism. Irrespective
of which of these is favoured, there are other precepts which ought
also to be considered, such as the rule of law, the principle of
equality,[1] and the requirements of "fair labelling".[2] These reflect the
need for the criminal law to approach the accused fairly, recognising
her rights and her status as a member of the polity while balancing
these against society's need to be protected from serious harm at her
hand.

4.2   THE RULE OF LAW

Liberalism entails allegiance to the rule of law.[3] In deciding whether   **4.2.1**
or not to criminalise certain behaviour, and in assessing whether
behaviour which is criminalised was rightfully proscribed, the rule
of law requires us to consider whether the criminal prohibition is of
general application, relatively certain in its ambit, clearly expressed,
adequately publicised, consistent with other laws, and prospectively
applied. A law is not of general application if it targets only a
particular section of society on unacceptable grounds, for example
on the basis solely of race or ethnic origin. It fails the requirement
of certainty if its parameters are ill defined.[4] It is not adequately

---

[1] See from section 4.4 below.
[2] See from section 4.6 below.
[3] See A V Dicey, *Introduction to the Study of the Law of the Constitution* (1885).
The "principle of legality" reflects similar ideals.
[4] According to Lon Fuller, "The desideratum of clarity represents one of the most
essential ingredients of legality": L L Fuller, *The Morality of Law* (1969), p 63.

publicised if citizens cannot easily find out its requirements.[5] It fails the "prospective" test if it is aimed at behaviour which took place before the proscription was enacted.[6] Lon Fuller noted:

> "The reason the retrospective criminal statute is so universally condemned does not arise merely from the fact that in criminal litigation the stakes are high. It arises also – and chiefly – because of all branches of law, the criminal law is most obviously and directly concerned with shaping and controlling human conduct. It is the retroactive criminal statute that calls most directly to mind the brutal absurdity of commanding a man today to do something yesterday."[7]

In continental European jurisdictions the rule of law has often been equated with that of *Rechtsstaat*, meaning a state in which the exercise of governmental power is constrained by law. As previously noted,[8] the enactment of the Human Rights Act 1998 gave further effect to the provisions of the ECHR in domestic law. Many of the Convention's provisions embody "rule of law" principles; for example, the requirement that criminal laws should not be retrospective is found in Article 7:

> "No one shall be held guilty of any criminal offence on account of any act or omission which did not constitute a criminal offence under national or international law at the time when it was committed."

The rule of law has particular resonance for criminal procedure since it chimes with requirements of "due process"; whether or not a person is guilty of a criminal charge should be determined according to established procedures and rules of evidence.[9] The ECHR reflects this in its emphasis on the presumption of innocence, the right to liberty, and to a fair trial without undue delay.[10]

4.3   THE RULE OF LAW AND SCOTS CRIMINAL LAW

4.3.1   In terms of the substantive law, we shall see that Scots criminal law has not always measured up to a strict application of "rule of law" requirements. This is especially so in relation to the criterion that crimes be defined with sufficient clarity and precision to enable

---

[5] See Fuller (1969), pp 49–51.
[6] See C Sypnowich, "Proceduralism and democracy" (1999) 19 *OJLS* 649.
[7] Fuller (1969) at p 59.
[8] See from section 1.4 below.
[9] Due process is considered further from section 5.2.1 below.
[10] Note, however, that the ECHR requirement of a fair trial may not be prayed in aid to address complaints directed at a perceived unfairness or inequity in the substantive law: see *Watson* v *King* 2009 SLT 228 at 231, para 11, per Lord Eassie; and *R* v *G* [2008] 1 WLR 1379 (HL).

citizens to know in advance whether their behaviour is liable to be subject to censure. Two notable examples of this are the uncertain ambit of the (now abolished) crime of "shameless indecency"[11] and the judicial acceptance of "causing real injury"[12] as a crime. The crime of shameless indecency was expanded in the 20th century because of a belief by senior judges that sexual immorality could be equated to criminality. This came about because of a tendency to treat broad statements by textbook writers as equivalent to axioms of general application. An assertion in Macdonald's *A Practical Treatise on the Criminal Law of Scotland*,[13] that all conduct which is "shamelessly indecent" is a fit subject for the criminal law, was endorsed by the then Lord Justice-General, Lord Clyde, in 1934.[14] This in turn led to the successful prosecution for "shameless indecency" of a range of behaviour, including: the showing of a pornographic film to consenting adults;[15] the selling of pornographic magazines;[16] and sexual contact (short of actual intercourse) between a father and his adult daughter.[17] It is not necessarily objectionable that these types of behaviour are proscribed by the criminal law; it may be that some (or indeed all) of these behaviours ought to be the subject of criminal law prohibitions.[18] What is objectionable is that the boundaries of the crime of shameless indecency were ill defined and remained so for nearly 70 years.[19] When it was finally abolished by the appeal court in 2003, Lord Justice-Clerk Gill referred to it as "a crime that had no basis in principle and was unconstrained by any clear

---

[11] This crime has now been replaced by "public indecency": see *Webster* v *Dominick* 2005 1 JC 65. This case is discussed further at section 11.20.1 below.

[12] See section 10.12.1 below.

[13] 4th edn (1929), p 221.

[14] In *McLaughlan* v *Boyd* 1934 JC 19 the Lord Justice-General stated: "In my opinion, the statement in Macdonald's *Criminal Law* ... that 'all shamelessly indecent conduct is criminal,' is sound, and correctly expresses the law of Scotland" (at 23).

[15] *Watt* v *Annan* 1978 JC 84. For a critique of the case, see G Maher, "The enforcement of morals continued" (1978) SLT (News) 281.

[16] *Robertson* v *Smith* 1980 JC 1.

[17] *R* v *HM Advocate* 1988 SLT 623. See also *HM Advocate* v *RK* 1994 SCCR 499, involving a man and his foster daughter. For a discussion of these cases, see the *Stair Memorial Encyclopaedia, Criminal Law Reissue 1*, para 13; and Gordon (2000) at para 1.31.

[18] The *Draft Criminal Code*, s 67 defines "incestuous conduct" in a more expansive way than the current law, to include sexual activity between close relatives which falls short of sexual intercourse, and also includes homosexual as well as heterosexual behaviours. Incest is discussed further in section 11.17 below.

[19] See Gordon: "*McLaughlan* v *Boyd* is open to the objections that it is a usurpation of the function of Parliament, and that its *ratio* is so wide as to infringe the principle of legality": Gordon (2000) at para 1.31.

or logical boundaries".[20] Furthermore, it exposed to prosecution "some forms of private conduct the legality of which should be a question for the legislature".[21]

4.3.2   In similar vein, a reference in Hume's *Commentaries*[22] to the need for an indictment libelling a charge of assault to describe conduct amounting to "real injury" led to judicial recognition of the proposition that it was a crime to "cause real injury". Unlike the charge of assault, "causing real injury" or "culpable and reckless conduct" leading to injury could be prosecuted in circumstances in which there had been no "attack" as such by the accused on the complainer. Hence in the case of *Khaliq* v *HM Advocate*[23] the indictment libelled that the accused did "culpably, wilfully and recklessly" supply quantities of solvents to several children and did "cause or procure the inhalation by said children of vapours from said quantities of solvents to the danger of their health and lives". This averment of a risk of causing real injury was held to constitute a relevant charge. It is not in conformity with the principle of legality for the boundary between criminal conduct and lawful behaviour to be so indeterminate, as a result of reliance on such broad, general statements.

4.4 EQUALITY ISSUES

4.4.1   As we noted above, one aspect of the rule of law is that crimes ought to be defined in general terms, in the sense of not targeting particular groups for what they are, as opposed to for what they have done. An historical example of the former is the Gypsies Act 1609, which banished "Egyptians" from Scotland, on pain of death.[24] Justice requires people to be treated fairly, with discrimination of individuals being for appropriate reasons rather than on specious grounds relating to factors outwith their control, such as race, colour, gender, sexual orientation or disability. It must be borne in mind, however, that "equality" has many meanings, and even an aim such as "equality of opportunity" is not free from controversy. As Lesley Jacobs has argued, equality of opportunity

> "amounts only to an ideal of formal equality; it is said to be empty of a commitment to substantive or genuine equality. Equality of opportunity

---

[20] *Webster* v *Dominick* 2005 1 JC 65.
[21] *Ibid* at 983.
[22] Hume, i, 328.
[23] 1984 JC 23. See also the case of *Ulhaq* v *HM Advocate* 1991 SLT 614. The *Khaliq* case is discussed further in section 7.3.7 below.
[24] See Hume, i, 472. The 1609 Act is no longer in force.

as a principle of law and legislation has generally targeted discriminatory practices and worked on the assumption that, apart from discrimination, there is presumptive equality between persons. The problem is that there exist genuine substantive inequalities between persons along, among other things, the lines of race, class, and gender, and equality of opportunity in practice seems to be blind to these very real inequalities".[25]

The Aristotelian view of equality[26] – that people who are alike ought   4.4.2
to be treated alike, and unalike people treated differently – has been attacked by Catharine MacKinnon, who points out that much depends on our initial assessment of what it means to be "alike":

> "While some progress has been made using this sameness/difference equality concept … some of the historical uses of this approach – applications, not misapplications – give one pause. Aristotle, his concept of equality apparently undisturbed, defended slavery and lived in a society in which prostitution (sexual slavery) thrived and no women were citizens. This approach readily supported official racial segregation by law in the United States, African Americans being construed as different from whites."[27]

An assessment that only like cases deserve to be treated alike may in fact serve to perpetuate social inequality.[28]

Issues of equality are also raised by the fact that the impact of   4.4.3
crime is not felt uniformly across society.[29] Those who argue that property crimes are designed to protect the more affluent members of society at the expense of its poorer citizens would do well to reflect on the fact that the poor are disproportionately the victims of theft. This point was well made by Hume, writing in the 19th century. In describing the aggravated crime of "theft by housebreaking", he referred to the types of place which benefit from this "high protection" and continued:

> "It is not disputed, that every dwelling-house, or tenement destined for habitation enjoys [the law's protection], how mean and fragile soever it be; as indeed the houses of the poor more especially require to be strengthened in this way, since they are generally weak in themselves, and are often left empty during the day, and unprovided with any defence, but that which they may borrow from the fear of the law."[30]

---

[25] L A Jacobs, *Pursuing Equal Opportunities: The Theory and Practice of Egalitarian Justice* (2004), p 11.
[26] See Aristotle, *Ethica Nichomachea* (Book V, iii, 112–116, translation by W D Ross, 1925).
[27] C A MacKinnon, *Women's Lives, Men's Laws* (2007), p 46 (footnote omitted).
[28] *Ibid*, p 47. For a discussion of the distinction between formal and substantive equality, see C McDiarmid, "A feminist perspective on children who kill" (1996) 2 *Res Publica* 3.
[29] See R Matthews and J Young, "Reflections of realism" in J Young and R Matthews (eds), *Rethinking Criminology: The Realist Debate* (1992) at p 2.
[30] Hume, i, 103.

The position is likely to be similar today.[31]

4.4.4   Andrew Ashworth considers the argument that there may be values or interests which could outweigh the principle of equal treatment.[32] He gives two examples of situations where it could be suggested "that the criminal law should be kept on the outer edges",[33] namely labour disputes and family situations. In relation to the former, there could be said to be a public interest in not prosecuting that which would otherwise be criminal, on the basis that labour relations mechanisms are arguably a more effective means of resolving these issues. Likewise, family law mechanisms (presumably mediation, counselling or social work intervention) might be said to be better able to resolve domestic disputes than using the blunt tool of the criminal law to prosecute offenders for assault, etc. Ashworth accepts that those favouring such exceptional treatment face an uphill struggle to justify this.[34] Another example where the principle of equal treatment is at issue relates to those who commit what would otherwise be an assault during a sporting event. It is sometimes suggested that players ought to be dealt with by the sport's own disciplinary body, rather than by the criminal courts. It is certainly the case that the fine imposed by the former often exceeds any penalty the courts are likely to impose. But the suggestion that footballers or rugby players ought to be exempt from the criminal law because of this is surely not a sound one. Physical contact and even a certain amount of (minor) injury is acceptable in many sports, but where one player intentionally injures another, this can be, and ought to be, treated as a criminal assault. Ashworth concludes that: "A system of criminal justice that allows the differential enforcement of its laws is not a system that honours the principle of equal treatment."[35]

4.5   EQUALITY OF ENFORCEMENT

4.5.1   In considering the types of behaviour which the law ought to proscribe, we must also be aware of the unevenness of its

---

[31] Other inequalities in relation to victimisation include the fact that younger adults are more likely to be victims of crime than older ones; according to the *Scottish Crime and Justice Survey 2012/13*, para 3.2.1, males aged between 16 and 24 are most likely to be the victims of violent crime: see http://www.scotland.gov.uk/Resource/0044/00447271.pdf.

[32] A Ashworth, "Is the criminal law a lost cause?" (2000) 116 *LQR* 225 at 245.

[33] *Ibid.*

[34] For a critique of the notion that the law should stay out of the domestic sphere, since this should be regarded as private, see K O'Donovan, *Sexual Divisions in Law* (1985); M Thornton (ed), *Public and Private Feminist Legal Debates* (1995); and C Pateman, "Feminist Critiques of the Public/Private Dichotomy" in C Pateman, *The Disorder of Women* (1989) at p 118.

[35] Ashworth (2000) at 246.

enforcement. While the law *stricto sensu* makes no distinction between theft of a tin of beans from a shop and theft of a laptop from one's workplace, in practice the shoplifter is more likely to face prosecution than is the employee, if only because the latter may be dealt with by disciplinary mechanisms, and the employer may not even inform the police or prosecuting authorities of the theft. The law may appear to apply equally to all, but this appearance masks the inequality in people's lives: "law, in its majestic equality, forbids the rich as well as the poor to sleep under bridges, to beg in the streets and to steal bread".[36] Until 1939, when Edwin Sutherland coined the term "white collar crime", and demonstrated its existence, it was generally believed that crime was predominantly committed by the working class.[37] Alan Norrie believes that the primary aim of the criminal law is to maintain the current social order by legitimising the coercion of the economically powerless by the state.[38] Noting that those from disadvantaged backgrounds are more likely than relatively affluent individuals to commit certain crimes, particularly property crimes, Norrie argues that the social background of offenders ought to be afforded greater weight by the courts – not just in relation to sentencing, but in the determination of whether or not to find them guilty of criminal acts.

This is similar to the distinction drawn by Seyla Benhabib between what she calls the "generalized other" and the "concrete other":[39] **4.5.2**

> "The standpoint of the generalized other requires us to view each and every individual as a rational being entitled to the same rights and duties we would want to ascribe to ourselves. In assuming the standpoint, we abstract from the individuality and concrete identity of the other. ... Our relation to each other is governed by the norms of *formal equality* and *reciprocity*: each is entitled to expect and to assume from us what we can expect and assume from him or her. The norms of our interactions are primarily public and institutional ones. If I have a right to X, then you have a duty not to hinder me from enjoying X and conversely.
> ... The moral categories that accompany such interactions are those of right, obligation and entitlement, and the corresponding moral feelings are those of respect, duty, worthiness and dignity."[40]

---

[36] Anatole France, cited in MacKinnon (2007) at p 49.

[37] See D Weisburd and E Waring, *White-Collar Crime & Criminal Careers* (2001). See also Chapter 18 below.

[38] A Norrie, *Punishment, Responsibility and Justice: A Relational Critique* (2000). See also, by the same author: *Crime, Reason and History: A Critical Introduction to Criminal Law* (2001), in which he writes that "the commission of crime, as it is defined and processed, remains the province in the main of the lower social classes ... and is primarily crime against property" (*ibid*, p 27).

[39] S Benhabib, "The generalized and the concrete other: the Kohlberg–Gilligan controversy and feminist theory" in S Benhabib and D Cornell (eds), *Feminism as Critique: Essays on the Politics of Gender in Late-Capitalist Societies* (1987) at p 86.

[40] *Ibid*, p 87 (emphases in original).

We can see that the law approaches the accused person from this generalised perspective. In contrast, the standpoint of the "concrete other"

"requires us to view each and every rational being as an individual with a concrete history, identity and affective-emotional constitution. In assuming this standpoint, we abstract from what constitutes our commonality. We seek to comprehend the needs of the other, his or her motivations, what s/he searches for, and what s/he desires. Our relation to the other is governed by the norms of *equity* and *complementary reciprocity*: each is entitled to expect and to assume from the other forms of behaviour through which the other feels recognized and confirmed as a concrete individual being with specific needs, talents and capacities".[41]

This form of approach would require a more "individualised" form of justice; one which focused on subjective approaches to liability, rather than objective ones.

4.5.3   It is certainly true that those members of society who are economically disadvantaged appear before the criminal courts proportionately more frequently than their more affluent neighbours, and that this reflects the priorities of the criminal justice system in pursuing, for example, petty thieves rather than insider dealers or tax evaders.[42] Ashworth has described the injustice of this:

"Would it not be – is it not – monstrously unfair and intolerable that people who steal from shops are dragged through the criminal courts and subjected to liberty-restricting penalties, when others (whether fraudsters or companies) who culpably inflict far greater harm are dealt with outside the criminal law? ... [I]f one person who wrongs another is convicted of a crime whilst another who commits an admittedly more serious wrong is not, this is manifestation of warped priorities and clear injustice. It is not appropriate that the criminal law should be either structured or enforced in such a discriminatory way."[43]

4.5.4   As well as discrimination in respect of social class, we must be alert for laws which discriminate on other spurious bases. Until the late 20th century, Scots criminal law discriminated against married women in relation to the protection offered by rape laws.[44] The plea of provocation may currently operate in a gendered fashion, such that women may find it more difficult to satisfy its requirements.[45] Until recently substantive law may have discriminated against men

---

[41] Benhabib (1987), p 87 (emphases in original).
[42] See J Lea and J Young, *What is to be Done about Law and Order?* (1984). This may also reflect the fact that it is easier to prosecute the former than the latter, since theft is a more straightforward crime than insider dealing.
[43] Ashworth (2000) at p 249.
[44] See section 11.2.6 below.
[45] See from section 21.10 below.

in relation to the so-called "wife's defence" in reset;[46] and may currently do so in limiting bestiality to male behaviours.[47] Although the enforcement of the criminal law is beyond the scope of this book, the criminalisation debate ought to consider whether any particular prohibition has been framed in such a way that its impact will be more keenly felt by certain categories of citizens than by others.

4.6 FAIR LABELLING

Closely allied to the rule of law/principle of legality is the concept of **4.6.1** "fair labelling".[48] This is concerned with ensuring

> "that widely felt distinctions between kinds of offences and degrees of wrongdoing are respected and signalled by the law, and that offences are subdivided and labelled so as to represent fairly the nature and magnitude of the law-breaking".[49]

James Chalmers and Fiona Leverick have identified several reasons why it is important that offences are fairly labelled. Clearly, the use of some sort of labels can be justified by expediency, since "it would be impractical to operate a purely descriptive system of criminal law whereby the offender's conduct is set out in narrative form without any attempt to categorise".[50] Having an accurate account of the nature of any previous convictions assists the court in determining the appropriate punishment for the offence for which the accused is currently being sentenced. This is required out of fairness to the accused, and also to the public.[51] Fair labelling also requires that the definition of an offence provides an accurate reflection of what the accused actually did that was reprehensible. Both the (genuine) mercy killer and the serial sexual sadist may kill deliberately but our moral sense is that the crime of the former is so much less serious

---

[46] See section 12.12.7 below.

[47] See section 16.4.1 below.

[48] The term seems to have been coined by Glanville Williams in "Convictions and fair labelling" (1983) 42 *CLJ* 85, based on an idea of "representative labelling" which was described by Andrew Ashworth, in "The elasticity of *mens rea*" in C Tapper (ed), *Crime, Proof and Punishment: Essays in Memory of Sir Rupert Cross* (1981) at p 45.

[49] A Ashworth and J Horder, *Principles of Criminal Law* (7th edn, 2013), p 77. See also J Chalmers and F Leverick, "Fair labelling in criminal law" (2008) 71 *MLR* 217.

[50] Chalmers and Leverick (2008) at 223.

[51] *Ibid* at 231. If the same offence label is employed to cover different types of wrongdoing, this can give a court too much discretion over the sentence to be passed. This argument has less force in a system such as the Scottish one, where most core offences continue to be defined by the common law, and the maximum sentence available is dependent on a court's general sentencing powers.

than those of the latter that it should be labelled differently: culpable homicide as opposed to murder.

4.6.2   It is worth considering whether Scots law conforms to the principle of fair labelling, given that crimes such as breach of the peace have been used to prosecute such a range of disparate behaviour – from fighting in the streets, and aggressively begging for money, to kerb-crawling, via kicking a ball in the street, and glue-sniffing.[52] Furthermore, since intentionally bringing about a consequence is generally regarded as more blameworthy than recklessly bringing it about, it may be that separate offences ought to be provided for each. For instance, "vandalism" is defined as the wilful (meaning "deliberate") or reckless destruction or damage of another person's property.[53] The authors can conceive of situations in which either of us might recklessly cause damage to someone else's property, but would balk at the suggestion that we would ever intentionally cause similar damage, yet the person who is merely reckless is branded a "vandal" in the same way as one who deliberately causes damage. This may not be in accordance with fair labelling. As Stuart Green has put it: "When legal rules fail to square with people's common understanding of what is wrong, the result is unfair labelling."[54]

4.7 CONCLUSIONS

4.7.1   The argument that the criminal law ought to be unambiguous and accessible, be applied without improper discrimination, and conform to the requirements of fair labelling is a persuasive one. We must, however, remain vigilant in ensuring that Scots law conforms to these ideals.

---

[52] See section 15.2.1 below.
[53] Criminal Law (Consolidation) (Scotland) Act 1995, s 52, discussed further from section 13.3 below.
[54] S P Green, *Lying, Cheating, and Stealing: A Moral Theory of White-Collar Crime* (2006) at p 42.

PART II

FOUNDATIONS

Parts III–VII consider the principal offences and defences recognised by Scots criminal law. Grouping offences into categories assists in articulating what it is about the prohibited behaviour that is reprehensible. As Peter Alldridge has stated:

> "... unless crimes are classified appropriately – that is, unless the exact wrong can be identified, which crimes it is like and which it is unlike – then, on a standard liberal account, it will be impossible to label, to compare or to sentence justifiably".[1]

For instance, is "robbery" primarily an offence of dishonesty, against property? Or is it better categorised as an offence of violence, against the person? If we put robbery in the former camp, what does this say about the value the criminal law puts on protection of persons, as opposed to property? Are "prostitution" and "soliciting" aimed at preventing the exploitation of vulnerable people (the prostitute)? Or are they more accurately portrayed as forms of "nuisance"? Perhaps some would regard them as offences against morality. If so, is it appropriate to have such a category of offences in the criminal law calendar? Before embarking on a classification of crimes in Scots law, we must consider some preliminary matters. Such is the remit of this part. We consider: aspects of criminal procedure and legal sources in Chapter 5, *actus reus* and *mens rea* in Chapter 6, general principles of liability in Chapter 7 and, since at least some of these are of general application, preventive offences in Chapter 8.

---

[1] P Alldridge, "The public, the private and the significance of payments" in P Alldridge and C Brants (eds), *Personal Autonomy, the Private Sphere and Criminal Law* (2001) 79 at p 80.

CHAPTER 5

PROCEDURAL FRAMEWORK AND SOURCES

5.1 INTRODUCTION

This chapter considers the origins of Scots criminal law, and of what **5.1.1**
that law consists. While this book, for example, contains as clear
a statement as we can provide of the rules of the criminal law it is,
necessarily, at one remove from the law itself. It is our gloss on the
law's sources and it can be no more than our opinion on its principles
both at a descriptive level (in terms of what it is)[1] and at a normative
level (as our notion of what it should be). The chapter identifies the
recognised bases of the law – the texts (because even court cases are
eventually pared down to a written case report) which constitute the
law.

These sources must be set in some kind of context. The chapter **5.1.2**
therefore looks at the history of the law – though, as we shall
see, there are particular difficulties in separating out the historical
from the current, given the status accorded to institutional
writings. It starts with a brief examination of the nature of the
criminal process since this provides a framework – or, perhaps
one of several frameworks[2] – into which the sources, and the
rules which they state, must fit. At one level, the criminal process
is not relevant to a work on substantive criminal law but the
latter does not exist in a vacuum. Indeed, Lindsay Farmer has
stated that "the principal characteristic of the modern common
law is that it is expressed through broad and flexible principles, the

---

[1] Criticism of the law's indeterminacy is made at various points in our discussion.
To some extent, this is unavoidable in a system whose development has, until very
recently, been concentrated in cases decided by the High Court of Justiciary. The
Scottish Parliament now has the power to legislate in the area of Scots criminal law.
So far, its approach has been piecemeal but it has enacted a legislative framework
for sexual offences (the Sexual Offences (Scotland) Act 2009, discussed further in
Chapter 11).

[2] For example, clearly the law also has a social context.

implementation of which are facilitated by a body of more precise procedural rules".[3] Similarly, Nicola Lacey "take[s] it as given that conceptions of criminal and other forms of responsibility take their colour from the institutions in which they are mobilized".[4] Thus, the criminal law both informs, and is informed by, the body of rules on criminal evidence and procedure which can be gathered together under the loose heading of the criminal process. That process is generally taken to be the route along which a suspect passes from arrest to eventual conviction or acquittal. It has been characterised as

> "all the complexes of activity that operate to bring the substantive law of crime to bear (or to avoid bringing it to bear) on persons who are suspected of having committed crimes. It can be described, but only partially and inadequately, by referring to the rules of law that govern the apprehension, screening, and trial of persons suspected of crime".[5]

A number of issues may be relevant to this process, some of which will not have taken place within this time frame. For example, aspects of the commission of the crime itself, the lawfulness of any search of the accused's person or property, and/or techniques of surveillance used to obtain initial evidence leading to the arrest might all be scrutinised as part of the criminal process. The criminal law, in the form of the body of rules governing the behaviour of a society, is engaged in different respects at some points in this process; certain of its leading cases are also intrinsically bound up with procedural points.[6] To some extent, then, the criminal process and the substantive criminal law operate together.

5.2   MODELS OF THE CRIMINAL PROCESS

5.2.1   In simplistic terms, the function of the criminal process is to issue authoritative declarations as to the guilt or "innocence" – though the latter term is not used[7] – of those individuals who are

---

[3] L Farmer, *Criminal Law, Tradition and Legal Order: Crime and the Genius of Scots Law, 1747 to the Present* (1997), p 145.

[4] N Lacey, "The resurgence of character: responsibility in the context of criminalization" in R A Duff and S P Green (eds), *Philosophical Foundations of Criminal Law* (2011) 151 at p 154.

[5] H L Packer, "Two models of the criminal process" (1964) 113 *U Pa L Rev* 1 at 2.

[6] See, for example, *Codona v HM Advocate* 1996 SLT 1100 which considered both substantive principles of art and part liability and the admissibility of evidence obtained from a confession to the police.

[7] Juries can return verdicts of "guilty", "not guilty" or, uniquely – and sometimes controversially – in Scotland, "not proven". See, for example, P Duff, "The not proven verdict: jury mythology and 'moral panics'" (1996) 1 *JR* 1, especially at 6.

prosecuted for the alleged commission of criminal offences. Fifty years ago, Herbert Packer conceptualised two possible models of the criminal process, which he labelled "due process" and "crime control".[8] These have remained influential.[9] Packer noted that, in strict theory, the (American) system was predicated on "due process" values which require that the accused should be treated with scrupulous fairness throughout the "course of justice". He described this as an "obstacle course" because "[e]ach of its successive stages is designed to present formidable impediments to carrying the accused any further along in the process".[10] For example, any search of a suspect's person or property should only be carried out in accordance with the appropriate authorisation; rules of evidence should operate at the trial to exclude improperly obtained material.[11] The presumption of innocence should apply strongly and, through pleading not guilty and thereby triggering a trial process, the accused should be allowed to force the state to prove its case against her.[12] This model fits well with the concept of liberalism outlined in Chapter 1. The individual's (private) sphere of autonomy is protected. If the state wishes to intervene – and particularly by such a draconian measure as the imposition of the criminal sanction – it can only do so by establishing its right to do so at every stage.

By contrast, the "crime control" model is concerned much more   5.2.2
with procedural efficiency than with any idealistic question of justice or presumed innocence. Packer likened it to "an assembly line or a conveyor belt",[13] the focus of which is on accelerating the progress of the guilty. His model recognised that the system would break down without a significant proportion of guilty pleas, in relation to at least some of which a "sentence" can be imposed administratively, without the need to take up court time.[14] The crime control model has a certain resonance with the concept of communitarianism which was examined in Chapter 1 as presenting

---

[8] Packer (1964). See also H L Packer, *The Limits of the Criminal Sanction* (1969).
[9] At one level, Packer's models have stood the test of time in that they are still a major point of reference in any discussion of these issues. However, they have also been heavily criticised as products of their time which do not take account of social forces, such as feminism, which only subsequently assumed importance in academic thought. There have been attempts to update Packer's models – see, for example, K Roach, "Four models of the criminal process" (1999) 89 *J Crim L and Criminol* 671.
[10] Packer (1964) at 13.
[11] *Ibid* at 18, n 16.
[12] *Ibid* at 17. See from section 5.4 below.
[13] *Ibid* at 11.
[14] *Ibid* at 13.

a challenge to the liberal orthodoxy which has pervaded criminal law. It requires a level of acceptance that officials, appointed to act on behalf of the community – police officers, prosecutors and judges – will do their jobs effectively, without the scrutiny which the due process model builds in. According to this model, when they arrest, charge, prosecute or convict, there can be some confidence that the systems which they have previously employed in investigation and evidence-gathering are sufficiently robust that the likelihood is that the individual suspect did commit the offence. The liberty and autonomy of that suspect and, by extension, of the individual generally, are seen as less important than the smooth progression of the system.

5.2.3   There are indications of the two models coming together with due process in some respects being subsumed within, or even swamped by, crime control. Lacey points to "the proliferation of overlapping criminal offences [which] has given increasing power to prosecutors through plea-bargaining", concluding that

> "a change in patterns of prosecution and criminalization amounts, in substance, to a change in the contours of criminal responsibility; that we cannot, in other words, separate the moment of responsibility-attribution from the moments of selection and case-processing which precede (and in most instances supplant) it, or indeed from the moments of penal execution which conclude the criminal process".[15]

It might be said, then, that the criminal law, while framed by criminal procedure and its institutions, has a reciprocal framing function in relation to process: law provides the process's trigger points. Without satisfaction of the definition of a crime – whether murder or operating as a property factor while unregistered[16] – the criminal process is not engaged. Once it has been, the model adopted may have a bearing on the ways in which the accused's criminal responsibility is drawn out.

5.3 PACKER'S MODELS AND SCOTS CRIMINAL LAW

5.3.1   Elements of both of Packer's models can be detected in the current Scottish criminal justice system. The "due process" model has assumed particular importance with the advent of the Human Rights Act 1998, which incorporates the European Convention on Human

---

[15] Lacey (2011), p 175.
[16] Property Factors (Scotland) Act 2011, s 12 – an example of a strict liability, regulatory offence which is considerably less morally repugnant than murder. Murder is *malum in se*; unregistered property factoring is *malum prohibitum*. See, further, from section 17.3.3 below.

Rights (ECHR, 1950) into the laws of all jurisdictions comprising the United Kingdom.[17] Article 6 of the Convention enshrines the right to a fair trial, allowing everyone accused of having committed a crime "a fair and public hearing within a reasonable time by an independent and impartial tribunal established by law".[18] It also embeds the presumption of innocence[19] and makes various provisions to ensure that those who are accused of crime are adequately and appropriately assisted in the preparation of their defence.[20] These are all recognisable "due process" values. These safeguards were in place in Scots law long before the Human Rights Act; more importantly for our purposes, the incorporation of Art 6 has generated new sources of criminal law in the form of case law in which the Scottish courts wrestle with interpretation of the broadly stated principles of the Convention.[21] While this has generally had a greater impact on the procedural framework, there is no doubt that the substantive criminal law has felt its reverberations.[22] Some scholars have suggested that "managerialism" is now the dominant model; changes to criminal procedure are based on concerns to cut costs and increase efficiency, rather than by any more profound philosophy of crime control or due process.[23] This is evidenced by the increase in the use of alternatives to prosecution, such as conditional offers of fixed penalties by the Crown Office and Procurator Fiscal Service.[24] Indeed, it has been estimated that three-quarters of all crime cleared up by the police is now diverted from the criminal trial process.[25]

5.4   THE PRESUMPTION OF INNOCENCE

At the time of writing, there are many issues of current interest in relation to criminal evidence and procedure in Scotland arising from   **5.4.1**

---

[17] See from section 1.4 above.
[18] Article 6(1).
[19] Article 6(2).
[20] Article 6(3).
[21] See, for example, *Starrs* v *Ruxton* 2000 JC 208, where the High Court determined that temporary sheriffs were not an "independent and impartial tribunal" for the purposes of Art 6, thereby throwing into doubt all convictions handed down by such judges.
[22] For example, where a child is accused of rape, there is a particular duty imposed on the Crown to bring the case to trial within a reasonable time, because of the impact of changes in the child's appearance and his understanding of sexual matters, if the delay is lengthy: *HM Advocate* v *P* 2001 SLT 924.
[23] See J McEwan, "From adversarialism to managerialism: criminal justice in transition" (2011) 31 *Legal Studies* 519.
[24] These are known as "fiscal fines". See the Criminal Procedure (Scotland) Act 1995, ss 302–303; and R M White, "Out of court and out of sight: how often are 'alternatives to prosecution' used?" (2008) 12 *Edin LR* 481.
[25] *Ibid* at 484–485.

the 2011 Carloway Review.[26] In particular, the recommendation to abolish the corroboration rule has attracted much discussion.[27] Such debate is largely beyond the scope of this book, which is concerned with substantive criminal law. Nonetheless, much of the criminal process, including criminal law itself, is concerned with balancing. The issues normally placed in the scales are broadly, the rights of the accused (possibly and certainly to a more limited extent, the rights of the victim) and the public interest in justice being done and being seen to be done. Discussion of an aspect of criminal procedure – the presumption of innocence – will be used to provide a point of entry into this issue.

5.4.2   It is a basic tenet of the criminal process that those accused of having committed crimes should be presumed innocent, the corollary of which is that the Crown must prove its case against them. An accused may sometimes be expected to place exculpatory evidence in issue, but it should be up to the prosecution to disprove this. The importance of the presumption of innocence has been well described by the Supreme Court of Canada:

> "The presumption of innocence protects the fundamental liberty and human dignity of any and every person accused by the State of criminal conduct. An individual charged with a criminal offence faces grave social and personal consequences, including potential loss of physical liberty, subjection to social stigma and ostracism from the community as well as other social, psychological and economic harms. In light of the gravity of these consequences, the presumption of innocence is crucial. It ensures that until the State proves an accused's guilt beyond all reasonable doubt, he or she is innocent. This is essential in a society committed to fairness and social justice. The presumption of innocence confirms our faith in humankind; it reflects our belief that individuals are decent and law-abiding members of the community until proven otherwise."[28]

5.4.3   An important facet of the presumption of innocence is that the reversal of the basic evidential presumption – that the Crown must prove the case against the accused beyond reasonable doubt – ought rarely to be employed. A reverse burden of proof means that an obligation is imposed on the accused to prove *an* element, usually a defence to the charge, but only on the civil standard of proof: the balance of probabilities. This is known as a "persuasive burden". If the state makes a serious allegation, proof of which

---

[26] *The Carloway Review: Report and Recommendations* (17 November 2011), available at: http://www.scotland.gov.uk/Resource/Doc/925/0122808.pdf.
[27] See, for example, J Chalmers and F Leverick, "'Substantial and radical change': a new dawn for Scottish criminal procedure" (2012) 75 *MLR* 837. This article provides a critical assessment of a number of aspects of the Carloway Review, including its recommendations on corroboration.
[28] *Oakes* (1986) 50 CR (3d) 1 (SCC) at 15, per Dickson CJ.

may lead to punishment, including in some cases the deprivation of the individual's liberty, then it must produce evidence to substantiate its claim. For this reason, as will be discussed in the following paragraphs, reverse burdens of proof are a contentious issue.

It is generally accepted in human rights jurisprudence, and also 5.4.4 by the English courts, before whom this matter has been more extensively debated, that reverse burdens are acceptable in some, strictly limited, circumstances. When a statutory provision is put in issue on this basis, the court considers what it is that the accused is required to prove, whether it is part of the *gravamen* of the offence and whether it is reasonable and proportionate. Thus, in one conjoined case,[29] the House of Lords found that requiring an accused person to prove, on the balance of probabilities, that there was no likelihood that he would drive a vehicle while intoxicated did not breach the presumption because this was a matter about which the accused knew so much more than the prosecutor. At the same time, it found that a provision under the Terrorism Act 2000 did contravene the presumption of innocence. Section 11 of that Act criminalises belonging to a proscribed organisation but provides a defence that the organisation had not been proscribed when the accused became a member, or that he had not taken part in any of its activities while it was proscribed. Had the provision been interpreted such that it imposed a legal burden on the accused, this would have meant that he would have had to establish the defence on the balance of probabilities. Instead, the court held that the defence should be interpreted such that it imposed only an evidential burden; the accused person had to lead some evidence, which the prosecution then had the burden of disproving.

The Scottish courts have found reverse burdens to be acceptable in 5.4.5 offensive weapons cases. The matter was examined in *Glancy* v *HM Advocate*.[30] The case considered the statutory defence of "reasonable excuse"[31] to the offence of having an article with a blade in a public place.[32] Section 49(4) of the Criminal Law (Consolidation) (Scotland) Act 1995 states specifically that it is for the accused to show that she had a reasonable excuse. In determining that the shifting of this onus onto the accused was acceptable, the appeal court observed that what was required was:

"a careful examination of (a) the relevant statutory provisions in each case, (b) the measures that are taken in those provisions directed at the activity in

---

[29] *Sheldrake* v *DPP; Att-Gen's Reference (No 4 of 2002)* [2005] 1 AC 264.
[30] 2012 SCCR 52.
[31] Criminal Law (Consolidation) (Scotland) Act 1995, s 49(4).
[32] *Ibid*, s 49(1).

question, which is made an offence, and (c) what justification can be made out for a departure from the presumption of innocence, balancing the interests of the public and the individual's fundamental rights".[33]

Paul Roberts has taken the view that Art 6(2) (the requirement that criminal trials be "fair") is "an exclusively *procedural* provision, which does not purport to regulate matters of substantive criminal law".[34] On this view, Parliament states the constituent elements of the offence which the prosecution must prove beyond reasonable doubt. It is not part of the courts' role to consider the terms of the offence. If its elements, as determined by Parliament, require to be proved by the prosecution, Art 6(2) is not engaged. However, others have argued that interpreting both that Article, and the legislative provisions which are measured by reference to it, in this way, is an unacceptable dilution of the protection of the presumption of innocence. Their view is that sometimes placing an onus, even if only a persuasive one, on the accused means that they are, in effect, being required to establish their innocence. Such provisions can only be identified by taking into account the *gravamen* of the offence – the evil which it proscribes – the ascertainment of which requires an investigation into what it was that Parliament sought to prohibit by creating the offence in the first place.[35] Here, then, a clear crossover is discernible between the procedural requirements of Art 6 and the content of the substantive criminal law. Before it can be ascertained whether the presumption of innocence is intact, the actual terms of the statute setting up the offence must be examined to ensure that those who are accused of breaching its provisions are not obliged to prove their innocence of any aspect of it.

5.4.6   In relation to serious crimes, with correspondingly severe penalties, there is considerable disquiet over reverse burdens generally. David Hamer would support them for regulatory provisions with little moral depth on the basis that "little censure, punishment or stigma" attaches to such offences.[36] A number of other commentators also take this view.[37] If, however, reverse burdens are generally unfair and contrary to Art 6(2), then restricting them to "minor breaches of

[33] *Glancy v HM Advocate* 2012 SCCR 52 at para [8], per Lord Clarke.
[34] P Roberts, "The presumption of innocence brought home?: *Kebilene* deconstructed" (2002) 118 *LQR* 41 at 48. See also *R v G* [2009] 1 AC 92 which supports Roberts' position.
[35] V Tadros and S Tierney, "The presumption of innocence and the Human Rights Act" (2004) 67 *MLR* 402 at 413–416.
[36] D Hamer, "The presumption of innocence and reverse burdens: a balancing act" (2007) 66 *CLJ* 142 at 170.
[37] See, for example, J R Spencer, "Case comment" (2004) *Archbold News* 5 at 6; N Padfield, "Case comment: the burden of proof unresolved" (2005) 64 *CLJ* 17 at 19–20.

regulations" may not help to make them any more just. Furthermore, the number of statutory offences which do not attract some degree of stigma is diminishing.[38] For example, motoring offences involving excess speed, alcohol or drugs now attract opprobrium; environmental crime is not tolerated; carrying knives or other weapons attracts, and has probably always attracted, moral condemnation, placing it on the line between *mala in se* (things which are wrong in themselves) and *mala prohibita* (things which are only wrong because a statute declares them to be so).[39]

As stated already, the presumption of innocence is a key aspect of Art 6 and the jurisprudence which flows from it. The ECHR is, in many respects, a unifying force since it applies in all signatory states whether their own systems of criminal procedure are "inquisitorial" or "adversarial". We will now consider these two concepts.   5.4.7

5.5 SYSTEMS OF CRIMINAL PROCEDURE

The inquisitorial system of criminal procedure, the main form used in continental Europe, attempts to seek "the truth" by employing a proactive and interventionist judiciary, particularly at the investigative stage of the proceedings. Adversarialism, on the other hand, is designed to reward the side which presents the better argument. In the latter, two interests are ranged against each other: the need to ensure that the accused is treated fairly – to ensure that her "due process" rights are respected – and the "public interest" in securing the conviction of those who are, in fact, guilty. In the adversarial system the trial assumes particular importance. The Scottish system is predominantly an adversarial one but it does contain some inquisitorial elements,[40] such as pre-trial judicial examination[41] and provisions for agreeing evidence in advance of the trial (which could have an adverse effect on the accused's right to have the prosecution prove its case against her, if pressure to agree was brought to bear). Indeed, on one view, the whole agreement mechanism comes closer to the inquisitorial "search for the truth".[42]   5.5.1

---

[38] Hamer (2007) at 149.

[39] See, further, section 17.3.3 below.

[40] See P Duff, "Intermediate diets and the agreement of evidence: a move towards inquisitorial culture?" (1998) *JR* 349; P Duff, "Disclosure in Scottish criminal procedure: another step in an inquisitorial direction?" (2007) 11 *E & P* 153.

[41] See the Criminal Procedure (Scotland) Act 1995, ss 35–39. See also Pt 6 of the Criminal Justice and Licensing (Scotland) Act 2010 which introduced a statutory scheme for the disclosure pre-trial of information relevant to the case, by both the prosecution and the defence.

[42] Duff (1998) at 359–360, considering the Scottish Law Commission's views as expressed in the Commission's *Responses to 1993 Review of Criminal Evidence and Criminal Procedure and Programming of Business in the Sheriff Courts* (1993).

5.6 SOLEMN AND SUMMARY PROCEDURE

5.6.1 The criminal process also has a mechanism for separating out more and less serious offences. "Solemn" procedure is used for the former; "summary" procedure for the latter. Solemn procedure involves trial by a jury (comprising 15 people), whereas in summary trials issues of both fact and law are determined by the judge. The procedure in the High Court is always solemn; the justice of the peace courts[43] employ summary procedure; and either type of procedure is competent in the sheriff courts. In solemn cases the charges are listed on an indictment, which runs in the name of the Lord Advocate. Such cases are reported as *"Her Majesty's Advocate* v *[name of the accused]"* (for example *HM Advocate* v *Purcell*,[44] *HM Advocate* v *Doherty*[45] and *HM Advocate* v *Forbes*[46]). In summary trials the charges take the form of a "complaint", and are prosecuted in the name of the local procurator fiscal. These cases are reported as *"[name of the fiscal]* v *[name of the accused]"* (for example *Crowe* v *Waugh*,[47] *Dean* v *John Menzies (Holdings) Ltd*[48] and *Dyer* v *Brady*[49]). If the accused appeals against conviction and/or sentence, the names of the parties are reversed (for example *Smart* v *HM Advocate*,[50] *Brennan* v *HM Advocate*[51] and *Drury* v *HM Advocate*[52]). If one knows that MacPhail, Lockhart and Donnelly are the names of current or former procurators fiscal, then it becomes apparent that the cases of *Thompson* v *MacPhail*,[53] *Stewart* v *Lockhart*[54] and *Smith* v *Donnelly*[55] were all appeals taken by the accused.

5.7 JURISDICTION

5.7.1 Before we proceed to consider the sources of Scots criminal law, a final aspect of the procedural context which requires consideration is the question of jurisdiction. Whether the court before which the accused has been ordered to appear has jurisdiction to try the case is one of the first aspects of an indictment or complaint which defence counsel

---

[43] Formerly the district courts: see the Criminal Proceedings etc (Reform) (Scotland) Act 2007, Pt 4.
[44] 2008 SLT 44.
[45] 1954 JC 1.
[46] 1994 SCCR 163.
[47] 1999 JC 292.
[48] 1981 JC 23.
[49] 2006 SLT 965.
[50] 1975 SLT 65.
[51] 1977 SLT 151.
[52] 2001 SLT 1013.
[53] 1989 SLT 637.
[54] 1991 SLT 835.
[55] 2002 JC 65.

must address. Much of this relates more to criminal procedure than to substantive law, but a few words on the jurisdiction of the Scottish courts, in general, are in order.[56] According to Hume:

> "A person domiciliated here, whether a Scotsman or a foreigner, for any crime he may have committed abroad, is not liable to be tried before our courts. They are not instituted to administer justice over the whole world, but in our country, or a particular district of it only; and, therefore, if the crime charged has been committed beyond those limits, they are neither called upon nor entitled to step forward for its correction."[57]

While it remains the case that our courts' jurisdiction is generally confined to crimes committed entirely in Scotland, there are now many statutory encroachments on this principle. These include crimes perpetrated in Scotland whose effects (or potential effects) occur in another jurisdiction[58] and crimes which have no connection to Scotland, by virtue of either the accused's nationality or the commission of the crime, but for which all courts have jurisdiction by virtue of these crimes being regarded as universally abhorrent.[59]

Overall, then, criminal procedure sets the parameters within which substantive criminal law operates. The latter also has a temporal dimension which is particularly pronounced because of the prominence of institutional writings (which will be considered subsequently in this chapter)[60] as a source. It is therefore necessary to place Scots criminal law in its historical context, as part of our examination of its sources. **5.7.2**

5.8 HISTORICAL CONTEXT

In relation to English law, Alan Norrie has argued that "the modern criminal law was formed in a particular historical epoch and derived its characteristic 'shape' from fundamental features of the social **5.8.1**

---

[56] For a more detailed account, see Gordon (2000), paras 3.41–3.50.

[57] Hume, ii, 52. (For Hume's role in Scots criminal law, see from section 5.10 below.) See also *HM Advocate* v *Hall* (1881) 4 Coup 438 per Lord Young: "The general rule is that criminal law is strictly territorial – so that a man is subject only to the criminal law of the country where he is, and that his conduct there, whether acting, speaking, or writing, shall be judged of as criminal or not by that law and no other."

[58] See, for example, the Criminal Procedure (Scotland) Act 1995, s 11A (inserted by the Criminal Justice (Terrorism and Conspiracy) Act 1998, s 7, and discussed further at section 8.6.8 below); and the Sexual Offences (Scotland) Act 2009, s 54. See also the War Crimes Act 1991, s 1; the Prohibition of Female Genital Mutilation (Scotland) Act 2005, s 4; and the International Criminal Court (Scotland) Act 2001, ss 1–3.

[59] For example, the Criminal Justice Act 1988, s 134 and the Geneva Conventions Act 1957, s 1(1) and (2).

[60] See from section 5.10 below.

relations of that epoch".[61] Much the same could be said of our law.[62] Its history suggests that Scotland struggled to distance itself from English law, as part of its desire to maintain legal independence. The Act and Treaty of Union with England of 1707 expressly provided that Scotland's laws generally remained intact and not subject to amendment by the British Parliament "except for the evident utility of the subjects within Scotland".[63] In the 20th century certain commentators sought to deploy the independence of the Scottish legal system as one of the insignia of Scottish nationalism.[64] There was no right of appeal to the House of Lords in Scottish criminal cases.[65] Accordingly, there is now no right of appeal to the Supreme Court (which, on 1 October 2009,[66] took over the appellate functions of the House of Lords)[67] other than in respect of devolution issues.[68]

5.8.2   There is room for debate as to whether this adherence to the status quo is justified.[69] One view has been that lack of appeal to the House of Lords has allowed Scots criminal law to remain true to its domestic principles, unadulterated by ill-thought-out transplants of English law.[70] Yet judges of the Supreme Court now have some involvement in issues which are purely Scottish, due to the right of appeal on devolution issues.[71] In two significant cases on Scottish criminal procedure[72] heard by the Judicial Committee of the Privy Council, there were two Scottish judges on the Board (Lords Hope and Rodger). The outcome of these cases had far-reaching implications for Crown practice on disclosure of its case to the defence prior to trial, and has not been universally welcomed,[73] but there was no failure on the part of the Board in understanding the underlying Scottish position.

---

[61] A Norrie, *Crime, Reason and History: A Critical Introduction to Criminal Law* (2001), p 8.

[62] Farmer (1997).

[63] Articles 18 and 19.

[64] See, for example, T B Smith, *A Short Commentary on the Law of Scotland* (1962) p vii.

[65] See *Mackintosh* v *Lord Advocate* (1876) 3 R (HL) 34.

[66] See the Supreme Court website: http:www//supremecourt.gov.uk/about/history/html.

[67] Constitutional Reform Act 2005, s 23.

[68] *Ibid*, Sch 9, Pt 2, para 103(8). See section 5.8.2 below for further discussion of "devolution issues".

[69] See T H Jones, "Splendid isolation: Scottish criminal law, the Privy Council and the Supreme Court" [2004] *Crim LR* 96.

[70] See, for example, Smith (1962) at p 119.

[71] Scotland Act 1998, Sch 6, para 11.

[72] *Holland* v *HM Advocate* 2005 SLT 563; and *Sinclair* v *HM Advocate* 2005 SLT 553.

[73] See, for example, R Johnston, "*McInnes* v *HM Advocate*: time for a(nother) definitive decision on disclosure" (2009) 13 *Edin LR* 108.

The matter cannot be left, however, without some discussion   5.8.3
of the Supreme Court's judgment in *Cadder* v *HM Advocate*,[74] in
which, again, Lords Hope and Rodger formed part of the seven-
strong Bench. This case has been described as "notorious"[75] and
the Court's decision as "flawed, mistaken and misconceived"[76] yet
it has also been said that "The Supreme Court had no real choice
in the matter[77] and cannot, therefore, be criticised for reaching the
conclusion it did".[78] The judgment applied Art 6 jurisprudence (on
the right to a fair trial[79]) to require that a person detained by the
police for questioning in Scotland should have the right to consult
with a solicitor. Under Scottish procedure before *Cadder*, suspects
could be questioned by the police for up to 6 hours without access to
legal assistance. Following *Cadder*, in any case where this aspect of
the Art 6 right had not been respected, admissions made during any
police interview could not be admitted in evidence in court.

As will be clear already, the case generated considerable   5.8.4
discussion.[80] It also had extensive and extremely sweeping practical
consequences in that, within 4 months of the decision, it had led to
the abandonment by the Crown of 867 prosecutions[81] of suspects
who had been questioned without being offered their right to legal
assistance. Perhaps here, then, we find a case where full account was
not taken of the Scottish position. Commentators have suggested
that there might have been scope for the Supreme Court to decide
the case in another way by applying slightly different interpretive
techniques[82] or by viewing Scottish criminal procedures in relation
to suspects' rights holistically.[83] It is certainly the case that the pre-
existing Scottish position, which had been carefully articulated and
supported in a seven-judge decision in the appeal court,[84] was set
aside. This was not, however, at any level, because English principles

---

[74] 2010 SLT 1125.

[75] F Leverick, "The right to legal assistance during detention" (2011) 15 *Edin LR*
352 at 353.

[76] J McCluskey, "Supreme error" (2011) 15 *Edin LR* 276 at 276.

[77] In that unanimous judgments of the ECHR Grand Chamber carry greater weight
in the hierarchy of precedent than judgments of the High Court of Justiciary.

[78] F Stark, "The consequences of *Cadder*" (2011) 15 *Edin LR* 293 at 293. Fiona
Leverick has expressed a similar view: F Leverick, "The Supreme Court strikes
back" (2011) 15 *Edin LR* 287 at 291 (henceforth Leverick 2011a).

[79] *Salduz* v *Turkey* (36391/02) (2009) 49 EHRR 19.

[80] See, for example, Leverick (2011); McCluskey (2011); Stark (2011).

[81] P R Ferguson, "Repercussion of the *Cadder* case: the ECHR's fair trial provisions
and Scottish criminal procedure" [2011] *Crim LR* 743 at 743.

[82] McCluskey (2011).

[83] Ferguson (2011).

[84] *HM Advocate* v *McLean* 2010 SLT 73. Following the Supreme Court's decision
in *Cadder* the appellant was given leave to appeal his conviction but the appeal was
unsuccessful: *McLean* v *HM Advocate* 2012 JC 91.

were unthinkingly taken to be of universal application. Rather, the decision was taken to reflect the binding nature of European human rights law. Indeed, Leverick notes that "even setting [the point that the decision was all but mandated by ECHR law] aside, the Supreme Court's reasoning is persuasive".[85] While *Cadder* has had major and difficult consequences for the Scottish criminal justice system, then, it is not, in any sense, legally unprincipled. Accordingly, it remains true to say that appeal to the Supreme Court does not appear to have resulted in the indiscriminate grafting of English principle onto Scots criminal law any more than did appeal to the House of Lords.

5.8.5 The fact that the jurisdiction of the Supreme Court of the United Kingdom is a controversial issue is an indication of the particular importance of case law in Scotland. The primary sources of Scots criminal law are: the common law, the works of institutional writers, and statute law, though the common law often makes resort to the institutional writers in defining its principles. The high value accorded to their work demonstrates the extent of the criminal law's reliance on its history. Law is hierarchical in its approach to source material. Primary sources constitute the law and carry greater authority than secondary ones, which merely explain it and have, at best, persuasive value.

5.9 THE NATURE OF THE COMMON LAW

5.9.1 The term "common law" is used to refer to law which has not been enacted by a legislative body, but rather is defined by the judges in the superior criminal courts, in deciding cases which come before them. Scotland's criminal law is based on the common law to a greater extent than other Western legal systems. Anyone wishing to find a definition of a range of crimes, including murder, culpable homicide, assault, theft, robbery, reset, breach of the peace, fire-raising and fraud, must look to the institutional writings, particularly Hume's *Commentaries*, and then at the case law, to see how the courts have applied Hume's text, in practice. It is clear that the judges of the High Court of Justiciary see themselves as the guardians of the common law. In the case of *Lord Advocate's Reference (No 1 of 2001)*[86] Lord Nimmo Smith referred to Lord Justice-General Emslie's comment in *S v HM Advocate*[87] that Scots criminal law is a "live system of law".[88] Lord Nimmo Smith continued:

---

[85] Leverick (2011a) at 291.
[86] 2002 SLT 466. (For an explanation of why such cases are reported as a "Lord Advocate's Reference", see n 229 of section 9.18.3 below.)
[87] 1989 SLT 469.
[88] *Ibid* at 473.

"it lies within the powers of this court, as custodians of the common law, to review it, and to correct the way in which it is stated, when it is necessary to do so in order to take account of developments in the law and to meet the needs of the community".[89]

It may, however, be argued that the job of defining crimes is better left to the legislature, which is democratically elected. If the law is perceived to be unsatisfactory – as was the case with the definition of rape prior to the ruling in *Lord Advocate's Reference (No 1 of 2001)*, then the courts should draw attention to this, and call on the Scottish Parliament to rectify the situation.[90] As against this view, it may be said that even when the courts do identify areas ripe for reform, the legislature does not generally respond swiftly to deal with the matter.[91]

5.10 INSTITUTIONAL WRITINGS

As previously noted, certain "institutional writings", produced in the 18th and 19th centuries, are a primary source of law and predominant among these in the criminal law context is Hume's *Commentaries on the Law of Scotland, Respecting Crimes*.[92] At one level, the degree of respect accorded by the High Court to these works is remarkable, given their antiquity and the differences in today's society. One reason for this may be that, given that most major crimes continue to be defined by the common law rather than by statute, there will simply be no law covering a particular issue. The institutional writers may be employed to fill in any gaps. For example, when faced for the first time with the question of whether purely patrimonial loss could constitute the *actus reus*

5.10.1

---

[89] 2002 SLT 466 at 481.

[90] Lord Gill has suggested that "a comprehensive re-examination of the mental element in homicide is long overdue", noting that this is "pre-eminently an exercise to be carried out by the normal processes of law reform" (*Petto v HM Advocate* 2012 JC 105 at 112). The Scottish Law Commission is currently undertaking a review of the law of homicide but it is not clear when it will report its recommendations.

[91] The Court in *Drury v HM Advocate* 2001 SLT 1013 (at 1032 per Lord Nimmo Smith) suggested that the legislature might wish to consider amending the law on provocation by sexual infidelity, but this has yet to be the subject of parliamentary scrutiny. This case is discussed further in section 9.11.1 below.

[92] Baron David Hume was the nephew of the philosopher of the same name. His *Commentaries* were first published in 1797. The latest (4th) edition was published in 1844, with supplementary notes by Benjamin R Bell. The courts occasionally refer to Archibald Alison's *Principles of the Criminal Law of Scotland* (1832) and *Practice of the Criminal Law of Scotland* (1833), but these are not as highly regarded as Hume's writings, and their status as "institutional" has been doubted – see "Sources of law (general and historical)" in *Stair Memorial Encyclopaedia*, vol 22, at para 537, n 9.

of the crime of malicious mischief, the court referred directly to Hume in holding that it could.[93] Nonetheless, although often consulted by the High Court of Justiciary, Hume's views are not always followed.[94] Lindsay Farmer has summarised the approach taken by the court:

> "If a line of precedent is leading away from the position the court desires to take, it may be able to disregard it by the invocation of Hume's statement of the 'true position' of the law. If, on the other hand, Hume does not appear to offer the desired solution then he can safely be regarded as a representative of an earlier age and a more 'up-to-date' solution preferred."[95]

The High Court makes reference to a wide variety of works on Scots criminal law and this statement would suggest that the relative weight which it attaches to these is a matter for its own discretion. In one influential murder case, for example, it regarded the statement in Gordon's *Criminal Law* on the *mens rea* for murder as correct, and relied upon this.[96] By the same token, Macdonald's *Practical Treatise on the Criminal Law of Scotland* has yielded the accepted definitions of "murder", "provocation" and "fraud". Despite this, there appears to be no suggestion that either Gordon or Macdonald should be regarded as a primary source.[97] Hume, therefore, must still be regarded as the pre-eminent

---

[93] *HM Advocate* v *Wilson* 1984 SLT 117 at 119, per LJ-C Wheatley.

[94] Examples include *Kelly* v *Vannet* 2000 SLT 75 at 78 (per LJ-C Cullen, where Hume was not followed because he was dealing with a "different procedure for the investigation of crime from that which is carried out in modern times"); *Justice* v *HM Advocate* 1995 SCCR 228 (where counsel's argument was unsuccessful on the basis of the facts of the case, with no discussion as to the relevance of the passage from Hume on which he relied); *S* v *HM Advocate* 1989 SLT 469 (Hume not followed in respect of rape in marriage); *Sneddon* v *HM Advocate* 2006 SCCR 103 (where the relevant passage from Hume dealt with art and part liability for homicide but the case was concerned with aggravated assault, allowing some departure from Hume's view); *Webster* v *Dominick* 2005 1 JC 65 (passages from Hume of tangential importance only); *Byrne* v *HM Advocate* 2000 SCCR 77 (Hume's distinction between wilful fire-raising and culpable and reckless fire-raising was "based on the fact that wilful fire raising was a capital crime and [therefore] outmoded" (per Lord Coulsfield at 83)). Hume's view that abduction could only be charged where this was done for the purpose of rape or marriage (Hume, i, 310–311) has not been followed: see *Brouillard* v *HM Advocate* 2004 JC 176, discussed further in section 10.17.1 below.

[95] Farmer (1997) at pp 39–40.

[96] *HM Advocate* v *Purcell* 2008 JC 131.

[97] David Walker simply states: "[o]n criminal law, the standard editions are Mackenzie's *Laws and Customs*, second edition, 1699 and his collected *Works* (two volumes 1716–22); Hume's *Commentaries*, fourth edition with supplement by B. R. Bell, two volumes, 1844 and Alison's *Principles* and *Practice*, only editions, 1832 and 1833": *The Scottish Legal System: An Introduction to the Study of Scots Law* (8th edn, 2001), p 506 (footnotes omitted).

institutional source. But is it acceptable for Scots law to place such store on a work first produced in 1797 and last updated in 1844? *Should* such an old statement of principle have the potential to be treated as the basis of modern law in any area on which it expresses an opinion?

John Cairns has pointed out that the current Scottish conception of institutional writers reflects "neither the aims of the institutional writers themselves nor the attitude of their contemporaries to their work".[98] He has argued that   5.10.2

> "the notion of institutional writers having special authority beyond that of other writers derives from a judicial recognition, even creation, of that authority ... In Scotland, an institutional work thus does not require to have a certain structure, to deal with certain topics, to be concerned with an exposition of national law; all it requires is to be recognised by the Scottish courts as specially authoritative".[99]

It has been suggested that:

> "recognition of the authority of certain authors or treatises has no other foundation than judicial recognition. As the judiciary is free to reformulate the doctrines of judicial precedent by which it will be bound, subject to subordination only to decisions of the judiciary higher in the hierarchy of courts, so presumably the courts may regulate and vary the recognition to be accorded to legal writing".[100]

Indeed, this is very far from Hume's own perception of the purpose of his work. He explained his motivations in writing the *Commentaries* as being

> "to initiate the young lawyer in the Elements of our Criminal Practice, and to lay before him such authorities and materials, as may serve to guide him in his future researches ... This, undoubtedly, and nothing higher, is the main bent and scope of my undertaking. I have no intention of bringing forward a Philosophical Treatise of Criminal Jurisprudence".[101]

It is also important to examine the ways in which, and the purposes for which, the High Court makes reference to Hume. Surveying a number of cases decided between 2009 and 2014, regular resort is apparent.[102] Issues raised include the definition

---

[98] J W Cairns, "Institutional writings in Scotland reconsidered" in A Kiralfy and H L MacQueen (eds), *New Perspectives in Scottish Legal History* (1984) at p 76.

[99] *Ibid* at p 102. See also J W Cairns, "Institutional writings in Scotland reconsidered" (1983) 4 *Journal of Legal History* 76.

[100] "Authoritative writings in Scots Law", in *Stair Memorial Encyclopaedia* (vol 22, para 440).

[101] Hume, i, 13–14.

[102] It should be noted that many references are made to Hume's pronouncements on criminal procedure which are not of immediate concern here.

of "murder",[103] "attempted murder"[104] and "culpable homicide"[105] separately and in relation to each other; the distinguishing of "theft" from "embezzlement";[106] endorsement of Hume's definition of "robbery"[107] (but by reference to its adoption in a more recent case[108]); and whether or not the crime of "attempting to pervert the course of justice" existed at all in Hume's time.[109] There is no doubt that the court's tendency to refer to his work is so frequent as to be routine. There is similarly little doubt that a work first written in 1797, which states specifically that it has no pretensions to any form of longevity, cannot reflect the nuances of a modern society. On the other hand, reference seems most often to be made to the *Commentaries* in relation to crimes which are strongly *mala in se* or wrong in themselves[110] – in other words, to crimes where the moral wrongness is so flagrant and so widely accepted that criminalisation of these behaviours is not contentious. We might quibble over the terminology used – in fact we will do so in a number of places in this book. We might, for example, find the use of the word "wicked" to define the mindset required for murder vague and anachronistic[111] but it is undeniable that murder, a heinous crime, ought to be set apart from less blameworthy forms of killing. *This* position is unlikely to have changed since 1797 even if the abolition of the death penalty renders its context different. If the courts are using Hume simply to reinforce the sense of the magnitude of the moral wrong of common law crimes, that seems acceptable. Rigid and dogmatic adherence to the literal interpretation of his words may, however, create significantly greater difficulties.

5.10.3 It is submitted, then, that there is a need to examine and revise the way in which common law crimes are defined and expressed at a detailed level and that the over-interpretation of Hume is not necessarily helpful for this purpose.[112] Without a detailed restatement, however, the use of Hume to reinforce the criminality

---

[103] *Elsherkisi* v *HM Advocate* 2012 SCL 181 and *Petto* v *HM Advocate* 2012 JC 105.
[104] *HM Advocate* v *Kerr* 2011 SLT 430.
[105] *Scott* v *HM Advocate* [2011] HCJAC 27 and *MacAngus and Kane* v *HM Advocate* 2009 SLT 137.
[106] *Moore* v *HM Advocate* 2010 SCL 843.
[107] *Morrison* v *HM Advocate* 2010 JC 174.
[108] *O'Neill* v *HM Advocate* 1934 JC 98.
[109] *HM Advocate* v *Harris* 2011 JC 125. See also *HM Advocate* v *Baillie* [2012] HCJAC 158 regarding the *mens rea* of "threats".
[110] See further from section 17.3.3 below.
[111] This point has also been made by the current Lord Justice-General (then Lord Justice-Clerk), Lord Gill, in *Petto* v *HM Advocate* 2012 JC 105 at 111–112, paras [21] and [22].
[112] See the discussion of *Drury* v *HM Advocate* 2001 SLT 1013 from section 9.11.1 below.

and unacceptability of such behaviours is less questionable. There is a level, then, at which Hume provides a cohesive backstop for the recognition of common law crimes so that they are not solely to be found in and between the *ratios* of individual cases. Indeed, in relation to sexual morality, where there is a clear mismatch between the mores of the 18th and 19th centuries and 20th- and 21st-century values the High Court did depart from his view, which had acquired the status of a principle, that a husband could not be guilty of the rape of his wife, noting that "this [was] the first time the Crown ha[d] sought to charge a cohabiting husband with the rape of his spouse".[113] The use of Hume has not been entirely unquestioning, then. Nonetheless it is submitted that there is a need for a modern restatement of the principles of Scots criminal law. This is one argument in favour of codification. Fifty years ago, Glanville Williams stressed the importance of the Latin maxims *nullum crimen sine lege/nulla poena sine lege* (that there should be no crimes or punishments except in accordance with fixed, predetermined law).[114] He stated:

> "A possible application of *nullum crimen* that has not received the attention it deserves is that penal laws should be accessible and intelligible. A system of penal law lying buried in many hundreds of volumes of statutes and reports can hardly be said to fulfil this requirement. Criminal law is not like the law of procedure, meant for lawyers only, but is addressed to all classes of society as the rules that they are bound to obey on pain of punishment. It might seem to follow that a compendious and authoritative statement of this law should generally be available."[115]

As previously noted,[116] there is a Scottish *Draft Criminal Code*, **5.10.4** prepared by a small group of law professors (including one of the authors of this book).[117] This was an unofficial exercise which seems unlikely to be enacted in the foreseeable future. Were this, or any other Code, to be enacted it would have legislative, and hence democratic, authority together with an inbuilt mechanism for updating (in that all legislation can be amended). This is entirely lacking in relation to institutional writings.[118]

---

[113] *HM Advocate* v *S* 1989 SLT 469, per L J-G Emslie at 471.

[114] See G Williams, *Criminal Law: The General Part* (1961).

[115] *Ibid*, p 582.

[116] See section 1.1.2, n 9 above.

[117] The Scottish code group comprised Professors Eric Clive, CBE (Edinburgh University); Pamela Ferguson (Dundee University); Chris Gane (Aberdeen University); and Sandy McCall Smith (Edinburgh University). Professor Sir Gerald Gordon also took part in the discussions of the group in the later stages. See E M Clive, "Submission of a Draft Criminal Code for Scotland to the Minister for Justice" (2003) 7 *Edin LR* 395; E Clive, "Codification of the criminal law" in J Chalmers, F Leverick and L Farmer (eds), *Essays in Criminal Law in Honour of Sir Gerald Gordon* (2010) at 54.

[118] The merits of a criminal code are discussed further at section 22.6.2 below.

5.11   CASE LAW

5.11.1   There is no doubt that case law is a primary source of Scots criminal law, with the hierarchical court structure, and the doctrine of precedent, according particular importance to decisions of the High Court sitting as a court of appeal. Earlier, we considered the use made of other writings on Scots criminal law in the courts' decision-making process.[119] Equally, there have been cases where the High Court has stated that particular behaviour is criminal without reference to any source, or by reference to a source with no recognised authority in the hierarchy. In *Kerr* v *Hill*,[120] for example, Lord Fleming simply announced that he was prepared to hold that "maliciously making a false statement to the police" was a crime.[121] Previously, such behaviour had been recognised as criminal only if the accused named another individual as the perpetrator.[122] In *Strathern* v *Seaforth*[123] all three judges held that "clandestinely taking and using" (in this case a motor car) was a competent charge, again on their own authority. In *McLaughlan* v *Boyd*[124] the court elevated a statement in Macdonald that "all shamelessly indecent conduct is criminal"[125] to the status of a legal principle of general application. Almost 70 years later, in the case of *Webster* v *Dominick*,[126] the appeal court determined that this was no longer appropriate. It therefore simply abolished the crime of "shameless indecency", substituting a new crime of "public indecency".[127]

5.11.2   This raises the question of the function fulfilled by the appeal court in relation to the development of Scots criminal law. In each of these four cases, its development or interpretation of the law changed the pre-existing position quite radically. In the first three cases this rendered criminal certain forms of behaviour which had not previously been so recognised or, at least, changed the basis on which criminalisation had hitherto been justified. This is also apparent in the malicious mischief case of *HM Advocate* v *Wilson*[128] where the court determined that the *actus reus* of the crime could be satisfied even if the loss which had been caused was a purely financial (or "patrimonial") one. Prior to this, it had been accepted

---

[119] See from section 5.10 above.
[120] 1936 JC 71.
[121] *Ibid* at 76.
[122] Hume, i, 341–343.
[123] 1926 SLT 445.
[124] 1934 JC 19.
[125] J H A Macdonald, *A Practical Treatise on the Criminal Law of Scotland* (4th edn, 1929) at p 221.
[126] 2005 1 JC 65.
[127] *Ibid* at paras 46 and 51.
[128] 1984 SLT 117. Malicious mischief is discussed from section 13.2 below.

that physical damage to property was an essential component. Wilson had pressed an emergency stop button at a power station, causing £147,000 worth of lost electricity, but no physical damage. Nonetheless, the court took the view that the *consequences* were the same as if he had hit the button with a hammer, hence the behaviour was criminal.[129] Despite its protestations to the contrary,[130] the court here extended the parameters of the existing law to the extent that it did, arguably, create a new crime. The consequences of Wilson's behaviour were amply covered by the civil law, one of the purposes of which is to place individuals in the position in which they would have been if others had fulfilled their obligations. There may be an argument that causing pure economic loss is a wrongful setback to another's interests, thereby satisfying the "harm principle", but it is not clear that this is the *type* of harm with which the criminal law should be concerned. In such cases, the constitutional principle of the separation of powers – that Parliament makes the law; the courts merely apply it – dictates that it should be for the legislature to make the final decision as to whether to criminalise such conduct at all.

5.12 THE DECLARATORY POWER

Hume stated that the High Court had "an inherent power ... com-   **5.12.1**
petently to punish ... every act which is obviously of a criminal nature; though it be such which in time past has never been the subject of prosecution".[131] This is known as the declaratory power. Its last overt use was in 1838 in the case of *Bernard Greenhuff*,[132] where the High Court declared for the first time that "keeping a common gaming house" was a criminal offence. In 1987, in the case of *Grant* v *Allan*,[133] the High Court confirmed the existence of this power but declined to use it to criminalise the dishonest exploitation of confidential material.[134] In fact, any punishment which resulted from the retrospective law-making which the power encapsulates would now be in direct contravention of Art 7(1) of the European Convention on Human Rights. It is not without significance that, in a lecture delivered on 3 December 2013, Lord Justice-General Gill

---

[129] 1984 SLT 117 at 119, per LJ-C Wheatley. The court also relied on a passage in Hume.
[130] Lord Wheatley specifically stated that this did not constitute introducing a new crime into Scots law (*ibid* at 120).
[131] Hume, i, 12.
[132] (1838) 2 Swin 236.
[133] 1987 JC 71.
[134] *Ibid* at 77–78, per LJ-C Ross.

called for the declaratory power "to be 'laid to rest' after warning of the dangers of 'judicial creativity'."[135]

5.13 INNOMINATE CRIMES

5.13.1 Further leeway in terms of the High Court's ability to expand the ambit of the criminal law arises from the fact that the Crown need not charge criminal behaviour as a particular named offence. The Criminal Procedure (Scotland) Act 1995 provides that:

> "It shall not be necessary to specify by any *nomen juris* the offence which is charged, but it shall be sufficient that the indictment … sets forth facts relevant and sufficient to constitute an indictable offence."[136]

The case of *Khaliq v HM Advocate*[137] has been described by Lord McCluskey as "the best-known recent example of an innominate crime charged without a *nomen juris*".[138] In *Khaliq*, Lord Justice-General Emslie quoted with approval the opinion of Lord Clyde in *McLaughlan v Boyd*,[139] to the effect that:

> "It would be a mistake to imagine that the criminal common law of Scotland countenances any precise and exact categorisation of the forms of conduct which amount to crime. It has been pointed out many times in this Court that such is not the nature or quality of the criminal law of Scotland. I need only refer to the well-known passage in the opening of Baron Hume's institutional work, in which the broad definition of crime – a doleful or wilful offence against society in the matter of 'violence, dishonesty, falsehood, indecency, or religion' is laid down."[140]

It does, however, seem unfair both to the accused and to the victim if the harm perpetrated is not accurately named. Four English authors have expressed this well:

> "The criminal law speaks to society as well as wrongdoers when it convicts them, and it should communicate its judgment with precision, by accurately naming the crime of which they are convicted".[141]

5.13.2 Even without expressly *declaring* new crimes, it is clear from the foregoing that the High Court can expand the boundaries of

---

[135] *Scottish Legal News*, 5 December 2013. With regard to certainty in the law, see from section 4.2.1 above.

[136] Schedule 3, para 2 (emphasis in original). The *nomen juris* of a crime is its legal label.

[137] 1984 JC 23.

[138] In *HM Advocate v Harris* 1993 JC 150 at 157.

[139] 1934 JC 19 at 22–23.

[140] *Khaliq v HM Advocate* 1984 JC 23 at 31.

[141] A P Simester, J R Spencer, G R Sullivan and G J Virgo, *Simester and Sullivan's Criminal Law: Theory and Doctrine* (5th edn, 2013), p 31.

criminal behaviour. This accords with Lord Cockburn's dissenting opinion in *Bernard Greenhuff*;[142] although he opposed the use of the declaratory power, he noted:

> "I am far from holding that the Court can never deal with any thing as a crime, unless there be a fixed *nomen juris* for the specific act, or unless there be a *direct precedent*. An old crime may certainly be committed in a new way; and a case, though never occurring before in its facts, may fall within the *spirit* of a previous decision, or within an established *general principle.*"[143]

Sweeping decisions like that in *McLaughlan* v *Boyd*,[144] and, indeed, its remediation in *Webster* v *Dominick*,[145] underline the dangers inherent in judicial law-making if the "general principles" relied on are overly vague, or the "spirit of a previous decision" interpreted too broadly.

5.14   STATUTE LAW

Legislative sources of Scots law comprise Acts of the (United Kingdom) Westminster Parliament and, since 1999, Acts of the Scottish Parliament.[146] In addition, both Parliaments have the authority to "delegate" their law-making powers to others who then pass subordinate legislation, usually in the form of statutory instruments. This is often done where the legislation required is particularly detailed or technical.[147] Legislation of the European Parliament has had only minimal impact in the area of criminal law, though any relevant Directive is binding.[148] Most aspects of Scots criminal law have been devolved to the Scottish Parliament, but some areas, currently governed by legislation which is common to Scotland and England, are not devolved matters. Referred to as

5.14.1

---

[142] (1838) 2 Swin 236.

[143] *Ibid* at 274 (emphases in original).

[144] 1934 JC 19.

[145] 2005 1 JC 65.

[146] By virtue of the Scotland Act 1998.

[147] For example, the Animal Health and Welfare (Scotland) Act 2006, s 27, delegated to the Scottish Ministers the authority to make regulations prohibiting the carrying on, without a licence, of certain activities involving animals. The Scottish Ministers duly passed the Licensing of Animal Dealers (Young Cats and Young Dogs) (Scotland) Regulations 2009 (SSI 2009/141) setting down the detail of the licensing system for such dealerships. It would have been impossible, without excessive complexity and consequent lack of clarity, for the 2006 Act itself to create detailed codes of conduct like this in perhaps several areas of activity coming under its aegis.

[148] For example, the Unfair Commercial Practices Directive (Directive 2005/29) has brought about the repeal of most of the key offences contained within the Trade Descriptions Act 1968 and the enactment, in their place, of the Consumer Protection from Unfair Trading Regulations 2008 (SI 2008/1277).

"reserved matters", these include offences relating to firearms,[149] misuse of drugs and road traffic legislation.[150] As a source, legislation is not much discussed in Scotland because its impact had been piecemeal and it has yet to impinge very much on any of the major crimes.[151] Certain specific crimes such as vandalism,[152] having an article with a blade or sharp point or, indeed, an offensive weapon in a public place[153] or being on premises in circumstances from which an intention to commit theft can be inferred[154] are part of the canon of criminal law courses in Scottish universities. Yet there is also a view that creating a criminal offence is a way for government to be seen to be taking decisive action about a perceived societal problem. Thus, for example, perhaps to demonstrate the taking of a firm stance against sectarianism, s 1 of the Offensive Behaviour at Football and Threatening Communications (Scotland) Act 2012 makes it an offence, in relation to certain football matches, to engage in behaviour which is, or would be, likely to incite public disorder where that behaviour is, *inter alia* expressing hatred of certain goups (including religious groups or groups identified by ethnic or national origins). Any new offence to deal instantly with a particular social issue like this will be created by legislation,[155] thus the number of statutory offences is likely to increase.[156] It is not clear that the creation of disparate provisions is beneficial for the criminal law as a whole, since it makes it more difficult for the lay-person (and indeed the lawyer) to know what it is that the law requires.[157]

5.14.2   The majority of legal systems have a codified system of criminal law.[158] As well as many continental European jurisdictions (including

---

[149] Recently "air weapons" have been made an exception to this reservation in terms of the Scotland Act 2012, s 10, which added a rider to the Scotland Act 1998, Sch 5, Pt 2, s B4. See now the Air Weapons and Licensing (Scotland) Bill which creates several new offences relating to the acquisition, possession and use of air weapons without a licence.

[150] See the Scotland Act 1998, s 29(2)(b) and Sch 5. The power to legislate in these areas has been reserved to the Westminster Parliament.

[151] Except for sexual offences, the majority of which became statutory offences by virtue of the Sexual Offences (Scotland) Act 2009. See Chapter 11 below for a fuller discussion.

[152] Criminal Law (Consolidation) (Scotland) Act 1995, s 52.

[153] *Ibid*, ss 49 and 47 respectively.

[154] Civic Government (Scotland) Act 1982, s 57.

[155] See C Wells and O Quick, *Lacey, Wells and Quick: Reconstructing Criminal Law: Text and Materials* (4th edn, 2010), p 13.

[156] For a fascinating account of the difficulties involved in quantifying the increasing numbers of statutory offences, see J Chalmers and F Leverick, "Tracking the creation of criminal offences" [2013] *Crim LR* 543.

[157] That the law should be knowable is a requirement of the rule of law- see from section 4.2 above.

[158] Smith (1962), p 116.

France, Italy and Germany) the criminal law has been codified in a range of jurisdictions which have traditionally been based on the common law, including Australia,[159] New Zealand[160] and many jurisdictions in the USA.[161] In 2002 the Irish Government established an Expert Group to explore the desirability and feasibility of codifying its substantive criminal law. Two years later, the Group recommended that codification be undertaken on a phased basis, and in 2007 an Advisory Committee was established to oversee the development of a programme for codification.[162] In July 2011 it published its draft Criminal Code but there is little sign that the Irish Parliament is planning to enact this any time soon.

Both the English and Scottish Law Commissions are under a statutory duty to codify the law.[163] A draft criminal code for England and Wales was prepared by the Law Commission in 1989[164] and the Government indicated in 2001 that codification of the criminal law in England and Wales was one of its primary objectives.[165] However, in its *Tenth Programme of Law Reform*,[166] the Law Commission specifically "removed ... mention of a codification project in relation to criminal law",[167] recognising that codification was becoming "ever more difficult".[168] Codification in England therefore seems a more distant prospect than hitherto. Nonetheless, much of English criminal law is contained in Acts of Parliament. If one wishes to find the definition of "rape", "theft" or "robbery" in England, the

5.14.3

---

[159] See the Commonwealth of Australia Criminal Code Act 1995; the Australian Capital Territory Criminal Code 2002; the New South Wales Crimes Act 1900; the Northern Territory Criminal Code Act 1983; the Queensland Criminal Code Act 1899; the South Australia Criminal Law Consolidation Act 1935; the Tasmania Criminal Code Act 1924; the Victoria Crimes Act 1958; and the Western Australia Criminal Code 1913. It should be noted that in some states, such as New South Wales, some common law crimes remain.

[160] Crimes Act 1961.

[161] For details of criminal codes in the USA, see http://research.lawyers.com/State-Criminal-Codes-and-Statutes.html.

[162] The Criminal Law Codification Advisory Committee, established under Pt 14 of the Criminal Justice Act 2006.

[163] The Law Commissions Act 1965, s 3(1) provides that both Commissions are "to take and keep under review all the law with which they are respectively concerned with a view to its systematic development and reform, *including in particular the codification of such law*" (emphasis added).

[164] Law Commission, *A Criminal Code for England and Wales* (Law Com No 177, 1989). The original English "code team", formed in March 1981, comprised Professors John Smith, Edward Griew, Peter Glazebrook and Ian Dennis.

[165] See the Government's White Paper on *Criminal Justice: The Way Ahead* (Cm 5074, 2001), paras 3.57–3.59.

[166] Law Com No 311, HC 605, June 2008.

[167] *Ibid*, para 1.6.

[168] *Ibid*, para 1.4. See also I Dennis, "RIP: The Criminal Code (1968–2008)" [2009] *Crim LR* 1.

starting point is a statutory one.[169] Scotland is unusual in still having the majority of its crimes based on the common law; it is perhaps the most "common law" based system in the world. Although criminal law is a largely devolved matter,[170] it remains the case that the Scottish Parliament has not seen fit to undertake its whole-scale reform, far less codification.[171]

5.15   THE ROLE OF THE CROWN OFFICE

5.15.1   Although case law, institutional writings and statutes constitute the only primary sources of Scots criminal law, the important role of the Crown Office and Procurator Fiscal Service (COPFS) in the development of the common law should not be overlooked. The Crown can shape the law in its drafting of indictments,[172] by accepting pleas to lesser crimes rather than insisting that the case be tried, and by deciding not to prosecute certain types of behaviour. For instance, in practice, culpable homicide is any blameworthy killing which the Crown holds insufficiently culpable to merit a conviction for murder; pleas to culpable homicide are routinely accepted without the basis for this concession being made explicit.[173] Thus, cases of assisted suicide and euthanasia have resulted in the Crown accepting a plea to culpable homicide, despite the fact that the accused had caused death, and had done so intentionally, thus arguably satisfying both the *actus reus* and *mens rea* of murder.[174] Sometimes the Crown simply decides to take no proceedings, even where there would seem to be *prima facie* evidence for a homicide charge.[175] Even before the age of consent for homosexual intercourse was lowered to 18 by statute, Crown Office policy was not to prosecute such cases without the agreement of Crown

---

[169] Sexual Offences Act 2003, s 1(1); and Theft Act 1968, ss 1 and 8, respectively.

[170] See from section 5.14 above.

[171] For the background to the (unofficial) *Draft Criminal Code for Scotland*, see section 5.10.4 above.

[172] See the innovative charge of conspiracy to participate in sexual offences (including lewd, indecent and libidinous practices and indecent assault) against children in *Strachan v HM Advocate* 2011 SCL 347. (M Wade, "'Paedophile conspiracy' trial jury deliberates", *The Times*, 5 May 2009.) Eight men were found guilty at trial.

[173] See C Connelly, "Women who kill violent men" (1996) *JR* 215.

[174] For example, the case of Paul Brady who killed his terminally ill brother. "Mercy killings" are considered further at section 9.16.4 below. Note that the more recent re-definition of the *mens rea* of murder as "wicked" intent to kill may serve to legitimise a lenient approach by the Crown in these types of cases – see section 9.11.6 below.

[175] See the case of Dr Michael Munro who admitted to the GMC that he had injected two dying babies in an Aberdeen hospital with a paralysing drug. The case is discussed further at section 6.10.2 below, at n 138.

Counsel.[176] In practice, prosecutions were rarely taken. The *skean-dhu*, a type of small dagger, is clearly within the definition of offensive weapons *per se*,[177] yet possession of such items was effectively decriminalised when the Lord Advocate at the time gave an undertaking to Parliament that no one would be prosecuted for having a *skean-dhu* in a public place, so long as they were wearing the dagger as part of Highland dress.[178]

5.16   CRITIQUE AND PROPOSALS FOR REFORM

Scots criminal law's heavy reliance on non-statutory sources of law means that in order to find an authoritative definition of core crimes such as murder, assault or theft, one has to consult the writings of Hume, then look at some of the leading cases which have been decided since Hume's time to see how he has been interpreted, applied and refined by the High Court. Farmer has likened Hume's *Commentaries* to "a millstone around the neck of the Scottish criminal law that chokes reasoned discussion about the type of law we want".[179] Few other Scots lawyers have been critical of Hume. Reliance on institutional writings may have been appropriate at a time when Scotland did not have her own legislature, and the Westminster Parliament had neither the time nor the inclination to reform Scotland's criminal law. Some view the common law nature of our criminal law as a positive good, since it allows the law to evolve and makes it sufficiently flexible to deal with new situations.[180] This is the approach which was taken by Lord Justice-General Cooper:

5.16.1

> "By the application of our native methods to our native principles, it has proved possible ... to keep the law sufficiently flexible and elastic to enable a just discrimination to be applied to the ascertained facts of each case, and

---

[176] Crown Office Circular 2025, issued to procurators fiscal by the Lord Advocate on 28 November 1991. See A Thorp, *"Age of consent" for Male Homosexual Acts*, House of Commons Research Paper 98/68, 19 June 1998, at p 22.

[177] See the Criminal Law (Consolidation) (Scotland) Act 1995, s 47, discussed further at section 8.11.2 below.

[178] See 1954 SLT (News) 67. That the debate on *skean-dhus* and Highland dress continues is clear from the parliamentary discussions of the Offensive Weapons Act 1996, which amended the Criminal Law (Consolidation) (Scotland) Act 1995 to introduce a prohibition on the carrying of knives in schools: see *Hansard*, 26 Apr 1996, col 676.

[179] L Farmer, "The boundaries of Scottish criminal law" (1989) 148 *SCOLAG* 9, at 11.

[180] A M Cubie, *Scots Criminal Law* (3rd edn, 2010), para 1.2: "The preponderance of common law offences in Scots criminal law has been regarded as one of its strong points." See also T H Jones, "Towards a good and complete criminal code for Scotland" (2005) 68 *MLR* 448, which considers some of these arguments; and T H Jones and M G A Christie, *Criminal Law* (5th edn, 2012), Ch 14.

sufficiently rigid to prevent proved guilt from escaping the just consequences on any mere technicality."[181]

Although Lord Cooper's statement was made more than 60 years ago, the attitude towards criminal law which it embodies can still be seen today. The High Court's description of the law as a "live system" presumably means that it is capable of growth in new directions.[182] In the post-devolution era, however, there is a strong argument that a mature legal system ought to have its core crimes and defences defined by the legislature in order to ensure clarity and certainty – if not in the form of a comprehensive code, then at least in statutory form. The Scottish Parliament has enacted criminal justice legislation, but this has tended to address procedural issues, rather than the substantive law. Forays into the latter have included the creation of new offences relating to mammals,[183] and to mammaries,[184] but until the enactment of the Sexual Offences (Scotland) Act 2009, little of significance had been achieved.[185]

5.16.2   It has been suggested that, at its base:

"law derives from the social group; legal rules express the way in which the group considers that social relations ought to be ordered. This point of view is quite different from that generally taught. The current doctrine ... applies its efforts to the different modalities in which the law appears (legislation, custom, judicial decisions ...), thus giving the impression that these modalities are radically different from one another. On the contrary, from a sociological point of view, these formal sources of law, which the jurists are concerned to distinguish, are simply different varieties of one single and unique source: the will of the social group".[186]

Can this be said to apply to Scots criminal law? To what extent is it a product of the will of the social group? To the extent that it has

---

[181] Memorandum of evidence to the *Royal Commission on Capital Punishment* (1949–53), p 428.

[182] *Lord Advocate's Reference (No 1 of 2001)* 2002 SLT 466, per Lady Cosgrove at 481.

[183] The Protection of Wild Mammals (Scotland) Act 2002, s 1(1) makes it an offence to hunt a wild mammal with a dog.

[184] The Breastfeeding etc (Scotland) Act 2005, s 1(1) makes it an offence deliberately to prevent a person from feeding milk (whether by breast or bottle) to a child under the age of 2 years in a public place or on licensed premises.

[185] An offence of smoking in enclosed public places has also been enacted – see the Smoking, Health and Social Care (Scotland) Act 2005, ss 1–4. For a critique, see P R Ferguson, "'Smoke gets in your eyes ...': the criminalisation of smoking in public places, the harm principle and the limits of the criminal sanction" (2011) 31 *Legal Studies* 259.

[186] L Lévy-Bruhl, Sociologie Du Droit (1964), pp 39–40, cited in (and translated by) L L Fuller, "Law as an instrument of social control and law as a facilitation of human interaction" (1975) *BYU L Rev* 89 at 94–95.

a legislature, society can influence the ambit of statutory offences. But as we have noted, many key offences remain defined by the common law, and the Scottish people have little control over its development.[187]

Although Art 7 of the ECHR requires crimes to be clearly defined, the European Court of Human Rights has made clear that a common law based system of criminal law is not in itself in breach of this requirement: **5.16.3**

> "However clearly drafted a legal provision may be, in any system of law, including criminal law, there is an inevitable element of judicial interpretation. There will always be a need for elucidation of doubtful points and for adaptation to changing circumstances. Indeed, in the United Kingdom, as in other Convention States, the progressive development of the criminal law through judicial law-making is a well-entrenched and necessary part of legal tradition. Article 7 of the Convention cannot be read as outlawing the gradual clarification of the rules of criminal liability through judicial interpretation from case to case, provided that the resultant development is consistent with the essence of the offence and could reasonably be foreseen."[188]

Historically, common law systems evolved because of the lack of effective legislative bodies, and continued heavy reliance on the common law may be seen by some as the hallmark of a primitive legal system. This has persisted longer in Scotland than elsewhere because of the historic lack of a legislature with the time and inclination to pass criminal legislation solely for Scotland. Devolution has rendered redundant the continuation of such an approach – at least in theory, since the Scottish Parliament has shown itself able and willing to pass legislation which affects the substantive criminal law, where it perceives there to be a need.[189] In a seminal article, written more than 30 years ago, Ian Willock criticised the "flexible and open-ended" nature of the common law, and concluded that:

> "the general principles of Scots criminal law and the definitions of some of its important criminal acts are in a needlessly ragged state, which leads to an unnecessary degree of uncertainty and inconsistency and can even be oppressive".[190]

---

[187] See, however, the arguments of Scott Styles, who has suggested, specifically in relation to supporting the use of the declaratory power, that judge-made law is no less responsive to public opinion than that made by the legislature. S C Styles, "Something to declare: a defence of the declaratory power of the High Court of Justiciary" in R F Hunter (ed), *Justice and Crime: Essays in Honour of the Right Honourable The Lord Emslie* (1993) at pp 213–218.

[188] *SW v United Kingdom; CR v United Kingdom* (1996) 21 EHRR 363 at 399.

[189] For example, the Sexual Offences (Scotland) Act 2009, and the Criminal Justice and Licensing (Scotland) Act 2010. Further examples are given in section 5.16.1 above.

[190] I Willock, "Scottish criminal law – does it exist?" (1981) 54 *SCOLAG* 225 at 228.

While the appeal court has filled in some of the gaps referred to in his article,[191] Willock's description remains an accurate one.

5.16.4   Jeremy Bentham was highly critical of the idea of the common law, referring to it as "a fiction from beginning to end".[192] As Brian Simpson explained:

> "Bentham's point depends upon the familiar fact that if six pundits of the profession, however sound and distinguished, are asked to write down what they conceive to be ... the definition of murder or manslaughter ... it is in the highest degree unlikely that they will fail to write down six different rules or sets of rules."[193]

There seems little doubt that, even today, six law professors or practising lawyers, if asked to define certain Scottish crimes such as assault or breach of the peace, may well devise differing definitions. In fact, prior to the decision in HM Advocate v Harris[194] in 1993, law students in Dundee University were being taught that an assault could not be committed recklessly, while those at Edinburgh University were being taught the opposite.[195]

5.16.5   Hume himself commented on the fact that, at the time he was writing, the leading work on Scots criminal law was Sir George Mackenzie's Treatise Concerning the Law of Scotland in Matters Criminal, published in 1678:

> "Thus, on the whole, the lawyer has to gain his knowledge of this, certainly the noblest and most interesting part of his profession [that is, criminal law], from the perusal of one work, composed upwards of a century ago, and in times so very different from the present, that, even if it were in every instance an accurate and faithful delineation of the law and practice as they then stood; still it would be found to give a very defective, and often an erroneous account of what is now the law, and to require a very ample commentary, to accommodate it to the uses of our day.
>
>   This will not appear surprising to any one who considers the great change which has taken place since the time of Sir George Mackenzie, in the manners, and temper, and way of thinking of the nation; by which the state of its Criminal Law, and its application to real business, must always, in a great measure, be affected.
>
>   ... the general spirit of [the] law will always, in some measure, be bent and accommodated to the temper and exigencies of the times".[196]

---

[191] For example, we now have Scottish case law on the defences of necessity, coercion and entrapment. See ibid at 225.

[192] J Bentham, Collected Works, IV, p 483.

[193] A W B Simpson, "The common law and legal theory", Ch 15 in Legal Theory and Legal History: Essays on the Common Law" (1987) at p 371.

[194] 1993 JC 150.

[195] See R A A McCall Smith and D Sheldon, Scots Criminal Law (2nd edn, 1997), at pp 158–159. It should be noted that the 3rd edition (by Andrew Cubie) contains a full discussion of the issue and states that "it is clear that assault cannot be committed negligently or recklessly". See Cubie (2010), para 9.5.

[196] Hume, i, 2.

He continued:

> "From this natural correspondence between the state of the Criminal Law, and the condition of the people as to its manners and ways of feeling, it will easily be understood why Sir George Mackenzie's treatise should be defective in its application to our present practice. For at the time of its publication, this country had advanced but little in any sort of improvement; and indeed, whether we consider it with respect to the administration of its Government, its internal discipline and economy, or the opinions, temper, and habits of the people, it was at that time utterly remote from what Scotland has since become."[197]

If Scotland had changed considerably between publication of Mackenzie's work, and Hume's own first edition, 120 years later, how much more has it changed in the 170 years since Hume's "latest edition"? Attitudes towards women, children, and people of different nationalities have changed considerably, as have notions of what is acceptable in the realms of behaviour, particularly sexual behaviour. In 1838, the operation of a gaming house was declared criminal because of its "tendency to corrupt public morals, and injure the interests of society".[198] Some 175 years later, we have a National Lottery.[199] We have moved from a society in which men who engaged in consensual sodomy were strangled and burned at the stake,[200] to one in which gay marriage is facilitated by the state.[201]

Hume referred to the close connection between a country's **5.16.6** criminal law and its inhabitants' "manners and habits, their religion, their state of Government".[202] To employ L P Hartley's observation that "the past is a foreign country",[203] it may be suggested that the Scotland of the early to mid-19th century was inhabited by a people in many respects foreign to the Scots of today. Our understanding of human psychology is far greater than in Hume's day. We know more about how people are likely to react in certain situations and can accommodate this in the law. Sometimes such findings are counter-intuitive. For example, one might expect that the victim of a serious sexual assault would immediately contact the police or, at the least, confide in a close relative or friend, but psychological studies show that this is not, in fact, the most common reaction. This knowledge has helped us to devise rules of criminal procedure and evidence to ensure that juries do not decide that failure to

---

[197] Hume, i, 3.
[198] *Bernard Greenhuff* (1838) 2 Swin 236 at 261, per LJ-C Boyle.
[199] See the National Lottery etc Act 1993.
[200] See Hume, i, 469.
[201] By virtue of the Marriage and Civil Partnership (Scotland) Act 2014.
[202] Hume, i, 3.
[203] L P Hartley's novel *The Go-Between* (1953) opens with these words.

reveal at an early stage that she has been attacked casts doubt on the veracity of a complainer's testimony.[204] Likewise, the knowledge that women who are provoked are generally less likely than men to lose control in a "blind fury" has implications for the reform of the law on provocation. Historical accounts of provocation envisaged a man who had been assaulted, or insulted, and whose honour was at stake,[205] and were unable to accommodate victims of domestic violence who killed their abusive partners.[206]

5.16.7   The common law aspects of Scots criminal law would benefit from being enacted in statutory form. Roscoe Pound put the case in favour of legislation more than a century ago:

> "It is fashionable to point out the deficiencies of legislation and to declare that there are things that legislators cannot do try how they will. It is fashionable to preach the superiority of judge-made law. It may be well, however, for judges and lawyers to remember that there is coming to be a science of legislation and that modern statutes are not to be disposed of lightly as off-hand products of a crude desire to do something, but represent long and patient study by experts, careful consideration by conferences or congresses or associations, press discussions in which public opinion is focussed upon all important details, and hearings before legislative committees. It may be well to remember also that while bench and bar are never weary of pointing out the deficiencies of legislation, to others the deficiencies of judge-made law are no less apparent."[207]

Criminal law statutes do not offer a panacea.[208] We must be wary of the tendency of legislatures to enact what some American

---

[204] See the Vulnerable Witnesses (Scotland) Act 2004, s 5, inserting s 275C into the Criminal Procedure (Scotland) Act 1995. In *D v Donnelly* 2009 SLT 476 the appeal court upheld a drunk-driving conviction of a woman who drove in order to escape a gang who had sexually assaulted her. The defence of necessity was rejected, on the basis that she ought not to have driven the car, but should instead have used her mobile phone to call for help. The view was taken that there was no immediate threat to her life or threat of serious injury. Cases such as this suggest that perhaps the courts could benefit from a greater understanding of human psychology.

[205] J Horder, *Provocation and Responsibility* (1992).

[206] Provocation is discussed further from section 21.10 below.

[207] R Pound, "Common law and legislation" (1907–8) 21 *Harv L R* 383 at 383–384.

[208] Even where a statute is enacted partly to correct a widely recognised weakness or anachronism in the pre-existing law, its application in practice may prove problematic. For example, s 54 of the Coroners and Justice Act 2009 provides, in England and Wales, for a partial defence to murder of loss of control where the accused kills as a result of a loss of her self-control arising from a qualifying trigger. Section 55 defines "qualifying trigger" such that a "thing done or said" leading to the loss of self-control which "constituted sexual infidelity is to be disregarded" (s 55(6)(c)). The provision is designed, rightly, to prevent extreme sexual jealousy or the notion of sexual ownership of another providing a legal defence. In *R v Clinton* [2012] 3 WLR 515, however, the court held that it was unrealistic always to exclude sexual infidelity from any consideration whatsoever. (This is discussed

commentators have referred to as "the crime *du jour*"[209] – the idea that a new crime must be enacted whenever there is public disquiet about some form of anti-social behaviour. If statutory offences are to be an improvement on the common law, they require to be carefully drafted and avoid unnecessarily convoluted language and excessive use of technical terms.[210] If ignorance of the law is to be no defence to a breach of criminal law, as is the case in Scotland,[211] then the law's requirements ought to be expressed in a way which makes sense even to the non-lawyer.

---

further from section 21.11.5 below.) Statutes, then, may reflect public and judicial opinion accumulated over a long period and undoubtedly offer greater certainty. They cannot necessarily, however, always take account of the justice of every individual set of circumstances. Judicial ingenuity still has a place in that respect.

[209] See, for example, S Sun Beale, "The many faces of overcriminalization: from morals and mattress tags to overfederalization" (2004–5) 54 *Am U L Rev* 747 at 755; P H Robinson and M T Cahill, "Can a Model Penal Code Second save the states from themselves?" (2003–4) 1 *Ohio St J Crim L* 169 at 171.

[210] See J R Spencer, "The drafting of criminal legislation: need it be so impenetrable?" [2008] 67 *CLJ* 585. For a criticism of the English Draft Criminal Law Bill (*Legislating the Criminal Code: Offences Against the Person and General Principles* (Law Com No 218, 1993)), see F Bennion, "The Law Commission's Criminal Law Bill: no way to draft a code" (1994) 15 *Stat LR* 108 at 109, in which he describes the draft as "over-technical, poor on exposition, and a sore puzzle from beginning to end". For a rebuttal in robust terms, see J C Smith, "The Law Commission's Criminal Law Bill: a good start for the criminal code" (1995) 16 *Stat LR* 105.

[211] See section 19.6.1 below.

CHAPTER 6

ACTUS REUS AND *MENS REA*

6.1 INTRODUCTION

In defining common law crimes, it is convenient to refer to them **6.1.1**
as having a "forbidden behaviour element or situation" and a
"mental element". The Latin terms *"actus reus"* and *"mens rea"*
are commonly employed to refer to these, respectively. The maxim
actus non facit reum nisi mens sit rea is sometimes translated as
meaning that the act is not criminal unless the mind is also criminal,
but a more accurate approach is to regard this as a requirement for
the prosecution to prove both a "forbidden behavioural element" or
"prohibited scenario" and a corresponding "mental element". Both
must be established beyond reasonable doubt for the prosecution to
secure a conviction. This does not, however, apply to all statutory
offences, many of which impose strict liability – that is, the accused
may be found guilty if the prosecution can establish the *actus reus*;
the offence has no *mens rea* in respect of at least one of its elements.
We discuss offences of strict liability in Chapter 17.[1]

6.2 *ACTUS REUS*

Each crime has its own *actus reus* – the "forbidden behavioural **6.2.1**
element" of assault includes making a physical attack on someone; in
theft it is the removal of property without authority; and in murder
that the accused has caused someone else's death. Behaviour may be
entirely neutral in itself but the circumstances may make it criminal.
For instance, undressing is not generally criminal, but it may be
in certain circumstances (for example, publicly exposing oneself).[2]
The *actus reus* of a crime may sometimes be an omission to act[3] or

---

[1] See from section 17.2 below.
[2] Consider the case of the "Naked Rambler", discussed at section 1.1.2 above, and
the Sexual Offences (Scotland) Act 2009, s 8, discussed in section 11.8 below.
[3] See from section 6.5 below.

(rarely) a state of affairs,[4] rather than positive behaviour on the part of the accused, hence the reference to "forbidden situation" rather than to "forbidden act" or "physical element".

6.2.2   The *actus reus* of some crimes is fulfilled by the accused behaving in a certain way. These are known as "conduct crimes".[5] Perjury is an example of a conduct crime, since it is committed as soon as a person who is under oath makes a statement knowing it to be false. Even if the perjury does not affect the outcome of the trial – even if it has not caused a miscarriage of justice – the charge of perjury is still competent.[6] Rape is also a conduct crime; it is completed by the act of sexual penetration.[7]

6.2.3   Commonly, the law requires some consequence to be caused by the initial conduct, and it is the forbidden result which is then the focus of the *actus reus*, rather than the conduct *per se*. Hence, in the crime of murder, the *actus reus* is that the accused has caused the death of a human being, and the law places little importance on the means by which the killing was committed – for example, whether this is achieved by punching, stabbing, shooting or drowning. Of course, there may be other legal consequences if the murder is committed in a certain way. If death is caused by shooting, there may a question as to whether the accused had a firearms licence, but the point is that, *in respect of the murder charge*, the mechanism for the causing of death is unimportant. The law's focus is instead on the result of the conduct, that is, with the fact that someone has been killed. Students commonly suppose that assault is a result crime, believing that it requires the accused to have caused some injury to the complainer. This is not the case, as we shall see when we examine the definition of assault in a later chapter.[8] Assault is in fact a conduct crime, since its *actus reus* consists in the accused having made a physical attack on someone. If the result of this attack is that the victim is injured (seriously or otherwise) then this can be libelled as an aggravation, but it is the accused's conduct in attacking the victim which in itself is sufficient for the crime to have been committed.

6.2.4   In result crimes it is necessary for the Crown to prove the conduct and its result, and that there is in fact a causal link between the two. This is illustrated by the English law case of *R v White*[9] in which the accused tried to murder his mother by putting poison in her drink. Mrs White died, but three-quarters of the drink was left untouched

---

[4] See from section 6.3 below.
[5] See Gordon (2000) from para 3.05.
[6] Perjury is discussed further from section 14.4 below.
[7] Rape is considered further from section 11.2 below.
[8] See from section 10.2 below.
[9] [1910] 2 KB 124.

and medical evidence showed that death had been caused by a heart attack, unrelated to the poison. The accused was not guilty of murder (but was guilty of the less serious charge of attempted murder) since he had not caused his mother's death.[10] While assault is a conduct crime (as noted above), the "aggravated" element of an aggravated assault is, however, a result which the Crown has to prove.[11]

As previously noted,[12] we can also subdivide the *actus reus* into three types: states of affairs; overt acts; and omissions.

6.3 STATES OF AFFAIRS

Michael Moore has suggested that a "state" differs from an "act" in two respects:

    6.3.1

> "(1) like all events, acts tend to be of short duration, while states can be quite long-lasting or even permanent; (2) human acts essentially involve the choice (or willing) of the actor in a way that states of that actor do not".[13]

In practice, criminalisation of "status" or "states of affairs" is less common than the proscription of acts or omissions. In the case of *Ramsay* v *HM Advocate*[14] the trial judge sentenced a man who had pled guilty to being in possession of a minute quantity of heroin to 4 years' imprisonment, saying that he treated the case as a "serious case of drug addiction". The appeal court substituted a sentence of 2 years' imprisonment, Lord Justice-General Emslie stressing that "drug addiction is not a crime".[15]

One example of a state of affairs proscribed by Scots criminal law is that of being "drunk and incapable" of looking after oneself in a public place, a statutory offence contained in the Civic Government (Scotland) Act 1982.[16] An accused person who is found in such a state fulfils the requirements of this offence – but does it matter how she came to be in the public place? In the English law case of *Winzar* v *Chief Constable of Kent*[17] the accused was found guilty of being drunk on a highway, despite the fact that the police had carried him there from a hospital. It is not certain that the Scottish courts would

    6.3.2

---

[10] Causation will be considered further, from section 7.2 below.
[11] See from section 10.3 below for a discussion of aggravated assaults.
[12] See section 6.2.1 above.
[13] M S Moore, *Act and Crime: The Philosophy of Action and its Implications for Criminal Law* (1993), p 19.
[14] 1984 SCCR 409.
[15] *Ibid* at 410.
[16] Civic Government (Scotland) Act 1982, s 50(1).
[17] (1983) *The Times*, 28 March, discussed in A Ashworth and J Horder, *Principles of Criminal Law* (7th edn, 2013), pp 96–97.

adopt a similar approach should such a case come before them, but the case of *Crowe* v *Waugh*,[18] which related to the accused's *inadvertent* possession of a knife, suggests that they might.[19] It is impossible to give a definitive answer to the approach a Scottish court would take to a *Winzar*-type case, since this has not been considered by the High Court, and indeed the offence of being drunk and incapable does not even merit a mention in Gordon's *Criminal Law.*

6.3.3   Difficulty arises in classifying offences in which bare possession is a sufficient *actus reus*. For example, there are statutory offences of being in possession of controlled drugs,[20] and housebreaking tools.[21] It is also an offence for a person to have an offensive weapon[22] or article with a blade or sharp point[23] (for example, a knife) in a public place. Is possession an "act"? And if not, do these offences involve merely a state of affairs? According to Moore, this conclusion can be avoided if we hold that

> "it is not the *state* of possessing that is being punished, but either the act of taking possession, or (in the cases where the defendant comes into possession without doing anything) the omission to rid oneself of possession. Possession crimes, so construed, present no counter-examples to the act requirement, or at least none greater than that presented by omissions generally".[24]

6.3.4   The offence of having housebreaking tools applies only to those who have two or more convictions for offences of dishonesty, hence the accused's "status" as belonging to a particular class or type of person requires to be proved. Scots criminal law does not generally criminalise status *per se*; it is not an offence to be a prostitute, a vagrant or a drunkard.[25] It may, however, be argued that vicarious liability, in which one person is held responsible for breach of certain statutory offences, committed by another, imposes liability for the status of being an "owner" or "employer".[26]

---

[18] 1999 JC 292.

[19] For further discussion of this case, see sections 8.11.8 and 8.13.2 below.

[20] Misuse of Drugs Act 1971, s 5(2). See also from section 8.9 below.

[21] Civic Government (Scotland) Act 1982, s 58(1), discussed further from section 8.18 below.

[22] Criminal Law (Consolidation) (Scotland) Act 1995, s 47(1), discussed further from section 8.11.1 below.

[23] *Ibid*, s 49, discussed further from section 8.11.7 below.

[24] Moore (1993) at p 21 (emphasis in original).

[25] The Supreme Court of the United States established in the case of *Robinson* v *California*, 370 US 660 (1962), that criminal offences required the accused to have committed an act or omission, and could not proscribe a mere status, such as being addicted to narcotic drugs. In *Powell* v *Texas* 392 US 514 (1968) the court distinguished *Robinson* v *California* in finding that an offence of public intoxication was not in breach of the Constitution.

[26] Vicarious liability is discussed further from section 17.8 below.

This is not to say, however, that the criminal law and the criminal   **6.3.5**
justice system ignore status altogether. In the 21st century, the
targets of societal disapproval are not – or certainly not so much –
prostitutes and vagrants but Nicola Lacey has suggested that we at
least come close, instead, to criminalising the status of "terrorist".[27]
Much of the activity coming under the heading of "terrorism"
already constitutes various criminal offences[28] – exploding a bomb
in a crowded street, causing death would, for example, constitute
murder. Following from this,

> "we see ... the idea that, on top of committing or planning acts of violence,
> there is something additionally and intrinsically wrong about being a certain
> kind of person, engaged in a certain kind of activity [ie a terrorist] – an
> aggravation of blameworthiness which justifies a special criminalization
> regime".[29]

The same sense of criminalisation of status may also apply to post-
release sex offenders whereby

> "certain sex offenders must render themselves visible to the police by providing
> details such as address, virtually ensuring that they will be investigated
> should any sexual (or perhaps other) offence be committed in the area. This
> amounts to a quasi-criminal status – indeed to a *prime facie* judgment of
> criminal propensity."[30]

In neither case does the criminal law reduce the issue to simple
criminalisation of status: "it shall be an offence to be a terrorist/
sex offender". In both, however, the legal rules applying within and
around the criminal law – the obligations imposed on sex offenders
are, for example, to some extent, administrative in nature – serve
to heap on the offender additional stigma arising directly from the
status. The criminal law itself has moved from its early roots in dole,
the attribution of which signified that the offender's whole character
was rotten (that she had a "corrupt and malignant disposition")[31]
to a judgment only upon the wrongness of the individual aspect of
conduct constituting the crime in question.[32] We should, therefore,
be wary about allowing such sweeping status-related judgements
to be made again, in these ways. This is particularly so where the
baseline for commission of an offence of terrorism is drawn so early
in the path from conception and preparation of a crime to actual

---

[27] Offences involving terrorism are described further from section 8.23 below.

[28] N Lacey, "The resurgence of character: responsibility in the context of
criminalization" in R A Duff and S P Green (eds), *Philosophical Foundations of
Criminal Law* (2011) 151 at p 164.

[29] *Ibid.*

[30] *Ibid* at p 169.

[31] Hume, i, 22.

[32] Dole is discussed further from section 6.9 below.

completion[33] – "where the conduct … is only suspected to be at the very furthest margins of terrorist activity".[34] Similarly, the range of offences in respect of which notification under Pt II of the Sexual Offences Act 2003[35] is required is very broad[36] so that, arguably, not all are of equal seriousness.

6.4 OVERT ACTS

6.4.1 The general principle here is that there must have been some conduct by the accused – the accused must have "done something" – and this must generally be voluntary. This is illustrated by the case of *Hogg* v *MacPherson*,[37] in 1928, in which a horse-drawn furniture van was blown over by a violent gust of wind. The van struck a lamp-post, flattening it and breaking the lantern. A demand for compensation was made against the driver of the van under a statute which allowed the municipality to recoup costs for "accidental or negligent damage" done to its streetlamp. The driver failed to pay, and was prosecuted as a result of this failure, as the statute provided. However, it was held on appeal that the breaking of the lantern was not an "act" of the accused at all, hence no compensation could be demanded. The case illustrates that the criminal law generally requires that the accused commit a voluntary act before it will hold her liable, since blame ought only to be attached to behaviours which have been freely chosen. As Oliver Wendell Holmes put it, many years ago:

> "The reason for requiring an act is, that an act implies a choice and that it is felt to be impolitic and unjust to make a man answerable for harm, unless he might have chosen otherwise."[38]

The requirement for a voluntary act reflects a liberal approach to criminal law, with its emphasis on individual autonomy.[39]

6.4.2 The accused's behaviour must be "willed" (the element which was absent in *Hogg* v *MacPherson*). There may have been an overt act, but the behaviour may not have been "voluntary" since the actor is not fully conscious of her conduct. Referred to as "automatism", this might be caused by epilepsy or hypoglycæmia (low blood sugar can, in

---

[33] See from section 8.23 below.
[34] V Tadros, "Justice and terrorism" (2007) 10 *New Crim L Rev* 658 at 665.
[35] Effectively, such notification is the practice commonly known as registration on the Sex Offenders Register. See section 11.21.1 below.
[36] Sexual Offences Act 2003, Sch 3, paras 36–60.
[37] 1928 JC 15. See also *HM Advocate* v *Mitchell* (1856) 2 Irv 488.
[38] O W Holmes, *The Common Law* (1882), p 35.
[39] See C Wells and O Quick, *Lacey, Wells and Quick: Reconstructing Criminal Law: Text and Materials* (4th edn, 2010), p 103. Liberalism was discussed in Chapter 1, from section 1.2.

rare cases, lead to aggressive behaviour in diabetics). It should follow that there is no criminal liability for acts that are not voluntary, such as the behaviour of someone who is sleep-walking or otherwise not conscious (at least where the accused is not at fault in bringing about her involuntary state). As we shall see, however, pragmatic concerns about public safety have resulted in the law being reluctant to allow such semi-conscious states to exonerate, in all circumstances.[40] For conduct to be voluntary it is enough that the actor can control the conduct; it is not necessary for the conduct to be desired or positively embraced. If A chooses to go to the dentist to have her tooth filled, her behaviour is voluntary, even though the pain involved in the process of having a filling is not something she desires.

6.5 OMISSIONS

What happens if someone fails to act? One can, for instance, bring about death by failing to act;[41] the driver of a car or train who fails to stop at a red light could cause death.[42] Of course, it is often the case that a situation can be looked at either as an omission or as a positive act. Is the train driver liable for failing to stop (an omission)? Or for the positive act of driving through a red light? If the driver did not even see the light, the former seems a better way of describing the situation: she failed to see the light, hence failed to stop. Gordon's *Criminal Law* divides omissions into two types: (1) crimes of omission; and (2) crimes of commission committed by means of omission.[43] The first category are conduct crimes, hence it is the failure to do something which constitutes the crime, such as failing to obey a traffic sign,[44] failure to wear a seat-belt[45] or failure to supply a sample of breath or blood when suspected of driving with an excess of alcohol in one's bloodstream.[46] In the second category, the *actus reus* is the result, and the omission is the cause of the result. For example, as we have seen, the *actus reus* of murder is the causing of

6.5.1

---

[40] This is discussed in more detail from section 20.16 below.

[41] For a case in which the accused was indicted for culpable homicide following an omission, see *Bone v HM Advocate* 2006 SLT 164, discussed further at section 6.7.6 below.

[42] Such events are not uncommon in the rail industry, to the extent that such a signal is known as a "SPAD" – a signal passed at danger. This was a major contributory factor in the Ladbroke Grove (or Paddington) rail crash on 5 October 1999. See Rt Hon Lord Cullen PC, *The Ladbroke Grove Rail Inquiry: Part 1 – Report* (2000) at pp 2–4, paras 1.7–1.13 and *passim*.

[43] Gordon (2000), para 3.30.

[44] See the Road Traffic Act 1988, s 36(1).

[45] For example, the Motor Vehicles (Wearing of Seatbelts) Regulations 1993 (SI 1993/176), reg 5.

[46] Road Traffic Act 1988, s 7(6).

death. This can be committed by an overt act (by stabbing, shooting, drowning, suffocating, hanging etc) or by an omission – Gordon gives the example of failing to feed a child, thereby causing its death.[47]

6.5.2   It is axiomatic that each of us "omits" to do thousands of things on a daily basis. By sitting at her computer typing a letter, A is "omitting" to read her e-mail, prepare a conference paper or make herself a cup of tea. However, it would be odd to refer to these as "omissions" or "failures". After all, no ill consequences result. Yet we do fail to do things, with important consequences. By failing to give more money to the victims of disasters, we allow many thousands of people to die, every day. It really only makes sense to say that in typing a letter A is omitting to give a lecture if she *ought* to have been giving the lecture. When we talk about omissions, we tend to refer to that which we are under an obligation to do. It would be senseless to upbraid a student for failing to hand in an assignment on Monday if that assignment was not due until the following Friday. The criminal law takes a similar approach, such that people are held liable for omitting to act in a certain way only if they are under a legal duty (not merely a moral duty) to act in that way.

6.5.3   In Scots law, people are not under any general duty to prevent crime, nor to rescue others in perilous situations. This is illustrated by the case of *HM Advocate* v *Kerr*[48] in 1871. Several youths were involved in assaulting a girl in a country lane, "with intent to ravish" (ie rape) her. One accused, by the name of Donald, did not participate in the assault, but watched the others through a hedge from a neighbouring field, and was charged with them. He was, however, acquitted on the basis that there was no legal duty on him to intervene. This case also serves to illustrate that legality and morality do not always coincide; it is clear that Donald was under a moral duty to assist the girl. As we shall see below, the law does impose certain duties on particular classes of people, and in such circumstances a failure to comply with the duty can result in criminal liability. Duties can be imposed by legislation, or can arise due to common law obligations. Sometimes liability is imposed for the omission itself, for example, if the legislature imposes a duty to do X then failure to do X is a pure omission. In some situations, however, the liability is referred to as commission by omission: in other words, it is the consequence of the omission, rather than the omission *per se*, which is important. As previously noted, one can cause the death of a dependent person, such as an elderly and ailing relative, or a child, by omitting to feed them.[49]

---

[47] Gordon (2000), para 3.30.
[48] (1871) 2 Coup 334.
[49] See Gordon (2000), para 3.30.

6.6 (1) BY STATUTE

Obligations can be imposed by statute – for example, road traffic 6.6.1
legislation imposes duties on motorists to display tax discs;[50] report
accidents to the police;[51] and provide a sample of breath, blood or
urine where it is suspected that they have been driving while under the
influence of alcohol.[52] Failure to do so – omitting to display the disc,
report the accident or provide the requested sample – is an offence. It
is likewise an offence for parents to fail, without reasonable excuse,
to ensure the attendance of their children at school.[53] Section 19 of
the Terrorism Act 2000 makes it an offence for certain people who
believe or suspect that someone has committed specific offences to fail
to disclose this to the police.[54] Specified offences include fundraising,[55]
using money or property[56] where these are done "for the purposes of
terrorism" and money laundering[57] in relation to terrorist property.

Liability for omissions based on status

Recently, the Scottish Government has passed legislation rendering 6.6.2
criminal specific omissions by holders of particular offices, namely
reservoir managers and police constables.[58] The Reservoirs (Scotland)
Act 2011 is designed to "introduce a new regime to better protect the
people of Scotland from the risk of flooding from reservoirs".[59] To
this end, it imposes requirements on reservoir managers[60] to ensure
engineer inspection of higher-risk reservoirs. Failure to comply, or to
act on the recommendations made by the engineer, is criminalised by
the creation of a number of new offences in terms of s 52.

Flooding is a contemporary issue of considerable social concern as 6.6.3
it becomes more frequent.[61] At this level, then, the stakes are high.
In this provision, an attempt is made to police one particular strand

---

[50] Vehicle Excise and Registration Act 1994, s 33.
[51] Road Traffic Act 1988, s 170.
[52] *Ibid*, s 7(6).
[53] Education (Scotland) Act 1980, s 35(1).
[54] This section applies to people who form such beliefs or suspicions in the course
of their trade, profession, business or employment.
[55] Terrorism Act 2000, s 15. See also s 17.
[56] *Ibid*, s 16. "Terrorism" is defined in s 1 of the Act.
[57] *Ibid*, s 18. See section 17.2.6 below.
[58] Though, at the time of writing, the legislation creating the offences relating
to reservoir managers has not yet been brought into force. In relation to the
responsibilities of police constables, see section 6.6.4 below.
[59] Richard Lochhead, MSP, Scottish Parliament Official Report, 27 January 2011
(available at: http://www.scottish.parliament.uk/parliamentarybusiness/28862.
aspx?r=6042&mode=html).
[60] See Pt I, Ch 6 of the Act.
[61] See, for example, the Scottish Flood Forum website: www.scottishfloodforum.
org.

of flood prevention arrangements, by imposing criminal liability for *failure* to act. The offences created are clearly stated so that reservoir managers should be able to establish, with relative ease, both their obligations and the consequences of omitting to carry these out. Perhaps the only outstanding question is the extent to which it is appropriate to criminalise individuals for, effectively, not performing their jobs particularly well. Provided that the obligations imposed are not excessively onerous, and where a pressing social issue is engaged, this seems acceptable.

6.6.4   The primary purpose of the Police and Fire Reform (Scotland) Act 2012 was to create one Scotland-wide police service and one Scotland-wide fire and rescue service to replace the several local forces which existed previously. The opportunity was also taken to create, in relation to police officers, a specific statutory offence of neglect of duty[62] or, in other words, criminally omitting to perform the obligations required of police constables.[63] It is also an offence for a constable to fail to return to the (new) Police Authority "any relevant item"[64] whether on being ordered to do so[65] or on ceasing to be a constable.[66] The first offence is broad in scope and, effectively, turns the obligation on police officers to perform their duties into a recognised legal duty backed by criminal sanction. As we shall see, similar liability is imposed by the common law for failure to perform duties arising by virtue of holding a particular office. Our view is that, where possible, it is generally better for duties of this nature to be set down in statutory form in the pursuit of clarity and certainty in the law.

6.7   (2) COMMON LAW OBLIGATIONS

6.7.1   Criminal liability for omissions may be imposed where the accused was required to act in a particular way through holding a particular office by virtue of a contract of employment. An early example of this is the case of *William Hardie*[67] in 1847. The accused was a poor-law inspector in Stirling. One of his duties was to acquaint himself with the circumstances of those in receipt of parish relief (rather like state benefits) and to respond to requests from such people for further sums. One woman made a number of such applications, and the indictment averred that Hardie had neglected his duties by ignoring

---

[62] Police and Fire Reform (Scotland) Act 2012, s 22(3).
[63] This term is used in the Act to refer to officers of all ranks. See *ibid*, s 99(1).
[64] "A relevant item is anything issued to a constable for the carrying out of the constable's functions, e.g. police uniform" (annotation to the Act).
[65] Police and Fire Reform (Scotland) Act 2012, s 23(1).
[66] *Ibid*, s 23(2).
[67] (1847) Ark 247.

this. Even when she became ill with dysentery and influenza, it seems that Hardie did not investigate the woman's case or advance her any further money. Eventually, she died of starvation. Hardie was charged with her culpable homicide and the High Court held that this was a relevant charge because of the duties imposed by his job.

A further mechanism by which omissions liability may arise, even **6.7.2** if there is no formal contract, nor any statutory provision, is through an (informal) agreement to look after someone which imposes a duty of reasonable care. This was at issue in the case of *Paterson* v *Lees*,[68] in which the appellant's conviction for "shameless indecency" was quashed on appeal. He had been babysitting two children, aged 9 and 11, and had originally been charged with having shown them "a film of an obscene and indecent nature". The evidence showed, however, that it was the children who had switched on the pornographic video, and that Paterson had failed to stop them watching it. The appeal court held that the accused was under no legal duty to prevent the viewing of the film. It does not, however, seem to have been doubted that he was under a duty to take reasonable care to safeguard their physical wellbeing.

Healthcare professionals are under a legal duty to treat and care **6.7.3** for their patients, but the Court of Session held in the case of *Law Hospital NHS Trust* v *Lord Advocate*[69] that there is no duty to provide treatment which is futile. This case involved a patient in a persistent vegetative state, a condition from which there was no possibility of recovery. "Treatment" was defined in this context to include artificial nutrition and hydration – in other words, providing sustenance by means of a naso-gastric tube.[70] Although this was a civil (ie non-criminal) case, it had the effect of de-criminalising passive euthanasia,[71] provided that the medical personnel have followed the procedure set up by the *Law Hospital* case.

Family relationships can also impose criminal liabilities for **6.7.4** omissions. It is clear that parents have a duty towards their children, and failure to exercise an appropriate level of care can result in criminal liability.[72] There is a dearth of Scottish cases which have considered liability for omissions by other family members,[73] but it

---

[68] 1999 JC 159.
[69] 1996 SC 301. The equivalent English law case is *Airedale National Health Service Trust* v *Bland* [1993] AC 789.
[70] 1996 SC 301.
[71] See from section 9.20 below.
[72] See *Bone* v *HM Advocate* 2006 SLT 164, discussed further at section 6.7.6 below.
[73] For a description of the case law of the 19th century, see R S Shiels, "Scots criminal law and liability for omissions" (2006) 70 *J Crim L* 413. See also the case of Brandon Muir (http://thescotsman.scotsman.com/scotland/Brandon-Muir-Another-child-left.5035018.jp).

is likely that the Scottish courts would define the parameters of this liability in a similar way to that of other common law jurisdictions. In the English case of *R v Gibbins and Proctor*,[74] both Proctor and her boyfriend, Gibbins, were charged with the murder of Mr Gibbins' 7-year-old daughter. They neglected to feed the girl or look after her and she died. Gibbins was held liable because the law imposes a duty on a parent, and Proctor was liable because she had acted as the child's mother and had been given money to feed her – in other words, she had assumed the role of mother. In *R v Instan*[75] a woman moved in with her aunt but failed to provide her with medical care or food, and as a result the older woman died. This was a duty, voluntarily assumed, by the niece, who was convicted of manslaughter (similar to the Scottish crime of culpable homicide). The accused had been living at the expense of her aunt.

6.7.5   In the Australian case of *R v Russell*[76] a man was charged with the murder of his wife and two children. The jury found on the evidence that the woman had decided to kill herself and drown her two children in the swimming pool. It found that the accused had stood by and had made no attempt to save them. The court held that he was under a duty to save his children, but not his wife. In *People v Beardsley*,[77] an American case, the accused was acquitted of manslaughter when his mistress collapsed, after having taken morphine tablets. The court held that he was under no legal duty to assist her, even though he knew her life was in danger, but that he would have had a legal duty to take care of her, had they been married. This decision has been criticised:

> "In its savage proclamation that the wages of sin is death, [the decision] ignores any impulse of charity and compassion. It proclaims a morality which is smug, ignorant and vindictive. In a civilised society, a man who finds himself with a helplessly ill person who has no other source of aid should be under a duty to summon help, whether the person is his wife, his mistress, a prostitute or a Chief Justice."[78]

6.7.6   One of the few Scottish cases to have considered a criminal omission by a parent is *Bone v HM Advocate*,[79] in which a child was murdered by her mother's boyfriend. The mother was convicted of culpable homicide by failing to protect the child, but this conviction was quashed on appeal. The appeal court held that the standard of behaviour required of the mother was whether "the particular parent, with all her personal characteristics and in the situation in

---

[74] (1919) 13 Cr App R 134.

[75] [1893] 1 QB 450. See also *R v Stone & Dobinson* [1977] QB 354.

[76] [1933] VLR 59.

[77] 113 NW 1128 (1907).

[78] G Hughes, "Criminal omissions" (1957–58) 67 *Yale LJ* 590 at 624.

[79] 2006 SLT 164.

which she found herself, could reasonably have intervened to prevent the assault".[80]

Liability for omissions by virtue of having created a dangerous situation

There may be a further category of omissions where the duty is   6.7.7
imposed because of the "creation of a dangerous situation" by the
accused. Someone who has exposed another person or another's
property to a risk of injury or damage, and then fails to take
reasonable steps to avert that risk, may be liable for failing to
remedy this. In *MacPhail* v *Clark*[81] the accused caused a road
accident by allowing a straw fire to spread to a roadside verge. The
court held that since the accused was a farmer, he ought to have
been aware of the danger and anticipated it, or at least, when the
danger occurred, to have tried to remedy it. The charge was of
"recklessly endangering safety and lives". The accused's failure to
act constituted the required *actus reus*. In the more recent case of
McCue v *Currie*[82] the accused broke into a caravan in order to steal
therefrom. He had been using a cigarette lighter for illumination,
but dropped it when it malfunctioned in his hand. This caused the
caravan to catch fire. He did not attempt to put out the fire, nor
did he call the fire brigade. The court held that the accused was not
liable for his omission to act, notwithstanding that the situation
was similar to that in *MacPhail* v *Clark*.

6.8   CRITIQUE OF THE LAW ON OMISSIONS AND PROPOSALS FOR REFORM

The decision in *McCue* v *Currie*[83] has left the law in a state of   6.8.1
uncertainty. If the circumstances of *MacPhail* v *Clark*[84] were to
arise again today, would the charge be regarded as a relevant one,
or would *McCue* v *Currie* be followed? Prior to the latter decision,
there was widespread academic agreement that failure to rectify a
dangerous situation could constitute a criminal omission.[85] People
must know what the criminal law requires of them if they are to be
able to choose to conform their behaviour to these requirements.
In respect of criminal liability for failing to attempt to limit harm

---

[80] 2006 SLT 164 at 167, per Lord Macfadyen.
[81] 1983 SLT (Sh Ct) 37.
[82] 2004 JC 73. See J Chalmers, "Fireraising by omission" 2004 SLT (News) 59.
(Henceforth "2004a".)
[83] 2004 JC 73.
[84] 1983 SLT (Sh Ct) 37.
[85] Chalmers (2004a) at 63.

resulting from a dangerous situation (which the accused has herself created) it is not acceptable for this to lack clarity. *McCue* v *Currie* is a surprising decision, not least for the court's refusal to criminalise the accused's behaviour, notwithstanding that the destruction of the caravan arose solely from his acts.

6.8.2   Scots law employs, at least in respect of assault, a doctrine of "transferred intent".[86] This means that where A throws a punch, intending to strike B, but the blow makes contact with C instead, A can be treated as having intended to assault C. The intention to injure B is "transferred" to C, making A liable for assaulting C. Transferred intent does not permit the fact that the accused had formed an intention to commit a particular crime to be employed to compensate for the lack of intent in relation to a wholly different crime; the fact that it can be shown that the accused intended to steal something from a shop cannot be substituted for an intention to damage property, should she stumble and accidentally break a window when leaving the premises. In *McCue* v *Currie*[87] the court may have been at pains to eschew any notion that transferred intent could be used here to find the accused guilty of fire-raising on the basis of his intent to steal. One can, however, vary the scenario slightly, so that the accused's initial behaviour is not tainted with blame. Let us imagine that a smoker attempts to light a cigarette, but the flame from her lighter is blown by a freak gust of wind onto curtains flapping nearby through an open caravan window. Prosecution of the smoker for the deliberate destruction of a caravan is clearly unwarranted. Yet were the smoker to see the fire take hold and simply walk away, we would surely have little difficulty in holding that, just like the farmer in *MacPhail* v *Clark*,[88] she had a moral responsibility to act, and that she should be subject to the sanctions of the criminal law for failing to take even minimal steps to rectify the damage she has caused, even if this was only by alerting the emergency services.

6.8.3   In the English law case of *R* v *Miller*[89] the defendant had been squatting in someone else's house, and had fallen asleep while smoking. His mattress caught fire and the fire spread to the house. Miller made no attempt to extinguish the flames, but instead moved to another room and went back to sleep. His conviction for arson (similar to the Scottish crime of fire-raising) was upheld by the House of Lords. According to Lord Diplock, there was

"no rational ground for excluding from conduct capable of giving rise to criminal liability, conduct which consists of failing to take measures that lie

---

[86] See also from section 6.13 below.
[87] 2004 JC 73.
[88] 1983 SLT (Sh Ct) 37.
[89] [1983] 2 AC 161 (HL).

within one's power to counteract a danger that one has oneself created, if at
the time of such conduct one's state of mind is such as constitutes a necessary
ingredient of the offence ...

I cannot see any good reason why, so far as liability under criminal law is
concerned, it should matter at what point of time before the resultant damage
is complete a person becomes aware that he has done a physical act which,
whether or not he appreciated that it would at the time when he did it, does
in fact create a risk that property of another will be damaged; provided that,
at the moment of awareness, it lies within his power to take steps, either by
himself or by calling for the assistance of the fire brigade if this be necessary,
to prevent or minimise the damage to the property at risk".[90]

There is much to be said for the Scottish courts adopting a similar
approach.

The court in *McCue* v *Currie*[91] suggested that there may be a **6.8.4**
case for enacting a new crime of "culpably failing to take appropriate steps" after having caused a dangerous situation to persons
or property.[92] This proposal seems to have been based on the
mistaken belief that such an offence existed in England. Mention has
been made of the (unofficial) *Draft Criminal Code for Scotland*.[93]
Section 14 of that *Code* establishes rules of causation and provides
that:

"A person is criminally liable for a result caused by omitting to act only if –
  (a) the legislation on a particular offence expressly so provides;
  (b) the person is under a duty to act (whether by operation of law, or under
      contract or by an assumption of responsibility) and in breach of that
      duty omits to act; or
  (c) *the person acts (whether lawfully or otherwise) so as to expose another
      person, or the property of another person, to a risk of injury or damage
      and then omits to take such steps as are reasonable to avert that risk.*"[94]

We suggest that a provision such as that contained in s 14(c) be
enacted. This would make clear that the behaviour of the accused
in *McCue* v *Currie* could be charged as reckless endangerment, and
remove the confusion which has resulted from that decision.

A more profound criticism can be made of Scots criminal law's **6.8.5**
approach to omissions, in that the law does not recognise a general
duty to rescue. While a parent or lifeguard is under a legal duty
to rescue a small child who is drowning in a shallow swimming
pool, no such duty is imposed on a mere passer-by or fellow bather
– and this is so even if the latter two could easily save the child,
without putting themselves at risk of harm. Since we recognise that

---

[90] [1983] 2 AC 161 at 176.
[91] 2004 JC 73.
[92] *Ibid* at 80, per Temporary Judge C G B Nicolson.
[93] See section 5.10.4 above.
[94] Emphasis added.

all parties in this scenario are under a *moral* duty to rescue the child, why does this translate into a *legal* obligation for some of the parties, but not others? Moore's response is based on a liberal philosophy:[95]

> "The answer lies in the value we accord to persons' *liberty* to make the wrong choice. To require parents to save their children diminishes their liberty to a certain extent; but to require strangers to save all children in peril diminishes their liberty to a greater extent. Furthermore, on the hard-to-justify but commonly felt assumption that we owe more to those near and dear to us than we owe to strangers, our positive duties towards our own children are stronger than they are to children as such; put another way, we do more wrong in failing to save our own child than we do in failing to save someone else's child."[96]

The lifeguard is taken to accept that her liberty will be curtailed in a way which is different from the passer-by; by choosing this form of employment, she puts herself under certain obligations to users of the swimming pool. According to William Wilson:

> "People could not be the authors of their own destiny if they were under an enforceable obligation to defer their own interests to those of others. Individual freedom takes priority over welfare as a vindication of the principle of autonomy. The exception to the rule, however, shows that welfare is a proper value to be pursued but only where this does not undermine autonomy. If one voluntarily assumes a responsibility of care over another, one may be punished for not discharging it if harm results. This is not considered a diminution of a person's autonomy because, by assuming the obligation, one is deemed already to have chosen to restrict the range of life choices available."[97]

We can again see a liberal philosophy at work here, and it is equally apparent in Peter Alldridge's comment that: "In a world peopled by atomised individuals ... there is no assumption that a helpless person in need or danger should be helped without some recompense."[98] Communitarianism would instead favour all citizens being under a duty of easy rescue.[99] This is indeed the approach taken in some

---

[95] See from section 1.2 above.

[96] Moore (1993) at p 57 (emphasis in original). There may be a genetic explanation for the "commonly felt assumption" to which Moore refers – see R Dawkins, *The Selfish Gene* (1989).

[97] W Wilson, *Central Issues in Criminal Theory* (2002), p 39.

[98] P Alldridge, *Relocating Criminal Law* (2000), p 51.

[99] See A Norrie, *Crime, Reason and History: A Critical Introduction to Criminal Law* (2001): "There are certain duties of citizenship which extend beyond those responsibilities that one has voluntarily undertaken on the basis of a contractual analogy. These derive from the social responsibility that comes from living in a community with others" (p 128). See also Alldridge (2000), p 53. Note, however, that Norrie cautions that there are dangers inherent in the communitarian approach (p 131).

continental jurisdictions.[100] Were Scots law to adopt a similar approach, this need not mean that a person whose omission causes death must be charged with murder or culpable homicide – a statutory offence of "failure to render aid" could be enacted. This could impose liability only where the accused could have acted to save life or prevent serious injury without putting herself at risk of harm.

6.9   MENS REA

It has been said that "[m]ore ink has been spilt over the guilty mind concept than any other substantive criminal law topic".[101] Despite this (or perhaps because of it?) Sanford Kadish has observed that: "The term '*mens rea*' is rivalled only by the term 'jurisdiction' for the varieties of senses in which it has been used and for the quantity of obfuscation it has created."[102] The expression can be used in at least two different ways. Stuart Green distinguishes between using *mens rea* in a "narrow 'elemental' sense" and in a "broad 'blameworthiness' sense":[103]

6.9.1

> "*Mens rea* in the former sense refers directly to the particular mental state either required in the definition of an offence, or with which the defendant actually committed the offence – such as purposely, intentionally, knowingly, and so forth. Used as such, *mens rea* has a fairly straightforward, technical meaning: the presence or absence of such mental states can typically be determined empirically, without the necessity of making a moral judgment about the defendant's conduct or character.
>
> The broader sense of *mens rea* is harder to characterize, in part because there are actually two separate sub-meanings at work here. The term has sometimes been used to refer to those conditions that must be satisfied in order for the criminal law to ascribe 'blameworthiness' to a defendant, including not only the mental elements of a particular offence but also the absence of any potentially applicable defences, such as insanity, duress, intoxication, or choice of evils. There is also a second, vaguer, 'blameworthiness' sense in which the term *mens rea* has been used: it can refer to a general 'immorality of motive' or 'evil will', rather than a specific mental state, with which the offender acted."[104]

---

[100] See M Menlowe and A McCall Smith (eds), *The Duty to Rescue: The Jurisprudence of Aid* (1993). When Princess Diana was fatally injured in a car accident in Paris in 1997, several photographers who were present at the scene of the crash were later investigated for violation of a French law which makes it a criminal offence deliberately to fail to assist a person who is in danger, the maximum penalty for which is 5 years' imprisonment and/or a €100,000 fine. Following the investigation, no charges were brought.

[101] D Stuart, *Canadian Criminal Law: A Treatise* (6th edn, 2011), p 167.

[102] S H Kadish, *Blame and Punishment: Essays in the Criminal Law* (1987), p 65.

[103] S P Green, "Six senses of strict liability: a plea for formalism" in A P Simester (ed), *Appraising Strict Liability* (2005) at p 11.

[104] *Ibid* (footnotes omitted).

In older criminal cases, particularly those in which the accused was charged with murder, the Scottish courts used the word "dole" meaning a "depraved disposition" or an "evil intent". Hence Hume referred to "dole" as "that corrupt and evil intention, which is essential ... to the guilt of any crime".[105] This approach employs "*mens rea*" as an umbrella term:

> "Just as all cars have different wheels, little cars little wheels and big cars big wheels and we are justified in referring to them collectively under the unifying concept wheels, so all crimes have a different mens rea and yet the concept of mens rea must be regarded as a unifying concept of various possible frames of mind."[106]

The High Court continues to use terms such as "wickedness" and to talk of "evil intent". It also sometimes refers to "dole".[107] It is not always clear whether, in modern times, this word is used as a substitute for the term "mental element" or *mens rea*, or in the sense in which Hume used the term.

6.9.2   Robert Shiels has questioned the relevance of dole in the 21st-century context,[108] suggesting that "modern commentators write of *dole* with a degree of uneasiness or even embarrassment".[109] He argues that a strong tone of moral condemnation, going beyond the finding of *mens rea* required for the offence actually charged, is found in the sentencing remarks of judges in particularly heinous cases where life sentences are imposed.[110] This leads him to state:

> "One view might be offered: *dole* and the general idea of malignancy and wickedness may well be relevant to what is now known as the punishment part in sentences that amount to great length for crimes of the utmost seriousness."[111]

---

[105] Hume, i, 21.

[106] G O W Mueller, "On common law *mens rea*" (1957–58) 42 *Minn L Rev* 1043, at 1055.

[107] See, for example *Lord Advocate's Reference (No 2 of 1992)* 1993 JC 43; *Merrin v S* 1987 SLT 193.

[108] R Shiels, "The unsettled relevance of dole" (2010) SCL 421.

[109] *Ibid* at 427. Dr Shiels comments that in the first edition of this book "The authors refer ... to the tendency of the judges of the High Court of Justiciary to use terms such as 'wickedness' and 'evil intent' as well as *dole* occasionally. No normative observations are made on this aspect of the law" (footnote omitted). We did, in fact, criticise the use of "wicked intent" and "wicked recklessness" and recommended their abolition: see P R Ferguson and C McDiarmid, *Scots Criminal Law: A Critical Analysis* (2009) at section 22.10.1.

[110] He cites, for example, *HM Advocate v Boyle* 2010 SLT 29, where the victim, having been subjected to a serious assault which involved, *inter alia*, stamping to his head, stabbing in the leg with a knife and being dragged down a flight of stairs, was eventually placed, alive, on a pyre and set alight. He died 5 days later (Shiels (2010) at 427).

[111] *Ibid* at 429.

It is widely accepted that one of the overarching functions of a criminal justice system is condemnatory[112] in that it expresses society's censure of the convicted person for breaching its norms as contained in the criminal law. The issues raised here are the way in which, and the extent to which, this is done. The criminal process, to the point of the jury verdict, determines only whether the accused carried out the crime, applying the narrow concept of *mens rea* as the specified mental state needed to make out the offence definition. Because dole constituted the mental element in Hume's time, however – it was a technical element "essential ... to the guilt of any crime"[113] – it would have been an element of the decision on guilt. Within the modern criminal process, sentencing (and the judge's remarks on sentence which may – and arguably should – express some form of societal condemnation) are kept separate from the determination of guilt. The fact that both dole and these remarks are grounded in moral considerations is not enough to allow us to regard the latter as a vestige of the former. This is not to say that the criminal process plays no role in passing judgement on character[114] nor is it to underestimate the role of the media in reflecting and disseminating moral condemnation,[115] but dole *per se* probably only persists in the tendency of certain judges to use it as a synonym for the mental element. Nonetheless, the resort by the courts to the terms and concepts of "wickedness" and "evil intent" was noted by Gerald Gordon in the preface to his second edition of *Criminal Law*, 30 years ago.[116] Gordon cited the cases of *Cawthorne* v *HM Advocate*,[117] *Smart* v *HM Advocate*[118] and *Brennan* v *HM Advocate*[119] as examples of this, but it is a trend which continues in the 21st century.[120]

It is submitted that loose use of terminology is particularly unhelpful **6.9.3** in this context. In Hume's time, because of the prevalence of capital punishment, the criminal law used the concept of dole to make an explicit moral judgement that an accused's whole character was

---

[112] See R Rodogno, "Shame, guilt and punishment" (2009) 28 *Law & Phil* 429 at 435–436.

[113] Hume, i, 21.

[114] Indeed, Nicola Lacey has argued strongly that there is a "resurgence" in this respect: Lacey (2011) at 153.

[115] See, for example, B Franklin and J Petley, "Killing the age of innocence: newspaper reporting of the death of James Bulger" in J Pilcher and S Wagg (eds), *Thatcher's Children? Politics, Childhood and Society in the 1980s and 1990s* (1996) at p 134.

[116] See now Gordon (2000), Preface, at p xv.

[117] 1968 JC 32.

[118] 1975 SLT 65.

[119] 1977 SLT 151.

[120] See, for example, *Drury* v *HM Advocate* 2001 SLT 1013.

flawed.[121] This allowed some comfort (if perhaps only theoretical) to be taken in the notion that only the truly bad were criminalised (and, at the extreme, executed). Today, it is not necessary for the Crown to prove the accused's *generalised* depravity. It must establish only that the precise and narrow terms of the *actus reus* and *mens rea* are made out. It is in this sense that the term *"mens rea"* ought to be used. As a concept, *mens rea* replaces dole; they are not synonymous. Even where a particular *mens rea* continues to require "wickedness,"[122] or to be "evil",[123] this is usually more specifically defined through case law.

6.9.4   The High Court has also demonstrated confusing imprecision in using terms such as "criminal intent" or "wilful intent" as a substitute for the generic term *"mens rea"*.[124] The lack of clarity created by this is evident from *Cawthorne* v *HM Advocate*;[125] in discussing the *mens rea* of wicked *recklessness* (for attempted murder) the judgments persist in identifying this as the "wilful *intent*"[126] or the "criminal *intent*"[127] necessary. Since *Cawthorne* is concerned with wicked recklessness *as an alternative to* "intention to kill" (as the *mens rea* of attempted murder), this can only make sense if "criminal intent" is being used simply to identify "the mental element" generally.

6.9.5   In many common law crimes such as murder, malicious mischief and theft, the conduct involved is seen not merely as criminal but morally wrong or wicked, hence it may be felt to be appropriate to equate *mens rea* with a "wicked" or "guilty" mind.[128] But this is not always the case. A person who acts from good motives may not have a "guilty mind" in a broad sense, but may well have sufficient *mens rea* to be guilty of a crime. If A kills B, her much-loved spouse, to prevent him from suffering a prolonged and painful terminal illness, few people would describe A's mindset as "wicked" or even "guilty", yet she does have the *mens rea* of a murderer.[129]

---

[121] See C McDiarmid, *Childhood and Crime* (2007), pp 106–107.

[122] See from section 9.11.1 below.

[123] See section 10.2.3 below, in relation to assault.

[124] Findlay Stark has referred to the "Scottish courts' abject failure to define mens rea terms consistently" – see "It's only words: on meaning and mens rea" (2013) *CLJ* 155 at 155 n 1.

[125] 1968 JC 32

[126] *Ibid* at 36, per LJ-G Clyde (emphasis added).

[127] *Ibid* at 38, per Lord Cameron (emphasis added).

[128] According to the Scottish Law Commission: "While this rather moralistic concept of general wickedness has to some extent disappeared from Scots law, no doubt largely because of the proliferation of statutory crimes using express words of *mens rea*, it still remains as the background against which the mental element necessary for most common law crimes is to be measured" (*The Mental Element in Crime* (Scot Law Com No 80, 1983), para 2.14).

[129] In practice, the Crown may well accept a plea to culpable homicide, on the ground of diminished responsibility, but there can be little doubt that in such cases the accused had the intention to kill, which is sufficient *mens rea* for murder. See,

Referring to *mens rea* as the "criminal mind/guilty mind", as **6.9.6**
many commentators do,[130] is far from ideal. Green correctly notes
that "determining whether a statute requires *mens rea* in the broader,
blameworthiness sense is likely to invite controversy, with judgments
varying from observer to observer".[131] It is more common nowadays
for *mens rea* to be used in Green's narrower sense. Viewed in this
way, the phrase *actus non facit reum nisi mens sit rea* means that the
accused's state of mind must have been such as to make the forbidden
situation/behavioural element criminal. Stephen explained:

> "the definition of all or nearly all crimes contains not only an outward and
> visible element, but a mental element, varying according to the different
> nature of different crimes ... Hence the only means of arriving at a full
> comprehension of the expression 'mens rea' is by a detailed examination of
> the definitions of particular crimes".[132]

As Glanville Williams succinctly put it, *mens rea* is the mental element
necessary for the particular crime.[133] This means that there is no one
"guilty mind" or "criminal mind" – the *mens rea* of murder is quite
distinct from that of theft, or of rape, or of assault. In summary,
then, the term *"mens rea"* should be used to denote only this narrow
concept, identified by Williams. Dole is an old concept reflecting
the overarching depravity of the accused's whole character. While
sometimes used interchangeably with *"mens rea"* in Scottish cases,
the two are not identical. The term "mental element" may be used
more generally to encompass either or both of the *mens rea* for the
specific offence and/or the moral fault element identified by Green.
"Mental element" also encompasses criminal capacity.[134] In our own
discussion, we will use the term *"mens rea"* in its narrow sense.

6.10 MOTIVE

"Motive" is the term used to describe the rationale underlying a **6.10.1**
decision to do something. In crime fiction, particularly "whodunits",
it is a common plot device to find that someone has been murdered,

---

however, the case of *Drury* v *HM Advocate* 2001 SLT 1013, discussed from section
9.11.1 below.
[130] See, for example, "Criminal Law", Chapter 16 in N Busby, B Clark, R Paisley
and P Spink, *Scots Law: A Student Guide* (3rd edn, 2006) at pp 634–635; Wilson
(2002) at p 4. Cubie refers to *actus reus* and *mens rea* as "a wrongful act" and "a
wrongful state of mind", respectively (A M Cubie, *Scots Criminal Law* (3rd edn,
2010), para 2.1).
[131] Green (2005) at p 12.
[132] J Fitzjames Stephen, *History of Criminal Law* 2 (1883), pp 94–95, quoted in
K J M Smith, *Lawyers, Legislators and Theorists: Developments in English
Criminal Jurisprudence 1800–1957* (1998) at p 145.
[133] G Williams, *Criminal Law: The General Part* (2nd edn, 1961), p 31.
[134] See from section 6.18 below.

and there are numerous suspects. Each suspect falls under the detective's spotlight because they have a motive for wanting the victim dead. Greed, hatred, jealousy, anger, envy – these are the motives which figure in crime novels. In reality, while it may assist the prosecution in establishing its case if the accused had a credible motive for committing a crime, there is no requirement for the Crown to establish this.[135] The *mens rea* for murder includes an intention to kill. The motive behind such an intention may be (and usually will be) a bad one, such as greed or hatred, but even a good motive, or a less bad one (for example, killing a blackmailer, or a dictator who plans to cause terrible misery) is still murder, since all that is required is that the accused intend the victim's death.[136]

6.10.2   This is, at least, the theory of the law. In practice, motive can make a difference in the decision whether to indict murder or culpable homicide, and anecdotal evidence suggests that the Crown frequently accepts pleas to culpable homicide where the accused's motive was to end suffering.[137] Indeed, it seems to be Crown practice not to prosecute some cases in which the accused's motive was a compassionate one – even where there is evidence that the accused may have intended to cause death.[138] Although motive will not affect conviction – A will be found guilty of theft whether she stole out of greed, or in order to give the money to charity – it can be used in mitigation of sentence. If the motive is good, the accused seems less blameworthy and will frequently receive a lesser sentence. A conviction on a charge of murder, of course, results in only one possible sentence – life imprisonment. As we shall see in Chapter 11, motive is an essential ingredient in some statutory sexual offences, where it must be shown that the accused acted for sexual gratification, or to humiliate, distress or alarm the complainer.[139] It is also of great importance in relation to a number of statutory offences in which prejudicial motives (based

---

[135] For a detailed discussion, see J Horder, "On the irrelevance of motive in criminal law", in J Horder (ed), *Oxford Essays in Jurisprudence* (4th series, 2000) at pp 173–191.

[136] There may now be an argument that an intention to kill such a dictator is not "wicked" as required by *Drury* v *HM Advocate* 2001 SLT 1013 (per LJ-G Rodger at 1016). See from section 9.11.1 below.

[137] See, for example, the case of Paul Brady, discussed at section 9.15.1 below.

[138] See, for example, the case of Dr Michael Munro, a consultant neonatologist at Aberdeen Maternity Hospital, who admitted to the GMC that he had injected two dying babies with a paralysing drug. One of the infants had been given 23 times the normal dose of a muscle relaxant. No prosecution was taken. See *BBC News*, "Baby doctor cleared of misconduct", 11 July 2007, available at: http://news.bbc.co.uk/1/hi/scotland/north_east/6291224.stm.

[139] Sexual Offences (Scotland) Act 2009, ss 5, 6, 9, 22–26 and 32–36.

on race, religion, disability or sexual orientation, for example)
are specified as a form of aggravation, meriting more severe
punishment.[140]

What if the motive is to amuse or entertain? Canadian author   **6.10.3**
Pierre Rainville argues that the law ought to distinguish between
conduct which is merely inappropriate and what he calls "true
criminal behaviour". He asks:

> "Is it appropriate to label practical jokers 'criminals'? There are numerous
> scenarios in which this question arises, some of the offenders in these cases
> being: a person who makes a phony bomb threat in an airport; someone who
> makes sexual contact as a form of inappropriate humour; an adolescent who
> points a gun at a friend and frightens him or her by giving the impression
> that he will shoot; the author of a threatening letter meant as a hoax; the
> pie-thrower; the exhibitionist who wrongly expects to make people laugh;
> individuals who hide other people's property as a joke; the joker who enjoys
> fooling a police officer by having the officer investigate an imaginary crime;
> the individual who suggests that another person commit a crime without
> suspecting that the person will take the advice seriously and will commit
> such a crime; the organizer of a military hazing or university initiation; the
> journalist or accused person who mocks a judge."[141]

While Rainville cautions that the law should hesitate to criminalise
some forms of behaviour which are intended to be humorous, he
also recognises that such behaviour can target "the very values
that criminal law seeks to protect", including "morality, safety,
property, human dignity, and the authority of the courts".[142] He
concludes: "When a joke does permanent damage, the magnitude
of the consequences of humour becomes such that criminal law
can no longer stand aside."[143] We can see the harm principle at
work here.[144] Don Stuart has suggested that the law ought not
to recognise what he calls a "defence of prank", arguing that it
confuses intent and motive.[145] We agree with his suggestion that
this should sometimes mitigate sentence, but should not provide a
complete defence.[146]

The approach taken to such forms of behaviour by Scots criminal   **6.10.4**
law is illustrated by the case of *Quinn* v *Lees*,[147] in which the accused
was charged with assaulting three boys by setting his dog on them.

---

[140] See from section 7.9 below.
[141] P Rainville, "From practical joker to offender: reflections on the concept of
'crime'", Ch 5 in Law Commission of Canada, *What Is a Crime? Defining Criminal
Conduct in Contemporary Society* (2004) at p 125.
[142] *Ibid* at p 126.
[143] *Ibid* at p 129.
[144] See Chapter 3.
[145] Stuart (2011) at pp 604–605.
[146] *Ibid* at p 583.
[147] 1994 SCCR 159.

He gave evidence that he had called on the dog to attack "as a joke". It was held that there had been sufficient evidence that he had intended the dog to attack the boys. If it had been a joke, this was merely his motive, and did not affect his *mens rea*.[148]

6.11   DEGREES OF *MENS REA*

6.11.1   There are different degrees of *mens rea*, reflecting degrees of moral disapprobation; some acts are more blameworthy than others, and this is reflected in criminal law. As Wendell Holmes famously remarked: "Even a dog distinguishes between being stumbled over and being kicked."[149] The three levels of *mens rea* employed in common law crimes are: intention (or knowledge); recklessness; and negligence. Green has suggested:

> "Assessments of *mens rea* are crucial to determining the extent to which an act entails fault and is therefore deserving of punishment. Other things being equal, we say that an offense committed purposefully is more blameworthy (and therefore more deserving of punishment, or perhaps deserving of more punishment) than an offense committed recklessly; and that an offense committed recklessly is more culpable than one committed negligently. And we say this even when the harm that the offense entails is precisely the same in each case."[150]

Suppose that A has caused B to sustain a broken arm. This may have been as a result of different scenarios:

(1) Alan intended to break Belinda's arm and so deliberately struck her with a baseball bat.

(2) Audrey had no intention of injuring anyone but, nonetheless, she swung the bat above her head in a reckless fashion (that is, in a way which made it likely that someone would be hurt) and broke Bob's arm.

(3) Albert had no intention of injuring anyone, nor was he reckless, but he was practising his swing near an open door, and struck Betty because he failed to take proper care (in other words, Albert behaved negligently).

In each of the three cases we have a person who has engaged in essentially similar conduct (that is, each person has swung a bat) and

---

[148] See also *Lord Advocate's Reference (No 2 of 1992)* 1993 JC 43. There are occasional instances where it could be said that motive does become important in Scots criminal law. For example, housebreaking is only a crime if the reason for it is the intent to steal. Motive is also important in establishing defences – see Part VII below.

[149] Holmes (1882), p 3.

[150] S P Green, *Lying, Cheating, and Stealing: A Moral Theory of White-Collar Crime* (2006), p 31 (footnote omitted).

we have harm being caused as a result (a person sustaining a broken arm) – yet we blame Alan more than Audrey, and Audrey more than Albert. This is because the *mens rea* of each one is different. This also makes clear that *mens rea* does not relate to one single state of mind. In all three scenarios, the injured parties can take a civil law action, for negligence, under the law of delict. This allows them to receive compensation for their injuries. In criminal law terms, Alan is likely to be charged with assault (which has the *mens rea* of intending to cause personal injury); Audrey could be charged with "culpable and reckless injury" which, as its name suggests, requires a *mens rea* of recklessness, and Albert is unlikely to face any criminal charges.

6.12   INTENTION

Those who cause harm to others intentionally are clearly more blameworthy than those who do so through recklessness, or mere negligence. As Antony Duff has put it: **6.12.1**

> "It is through the intentions with which I act that I engage in the world as an agent, and relate myself most closely to the actual and potential effects of my actions; and the central or fundamental kind of wrong-doing is to *direct* my actions towards evil – to *intend* and to *try* to do what is evil." [151]

As we saw in Chapter 3, a primary purpose of the criminal law is to prevent people from harming each other. It could do this most effectively if it proscribed the causing of harm in all circumstances, irrespective of whether the perpetrator acted intentionally, recklessly or negligently. However, the criminal law is also about ascribing blame, and as we have seen from our "broken arm" scenarios, we ascribe differing levels of blame to people depending on their mental state when causing injury. The criminal law is also in the business of punishing people who have infringed its prohibitions, and punishment is generally felt to be most justified where people have deliberately (that is, intentionally) caused injury, occasionally justified where the injury was caused recklessly, and generally not justified where the injury was negligently caused.[152] It follows from this that most crimes are defined in such a way as to strike at the intentional causing of harm:

> "If we accept that whatever utility punishment might have it must also be deserved, the centrality of intention in criminal liability will be appreciated.

---

[151] R A Duff, *Intention, Agency and Criminal Liability* (1990), p 113 (emphases in original).
[152] Negligently caused injuries are generally the focus of the law of delict, which is concerned to award compensation for losses wrongfully caused, rather than to punish those who have caused such losses.

Whether we take the view that responsibility for harmful outcomes depends upon one's capacity to have avoided the outcome or having the kind of (bad) character which disposes to such outcomes, intention creates a linkage between outcome and action which could not create a closer association, making the outcome all the actor's own".[153]

6.12.2 Intention is, however, much harder to define than one might imagine. It has been described as follows:

"An 'intention' to my mind connotes a state of affairs which the party 'intending' ... does more than merely contemplate; it connotes a state of affairs which, on the contrary, he decides, so far as in him lies, to bring about, and which, in point of possibility, he has a reasonable prospect of being able to bring about, by his own act of volition."[154]

This seems to suggest that one cannot "intend" to do that which is in fact impossible. But if A shoots at B in an attempt to kill him, would the fact that (unbeknown to A) B is already dead necessarily lead us to say that A did not "intend" to kill B?[155]

6.12.3 Intention has also been described as involving "a decision to bring about, insofar as it lies within the accused's power, the commission of the offence which it is alleged the accused attempted to commit, no matter whether the accused desired that consequence of his act or not".[156] Some crimes, such as assault and theft, can only be committed intentionally, where "intention" means a decision or determination to bring about a particular result. This means merely that the accused has decided to act in a particular way at the time of the *actus reus*. The prosecution need not prove that the accused had determined to act in a particular way in advance of that point. The crime of theft requires the accused to have an intention to deprive the owner of her property. If A takes someone else's coat home from a party, this is not theft if she takes the wrong coat by accident, or even if she is negligent in not looking at it properly and checking that it is hers. Even if A is reckless – she is in a hurry and it crosses her mind that this might not, in fact, be her coat – this is not theft. It is only theft if A *intends* to steal it: that is, if she intends to deprive its owner.

6.12.4 How can we ever tell what someone intends? One of the authors can recall telling a jury that they had to determine what the accused intended – what was going on in her head at the time of the crime; and pointing out that while we cannot unscrew the top of a person's head and look inside it, intention could be inferred from what the

---

[153] Wilson (2002) at pp 135–136.
[154] Asquith LJ in *Cunliffe v Goodman* [1950] 2 KB 237 at 253, adopted by Lord Ross in *Sayers v HM Advocate* 1981 SCCR 312 at 318.
[155] See from section 8.3 below for a discussion of "impossible attempts".
[156] *R v Mohan* [1975] 2 All ER 193 at 200, per James LJ.

accused did, or said, and from the general circumstances surrounding the crime.[157] An intention to kill, required for murder, could easily be inferred if the accused had stabbed her victim through the heart while shouting "Die! Die! I want to kill you!". Of course, in reality matters are rarely so straightforward. In the scenarios we looked at earlier, where A broke B's arm with a baseball bat,[158] it will generally be easy to determine from the manner in which the blow was struck, and the surrounding circumstances, whether the blow was a deliberate one, or not. What about the example of taking someone else's coat from a party? Since the *actus reus* is the same whether A put on the coat knowing that it belonged to someone else, and *intending* to steal it, or whether she took it by mistake, how can we know what was going on in her mind? In such cases, the *actus reus* is equivocal – her acting may be equally consistent with an innocent interpretation. But an intent to steal may be determined from other circumstances, such as how she takes the coat (does she wear it openly, or hide it in a bag?) and whether she does in fact own a similar coat. In order to ascertain whether the accused has *mens rea*, then, the court will examine all of the available evidence and use this to infer her actual mental attitude.

While working in the Appeals Division of the Crown Office, 6.12.5 one of the authors had to prepare arguments for the prosecution in relation to an appeal by a medical student against a conviction for theft. The appellant's letter of appeal stated that he had been under a lot of stress from his final examinations and had taken something from a shop while suffering from this stress, and a lack of sleep. In effect, he was suggesting that he lacked the *mens rea* of intention to steal. Initial sympathy for the student soon vanished when the circumstances of the case were considered. The item in question was a video recorder (a heavy thing to remove from a shop "accidentally") and when the student was arrested the recorder was found in a large false lining which had been sewn into his coat.

6.13   TRANSFERRED INTENT

Where one person aims a blow at another, but misses that other 6.13.1 and strikes a different person instead, this constitutes an assault on the person who is struck, even though the attacker did not intend to hit that particular person.[159] It was at one time thought that this

---

[157] See R v *Moloney* [1985] AC 905 (HL) at 918 (quoting the trial judge's directions to the jury).
[158] See section 6.11.1 above.
[159] This is illustrated by *Roberts* v *Hamilton* 1989 JC 91. An assault is an attack on the person of another, thus the accused had in fact assaulted both parties. See from section 10.2.7 below.

was because the accused had recklessly injured the victim, but the appeal court has confirmed that assault is a crime which can only be committed intentionally, hence the rationale for such cases is that A's intention to assault B is transferred to the ultimate victim, C. As we have seen,[160] this doctrine of transferred intent will only operate when the *mens rea* for a particular crime is present. Hence it will not apply where the accused has *mens rea* for one offence but in fact commits a different offence, requiring a different *mens rea*.[161] For example, let us suppose that A intends to steal from a shop, so tries to smash a window by throwing a stone at it. If the window is made of toughened glass and the stone bounces off it and hits a passer-by, A has not committed assault. Her intention was to damage property, not to cause personal injury. This echoes what we noted earlier about *mens rea* relating to a specific state of mind.[162] If we equated *mens rea* with Hume's idea of "dole" then we could convict A since she did display "wickedness" and an "evil disposition" by intending to break the window. Dole is a pervasive wickedness of character and committing any crime which has moral content (as both theft and assault do) could provide evidence of this. The High Court has held that the doctrine of transferred intent does not operate in relation to wilful fire-raising,[163] and it may be that its only application nowadays is in relation to the crime of assault.

6.14 CRITIQUE OF THE LAW ON TRANSFERRED INTENT AND PROPOSALS FOR REFORM

6.14.1 It may be argued that the doctrine of transferred intent ought not to operate in Scots criminal law, even in respect of the crime of assault. Assault requires an intention to inflict immediate bodily harm or the fear of such harm. This is not a generalised idea; the intention is directed towards a particular individual. Transferred intent in assault transgresses the modern approach which is to regard *mens rea* as the specific mental state required for a particular crime. A's intention was to hit B but she actually hit C and, her aim being poor, she might instead have hit D, E or F, depending on where any of them happened to be standing when the blow was mobilised. The argument in favour of transferred intent is that, simply because the blow hit C, the accused's initial intention to cause immediate bodily harm was not dissipated. Accordingly, since

---

[160] Section 6.8.2 above.
[161] *Ibid.*
[162] See section 6.9.6 above.
[163] *Byrne* v *HM Advocate* 2000 JC 155. See section 13.5.3 below.

the *actus reus* and the *mens rea* of assault occurred simultaneously, she is guilty of assault. This seems to require an acceptance that having an intention to inflict immediate bodily harm generally, on anyone who comes within striking distance, is sufficient, because that intention *vis-à-vis* B never comes together with the actual attack. The idea that the accused could simply hold the intention against B in her mind and execute it against C seems to reify the concept of intention too much. As a *mens rea*, intention has to be that which was actually in the accused's mind. This related to B, and only to B. The state of mind which accompanied the actual attack on C seems more like taking a risk. In our earlier example, it equates better to the individual waving the baseball bat around in an uncontrolled and indiscriminate fashion above her head, rather than to her counterpart who strikes the victim on the arm, intending to cause that victim personal injury.[164] If the accused's aim is so poor that a third party is struck, then the fact that the blow was initially directed towards a particular victim is treated by the law as irrelevant. There is certainly an argument, then, that transferred intent in assault simply collapses into recklessness.[165] If this is so then it would be preferable to recognise that when A attempts to strike B but misses and hits C instead, A is guilty of assaulting B, but of "recklessly causing injury" to C, rather than of assaulting her.[166]

We have posited that transferred intent may apply only in relation **6.14.2** to assault in Scots law. By contrast, theoretical literature on the topic is concerned primarily with the murder context.[167] Until recently, this would not have been an issue in Scotland because of its use of the concept of "wicked recklessness" as an alternative and sufficient form of the *mens rea* for murder.[168] However, the case of *HM Advocate* v *Purcell*[169] may now have introduced an intention (to cause personal injury) requirement into this form of the mental element of murder.[170] Accordingly, it becomes all the more important to be clear as to the doctrine's applicability – or

---

[164] See section 6.11.1 above.

[165] See Cubie (2010) at para 9.5. See also the commentary on *Connor* v *Jessop* 1988 SCCR 624.

[166] A blow which misses its intended target is nonetheless an attack, hence fulfilling the requirements of the *actus reus* of assault – see section 10.2.7 below. The crime of "recklessly causing injury" is discussed further at section 10.12.1 below.

[167] See, for example, D N Husak, "Transferred intent" (1996) 10 *Notre Dame J L Ethics & Pub Policy* 65; A M Dillof, "Transferred intent: an inquiry into the nature of criminal culpability" (1997–98) 1 *Buff Crim L Rev* 501.

[168] This constitutes a form of "depraved-heart murder". See Husak (1996) at 72; Dillof (1997–98) at 506.

[169] 2008 SLT 44.

[170] Discussed in detail from section 9.12.7 below.

otherwise. Douglas Husak considers the doctrine and ultimately concludes that it can only be a legal fiction.[171] It exists to satisfy our intuitive sense that to aim a blow at B which, in fact, injures C is just as culpable as intending to hit C in the first place. The doctrine cannot, however, be rationalised.[172] Husak therefore takes the view that the matter is best dealt with by ensuring that *sentencing* is proportionate and reflects the actual harm and culpability which the conduct carried with it.[173] This formulation seems to miss issues of fair labelling.[174] Of course, a particular instance of the crime of "recklessly causing injury" may be identically "serious" to an assault, in respect of the physical harm actually caused, but there is greater stigma in an assault conviction. This applies all the more strongly where the line to be drawn is between murder and culpable homicide.

6.15   RECKLESSNESS

6.15.1   A person who takes an unacceptable risk acts recklessly. A risk is regarded as unacceptable if it is one which the reasonable person would not have taken. Recklessness can be assessed either subjectively or objectively.[175] Scots law holds as reckless the person who knowingly takes a risk (subjective recklessness), and sometimes also the person who did not realise that her behaviour involved such a risk, but ought to have done so (objective recklessness). When it is assessed objectively, the accused's mind-set is judged according to the "reasonable person test". Here, a conviction is possible when it can be reasonably said that the accused *ought* to have foreseen the consequences of her behaviour (whether or not she actually did). In contrast, the subjective approach concentrates on what the accused actually intended or foresaw. Since the onus is on the prosecution to prove its case, it is clearly more difficult for it to prove recklessness by a subjective test. For example, it is easier to establish that a reasonable person would know that battering a child's head on the floor is likely to cause injury – considerable injury, even. It is much harder to show that a particular accused was aware of this.

6.15.2   The danger with an objective approach is that it holds a person liable for failing to behave in the way that a hypothetical "reasonable person" would have done. In reality none of us behaves as this fully

---

[171] Husak (1996) at 68 and 84.

[172] *Ibid* at 84–86.

[173] *Ibid* at 91–96.

[174] See from section 4.6 above.

[175] For an analysis of the Scottish approach see J Chalmers, "*Lieser* and misconceptions" (2008) SCL 1115.

rational, fictional figure, all of the time. Particularly in situations of extreme fear or stress, it may be unfair to blame, and punish, a person for failing to attain the standard of the reasonable person. It also fails to take account of the individual accused's *actual* innate capacity to conform her behaviour to the requisite standard. In the English law case of *Elliott* v *C (a minor)*,[176] the defendant was a 14-year-old girl who was in a "remedial class" at school. She had been out all night and, at 5 am, went into a garden shed, poured some white spirit which she found there onto a carpet and set fire to it. The shed was destroyed. At that time, English law endorsed a wholly objective approach to recklessness, hence the accused was convicted, despite doubts over her understanding of the properties of white spirit and the likely effects of igniting it.[177]

Justice may require a more individualised approach, which 6.15.3 recognises that people have their weaknesses, and that some are capable of greater fortitude, resilience, tolerance etc than others.[178] The counter-argument, of course, is that an individualised approach, which employs the subjective test, expects no more of accused persons than what they have actually achieved. It is in danger of allowing people to fail to conform to any real standard. Concerns that those who are deserving of punishment will exploit subjective standards and escape liability lie behind support for the objective standard. In the United States of America, such fears have led 23 states to introduce an objective standard in the defence of provocation.[179] It is often said that Scots criminal law generally adopts an objective approach to recklessness,[180] but it does not always do so. In *McDowall* v *HM Advocate*,[181] a case involving culpable homicide by reckless driving, the High Court stated: "the fact that immediately after the accident the appellant showed utter disregard for the victims and the fact that he drove with the bonnet in an upright position are factors which the jury were entitled to take into account ... when assessing his state of mind at the time of the accident".[182] This case also shows that a subjective approach does not necessarily favour the accused.

---

[176] [1983] 1 WLR 939.

[177] See S Field and M Lynn, "The capacity for recklessness" (1992) 12 *Legal Studies* 74; M Lynn and S Field, "Capacity, recklessness and the House of Lords" [1993] *Crim LR* 127.

[178] See Alan Norrie's argument on this point in section 4.5.1 above.

[179] See P H Robinson and M T Cahill, *Law Without Justice: Why Criminal Law Doesn't Give People What They Deserve* (2006), p 48.

[180] T H Jones and M G A Christie, *Criminal Law* (5th edn, 2012), para 3–30; Cubie (2010), para 2.24; J Barton, "Recklessness in Scots criminal law: subjective or objective?" (2011) *JR* 143.

[181] 1998 SCCR 343.

[182] *Ibid* at 349.

6.15.4   Objective recklessness raises the question of whether it is fair that people can be punished for harm caused by a risk of which they were unaware. Since one of the purposes served by the mental element in crime is to allocate blame appropriately, this is of some importance. By adopting an objective approach the law is making the normative assumption that individuals *should* recognise certain risks, even if, in fact, they do not. It is also, arguably, prioritising the public interest in safety over the principle that individuals are criminally responsible only where they freely choose to break the law. If A thinks tobogganing will be easy but, never having done it before, careers into another person and injures them, A may well meet an objective standard of recklessness, though it had simply not occurred to her that there would, or even might, be any risk. In some respects, recklessness is a nebulous concept, perhaps easier to identify in practice than to define. The High Court has dealt with a case of individuals chasing bulls out of their field and along a road and a railway line,[183] and with an experienced firearms user firing a weapon thoughtlessly.[184] In both cases, it seems fairly clear that such acts involve a great deal of risk. Since, by definition, recklessness deals only with dangerous situations, it may be acceptable for the balance to be towards the protection of the public.

6.15.5   To lessen potential unfairness, the courts generally insist on a high degree of culpability before recklessness can be established. In the case of W v *HM Advocate*[185] the court referred to the accused's "total indifference to and disregard for the safety of the public".[186] This led to a charge of "reckless endangerment" when the accused dropped or threw a bottle from the window of a 15th-floor flat. He had been warned of the danger, and it was this disregard of the consequences which was reckless. In *Cameron* v *Maguire*[187] the appellant was charged with the reckless discharge of a loaded rifle, to the danger of the lieges. It was emphasised that the appropriate test was that employed in *Quinn* v *Cunningham*,[188] namely whether there had been an "utter disregard of what the consequences of the act in question may be so far as the public are concerned"; a "recklessness so high as to involve an indifference to the consequences for the public generally".[189] In *HM Advocate* v *Harris*,[190] Lord Prosser stated:

---

[183] *Robson* v *Spiers* 1999 SLT 1141.
[184] *Cameron* v *Maguire* 1999 JC 63. The case is discussed further in section 6.15.5 below.
[185] 1982 SCCR 152.
[186] *Ibid* at 155.
[187] 1999 JC 63.
[188] 1956 JC 22.
[189] *Cameron* v *Maguire* 1999 JC 63 at 66, per Lord Marnoch, quoting LJ-G Clyde in *Quinn* v *Cunningham* 1956 JC 22 at 24 and 25.
[190] 1993 SCCR 559.

"in deciding that some conduct has been reckless, one will always be at least very close to saying that it involved a failure to pay due regard to foreseeable consequences of that conduct, which were foreseeably likely to cause injury to others, and which could correspondingly reasonably be called dangerous in relation to them".[191]

The case of *Transco plc* v *HM Advocate (No 1)*[192] involved an (unsuccessful) attempt to prosecute a corporation for "involuntary, lawful act culpable homicide", the *mens rea* for which is recklessness.[193] The judgment states specifically that recklessness, in this context, is a state of mind.[194] While this may seem obvious, it is also possible to *behave* recklessly – and it may be easier to identify this quality in actions. The case of *Allan* v *Patterson*[195] has been criticised for defining recklessness for the purposes of a statutory road traffic offence as a way of behaving as much as a mental attitude.[196] A state of mind would appear to require thought concerning the behaviour in question. Consequently, this moves towards a subjective concept of recklessness. James Chalmers has suggested that an "awareness of risk" is required.[197] In terms of the actual meaning of recklessness, Lord Osborne, as well as endorsing the definitions from *Quinn* v *Cunningham*,[198] cited above, took the view that "gross or wicked ... indifference to consequences"[199] was a reasonable statement of the concept. Lord Hamilton took as the essential element of recklessness, "a degree of want of care which is grave [and] ... a state of mind on the part of the accused which is 'wicked' or amounts, or is equivalent, to a complete indifference to the consequences of his conduct".[200] The use of the term "wicked" is less than helpful[201] and it is also not entirely clear what the accused has to be thinking to constitute "indifference to consequences", whether "gross" or

6.15.6

---

[191] 1993 SCCR 559 at 574.
[192] 2004 JC 29.
[193] This is discussed in more detail at section 18.5.7 below.
[194] 2004 JC 29 at 36, per Lord Osborne.
[195] 1980 JC 57. See section 9.24.3 below.
[196] See *Carr* v *HM Advocate* 1994 JC 203 at 207–208, per LJ-G Hope; *Transco plc* v *HM Advocate (No 1)* 2004 JC 29 at 49 per Lord Hamilton.
[197] J Chalmers, "Corporate culpable homicide: *Transco plc* v *HM Advocate*" (2004) 8 *Edin LR* 262 at 264.
[198] 1956 JC 22.
[199] *Transco plc* v *HM Advocate (No 1)* 2004 JC 29 at 33. This definition was derived from that given in *Paton* v *HM Advocate* 1936 JC 19, which had been relied upon in a number of cases but which was circular in that it defined recklessness for the purposes of the criminal law by reference to "criminal negligence" and "criminal indifference to consequences".
[200] *Transco plc* v *HM Advocate (No 1)* 2004 JC 29 at 48–49.
[201] See from section 6.9.4 above and Chapter 9 below.

"complete". It still seems possible that not thinking about the risk at all would meet this requirement, but that seems to amount to neither a state of mind nor an awareness.

6.16   CRITIQUE OF THE LAW ON RECKLESSNESS AND PROPOSALS FOR REFORM

6.16.1   It has been suggested that "the problem with recklessness in Scots law is its definition".[202] An in-depth examination has been conducted by Findlay Stark, who has identified "five *distinct* forms".[203] From this analysis, he takes the view that the attempt to examine recklessness as a "monolithic"[204] concept, applicable in the same mode to all crimes involving recklessness, is "misguided".[205] His conclusion is that the "'subjective/objective' dichotomy ... does little useful work in discussing recklessness in Scots criminal law".[206] Instead, he argues that Scots law needs to develop a theory of "culpable carelessness".[207] It is certainly true, as this chapter itself demonstrates, that there is slippage between subjective and objective definitions of recklessness in the current law, and that attempts to characterise it as *either* subjective *or* objective, in its entirety, always come up against contradictory *dicta*. Joshua Barton, for example, who argues that Scots law applies, and has always applied, an *objective* concept, is still not entirely able to explain such contradictions away.[208] Nonetheless, until there is greater theoretical clarity – and Stark is to be commended for his work in this area – some attempt needs to be made to work within the existing concepts.

6.16.2   Objective recklessness punishes the person who ought to have been aware of a risk. If the accused really gave no thought to the possibility that her conduct might cause harm or loss, it can seem unjust to hold her liable for the consequences. Objective recklessness notionally holds everyone to the same standard – that of the reasonable person

---

[202] Peter Ferguson, QC, "The mental element in modern criminal law" in J Chalmers, F Leverick and L Farmer (eds), *Essays in Criminal Law in Honour of Sir Gerald Gordon* (2010) 141 at p 153.

[203] F Stark, "Rethinking recklessness" (2011) *JR* 163 at 164 (emphasis in original). Three of these are applicable in relation to specific areas – murder, common law rape and intoxication. The other two (*Allan* v *Patterson* recklessness and *Quinn* v *Cunningham* recklessness) are discussed in this chapter.

[204] *Ibid* at 202.

[205] *Ibid.*

[206] *Ibid.*

[207] *Ibid.*

[208] Barton (2011). For example, in discussing a *dictum* of Lord Prosser in *HM Advocate* v *Harris* 1993 JC 150 at 165 he finds it necessary to read in the word "reasonably" to support the objective "reasonable person" concept (at 153).

– in taking account of risk in their behaviour. On the one hand, if taken to the extreme, this may operate harshly: some may simply be *unable* to conform as required because they lack criminal capacity.[209] For others, there may have been a particular circumstance preventing their appreciation of that specific risk. To be reckless, an individual must have been at least cavalier in her assessment of that risk, if not entirely oblivious of it. Recklessness is a particularly serious failure to accommodate risk – simple carelessness is not sufficient for *criminal* liability. While, undoubtedly, subjective recklessness is often fairer to the accused, an objective concept may be necessary in order properly to protect the public. The balancing process – one with which the criminal law is particularly familiar – should in this instance favour the public interest.

6.17   NEGLIGENCE

A person is said to have been negligent when her conduct has failed   **6.17.1** to reach the standard of the reasonably competent or careful person. The distinction between recklessness and negligence lies in the degree of carelessness since, as we have seen, a negligent act is less blameworthy than a reckless or an intentional one.[210] In *Johnston* v *National Coal Board*,[211] a civil action, a fly flew into the eye of an employee of the National Coal Board while he was driving. He lost control of his van and swerved into the path of an oncoming vehicle. The court determined that he had been negligent for the purposes of the civil case against him, but stated that the issue was a narrow one and no question of criminal liability under road traffic legislation could have arisen.[212] Simple negligence, then, is generally insufficient for the imposition of criminal liability. While it may suffice for some road traffic offences,[213] the common law categorises negligent conduct as criminal only where that negligence is gross. Indeed, while the matter is not uncontroversial, recklessness as a *mens rea*, has sometimes been defined specifically as "gross ... negligence".[214] In practice, therefore, there is often little or no difference between

---

[209] See from section 6.18 below.

[210] See section 6.11.1 above.

[211] 1960 SLT (Notes) 84.

[212] *Ibid* per Lord Kilbrandon.

[213] The Road Traffic Act 1988, s 3 makes it an offence to drive a motor vehicle on a road without due care and attention, or without reasonable consideration for other persons using the road, and s 29 contains a similar offence in relation to cycling.

[214] For example, *Paton* v *HM Advocate* 1936 JC 19 at 22, per LJ-C Aitchison. This definition was criticised by Lord Osborne in *Transco plc* v *HM Advocate (No 1)* 2004 JC 29 at 33. He preferred "gross ... indifference to consequences".

the concepts of recklessness and (gross) negligence. Given that this is the case, it would be preferable for the criminal courts to eschew the use of the term "negligence" altogether.[215]

6.18   CRIMINAL CAPACITY

6.18.1   The issue raised in *Elliott* v *C (a minor)*,[216] concerning the defendant's *ability* to conform her actions to the criminal law, brings us back to the question of criminal capacity. Our discussion of liberalism in Chapter 1 demonstrated the importance placed on personal autonomy. The corollary of this is that those who, for some reason personal to them, are *unable* to conform their behaviour to the dictates of the criminal law should not be held criminally responsible. Criminal liability should apply only where the accused, with understanding of her actions, has exercised a choice to commit an offence.[217]

6.18.2   Young children may lack criminal capacity. They may not have sufficient understanding of their acts in their context and of the consequences to be held criminally responsible. They may not have developed cognitively such that they can exercise control over their actions and bring these fully into line with their intentions. Scots criminal law currently deems those aged 7 years and under to be incapable of committing crime.[218] Similar considerations may apply to those suffering from some forms of mental disorder at the time of the crime. These two groups are considered to lack criminal capacity. This issue of understanding and volition generally does not even arise in most cases in which a "sane" adult is charged with an offence. It is separate from *mens rea* (in the narrow sense of that term) and, indeed, it may be possible for an accused who lacks criminal capacity to formulate the specific *mens rea* for a particular crime. Accordingly, criminal capacity is an important, if sometimes overlooked, aspect of the mental element generally.[219]

---

[215] Stark's view is that Scots criminal law needs to "better explain the role of negligence" which he describes as "the elephant in the room in some discussions of 'recklessness'" (Stark (2011) at 202).

[216] [1983] 1 WLR 939. See section 6.15.2 above.

[217] See H L A Hart, *Punishment and Responsibility: Essays in the Philosophy of Law* (1968), especially Chapter 1. Also N Lacey, *State Punishment: Political Principles and Community Values* (1988), pp 62–63.

[218] Criminal Procedure (Scotland) Act 1995, s 41. In terms of s 41A(1) of the Act, no child under the age of 12 years may be *prosecuted* for an offence. Children aged 8, 9, 10 and 11 (as well as older children) may be referred to a children's hearing on the ground of having committed an offence: Children's Hearings (Scotland) Act 2011, s 67(2)(j).

[219] For a full discussion, see McDiarmid (2007), Chapter 3.

6.19   CONCURRENCE OF *MENS REA* AND *ACTUS REUS*

As we have already noted, the maxim *actus non facit reum nisi*   **6.19.1**
mens sit rea requires there to be a "forbidden behaviour element
or situation" (*actus reus*) and a "mental element" (*mens rea*). For
conduct crimes, the law requires that these co-exist;[220] it is not the
crime of assault to form an intention to injure someone by beating
them up, then accidentally to knock them down while driving to
their house. Textbooks on criminal law generally explain that
the *actus reus* and the *mens rea* of a criminal offence must occur
simultaneously.[221] Andrew Ashworth and Jeremy Horder call this
"the principle of contemporaneity".[222] The corollary of this is that
the existence of *mens rea* is, or certainly ought to be, judged at the
moment of commission of the *actus reus*. In other words, *actus reus*
and *mens rea* must come together, and only require to come together,
at the point at which the crime itself is committed. This point may
last but a few seconds. In Scots criminal law, this principle may
also serve to create distance between Hume's concept of dole (the
wickedness of character which permeated the accused, the existence
of which was evidenced by the crime) and *mens rea* (the specific
mental attitude which must exist simultaneously with the accused's
commission of specific elements of proscribed behaviour). Dole did
not necessarily either arrive or depart with the commission of the
crime, as it pervaded the accused. *Mens rea* is only of any relevance
at the time of perpetration.

Although the contemporaneity principle seems a simple one,   **6.19.2**
McCue v Currie[223] illustrates a difficulty which it may create in
Scots law. We already discussed this case in relation to criminal
omissions: the accused set fire to, and ultimately destroyed, a
caravan by dropping a defective lighter. He was charged with
culpable and reckless fire-raising. At first instance, the sheriff treated
the matter as one of liability for a continuing act – in other words,
that the accused was not only liable for starting the fire but for "the
immediate consequences"[224] of so doing. By leaving, the accused had
demonstrated an "utter disregard for the obvious consequence of
the fire spreading".[225] On that basis, it was appropriate to convict
of culpable and reckless fire-raising. This ruling was overturned on

---

[220] Conduct crimes are defined at section 6.2.2 above.
[221] For example, C M V Clarkson, H M Keating and S R Cunningham, *Clarkson and Keating: Criminal Law* (7th edn, 2010) at pp 187–190.
[222] Ashworth and Horder (2013) at pp 80 and 157–159.
[223] 2004 JC 73. See section 6.8.1 above.
[224] *Ibid* at 76.
[225] *Ibid*. In *Byrne v HM Advocate* 2000 JC 155, the High Court had stated that the *mens rea* of culpable and reckless fire-raising was "a reckless disregard as to what the result of [the] act would be" (per Lord Coulsfield at 163).

appeal, the court holding that, at least in relation to fire-raising, "*mens rea* has always been determined by reference to the act of starting the fire and not by reference to something which took place thereafter".[226] In other words, the *mens rea* should occur at the moment of setting fire to the property, which constitutes the *actus reus* of the offence.

6.19.3   On a strict interpretation of the contemporaneity principle, then, *McCue* v *Currie*[227] was correctly decided, yet this approach does not seem to meet the justice of the situation. The sheriff accepted that the dropping of the lighter was an accident – a ruling that, by definition, excludes the application of criminal liability. Other than in homicide – and even there the extent is debatable[228] – there is no constructive liability[229] in Scots criminal law. Accordingly, the fact that McCue was in the caravan for a criminal purpose had to be disregarded. However, there seems to be no doubt that he did display "reckless disregard as to what the result of his act would be",[230] if not at the second of dropping the lighter, then certainly immediately thereafter. In this instance, then, a strict application of the contemporaneity principle seems to have served the public interest badly. If the appeal court had accepted that the *actus reus* extended to the point at which the fire took hold, the outcome would have been different.

6.19.4   The particular complexity and importance of the issue are also illustrated by the (common law) rape case of *McKearney* v *HM Advocate*.[231] The complainer was McKearney's former girlfriend. He broke into her flat in the early hours of the morning and terrorised her. McKearney repeatedly threatened to kill her, putting his hands round her throat. The complainer managed to calm him down and he then had sexual intercourse with her. These events took place over a period of some hours and there was a 4-hour interval between the initial violence and the moment when the accused penetrated the complainer. She testified that she gave him no indication as to whether or not she consented because she was terrified. The jury determined that the accused had committed rape. On appeal, the court took the view that the sexual intercourse could be treated as a separate event from the breaking in and the threatening behaviour,

---

[226] 2004 JC 73 at 79.
[227] *Ibid.*
[228] See Chapter 9 below.
[229] Constructive liability arises where an accused, while involved in committing one crime, inadvertently commits another, quite separate, crime. The commission of the first crime renders her constructively liable for the second.
[230] This is the *mens rea* of culpable and reckless fire-raising as set down in *Byrne* v *HM Advocate* 2000 JC 155 at 163.
[231] 2004 JC 87.

because of the time interval. The jury had not been instructed that an honest belief in consent negated *mens rea*[232] and it was possible that, at the time of the intercourse, the accused had held such a belief, based on the complainer's passivity, hence the conviction had to be overturned.

This decision was subject to much debate in Scotland.[233] Here, the **6.19.5** moment of commission of the crime of rape was, clearly, at the point of sexual penetration. The appeal court judged the accused's *mens rea* at that moment, hiving it off from all that had gone before. The crime of rape presents particular difficulties of proof, partly because the complainer's mental attitude – whether she consented – is as important as the belief the accused formed of this.[234] In this instance, surely the accused's belief in consent must have been influenced by the complainer's response to his earlier actions? In order to convict of rape in the first place, the jury must have been convinced that there was in fact no consent. It may be technically correct to judge the *mens rea* of rape by reference only to the instant of penetration but, as with *McCue* v *Currie*,[235] it does not necessarily promote a just decision.

In result crimes, the situation is looked at as a continuum. The **6.19.6** requirement that *mens rea* and *actus reus* occur simultaneously does not mean that the accused must continue to have the requisite *mens rea* until the result actually occurs. In *Meli* v *R*[236] the appellants appealed from Lesotho to the Privy Council against their convictions for murder, claiming that the necessary elements of a murder charge were absent.[237] They had assaulted their victim, and had rolled the body over a low cliff. At that point, they had thought that the victim was dead, but this was not in fact the case and he died, thereafter, of exposure. The appellants' argument was that they had the *mens rea* for murder – that is, the intention to kill – only during the assault, but not when they committed the act which actually caused death – that is, the rolling of the body from the cliff and the abandoning of the victim. Upholding their conviction for murder, the Privy Council held that it was not possible to analyse

---

[232] *Jamieson* v *HM Advocate* 1994 JC 88. This is no longer the law. See the Sexual Offences (Scotland) Act 2009, s 1(1)(b), which indicates that the accused's belief in consent must be "reasonable" to negate a rape charge. The matter is discussed further at section 11.2.4 below.

[233] J Chalmers, "Distress as corroboration of *mens rea*" (2004) SLT 141; M E Scott, "Redefined rape and the difficulties of proof" (2005) SLT 65; P R Ferguson and F E Raitt, "Reforming the Scots law of rape: redefining the offence" (2006) 10 *Edin LR* 185.

[234] See from section 11.3.3 below.

[235] 2004 JC 73.

[236] [1954] 1 WLR 228.

[237] Lesotho was at that time named Basutoland.

their conduct in this way, and that their behaviour should be regarded as a series of acts.[238]

6.20 GENERAL CRITIQUE AND PROPOSALS FOR REFORM

6.20.1 Throughout this book we argue that the criminal law should strive for certainty – something which the contemporaneity principle provides. Yet the main purpose of certainty is to ensure that individuals can know when their behaviour will be criminal and when it will not. Allowing a caravan to be destroyed by burning, or having sexual intercourse with a woman having threatened to kill her some hours before, are both circumstances in which the hypothetical "reasonable person" might well expect criminal consequences. As Chalmers points out, criminalising the behaviour in *McCue* v *Currie*[239] would be unlikely to fall foul of Art 7 of the European Convention on Human Rights because this "could hardly be described as an unforeseeable development of the law".[240] Peter Alldridge has summed up the contemporaneity doctrine in the memorable phrase that "the criminal law takes snapshots and does not make videos".[241] He points out that this approach makes it difficult for women who kill their violent and abusive partners to argue that they were acting in self-defence, or that they were provoked, since both these defences require the courts to employ the "snapshot" technique.[242] It seems that *McCue* v *Currie* and *McKearney* v *HM Advocate*[243] are also examples of this "snapshot" technique.

---

[238] The judgment has recently been criticised as an example of an instance where the court "usurped the power entrusted to Parliament" because of the judges' personal views that "a strict application of the existing law would lead to results that offend[ed] their personal notions of what is fair and just". It is argued that, instead of straining the contemporaneity principle, greater resort should have been made to existing legal rules on causation (K J Arenson, "*Thabo Meli* revisited: the pernicious effects of result-driven decisions" (2013) 77 *J Crim L* 41 at 41). In relation to the contemporaneity principle, see also the New Zealand case of *Ramsay* [1967] NZLR 1005.

[239] 2004 JC 73.

[240] Chalmers (2004a) at 63.

[241] Alldridge (2000) at p 87.

[242] *Ibid*. See from section 21.11.9 below for a discussion of provocation in respect of battered women who kill their partners.

[243] 2004 JC 87.

CHAPTER 7

GENERAL PRINCIPLES OF LIABILITY

7.1   INTRODUCTION

Scots law criminalises many forms of behaviour – from killing, **7.1.1** stealing and raping to driving at excess speed. Each proscribed practice constitutes a separate crime and we will consider in subsequent chapters the specific elements of the *actus reus* and, where appropriate, the *mens rea*, which these individual crimes require. Before doing so, however, it is necessary to turn our attention to certain aspects of the criminal law which apply, or which could apply, to all crimes or, in the case of causation, to all result crimes. Consideration of these generalities emphasises some of the unifying principles of the criminal law, which should be borne in mind when we move to our consideration of particular offences.

7.2   CAUSATION

As previously noted,[1] sometimes the law imposes liability for **7.2.1** particular conduct or behaviour, irrespective of the outcome of that behaviour. Hence it is an offence to attempt to kick someone even if no injury results,[2] or to have a knife in a public place even if the knife is at no time taken out of the accused's pocket.[3] In other crimes, the law is more concerned with the result of certain behaviour, rather than with the behaviour itself.[4] In the civil law case of *Blaikie* v *British Transport Commission*,[5] Lord Justice-Clerk Thomson stated:

---

[1] See section 6.2.2 above.
[2] Assault is discussed in more detail, from section 10.2 below.
[3] By virtue of the Criminal Law (Consolidation) (Scotland) Act 1995, s 49. See further at section 8.11.7 below.
[4] See section 6.2.3 above.
[5] 1961 SC 44.

"The law has always had to come to some kind of compromise with the doctrine of causation. The problem is a practical rather than an intellectual one. It is easy and usual to bedevil it with subtleties, but the attitude of the law is that expediency and good sense dictate that for practical purposes a line has to be drawn somewhere, and that, in drawing it, the Court is to be guided by the practical experience of the reasonable man rather than by the theoretical speculations of the philosopher."[6]

Crimes where causation can be important include fraud, aggravated assault, murder and culpable homicide.[7] We will look briefly at the causal link in each of those. It should be noted that, sometimes, the determination that the accused "caused" the proscribed outcome is made where his or her part in the harm arising is, in fact, minimal.[8]

Fraud

7.2.2 Fraud occurs where the accused makes a false pretence (usually a false statement) in order to gain some advantage. There must be a causal connection between the false pretence and the actions of the dupe, or victim. Put simply, it is not enough for the prosecution to establish that the accused made some false pretence to the victim – for example, pretended that her car was in a good condition when it was not – and to show that the victim bought the car and lost out. The Crown must also show that the false pretence *caused* the victim to buy the car, hence caused her loss.

Assault

7.2.3 This is primarily a conduct crime, but it may be libelled to include various aggravations – results or conditions which render it more serious. A person can be charged with simple assault (for example, "you did assault AB and did strike her on the face") or there may be aggravations such as "you did assault AB and did strike her on the face to her severe injury" or "... to her permanent disfigurement", or "... to the permanent impairment of her sight". The accused can be convicted of the aggravation only if the causal link between the charge and the aggravation can be established.

Culpable homicide and murder

7.2.4 In relation to both of these crimes, the accused must have caused the death of the victim. If there is a delay between the attack and the death, the defence may contend that death was caused by someone,

---

[6] 1961 SC 44 at 49.
[7] These crimes are discussed in more detail below, from sections 12.16, 10.3, 9.11 and 9.15, respectively.
[8] For a critique of certain road traffic offences where this phenomenon can be observed, see from section 9.25.1 below.

or something, other than the attack by the accused. This is considered further, below.[9]

In many cases, the causal link will be quite straightforward. For **7.2.5** instance, if A kicks B on the leg, and B's leg immediately breaks, it is not too difficult to establish the causal connection between the kick and the broken leg. However, problems can occur when events intervene between the kicking and the leg being broken; if A kicks C on the body and C falls, and her leg breaks in the fall, did A cause that broken leg? It is probably easy to conclude that this was the case. But what if A kicks D, breaking D's leg, but while being taken to hospital D falls off a stretcher and breaks her arm? Can it be said that A caused *that* injury?

In *HM Advocate v Robertson and Donoghue*,[10] the two accused **7.2.6** had struggled with an elderly shopkeeper, a Mr Demarco, and he had died of heart failure. He had, in fact, a very weak heart. The Lord Justice-Clerk (Lord Cooper) charged the jury regarding causation:

> "whether the criminal taking of life is charged as murder or culpable homicide, in either event it is indispensable that the victim should have died as a result of the injury inflicted – obviously so. The death must result from real violence used against the victim. To take obvious examples, if in any case death was due to, say, natural causes, or to some subsequent accident or maltreatment or neglect, which broke the chain of causation between the so-called crime and the death, then the death cannot be laid to the door of the assailant".[11]

He later advised the jury that they had to consider whether the violence inflicted on Mr Demarco by the accused "was or was not the direct cause of his death, or whether, to put it from the opposite standpoint, Mr Demarco's death was a pure mischance and an act of God".[12] He emphasised that the jury must be satisfied that the violence was the effective cause of the death.

The vast majority of cases involving issues of causation are in **7.2.7** the area of homicide, where there can be a lapse of time between the initial attack by the accused and the death of the victim. Since everyone dies sooner or later, we have to decide whether the accused did in fact cause the death. The fact that a victim may have been on the point of dying before the accused's attack is treated as irrelevant. Hence, in the English law case of *Dyson*,[13] Lord Alverstone stated:

---

[9] See from section 7.3 below.
[10] 1945 (unreported). See C H W Gane, C N Stoddart and J Chalmers, *A Casebook on Scottish Criminal Law* (4th edn, 2009), para 4.05 at p 106.
[11] *Ibid*.
[12] *Ibid*, p 107.
[13] [1908] 2 KB 454.

"The proper question to have been submitted to the jury was whether the accused accelerated the child's death by the injuries which he inflicted ... For if he did, the fact that the child was already suffering from meningitis, from which it would in any event have died before long, would afford no answer to the charge of causing its death."[14]

7.2.8   Reference is sometimes made to the "but for" test, the *sine qua non* – which is Latin for "without which not". The accused's conduct does not have to be the only cause or even the most substantial cause; it need only be a material cause, a more than a minimal cause.[15] We have already mentioned the case of *R v White*,[16] in which the accused tried to murder his mother by putting poison in her drink. He had the *mens rea* (the intention to kill), and the *actus reus* of attempted murder (poisoning the drink was an act of trying to kill his mother) but the mother died of a heart attack so we cannot say: "but for the accused's acts his mother would not have died at that time." White was convicted of attempted murder but not murder, since he had not caused her death.

7.2.9   Of course, the "but for" test is only a starting point. So far, it looks as though causation is a question of fact, but it is also a legal issue, in that it is for the law to determine the point at which a person has behaved in a fashion which is sufficiently blameworthy, such that she ought to be held criminally liable. The conduct has to be the factual cause of death, but this is not sufficient, since the "but for" test can be extrapolated *ad infinitum*. If A invites B for dinner and B is run over by a drunk driver on the way to A's house, one could say that the death would not have occurred if B had not been coming to A's house at that time. "But for" the invitation, the accident would not have occurred. This is obviously an insufficient basis on which to hold A criminally liable for causing B's death. A basic legal requirement is that the cause must be proximate: that is, the law is only concerned with causal factors closely related to the result. Where there is more than one cause, the law must decide whom to blame (and punish) for causing the death.

7.3 BREAKING THE CAUSAL CHAIN

7.3.1   An accused may be able to escape criminal liability if something happens to cut off the flow of consequences from the accused's initial act. Such an event, which breaks the causal chain, is referred to as a

---

[14] [1908] 2 KB 454 at 457.
[15] See also *Rai v HM Advocate* 2012 SCL 283 at 286–287, per Lord Clarke, citing with approval *R v Williams* [2011] 3 All ER 969. For a discussion of the legislation to which these cases relate, including subsequent case law, see from section 9.25.1 below.
[16] [1910] 2 KB 124. See section 6.2.4 above.

novus actus interveniens – a new, intervening act. A brief example may clarify the point, though since the case is drawn from the civil law of delict it is of value only as an illustration, not as a precedent. A man injured his left leg at work. His employers were liable to compensate him for this. Subsequently, he experienced a weakness in this leg while descending the stairs of a tenement building. Apparently in an attempt to save his left leg, he jumped from one landing in the close to the one below, down ten steps, thereby seriously injuring his right ankle. His employers were not liable for this second injury. The chain of causation was broken by his own voluntary, stupid and completely unexpected act. The flow of consequences from his employers' negligence, which caused the first injury, ceased when he jumped.[17]

The courts are reluctant to recognise that events subsequent to the accused's acts have broken the causal chain; importance is attached to the fact that the victim is placed in less favourable circumstances in the first place (whether in terms of needing hospital treatment or being exposed to a particular risk) because of the accused's initial wrongful act. Thus, the appeal court has rightly determined that switching off a life-support machine does not constitute a *novus actus interveniens* because the initial injection of harmful drugs by the accused remained the operating cause of the victim's death.[18]   7.3.2

Certain types of circumstance exist in which it is recognised that a *novus actus interveniens* might arise (although, in fact, breaks in the chain of causation are seldom established). The courts have developed guidelines to assist in ascribing liability for certain events. One type of case occurs where the hospital treatment itself contributes to the victim's death. This is called "malregimen". Such cases are categorised differently, depending upon whether the infection is unpredictable or not, and whether or not the original wound was potentially fatal. Generally, if even a non-fatal wound becomes infected, leading to death, then the assailant is still held liable, since the original wound is regarded as the proximate cause of death.[19]   7.3.3

Another guideline concerns characteristics of the victim. This is embodied in the phrase that "accused persons must take their victims as they find them". This is also known as the "thin skull" rule – if A attacks B, striking her on the head, and B dies as a result, then A may be liable for murder, or at least culpable homicide, and this   7.3.4

---

[17] *McKew v Holland Hannen & Cubitts (Scotland) Ltd* 1970 SC (HL) 20.
[18] *Finlayson v HM Advocate* 1979 JC 33. This case is discussed further at section 9.9.3 below.
[19] See the old case of *Heinrich Heidmesser* (1879) 17 SLR 266 (see Gane, Stoddart and Chalmers (2009), para 4.35), which clearly expresses these principles.

is so even if it can be shown that B had an abnormally "thin skull" and that most people would not have died from such a blow. This is illustrated by *HM Advocate* v *Robertson and Donoghue*,[20] above. A similar case is *Bird* v *HM Advocate*,[21] in which Lord Jamieson stressed in his charge to the jury that it is no defence:

> "that the victim was an old person, an infirm person, or a person that suffered from a bad heart, and that if he had been young and healthy the consequences would not have happened. If a person commits an assault, he must take his victim as he finds him".[22]

Bird had chased a woman along a road and had tried to grab her. He caused her such apprehension and alarm that she tried to enter a passing car, whereupon she collapsed and died of shock. Bird was convicted of culpable homicide as a result. He did not intend to kill the woman but, as a matter of public policy, the law holds that accused persons must accept liability for the consequences of their actions. An accused might not know that a victim has a thin skull, a weak heart or other physical disability, but is deemed to have taken the risk of liability for death by assaulting such a person.

7.3.5   So much for physical characteristics. What about any emotional or psychological aspects of the victim's character? An interesting English law case is *R* v *Blaue*,[23] in which the accused attacked a woman with a knife. The victim would ordinarily have been saved by medical intervention, but she refused the necessary blood transfusion since she was a Jehovah's Witness. The defence tried to argue that the victim's refusal of the transfusion was so unreasonable as to breach the chain of causation between the accused's attack and the victim's death. This approach was rejected by the English Court of Appeal on the basis that persons who resort to violence must take their victims as they find them, and that this refers to the whole victim. The court ruled that the knife attack was the legal cause of the victim's death.

7.3.6   The cases of *Bird*[24] and *Blaue*[25] suggest that neither physical nor psychological characteristics of the victim can be used by assailants to evade criminal liability. Such characteristics do not "break the causal chain" between the accused's acts and the death or injury of the victim. Of course, the question must be asked: how far does this go? As Gane, Stoddart and Chalmers ask, would the rule apply if a racial bigot refused treatment from a doctor who is not of her race?[26]

---

[20] 1945 (unreported). See section 7.2.6 above.
[21] 1952 JC 23.
[22] *Ibid* at 25.
[23] [1975] 3 ALL ER 446.
[24] 1952 JC 23.
[25] [1975] 3 ALL ER 446.
[26] Gane, Stoddart and Chalmers (2009), para 4.08.

What if a misogynist refused life-saving treatment from a female doctor? While a court might be reluctant to enter into debate about the reasonableness of a person's religious beliefs, which by definition depend on faith more than reason, it may well take a different approach to other characteristics of the victim. We can clearly see the operation of public policy interests at play here; even in cases in which the victim's physical condition is not an obvious one – indeed, it may even include conditions of which the victim herself is unaware – the accused is nonetheless held liable for causing death. Don Stuart has argued that the "thin skull" rule is "unnecessary and potentially productive of grave injustice".[27] If we focus on what *Blaue* and *Bird* actually did – what they can reasonably be held responsible for – it can be argued that they are guilty of aggravated assault, but not of culpable homicide.

What about harm which results, not so much from characteristics of the victim, but from the victim's own positive conduct? What if the victim is harmed when trying to escape? If A chases B with a meat cleaver, and B jumps out of the window in fright, breaking both legs, is A criminally liable for these injuries? Or have B's actions "broken the chain of causation" so that A is not to be held responsible for them? In the English law case of *R v Roberts*,[28] it was held that where the victim does something "daft" (as the defence counsel in that case put it) this might break the chain of causation.[29] According to Glanville Williams:

7.3.7

> "What a person does (if he has reached adult years, is of sound mind and is not acting under mistake, intimidation or other similar pressure) is his own personal responsibility, and is not to be regarded as having been caused by other people."[30]

The Scottish courts have taken a different approach. In *Khaliq v HM Advocate*,[31] the two accused were charged with causing a risk of injury to children by supplying them with "glue sniffing kits" (glue decanted into plastic bags).[32] They took a plea to the relevancy of the charge, on the ground that a causal link between their actions and the injuries sustained by the children could not be established. They argued that since the children required to inhale the solvents before injury would occur, this unreasonable behaviour broke the chain of causation between the accused's acts of selling the glue-sniffing kits

---

[27] D Stuart, *Canadian Criminal Law: A Treatise* (6th edn, 2011), p 157.
[28] (1972) 56 Cr App R 95.
[29] See n 44, in section 7.3.11 below.
[30] G Williams, *Textbook of Criminal Law* (2nd edn, 1983), p 391.
[31] 1984 JC 23.
[32] The crime of "causing real injury" is discussed further at section 10.12.1 below.

and the injuries. The court dismissed this line of argument, holding that a victim's acts could amount to a *novus actus interveniens* only if these were out of the ordinary, and in no way related to the accused's conduct.

7.3.8   It is apparent from our discussion that causation assumes particular importance in relation to homicide cases: unless the death results from the accused's actions, no homicide offence has been committed. At one level, this is purely a question of fact. If A shoots B in the head at point-blank range and B dies from the resulting gunshot wound, there will be no debate as to the "cause" of the death. However, the matter becomes more complicated where a number of different "causes" have together culminated in death. In *Johnston* v *HM Advocate*,[33] for example, two accused were convicted of the murder of the victim even though the jury determined that each had acted separately and not "in concert"[34] with one another. One had "knocked the deceased to the floor and then delivered eight powerful punches to his head",[35] rendering him unconscious. The second accused had then kicked the victim's head, "as if he were taking a penalty kick with a football".[36] It was impossible to determine which blow was the cause of death. In circumstances like this, where a number of causes have operated together, the courts usually apply the *sine qua non* or "but for" test: can it be said that, but for the accused's actions, the victim would not have died at that time? In addition, the part played by the accused must have been the, or at least a, direct cause of the death. As Jeremy Horder and Laura McGowan have stated: "[a] cause of death is still a cause, in law, even if it is only one of a number of operating causes".[37] It ceases to be relevant in criminal law only if it is deemed too "remote" from the death. As in other aspects of the law on homicide, this gives the courts scope to allow criminal liability to follow moral blameworthiness.[38]

7.3.9   This is another instance where the edifice of law, as a discipline which identifies and applies pre-determined rules, crumbles slightly. Facts, particularly in relation to causation, do not always

---

[33] [2009] HCJAC 38.

[34] For a discussion of art and part liability (or acting in concert), see from section 7.5 below.

[35] *Johnston* v *HM Advocate* [2009] HCJAC 38 at para 29, per Lord Reed.

[36] *Ibid.*

[37] J Horder and L McGowan, "Manslaughter by causing another's suicide" [2006] *Crim LR* 1035, at 1039. For a Scottish perspective, see P R Ferguson, "Killing 'without getting into trouble'? Assisted suicide and Scots criminal law" (1998) 2 *Edin LR* 288.

[38] Gordon discusses this in relation to the decision as to whether the accused should be convicted of murder or culpable homicide: Gordon (2001), para 23.21.

lend themselves to such an analysis. It may be difficult to determine the relative importance of several competing causes in terms of actually bringing about death. Accordingly, there is some scope to make a decision as to whether the accused should be blamed for the death and then to apply a view of causation designed to draw this out. Thus, while in theory causation may be regarded as purely factual – (if A's act, committed with an appropriate mental attitude, caused B's death, other than accidentally or justifiably, then A is responsible for an offence of homicide) – in practice, causation may be more appropriately characterised as a condition of criminal liability which the court deems satisfied by reference to its assessment that the accused is *morally blameworthy* for the death.[39]

In *McDonald* v *HM Advocate*,[40] the victim had been seriously assaulted by the two accused, who had punched and kicked him repeatedly on his head and body, and locked him in his third-floor flat, taking the key with them. There was no telephone in the flat. Within 30 minutes of both accused leaving, the victim climbed out of his window, apparently in an attempt to escape, either from his attackers or from the flat itself and to reach the street. The lintel of a second-floor window broke when he stood on it, and he fell to his death. The victim was a drug addict who had consumed a large quantity of amphetamine on the day he died. Both accused were convicted of culpable homicide, but McDonald appealed on the ground that since it was his co-accused, not he, who had locked the door, he could not be said to have caused the victim's death. The trial judge had given the jury a very detailed account of causation, which drew on the facts of some of the classic causation cases, and bears repeating:

7.3.10

> "[T]o find an accused guilty of culpable homicide you must be satisfied that there is a direct causal link between the unlawful act, in this case the alleged assault, and the victim's death. ... To find a causal link you must be satisfied that but for the unlawful act, in this case the alleged assault, the victim would not have died. The unlawful act need not be the only cause of death but it must be one of the causes. In other words, in this case if you were not satisfied that the assault contributed significantly to the deceased's decision to climb out the window, then there would be no causal link and the accused, if guilty of a serious assault, would not be guilty of culpable homicide, but if

---

[39] See from section 2.6 above, for further discussion of moral blame and criminal liability. If such a practice were to go so far that it could be said to *distort* the applicable legal principles, it would rightly be criticised as "usurping the power of the legislature": K J Arenson, "*Thabo Meli* revisited: the pernicious effects of result-driven decisions" (2013) *J Crim L* 41 at 42. The position is, rather, that the principles of causation are so broad that they permit of a wide variety of possible outcomes.

[40] 2007 SCCR 10.

you were so satisfied you would then need to go on and to consider whether the causal link was direct or indirect. Some acts may pass the 'but for' test but be considered too remote in time or other circumstances to be direct causes. Thus, suppose a blacksmith fails to put a nail in a horse's shoe and the horseshoe comes off in a battle, the king who is riding the horse finds that his horse goes lame for lack of a shoe. As a result of the horse's lameness the king is captured and the battle is lost. As a result of the loss of the battle the kingdom is lost. Now, the blacksmith's mistake meets the 'but for' test, but for the lack of the nail the kingdom would not have been lost, but the blacksmith's mistake was not the direct cause of the loss of the kingdom. Or suppose a ship is seriously damaged as a result of the criminal negligence of her captain. It is reasonably safe to stay on board in the meantime while awaiting rescue, but some passengers choose, when it is very imprudent to do so, to jump into the water and are drowned. But for the shipwreck they would not have died but the wreck was not the direct cause of their death. Their voluntary act would break the chain of causation and the captain would not be guilty of culpable homicide. Or suppose a man beats up his wife and as a result she leaves the family home in winter to walk two miles to her father's house to spend the night. When almost there, with only a couple of hundred yards to go, she decides that she is tired and lies down in the wood to rest, intending to go on in the morning. She then dies of exposure. Her voluntary decision to rest breaks the chain of causation and the husband isn't guilty of culpable homicide. But not every voluntary act by a victim breaks the chain of causation in law. In law the person who attacks another person takes his victim as he finds him. In other words, if the victim is old or infirm or has a weak heart and dies as a result of an assault which would not seriously injure a person in robust health, the victim's weakness is no defence to the charge of culpable homicide. Similarly, if the victim is mentally ill or is under the influence of alcohol or drugs when assaulted or is disoriented by the assault and does something directly in response to the assault which a more rational person would not do, the fact that his act was voluntary in the sense that it was done intentionally would not necessarily break the chain of causation."[41]

He later stated:

"In summary I wish to make four points in relation to the question of the causal link in this context. First, the 'but for' test must be met, but if it is met it is not enough. The unlawful act must be the direct cause of the death. Secondly, the attacker takes his victim as he finds him. Thirdly, where there is a direct link it does not matter if the attacker could not reasonably have foreseen that death would result from his attack or how the death would occur but, fourthly, in deciding whether there is a direct link where the victim has responded in a particular way to an attack you must consider whether that response was unforeseeable or wholly unreasonable as, if it was, the attack would not be the direct cause of the death."[42]

7.3.11   The decision in *McDonald*[43] rests on the inference that the victim was trying to escape. Accordingly, his death was a direct result of

---

[41] 2007 SCCR 10 at 11–12.
[42] *Ibid* at 12.
[43] 2007 SCCR 10.

the initial assault – he would not have died "but for" that assault. In fact, however, the medical evidence indicated that the injuries inflicted by the assault would not in themselves have caused death and it was unclear whether the injuries together with the fall would have been sufficient. The victim suffered exposure because he was not discovered until several hours after the fall, without which he would not have died. It would have been possible for the court to hold that the only injuries which the accused actually *caused*, physically and directly, were those inflicted during the attack. The victim's decision to try to climb to the ground from the third floor, presented in the case as entirely rational in the circumstances, could equally have been construed by the court as demonstrating the level of "daftness" which has, on occasion, been held sufficient in English law to break the chain of causation.[44] In *McDonald*, the view seems to have been taken that the appellant was blameworthy for the death and the court's reasoning tailored to allow liability to follow in law.

This appears to be part of a growing trend by the appeal court to elide any responsibility by the victim where it is clear that the accused's conduct was, in a broader view, culpable. The law has been protecting glue-sniffers in this way since 1984[45] and has controversially extended its protection to recreational drug-users,[46] a route not favoured in the English law case of *R v Kennedy (No 2)*.[47] Lord Bingham rejected the argument that the accused could be said to have caused the victim's death by supplying him with a syringe of heroin. His approach reflects a liberal perspective:

7.3.12

> "The criminal law generally assumes the existence of free will. The law recognises certain exceptions, in the case of the young, those who for any reason are not fully responsible for their actions, and the vulnerable, and it acknowledges situations of duress and necessity, as also of deception and mistake. But, generally speaking, informed adults of sound mind are treated as autonomous beings able to make their own decisions how they will act, and none of the exceptions is relied on as possibly applicable in this case.

---

[44] See *R v Roberts* (1972) 56 Cr App R 95, concerning the (justified) action of a young woman in jumping out of a moving car, where Lord Justice Stephenson stated (at 102): "if of course the victim does something so 'daft,' in the words of the appellant in this case, or so unexpected, not that this particular assailant did not actually foresee it but that no reasonable man could be expected to foresee it, then it is only in a very remote and unreal sense a consequence of his assault, it is really occasioned by a voluntary act on the part of the victim which could not reasonably be foreseen and which breaks the chain of causation between the assault and the harm or injury." See also R Williams, "Policy and principle in drugs manslaughter cases" (2005) *CLJ* 66 at 68–70.

[45] See *Khaliq v HM Advocate* 1984 JC 23; *Ulhaq v HM Advocate* 1991 SLT 614.

[46] *Lord Advocate's Reference (No 1 of 1994)* 1996 JC 76; *Paxton v HM Advocate* 1999 SCCR 895.

[47] [2007] 3 WLR 612. See also *R v Khan* [1998] *Crim LR* 830.

Thus [the accused] is not to be treated as causing [the victim] to act in a certain way if [the victim] makes a voluntary and informed decision to act in that way rather than another."[48]

The question for the court was:

"When is it appropriate to find someone guilty of manslaughter where that person has been involved in the supply of a class A controlled drug, which is then freely and voluntarily self-administered by the person to whom it was supplied, and the administration of the drug then causes his death?"[49]

In respect of a "fully-informed and responsible adult",[50] the House of Lords' reply to this question was "never".[51]

7.3.13   That Scots law takes a different approach is illustrated by the case of *MacAngus and Kane* v *HM Advocate*.[52] A Bench of Five Judges held that indictments libelling culpable homicide in the context of the supplying of a controlled drug were relevant, so long as the Crown specified that the supplying/administration of the drug was in the circumstances reckless. Lord Justice-General Hamilton concluded:

"The adult status and the deliberate conduct of a person to whom a controlled drug is recklessly supplied by another will be important, in some cases crucial, factors in determining whether that other's act was or was not, for the purposes of criminal responsibility, a cause of any death which follows upon ingestion of the drug. But a deliberate decision by the victim of the reckless conduct to ingest the drug will not necessarily break the chain of causation."[53]

7.4   CRITIQUE OF THE LAW ON CAUSATION AND PROPOSALS FOR REFORM

7.4.1   It is obvious from the foregoing discussion that policy plays a major role in ascribing the behaviour of the accused as a cause of an event. The law's approach to causation issues reflects a liberal philosophy in which individuals are responsible for their autonomous choices. In relation to the supply of narcotic drugs, leading to fatalities, it seems

---

[48] *R* v *Kennedy (No 2)* [2007] 3 WLR 612 at 616; [2007] 4 All ER 1083 at 1088.
[49] This was the question certified by the Court of Appeal Criminal Division: *ibid* at 613.
[50] *Ibid* at 620.
[51] *Ibid*. The subsequent case of *R* v *Evans* [2009] 1 WLR 1999 "does not disturb this principle, but holds that even when [the victim] self-injects, the supplier of the drugs will be liable if she does not summon help": D J Baker, "Omissions liability for homicide offences: reconciling *R* v *Kennedy* with *R* v *Evans*" (2010) 74 *J Crim L* 310 at 319.
[52] 2009 SLT 137. See also section 9.18.1 below.
[53] *Ibid* at 151, para 48.

that the "responsible individual" in English law is the victim, who chooses to take the illegal drugs, while in Scots law it is the accused, who chooses to supply such drugs. The Scottish approach is harsh; it can be argued that the "wrong" committed by the accused in cases such as *MacAngus and Kane* v *HM Advocate*[54] is the supply of drugs, and not the subsequent death. Counsel for the accused in that case argued that it was a fundamental principle of the common law that the drug users ought to be held responsible for the consequences of their own actions; if greater protection and sanction were required for drug-related deaths, it was more appropriate that Parliament, rather than the courts, rectify the issue. There is much to be said for this argument.

7.5 ART AND PART LIABILITY

Normally a person is criminally liable for her own acts or omissions, only. Where people act as a group, however, the whole group may be held responsible for the actions of each person. This is referred to as "art and part" liability – all those concerned in the crime are equally guilty, whatever their part in the criminal conduct. Art and part liability requires the participation of at least two people, and is essentially a form of derivative liability; where two or more people engage in crime, each is liable for the whole crime regardless of the actual part each played.[55] Judges often explain this concept to a jury by use of a bank robbery example. If the charge is that "A, B, C, D and E did rob a bank", then there may be evidence that A was the lookout, B simply drove the getaway car and did not go into the bank, C and D actually robbed the bank and E's role was to transport the stolen money out of the country. In this scenario, if the jury is satisfied that all the accused were acting as part of a common plan, then liability is said to be art and part and each may be convicted of the robbery. If F lent the gang some equipment (perhaps a gun or some explosives) in the knowledge that this was to be used in the robbery, then F would also be art and part liable for robbery, even though she was nowhere near the bank at the time of the crime.[56]

Even instigating a crime or giving advice to a person can make 7.5.2 one art and part liable if this has the effect of inducing the crime. The advice must be more than a general vague remark: it must be

7.5.1

---

[54] 2009 SLT 137.
[55] See *McKinnon* v *HM Advocate* 2003 JC 29, per LJ-G Cullen at 39, para 27. This case is considered further at section 7.6.4 below.
[56] See Lord Patrick's charge to the jury in *HM Advocate* v *Lappen* 1956 SLT 109 for a particularly clear statement, in this form, of the principle of art and part liability.

likely to lead to the commission of the crime. In many cases of art
and part liability there will have been prior agreement to commit
the crime, such as in the bank robbery example. This common plan
is sometimes referred to as "antecedent concert". A case illustrating
this is *HM Advocate* v *Fraser and Rollins*,[57] in which a woman
enticed the victim into a park where her two associates attacked,
robbed and killed him. The basis of her homicide conviction was
that, even though she had not actually attacked the victim, there had
been prior agreement to do this, among the three of them.

7.5.3   As mentioned previously,[58] instigating a crime can constitute a
form of art and part liability. Procuring another person to commit
a crime is one illustration of this form which is sometimes known
as art and part liability "by counsel and instigation". An example
of this is that staple of crime fiction: the contract killing. In such
a situation both the actual killer and the prson who procurred her
services will be guilty of an offence of homicide (most likely, murder).
The circumstances which underlie the procedural decision in *HM
Advocate* v *Meikleham*[59] are an example of such an arrangement,
where the actual killer had not been identified and was not on trial.

7.5.4   It is against the background of these forms of art and part
liability that we will examine ss 28 and 30 of the Criminal Justice
and Licensing (Scotland) Act 2010. These provisions respectively
criminalise agreeing to commit, and directing another person to
commit, serious organised crime.[60] Both Westminster and Scottish
Governments have, in recent years, demonstrated a commitment
to "respond[ing] robustly to the threat posed by organised cime".[61]
To this end, the Serious Organised Crime Agency set up by s 1 of
the Serious Organised Crime and Police Act 2005, may operate in
both jurisdictions, *inter alia* to prevent and detect serious organised
crime[62] and "to contribut[e] to the reduction of such crime in other
ways".[63] The Scottish Justice Secretary has spoken of targeting
"gangsters".[64] The activities covered include drug crimes, serious

---

[57] 1920 JC 60.

[58] At section 7.5.2 above.

[59] 1998 SCCR 621.

[60] It also includes directing someone to direct someone else to commit such a crime:
Criminal Justice and Licensing (Scotland) Act 2010, s 30(2).

[61] Scottish Government website: http://www.scotland.gov.uk/Topics/Justice/crimes
/organised-crime/soc/taskforce.

[62] Serious Organised Crime and Police Act 2005, s 2(1)(a).

[63] *Ibid*, s 2 (1)(b).

[64] See, for example, press release: "Turning the screw on the gangsters", 13 December
2010, available at: http://www.scotland.gov.uk/News/Releases/2010/12/12171051.
Press release: "Serious organised crime", 7 March 2011, available at: http://www.
scotland.gov.uk/News/Releases/2011/03/04151145.

violence, counterfeiting, human trafficking, e-crime and money laundering.[65] In principle, then, the prevention and criminalisation of serious organised crime is unobjectionable. We might, however, question the mechanism by which this has been done within the 2010 Act. Given the breadth, and type, of circumstances to which the common law on art and part liability is applicable, it is important to look carefully at the behaviour which is directly criminalised by the Act.

Section 28(1) of the Act creates a new offence of "agree[ing] with   7.5.5
at least one other person to become involved in serious organised crime".[66] "Become involved" is not defined and, in fact, the accused does not even have to have "*become* involved": she merely has to have agreed to do so. Currently, where such an agreement is found, the possibility of conviction *for offences committed pursuant to it*, on an art and part basis, already exists. Furthermore, entering into an agreement to commit an offence also constitutes *per se* the existing crime of conspiracy.[67] The definition of "serious organised crime" is vague but it requires, as its focus, the commission of (or conspiracy to commit) a serious offence(s). We would suggest, therefore, that the behaviour proscribed by s 28(1) is already criminalised in Scotland in terms of either conspiracy or, when further crimes are committed in pursuance of the conspiracy, art and part liability for those crimes. Thus the provision is unnecessary. Like the terrorism legislation,[68] s 28 criminalises at such an early stage in the process towards actual commision of a crime that the accused may have done very little. While there is no doubt that serious organised crime requires a robust response, the enactment of vague, over-inclusive offences is not the best mechanism by which to achieve this.

Section 30 may operate more productively, though similar   7.5.6
criticisms may be made. The essence of the offence is directing another person to commit a serious offence (as defined in s 28)

---

[65] Kenny MacAskill, "Tackling serious organised crime", 11 March 2010, available at: http://www.scotland.gov.uk/News/Speeches/Speeches/Safer-and-stronger/soc.

[66] "Serious organised crime" is defined by the Criminal Justice and Licensing (Scotland) Act 2010, s 28(3) to mean "crime involving two or more persons acting together for the principal purpose of committing or conspiring to commit a serious offence or a series of serious offences". "Serious offence" means an indictable offence "(a) committed with the intention of obtaining a material benefit for any person, or (b) which is an act of violence committed or a threat made with the intention of obtaining such a benefit in the future", and "material benefit" means "a right or interest of any description in any property, whether heritable or moveable and whether corporeal or incorporeal."

[67] Conspiracy is discussed further from section 8.6 below.

[68] See from section 8.23 below.

or any offence aggravated by a connection with serious organised crime.[69] Where the crime was carried out as directed, such behaviour could already be criminalised by applying the principles of art and part liability by counsel and instigation to the person directing this. The directing itself could also be caught by the common law crime of incitement.[70] It may be, however, that this provision will make easier the prosecution of a key player who orders the commission of the crime by another person but takes no further part in the perpetration. "Directing" may have slightly different connotations to "instigating" or "inciting".

7.5.7   In some cases there is no evidence of any prior agreement yet still the accused is found liable for the actions of a group. This is where there seems to have been a "spontaneous coming together" at the time of the offence. The case of *Gallacher v HM Advocate*[71] is an example of this. The background to the case is that there was an ongoing feud between members of a circus and some of the local residents of Hamilton. The victim was mistakenly taken to be a member of that circus and a fight ensued between the victim and one of the accused. A group of other people subsequently joined in the fight, and the victim was kicked to death. Three people were convicted of murder, despite the fact that there was no evidence of any prior agreement. The accused were art and part liable because they were said to have been animated by a common criminal purpose, which in this case was murderous. Where the jury is not satisfied that there was either prior agreement or a spontaneous coming together, each accused is held responsible for her own acts, only.[72]

7.5.8   Assistance in the crime is required for art and part guilt, and this must be distinguished from the situation in which the accused is present at the scene of a crime, but has no involvement in its commission. This is clear from the case of *HM Advocate v George Kerr and Others*,[73] in which the court held that observing an attempted rape, and failing to intervene to assist the victim, was not sufficient for art and part liability.

7.5.9   The art and part doctrine makes it possible, in certain circumstances, for an accused to be found criminally responsible for a crime which, in practice, she could not have committed individually. Thus, in *Petch v HM Advocate*,[74] the indictment charged a woman with

---

[69] Criminal Justice and Licensing (Scotland) Act 2010, s 30(1).
[70] Discussed further from section 8.6.6 below.
[71] 1951 JC 38.
[72] See *Johnston v HM Advocate* [2009] HCJAC 38, discussed further at section 7.3.8 above.
[73] (1871) 2 Coup 334, discussed in section 6.5.3 above.
[74] 2011 SLT 526 (an appeal in relation to the severity of the sentence imposed).

rape on an art and part basis, along with two male co-accused.[75] There have been cases where the principal offender was acquitted of the charge but a co-accused was convicted for art and part involvement.[76] Since the purpose of the art and part doctrine is to render co-accused liable for their involvement in an overall criminal enterprise, such an outcome should be reasonably foreseeable (to such co-accused) and therefore is not obviously unfair.

7.6 THE LIMITS OF ART AND PART

We have said that this form of liability occurs where people act as a group, and that there has often been prior planning to commit the crime. What happens if one member of the group steps outside the agreed plan? Are the others liable for *this* conduct? Once the Crown proves that there was a common plan or common criminal purpose, the accused will be held responsible (in the sense of liable to punishment under the criminal law) for any foreseeable consequences of the crime, and this is so whether or not a particular accused intended those consequences. If, however, one member of the group had stepped outside the common plan in an unforeseeable way, then the others will not be liable for that result. In the case of *HM Advocate* v *Welsh and McLachlan*,[77] the two accused broke into a house, intending to steal. One of them beat the occupant of the house to death with a crowbar, but the prosecution was unable to establish which accused had done so. Indeed, there was little evidence at all as to what had happened in the house. The forensic evidence indicated that the violence was sudden and unexpected, hence it was unlikely that there had been any agreement to use such violence. Accordingly, art and part liability could not apply and each accused could be held liable only for his own actions. As a result, both were acquitted of homicide. While this result is far from satisfactory – one of these two accused beat someone to death, with impunity – to hold them both liable would be grossly unjust to the one who was in fact innocent.

In *Boyne* v *HM Advocate*,[78] several people were involved in an assault and robbery and the victim was killed from a stab wound

7.6.1

7.6.2

---

[75] The charge pre-dated the coming into force of the Sexual Offences (Scotland) Act 2009, s 1, so was common law rape, which could only be committed by a male person as principal.

[76] See *Capuano* v *HM Advocate* 1984 SCCR 415. Where only holders of a particular office (such as company director) can commit the offence charged, it has been held that it is inconsistent to hold someone else liable on an art and part basis, when all actual holders of the office had been acquitted: *Young and Todd* v *HM Advocate* 1932 JC 63.

[77] (1897) 5 SLT 137.

[78] 1980 SLT 56.

inflicted by one of the assailants. The others could be held liable for the death if the Crown established either that they knew about the knife and that it was liable to be used (that is, that use of the knife was part of the common plan) or, if they did not know that one of them had a knife or that it might be used, that when the knife was in fact used, they continued their attack on the victim. The second of these is similar to the idea of art and part liability based on the accused having been "animated by a common purpose". In fact, in this case, the appeal court held that the use of the knife went beyond the common plan and was unforeseeable by two of the accused. It quashed their murder convictions, substituting convictions for assault and robbery.

7.6.3   In *Codona* v *HM Advocate*,[79] the appellant was a teenage girl, involved with a group of young men who were engaged in a campaign of assaulting men whom they believed to be homosexuals. The gang committed two separate assaults, resulting in minor injuries. During the next assault, Codona kicked the victim on the back of the leg. Thereafter, the other members of the gang assaulted the victim by repeatedly kicking and stamping on his head, ultimately killing him. Codona was found guilty of murder on the basis of art and part liability, but her conviction was quashed on appeal, the court holding that the nature and severity of the third assault were not foreseeable, and that she could not be held liable for its fatal consequences.[80]

7.6.4   In *McKinnon* v *HM Advocate*,[81] the Crown sought a conviction for murder on the basis that the victim's death was the outcome of an agreement between the accused to commit the crime of assault and robbery. The appeal was remitted to a Full Bench (five judges), in which the Lord Justice-General quoted from Hume:

> "One thing is plainly reasonable and is allowed by all authorities: That if a number conspire and lie in wait, to kill a certain person ... it signifies nothing who gives the mortal blow, or how few blows are given. Though but one of the party strike, and dispatch with one blow of a lethal weapon, he is not therefore the one actor on the occasion, but executioner, for all of them, of their common resolution".[82]

---

[79] 1996 SLT 1100.

[80] See also *Kabalu* v *HM Advocate* 1999 SCCR 348 in which two of the accused joined a gang at the end stages of an assault, and were held not to be responsible for the fatal blows which had been inflicted prior to their arrival. Their late arrival meant that they had not witnessed the level of violence used initially and they could not be held to have shared the common (murderous) purpose because it was not clear that they knew how violent the assault had been.

[81] 2003 JC 29.

[82] Hume, i, 264 (quoted in *McKinnon* v *HM Advocate* 2003 JC 29 at 32, para 9).

Hume continued:

"This rule is to be understood as applicable not only to those comparatively rare cases, where an express and formal compact to kill can be proved, but equally to all, in which, from the number, arms, words and behaviour of the persons engaged, an implied and tacit confederacy may reasonably be inferred ...[83]

What is true of homicide committed in pursuance of a concert to kill, or to do some grievous bodily harm, seems to be equally so of homicide done in prosecution of any other felony; provided the nature of the attempt imply, or the behaviour and proceedings of the parties indicate, an unity of purpose in all concerned, and a resolution to control all resistance by numbers and force. If several go out together, armed, to rob on the highway, and one of them kill in the assault, it is murder in all those of the party who are anywise aiding in the robbery, whether present or not on the spot. For they are all there under a compact of mutual support; and the homicide is an obvious and not unforeseen consequence of the assault, to rob: Else why do they go out provided with arms? The like judgment is due, if a number are engaged in a housebreaking and one of them kills a person in the house, whether to subdue resistance, or make good his own escape: Even those who never enter the house, but watch only without, to prevent surprise, are here guilty art and part of the murder".[84]

The Lord Justice-General then stated:

"There is no reason to think that what was said by Hume ... does not or should not represent a correct statement of the law in regard to guilt of murder on the basis of antecedent concert. While there may be cases in which no other conclusion can reasonably be reached, it is for the jury to decide whether a person who participates in the carrying out of a common criminal purpose which leads to a fellow participant committing murder should be held criminally responsible for the murder on the basis that he knew that a weapon which could readily be used to kill was being carried for use in furtherance of that purpose, so that there was an obvious risk of murder. In such a situation it would be immaterial whether he knowingly ran that risk or was recklessly blind to it."[85]

The court in *MacKinnon* departed from the decision in the case of *Brown* v *HM Advocate*[86] in which it had been held that in a homicidal attack the court should attempt to ascertain the *mens rea* of each accused, and that it was possible for some to be guilty of murder, while other were guilty of culpable homicide.[87]

Homicide constitutes a special application of the rules on art 7.6.5 and part because it allows, at the stage of conviction, a judgment

---

[83] Hume, i, 265 (quoted *ibid*).
[84] Hume, i, 268–269 (quoted in *McKinnon* v *HM Advocate* 2003 JC 29 at 32–33, para 10).
[85] *McKinnon* v *HM Advocate* 2003 JC 29 at 38, para 25.
[86] 1993 SCCR 382.
[87] See section 7.8.3 below, for a critique of this approach.

to be made on seriousness in terms of whether a verdict of murder or culpable homicide will be returned. Much of the judgment in *McKinnon* is concerned with this and the rules will be considered, below, in their own right.[88] In relation to all crimes, where there is a pre-arranged common plan, however, the judgment also makes clear that the inference of guilt arising throught concert will be made on an objective basis – the question therefore becoming what crime(s) a reasonable person would have foreseen as flowing directly from the common criminal purpose rather than what was actually within the individual accused's own contemplation.[89]

7.6.6   Whether one member of a gang can withdraw from the common plan and thereby avoid conviction for the ultimate crime is an issue which has not been subject to much discussion by the Scottish courts. Some writers take the view that withdrawal at the planning stage may avoid liability, but that once the crime is actually being perpetrated, withdrawal will be insufficient in itself.[90] According to this view, the accused who changes her mind once the plan is being put into operation must do more than simply withdraw; she must take positive steps to prevent the successful completion of the crime, or notify the police. This is given some support by the case of *MacNeil* v *HM Advocate*[91] in which one of eight men accused of importing cannabis had helped to store the cannabis on a ship, but took no further part in the venture, and claimed on appeal that he had dissociated himself from the common plan and should therefore have been acquitted. The appeal court held that once a common plan has been put into operation, there is no defence of dissociation.

7.7   ART AND PART LIABILITY IN (ANTECEDENT CONCERT) HOMICIDE

7.7.1   *McKinnon* v *HM Advocate*[92] was a case of homicide arising from a common plan to commit robbery for which a number of the co-accused armed themselves in advance with chef's knives. Clearly, then, there was antecedent concert. The evidence was that the fatal stab wound (to the victim's heart) had most likely been inflicted by only one of the co-accused but it was not known which one. The question was whether, in those circumstances, it was appropriate to hold *all* the co-accused liable for murder. A five-judge Bench held that it was, stating:

[88] See from section 7.8 below, for a critique of this approach.
[89] *McKinnon* v *HM Advocate* 2003 JC 29, per LJ-G Cullen at 37, para 22, and 39, para 29.
[90] For example, A M Cubie, *Scots Criminal Law* (3rd edn, 2010), para 6.16.
[91] 1986 JC 146.
[92] 2003 JC 29.

"an accused is guilty of murder art and part where, first, by his conduct, for example his words or actions, he actively associates himself with a common criminal purpose which is or includes the taking of human life or carries the obvious risk that human life will be taken, and, secondly, in the carrying out of that purpose murder is committed by someone else".[93]

Individual co-accused therefore do not require to have the specific *mens rea* of murder. In *Poole* v *HM Advocate*,[94] it was stated that, in cases of antecedent concert:

"The question, following *McKinnon v HM Advocate*, comes to be whether there was evidence entitling the jury to find that it was objectively foreseeable to the appellant that such violence was liable to be used as carried an obvious risk of life being taken. The question is not ... whether there was evidence from which it could be said that the appellant had the mens rea necessary for murder."[95]

This indicates that an accused may be found guilty of murder on an art and part basis where a reasonable person would have foreseen "an obvious risk of life being taken" but where that individual did not. This therefore raises all of the potential unfairness of a wholly objective approach to criminal liability which we discussed in more detail in relation to the concept of recklessness.[96] Fiona Leverick has noted this unfairness, particularly in relation to convicting of murder an accused who did not wish the fatal consequences to ensue and had not even foreseen the possibility that death would occur, though a reasonable person would have done so.[97] The law has continued to develop with the subsequent case of *Hopkinson* v *HM Advocate*[98] which, perhaps surprisingly, given the authority and clarity of *McKinnon*, at least re-opened the door to the possibility of the return of different verdicts in cases of homicide arising out of antecedent conduct.

In *Hopkinson*, the victim had been stabbed to death in the   7.7.2 course of a robbery. He died from a single stab wound to the top of his leg which severed his femoral artery. This was inflicted by Hopkinson's co-accused, a woman named Stewart. The victim bled to death after both co-accused ran away from the locus. Both were convicted of murder at first instance. Hopkinson had himself gone to the scene armed with a knife but with the intention only of threatening the victim if he refused to hand over his money. His

---

[93] 2003 JC 29, per LJ-G Cullen at 40, para 32.
[94] 2009 SCCR 577.
[95] *Ibid* at 586, para [11], per Lord Kingarth.
[96] See from section 6.15.1 above.
[97] F Leverick, "The (art and) parting of the ways: joint criminal liability for homicide" 2012 SLT 227 at 230–231.
[98] 2009 SLT 292.

evidence was that he had not known until he was on his way to the
locus that his co-accused also had a knife and he had had no reason
to anticipate that she would use it to stab the victim, let alone in
such a way as to cause his death. He was initially convicted of
murder on an art and part basis but his appeal was successful. The
appeal court held that the possibility that the *common* criminal
purpose did *not* include the taking of life or the material risk of life
being taken should have been presented to the jury. If the common
criminal purpose did not encompass such a risk then Stewart had
gone beyond the common plan. Her actions were not foreseeable
in terms of that plan. The fact that Hopkinson had himself gone
armed with a knife was not conclusive. It was the purpose for which
he thought it would be used which was important. In the end, the
Crown did not seek a re-trial and a verdict of culpable homicide
was substituted for Hopkinson.[99]

7.7.3   In some respects, *Hopkinson* is difficult to reconcile with
McKinnon. Like *McKinnon*, *Hopkinson* was a case of antecedent
concert in terms of a common plan to commit robbery. Hopkinson
pre-armed himself with a kitchen knife. He held this knife to the
victim's throat to effect the robbery itself. He did know prior to the
attack – if only just prior – that the co-accused also had a knife.
Might not a reasonable person have found that there was a "material
risk of life being taken" in these circumstances? The judgment in
Hopkinson also states that if any agreement between the two co-
accused regarding the use of knives had been "restricted to the
limited purpose of scaring the deceased, without there having been
any foreseeable risk of injury being inflicted" then "the appellant
could not [even] have been convicted of culpable homicide".[100] This
seems to accord neither with the law on art and part homicide as set
down in *McKinnon*,[101] nor with the general law which would treat as
culpable homicide any death arising from an assault.[102]

7.7.4   Nonetheless, it is possible to find some support for this stance in
the judgment in *McKinnon*, albeit that the comment is *obiter* and it
is not clear that the court in *Hopkinson* sought to apply it:

> "Where an individual accused knows that weapons are being carried for use
> in order to carry out a common criminal purpose, and these are weapons of

---

[99] Commentary on *Hopkinson v HM Advocate* 2009 SCCR 225 at 237.

[100] *Hopkinson v HM Advocate* 2009 SLT 292 per Lord Mackay of Drumadoon at
299 para [22].

[101] See Leverick (2012) at 229.

[102] Following the rules of causation, including those requiring accused persons to
take their victims as they find them. See from section 7.3.4 above. See also *Bird v
HM Advocate* 1952 JC 23. Following *Atkinson v HM Advocate* 1987 SCCR 534,
it is accepted that threatening gestures are sufficient to constitute the *actus reus* of
assault.

such a nature that they can readily be used to kill, it is open to the jury to convict him or her of murder on the basis that it was foreseeable that such weapons were liable to be used with lethal effect. That is, however, dependent on the circumstances, including the way in which it was envisaged that the weapons were to be or might be used. There is no rule of law that the jury must convict. In particular it is not a rule of law that homicide in pursuance of the commission of a crime involving the use of violence is necessarily a murder. The jury may conclude that they are not satisfied, in regard to an individual accused, that it was obvious that ... such weapons might be used to kill the victim. If, for example, one of two accused is carrying a stick or even a penknife which, so far as the other accused is concerned, is intended to frighten a shopkeeper whom they intend to rob, the latter might well not be guilty of murder perpetrated by the former even though he had reason to anticipate that such a weapon would or might be used for that limited purpose. Much will depend on whether the participant is reckless as to the consequences of proceeding."[103]

The judgment in *Hopkinson* was *not* to the effect that the common plan in that case carried no material risk of life being taken. The issue was rather that the possibility that this might be the case had not been properly put to the jury. On that basis, Hopkinson's conviction fell to be quashed. The judgment does, however, expressly, canvass the possibility of one co-accused being convicted of murder, and the other of culpable homicide in a case of antecedent concert robbery where both accused pre-arm themselves with knives. This can only be explained by reference to the terms of the common plan, proof of which is often difficult.[104]

7.8 CRITIQUE OF THE LAW ON ART AND PART AND PROPOSALS FOR REFORM

While the ambit of art and part liability in Scots law is potentially 7.8.1 very wide, the need for proof that all of the co-accused shared a common criminal aim serves a unifying purpose. In the (pre-planned) bank robbery scenario, the getaway driver and the lookout, for example, are criminalised because they have associated themselves with that crime of robbery. They cannot be art and part liable unless the Crown proves beyond reasonable doubt that they knew the extent of the criminality planned and decided to go along with it. In cases where there is a spontaneous coming together of individuals to commit a crime, the common criminal purpose – the purpose to commit the crime with which they are charged – must have animated the group. In *Gallacher*,[105] there was no particular evidence that those eventually convicted of murder had actually inflicted the fatal

---

[103] *McKinnon v HM Advocate* 2003 JC 29 per LJ-G Cullen at 39–40, para 31.
[104] See Leverick (2012) at 227.
[105] 1951 JC 38. See section 7.5.7 above.

blows on the victim. Their convictions rested on the fact that it was proved that they were part of the group which acted with murderous purpose. This is in accordance with the liberal basis of the criminal law. In both situations, autonomous individuals exercise freewill to decide to associate themselves with criminal conduct. Nor is art and part liability limitless. Going beyond the common plan by one co-accused may serve to terminate the liability of the others. Where the ultimate offence, which is committed spontaneously, is not one which a co-accused had anticipated, she may escape liability for the more serious crime, as in *Codona*.[106]

7.8.2   *McKinnon*[107] sets down a robust and objective formulation of art and part liability in homicide cases involving pre-concert. If there is an obvious and material risk of taking life *within the corners of the common plan*, and life is taken, the crime will be murder. *Hopkinson*[108] does not directly depart from this but it does indicate a greater willingness to focus on the exact terms of the common plan so as to be clear as to its extent. Much of the evidence of this, in that case, was Hopkinson's own. While this merely assists the jury in forming its own, objective view of the nature of the plan, it also provides some mechanism by which an accused can feed her own understanding of the situation into the process. It is, however, still a long way from making an individual determination as to the mental attitude of each co-accused towards the attack at the moment of carrying it out. Given the stigma, and the mandatory sentence attaching to a conviction of murder, this is an area where the potential for unfairness is high. Lethal weapons raise an inference of wicked recklessness[109] (though this is not conclusive). The extent to which a co-accused believes such weapons will be used during the crime forms a continuum from "only as a threat" to "for intentional killing". *Hopkinson* seems at least to focus attention on this. The deciding factor remains the jury's objective construction of the contours of the common plan. It was this which had not been properly put to them in *Hopkinson*. *McKinnon* also draws a distinction between cases in which the perpetrator of the fatal violence is known (like *Hopkinson*) and those, like *McKinnon* itself, where this is not clear. In the former, the court seeks to establish whether any co-accused shared with the perpetrator the criminal purpose for the crime which she is held to have committed. However, where the actual killer is not known the court must first decide which crime has been committed. It will

---

[106] 1996 SLT 1100. See section 7.6.3 above.
[107] 2003 JC 29.
[108] 2009 SLT 292.
[109] See, for example, LJ-C Aitchison's charge to the jury in *HM Advocate* v *McGuinness* 1937 JC 37.

then hold all who were parties to the common plan accountable for that crime.[110] It is not, however, clear that this forms any part of the basis of the *Hopkinson* decision.

In homicide cases generally in Scots law the view is taken that it **7.8.3** is important to convict an accused at the appropriate *level*, that is, either as a murderer or as the perpetrator of a culpable homicide.[111] This also accords with the principle of fair labelling.[112] In art and part homicide, these principles are attenuated in favour of punishing the group as a group, yet Scots law has not consistently held to this rule. There are obvious advantages to the decision in *McKinnon*:[113] the law is relatively clear and, given that the ascertainment of an accused's *mens rea* is not an exact science, an objective test as to the crime of which all co-accused are to be convicted makes the jury's task easier. The moral argument on which the judgment is based is also discernible: murder was committed therefore murder should be punished. Nonetheless, the basis of the decision in *Brown v HM Advocate*[114] deserves further consideration, despite the fact that in *MacKinnon*[115] the court stated that the points made in *Brown* on antecedent conduct "should not be regarded as authoritative".[116] If it is possible to ensure that all co-accused are convicted by reference to their level of fault, as is the case where homicide occurs without pre-concert,[117] then this may ensure greater fairness, with no diminution in either public protection or the denunciatory power of the criminal law. In our view, therefore, liability for homicide, even where there is a pre-arranged common plan, should be established by considering the *mens rea* of each co-accused on an individual basis. Indeed, as Leverick has also indicated, it is not entirely clear why there should be such a distinction between a spontaneous coming together resulting in the death of the victim and a pre-arranged common plan where the outcome is the same.[118] It is true that Hume categorised art and part cases differently on this basis,[119] but if the current distinction offers no principled reason for imposing differing levels of blameworthiness for similar acts then that is not, in itself, a good enough reason for continuing to do so.

---

[110] *McKinnon* v *HM Advocate* 2003 JC 29, per LJ-G Cullen at 39, para 28.
[111] *Ferguson* v *HM Advocate* 2009 SLT 67; and see C McDiarmid, "Withholding culpable homicide: *Ferguson* v *HM Advocate*" (2009) 13 *Edin LR* 316.
[112] See from section 4.6 above.
[113] 2003 JC 29.
[114] 1993 SCCR 382.
[115] See section 7.6.4 above.
[116] *McKinnon* v *HM Advocate* 2003 JC 29, per LJ-G Cullen at 38, para 24.
[117] *Docherty* v *HM Advocate* 2003 SLT 1337.
[118] Leverick (2012) at 231.
[119] Hume, i, 264–268, 270–272 and 274–277.

7.8.4　We have seen that it is uncertain whether the law recognises a defence of dissociation.[120] We suggest that it ought to do so. This would provide an incentive for those who have embarked on a criminal enterprise to think again, in the knowledge that they will at least receive a lesser punishment if they go no further.[121] The onus of establishing this defence should lie with the accused.

7.9 STATUTORY AGGRAVATIONS

7.9.1　Continuing our examination of general principles of liability, we turn now to statutory aggravations, most of which are applicable to a range of offences.[122] Section 96 of the Crime and Disorder Act 1998 provides that where an offence is motivated by racial prejudice, or involves a display of such prejudice, this is an aggravation which must be taken into account in sentencing.[123] Religious prejudice is also an aggravating factor, by s 74 of the Criminal Justice (Scotland) Act 2003.[124] In relation to both of these aggravations, the court must now record the difference, because of the aggravation, in the sentence actually imposed (or give its reason why there was no difference).[125] Furthermore, it is an offence under s 50A of the Criminal Law (Consolidation) (Scotland) Act 1995 for a person to pursue a racially aggravated course of conduct which amounts to harassment, or to act in a manner which is racially aggravated and which causes, or is intended to cause, a person alarm or distress. "Racially aggravated" has been interpreted strictly. In *Sennels* v *McGowan*,[126] the appeal court quashed the appellant's conviction for shouting the word "Afro" "in an insulting and threatening manner".[127] This was on the basis that the term could equally refer

---

[120] Section 7.6.6 above.
[121] See Law Commission Consultation Paper 131, *Assisting and Encouraging Crime* (1993), para 4.133.
[122] Common law aggravations are considered elsewhere – see from section 10.3 below in respect of aggravated assaults, and from section 12.8 below in relation to aggravated forms of theft.
[123] Crime and Disorder Act 1998, s 96(6) defines "racial group" to include persons defined by reference to race, colour, nationality (including citizenship) or ethnic or national origins.
[124] "Religious group" includes a group of persons defined by reference to their religious belief, or lack of religious belief (Criminal Justice (Scotland) Act 2003, s 74(7)).
[125] Crime and Disorder Act 1998, s 96(5), as inserted by the Criminal Justice and Licensing (Scotland) Act 2010, s 25(1); Criminal Justice (Scotland) Act 2003, s 74(4A), as inserted by Criminal Justice and Licensing (Scotland) Act 2010, s 25(2)(c).
[126] 2011 SCCR 180.
[127] *Ibid* at 181, para [4], per Lord Osborne.

to a hairstyle and that the sheriff had not explained why he had determined that, in this case, it related to the complainer's racial origins. In the case of *Martin* v *Bott*[128] the appeal court held that the complainer in a charge under s 50A must be the person whom the accused intended to alarm or distress, rather than a mere spectator. Although the appeal court quashed the appellant's conviction for acting in a manner which is racially aggravated, contrary to s 50A, it held that since s 96 of the Crime and Disorder Act 1998 enables *any* charge to be racially aggravated, it could substitute a conviction for a racially aggravated breach of the peace.[129] The Offences (Aggravation by Prejudice) (Scotland) Act 2009 provides further statutory aggravations which may be applied where there is evidence that a crime has been motivated by malice and ill-will based on a victim's actual or presumed disability,[130] sexual orientation[131] or transgender identity.[132]

All of the foregoing relate to offensive attitudes on the accused's behalf. In a departure from this unifying factor, the Scottish Government has also enacted an aggravation by connection with serious organised crime.[133] Thus: **7.9.2**

> "An offence is aggravated [in this way] if the person committing the offence is motivated (wholly or partly) by the objective of committing or conspiring to commit serious organised crime."[134]

7.10 CRITIQUE OF THE LAW ON STATUTORY AGGRAVATIONS AND PROPOSALS FOR REFORM

The English law offence of incitement to racial hatred has been criticised: few prosecutions have been taken, leading to the accusation that the creation of the offence was **7.10.1**

> "a costless (for government) sop to concern about racism which merely serves to legitimate government's relative inaction in other more potentially fruitful areas. In addition, each unsuccessful prosecution implies the *legitimacy* of the racist conduct thereby condoned".[135]

---

[128] 2005 SCCR 554.

[129] By virtue of the Criminal Procedure (Scotland) Act 1995, s 183 and Sch 3, para 14.

[130] Offences (Aggravation by Prejudice) (Scotland) Act 2009, s 1.

[131] *Ibid*, s 2.

[132] *Ibid*. The Act came into force on 24 March 2010. It has been held in relation to similarly worded aggravations under English law that paedophilia is not a form of "sexual orientation" (*R* v *B* [2013] Crim LR 614).

[133] Criminal Justice and Licensing (Scotland) Act 2010, s 29.

[134] *Ibid*, s 29(2).

[135] N Lacey, *Unspeakable Subjects: Feminist Essays in Legal and Social Theory* (1998) at 94 (emphasis in original).

The latter point is not necessarily accurate, so far as the Scottish position is concerned. A prosecution for an offence aggravated by racial prejudice could fail because of a lack of corroborated evidence that the accused was the perpetrator, or that the offence was committed at all, neither of which necessarily suggests that the victim's testimony was not accepted, or that racism was condoned.

7.10.2   We are concerned here with aggravations of other offences, rather than specific crimes, like incitement to racial hatred which criminalise directly certain aspects of public discourse. The drafting of the statutory provisions on these aggravations focuses attention on the accused's pre-existing attitude to members of the groups covered by the relevant sections, drawing out the risk of harm towards such group members. Before the aggravation is established, the Crown must prove either that the accused has "evince[d] ... malice and ill-will" towards the victim based on the victim's membership of the group, or that the offence is "motivated ... by malice and ill-will towards" such members.[136] Accordingly, the aggravation will not be established unless there is evidence that the accused's proven attitude is such that unpleasant consequences for group members are likely to flow from it. This view is strengthened by the fact that many indictments in cases of murder also aver that the accused had previously evinced malice and ill-will towards the victim.[137] By contrast, the Public Order Act 1986 (the source of the offence of incitement to racial hatred) criminalises, *inter alia*, the use of "threatening, abusive or insulting words" if there is an intention to "stir up racial hatred" or "racial hatred is likely to be stirred up thereby."[138] There is, therefore, more of a direct conflict with the right to freedom of expression under Art 10 of the ECHR and less recognition of the likelihood of actual harm, certainly in physical terms, to members of the group.

7.10.3   Nonetheless, it remains important to be vigilant as to the groups selected to be protected. Eric Barendt, for example, has carefully examined the extension of the English offence[139] to include, in a more limited way, the incitement of hatred against *religious* groups.[140] His view is that it is important not to criminalise legitimate, even if

---

[136] Crime and Disorder Act 1998, s 96(2); Criminal Justice (Scotland) Act 2003, s 74(2); Criminal Law (Consolidation) (Scotland) Act, s 50A(2); and Offences (Aggravation by Prejudice) (Scotland) Act 2009, ss 1(2) and 2(2).

[137] See, for example, *Stewart v HM Advocate* 2012 SCL 1054; *HM Advocate v McNamara* 2012 SLT 1037.

[138] Public Order Act 1986, s 18(1).

[139] *Ibid*, ss 29A and 29B-29F.

[140] E Barendt, "Religious hatred laws: protecting groups or belief?" (2011) 17 *Res Publica* 41.

forcefully expressed, criticism of religious *practices*.[141] Freedom of expression requires that this should be permitted. In a largely secular society, however, religious *groups* may need greater protection.[142]

As we shall see when we examine the crime of breach of the **7.10.4** peace in more detail, *Martin v Bott*[143] is but one example of that common law crime being applied to a wide range of conduct.[144] This is arguably contrary to the principle of fair labelling.[145] Furthermore, having three separate offences of aggravations evincing racial or religious prejudice seems unnecessary. The *Draft Criminal Code* provides a general provision on aggravations, such that any offence may be aggravated

> "by the intent or motivation with which it is committed, by the manner or circumstances in which it is committed, by the serious nature of the effects produced, by the special vulnerability of the victim; or by the abuse of a special relationship between the perpetrator and the victim".[146]

Specific aggravations include, *inter alia*, offences "motivated by hatred or contempt for, or malice or ill-will towards, a group of persons defined by reference to race, colour, religion, gender, sexual orientation, nationality, citizenship or ethnic or national origins".[147] Enactment of a single provision such as this which includes a variety of aggravations – whether based on prejudice or otherwise – would help to de-clutter the statute books.

The newer aggravation (by a connection with serious organised **7.10.5** crime) is rather different. The accused's own attitudes are irrelevant, at least in the sense of previously evinced ill-will against certain societal groups. Her motivation is, however, important, despite the general view in Scots law that motive is separate from intention and relevant only to sentence.[148] The aggravation is made out if the accused "is motivated (wholly or partly) by the objective of committing or conspiring to commit serious organised crime."[149] The definition of serious organised crime[150] might, however, be criticised

---

[141] Barendt (2011), especially at 41–43.
[142] *Religiously Aggravated Offending in Scotland 2012–13* (Scottish Government Social Research), available at: http://www.scotland.gov.uk/Resource/0042/00424865.pdf.
[143] 2005 SCCR 554, described in section 7.9.1 above.
[144] See section 15.2 below.
[145] See from section 4.6 above.
[146] *Draft Criminal Code*, s 7(1).
[147] *Ibid*, s 7(2)(b). What it means for a group of persons to be defined by reference to religion is specified in s 7(4). The wording in the 2003 Act is notably similar to that in the *Code*.
[148] Motive is discussed further from section 6.10.1 above.
[149] Criminal Justice and Licensing (Scotland) Act 2010, s 29(2).
[150] Section 28(3). This is quoted in full at section 7.5.5 above.

for being over-inclusive or perhaps simply reliant on an underlying assumption that the concept will be recognised when encountered. In summary, it requires two or more people to act together for the principal purpose of committing (or conspiring to commit) an indictable offence (or a series of such offences) with the intention of obtaining a material benefit. Acts of violence or threats made with such an intention are specifically included. Thus, if two people agree to commit a bank robbery to pay off their debts, it appears that this would be caught by the definition, even where the crime is a one-off and neither has any connection to any criminal organisation. In principle, an aggravation of this nature is unobjectionable, given the "far-reaching and devastating"[151] effects which serious organised crime may cause.[152] Precision in defining the concept should not, however, be sacrificed to the attempt to catch *all* such behaviour.

---

[151] Scottish Serious Organised Crime Group Mapping Project, *Preliminary Findings on the Scale and Extent of Serious Organised Crime in Scotland* (2010), p 2.
[152] For examples of the nature of serious organised criminality in Scotland see *ibid*, p 3.

CHAPTER 8

PREVENTIVE OFFENCES

"Prevention is an important facet of criminalization, but one that must be subject to principled constraint if it is not to result in overextension of the criminal law."[1]

8.1 INTRODUCTION

According to Joel Feinberg, the class of "properly prohibited" **8.1.1** behaviours can include those which threaten harm. These are proscribed "not because they necessarily cause harm in every case, but rather because they create *unreasonable risks* of harm to other persons".[2] The criminal law at times proscribes the creation of even quite remote harms. Herbert Packer described how this operates:

> "The conduct proscribed by any criminal code can be ranked in a hierarchy of remoteness from the ultimate harm that the law seeks to prevent. We prohibit the sale of liquor to an intoxicated person to lessen the likelihood that he will drive while drunk (an offense), crash into another car (an offense), injure an occupant of the other car (an offense), or cause the death of someone in the other car (an offense). There we have a spectrum of remoteness ranging from the illegal sale of liquor to manslaughter."[3]

Preventive offences criminalise behaviour which takes place **8.1.2** in preparation for the commission of (some other) crime. The paradigm example of this is that an attempt to commit a crime is in itself a crime.[4] While the harm principle[5] may be invoked to justify the criminalisation of some attempted crimes, since the principle

---

[1] A Ashworth and L Zedner, "Prevention and criminalization: justifications and limits" (2012) 15 *New Crim L Rev* 542 at 542.
[2] J Feinberg, *The Moral Limits of the Criminal Law: Harm to Others* (1984), p 11 (emphasis added).
[3] H L Packer, *The Limits of the Criminal Sanction* (1969), p 270.
[4] Criminal Procedure (Scotland) Act 1995, s 294.
[5] See Chapter 3 above.

embraces conduct which merely threatens harm to others, other attempts may not risk harm at all; attempts to do something which is in fact impossible to achieve is the paradigm example of this.[6] Perhaps the most that can be said is that the *failure* to criminalise attempted crimes would risk harm, but that is not quite the same thing. There is also a difficulty in determining where the law ought to draw the line between acts which are too remote to merit being branded as an attempt, and acts which are so close to the completed act that the law has failed to intervene early enough to prevent harm being caused. One way of circumventing the problem of attempted crimes is to criminalise the earlier, preparatory behaviour in its own right. This chapter examines some such offences, designed to prevent crimes involving personal violence (such as assault, culpable homicide or even murder) and crimes of dishonesty (such as theft, theft by housebreaking, etc). Prohibition of possession of certain items, innocuous in themselves, makes it easier for the prosecution to secure a conviction since it is easier to prove a relationship of physical control over an object than to prove that the accused has some nefarious intention to use that object.[7]

8.2   CRIMINAL ATTEMPTS

8.2.1   The law relating to attempted crimes considers what happens when the crime does not come to fruition. We have seen that a primary purpose of the criminal law is to deter people from harming others in a wrongful fashion, and to punish those who do cause such harm. Yet, by definition, those charged with attempted crimes have not caused the intended harm: A attempts to kill B but does not succeed in causing death; A attempts to steal from B's pocket, but does not deprive B of any property since the pocket is in fact empty. Of course, some other harm may have been caused – in attempting to kill B, A may have wounded her, seriously or otherwise. That will constitute the separate crime of assault, so why do we need a charge of attempted murder? Since the harms which the criminal law wants to prevent (causing death, deprivation of property, etc) have not materialised, the unsuccessful attempter can only be the subject of a criminal prohibition on the basis that to threaten harm is *itself* a species of harm. As Antony Duff has put it, "a law that condemned and punished actually harm-causing conduct as wrong, but was utterly silent on attempts to cause such harms ...

---

[6] See from section 8.3 below.
[7] A point made in P Charleton, P A McDermott and M Bolger, *Criminal Law* (1999) at para 1.36.

would speak with a strange moral voice".[8] Gordon's *Criminal Law* suggests that in punishing people who have attempted to commit crimes "the law is punishing them for something they did not do, for an unfulfilled intention".[9] At first sight, this seems puzzling; surely they are being punished for what they *did* do, not for what they did not do? A person who fires a gun at her victim, intending to cause death, but who does not kill him is punished for what she did (for shooting at or injuring someone). The point, however, is that the charge may not be restricted to the shooting of the gun, or even for causing injury (assault) but will be for attempted murder. Even if the bullet missed the victim altogether, the charge is still attempted *murder*.

The two elements of *mens rea* and *actus reus* are equally necessary in attempts, as in completed crimes, though Sarah Christie argues that "it is the mental element which makes [the] conduct criminal and which is therefore at the very heart of inchoate liability".[10] However, since the general rule is that the *mens rea* of an attempted crime is the same as for a completed crime,[11] and it is only the *actus reus* of the *completed crime* which is missing, this tends to suggest that the *actus reus* is the central issue. If A intends to kill someone, A has the *mens rea* for murder, whether she succeeds in causing death, or not. But since the law does not criminalise our thoughts and emotions, an intent to kill is not enough by itself; A must also have fulfilled the *actus reus* of attempted murder – she must have tried to kill the victim.

8.2.2

The *Scottish Crime and Victimisation Survey 2006* estimated that in 6 out of 10 cases in which would-be housebreakers have attempted to steal, no items were actually taken.[12] It is clear that theft has not occurred in these cases, far less the aggravated offence of theft by housebreaking, yet given the scale of the problem it would seem unwise for such attempts to go unpunished. The difficulty lies in determining the point at which we are prepared to hold a person liable for an attempted crime. For example, suppose that on Monday A makes the decision to murder B, later that week. On Tuesday, A buys a gun and, on Wednesday,

8.2.3

---

[8] R A Duff, *Criminal Attempts* (1996), p 134. See also Christie: the harm of attempted crimes "may be restricted to causing a sense of insecurity within the community, but it is yet perceived as sufficient to justify punishment": S Christie, *Inchoate Crimes: Incitement, Conspiracy and Attempts in Scottish Criminal Law* (2001), para 1.01.

[9] Gordon (2001), para 6.02.

[10] Christie (2001), para 6.01.

[11] *Cawthorne* v *HM Advocate* 1968 JC 32.

[12] 2006 *Scottish Crime and Victimisation Survey*, para 2.24. The *Scottish Crime and Justice Survey 2012/13* did not directly address this issue.

she buys ammunition. On Thursday, she stakes out the victim's house and notes his routine. At 3.30 pm on Friday, A sees her target walking his dog. At 3.40 pm, A takes out the gun. She loads it at 3.45 pm, and aims carefully at the victim. At 3.47 pm, she fires the gun. At what stage is A guilty of attempted murder? She had been preparing the crime all week, but only attempted to kill the victim on Friday afternoon. But even on Friday, a line has to be drawn. Should A be charged with attempted murder the moment she gets into her car? Or when she sees the victim? When she takes out the gun? Or when she loads it? Does she attempt murder when she aims the loaded gun at the victim? Or do we need to go one step further and say that it is not attempted murder until A pulls the trigger?

8.2.4   When first-year law students are asked to suggest when A ought to be regarded as having attempted to kill her victim, the majority plump either for Friday at 3.45 pm (when the gun is loaded) or for 3.47 pm (when the gun is fired). However, a small minority see little problem in opting for an earlier point, in some cases as far back as Monday – after all, they argue, we are told that it is on Monday that A *decides* to murder someone. They recognise the practical problems involved in the prosecution being able to prove what A had decided on Monday. Perhaps A tells the gun shop owner "I need a gun because I want to kill someone". Or, slightly more plausibly, tells a friend, "I've finally decided. I'm going to kill B this week". If we can prove that A resolved to kill on Monday, then (for some students) A ought to be regarded as guilty of attempted murder at that point. For most people, however, this does not seem just. As William Wilson has argued:

> "Penal policy must in such cases be able to reconcile its retributive and preventative functions. Clearly it is better for harm to be prevented but there must nevertheless be a critical point before which official intervention is discounted to reflect the law's overriding commitment to freedom and autonomy, displayed in such features as the presumption of innocence and the act requirement. The overriding concern here, therefore, is to devise a secure benchmark for when the criminal attempt actually begins."[13]

One can see a liberal philosophy here.[14]

8.2.5   Historically, the Scottish courts have drawn the line for attempted crimes at various stages. In some cases the courts have held that an attempted crime can be said to have been committed only when the situation is "beyond the recall" of the accused (that

---

[13] W Wilson, *Central Issues in Criminal Theory* (2002), p 231.
[14] See from section 1.2 above.

is, incapable of being remedied by the accused).[15] Few cases support this[16] and it is a theory which is far from satisfactory. For instance, if A decides to kill B and puts poison in his tea, A may then sit back and wait for B to drink the tea. But A has not really gone beyond the stage of recall as she could, at any stage prior to B swallowing sufficient tea, take the teapot away or otherwise prevent him from drinking. It would, however, be most unsatisfactory if A could not be charged with attempted murder until her victim had actually swallowed some tea. At one time it was felt that there should be no criminal liability for unsuccessful attempts unless the accused had performed the last act necessary for the crime to be fulfilled. This is illustrated by the case of *Janet Ramage*[17] in which the facts were similar to the scenario described above; the accused had placed poison in a teapot, in order to kill her victim.[18] The court held that a charge of attempted murder was relevant in such circumstances, even though the consequences were capable of being recalled by the accused. Crucially, she had performed the last act which she needed to do to kill her victim.

The modern approach is that a person is guilty of an attempted crime at the stage at which she has progressed from *preparing* to commit the crime, to actually *perpetrating* it. This is the test which seems to have the most persuasive judicial authority. It is regarded as a factual question, and therefore an issue for the trier of facts, which in solemn cases means the jury. The leading case is *HM Advocate* v *Camerons*,[19] in which a husband and wife pretended that they had been robbed, intending to commit an insurance fraud. The jury was directed that its task was to determine whether the couple had advanced from the stage of preparing a fraud to its actual perpetration. The trial judge emphasised that this was a question of degree, and hence was properly a question for the jury to decide. The couple had reported the alleged robbery to the police, and had notified their insurance company, but had not made any claim to the company. The "beyond recall" test would not result in a conviction since the Camerons could still have repented. The "last act" test of *Janet Ramage* would not work either, since the insurance claim form had not been completed. Since it was a matter for the jury

8.2.6

---

[15] This is also referred to as the "irrevocability" theory – see T H Jones and M G A Christie, *Criminal Law* (5th edn, 2012), para 6.15; C McDiarmid, *Criminal Law* (2nd edn, 2010), p 53; and (in England) the "Rubicon test"– see *DPP* v *Stonehouse* [1977] 2 All ER 909.

[16] See, however, *HM Advocate* v *Baxter* (1908) 5 Adam 609.

[17] (1825) cited in Hume, i, 28.

[18] See also *Samuel Tumbleson* (1863) 4 Irv 426.

[19] 1911 SC (J) 110.

to decide, it became a value judgement, depending on the jury's assessment of the blameworthiness of the accused. The couple were convicted. More recent cases include *Hamilton* v *Vannet*,[20] in which "preparation" and "perpetration" were described by Lord Prosser as "the classic terms used in identifying the offence of attempt", and *Ford* v *HM Advocate*,[21] where Lord Nimmo Smith referred to attempted rape as having been committed when the accused "engaged in conduct which passed from the stage of preparation for the crime into the stage of perpetration of the crime".[22]

8.2.7   It may be argued that this test is sufficiently flexible to allow for rationalising the decisions in different cases. It has, however, been criticised by some commentators on the basis that it is unsatisfactory that a major element in the definition of a crime (which should surely be a legal matter) should be treated as a matter of fact.[23] It is difficult to know whether, in the scenario described in section 8.2.3 above, A would be guilty of attempted murder as soon as she loads the gun, or whether we need to wait until the gun is actually fired. If the latter, it should be borne in mind that earlier actions may amount to a different crime: for example, breach of the peace (causing alarm by displaying a gun in public), assault (aiming a gun at someone), or a contravention of the Firearms Act 1968 (having a firearm, whether loaded or not, together with ammunition in a public place).[24]

8.2.8   A case which illustrates the difficulty of determining whether an accused person has indeed progressed from preparing to commit a crime to actually perpetrating it is *Barrett* v *Allan*.[25] The appellant had been convicted of a statutory offence of attempting to enter a sports ground when drunk.[26] He had initially been warned off by police and had appeared to heed this warning. He went away, but came back and was arrested while waiting in the queue to the ground. He appealed on the basis that at the time of his arrest he had not begun to "attempt to enter" the sports ground. The court decided that joining the queue constituted an attempt.

8.2.9   We can see, then, that there may be some difficulty in establishing that the accused's actions have reached the perpetration stage: "[t]he line of demarcation between preparation and perpetration

---

[20] 1999 GWD 8–406.
[21] 2001 Scot (D) 31/10.
[22] *Ibid* at para [13].
[23] See Gordon (2000), para 6.26, in which the theory is described as "meaning-less".
[24] Firearms Act 1968, s 19.
[25] 1986 SCCR 479.
[26] For the current prohibition, see the Criminal Law (Consolidation) (Scotland) Act 1995, s 20(7).

cannot be defined in any general proposition".[27] In one case it was emphasised that: "Acts remotely leading towards the commission of the offence are not to be considered as attempts to commit it, but acts immediately connected with it are".[28] Drawing the line at actual perpetration, a late stage in the proceedings, makes it more likely that the accused will succeed in achieving a completed crime. This is one reason why legislatures often devise offences which criminalise mere possession of firearms or offensive weapons; these allow the police to arrest and charge people with something less serious than assault or attempted murder, in order to prevent such crimes from taking place.[29]

8.3 IMPOSSIBLE ATTEMPTS

The leading case here is *Docherty* v *Brown*,[30] in which the accused was charged with attempting to possess a controlled drug, with intent to supply it to others. This is a statutory offence, under s 5(3) of the Misuse of Drugs Act 1971.[31] He had tablets which he thought were Ecstasy, but which were not drugs at all, hence he was attempting something which was, in fact, impossible. Was this a crime? There had been some debate over this, with earlier, conflicting cases, but in *Docherty* v *Brown* it was held that one could be charged with attempting to do something which was, in fact, impossible to achieve. Lord Justice-General Hope expressed his opinion, albeit *obiter*,[32] on several hypothetical scenarios, including

8.3.1

> "a pickpocket who puts his hand into another man's pocket only to find it empty; a man who attempts to assassinate a corpse, or a bolster in a bed, believing it to be the living body of his enemy; or a man who fires into an empty room believing that it contained an intended victim; and a man who takes away an umbrella from a stand with intent to steal it believing it not to be his own, although it turns out to be his own."[33]

He concluded:

> "I am satisfied that all these instances would constitute relevant charges of attempt to commit the complete offence because the accused had the necessary *mens rea*, and had taken positive steps to carry out his purpose. The only reason that his purpose was not carried fully into effect was that it

---

[27] LJ-G Normand in *Coventry* v *Douglas* 1944 JC 13 at 20.
[28] *R* v *Eagleton* (1855) Dears 515.
[29] See from section 8.8 below.
[30] 1996 JC 48. For a useful summary, see S A Christie, "The relevance of harm as the criterion for the punishment of impossible attempts" (2009) 73 *J Crim L* 153.
[31] See from section 8.9 below.
[32] *Obiter dicta* are remarks made by a judge which are not logically necessary for deciding the issue before the court.
[33] 1996 JC 48 at 58.

was impossible to commit the complete crime. I am not persuaded that the fact that it was impossible to commit the complete crime would prevent a relevant charge of attempt to commit that crime being laid."[34]

8.4   CRITIQUE OF THE LAW ON ATTEMPTS AND PROPOSALS FOR REFORM

8.4.1   The main difficulty with attempted crimes lies in determining how advanced a person's conduct has to be to suffice for liability. The "preparation to perpetration" test is easily stated but difficult to apply in practice. It leaves a great deal (perhaps more than is desirable) to the jury's intuitive moral sense of what is – or ought to be – criminal. According to Christie, at least six possible tests have been applied in various jurisdictions: "the first act, a substantial step, conduct amounting to perpetration, proximate conduct, an unequivocal act, or the last act which the accused needs to perform".[35] In *Barrett* v *Allan*,[36] the trial judge dismissed the argument that going to a railway station in Glasgow in order to catch a train to Edinburgh (where the football match was taking place) could constitute an "attempt to enter a football ground". This was simply too early to constitute an attempt. Paul Robinson and John Darley have noted a shift in the United States from the objective approach to attempted crimes taken by common law to a more subjective position in modern American criminal codes.[37] The objective approach looked at the "*proximity*" of completion of the actual offence, a matter which could be determined by external evaluation. By contrast, subjective approaches consider how far the accused has moved along the "preparation to perpetration" continuum. A "substantial step" is sufficient to concretise the accused's *mens rea* so that she can be convicted of a criminal attempt.[38] At one level, the decision as to whether there has been enough of a shift from preparation to perpetration is always going to be a question of degree in all the circumstances and the formulation of the test in words a matter of semantics. Scots law could, however, recognise more clearly that a continuum exists in this context – from "first act" to "last act" – and seek to situate itself, rather more definitely, at a point on that line.

8.4.2   In contrast to the difficult issue of determining the point at which the accused has done sufficient to constitute an *actus reus*,

---

[34] 1996 JC 48 at 58.
[35] Christie (2001), para 1.13.
[36] 1986 SCCR 479. See section 8.2.8 above.
[37] P H Robinson and J M Darley, "Objectivist versus subjectivist views of criminality: a study in the role of social science in criminal law theory" (1998) 18 *OJLS* 409.
[38] *Ibid* at 411–412.

the *mens rea* of criminal attempts is easily stated in Scots law: it is identical to that of the completed crime. In relation specifically to attempted murder, however, it seems that many, if not most, other jurisdictions accept only an *intention to kill*,[39] whatever alternative formulations exist for murder itself. Christie's view is that this is preferable:

> "Since, in practice, it is possible to require intention to kill for attempted murder and deal with serious assaults which have not involved an intent to murder under the general rubric of assault, it falls to be asked whether this is not a better approach, avoiding the complications of asserting that the accused can attempt something so serious without actually intending it."[40]

This might preclude any possibility of attempted murder being charged simply because an assault has been particularly ferocious, or where its consequences are very serious, but where the accused did not have either of the alternative mental states required for murder.[41]

A further difficulty with the current law relates to voluntary abandonment by the accused. It is unclear whether Scots law recognises this as a defence to an attempted crime. The *Draft Criminal Code* provides for this possibility.[42] As its *Commentary* explains, under this provision: 8.4.3

> "Lady Macbeth is not guilty of attempting to murder the sleeping Duncan even after she stands over his bed with a knife in her hand, since she is unable to proceed due to the King's resemblance to her father."

This uncertainty ought to be removed, and the defence recognised.

8.5 COMMON LAW PREVENTIVE OFFENCES

Several common law crimes are essentially preventive in nature, sometimes focusing on quite remote harms. For instance, the offence of "reckless endangerment" strikes at the potential harm which the accused's behaviour may cause, rather than actual harm having been caused.[43] As we shall see when we consider the crime of breach of the peace, this has often been charged where the accused's conduct is assessed by the police as being likely to cause *others* to react to it in a way which itself breaches the peace. Hence A is arrested in order to prevent B from breaching the peace.[44] 8.5.1

---

[39] Christie (2001), paras 6.14–6.18.
[40] *Ibid*, para 6.18.
[41] Both murder and culpable homicide are discussed further in Chapter 9.
[42] *Draft Criminal Code*, s 18(2).
[43] See section 10.12.1 below.
[44] See section 15.2.1 below.

8.6   CONSPIRACY

8.6.1   The principal common law preventive offence is conspiracy. The word comes from the Latin "con" and "spirare" which means "to breathe together". It was described in the case of *Maxwell and Others* v *HM Advocate*[45] as being

> "constituted by the agreement of two or more persons to further or achieve a criminal purpose. A criminal purpose is one which if attempted or achieved by action on the part of an individual would itself constitute a crime by the law of Scotland. It is the criminality of the purpose and not the result which may or may not follow from the execution of the purpose which makes the crime a criminal conspiracy".[46]

8.6.2   As this makes clear, in Scots law, the crime of conspiracy is committed as soon as two or more people agree to commit a crime.[47] The crime is a continuing one; the conspiracy continues even if the crime with which it is concerned is completed (or abandoned). Hence agreement to commit a crime in Scotland can be prosecuted before the Scottish courts, even if the agreement itself was made in another jurisdiction.[48] The Supreme Court of Canada has offered a convincing rationale for the crime of conspiracy:

> "Society is properly concerned with conspiracies since two or more persons working together can achieve evil results that would be impossible for an individual working alone. For example, it usually takes two or more conspirators to manufacture and secrete explosives or to arrange for the purchase, importation and sale of heroin. The very fact that several persons in combination agree to do something has for many years been considered to constitute 'a menace to society' ... In fact, the scale of injury that might be caused to the fabric of society can be far greater when two or more persons conspire to commit a crime than when an individual sets out alone to do an unlawful act."[49]

8.6.3   In the case of *Cochrane* v *HM Advocate*,[50] the appellant had been convicted on an indictment which libelled:

> "you did conspire [with C and M] ... to break into 'Langside Farmhouse' ..., and in furtherance of said conspiracy you did provide ... [C and M] with a motor van and said [C and M] did break into said premises and there rob [S]".

The appeal court held that this charge was irrelevant; the purported conspiracy charge did not disclose a crime, since it is not a crime to

---

[45] 1980 JC 40.
[46] *Ibid* at 43.
[47] See also *HM Advocate* v *Al Megrahi (No 1)* 2000 SCCR 177.
[48] *Ibid*.
[49] *United States of America* v *Dynar* (1997) 3 LRC 265 at 291, per Cory and Iacobucci JJ.
[50] 2002 SCCR 1051.

break into a house, *per se*.[51] The charge ought to have been worded as conspiracy to commit robbery.

Gordon's *Criminal Law* suggests that Scottish conspiracy charges **8.6.4** may be divided into three categories, namely: (1) where a specific crime (or crimes) has been carried out in pursuance of a conspiracy; (2) where no other specific crime is charged; and (3) where a charge of conspiracy is a substitute for a charge of "attempt".[52] An example of the first category is the case of *HM Advocate* v *Al-Megrahi (No 1)*,[53] which arose from the Lockerbie bombing,[54] in which the indictment against the accused contained a charge of conspiracy to murder and within that charge were other offences, including multiple murders. Although two men were prosecuted, only one was convicted; one can be found guilty of conspiring with a person or persons "unknown". As Gordon notes, sometimes conspiracy is the only crime charged, although the indictment may libel that the accused have done certain things, or planned certain things, as part of the conspiracy. These cases are generally directed against terrorist activities. In *HM Advocate* v *Walsh and Others*[55] the accused were charged with conspiring to further the purposes of the IRA. The means libelled was "by use of violence and explosives". In such cases, if the Crown is unable to prove to the satisfaction of the jury that there was a conspiracy then the accused will have to be acquitted, since that is the only crime with which they have been charged.

According to Gordon: "Conspiracy charges are arguably **8.6.5** prejudicial, they are certainly confusing, and it may be doubted whether they achieve any purpose".[56] One purpose they can achieve is allowing the Crown to obtain a conviction for conspiracy to commit a particular crime when a charge of attempting that crime would not succeed. As we have seen, the law generally holds that an attempted crime has not been committed until the accused's actions have gone beyond "preparation" for the crime and have reached actual "perpetration".[57] Conspiracy may be charged when several

---

[51] See the case of *HM Advocate* v *Forbes* 1994 SCCR 163, discussed further in section 12.9.2 below. Cochrane's conviction was not, however, quashed, since he had failed to take a plea to relevancy of the charge at the trial (as required by the Criminal Procedure (Scotland) Act 1995, s 118(8)). See also *Cochrane* v *HM Advocate* 2006 JC 135.

[52] Gordon (2000), para 6.57 onwards.

[53] 2000 JC 555.

[54] On 21 December 1988, a Boeing 747 was destroyed by a bomb which exploded as the plane flew across Scotland. All of the 259 people on board were killed, as were 11 people in Lockerbie, as a result of large parts of the plane landing on the town.

[55] 1922 JC 82. See Gordon (2000), para 6.64.

[56] *Ibid*, para 6.59.

[57] See from section 8.2.6 to section 8.2.9 above.

people act together in the preparation of a crime, but have not yet reached the perpetration stage. This is illustrated by the case of *West* v *HM Advocate*,[58] in which the accused were charged with conspiracy to assault and rob. They had been loitering suspiciously, and had a blade and an open razor with them. This conspiracy conviction was upheld on appeal. Clearly, there had been no "attempt" to rob anyone. Had only one accused acted in a similar way there could have been no conspiracy charge, nor would the requirements of a charge of attempted robbery have been fulfilled at that stage. By contrast, where two or more people are charged with conspiracy all that needs to be proved is their agreement to commit a crime. Even if they do not act further, this will still be a conspiracy.

8.6.6   It is possible to charge attempted conspiracy when A tries to involve B in a crime, but fails. Attempted conspiracy is called incitement or instigation. According to the case of *Baxter* v *HM Advocate*,[59] it is sufficient in a charge of incitement that the accused person was serious in inviting another to commit a crime: in the words of the court, "the decisive question in each case is whether the accused reached and sought to influence the mind of the other person towards the commission of a crime".[60] The details of the crime need not have been finalised. Incitement can also involve persuading or intimidating someone into committing a crime.

8.6.7   Students often become confused about the difference between "art and part" and conspiracy. "Art and part" can apply to any crime and is a form of liability, not a crime in its own right. One has to be art and part liable *for something*. By contrast, conspiracy is itself a crime. It is commonly charged when the accused have agreed to commit a crime, but matters have gone no further than this, whereas "art and part" is charged when the planned crime has been carried out, or at least attempted.

8.6.8   The Criminal Procedure (Scotland) Act 1995, s 11A[61] provides that it is conspiracy for a person in Scotland to do an act which would amount to conspiracy but for the fact that the criminal purpose is intended to occur outwith Scotland. The criminal purpose must involve an act by the accused or a co-conspirator or the happening of some other event which constitutes an offence under the relevant law – ie the law in force in the place where the act or event would take place, whether that is another part of the UK[62] or a country

---

[58] 1985 SCCR 248.
[59] 1998 JC 219.
[60] *Ibid* at 221, per LJ-G Rodger, citing *S* v *Nkosiyana* 1966 (4) SA 655 at 658H–659A.
[61] Inserted by the Criminal Justice (Terrorism and Conspiracy) Act 1998, s 7 and amended by the Criminal Justice and Licensing (Scotland) Act 2010, s 50.
[62] Criminal Procedure (Scotland) Act 1995, s 11A(3A)(a).

or territory outwith the UK.[63] A statutory offence of conspiracy is provided by s 28(1) of the Criminal Justice and Licensing (Scotland) Act 2010: "A person who agrees with at least one other person to become involved in serious organised crime commits an offence."[64] What this adds to the common law crime is far from clear. Unlike the Scottish provision, similar legislation in Ireland, and case law in Canada, require the involvement of at least three people.[65]

8.7 CRITIQUE OF THE LAW ON CONSPIRACY AND PROPOSALS FOR REFORM

The crime of conspiracy is underdeveloped in Scots law, and it is arguable that bare agreement to commit a crime should not be a sufficient *actus reus*. Instead, there ought to be evidence that the accused had, at the very least, embarked on the crime which is the subject of the conspiracy. Gordon's *Criminal Law* suggests that it is unclear whether it is a common law crime to conspire to commit a statutory offence.[66] There seems to be no reason why it should not be, but it is nonetheless regrettable that such uncertainty should persist in our criminal law. Some crimes previously governed by the common law, such as rape and some forms of sexual assault, have now become statutory offences,[67] making it imperative that the position in respect of conspiracy be clarified. Imagine that a group of men have raped someone and are caught with a list of potential victims, and dates and times of future attacks which they have agreed to carry out. It would be a travesty if the Crown were unable to charge "conspiracy with intent to rape" in such circumstances merely because rape is now a statutory offence. The 2009 Act does, however, seem to accept, if rather indirectly, that it is possible to conspire to commit some of the offences which it creates. In relation to offences against older children,[68] there is a defence of reasonable belief that the complainer was 16 years old or over.[69] This defence is not available where the accused has previously been charged by

8.7.1

---

[63] Criminal Procedure (Scotland) Act 1995, s 11A(3A)(b).

[64] "Serious organised crime" is defined in s 28(3) of the 2010 Act. For a critique of the law, see L Campbell, *Organised Crime and the Law: A Comparative Analysis* (2013), especially pp 26–27. Dr Campbell has argued that "the definition in the 2010 Act is misguided due to its inconsistency with the core wrongs of serious organised criminality, which relate to the entity rather than the behaviour alone": "Organised crime and the Criminal Justice and Licensing (Scotland) Act 2010" (2014) 18 *Edin LR* 225 at 229.

[65] *Ibid* at p 27.

[66] Gordon (2000), para 6.66.

[67] See the Sexual Offences (Scotland) Act 2009, discussed from section 11.1.2 below.

[68] Those found in ss 28–37 of the Sexual Offences (Scotland) Act 2009.

[69] *Ibid*, s 39(1).

the police with certain other offences.[70] The relevant offences for this purpose (some of which are created by the Act) are listed in its Sch 1. These include "conspiracy … to commit an offence in Part 1 of [the] schedule".[71] Here, then, is some recognition that a crime of conspiracy to commit a statutory offence does exist in Scots law.

8.7.2   Since "agreement" is essential to the charge of conspiracy, we must consider the position where there are two parties to a conspiracy but one of them only pretended to agree. This could occur where one of the parties is in fact an undercover police officer. Robinson and Darley have suggested that the lack of genuine agreement would preclude any conviction for conspiracy in many common law jurisdictions.[72] This was the approach taken by the Canadian Supreme Court in the case of *O'Brien*.[73] The American Model Penal Code makes it clear that "unilateral agreement" will suffice.[74] Despite sounding like an oxymoron, this means in essence that a person who conspires with an undercover agent to commit a crime cannot escape liability due to the latter's lack of genuine agreement. This is another aspect of the Scots law of conspiracy which would benefit from greater clarity.

8.8   POSSESSION OFFENCES

8.8.1   As well as these inchoate forms of liability (attempts, conspiracy, incitement) many statutes proscribe offences whose *actus reus* involves the possession of a prohibited article, such as firearms,[75] explosives,[76] knives[77] or other weapons.[78] Often these are aimed at preventing future harm.[79] Indeed, the 1953 statute which initially proscribed the carrying of offensive weapons in public was entitled the "Prevention of Crime Act". Other possession offences are aimed at past conduct as well as, or sometimes instead of, future behaviour. For example, the criminalisation of possession of certain drugs[80] is in part to avoid the future harm that could be occasioned by the use

---

[70] Sexual Offences (Scotland) Act 2009, s 39(2)(a)(i) and (b)(i). See section 11.12.3 below.
[71] *Ibid*, Sch 1, Pt 1, para 13.
[72] Robinson and Darley (1998) at 411.
[73] [1954] SCR 666.
[74] MPC, s 5.03(1)(a) and (b).
[75] The Firearms Act 1968, s 1 makes it an offence for a person to possess, purchase or acquire a firearm or ammunition without holding a firearm certificate.
[76] Explosive Substances Act 1883, s 4(1).
[77] Criminal Law (Consolidation) (Scotland) Act 1995, s 49, as amended by the Criminal Justice and Licensing (Scotland) Act 2010, s 37.
[78] Criminal Law (Consolidation) (Scotland) Act 1995, s 47(1), as amended by the Criminal Justice and Licensing (Scotland) Act 2010, s 37. Both these provisions are discussed further from section 8.11 below.
[79] This was acknowledged in *Lister* v *Lees* 1994 SCCR 548 at 552.
[80] See the Misuse of Drugs Act 1971, discussed from section 8.9 below.

or distribution of these drugs, but the fact that it is an offence to possess even minute quantities strikes at their past use or supply.[81] Similarly with the possession of housebreaking tools; the legislation is intended to catch the person who intends to commit theft, or who *has committed theft*, using these tools.[82] As we shall see below,[83] the rationale behind the criminalisation of those in possession of "extreme pornography" is more difficult to discern. It may strike at the past harm done to those who are involved in the making of such images; it may be an attempt to prevent others (mainly children and women) from being assaulted due to some possessors emulating the violence they have seen in such images; or it may even be designed to protect the viewers of the images from self-debasement.

In respect of tools, knives, and some types of offensive weapon, **8.8.2** the items themselves may well have a legitimate use, but it is the circumstances of the possession – for example, in a public place – which gives rise to criminal liability. This is particularly so in relation to terrorism offences.[84] Section 57(1) of the Terrorism Act 2000 is worded in a very broad fashion:

> "A person commits an offence if he possesses an article in circumstances which give rise to a reasonable suspicion that his possession is for a purpose connected with the commission, preparation or instigation of an act of terrorism."

Section 57(2) provides a defence where the accused is able "to prove that his possession of the article was not for a purpose connected with the commission, preparation or instigation of an act of terrorism". In holding that there required to be a direct connection between the object possessed and the act of terrorism, the appeal court pointed out that

> "if [a] jury had previously been instructed that the requirement of sec 57(1) was that the offence consisted in possession of an article for a purpose connected with the commission, preparation or instigation of an act of terrorism, it is logically impossible to see how the defence could ever be established."[85]

John Scott, a leading human rights advocate, has argued:

> "the law is attempting to achieve the conviction of those who have not yet been involved in any terrorist activity. The consequences of successful acts of

---

[81] See, for example, *Keane* v *Gallacher* 1980 JC 77; *McCleary* v *Walkingshaw* 1996 SCCR 13.

[82] See from section 8.18 below.

[83] See the Civic Government (Scotland) Act 1982, s 51A, discussed at section 11.15.2 below.

[84] Terrorism legislation is discussed further from section 8.23 below.

[85] *Siddique* v *HM Advocate* 2010 JC 110 at 138, para [81] per Lord Osborne, citing *R* v *Zafar* [2008] 2 WLR 1013.

terrorism are considered so severe that the law allows for a greater element of crystal ball gazing. Conviction can follow where the matter has not proceeded even as far as an attempt to do anything."[86]

The pre-emptive nature of many possession offences should be borne in mind as we describe them in more detail in the following sections.

8.9 MISUSE OF DRUGS

8.9.1 This is a highly specialised area of the law, and as such justice cannot be done to its intricacies by a general text such as this.[87] This section attempts to provide a brief outline, and concentrates on those offences which may be categorised as preventive.[88] The Misuse of Drugs Act 1971 proscribes, *inter alia*, the possession of any "controlled drugs".[89] It is also an offence to possess such drugs with intent to supply them to another.[90] Controlled drugs are grouped into three classes. Class A drugs include Ecstasy, LSD, heroin, cocaine, crack, "magic mushrooms", methylamphetamine ("crystal meth"), and other amphetamines if prepared for injection. Class B contains cannabis, cannabis resin, amphetamines, Methylphenidate (Ritalin) and Pholcodine (a cough medicine); and Class C lists tranquillisers, some painkillers, GHB (Gamma hydroxybutyrate) and ketamine. The penalties for possession or supply of a Class A drug are more severe than for those in Class B, which in turn are more serious than for drugs in Class C.[91] It has been reported that the UK has the largest market in Europe for so-called "legal highs". Since many of these drugs are as dangerous as, if not more dangerous than, controlled drugs, this legislation requires regular updating.[92]

8.9.2 As Peter Alldridge has pointed out, once possession of drugs is criminalised, a variety of other preventive offences, such as manufacturing and importing drugs, is also required.[93] Thus, as well as it being an offence to supply, or even to offer to supply, such a drug to another person,[94] an offence is committed at an earlier stage, merely

---

[86] J Scott, "*Siddique (Mohammed Atif) v HM Advocate*: what are you thinking?"(2010) SCL 315 at 317.
[87] For a more detailed account, see K S Bovey, *Misuse of Drugs: A Handbook for Lawyers* (2nd edn, 1986).
[88] See also section 17.3.12 below.
[89] Misuse of Drugs Act 1971, s 5(2).
[90] *Ibid*, s 5(3).
[91] For example, the production or supply of a Class A drug has a maximum penalty of life imprisonment – see Misuse of Drugs Act 1971, Sch 4.
[92] See B Bell, "UK legal high market is EU's largest, UN report says", *BBC News*, 26 June 2013, available at: http://www.bbc.co.uk/news/uk-23048267.
[93] P Alldridge, *Relocating Criminal Law* (2000), p 200.
[94] Misuse of Drugs Act 1971, s 4(1)(b).

by producing a controlled drug.[95] A person who is the occupier, or
who is concerned in the management, of any premises, commits an
offence by knowingly permitting or suffering a variety of activities to
take place on those premises, including the production of a controlled
drug, the supplying of such drugs to another person; preparing opium
for smoking; or the smoking of cannabis, cannabis resin or prepared
opium.[96] In addition to proscribing the smoking or using of prepared
opium, the legislation also makes it an offence to frequent a place
which is used for opium smoking, or to possess pipes or other utensils
which have been made or adapted for use in connection with the
smoking of opium.[97] These provisions require to be updated; opium
is surely less of a problem nowadays than heroin or ecstasy.

8.10   CRITIQUE OF DRUG OFFENCES AND PROPOSALS
         FOR REFORM

Some of these ancillary offences may be justified by the harm   8.10.1
principle, but only if the law is justified in prohibiting the *possession*
of certain drugs, in the first place. Drug possession and use *per se*
are classic examples of behaviours which many liberals favour being
decriminalised, on the basis that they constitute victimless crimes.
By this they mean that they harm no one other than the drug user.
Of course, drug users commonly commit other crimes, particularly
theft, in order to finance their habit, and this creates secondary
victims. But this is in large part a side-effect of criminalisation: as
with black markets, generally, the price of drugs would decrease
if they were legalised. Furthermore, it is difficult to justify the
criminalisation of the possession of cannabis, heroin etc, on the
basis of their potential harm, but not alcohol and tobacco, since
the number of people dying from drug-related deaths is a small
fraction of those killed from alcohol or tobacco misuse.[98]

8.11   OFFENSIVE WEAPONS AND ARTICLES WITH A BLADE
         OR SHARP POINT

By virtue of ss 47(1) and 49(1) of the Criminal Law (Consolidation)   8.11.1
(Scotland) Act 1995 it is an offence for a person to have an "offensive
weapon" or an article with a blade or sharp point in a public place.

---

[95] Misuse of Drugs Act 1971, s 4(1)(a). It is also an offence to manufacture or supply
certain substances, knowing or suspecting that these are to be used in or for the
unlawful production of a controlled drug – see the Criminal Justice (International
Co-operation) Act 1990, s 12.
[96] Misuse of Drugs Act 1971, s 8.
[97] *Ibid*, s 9.
[98] Alldridge (2000), p 203.

"Public place" is defined for both these offences as any place other than domestic premises, school premises or a prison.[99] "Domestic premises" are those occupied as a private dwelling and include any stair, passage, garden, yard, garage, outhouse etc which is not used in common by the occupants of more than one dwelling.[100] Paul Roberts has explained the rationale for the equivalent (and similarly worded) English legislation[101] as follows:

> "Merely carrying a knife is not harmful in itself nor even inherently immoral, yet experience shows that people armed with knives in public have a tendency to get involved in fights or confrontations, or to intimidate others. Criminal offences are more likely to be perpetrated and, sooner or later, somebody will end up getting seriously hurt or even killed. The ... prohibition on being in possession of a knife (or similar bladed or pointed object) in a public place is justified by reference to *the harm that would probably result* if people were entitled to carry dangerous weapons with them wherever they went."[102]

Offensive weapons

8.11.2   In respect of offensive weapons, s 47 refers to three categories: those *made for* causing personal injury; those *adapted for* use for causing personal injury; and all other weapons.[103] The last category comprises items which have been neither made nor adapted for causing injury, but which are *intended* for such use, and it is this intention – to use something to cause personal injury – which makes that object an offensive weapon. Weapons "made for causing personal injury" include knuckledusters, flick knives, coshes and bayonets.[104] Gordon's *Criminal Law* gives as examples of "adapted" weapons razor blades stuck into potatoes, and sharpened kitchen tools.[105] This category includes an innocent object which is "adapted" as an

---

[99] Criminal Law (Consolidation) (Scotland) Act 1995, s 47(4), as amended by the Criminal Justice and Licensing (Scotland) Act 2010, s 37. There are separate prohibitions on having such items in schools or prisons: see section 8.11.10 below.
[100] *Ibid.*
[101] That is, the Prevention of Crime Act 1953, s 1 (offensive weapons), and the Criminal Justice Act 1988, s 139 (articles with a blade or sharp point). The English legislation provides for a defence of "good reason" in respect of articles with a blade or point, and "reasonable excuse" in respect of offensive weapons, but these have in practice been treated as synonymous: see *McAulay* [2010] 1 Cr App R 11.
[102] P Roberts, "Strict liability and the presumption of innocence: an exposé of functionalist assumptions" in A P Simester (ed), *Appraising Strict Liability* (2005) 151 at pp 166–167 (emphasis added). Roberts calls these types of offences "substantive–inchoate" (at p 166).
[103] Both the English and Scottish courts have affirmed that there are three categories: see *R v Williamson* (1978) 67 Cr App R 35; [1978] Crim LR 229; and *Ashton v HM Advocate* 2012 JC 213, respectively.
[104] Gordon (2001), para 30.44 onwards.
[105] *Ibid.*

offensive weapon on the spur of the moment – for example, if the accused smashes a bottle and uses it as a weapon.

The importance of the division is that in relation to weapons which **8.11.3** are made or adapted for causing personal injury, the offence is one of strict liability.[106] That is, there is no requirement for the Crown to prove that the accused intended to do anything in particular with the item. Establishing the *actus reus* – that the accused had the item in a public place – is sufficient for a conviction (unless the accused can establish one of the statutory defences)[107] in respect of *per se* weapons. In relation to the second category – adapted weapons – it seems that the Crown must prove that the adaptation was made by someone (not necessarily the accused) for the purpose of causing injury, but need not show that the accused had that specific intention.[108] With the third group, as well as proving that the accused had the item in a public place, the Crown must also prove that the accused intended to use the object to cause personal injury (as opposed to having some other unlawful intention, such as to use it to steal, or to cause property damage). The Irish legislation on offensive weapons specifies that the court may have regard to "all the circumstances" in determining whether there is evidence that the accused intended to cause injury, such circumstances to include "the type of the article ... the time of the day or night, and the place".[109] While such considerations are not made explicit in the Scottish legislation, it is clear that the courts will take such matters into account.[110]

The legislation provides two defences, namely "lawful authority" **8.11.4** and "reasonable excuse". The former would allow a soldier to carry a gun in certain circumstances, or a policeman to carry a truncheon. Fiscals carrying offensive weapons to court for use as Crown productions could presumably use this excuse (which gave one of the authors some comfort when she walked through the streets of Kirkcaldy, carrying in her briefcase a baseball bat wrapped in barbed wire, and a golf ball tied in a sock).

In *Frame* v *Kennedy*,[111] having two police batons as part of a **8.11.5** "strip-o-gram" costume was held to be a reasonable excuse.[112] The accused was dressed as a police sergeant, and the court held that the reason for having the batons on his person was "to add

---

[106] Strict liability is described further from section 17.2 to section 17.7.3 below.

[107] See from section 18.11.4 below.

[108] *Ashton* v *HM Advocate* 2012 JC 213. For a commentary on the case, see (2012) *Scottish Criminal Law* 455.

[109] Firearms and Offensive Weapons Act 1990, s 9.

[110] See, for example, *Smith* v *Vannet* 1999 SLT 435.

[111] 2008 JC 317.

[112] Such batons were held to have been made for causing injury in *Latham* v *Vannet* 1999 SCCR 119.

verisimilitude to his fancy dress".[113] Picking up a weapon in self-
defence may be a reasonable excuse, but only if an attack is
imminent.[114] In *Grieve v MacLeod*,[115] the accused was a taxi driver
who was found to have in his cab a rubber hose with a lump of
metal at its end. He argued that this was for defensive purposes, but
was held not to have a reasonable excuse. This suggests that "pepper
sprays" or other "anti-attack" devices are offensive weapons. The
object of the prohibition is to ensure that people do not, unless in
exceptional circumstances, take the law into their own hands.

8.11.6   If the weapon is actually used, the Crown will generally charge
the accused with assault rather than a breach of s 47. It will not
charge both offences (except as alternatives) as this would amount
to double jeopardy.[116] If the accused is convicted, then the Crown
will ask for forfeiture of the weapon, which will then be destroyed.
As noted previously,[117] *skean-dhus* are small daggers, often worn
in the socks of Scotsmen at ceremonial occasions such as dinner
dances or weddings. Clearly a *skean-dhu is* an offensive weapon.
But there was an outcry at the passing of the original offensive
weapons legislation,[118] with Scottish politicians arguing that the
legislation would prohibit Scots from wearing their national dress.
As a result, the Lord Advocate at the time gave an undertaking that
a person wearing a *skean-dhu* as part of ceremonial dress would
not be prosecuted.[119] Of course, if someone actually used the *skean-
dhu* – or even took it out and waved it about – then that might well
be an offence. It should be noted that the legislation on carrying
knives *per se*, to which we now turn our attention, includes a specific
defence that the bladed article is part of a national costume.[120] Any
Scotsman prosecuted under s 47(1) would, however, simply have to
fall back on the Lord Advocate's undertaking.

Articles with a blade or sharp point

8.11.7   According to a report on homicide produced by the Scottish
Government in 2013, the "most common [main] method of killing
in each of the last ten years was with a sharp instrument".[121] Most
sharp instruments have a legitimate purpose; when persons are

---

[113] *Frame v Kennedy* 2008 JC 317 at para 24.
[114] *Miller v Douglas* 1988 SCCR 565.
[115] 1967 JC 32.
[116] See *McLean v Higson* 2000 SCCR 764.
[117] At section 5.15.1 above.
[118] Prevention of Crime Act 1953.
[119] See 1954 SLT (News) 67; and also *McLean v Higson* 2000 SCCR 764.
[120] Criminal Law (Consolidation) (Scotland) Act 1995, s 49(5)(c).
[121] *Homicide in Scotland, 2012–13* at p 4, available at: http://www.scotland.gov.uk/Resource/0043/00435280.pdf.

apprehended with bread knives, screwdrivers etc in public places, the Crown will generally only secure a conviction for breach of s 47 if it can establish that the accused had these items with intent to use them to cause personal injury. Such proof can be difficult, so legislation was enacted to make it a strict liability offence to have in public "any article which has a blade or is sharply pointed". This is now contained in s 49 of the Criminal Law (Consolidation) (Scotland) Act 1995.[122] There are defences available to an accused, such as having the item for use at work,[123] for religious reasons[124] or as part of any national costume.[125] An exception is also made for folding pocket knives whose blades do not exceed 3 inches/7.62 cm.[126]

When s 49 was originally enacted, it was a defence for someone **8.11.8** charged with a breach of this section to prove that she had either "lawful authority" or "good reason" for having the knife in a public place. It seemed anomalous to provide a defence of "good reason" in respect of knives, but one of "reasonable excuse" for all other weapons, and this had been criticised.[127] The Criminal Justice and Licensing (Scotland) Act 2010 has now rectified this such that for both ss 47 and 49 the defence is one of "reasonable excuse".[128] The two are not synonymous; as the appeal court has stated: "There may, in certain situations, be a reasonable excuse for something, although there may be no good reason for it."[129] In *Crowe* v *Waugh*[130] in 1999, the accused had committed a breach of the peace in the street near his house. He then went home and put on his fishing jacket. When he was later arrested by police outside his house, he told them that he had a knife in his jacket pocket. The accused explained that he had fetched the jacket because it was raining, and that he had no recollection that the knife, which he used when he went fishing, was in the pocket. The appeal court held that his forgetfulness could not amount to a good reason:

---

[122] As amended by the Criminal Justice and Licensing (Scotland) Act 2010, s 37.
[123] Criminal Law (Consolidation) (Scotland) Act, s 49(5)(a).
[124] *Ibid*, s 49(5)(b).
[125] *Ibid*, s 49(5)(c).
[126] *Ibid*, s 49(3).
[127] See P R Ferguson and C McDiarmid, *Scots Criminal Law: A Critical Analysis* (1st edn, 2009) at section 22.9.1, and P R Ferguson, "Criminal law and criminal justice: an exercise in ad hocery" in E E Sutherland *et al* (eds), *Law Making and the Scottish Parliament: The Early Years* (2011) 208 at p 220.
[128] Criminal Law (Consolidation) (Scotland) Act 1995, s 49(4), as amended by the Criminal Justice and Licensing (Scotland) Act 2010, s 37. The differing defences for the two offences persists under English law: see the Prevention of Crime Act 1953, s 1 and the Criminal Justice Act 1988, s 139(1).
[129] *Thomas* v *HM Advocate* 2012 SCCR 762 at 766, para [14] per LJ-C Carloway.

"If one owns a garment which one is likely, or even liable on occasion, to wear in a public place, then the pockets of that garment are not a suitable place to keep something like a knife. Whether or not one will be thinking of the knife when putting on the garment and going to a public place, sec 49 appears to us to require that one simply should not have the knife in that garment, and that the fact of ordinarily keeping it in the garment cannot constitute a good reason for having it on the particular occasion in a public place, whatever one's state of mind or awareness at that later time".[131]

Such forgetfulness may not be a "good reason" for having a knife in a public place but it is possible that it may amount to a "reasonable excuse".

8.11.9 Previously, both ss 47 and 49 specified that it was for the accused to "prove" these defences. This was changed by the 2010 Act, such that the accused must now "show" lawful authority or reasonable excuse. If this was intended to reduce the burden of proof on the accused, it has not succeeded. In *Glancy* v *HM Advocate*[132] the appellant argued that requiring him to establish, on the balance of probabilities, that he had a reasonable excuse for having a knife in public was incompatible with the principles of Art 6(2) of the European Convention on Human Rights (ECHR) with regard to the presumption of innocence. This was rejected by the appeal court, which held that placing the onus on the accused struck a fair balance between the rights of the accused and the interests of the public.[133]

8.11.10 Subsequent to the enactment of s 49 it was realised that there was a problem with children taking knives and other weapons to school. Since schools are not public places s 49A was added to the 1995 Act, to proscribe the carrying of offensive weapons and articles with a blade or sharp point on school premises.[134] Defences include those available under s 49, but also that the item was for educational purposes.[135] Section 49C repeats the provisions of ss 47 and 49 and applies them to prisons.[136]

---

[130] 1999 JC 292.

[131] *Ibid* at 296, per Lord Prosser. Taking home a recently purchased item (a knife) was held to amount to a "good reason" in *McGuire* v *Higson* 2003 SLT 890 and to a "reasonable excuse" (in relation to a baton and a knuckleduster) in *Smith* v *Shanks* [2014] HCJAC 25.

[132] 2012 SCCR 52.

[133] See also *Robertson* v *HM Advocate* [2012] HCJAC 63: a trial judge need not attempt to define the expression "on the balance of probabilities", but should make clear to a jury that this was lower than the criminal law standard of proof beyond reasonable doubt.

[134] Added by the Offensive Weapons Act 1996, s 4(3).

[135] Criminal Law (Consolidation) (Scotland) Act 1995, s 49A(4)(b).

[136] Added by the Custodial Sentences and Weapons (Scotland) Act 2007, s 63. See section 8.14 below for further discussion of articles prohibited in prisons.

8.12 OTHER WEAPONS OFFENCES

Although they are not, strictly speaking, offences of possession, a   **8.12.1**
short summary of other weapons offences may be included here.
Section 141A of the Criminal Justice Act 1988[137] prohibits the
sale or hire of knives, knife blades, razor blades, axes and swords
to anyone aged under the age of 18. An exception is made for
knives and blades designed for domestic use which can be sold to
persons aged between 16 and 18.[138] In addition, the section makes
it an offence to sell or hire to someone aged under 18 "any other
article which has a blade or which is sharply pointed *and* which
is made or adapted for use for causing injury to the person".[139]
The sale or hire of crossbows to a person aged under 18 is proscribed
by s 1 of the Crossbows Act 1987.[140] Possession offences are
one step removed from behaviours which actually cause harm.
Offences involving sale or hire are a further step removed from
such harm.

8.13 CRITIQUE OF THE LAW ON POSSESSION OF WEAPONS AND PROPOSALS FOR REFORM

The 2010 Act has improved the law in this area by providing the   **8.13.1**
same defences for ss 47 and 49 (as described above), but there could
be yet greater consolidation of these offences. It would be preferable
for there to be one offence of carrying a weapon or bladed article
in a public place, school, or prison. This would allow for repeal of
sections 47, 49, 49A, and 49C of the 1995 Act and would greatly
simplify the law.[141]

Andrew Ashworth has criticised these types of offences: **8.13.2**

---

[137] Added by the Offensive Weapons Act 1996, s 6(1), and amended by the Police, Public Order and Criminal Justice (Scotland) Act 2006, s 75 and the Criminal Justice and Licensing (Scotland) Act 2010, s 36.

[138] Criminal Justice Act 1988, s 141A(3A).

[139] *Ibid*, s 141A(2)(c) (emphasis added). There is a defence in s 141A(4) for sellers who are able to prove that they believed the person to whom the article was sold or let on hire to be aged 18 or older and that they had taken "reasonable steps" to establish that person's age, or that "no reasonable person could have suspected" from the person's appearance that she was under age.

[140] As amended by the Custodial Sentences and Weapons (Scotland) Act 2007, s 62(1) and (2)(a). Similar defences to those described *ibid* are to be found in the Crossbows Act 1987, s 1A.

[141] For an indication of how such consolidation might be achieved, see the *Draft Criminal Code*, s 91. That section would also extend the ambit of these offences to include medical premises, defined to include doctors' surgeries and hospitals.

"In view of the remoteness of the harm from the actual possession of an article, there is a strong case for arguing that [such] offenses should include a requirement of intention or willingness to engage in unlawful use of the article."[142]

Given the prevalence of knife crime in Scotland, we believe that the imposition of strict liability is justified in relation to *per se* weapons and articles with a blade or sharp point. However, a more generous interpretation ought to be given to defences. The first edition of this book criticised the case of *Crowe* v *Waugh*[143] in which the accused had forgotten that there was a knife in the pocket of his fishing jacket. That decision can be justified only on the grounds of general deterrence – ie that individuals would be deterred from carrying knives in public places if it were known that simple possession, without proof of fault, was sufficient for liability. We argued that it was surely not the purpose of the criminal law to stigmatise and punish "the careless and the casual and the thoughtless and the forgetful".[144] The maximum penalty for having a knife or offensive weapon in a public place is now 4 years' imprisonment.[145] The replacement of "good reason" by "reasonable excuse" in s 49 is to be commended, but given this high potential penalty, the latter defence ought to be applied in a way which is more favourable to the accused than has been the case with the former. In circumstances such as that of Mr Waugh, if the accused's story is not believed by the court, then a conviction is merited. But if the court accepts that an accused had a knife in a coat pocket out of sheer forgetfulness, then neither the harm principle nor any other principle of criminalisation can justify conviction.

8.14 POSSESSION OR USE OF BANNED ARTICLES IN PRISON

8.14.1 Section 41 of the Prisons (Scotland) Act 1989 was amended in 2010 to make it an offence to bring a "proscribed article" into a prison, without reasonable excuse.[146] A proscribed article is defined as any "personal communication device" (which includes a mobile phone, and other portable electronic devices capable of transmitting or receiving a communication of any kind); any drug, firearm or

---

[142] A Ashworth, "Conceptions of overcriminalization" (2008) 5 *Ohio St J Crim L* 407 at 416.

[143] 1999 JC 292. See section 8.11.8 above.

[144] *Ibid* at 296, per Lord Prosser. See Ferguson and McDiarmid (2009) section 8.12.2.

[145] Criminal Law (Consolidation) (Scotland) Act 1995, s 47(1)(b), as amended by the Offensive Weapons Act 1996, s 2(2).

[146] By the Criminal Justice and Licensing (Scotland) Act 2010, s 34. It is also an offence to take a proscribed article out of prison: Prisons (Scotland) Act 1989, s 41(1)(b).

ammunition, offensive weapon, article which has a blade or is sharply pointed, or other article prohibited by rules made under s 39.[147] It is an offence to use a personal communication device inside a prison, either to make or receive calls,[148] and also to be in possession of such a device inside a prison.[149] (No offence is committed in relation to mobile communication devices where these are brought into or used within a "designated area" of a prison.[150]) Some of these offences do not apply to prison officers, or to persons who are otherwise authorised.[151] It is also specifically provided that it is a defence to show that "there was an overriding public interest which justified the person's actions".[152] This would allow for an acquittal where the accused had used her mobile phone to contact the emergency services, for example if there were a fire in the prison, and embodies the defence of necessity.[153]

8.15 CRITIQUE OF THE LAW ON POSSESSION OR USE OF BANNED ARTICLES IN PRISON

As previously described in this chapter, there are several other statutory provisions which already made it an offence to have many of the articles listed in s 41 (above) in a public place: controlled drugs; firearms; offensive weapons; bladed or sharply pointed articles. It is clearly undesirable for persons who have been sentenced to imprisonment to have such things, and it seems reasonable to apply similar restrictions to prisons. One can also understand that prisoners who are able to use mobile phones during their term of imprisonment may abuse this in order to organise or engage in further criminal activity, inside or outside the prison. However, the harms which the prohibition of their possession or use in prisons is intended to prevent are fairly remote; unlike drugs, firearms or other weapons, mobile phones are not intrinsically dangerous. If one considers the chain of events needed for harm to be caused – the possessor of the phone has to use it to contact a third party outside the prison, who then has to engage in some kind of harmful activity – it is apparent that this requires the "harm principle" to be given a broad interpretation.

8.15.1

---

[147] Prisons (Scotland) Act 1989, s 41(9A).

[148] *Ibid*, s 41ZA(2).

[149] *Ibid*, s 41ZA(3).

[150] *Ibid*, s 41ZB(1) and (2)(a). "A designated area ... is any part of the prison, used solely or principally for an administrative or similar purpose, that is specified as such by a written designation given under this paragraph by the governor or director of the prison" (*ibid*, s 41ZB(9)).

[151] *Ibid*, s 41ZB(2)(b), (3) and (4).

[152] *Ibid*, s 41ZB(7)(b).

[153] The necessity defence is discussed more fully from section 21.4 below.

8.16   PREVENTING OFFENCES OF DISHONESTY

8.16.1   Hume refers to the difficulties associated with convicting for house-breaking the would-be thief who is "caught lurking in the night, hard by his neighbour's shop, with a ladder, picklock, and dark lanthorn",[154] having noted that

> "the law does not ordinarily take cognisance of those remote acts of preparation, such as procuring the instrument of ... house-breaking ... which serve indeed to disclose a wicked purpose".[155]

Parliament has now changed this. Two of the main preventive offences are found in ss 57 and 58 of the Civic Government (Scotland) Act 1982.

8.17   BEING FOUND IN PREMISES, WITH INTENT TO COMMIT THEFT

8.17.1   To catch potential thieves at an early stage, s 57(1) of the Civic Government (Scotland) Act 1982 provides that:

> "Any person who, without lawful authority to be there, is found in or on a building or other premises, whether enclosed or not, or in its curtilage or in a vehicle or vessel so that, in all the circumstances, it may reasonably be inferred that he intended to commit theft there shall be guilty of an offence."

The accused must be "found" in or on the premises, vehicle or vessel, or in their curtilage, though not necessarily arrested there. The section refers to the accused being on premises "without lawful authority". In *Marr* v *Heywood*,[156] a burglar alarm went off, alerting the householder to an attempted break-in. He found the accused scrambling into the garden of a neighbouring house. When arrested, the accused said "I didn't get into the house; you can't do me with this". The intent to steal was inferred, and the accused convicted. In *Scott* v *Friel*[157] it was emphasised that a lack of lawful authority to be in a particular place cannot properly be inferred from the mere fact that intention to commit theft has been established. The Crown must prove that there was no lawful authority.[158]

8.18   CONVICTED THIEF IN POSSESSION OF TOOLS

8.18.1   Section 58 of the Civic Government (Scotland) Act 1982 concerns the tools used by thieves. It is an offence for a person who has

---

154 Hume, i, 29.
155 *Ibid* at 28.
156 1993 SCCR 441.
157 1999 SLT 930.
158 See also *Hamilton* v *Donnelly* 1994 SLT 127.

two or more previous convictions for theft (or any aggravation of theft) to have "any tool or other object" from the possession of which it may reasonably be inferred that she intends to commit, or has committed, theft. In *Allan* v *Bree*[159] the police observed the accused in and near a car park on two occasions. He was skulking in undergrowth and scrutinising cars through binoculars, and had with him two torches and a pair of gloves. The court held that he had no case to answer. The "theftuous intention" had to be inferred from the tools themselves – not from the surrounding circumstances – and binoculars, torches and gloves are not suspicious in themselves.[160] The legislation provides that a person who is found with such tools or objects commits the offence if "unable to demonstrate satisfactorily" that this possession was not for the purposes of theft. One might imagine that this places a legal burden on the accused to provide a satisfactory explanation, however, in *Mathieson* v *Crowe*[161] the appeal court held that it was for the Crown to prove that there was no reasonable explanation. This approach is in line with other cases concerning so-called "reverse onus" provisions.[162]

8.19 POSSESSION OF ARTICLES FOR USE IN FRAUD

Section 49(1) of the Criminal Justice and Licensing (Scotland) Act 2010 makes it an offence for a person to have in her possession or control an article for use in, or in connection with, the commission of fraud. The Crown will have to prove that the accused had the article, and that it was to be used in perpetrating a fraud, but this use could be by the accused or by some other person. It is also an offence to make, adapt, supply or offer to supply an article, knowing that it is designed or adapted for fraud, or intending that it be so used.[163] "Article" is defined to include a program or data held in electronic form.[164] **8.19.1**

---

[159] 1987 SCCR 228.

[160] This seems a surprising decision, until it is realised that the locus was a place frequented by homosexuals, and that the accused eventually entered a car driven by another man. The sheriff concluded that "the only reasonable inference to be drawn is that whatever purpose lay behind the accused's bizarre conduct it was not theft" (*ibid* at 230).

[161] 1993 SCCR 1100. See also *Phillips* v *Macleod* 1995 SCCR 319; *Docherty* v *Normand* 1996 JC 207; and *Thomson* v *McLaughlin* 2012 JC 37.

[162] Compare, however, the Criminal Law (Consolidation) (Scotland) Act 1995, ss 47(1A) and 49(4). As discussed at section 8.11.9 above, the onus of establishing these defences on the balance of probabilities lies with the accused. For further discussion of reverse onus provisions, see from section 5.4.3 above.

[163] Criminal Justice and Licensing (Scotland) Act 1010, s 49(3).

[164] *Ibid*, s 49(5).

8.20   POSSESSION OF POLICE UNIFORM

8.20.1   Section 92(2) of the Police and Fire Reform (Scotland) Act 2012 makes it an offence for a person who is not a constable to possess any article of police uniform without permission from the Scottish Police Authority. It is a defence for the accused to prove that the article was lawfully obtained and was for a lawful purpose.[165] It may be supposed that a constable's spouse, or a dry cleaner, are among those who could lawfully possess a police uniform, as could an actor playing the part of a police constable.[166] An "article of police uniform" is defined in the 2012 Act to include any distinctive badge or mark usually issued to constables, or any article which has the appearance of any article of uniform, badge or mark.[167] Section 92(4) makes it an offence

> "for a person (other than a constable) to wear, without the prior permission of the Authority, any article of police uniform in circumstances where it gives an appearance so nearly resembling that of a constable as to be calculated to deceive."

These offences seem designed to prevent the possessor from engaging in crimes of dishonesty, such as fraud, but it should be noted that while there is a requirement for the accused's appearance to be "calculated to deceive" in respect of the wearing of the uniform or article, no such requirement is necessary for the possession offence in s 92(2).

8.21   CRITIQUE OF THE LAW ON POSSESSION OF POLICE ITEMS

8.21.1   Our criticism here is similar to that made in respect of possession of articles banned in prisons: the harms which the prohibition of possession (or indeed wearing) of a police uniform, or article of police uniform, are intended to prevent will generally involve some form of fraud. But since police apparel is not inherently dangerous, this is criminalising conduct far in advance of behaviour(s) which could actually cause harm. As Ashworth and Zedner have argued:

> "To hold a person responsible now for her possible future actions (i.e., without proof of an intent to do the actions), as may occur with respect to … crimes of possession, is objectionable in principle".[168]

They endorse Antony Duff's view that such predictions of future conduct deny individuals their responsible agency by treating them as if they "cannot be trusted to guide [their] actions by the

---

[165] Police and Fire Reform (Scotland) Act 2012, s 92(3).
[166] These offences replace similarly worded provisions in the Police (Scotland) Act 1967, s 43(1).
[167] Police and Fire Reform (Scotland) Act 2012, s 92(6).
[168] Ashworth and Zedner (2012) at 556.

appropriate reasons".[169] Since the wearing of a police uniform in order to achieve a practical result (for example, entry into a person's home, or other place not generally accessible to the public) would be the common law crime of attempted fraud, it is suggested that these statutory offences are not justifiable.

8.22   ROAD TRAFFIC OFFENCES

Many road traffic offences fall into the category of preventive offences. Drivers are required to drive within the speed limit,[170] maintain the depth of their tyres' tread,[171] drive on the left-hand side of the road,[172] obey traffic signs,[173] etc in order to prevent the harmful consequences which can ensue when these requirements are disregarded. The offence of driving with excess alcohol in one's blood stream is another example.[174] Inevitably, drink-driving offences employ what Paul Robinson and Michael Cahill have called "bright-line" rules, since they "effectively impute an intoxicated state where none might be present – a person's blood-alcohol level might be elevated without any significant attendant impairment of physical skills or psychological awareness".[175] Moreover, they are based on the fact that drunk drivers have the potential to cause harm to other people, or other people's property, but no harm need actually have been caused, nor need the prosecution even prove that, in the particular case before the court, there was any danger of harm actually being caused.

8.22.1

8.23   TERRORISM

Since the 9/11 attacks on the World Trade Center in New York in 2001, terrorism has assumed a greater importance on the global stage than before.[176] The attacks on London transport on 7 July

8.23.1

---

[169] R A Duff, *Answering For Crime: Responsibility and Liability in the Criminal Law* (2007), p 165, cited *ibid* at 556.

[170] Road Traffic Regulation Act 1984, s 89(1).

[171] Road Vehicles (Construction and Use) Regulations 1986 (SI 1986/1078), reg 27(1)(f) and (g) and Road Traffic Act 1988, s 41A.

[172] See, for example, Motorways Traffic (Scotland) Regulations 1995 (SI 1995/2507), reg 5.

[173] Road Traffic Act 1988, s 36.

[174] *Ibid*, ss 4 and 5.

[175] P H Robinson and M T Cahill, *Law Without Justice: Why Criminal Law Doesn't Give People What They Deserve* (2006), p 115.

[176] Al-Qa'ida terrorists hijacked four passenger planes and deliberately crashed them into buildings, including the Twin Towers in New York. Almost 3,000 people were killed. See T H Keen, L H Hamilton *et al*, *The 9/11 Commission Report: Final Report of the National Commission on the Terrorist Attacks upon the United States: Executive Summary* (2004), 1–2.

2005[177] and on Glasgow Airport 2 years later[178] brought the issues raised by this new form of terrorism, and, in particular, the use of suicide bombers, closer to home. This chapter's focus is on ":preventive offences" – behaviour which has been criminalised at an early stage in order to prevent the commission of a greater wrong. Thus, we saw that theft, for example, may be prevented if an accused person is arrested at the locus, in suspicious circumstances, before having actually stolen anything.[179] In the terrorism context, this notion of "prevention" takes on huge significance. It is clearly desirable to prevent crimes of dishonesty, where possible, but it may be regarded as a moral imperative to prevent acts which have the potential to cause the deaths of hundreds, if not thousands, of people. In the United Kingdom, this moral obligation is backed by international obligations.[180]

8.23.2   Accommodating the prevention of terrorism in criminal law requires a particularly nuanced approach to the balance between the rights of the accused and the protection of the public. Indeed, "suspect" may be a better term than "accused", since the state has taken powers to detain individuals for lengthy periods without bringing charges.[181] The stakes are high. The legislature may wish to err on the side of prevention of terrorism but this ought not to be allowed to compromise excessively either the suspect's right to liberty or the need for certainty in the law, reflected in Arts 5 and 7 of the European Convention on Human Rights (ECHR) respectively.[182] How, then, has this balancing act been approached?

---

[177] Three bombs exploded in the London Underground, and a fourth bomb exploded on a bus: 56 people were killed and more than 700 injured. See the House of Commons *Report of the Official Account of the Bombings in London on 7th July 2005* (HC1087) (2006) at 2, para 2.

[178] On 30 June 2007 a jeep loaded with propane was driven through the doors of Glasgow Airport in an attempt to blow up the building. Five members of the public received minor injuries, and one of the two suicide bombers died from burns received in the explosion. The other was found guilty of conspiracy to commit murder and sentenced to life imprisonment with a minimum term of 32 years. See H Siddique, "Glasgow airport car bomber jailed for 32 years" *The Guardian* 17 Dec 2008.

[179] Civic Government (Scotland) Act 1982, s 57 – see from section 8.16 above.

[180] The UK is a signatory to the Council of Europe Convention on the Prevention of Terrorism (2005). It has not, however, ratified the treaty as yet. The United Nations Security Council Resolution (No 1373) (2001) provides further international backing for laws suppressing terrorism.

[181] See Terrorism Act 2000, s 41 and Sch 8.

[182] It has been said that the justification of preventing terrorism "seems to conduce towards vaguer than normal legal grounds for intervention by the security agencies": C Walker, "Case comment: terrorism: Terrorism Act 2000, ss 1 and 58 – possession of terrorist documents" [2008] *Crim LR* 160 at 162. For a list of the Convention rights, see from section 1.4, above.

The first point to note is that terrorism is a reserved matter **8.23.3** under the Scotland Act 1998.[183] Terrorist legislation therefore applies to the whole of the UK. Since 2000, six major statutes have been passed in this area.[184] It is possible to give only a flavour of these provisions. According to the Terrorism Act 2000, terrorism involves

> "the use or threat of action where–
> (a) the action falls within subsection (2),
> (b) the use or threat is designed to influence the government or an international governmental organisation or to intimidate the public or a section of the public, and
> (c) the use or threat is made for the purpose of advancing a political, religious, racial or ideological cause".[185]

An action falls within subs (2) if it–

> "(a) involves serious violence against a person,
> (b) involves serious damage to property,
> (c) endangers a person's life, other than that of the person committing the action,
> (d) creates a serious risk to the health or safety of the public or a section of the public, or
> (e) is designed seriously to interfere with or seriously to disrupt an electronic system."

In addition: "The use or threat of action falling within subsection (2) which involves the use of firearms or explosives is terrorism whether or not subsection (1)(b) is satisfied."[186]

This has been described as "notoriously broad".[187] It is also **8.23.4** complex. The types of action listed in s 1(2) are all related to pre-existing criminal offences but, as Adrian Hunt points out, do not necessarily satisfy the definition of any discrete crime.[188] The relevant action must be designed to influence the government, or an international governmental organisation or to intimidate the public or a section thereof. Finally, the use or threat must be made for the purpose of advancing a political, racial, religious or ideological

---

[183] Sch 5, Pt II, para B8. It is thus a matter for the Westminster Parliament – see from section 5.14 above.

[184] Terrorism Act 2000, Anti-Terrorism, Crime and Security Act 2001, Prevention of Terrorism Act 2005 (now repealed), Terrorism Act 2006, Counter-Terrorism Act 2008, and Terrorism Prevention and Investigation Measures Act 2011.

[185] Terrorism Act 2000, s 1(1). This section has been amended by the Terrorism Act 2006, s 34(a) and the Counter-Terrorism Act 2008, s 75(2)(a).

[186] Terrorism Act 2000, s 1(3).

[187] A Tomkins, "Legislating against terror: the Anti-terrorism, Crime and Security Act 2001" (2002) *Public Law* 205 at 211.

[188] A Hunt, "Criminal prohibitions on direct and indirect encouragement of terrorism" [2007] *Crim LR* 441 at 447.

cause. Concern has been expressed that this definition would have captured action taken by, for example, the suffragettes or those who opposed apartheid in South Africa.[189]

8.23.5   Section 3 of the Terrorism Act 2000 allows the proscription of certain organisations.[190] The current list of such organisations is set down in Sch 2, para 1.[191] The inclusion of Al-Qa'ida and the IRA[192] might be expected. Others are less well known.[193] It is an offence to profess membership of a proscribed organisation,[194] to seek support for one[195] or to wear clothes or carry articles in such a way as to arouse reasonable suspicion of membership.[196] The balancing function performed by the courts between the need to prevent acts of terrorism on the one hand, and to ensure that the defendant's rights are properly respected is apparent from *Attorney-General's Reference (No 4 of 2002)*[197] which considered the offence of professing membership of a proscribed organisation in relation to the defendant's Art 6 rights to a fair trial. The House of Lords determined that the statute had to be interpreted in a manner which would not breach the presumption of innocence by creating a situation where a defendant might actually be innocent but be unable to prove that.[198]

8.23.6   The Prevention of Terrorism Act 2005 introduced the concept of the Control Order[199] – a paradigm example of preventive law-making in that it was "accepted that it would be wholly inappropriate, if the necessary evidence were available, for a suspect to be restricted under a control order instead of being prosecuted before the courts".[200] The relevant sections of the 2005 Act were due to expire one year after they came into force[201] but were continued by statutory instrument[202] before being repealed by the Terrorism

---

[189] Walker (2008) at 162.

[190] For a critique of these types of status offences, see section 6.3.5 above.

[191] The Secretary of State may amend the list by Order: Terrorism Act 2000, s 3(3).

[192] It has been held that this proscription includes the Real IRA and any other schism of the Irish Republican Army organisation: *R v Z* [2005] 2 AC 645.

[193] For example, the International Sikh Youth Federation, and the Islamic Movement of Uzbekistan.

[194] Terrorism Act 2000, s 11.

[195] *Ibid*, s 12.

[196] *Ibid*, s 13. See *Rankin v Murray* 2004 SLT 1164.

[197] This was conjoined with the (road traffic) case of *Sheldrake v Director of Public Prosecutions* [2005] 1 AC 264.

[198] See from section 5.4 above for a discussion of the presumption of innocence.

[199] Prevention of Terrorism Act 2005, ss 1–9.

[200] C Forsyth, "Control orders, conditions precedent and compliance with Article 6(1)" (2008) 67 *CLJ* 1 at 2.

[201] Prevention of Terrorism Act 2005 Act, s 13(1).

[202] Prevention of Terrorism Act 2005 (Continuance in force of sections 1 to 9) Order 2009 (SI 2009/554).

Prevention and Investigation Measures Act 2011 (TPIMA). The possible obligations which could form the basis of a Control Order were wide-ranging[203] and had the potential to be exceptionally restrictive.[204] As a form of preventive offence, Control Orders did not so much intervene very early in the process towards the commission of a completed crime, as create a bespoke, personal, and often highly restrictive, criminal code for the individuals affected by them. The 2011 Act replaced such Orders with TPIM notices ("terrorism prevention and investigation measures").[205] Before imposing such a notice the Secretary of State must be satisfied that certain conditions have been met.[206] These include that he reasonably believes that the individual is, or has been, involved in terrorism-related activity, and considers that it is necessary to impose a TPIM to protect the public from a risk of terrorism. The requirement for "reasonable belief" is a higher standard than that of "reasonable suspicion" which sufficed for the making of a control order.[207] Crucially, the Secretary of State needs permission from a court to issue a TPIM, unless the case is so urgent that the measures require to be imposed without obtaining such permission.[208] These measures last for one year. They may be extended for a second year, but no further.[209]

Finally, we will briefly consider ss 1 and 5 of the Terrorism Act 2006, both of which are drafted broadly. Section 1 seeks to prohibit the "encouragement" of terrorism and, in so doing, creates one of the least well-defined offences in an already vague area. The section renders it criminal to publish statements which "encourage terrorism", defining "encouragement" as including:

8.23.7

---

[203] For example, to surrender one's passport (s 1(4)(i)); to co-operate with specified arrangements to monitor movements or communications (s 1(4)(n)); and restrictions on place of residence (s 1(4)(e)).

[204] In *Secretary of State for the Home Department* v *JJ* [2008] 1 AC 385, the House of Lords held that the restrictions imposed on six individuals, which included an 18-hour curfew, the wearing of an electronic tag and restrictions on pre-arranged meetings with anyone, were so restrictive that they constituted a breach of Art 5 of the ECHR and were therefore unlawful in terms of the Prevention of Terrorism Act 2005, s 1(2)(a). For a critique of control orders see: HM Government, *Review of Counter-Terrorism and Security Powers: Review Findings and Recommendations* (CM 8004), January 2011).

[205] Terrorism Prevention and Investigation Measures Act 2011, s 2(1). For a critique of TPIM, see B Middleton, "Terrorism prevention and investigation measures: constitutional evolution, not revolution?" (2013) 77 *J Crim L* 562.

[206] Terrorism Prevention and Investigation Measures Act 2011, ss 2(1) and 3.

[207] In the words of Lord Brown: "To suspect something to be so is by no means to believe it to be so: it is to believe only that it may be so." (*R v Saik* [2007] 1 AC 18 at 61, para [120].)

[208] Terrorism Prevention and Investigation Measures Act 2011, s 3(5). See also s 6 for the role of the courts.

[209] *Ibid*, s 5.

"every statement which–
  (a) glorifies the commission or preparation (whether in the past, in the future or generally) of such acts or offences; and
  (b) is a statement from which those members of the public [to whom the statement is published] could reasonably be expected to infer that what is being glorified is being glorified as conduct that should be emulated by them in existing circumstances."[210]

Prior to the enactment of this section, the Parliamentary Joint Committee on Human Rights had been critical of the use of the term "glorification" because it was so vague.[211] The Government's Explanatory Notes to the Terrorism Act 2006 provide as an example a statement glorifying the bomb attacks on the London Underground in 2005. If such a statement were reasonably likely to cause members of the public to infer that similar action ought to be emulated, this would be an offence under the provision.

8.23.8   It is particularly difficult to achieve an appropriate balance, here. As David Barnum states:

"Courts and commentators in both the United Kingdom and the United States have generally endorsed the proposition that government should not be allowed to punish anything other than 'direct incitement' to unlawful action nor to do so in circumstances other than those presenting a 'clear and present danger' of the occurrence of such action. This hard-won limitation on the power of government to punish its critics has been sorely tested, however, by the emergence of religious and ideological divisions of unprecedented persistence and depth and by the recent perpetration of unimaginable acts of terrorist violence. In the United Kingdom, as elsewhere, it now seems obvious to many that if the only thing that government is entitled to punish is 'direct incitement to violence', and if the only thing that qualifies as such incitement is a declarative sentence that others are commanded to commit a particular act of violence, then government will be inexplicably precluded from punishing a broad spectrum of messages that are both intended and highly likely to bring about various kinds of unlawful action, including horrific violence."[212]

There is limited acceptance of a need to criminalise some forms of indirect incitement.[213] The difficulty is finding a form of words which does not interfere unreasonably with the right to freedom of expression under Art 10 of the ECHR. Hunt suggests that this could be partly achieved by making it clear that the offence is only committed where "what is said/published cause[s] a danger that persons might be encouraged to engage in terrorism as a

[210] Terrorism Act 2006, s 1(3).
[211] (Session 2005–06) *Third Report: Counter-Terrorism Policy and Human Rights: Terrorism Bill and Related Matters* (HL 75-I / HC 561-I) at 3.
[212] D G Barnum, "Indirect incitement and freedom of speech in Anglo-American law" (2006) 3 *EHRLR* 258, at 277–278.
[213] Parliamentary Joint Committee on Human Rights (2005–06) at 17–18.

consequence".[214] It is unclear whether the same need for a new offence existed under Scots law, where the common law crime of incitement can be committed without the need for a direct order or instruction.[215] Mark Stephens is one of many critics:

> "When there are already laws in place which deal with those seeking to incite violence, the question is whether the aim of [the Terrorism Act 2006] is legitimate or simply a dose of legislative valium to placate the electorate."[216]

While many aspects of anti-terrorism legislation may constitute little more than calming measures (or even placebos) for the great majority, they constitute powerful and unpleasant medicine for those who are the subject of some of their provisions.

Section 5(1) of the 2006 Act is headed "preparation of terrorist acts" and provides: **8.23.9**

> "A person commits an offence if, with the intention of–
> (a) committing acts of terrorism, or
> (b) assisting another to commit such acts,
> he engages in any conduct in preparation for giving effect to his intention."

The maximum penalty for breach of this provision is life imprisonment.[217]

8.24 CONCLUSION

Preventive crimes are not uncontroversial. Michael Moore is critical of them, particularly where they criminalise mere possession: **8.24.1**

> "Faced openly, impatience (for future crimes) and inability to prove guilt (for past crimes) are not comfortable rationales for criminalizing conduct. Faced openly, most crimes of possession perhaps should not be crimes ... because there is no *wrongful* act being punished."[218]

He suggests

> "if there is no *wrongful* act in acquiring, maintaining, or failing to rid oneself of possession of items like guns, drugs, obscene materials, etc., then on one well-regarded theory of criminal legislation these acts should not be made criminal".[219]

Such offences should be used with caution, lest they criminalise a great deal of behaviour which is in itself innocuous. One can readily

---

[214] Hunt (2007) at 458.

[215] See *Baxter* v *HM Advocate* 1998 JC 219, discussed at section 8.6.6 above.

[216] M Stephens, "Pushing for glory?" (2006) 156 *NLJ* 469.

[217] Terrorism Act 2006, s 5(3).

[218] M S Moore, *Act and Crime: The Philosophy of Action and its Implications for Criminal Law* (1993), p 22 (emphasis in original).

[219] *Ibid* (emphasis in original).

see the harm which can result from possession of guns or explosives. As previously suggested, while one can imagine various scenarios in which harm could be caused by possession of a mobile phone while in a prison, or article of police uniform, the link between the harm and the mere possession of the phone or uniform seems a more tenuous one.[220] Furthermore, some of the provisions in the recent anti-terrorism legislation have arguably failed to strike an appropriate balance between the prevention of harm and the rights of individuals. Long before this legislation was conceived, Packer cautioned that

> "increasing the radius of the criminal law in the interest of early intervention is a very risky business. The first question in every case is, or should be: how high is the probability that the preparatory conduct, if not inhibited by the threat of criminal punishment, will result in an ultimate harm of the sort that the law should try to prevent? A related consideration is whether the preparatory conduct is itself socially useful, or at least neutral, so that its proscription or curtailment might unduly inhibit people from doing what they should otherwise be free to do ... is the risk substantial and is it justifiable?"[221]

It is submitted that in respect of several of the offences which we have looked at in this chapter, no convincing case has yet been made that these types of preparatory conduct have a high probability of resulting in ultimate harm.

---

[220] See section 8.14.1 above.
[221] Packer (1969) at pp 270–271.

PART III

OFFENCES WHICH THREATEN
OR HARM BODILY INTEGRITY

References to "offences against the person" in Scots criminal law are to those crimes which impact on the physical person, as opposed to property, or indeed reputation. Crimes which cause physical injury to other people are clearly within the "harm principle". As Joel Feinberg put it:

> "About the propriety of one class of crimes there can be no controversy. Wilful homicide, forcible rape, aggravated assault, and battery are crimes (under one name or another) everywhere in the civilized world, and no reasonable person could advocate their 'decriminalization'."[1]

The safeguarding of bodily integrity – attempting to protect individuals from physical harm – is obviously an important aim of the criminal law. As Victor Tadros has so vividly described it:

> "Violence is the food and drink of criminal law. But as violence comes in different forms and degrees, there is a question about how the criminal law should distinguish between different forms of violence."[2]

Offences against bodily integrity could be sub-divided in a number of ways; we have separated fatal offences (Chapter 9) from those which are not fatal, and separated the latter into non-sexual offences (Chapter 10) and sexual offences (Chapter 11).

---

[1] J Feinberg, *The Moral Limits of the Criminal Law: Harm to Others* (1984), p 10.
[2] V Tadros, "The distinctiveness of domestic abuse: a freedom based account" (2004–05) 65 *Louisiana Law Review* 989.

CHAPTER 9

HOMICIDE

9.1 INTRODUCTION

The sanctity of life is one of the highest values protected by **9.1.1** most societies. It has a long history in Judeo–Christian doctrine, a prohibition on killing constituting the sixth of the Ten Commandments,[1] and is also a fundamental concept in Islam.[2] The principle assumes particular importance in a legal context in relation to some of the vexed questions with which medical law has had to grapple.[3] It is obvious that the criminal law interacts with the sanctity principle primarily in relation to homicide offences. Indeed, in its Consultation Paper, *A New Homicide Act for England and Wales*,[4] the Law Commission specifically engaged with the way in which this value in both its religious and its secular formulation underlies homicide law,[5] though it took the view that the relationship was primary only in relation to intentional killing.

The value to be attached to the principle is not, however, absolute, **9.1.2** either in criminal law or more generally.[6] Not all homicides are criminal. It is not generally criminal to kill someone accidentally, or for a soldier to kill in times of war. Killing in self-defence is regarded as justifiable and therefore not blameworthy.[7] In a genuine "mercy"

---

[1] Book of Exodus, Chapter 20, verse 13.

[2] The *Qur'an*, Chapter 6, verse 151. See also Chapter 5, verse 32: "Whosoever has spared the life of a soul, it is as though he has spared the life of all people. Whosoever has killed a soul, it is as though he has murdered all of mankind."

[3] For example in relation to discontinuing life support for patients in a persistent vegetative state. See, for example, *Airedale NHS Trust* v *Bland* [1993] AC 789 per Lord Hoffmann at 826, and *Law Hospital NHS Trust* v *Lord Advocate* 1996 SC 301, discussed at section 9.9.4 below.

[4] Law Commission, Consultation Paper No 177 (2005).

[5] *Ibid*, paras 2.20–2.31.

[6] See A Norrie, "Between orthodox subjectivism and moral contextualism: intention and the Consultation Paper" [2006] *Crim LR* 486 at 489–490.

[7] Self-defence is discussed from section 21.8 below.

killing, a utilitarian would argue that ending suffering represents a greater good.[8] Nonetheless, the sanctity of life is recognised by Art 2 of the ECHR which states that: "Everyone's right to life shall be protected by law." One obvious way in which a state can accord this protection is to ensure that it has robust laws, prohibiting the killing of one citizen by another. Nor is this an empty guarantee.[9] Case law from the European Court of Human Rights[10] has emphasised the importance of ensuring that a state's laws on self-defence do not undermine the right to life.[11] While this jurisprudence has to date related primarily to killings of citizens by state agents such as the police, it is within the European Court's power to declare that a state's application of its domestic law does not adequately protect its own citizens.[12] Accordingly, the principles of criminal offences premised on the unlawful taking of life require to accord both with the prevailing views of the society on which they are imposed[13] and with the overarching legal framework represented by human rights legislation.

9.1.3   The categorisation of homicide presents difficulties in all legal systems. The (English) Law Commission's *Report on Murder, Manslaughter and Infanticide*[14] demonstrates the complexities – moral and social as well as legal – encountered in trying to determine where particular types of homicide should sit within this framework. Until recently, at least, this had been less of a problem in Scots law where the concept of "wicked recklessness" had been invoked to allow conviction of murder in circumstances where the accused had

---

[8] It should be noted that the (English) Law Commission has been sceptical about the use of the term "mercy killing" in the context of suicide pacts entered into by older couples, where one survives, taking the view that these may arise from the carer's need to be free of the burden of caring: Law Commission (2005) at para 1.84.

[9] See A Ashworth, "Case comment: Human rights – right to life – exception for defensive force where 'absolutely necessary'" [1998] *Crim LR* 823 at 825; F Leverick, "Is English self-defence law incompatible with Article 2 of the ECHR?" [2002] *Crim LR* 347 at 358–359.

[10] For example, *R (on the application of Bennett) v HM Coroner for Inner South London* [2006] HRLR 22; *Bubbins v United Kingdom* (2005) 41 EHRR 24; and *McCann v United Kingdom* (1996) 21 EHRR 97.

[11] See F Leverick, "Mistake in self-defence after *Drury*" (2002) 1 *Jur Rev* 35 at 45.

[12] This has happened in relation to the use of the defence of reasonable chastisement to a charge of assaulting a child. See the case of *A v United Kingdom* (1999) 27 EHRR 611, discussed at n 41 in section 1.4.1 above.

[13] In this regard Barry Mitchell has carried out quantitative research on public opinion in relation to homicide offences in England and Wales: see "Public perceptions of homicide and criminal justice" (1998) 38 *Brit J Criminology* 453.

[14] Law Commission, *Murder, Manslaughter and Infanticide* (Law Com No 304, 2006).

killed callously,[15] but without *intention* to kill.[16] However, as will
be discussed subsequently, the case of *HM Advocate* v *Purcell*[17] has
brought to the forefront of the debate in Scotland the issue of a need
for at least an intention to cause personal injury before the *mens
rea* for murder can be satisfied, as opposed to the view that total
indifference as to whether the victim lived or died, absent any such
intention, would suffice.

9.2 NON-CRIMINAL ("CASUAL") HOMICIDE

In the criminal law context, it is perhaps particularly important **9.2.1**
not to lose sight of the fact that a death may have been caused
by a pure accident. In those circumstances, no criminal liability
attaches, even where, *prima facie*, an individual appears to have
been involved in bringing about the death. This category was
recognised by Hume under the heading of "casual homicide"
which he defined as "that which happens by pure misadventure,
without any act of the killer's will".[18] He cited the case in 1682 of
John Leper, town-officer, who had apprehended a person in the
course of his duties and was escorting him to his cell in Straven
[*sic*] Castle. Despite Leper's warnings about the dangerous and
dilapidated state of much of the building, the prisoner went ahead
and, going through the wrong door, fell 20 feet to his death. Leper
had no criminal liability whatsoever for this outcome.[19] While
the criminal justice system needs to be alive to the possibility that
no liability may attach to someone accused of homicide because
she did not cause the death in question, the substantive criminal
law is, obviously, concerned mainly with the conditions in which
criminal responsibility should apply. From a historical perspective,
Lindsay Farmer has argued that "the 'general part' of the criminal
law, comprising the definitions of responsibility, causation, excuse,
justification and so on, derives almost exclusively from the law
of homicide".[20] He does, however, question the crime's status as,

---

[15] "Callous" is the term favoured in the *Draft Criminal Code* (s 37(1)) in relation
to killings of this nature.
[16] See *Brennan* v *HM Advocate* 1977 JC 38. Also *Cawthorne* v *HM Advocate*
1968 JC 32, where the charge was *attempted* murder but the *mens rea* of wicked
recklessness is discussed.
[17] 2008 JC 131. See sections 9.12.7 and 20.14.2 below. A five-judge Bench has
considered this issue again more recently, though rather inconclusively, in the case
of *Petto* v *HM Advocate* 2012 JC 105.
[18] Hume, i, 191.
[19] *Ibid*, 194.
[20] L Farmer, *Criminal Law, Tradition and Legal Order: Crime and the Genius of
Scots Law 1747 to the Present* (1997), p 143.

simultaneously "atypical" and "paradigmatic".[21] A crime to which all of these viewpoints could be applied is clearly deserving of close analysis.

9.3   CRIMINAL HOMICIDE

9.3.1   There are two categories of homicide at common law, as well as several statutory offences.[22] We distinguish between these on the basis of the differing *mens rea* (and hence blameworthiness) of the accused. The *actus reus* is the same in that in each case the accused has caused the death of another person. [23] The importance of the distinction between murder and culpable homicide is that a conviction for murder results in a sentence of life imprisonment[24] – this is a mandatory penalty – while the sentence for culpable homicide is more flexible.[25] Let us first consider the *actus reus* in more detail.

9.3.2   The forbidden behavioural element of both murder and culpable homicide is the same: "the destruction of life".[26] The accused must have caused the death of a person, but this must be someone other than the accused herself. Hume discussed "self-murder" only in relation to the penalty – confiscation of the deceased's moveable goods – a practice of which he did not approve.[27] Nonetheless, he seems to have accepted that it constituted "an offence" albeit "of a quite different nature from any other homicide".[28] It is no longer a crime to commit suicide. The crime seems to have fallen into desuetude.[29]

9.3.3   Suicide *attempts* which alarm other people could be charged as a breach of the peace.[30] One of the authors was involved in two

---

[21] Farmer, *Criminal Law*, p 143.

[22] Road traffic homicide is discussed from section 9.23, and corporate homicide from section 18.5.14 below.

[23] See section 9.3.3 below for the law's approach to attempted suicide.

[24] This is in terms of the Criminal Procedure (Scotland) Act 1995, s 205. Those aged under 18 at the time of conviction are not sentenced to life imprisonment but rather sentenced to be detained without limit of time.

[25] See section 9.15.1 below.

[26] J H A Macdonald, *A Practical Treatise on the Criminal Law of Scotland* (5th edn by J Walker and D J Stevenson, 1948), p 89.

[27] Hume, i, 300. Suicide was a crime in Ireland until the enactment of the Criminal Law (Suicide) Act 1993.

[28] Hume, i, 300. See also J Chalmers, "Assisted suicide: jurisdiction and discretion" (2010) 14 *Edin LR* 295.

[29] Desuetude is a doctrine that has the effect of rendering inoperative legal principles which have not been enforced for a considerable period. The Latin phrase *cessante ratione legis, cesssat ipsa lex* means that once the public policy objective or rationale for a law has ceased to apply, the law itself ceases to apply. This fate may also have befallen the crime of blasphemy – see from section 16.8 below.

[30] For examples of this, see M G A Christie, *Breach of the Peace* (1990), para 3.33.

such cases while in the Procurator Fiscal Service. In one case, a
woman threatened to throw herself from the roof of a supermarket.
In another, a young man locked himself in the toilet of his mother's
house, and told his mother that he was going to take an overdose
of paracetamol. In both cases, the police were able to prevent the
suicide by arresting the accused for breach of the peace.[31] It seems
that current practice is for would-be suicides to be arrested for
breach of the peace, but then dealt with under the mental health
legislation, rather than being prosecuted. The situation is different
where two or more people agree to commit suicide together; those
who survive such suicide pacts are likely to be prosecuted for
culpable homicide.[32]

9.4   WHEN DOES LIFE BEGIN?

Homicide involves causing the death of a *person*; homicide laws   9.4.1
are directed at the killing of human beings, rather than non-
human animals. This raises the question: how is a person/
human being defined for the purposes of the criminal law? In his
general exposition of the category of "homicide", Macdonald
states: "Homicide is committed only where a self-existent human
life has been destroyed."[33] One implication of this definition is
that Scots criminal law has not involved itself in complex
moral and ethical issues as to when life begins.[34] Many people
believe that a foetus is a human being,[35] hence that abortion is
tantamount to murder. Such people are passing comment on
their perceptions of the morality of the situation, but it is
clear that, so far as the criminal law is concerned, a foetus is (at
most) a potential human being; terminating its life is not homicide
in Scots law. Such killings are defined as the separate crime of
abortion.

---

[31] Breach of the peace is discussed further from section 15.2 below.
[32] See Gordon (2000), para 7.07 and (2001), para 25.04. Nothing is said about
attempted suicide, *per se*.
[33] Macdonald (1948), p 87. See also Hume, i, 186.
[34] In *Evans* v *UK* (2008) 46 EHRR 34 (NB: case reports starts at p 728), it was
noted by the European Court of Human Rights (ECtHR) that there is no European
consensus on the scientific and legal definition of the beginning of life (at 747, para
54).
[35] The ECtHR considered the right to life of a foetus, under Art 2, in *Vo* v
France (2005) 40 EHRR 12, a case arising from medical negligence. It held that
there had been no violation but did not commit itself on the issue of the foetus's
status as a person. It stated: "the Court is convinced that it is neither desirable,
nor even possible as matters stand, to answer in the abstract the question whether
the unborn child is a person for the purposes of Art 2 of the Convention"
(at 295).

9.5   ABORTION

9.5.1   Abortion remains a common law offence in Scots law. Since the enactment of the Abortion Act 1967, however, the law has provided a defence to doctors who terminate pregnancies, so long as they comply with the requirements of that legislation.[36] These are that the pregnant woman consents to the procedure, and that two registered medical practitioner are of the opinion, formed in good faith, that one of the following sets of circumstances applies:

> "(a) that the pregnancy has not exceeded its twenty-fourth week and that the continuance of the pregnancy would involve risk, greater than if the pregnancy were terminated, of injury to the physical or mental health of the pregnant woman or any existing children of her family; or
> (b) that the termination is necessary to prevent grave permanent injury to the physical or mental health of the pregnant woman; or
> (c) that the continuance of the pregnancy would involve risk to the life of the pregnant woman, greater than if the pregnancy were terminated; or
> (d) that there is a substantial risk that if the child were born it would suffer from such physical or mental abnormalities as to be seriously handicapped."[37]

What amounts to a "substantial" risk or a "serious" handicap is not defined. In 2012, 12,447 legal abortions were performed in Scotland.[38]

9.6   CRITIQUE OF THE LAW ON ABORTION AND PROPOSALS FOR REFORM

9.6.1   As Catharine MacKinnon has argued: "Abortion *is* a sex equality issue. Everyone knows it."[39] She points out that denying access to abortion prevents women from controlling their lives, and "largely seals women's lack of control over their time, which is what a life is made of".[40] While the decriminalisation of abortion in the circumstances specified in section 9.5.1 is in keeping with a liberal perspective, it is noteworthy that the legislation does not confer any rights to pregnant women who are seeking an abortion.

---

[36] The law on abortion is not a devolved matter, hence may not be amended by the Scottish Parliament: Scotland Act 1998, Sch 5, Pt II, para J1. This is presumably intended to ensure that the law remains the same in Scotland and in England, to prevent women travelling from whichever jurisdiction has more stringent requirements to the other jurisdiction in order to have abortions.

[37] Abortion Act 1967, s 1(1), as amended by the Human Fertilisation and Embryology Act 1990, s 37.

[38] Abortion statistics available at: http://www.isdscotland.org./Health-Topics/Sexual-Health/Publications/2013-05-28/2013-05-28-Abortions-Report.pdf (p 4).

[39] C A MacKinnon, *Women's Lives, Men's Laws* (2007), p 19 (emphasis in original).

[40] *Ibid.*

Rather, the wording of the section makes clear that its primary purpose is to provide doctors with a defence to the criminal charge. Abortion is a highly charged moral issue. The 1967 Act occupies the middle ground. On the one hand, abortion is available, legally and safely, in certain circumstances; on the other, it is not provided on demand. As we have seen, there is a lack of clarity in some of the terminology used in the abortion legislation. Section 1(1)(d) of the 1967 Act has been particularly criticised in this respect.[41] This ought to be amended to tighten up the meanings of "serious handicap" and "substantial risk". As Rosamund Scott has said:

> "As for our perceptions about the seriousness of an impairment a prospective child would have, there is a need for better information in prenatal screening practices, in particular that which includes the views of those who live with certain impairments or disabilities. Consideration of such views will likely expose, though not necessarily expunge, presumptions about suffering. At the same time, it will lead to more open reflection about whose interests may be most at stake when we reflect on the legality of abortion in cases where a child would have an impairment the seriousness of which is a matter of reasonable disagreement."[42]

9.7   INFANTICIDE?

Where a baby is harmed at birth, at issue is the question of whether **9.7.1** or not the child has lived and breathed unaided. The authorities on this are contradictory. In *HM Advocate* v *Jean (or Jane) McAllum*,[43] the court stated expressly that only a "living child" could be the victim of murder.

> "As to what is a living child, there is no difficulty about the law. A child that is not fully born has no separate existence from the mother, and is not, in the eye of the law, a living human being. It is in a state of transition from a *foetus in utero* to a living human being, and it does not become a living human being until it is fully born, and has a separate existence of its own."[44]

In this case, it was alleged that the child's mother had tied a ligature, apparently made from her garter, tightly around the child's neck at, or immediately after, birth. The Lord Justice-Clerk laboured the point that no question of murder could arise unless the child had been fully born. The medical evidence was inconclusive and a

---

[41] See, for example, S McGuinness, "Law, reproduction, and disability: fatally 'handicapped'"? (2013) 21 *Med Law Rev* 213.
[42] R Scott, "Interpreting the disability ground of the Abortion Act" 2005 64 *CLJ* 388 at 412 (footnote omitted).
[43] (1858) 3 Irv 187.
[44] *Ibid* at 199–200 per LJ-C Inglis.

verdict of not proven was returned. In contrast, in *HM Advocate* v *Elizabeth Scott*[45] Lord Young's view was that

> "in the death of a child which has both cried and breathed [, i]t does not matter in the least, so far as the criminality of the accused is concerned if the injuries were inflicted when the child was partly in its mother's body".[46]

Here it was alleged that the accused had brought about the death of her new-born baby by compressing his throat.

9.7.2 Gordon's *Criminal Law*, following Macdonald,[47] prefers the latter view. In both types of case the accused's mental attitude, if proven, would be identical – the intention to destroy the child's life – hence it is submitted that the actual moment in the birthing process at which this is achieved should, generally, be irrelevant. Nonetheless, it is interesting to note that the jury acquitted the accused in both of these cases: in *McAllum*,[48] in response to Lord Inglis's assertion that they had to be convinced that the child had been fully born and in *Scott*,[49] apparently because they accepted that no blame attached to the accused, an option expressly put to them in the judge's charge. It is not surprising that this matter has received no consideration in the modern case law, given the relative lack of stigma which now surrounds extra-marital pregnancy, and the availability of lawful abortions.

9.7.3 In some jurisdictions, special rules govern the killing shortly after birth of a child by the child's mother. In Ireland, for example, the court has discretion in the sentencing of mothers who commit infanticide where the child is less than a year old, and

> "the balance of [the accused's] mind was disturbed by reason of her not having fully recovered from the effect of giving birth to the child or by reason of the effect of lactation consequent upon the birth of the child".[50]

There are few cases in which it could be said that the killing of a young child was due to mental imbalance caused by lactation[51] or the delivery process itself, and it might be preferable to subsume infanticide into manslaughter/culpable homicide provisions in these

---

[45] (1892) 3 White 240.
[46] *Ibid* at 244.
[47] Macdonald (1948), p 87.
[48] (1858) 3 Irv 187.
[49] (1892) 3 White 240.
[50] Infanticide Act 1949, s 1. See also the (English) Infanticide Act 1938, s 1(1), and the Canadian Criminal Code, s 233.
[51] Indeed, the law relating to infanticide in England and Wales has been described as "unsatisfactory and outdated" in *R v Kai-Whitewind* [2005] 2 Cr App R 31 (NB: case reports starts at p 457) at 484 per Judge LJ.

jurisdictions.[52] In England, the Criminal Law Revision Committee has recommended that the crime be defined to include consideration of environmental or other stresses on the mother.[53] As Peter Alldridge notes, "by having a separate category of infanticide, the law *creates* as much as reflects a whole series of attitudes towards the killing of young children by their mothers".[54] Scotland does not have a separate crime of infanticide, but it is possible that a mother who killed her young child may be able to demonstrate that hormonal imbalances or environmental stresses caused her to be of diminished responsibility.[55] While in practice it may be easier for mothers to prove this, Scots law does not discriminate against fathers in this respect.

9.8   DEATH FOLLOWING INJURIES RECEIVED *IN UTERO*

The question of the consequences of injury inflicted on a foetus *in   9.8.1 utero*, which causes its death shortly after birth, arose in *McCluskey* v *HM Advocate*.[56] The case concerned the statutory offence of causing death by reckless driving.[57] Here, the accused caused a road traffic accident in which a foetus of 35 weeks' gestation was injured in the womb. The baby was delivered by emergency Caesarean section but died shortly thereafter. The accused was convicted. The appeal court stated that there was no authority in Scots law to say that such facts, divorced from the road traffic context, could not constitute culpable homicide.[58] The issue has received slightly more analysis in English law, where it was determined that the fact that the foetus was not living independently at the time of the relevant attack was not a bar to a subsequent prosecution for manslaughter where the baby was born alive but died as a result of the injuries sustained *in utero*. The House of Lords simply applied the principles of the crimes of murder and manslaughter: the defendant had intentionally stabbed the mother, and reasonable

---

[52] R D Mackay, "The consequences of killing very young children" [1993] *Crim LR* 21.
[53] CLRC 14th Report on *Offences Against the Person* (1980), p 103. See also the English Draft Criminal Code Bill, cl 64(1).
[54] P Alldridge, *Relocating Criminal Law* (2000), p 12 (emphasis in original).
[55] Diminished responsibility is discussed from section 20.10 below.
[56] 1989 SLT 175.
[57] Road Traffic Act 1972, s 1, as substituted by the Criminal Law Act 1977, s 50(1). The relevant charge would now be causing death by dangerous driving under the Road Traffic Act 1988, s 1, as substituted by the Road Traffic Act 1991, s 1.
[58] *McCluskey* v *HM Advocate* 1989 SLT 175 at 176–177. But note that the case expressly provides that this does not amount to a positive statement that a charge of culpable homicide *would* lie in these circumstances.

people would have realised that harm would result to the baby. These facts were sufficient to bring the matter within the ambit of the crime of "manslaughter from an unlawful and dangerous act".[59]

9.9   END-OF-LIFE ISSUES

9.9.1   For the criminal law, the corollary of the question "When does life begin?" ought to be "When does life end?" but the only point of real significance in relation to homicide is that death has, in fact, occurred. Accordingly, no principles exist on the timing of the end of life and it is submitted that, if it assumed importance in specific circumstances, the moment at which life ends would be deemed a question of fact in every case. This is not to say that the law on criminal homicide has never been confronted with any "end-of-life" issues, and some of these will now be considered.

9.9.2   The first point to note is that the length of the period between an initial assault and the death is of no consequence, provided causation can be established. A homicide charge remains competent no matter how long after the initial attack the death occurs. The principle that formerly operated in England, such that there was a conclusive presumption that a death which occurred more than a year and one day after the initial assault could not have been caused by that assault,[60] has never applied in Scotland. Conviction of assault *and* homicide arising out of the same incident is, therefore, possible. The conclusion can be drawn that murder and culpable homicide are not just forms of aggravated assault but crimes in their own right. In *Tees* v *HM Advocate*[61] the appellant had received a sentence of 7 years' imprisonment in July 1991, for the aggravated assault of his victim. Tees and another person had kicked the victim on the head and body, putting him into a coma. The victim died in October 1991 as a direct result of the injuries inflicted in that attack. It was held to be competent, at that point, for the Crown to charge the accused with culpable homicide because it was a separate crime from aggravated assault, even though both charges arose from the same incident.

9.9.3   It has been held that switching off a life-support machine does not constitute a *novus actus interveniens* between the accused's culpable act and the victim's death. In *Finlayson* v *HM Advocate*[62]

---

[59] *Re Attorney-General's Reference (No 3 of 1994)* [1998] AC 245.
[60] The principle was abolished in England by the Law Reform (Year and a Day Rule) Act 1996, s 1.
[61] 1994 JC 12.
[62] 1979 JC 33.

the accused had injected a noxious mixture of morphine and diazepam into the victim, which caused immediate brain death and would have caused heart failure had the victim not been placed on a life-support machine. The initial injection of the morphine mixture was done with the latter's consent, but the accused was nonetheless found guilty of culpable homicide, when the life-support machine was turned off, following discussion between the victim's parents and medical personnel.

Finally, it is competent to make an application under civil law to the Court of Session for permission to stop feeding and hydrating a person who is in a persistent vegetative state. This point arose in *Law Hospital NHS Trust* v *Lord Advocate*,[63] following which the Lord Advocate issued a policy statement to the effect that no prosecution would be authorised in such cases so long as medical practitioners had followed the guidelines set down there – more specifically where medical personnel have acted "in good faith and with the authority of the Court of Session".[64] **9.9.4**

9.10 MURDER AND CULPABLE HOMICIDE

"[I]n Scotland ... it is degrees of moral heinousness generally rather than intention specifically which police the line between murder and lesser killings."[65] **9.10.1**

As noted previously,[66] the *actus reus* of both murder and culpable homicide is causing the death of a human being other than the accused. This may be done by an overt act (for example, shooting, stabbing, suffocating, drowning, striking) or by an omission, if the accused was under a legal duty towards the victim,[67] as in the case of *Bone* v *HM Advocate*,[68] where a mother was charged with culpable homicide, partly for failing to protect her daughter from assaults carried out by the mother's partner.

The dividing line between murder and culpable homicide is the *mens rea*. In relation to all crimes, the purpose of *mens rea* is to attach blameworthiness to the wrongdoer. Thus, as we have seen,[69] one of the most basic maxims of the criminal law is *actus non* **9.10.2**

---

[63] 1996 SC 301.
[64] These are set out in full in the commentary to the case to be found at 1996 SCLR 518. See also section 6.7.3 above.
[65] W Wilson, *Central Issues in Criminal Theory* (2002), p 144.
[66] See section 9.3.1 above.
[67] See from section 6.5.1 above.
[68] 2006 SLT 164.
[69] See Chapter 6 above.

facit reum nisi mens sit rea[70] – which can be translated to mean that "forbidden behaviour" is not criminal unless it is performed with the requisite mental state. The *mens rea* of murder, however, requires not only to fulfil this function but also to establish that the individual's conduct is so blameworthy that a conviction for culpable homicide would not reflect its gravity. In other words, the *mens rea* for murder has to do more work than that of other crimes. It must demonstrate not only that the accused is blameworthy in relation to the victim's death but also that she is *so* culpable that it is appropriate to place her crime in the higher category represented by murder (vis-à-vis culpable homicide). If the *mens rea* is *not* fulfilling this function then it must be questioned whether there is any point in having a separate crime called "murder", rather than a generic homicide offence. The *mens rea* is the dividing line but frequently it can only be established by inference from the facts. In this way, *actus reus* and *mens rea* are, to some extent, intertwined. Some acts causing death are so extreme that it is accepted, assuming proof that the accused carried these out, that the only possible verdict is murder. The mental element – intention to kill, which failing, wicked recklessness – is regarded as the necessary inference. This was the position in *Parr* v *HM Advocate*,[71] in which the accused assaulted his elderly mother with a hammer, inflicting around eight blows to the head. Similarly, in *Broadley* v *HM Advocate*[72] the accused stabbed the victim repeatedly on the head, throat and body, an act described as "an attack of great determination involving the use of a lethal weapon with which repeated blows were delivered upon the body of the victim".[73] If the act is equivocal, however, so that a verdict of culpable homicide is reasonably available on the evidence then it is the trial judge's responsibility to charge the jury to ensure that it is aware that it has the option of returning such a verdict. This was stated in *Ferguson* v *HM Advocate*[74] where death was caused by a single stab wound to the victim's back so deep that it almost penetrated to the front of his body. Of course, this calls for the exercise of judicial discretion. Both of the subsequent cases of *Anderson* v *HM Advocate*[75] and *Dearie* v *HM Advocate*[76] have indicated that the mere fact that death arose from a single stab wound is not, in itself, sufficient to require a specific direction on culpable

---

[70] See Gordon (2000), para 7.01.

[71] 1991 JC 39.

[72] 1991 JC 108.

[73] *Ibid* at 114, per LJ-C Ross.

[74] 2009 SLT 67.

[75] 2010 SCCR 270.

[76] 2011 SCCR 727.

homicide if this is not otherwise raised.[77] As ever, the criminal law is required to balance fairness to the accused with the public interest.

It is still not entirely clear whether culpable homicide and murder **9.10.3** are best viewed as being on a continuum, so that, once a particular level of seriousness is reached, the crime becomes categorised as murder, or whether they are, definitively, two separate crimes. This issue may turn on the tightness of the definition of the murder *mens rea*. In English law, for example, strenuous efforts have been made to identify the exact meaning of "intention to kill". The presence of such an intention, as rigidly so defined, renders the crime murder. Here, then, murder is a separate crime, committed only where its highly specific and, arguably, certain, definition, is satisfied. Until the case óf *HM Advocate* v *Purcell*,[78] Scots law had been regarded as more fluid in its deployment of the *mens rea* of wicked recklessness, so that categorisation as murder could arise because the jury deemed the accused deserving of it.[79] As will be discussed subsequently, this more flexible approach has benefits, though it does raise issues of fair labelling.[80] It also seems important that the *mens rea* for murder should, at least notionally, reflect the crime's additional blameworthiness to culpable homicide. Its principles will be examined on this basis.

9.11 MURDER

As Antony Duff makes clear, the harm caused in murder is not solely **9.11.1** that the victim suffers death:

> "Both the murder victim and the victim of natural causes suffer death: but the character of the harm that they suffer surely also depends on the way in which they die. One who tries to kill me ... *attacks* my life and my most basic rights; and the harm which I suffer in being murdered ... essentially involves this wrongful attack on me ... The 'harm' at which the law of murder is aimed is thus not just the *consequential* harm of death, but the harm which is *intrinsic* to an attack on another's life."[81]

Until the decision in the case of *Drury* v *HM Advocate*[82] in 2001, the accepted definition in Scots law was that of Macdonald:

---

[77] For a fuller discussion, see C McDiarmid, "Withholding culpable homicide: *Ferguson* v *HM Advocate*" (2009) 13 *Edin LR* 316.

[78] 2008 JC 131.

[79] See Gordon (2001), para 23.21.

[80] See from section 4.6 above.

[81] R A Duff, *Intention, Agency and Criminal Liability* (1990), pp 112–113 (emphases in original).

[82] 2001 SLT 1013. This case involved a plea of provocation, and is described in more detail in section 21.10.11 below.

> "Murder is constituted by any wilful act causing the destruction of life, whether intended to kill, or displaying such wicked recklessness as to imply a disposition depraved enough to be regardless of consequences".[83]

This made clear that it was murder if the accused either (a) intended to cause death, or (b) reached the point of being indifferent to whether the victim lived or died. In the latter case, the accused was said to have the *mens rea* of "wicked recklessness".[84] However, the five-judge Bench in *Drury* held that murder required a *wicked* intention to kill: Macdonald's definition was described by Lord Justice-General Rodger as "somewhat elliptical"[85] because it did not describe the relevant intention. He continued: "In truth, just as the recklessness has to be wicked so also must the intention be wicked."[86] *Drury*'s case involved an allegation of provocation – a factor which is recognised as being capable of exculpating for murder, leading to a conviction for culpable homicide, instead.[87] Thus Lord Rodger concluded that "the person who kills under provocation is to be convicted of culpable homicide rather than of murder because, even if he intentionally kills his victim, he does not have that wicked intention which is required for murder".[88] According to the Lord Justice-General:

> "In this case, the question for the jury was whether the Crown had proved beyond a reasonable doubt that the appellant had acted with the necessary mens rea for murder. If so, the jury would convict him of murder. If not, they would convict him of culpable homicide. In reaching their conclusion the jury had, of course, to draw inferences from all the relevant evidence, including the appellant's evidence relating to provocation. In effect, that evidence was simply one of the factors – the principal factor, perhaps – upon which the defence invited the jury to infer that the appellant had not had either the wicked intention to kill the deceased or the necessary wickedly reckless indifference as to whether she lived or died, to justify a conviction of murder. Rather, taking all the relevant factors into account, they should conclude *that his action, though culpable, was not wicked* or, at least, that they had a reasonable doubt as to whether it was wicked: they should therefore convict him of culpable homicide."[89]

9.11.2 What does it mean to say that the intention to kill must be shown to have been a "wicked" one? It does not mean that the killing must be premeditated; this has not been a prerequisite since at

---

[83] Macdonald (1948), p 89.

[84] Wicked recklessness is described in more detail from section 9.12 below.

[85] 2001 SLT 1013 at 1016.

[86] *Ibid*. See also the case of *HM Advocate v Purcell* 2008 JC 131: "the definition is now usually qualified by the insertion of the adverb 'wickedly' before 'intended'" (*ibid* at para 9 per Lord Eassie).

[87] Provocation is discussed further from section 21.10 below.

[88] 2001 SLT 1013 at 1019, para 20.

[89] *Ibid* at 1018, para 18 (emphasis added).

least 1867[90] and *Drury*[91] does not change this. It remains sufficient to satisfy the "intention" arm of the definition that the accused intended to kill the victim *at the time when the attack took place.* Lord Rodger may have meant only that the Crown requires to prove intent to kill, and that this is "wicked" if there are no mitigating factors, such as provocation, preventing it from being murder.[92] Some support for this view may be obtained from the case of *Elsherkisi v HM Advocate*,[93] where, in interpreting Hume,[94] Lord Hardie stated:

> "Properly understood the passage at p 254 of Hume is designed to emphasise that, where a homicide follows upon an intention to kill, the necessary wickedness of the intention can be implied in the absence of any other circumstances which would justify or mitigate the actions of the accused in killing his victim."[95]

Nevertheless the decision in *Drury* has caused some confusion and there is little doubt in the minds of academic commentators that it constituted a change to the pre-existing *mens rea* for murder – and one which muddied the waters of its basic requirements.[96] This is somewhat ironic, given that the judgments in *Drury* suggest that the appeal court's reformulation was intended to provide greater clarity. Lord Rodger stated, for example, that:

> "One cannot help feeling that some at least of the difficulties of the subject have arisen because provocation has sometimes tended to be treated as an isolated topic rather than in its proper place within [the] wider context [of the overall scheme of our law on murder and culpable homicide]."[97]

---

[90] *HM Advocate v Macdonald* (1867) 5 Irv 525 in which the accused had killed his wife by battering her to death. At that time, the penalty for murder was hanging. The jury attached to its decision a recommendation for mercy because there had been no premeditation. In clarifying the meaning of the jury's recommendation, the case separated out premeditation from intention and indicated that only intention is necessary.

[91] 2001 SLT 1013.

[92] The expression "wicked intent" had been used by the High Court on at least one previous occasion: see *Dean v John Menzies (Holdings) Ltd* 1981 JC 23 at 35, per Lord Stott. The courts have also used the expression "evil intention" to mean *mens rea*, generally. See, for example, *HM Advocate v Raiker* 1989 SCCR 149 (discussed also at section 21.2.5 below).

[93] 2011 SCCR 735.

[94] Hume, i, 254.

[95] *Elsherkisi v HM Advocate* 2011 SCCR 735 at 741–742, para [11].

[96] For example, see J Chalmers, "Collapsing the structure of criminal law" 2001 SLT 241; Leverick (2002); and the commentary on *Drury* by Gerald Gordon in 2001 SCCR 583. In his commentary to *Ferguson v HM Advocate* 2009 SCCR 78, Gordon refers to "what many of us regard as the unfortunate addition of 'wicked' to the definition of intentional murder in *Drury*" (at 92).

[97] *Drury v HM Advocate* 2001 SLT 1013 at 1016.

Similarly, Lord Nimmo Smith's view was that in cases "where the mens rea of the accused is put in issue the [pre-existing] definition is incomplete and to that extent misleading".[98]

9.11.3   What, then, are the difficulties perceived by academic commentators, in the face of this judicial endorsement of the need for the intention to be wicked? First, and most cogently, James Chalmers has suggested that altering the definition in this way threatens to collapse the definitional structure of the law.[99] As we have seen, the basic pattern of Scots criminal law is, in general, to define a crime in terms of *actus reus* and *mens rea*. Defences have their own definitions which, at least in these classificatory terms, come into play subsequent to, and independently of, the definitions of the crimes. The appeal court's criticism of Macdonald's definition of "murder" was that it was incomplete and insufficient since it failed to take account of the role of the defences of provocation and self-defence. This is tantamount to using the exception (cases of murder where there is a valid defence) as the standard by which to set the overarching rule (that murder has specific and unchanging mental and behavioural elements). While the effect of certain defences (namely automatism[100] and coercion[101]) has been a finding that the accused did not have the *mens rea* for the crime in the first place, there has never been any suggestion that the definitions of the crimes in relation to which these defences were pled were deficient because they did not take account of the possibility that these defences could be used. Provocation has a certain uniqueness, in that it can only be pled in relation to murder,[102] but this does not apply to self-defence, which is also considered in the judgments in *Drury*.[103] Chalmers's view is that the invocation of "wickedness" refers to "the absence of any applicable justification or excuse".[104] This is echoed by Gerald Gordon, who concluded that "what the court has done has been to incorporate the defences to the crime of murder into the definition of the crime by using the word 'wicked' as a shorthand for all of them".[105]

---

[98] *Drury* v *HM Advocate* 2001 SLT 1013 at 1030.
[99] Chalmers (2001).
[100] *Ross* v *HM Advocate* 1991 JC 210.
[101] In *HM Advocate* v *Raiker* 1989 SCCR 149 the view that coercion negates *mens rea* was expressed at first instance, in the trial judge's charge to the jury, but this has been criticised: see J Chalmers and F Leverick, *Criminal Defences and Pleas in Bar of Trial* (2006) at para 5.04.
[102] It can also be pled in assault cases, but only in mitigation, not in relation to responsibility for the crime itself.
[103] 2001 SLT 1013.
[104] Chalmers (2001) at 242.
[105] Commentary on *Drury* v *HM Advocate* 2001 SCCR 583 at 618–619, para 2.

Why was this necessary? At one level, it might seem that adding   **9.11.4**
a "wickedness" requirement assists in ensuring that the *mens rea*
of murder delivers the "added blameworthiness" which is required
to differentiate it from culpable homicide. Unfortunately, however,
it is difficult to reduce the criminal law to a mathematical formula
such that, if recklessness requires wickedness so also must intention
if they are to equate.[106] As will be discussed subsequently,[107] the
term "wicked recklessness" has been given content through its
interpretation by the courts. If "wicked intention" is to mean
something other than "intention to kill", this too needs to be filled
in by the appeal court. Moreover, the term "wicked" was chosen for
its fit with the historical position in Scots criminal law; Lord Rodger
stated that he

> "would not think it right to accord to [Hume and Alison's] writings any
> superstitious reverence which left no room for evaluating their exposition of
> the law in the light of later experience, later developments or more modern
> analysis".[108]

yet his judgement seeks continuity between the views of these
institutional writers and the current law.

There are several difficulties with this. First, the concept of   **9.11.5**
"wickedness" applied by Hume on a generalised basis in the form
of dole cannot simply be translated into the 21st-century context
and, particularly, not slotted into the *mens rea* of any specific crime.
As previously noted, Hume defined dole as "that corrupt and evil
intention, which is essential ... to the guilt of any crime".[109] He
expanded on this by stating "that the act must be attended with
such circumstances, as indicate a corrupt and malignant disposition,
a heart contemptuous of order, and regardless of social duty".[110] In
modern Scots criminal law, the proscribed behaviour for a particular
crime must be accompanied by a specific mental element, unique
to each offence. Even in Alison's time in the early 19th century,
a definitional framework in terms of a behavioural element and
accompanying mental state was apparent.[111] In contrast, for Hume,
and Mackenzie before him, the purpose, and proof, of the mental
element was all but turned on its head. Dole was a wickedness of
character which suffused the accused. The issue for proof was not,

---

[106] As Chalmers points out, the case of *Scott v HM Advocate* 1996 JC 1 had
previously indicated that any such endeavour was futile (Chalmers (2001) at 242).
[107] See from section 9.12 below.
[108] LJ-G Rodger in *Drury* at 1016. The reference to Alison is to his *Principles of the
Criminal Law of Scotland* (1832).
[109] Hume, i, 21. See also section 6.9.1 above.
[110] Hume, i, 22.
[111] Alison (1832).

as a contemporary criminal lawyer would expect: "Can the Crown prove beyond reasonable doubt that the accused's attitude to the criminal act matches the elements of the *mens rea* set down in the crime's definition?" Rather, it amounted to a view that only a thoroughly wicked person would carry out the relevant criminal act, and looked to the accused to disprove this, if she could.[112]

9.11.6   It has been a particular criticism of the change in the *mens rea* wrought by *Drury*[113] that the word "wicked" does not convey much to members of a modern jury.[114] The use of the term is arguably not even in keeping with Hume's approach because it has been taken by itself, shorn of the context and purpose which it served in his day. While it is clearly the case that Hume looked for wickedness as a prerequisite of conviction for any criminal charge, it is not self-evident that the idea of a thoroughly wicked character can, or should, be added into the *mens rea* – a specific and subjective attitude – for any crime, let alone murder. It could be argued that "wicked recklessness", the alternative *mens rea* for murder, has incorporated a shadowy form of dole into the modern law but it is submitted that it is not the use of the word "wicked" which achieves this but, rather, the rest of Macdonald's extended definition – "a disposition depraved enough to be regardless of consequences". In any event, as will be discussed below, "wicked recklessness" has come to have a particular technical definition. It can be argued that the term "wicked" in that context serves primarily to indicate that the *mens rea* required for murder is different from the "recklessness" of other crimes of recklessness committed against the person, such as "involuntary lawful act culpable homicide", and "culpably and recklessly endangering the lieges". In fact, the only crimes in relation to which the addition of the word "wicked" may provide assistance are so-called "mercy killings" where the accused clearly *does* intend to kill, but for benign reasons.[115]

9.11.7   Murder and culpable homicide are separated only by their respective forms of *mens rea*. That line should be drawn not by reference to a judgement on the underlying character of the accused but by the blameworthiness to be attached to the offence. In *technical* terms, "wicked intention" may simply mean an intention

[112] Thus, in Hume's view, there was a particular difficulty in holding young children responsible for criminal offences because their characters were unlikely to be sufficiently settled to allow an automatic inference of dole to be drawn from their acts (Hume, i, 30).
[113] 2001 SLT 1013.
[114] See Gordon (2001), para 23.13.
[115] See M G A Christie, "The coherence of Scots criminal law: some aspects of *Drury v HM Advocate*" (2002) *Jur Rev* 273 at 283–284. Euthanasia is discussed further from section 9.20 below.

to kill when neither provoked nor acting in self-defence; in *historical* terms, the transposition of the term "wicked" is too anachronistic to be "slotted into" a modern definition of the mental element, and in terms of *clarity*, the word "wicked" is imprecise and there is difficulty in tying down its meaning. If this is so, then the appeal court's redefinition is less than helpful.

9.12 "WICKED RECKLESSNESS"

What, then, of the "wicked recklessness" strand of the *mens rea* of murder? That this constitutes a separate and alternative *mens rea* was determined in *Cawthorne* v *HM Advocate*.[116] In that case, the accused fired a high-velocity rifle into a room where he knew that four people had retreated to take refuge from him. He made no attempt to mitigate the danger but fired five shots at a height where he might reasonably have been expected to cause serious injury. It was held that the *mens rea* of murder (or, in this specific case, attempted murder) could be proved by evidence of a deliberate intention to kill *or* by such recklessness as to show that the accused was regardless of the consequences of his actions – in other words, that he was completely indifferent as to whether death resulted from his actions. In the context of attempted murder, this was of particular importance, a view having been put forward strongly by defence counsel that the Crown had to prove intention to kill before a conviction for attempted murder could be returned.[117] This argument was rejected by the court and *Cawthorne* is now a clear precedent both that the *mens rea* of a criminal attempt is exactly the same as that for the completed crime and that wicked recklessness is a separate and sufficient form of the *means rea* of murder.

It is fair to say that, as a *mens rea* for murder, wicked recklessness has been defined in a way which gives it more content than "wicked intention" currently has. It is, however, important not to lose sight of the view expressed in Gordon's *Criminal Law* that the work done by the term "wicked" in this context is primarily to allow flexibility, so that juries can convict of murder only those who morally seem to deserve this.[118] The essence of the modern understanding of the term is to be found in Alison's definition of the crime. He stated:

9.12.1

9.12.2

---

[116] 1968 JC 32.
[117] *Ibid* at 34–35. As a point of principle, the view that intention to commit the crime ought to be a prerequisite of the *mens rea* of a criminal attempt is held by some commentators – for a discussion, see, for instance, V Tadros, *Criminal Responsibility* (2005), p 234.
[118] Gordon (2001), para 23.21.

"Murder, the greatest crime known in the law, consists in the act which produces death, in consequence either of a deliberate intention to kill, or to inflict a minor injury of such a kind as indicates *an utter recklessness as to the life of the sufferer, whether he live or die.*"[119]

9.12.3   Gordon describes "wicked recklessness" as recklessness which is "so gross that it indicates a state of mind which falls to be treated as being as wicked and depraved as the state of mind of a deliberate killer".[120] We can envisage the situation where A is repeatedly stabbing B, or perhaps kicking and punching B on the head. A does not intend to kill B, but if one were to say "Watch you don't go too far or you'll end up killing B", A might reply "So what?" or "Who cares? What if I do?". This attitude typifies the indifference to consequences encapsulated by the expression "wicked recklessness". Lord Goff of Chievely, at that time a judge in the English Court of Appeal, discussed the meaning of "wicked recklessness" in some depth in an article published in 1988.[121] He quoted the charge to the jury in the unreported case of *HM Advocate* v *Byfield* (1976) that, to constitute wicked recklessness, the accused had to be "totally regardless of the consequences, whether the victim lived or died".[122] More recently, in *Cowie* v *HM Advocate*,[123] the appeal court endorsed the trial judge's charge to the jury on wicked recklessness as follows:

"It is sufficient to say that the trial judge left the jury in no doubt that for the *mens rea* of murder there had to be either a deliberate intention to kill or wicked recklessness; *and that there was wicked recklessness where the conduct of the accused demonstrated that he did not care whether the victim lived or died.* ... The trial judge gave accurate directions on the point."[124]

Lord Goff argued that importation of such a concept into English law might resolve a number of difficult issues and, indeed, difficult cases in homicide with which the English courts have had to wrestle.[125]

---

[119] Alison (1832), p 1 (emphasis added).
[120] Gordon (2001), para 23.19. This description was endorsed by the appeal court at the first hearing of the appeal in *Petto* v *HM Advocate* 2009 SLT 509 at 512, para [14] per Lord Wheatley.
[121] R Goff, "The mental element in the crime of murder" (1988) *LQR* 30. Note, however, that his understanding of the concept is not supported by the definition of wicked recklessness presented in *HM Advocate* v *Purcell* 2008 JC 131. See P W Ferguson, "Wicked Recklessness" (2008) *Jur Rev* 1 at 8.
[122] Goff (1988) at 54.
[123] 2010 JC 51.
[124] *Ibid* at para [21] per LJ-C Gill (second emphasis added).
[125] Goff (1988) at 55–58. For a discussion of some of the English cases, see section 9.12.9 below. See also M C Kaveny, "Inferring intention from foresight" (2004) *LQR* 81 at 82 and 86.

Halliday v *HM Advocate*[126] is a good example of the appeal   **9.12.4**
court's approach to wicked recklessness in practice, making it
clear that what is sought is a display of utter indifference towards
the life of the victim. This is described in *Halliday* as "complete,
utter and wicked disregard of the consequences of [the] attack on
the deceased".[127] The only issue both at the trial and on appeal was
whether the killing amounted to murder or culpable homicide. The
deceased had been kicked by the appellants and left motionless. The
appellants moved away, shook hands, said what great brothers they
were, then returned and kicked the deceased again and stamped on
his head. They then put him in the recovery position and went home
and washed their clothes. Some time later, they returned to their
victim, were unable to find a pulse, and called an ambulance. It was
held that the evidence of what happened *after* the attack (leaving the
victim, and washing their clothes) could cast light on the appellants'
attitude at the time of the attack. Their actions tended to show
that they had been wickedly indifferent to the consequences of that
attack, and their convictions for murder were upheld on appeal.

If an accused has carried and used a lethal weapon in the killing,   **9.12.5**
this is likely to found an inference that there was a total disregard of
the consequences for the victim and that the accused was indifferent
as to whether death resulted. In *HM Advocate* v *McGuinness*,[128]
Lord Justice-Clerk Aitchison stated:

> "People who use knives and pokers and hatchets against a fellow citizen are
> not entitled to say 'we did not mean to kill,' if death results. If people resort
> to the use of deadly weapons of this kind, they are guilty of murder, whether
> or not they intended to kill."[129]

This cannot be taken as a blanket pronouncement that use of a
lethal weapon automatically transforms any killing into murder.
As Gordon has pointed out, the term "deadly weapon" is not
helpful because people can be killed by, for example, being kicked
to death (as in *Halliday*).[130] The issue is always, therefore, whether
there was wicked recklessness in relation to the particular set of
events charged. When the accused causes death during a robbery,
the Crown will generally charge murder, rather than culpable
homicide, as a matter of policy. It could be said that the very act
of attempting to rob – that is, to steal using personal violence or
threats of such violence – is in itself wickedly reckless. We have

[126]   1999 SLT 485.
[127]   *Ibid* at 487, per LJ-G Rodger.
[128]   1937 JC 37.
[129]   *Ibid* at 40.
[130]   Gordon (2001), para 23.23.

already looked at the case of *HM Advocate* v *Fraser and Rollins*,[131] in relation to art and part liability. Here, a woman enticed the victim into a park where her two associates attacked, robbed and killed him. Lord Sands stated:

"If a person attempts a crime of serious violence, although his object may not be murder, and if the result of that violence is death, then the jury are bound to convict of murder."[132]

It is now clear that, if this doctrine of "constructive malice" applies at all, an issue which is not free from doubt,[133] then it only applies to deaths occurring in the course of robbery.[134] If death occurs in the course of a different crime, this may be murder, but not necessarily so.

9.12.6   In English criminal law, the crime of murder requires an intention to kill or to cause "grievous bodily harm". This has led to considerable complexity in cases in which the accused appears to have had no such intention *per se*, but had, at the very least, embraced the possibility that death would result. As noted above, there is an ongoing debate[135] in Scots law concerning the provenance of the current requirement that the accused has to have intended to cause personal injury to the victim, as a necessary part of the wicked recklessness *mens rea*.[136] However, we would argue that, prior to *HM Advocate* v *Purcell*[137] (discussed further below), utter indifference as to the victim's life could have been regarded as enough in itself, no matter how it was manifested, without a definite intention either to kill or to cause bodily harm.[138] On this basis, then, Scots law could extricate itself from such issues, it being sufficient for the Crown to demonstrate that the accused showed this utter indifference as to whether the victim lived or died, whether or not bodily harm was actually *intended*. Thus Pearl Hyam, who set fire to the home of her ex-lover's new partner, killing two children, but who intended

---

[131] (1920) 2 SLT 77. See section 7.5.2 above.
[132] *Ibid* at 79.
[133] See Gordon (2001), para 23.28 for a discussion of relevant cases.
[134] In *Petto* v *HM Advocate* 2009 SLT 509, the appeal court stated: "That the doctrine of constructive malice has been discarded was confirmed by Lord Eassie in *HM Advocate* v *Purcell* ... , subject to a possible surviving trace in the case of death caused in the course of an assault and robbery" (at para 7 per Lord Wheatley).
[135] For an overview and discussion of the issues, see M Plaxton, "Foreseeing the consequences of *Purcell*" 2008 SLT 21.
[136] See section 9.1.3.
[137] 2008 JC 131.
[138] For statements of wicked recklessness which support this view, see, for example, *Scott* v *HM Advocate* 1996 JC 1 at 5 per LJ-C Ross; *Byrne* v *HM Advocate* 2000 JC 155 at 163 per Lord Coulsfield. See also from section 9.12.3 above.

only to frighten the occupants, would not have presented Scots law with the same level of difficulty as the English courts experienced in determining whether her crime was murder or manslaughter.[139]

However, this inherent flexibility, and the ability to follow blameworthiness which wicked recklessness in this form presented, has been called into question by the appeal court's decision in *HM Advocate* v *Purcell*.[140] In this case, a motorist knocked down a 10-year-old boy at a pedestrian crossing in Edinburgh, following a spree of extremely dangerous driving. The victim subsequently died from the injuries which he had sustained and the Crown sought to charge the accused with murder. Purcell had pulled on to the wrong side of the road to overtake traffic which had stopped in obedience to the pedestrian-crossing signal. This showed a "green man" for pedestrians (the victim was crossing in response to this) and, consequently, a red light for vehicles. The accused then made a chicane manoeuvre – driving diagonally through the crossing to avoid the cars stopped at the other side – in the course of which his car struck the child. Indicting for murder in such circumstances was an innovation on the part of the Crown, but from the point of view of the victim's family, fair labelling requirements might suggest that the callous disregard of public safety averred in the indictment *ought* to be regarded as "murder", rather than merely the statutory offence of "causing death by dangerous driving".[141]

9.12.7

The appeal court considered previous authorities on wicked recklessness and concluded that an accused's actions must have been intended to cause *some* personal injury before there could be a conviction for murder. Purcell's actions were not so intended, therefore only a charge of culpable homicide was appropriate.[142] The court explicitly followed the view expressed in Gordon's *Criminal Law* on *mens rea* in this area.[143] Perhaps more importantly, it proceeded on the assumption that Gordon's statement of the pre-existing (and long-standing) law of Scotland was correct on this point. The judgment has been welcomed by James Chalmers on this basis.[144] Peter Ferguson also regarded this interpretation of the law as a positive step, though he hinted that Gordon himself was responsible for the creation of the principle, in that it may well *not*

9.12.8

---

[139] *R* v *Hyam* [1975] AC 55.

[140] 2008 JC 131.

[141] Fair labelling is discussed from section 4.6 above, and the statutory offence of causing death by dangerous driving from section 9.24 below.

[142] The accused was ultimately convicted of culpable homicide and was sentenced to 12 years' imprisonment.

[143] *HM Advocate* v *Purcell* 2008 JC 131 at 141, para 16 per Lord Eassie.

[144] See "Criminal Letters" blog: http://criminalletters.blogspot.com/2007/11/murder-no-safety-in-numbers.html.

have been part of Scots law prior to the first edition of *Criminal Law*, in 1967.[145]

9.12.9   As Michael Plaxton has noted, albeit without conceding the point, if *Purcell*[146] does nothing more than present a clearer statement of the law as it has been for a number of decades, it may not have any practical consequences in its own right.[147] Nonetheless, it is at least possible to argue, as Plaxton does,[148] that the need for an intention to cause personal injury was controversial before *Purcell*. Accordingly, it is important to question the benefits of this requirement. First, it was perhaps unnecessary to be as prescriptive as this. One of the defence arguments in the case was that

> "it had been the accepted position in Scots law since at least the advent of the motorcar that reckless driving, however appalling, which resulted in death might found a charge of culpable homicide but not murder. (Plainly there could be cases of murder where the driver had deliberately driven the car at the victim, thus using the car as a weapon to assault the victim, but this was not alleged in the present case.)"[149]

This view is supported by Gordon.[150] The appeal court could, therefore, have found the murder charge oppressive simply on this basis. Second, the requirement of an intention to cause personal injury as a prerequisite of a finding of wicked recklessness can be questioned in its own right. In many cases it will not be difficult to satisfy this requirement – it would not have been in any doubt, for example, in *Halliday*[151] or in *Cowie*[152] (where the accused, *inter alia*, kicked, stamped on and stabbed the victim). However, there will always be cases at the margins, where the accused appears to show an utter indifference as to whether the victim lives or dies, without, necessarily, *intending* to cause injury. The "hard" cases with which English law has struggled in recent years – *Hyam*,[153] *Hancock and Shankland*,[154] *Nedrick*[155] and *Woollin*[156] – are examples of

---

[145] Ferguson (2008) at 5.
[146] 2008 JC 131.
[147] Plaxton (2008) at 22.
[148] *Ibid* at 23.
[149] 2008 JC 131 at para 5.
[150] (2001), para 23.17.
[151] 1999 SLT 485.
[152] 2010 JC 51.
[153] [1975] AC 55. See also section 9.12.6 above.
[154] [1985] 3 WLR 1014. Two striking miners pushed a block of concrete onto a motorway from an overhead bridge, into the path of a taxi carrying another miner to work. Their intention was merely to frighten and they expected the concrete to land in the middle lane, when the taxi was in the nearside lane.
[155] [1986] 1 WLR 1025. The defendant poured paraffin though the letter box of a house and set it alight, causing the death of a child. He had no intention to kill.
[156] [1998] 3 WLR 382. The appellant lost his temper and threw his 3-month-old baby onto a hard surface. He did not intend to kill.

this. Although all of these cases are concerned with the inference of intention *to kill*, each could equally be analysed similarly as to whether an intention to cause personal injury can be discerned.

The judges in *Purcell*[157] seem to have been influenced by the   **9.12.10** Crown's inability to differentiate the recklessness required to constitute the *mens rea* of involuntary, lawful act culpable homicide from the *wicked* recklessness required for murder. In delivering the judgment of the court, Lord Eassie stated:

> "Indeed, when asked how the jury could meaningfully and usefully be directed by the presiding judge as to the distinction between 'utter disregard' for culpable homicide purposes and 'wicked recklessness amounting to utter disregard' for murder purposes the Advocate-depute was at some very evident difficulty in providing any answer."[158]

In fact, however, it is submitted that there *is* a clear distinction between the *mens rea* of "recklessness" for crimes other than murder,[159] and murder's "wicked recklessness". The "utter indifference" required in murder is as to the victim's life. The accused, in colloquial terms, could not care less whether the victim lives or dies. Other crimes of recklessness, including culpable homicide, do not prioritise the accused's approach to the risk *of death* which she creates. Unacceptable risk-taking in relation to the consequences more generally will be sufficient. Of course, this is always related to the circumstances of the individual case.

Following *Purcell*, Scots law has continued to wrestle with the role   **9.12.11** of an intention to cause personal injury in wicked recklessness, most notably in the case of *Petto* v *HM Advocate*.[160] Here, the accused had killed a man named Arthur Rawlinson by stabbing him. He pled guilty to a charge of culpable homicide in that respect. Following this killing, Petto had formulated a plan to dispose of the body by burning it. With three others, he had obtained a quantity of petrol and poured it throughout the flat, situated on the ground floor of a tenement in Glasgow, where the body lay. They then ignited the petrol, causing an explosion and a subsequent fire which affected the whole building. The resident of an upstairs flat, Myra Donachie, was killed in the blaze. Petto initially pled guilty to her murder. Subsequently, he sought to withdraw this plea on the basis that he did not satisfy the *mens rea* of wicked recklessness as set down in

---

[157] 2008 JC 131.
[158] *Ibid* at 139, para 12.
[159] As defined in *Paton* v *HM Advocate* 1936 JC 19, and refined in *Transco plc* v *HM Advocate (No 1)* 2004 JC 29. This is discussed further in section 13.6.2 below.
[160] 2009 SLT 509: a three-judge Bench which, on the basis of lack of authority for the view which it had taken on this aspect of wicked recklessness, referred the matter to a larger court (at 513, para [16] per Lord Wheatley). This second (procedural) hearing (before five judges) is reported at 2012 JC 105.

Purcell,[161] in particular, that there had been no intention to cause Mrs Donachie any injury.

9.12.12   Here, then, would appear to be a perfect test case for the issue of the need for an intention to cause personal injury (or not) as a constituent element of wicked recklessness.[162] It had long been accepted in Scots law that causing death by wilful fire-raising constituted murder;[163] Petto's initial plea of guilty suggests that he accepted that his conduct was sufficiently blameworthy to be so labelled. On the other hand, if we are to focus on Petto's actual intentions, as far as these are discernible, then it appears that these extended to burning a dead body, and to burning the property in which that corpse was situated. He had no intention to cause personal injury to anyone. He did, however, know when he ignited the fire that other flats in the building were likely to be occupied. On the face of it, this is insufficient. As adopted by the appeal court in *Purcell*,[164] Gordon's definition of wicked recklessness requires "an act intended to cause physical injury and displaying a wicked disregard of fatal consequences".[165] Petto may have known that there was a very strong likelihood that his act would cause physical injury to an unknown person. At least in ordinary parlance, this is not the same as "intending" that outcome.

9.12.13   In the event, and rather disappointingly, the five-judge decision in *Petto* turns on the circumstances in which it is acceptable to withdraw a guilty plea.[166] Such circumstances were not present in this case. In relation to the meaning of "wicked recklessness", Lord Justice-Clerk Gill ultimately states that

> "a comprehensive re-examination of the mental element in homicide is long overdue [but t]hat is not the sort of exercise that should be done by *ad hoc* decisions of this court in fact-specific appeals. It is pre-eminently an exercise to be carried out by the normal processes of law reform".[167]

9.12.14   Beyond this, we have only *obiter* statements though these indicate the difficulty of defining intention for these purposes.[168] Lord Justice-Clerk Gill expresses, as his own opinion, that since a person

---

[161] *HM Advocate* v *Purcell* 2008 JC 131.
[162] For a full discussion, see C McDiarmid, "'Something wicked this way comes': the *mens rea* of murder in Scots law" 2012 *Jur Rev* 283.
[163] See *Petto* v *HM Advocate* 2012 JC 105 at 109–110, paras [15]–[17] per LJ-C Gill for a summary of the views of historical writers (Hume, Alison, Burnett and Macdonald).
[164] 2008 JC 131 at 141 para [16] per Lord Eassie.
[165] Gordon (2001), para 23.33.
[166] *Petto* v *HM Advocate* 2012 JC 105 at 108–109, para [10] per LJ-C Gill; at 112, para [26] per Lord Eassie and at 113, para [30] per Lord Carloway.
[167] *Ibid* at 112, para [22].
[168] See sections 9.12.6 and 9.12.9 above.

who sets fire to a tenement building must have an "appreciation of the virtual certainty" that "a risk [of death or serious injury] will eventuate [then] ... his deliberate acceptance of it should ... be rightly equiparated with an intention that such consequences should occur".[169] Lord Eassie states that Petto "must be held to have had foresight of the virtual certainty, or obviousness, of the adverse consequences of that wilful fire-setting activity for the safety of those known by him to be in the tenement building".[170] "Virtual certainty" is the concept utilised by English law in instructing a jury in a murder trial where a simple instruction on intention to kill or intention to cause serious bodily injury does not meet the circumstances of the case.[171] Provided that the defendant appreciated this virtual certainty, it can equate to – or constitute – the necessary intention. In Scots law, wicked recklessness stands as an alternative to (wicked) intention to kill.[172] Incorporating the "virtual certainty" formulation threatens to elide the distinction between the two forms of the *mens rea* of murder.[173]

It is notable that, in the subsequent case of *Scott* v *HM Advocate*,[174]   **9.12.15** the appeal court placed some emphasis on the need for the, more broadly stated, concept of a "wilful act" rather than, specifically, an intention to cause physical injury. Lord Bonomy stated:

> "The solicitor advocate for the appellant recognised that, if ... the jury had acquitted the appellant of assault, the jury would still have had to address the question whether murder had been proved or the conviction should be for culpable homicide. As was fully explained in the recent Full Bench case of Petto v HM Advocate, a *wilful act* such as injecting another with heroin can amount to murder as long as it is shown to be committed with intent to kill or with such a degree of wicked recklessness as to amount to reckless indifference to the consequences."[175]

While there was no doubt that the initial act of the accused in *Scott* amounted to an assault[176] and therefore, by definition, incorporated an intention to cause physical injury, this was less clear in *Petto*, on which *Scott* relies in explaining its use of the term "wilful act". There is also the suggestion that, even if there was no assault as such, a murder conviction would be competent provided that there was a wilful act carried out with wicked recklessness.

---

[169] *Petto* v *HM Advocate* 2012 JC 105 at 109, para [13].
[170] *Ibid* at 112–113, para [28].
[171] *R* v *Woollin* [1999] 1 AC 82 at 94 per Lord Steyn.
[172] *Cawthorne* v *HM Advocate* 1968 JC 32. See section 9.12.1 above.
[173] See McDiarmid (2012) at 296–297.
[174] 2012 SCL 153.
[175] *Ibid* at 159, para [18] (emphasis added).
[176] Scott injected the victim, who was not a drug user, with a quantity of heroin from a batch which he knew to be of a higher than normal strength.

9.13   *DOLUS EVENTUALIS*

9.13.1   Perhaps light can be shed on this in a normative sense by reference to the concept of *dolus eventualis* discussed by George Fletcher in relation to the scope of intention.[177] In the context of homicide, *dolus eventualis* requires that the accused, in some way, embraced the possibility that death might result from her actions. Fletcher gives the example of the rapist who puts his hand over his victim's mouth "with indifference to her fate" and she suffocates.[178] According to Fletcher, in the German and the former Soviet legal systems, which employ this concept, this would amount to an intentional killing. In systems with a more narrowly drawn definition of intention, it would not. To hold the rapist liable for murder in these other systems would come close to enshrining the felony murder rule (similar to constructive malice).[179] That rule holds that where the accused is involved in the commission of *any* other (serious) crime and death results, that death should be treated as murder. It has fallen into disuse in both Scottish and English law.[180]

9.13.2   *Dolus eventualis* may, however, give a clearer indication of the level of fault which wicked recklessness seeks to encapsulate. The accused who accepts that her actions might cause death, and is comfortable with that, whether or not she intends death or personal injury, has done enough to meet the *mens rea* for murder. In "pure" *dolus eventualis* systems, such as Germany, this in itself would suffice. Fletcher considers it in terms of "the lust for death compensat[ing] for a low risk of harm".[181] In Scotland, the need for "utter indifference" as to the victim's life almost certainly means that this would have to be combined with a high level of risk-taking. Indeed, we may be able to see some indication of a move in this direction. As already noted, in *Petto*, Lord Justice-Clerk Gill makes reference to the accused's "appreciation of the virtual certainty that ... a risk [of death or serious injury] will eventuate and his deliberate acceptance of it".[182] While this comment relates specifically to the circumstances of *Petto*, it overtly imports an element of subjectivity into that determination of wicked recklessness in its insistence on a "deliberate acceptance of" such a very serious risk.

9.13.3   There may be a difficulty in marrying the subjective question of the accused's attitude to the possibility of death, with an objective

---

[177] G P Fletcher, *Rethinking Criminal Law* (2000), pp 445–449.

[178] *Ibid*, p 447.

[179] See section 9.12.5 above.

[180] But note that the causing of death in the course of a robbery is often treated by the Crown as murder, which comes close to a felony murder rule: see section 9.12.5 above.

[181] Fletcher (2000) at p 448.

[182] *Petto* v *HM Advocate* 2012 JC 105 at 109, para [13].

assessment of the nature of the risk which the accused created. Gordon suggests that the decision as to whether an accused displayed wicked recklessness

> "depends on a moral judgement which, so far as capital murder was concerned, and the law grew up when all murders were capital, could be summed up in the question: 'Does A deserve hanging?'"[183]

Now that the death penalty is no longer competent, a more apposite question might be whether A deserves to be branded a murderer and sentenced to life imprisonment. The concept of "wicked recklessness" may work quite effectively in answering this question.

9.14 CRITIQUE OF THE LAW ON MURDER AND PROPOSALS FOR REFORM

There is, undoubtedly, an issue as to whether anything other than an intention to kill *ought* to be sufficient to constitute the *mens rea* of murder. The (English) Law Commission ultimately answered that question by dividing murder into two categories of seriousness.[184] "First degree murder" would require such an intention or intent to do serious injury in the awareness of a serious risk of causing death. "Second degree murder" would include killing with an intention to cause serious bodily harm, killing through intention to cause injury or fear or risk of injury in the awareness of a serious risk of causing death, and killing where there is a partial defence available, such as provocation. Thus, an intention to kill separates off the most serious crime, yet several other forms of killing are still labelled as murder, including those which would not previously have so ranked. **9.14.1**

The *Draft Criminal Code* defines the *mens rea* of murder without using "wicked intent" or "wicked recklessness". Under the *Code's* provisions, murder requires intention to cause death, or "callous recklessness" as to whether death is caused.[185] "Callous recklessness" is intended to suggest an extreme disregard for human life. There is a strong element of objectivity; a person who *ought to* have foreseen that her behaviour could prove fatal will, *prima facie*, have satisfied the *mens rea* for murder, but the term does not necessarily exclude recognition of some level of (subjective) acceptance of the risk of death. The matter would turn on the court's interpretation. The *Code* also proposes a change in the penalty on conviction for murder: "life imprisonment" becomes the maximum, rather than the mandatory, **9.14.2**

---

[183] Gordon (2001), para 23.21.
[184] Law Commission (2006), particularly paras 2.23–2.116.
[185] *Draft Criminal Code*, s 37.

penalty.[186] If the mandatory penalty for murder were abolished, many of the law's problems with determining how to distinguish between murder and culpable homicide would be greatly reduced.[187] It should be noted that some differentiation is currently possible *within* the mandatory life sentence in that the court must set a "punishment part"[188] of the life sentence for individuals convicted of murder. This constitutes "such part as the court considers appropriate to satisfy the requirements for retribution and deterrence".[189] The life prisoner will not be considered for parole until this part of the sentence has expired. Nonetheless, and however short this tariff, the sentence will always be a custodial one. It also remains the case that whenever a life prisoner is released, that release will be on life licence, thereby subjecting the individual to a heightened level of state surveillance for the rest of her life.[190]

9.15   CULPABLE HOMICIDE

9.15.1   Culpable homicide is often defined in terms of what it is not: it is the causing of death in circumstances which, though blameworthy, fall short of the degree of disapprobation required for murder. Clearly, there is a moral judgement being made when a jury has to determine whether the accused is guilty of murder or the lesser crime of culpable homicide. All those convicted of murder are sentenced to life imprisonment. The sentence for culpable homicide is much more flexible, as was shown by the case of Paul Brady who pled guilty to the culpable homicide of his brother, but was admonished (that is, given a warning, only).[191] It is the appropriate charge for killings which are neither accidental nor justifiable, but which are not sufficiently

---

[186] *Draft Criminal Code*, s 37, Sch 1, Pt 1, and s 36. The abolition of the mandatory sentence for murder was also recommended by the Nathan Committee, HL Paper 78-1 (1989).

[187] Jeremy Horder has argued that abolition of the mandatory penalty would allow provocation in murder cases to be a matter of mitigation in sentence: *Provocation and Responsibility* (1992), p 197. The mandatory sentence has been referred to as "[p]erhaps the key issue in debates on homicide": G Maher, "'The most heinous of all crimes': reflections on the structure of homicide in Scots law" in J Chalmers, F Leverick and L Farmer (eds), *Essays in Criminal Law in Honour of Sir Gerald Gordon* (2010) 218 at p 229.

[188] Prisoners and Criminal Proceedings (Scotland) Act 1993, s 2(2).

[189] *Ibid.*

[190] See section 9.21.2 below.

[191] B Christie, "Man walks free in Scottish euthanasia case" (1996) 313 *BMJ* 961. The case is discussed further in section 9.16.5 below. Kenneth Edge, who pled guilty in April 2005 to the culpable homicide of his wife, was similarly admonished. The couple had been married for 50 years, and the accused had struggled to cope with his wife's dementia. See http://news.bbc.co.uk/1/hi/scotland/4498513.stm.

blameworthy to amount to murder. Assuming, therefore, that the
mens rea for murder is appropriately drawn, and that effective
mechanisms exist to determine when no blame whatsoever should
be ascribed in relation to a killing, culpable homicide should operate
to "catch" all other deaths. In *Drury* v *HM Advocate*,[192] the Lord
Justice-General stated that it "covers the killing of human beings in
all circumstances, short of murder, where the criminal law attaches
a relevant measure of blame to the person who kills".[193] It can be
divided into "voluntary" and "involuntary" culpable homicide,
and this makes clearer the rationale behind its different forms, but
it should be noted that, in practice, the charge or conviction is for
culpable homicide, not for "voluntary" or "involuntary" culpable
homicide.

9.16 VOLUNTARY CULPABLE HOMICIDE

To understand the rationale behind voluntary culpable homicide it **9.16.1**
is important to appreciate that until 1965 a conviction for murder
automatically resulted in the death penalty. There were circumstances
in which a person had taken life, and was deserving of punishment,
but it was felt that the death penalty was not appropriate. Following
the case of *Drury* v *HM Advocate*,[194] however, it has become rather
more difficult to define this form of culpable homicide. Previously,
it was possible to state that it existed where the crime committed
would satisfy the definition of murder but, for some reason, it was
appropriate to "reduce" it to culpable homicide. In almost all cases,
the successful operation of the defence of either provocation or
diminished responsibility constituted the reason for the reduction.
Drury is itself an example of a killing in which the accused claimed to
have been provoked. Diminished responsibility is a mitigating factor
where the accused was suffering from mental impairment at the time
of the crime. This degree of mental impairment is less than full-blown
"mental disorder"[195] (a defence that results in an acquittal) but, as its
name suggests, is nonetheless regarded as being capable of lessening
the accused's criminal liability. Both pleas will be considered in more
detail later.[196] In "provocation" and "diminished responsibility"

---

[192] 2001 SLT 1013.

[193] *Ibid* at 1017.

[194] *Ibid*.

[195] Until June 2012, this defence was known as "insanity". See now the Criminal
Procedure (Scotland) Act 1995, s 51A, inserted by the Criminal Justice and
Licensing (Scotland) Act 2010, s 168.

[196] Provocation and diminished responsibility are discussed from sections 21.10
and 20.10 below, respectively. It is also theoretically possible that a successful
defence of necessity or coercion could have the same effect, although this has never

cases, the killings are "voluntary", that is, death was the intended outcome, but the mitigating factor means that the accused ought not to be equated with a murderer. In *Drury*, however, Lord Justice-General Rodger indicated that both the notion and the terminology of "reduction" were "essentially misleading", at least in relation to provocation.[197] According to Lord Rodger,

> "evidence relating to provocation is simply one of the factors which the jury should take into account in performing their general task of determining the accused's state of mind at the time when he killed his victim".[198]

On this analysis, then, provocation's only function is to assist in determining whether the accused had the *mens rea* necessary for murder. In other words, was there a *wicked* intention to kill rather than a simple intention so to do?

9.16.2   Even this apparently straightforward pronouncement merits further explanation. Where the accused has been provoked, it seems likely that her intention, fuelled by the anger invoked by the provoking act, will, at the time of the killing, be "wicked". It is only because provocation constitutes the criminal law's concession to "human frailty" that the accused is not to be convicted of murder. Provocation may render the accused less culpable, for reasons which will be examined subsequently, but it is submitted that it does not necessarily affect the "wickedness" of intention at the moment of killing. As already discussed, if it is "not wicked", this can only be because wickedness has been circularly defined in this context as the absence of certain defences (namely, provocation and self-defence). In fact, in such circumstances, the intent of the accused, at the moment of killing, is surely to see the victim dead at all costs. At one level, then, provoked killings could be said to constitute the paradigm example of "wicked intention". Thus, it would have been altogether less complicated to adhere to the notion of "reduction" – as the then leading case on diminished responsibility – *Galbraith* v *HM Advocate*[199] – appears to have done. The judgement in that case states:

> "In our law diminished responsibility applies in cases where, because the accused's ability to determine and control his actings is impaired as a result of some mental abnormality, his responsibility for any killing can properly

---

been tested in the Scottish courts and, where such defences are used in relation to lesser crimes than murder, they usually afford a complete defence, leading to acquittal.

[197] 2001 SLT 1013 at 1018, para 17.

[198] *Ibid*.

[199] 2002 JC 1. Diminished responsibility is now a statutory defence: Criminal Procedure (Scotland) Act 1995, s 51B, as inserted by the Criminal Justice and Licensing (Scotland) Act 2010, s 168. See further section 20.10 below.

be regarded as correspondingly reduced. The accused should, accordingly, be convicted of culpable homicide rather than of murder."[200]

It is fair to say that *Drury*[201] has, at the very least, rendered voluntary culpable homicide a more nebulous concept than was previously the case. As with all homicide, its *actus reus* is the destruction of human life but its *mens rea* is not so easy to state. *Drury* addresses only the *mens rea* of murder; it says nothing about the mental element of culpable homicide. It would appear therefore that voluntary culpable homicide arises, by default rather than by virtue of clear judicial pronouncement, where there is intention to kill but that intention is not deemed to be "wicked". Since the need for wickedness to constitute the *mens rea* of murder applies generally,[202] not only in relation to provocation cases, it would appear that this principle – of intentional but not wickedly intentional killing constituting culpable homicide – must also apply generally. Thus, the successful operation of the defence of provocation is only one mechanism by which an intention to kill may be divested of its wickedness. Gordon states

> "The opinions in *Drury* may be read, ... , as suggesting that such wickedness as is required is not to be presumed even rebuttably from a proved or admitted intention to kill, but rather is to be considered independently in each case by the jury according to the whole of the relevant evidence and the jury's moral judgment of the accused's intentional conduct in the circumstances of the case."[203]

The question therefore arises as to whether a further unanticipated consequence of *Drury* has been the creation of a new, ill-defined defence to a murder charge of "absence of wickedness".[204] Of course this is not a defence as such – it is a failure of proof of an essential element of the crime.[205] Generally in such circumstances the accused would simply be acquitted. In relation to murder, however, the accused may instead be convicted of voluntary culpable homicide.

This issue was raised in the case of *Elsherkisi* v *HM Advocate*[206] where the court was dismissive, stating "We reject any suggestion that the question of the wickedness of an intention to kill is at large

9.16.3

9.16.4

---

[200] *Galbraith* v *HM Advocate* 2002 JC 1 at 16, para 41 per LJ-G Rodger.
[201] 2001 SLT 1013.
[202] *Ibid* at 1018, para 18. LJ-G Rodger states that the jury should take "*all* the relevant factors into account" (emphasis added) in determining whether the action was "wicked". Evidence of provocation was "simply one of the factors – the principal factor, perhaps".
[203] Gordon (2001), para 23.13 (footnotes omitted).
[204] Where the accused effected the destruction of a life recklessly, but not wickedly recklessly, that would always have constituted the crime of involuntary lawful act culpable homicide.
[205] Chalmers and Leverick (2006), para 1.06.
[206] 2011 SCCR 735.

for the jury in every case, or that the determination of that question is not constrained by any legal limits."[207] Subsequently, in addressing "the appropriate direction where intention to kill is either admitted or proved" the court said

> "In such a case, in the absence of any legally relevant factor capable of justifying or mitigating the accused's actions, the jury should be directed that they must convict of murder. Any other direction leaving the matter to the discretion of the jury would have the effect of enabling them to ignore the boundaries set by legal relevancy and to determine the issue on the basis of irrelevant considerations. Not only does that discretionary approach defy the common-sense view mentioned by [Gordon] but it would place an unduly onerous burden upon the Crown in murder cases where the killing was intentional and could result in verdicts that brought the law into disrepute for failing to provide adequate protection to society as a whole."[208]

If the definition of a "legally relevant factor capable of justifying or mitigating the accused's actions" is confined to the recognised defences such as self-defence and provocation, the matter may now be settled. It is submitted that a question may still arise, however, as to whether, for example, proof beyond reasonable doubt that the accused killed for compassionate reasons, as in a "mercy killing", is "legally relevant" such as to negate the wickedness of the intention to kill.

9.16.5   Indeed, prior to *Elsherkisi* it had been suggested that such "mercy killings" might be *better* accommodated under the post-*Drury* law because the accused in such cases acts intentionally to bring about death, but not wickedly.[209] Mention has already been made of *HM Advocate* v *Brady*.[210] The accused, Paul Brady, had killed his brother, James, who was in the advanced stages of Huntington's disease, a progressive, degenerative condition. He had done this by serving him a cocktail of alcohol and very high doses of his prescription drugs, and then smothering him with a pillow while he slept. James, who was described by his sister as the "most miserable picture of misery",[211] had asked Paul to kill him. Press reports suggest that family members considered Paul's act to be both brave and (morally) right.[212] The Crown initially charged Paul with murder but accepted a plea of guilty to culpable homicide. He was later admonished. It may be that

---

[207] 2011 SCCR 735 at 742, para [12] per Lord Hardie.
[208] *Ibid* at 743, para [12] per Lord Hardie.
[209] Christie (2002) at 283–284.
[210] 1997 GWD 1–18. See section 9.15.1 above. See also "Mercy killing brother admonished", *The Herald*, 15 October 1996.
[211] K Mcveigh, "Family speak of mercy death ordeal", *The Scotsman*, 1 October 1996 at 6.
[212] K Sinclair, "Family declare support for brother's mercy killer", *The Herald*, 1 October 1996 at 3.

this decision reflects the gravity of the case but, certainly at the time, there was no legally principled basis for the "reduction" to culpable homicide.[213] In any future case, the absence of wickedness may now supply that principle but, nonetheless, it remains very open-ended and vague. What should happen, for example, in the "mercy killing/ suicide pact" cases identified by the English Law Commission where the accused's purpose arises as much from the strain on herself as carer as to bring the deceased's suffering to an end?[214] If voluntary culpable homicide is no longer "murder reduced" then its own *mens rea* requires sharper definition. It cannot cease to exist as a category since diminished responsibility cases do not easily fit either of the other two culpable homicide categories.[215] In fact, it is perhaps the mandatory life sentence for murder which is implicated here. Without it, while the stigma of a murder conviction would remain, the consequences could be tailored to the seriousness of the crime.

9.17   INVOLUNTARY CULPABLE HOMICIDE

Scots criminal law recognises two forms of *in*voluntary culpable   **9.17.1**
homicide – where culpable homicide is seen as a crime in its own right and not as mitigated murder. These are: (a) involuntary culpable homicide in the course of an *unlawful* act; and (b) involuntary culpable homicide in the course of a *lawful* act.

9.18   INVOLUNTARY CULPABLE HOMICIDE IN THE COURSE OF AN UNLAWFUL ACT[216]

This first, "unlawful act", type arises where the accused is engaged   **9.18.1**
in committing a crime and, through her criminal actions, causes someone else's death, though the death itself is unintentional. It is no longer the law that an accused who causes death while engaged in any criminal enterprise whatsoever is guilty of this form of culpable homicide. It seems that it is only those crimes in which causing some injury to others is intended or, at least, the action can be seen as, in some way, directed against the deceased which will form the foundation of this type of culpable homicide. The case of *MacAngus and Kane v HM Advocate*[217] has now confirmed that this is the

---

[213] Paul took James's life intending to do so, thereby *prima facie* satisfying the essential elements of the crime of murder at the time.
[214] Law Commission (2005), para 1.84. See also n 8 in section 9.1.2 above.
[215] That is, involuntary culpable homicide in the course of an *unlawful act* (discussed from section 9.18 below) and involuntary culpable homicide in the course of a *lawful act* (discussed from section 9.19 below).
[216] This is also referred to as "unintentional unlawful act culpable homicide".
[217] 2009 SLT 137.

position.[218] Gordon discusses cases where there was a finding of culpable homicide without such an intention,[219] but the authorities are, at best, patchy. As with all homicide in Scots law, the *actus reus* here is the destruction of human life. The *mens rea* is that of the underlying crime, the crime in which the accused was engaged when death resulted. It is not, however, clear to which crimes other than assault this principle now applies.

Assault[220]

9.18.2 The crime of assault can underlie involuntary unlawful act culpable homicide because accused persons are required to take responsibility for all the consequences of their actions and to take their victims as they find them.[221] Thus, where the Crown can prove the assault *and* that the assault has caused death then the accused will be convicted of this type of culpable homicide. This applies even if the assault itself is a minor one.[222] The relevant *mens rea* is that of assault. In the case of *HM Advocate* v *Hartley*[223] the trial judge (Lord Sutherland) charged the jury as follows:

> "Culpable homicide is simply the causing of death by any unlawful act. The unlawful act must be intentional, but it is quite immaterial whether death was the foreseeable result of that act. So, to take an example, if you are having an argument with somebody and give him a punch on the chin, not a very hard one, but a punch on the chin, and he is taken aback and stumbles backwards, catches his heel on the kerb of the pavement, falls over, cracks his skull and dies, you would be guilty of culpable homicide because you have committed an unlawful act, an assault by punching him, and as a direct consequence of that act he sustained injuries from which he died. So even though you had not the slightest intention of causing him any serious harm at all, you are responsible for his death; and the crime is not murder, because there was no question of wicked recklessness, the crime is one of culpable homicide."[224]

This principle is demonstrated in *McDade* v *HM Advocate*[225] where the accused, the deceased and a third party were all involved in a scuffle which resulted in them falling down a flight of stairs. It was not proved that the accused *caused* the deceased to fall. The jury

---

[218] See section 7.3.13 above.
[219] Gordon (2001), para 26.27.
[220] Assault is discussed further from section 10.2 below.
[221] This is also known as the "thin skull" rule – see section 7.3.4 above.
[222] See, for example, *Bird* v *HM Advocate* 1952 JC 23, discussed in section 7.3.4 above.
[223] 1989 SLT 135.
[224] *Ibid* at 136. See the Australian case of *Holzer* [1968] VR 481. The assault consisted of a punch to the mouth, which caused a small cut on the victim's lip. Unfortunately, the victim fell backwards, hit his head on the roadway and died. This was sufficient for a conviction for manslaughter.
[225] [2012] HCJAC 38.

did accept that he had inflicted three, relatively minor, stab wounds on the deceased, about which the deceased had shown anxiety. The deceased had underlying health conditions, including high blood pressure, and died from a heart attack immediately after the incident. The appeal court held that the accused had been properly convicted of culpable homicide because the use of the knife was held to be a "substantial direct cause of [the victim's] death".[226] It will be clear, then, that culpable homicide is a crime which applies to a spectrum of behaviour:

> "culpable homicide is the sort of crime which covers everything from the most minor unlawful act which unfortunately and quite unforeseeably causes death, right up to and including the sort of attack, a fairly severe, vicious attack, which only just fails to meet the wicked recklessness which is required for murder".[227]

Deaths arising from the supply of noxious substances – the status of causing real injury?

In *Lord Advocate's Reference (No 1 of 1994)*[228] the accused was 9.18.3 charged with supplying a controlled and potentially lethal drug and thereby killing the victim. The facts were that the accused's friend had asked him to obtain a quantity of the drug to be shared among a group of people. He did so, and gave her the drug. The victim divided it up and decided exactly which quantity she herself would take. When this dose ultimately proved fatal, the accused was charged with culpable homicide. At first instance, the trial judge ruled that the deceased's behaviour constituted a *novus actus interveniens* in the chain of causation between the accused's supply of the drugs and the death and that, accordingly, the accused was not liable for causing the death. The Crown appealed on a point of law[229] and the court ruled that the trial judge had been in error; the accused knew that the drug could be harmful. The victim's interventions – in dividing up the drug and determining her own dose – did not break the chain of causation between the supply by the accused and the death of his friend. Although the charge itself makes reference only

---

[226] [2012] HCJAC 38, at para [11] per Lord Carloway.
[227] *HM Advocate* v *Hartley* 1989 SLT 135 at 136 per Lord Sutherland.
[228] 1996 JC 76.
[229] Where an accused person has been acquitted following trial under solemn procedure the Criminal Procedure (Scotland) Act 1995, s 123(1) provides that the Lord Advocate may refer to the High Court a point of law which has arisen in relation to the charge. This is designed to clarify the law for future cases, but does not change the outcome of the case so far as the accused person is concerned; the accused remains acquitted irrespective of how the point of law is decided by the High Court.

to supplying a "class B" substance in a lethal quantity, the appeal court analysed the matter in terms of the decision in *Khaliq* v *HM Advocate*,[230] noting that the accused's conduct was "the equivalent of culpable and reckless conduct".[231] In *Khaliq* (where the accused had supplied glue-sniffing kits), Lord Justice-General Emslie stated "the question is simply whether the accused has, by wilful and reckless conduct on his part, caused real injury to a third party".[232] It appeared, therefore, immediately following this *Lord Advocate's Reference* that "causing real injury" was a crime which could form the basis of involuntary unlawful act culpable homicide.

9.18.4   It is implicit in this judgement that, without recklessness, there could be no charge of culpable homicide in these circumstances. The appeal court arrived at this view rather circuitously, by equating the simple supply of a substance to culpable and reckless conduct. It has subsequently reviewed the law in this area in the case of *MacAngus and Kane* v *HM Advocate*.[233] Here, in relation to causation, it held to its view that "a deliberate decision by the victim of the reckless conduct to ingest the drug will not necessarily break the chain of causation".[234] With regard to charges of culpable homicide in supply of controlled drugs cases, it has clearly expressed the view that such supplies can only ground such a charge where they were reckless. While a charge of causing real injury, or of risking such injury, as in *Khaliq*, cannot be established without recklessness as to the supply of the noxious substance, the decision in *MacAngus* seems rather to place cases of death resulting from the supply of a controlled drug into the involuntary *lawful* act category of culpable homicide.[235]

Other crimes

9.18.5   It is unclear which other crimes automatically incur a culpable homicide charge where the victim dies. It applies to wilful fire-raising and to culpable and reckless fire-raising "because of the dangerous nature of the crime and the consequent very high duty to take care not to injure anyone".[236] This is borne out by the case of *Mathieson* v *HM Advocate*.[237] Overall, it appears that this category will be limited to those crimes where either there is some evidence of intention to cause physical harm to the victim or where, at least, the accused's

---

[230] 1984 JC 23. This case is discussed further in sections 4.3.2 and 7.3.7 above.

[231] *Lord Advocate's Reference (No 1 of 1994)* 1996 JC 76 at 81, per LJ-C Ross.

[232] *Khaliq* v *HM Advocate* 1984 JC 23 at 33.

[233] 2009 SLT 137.

[234] *Ibid* at para 48 per LJ-G Hamilton. See also section 7.3.13 above.

[235] The issues of causation in this area are discussed from section 7.3.12 above.

[236] Gordon (2001), para 26–27, n 53.

[237] 1981 SCCR 196. Fire-raising is discussed further from section 13.5 below.

actions can be seen as in some way directed against the deceased. This position was affirmed by the appeal court in *MacAngus and Kane*,[238] where Lord Justice-General Hamilton stated "there appears to be no support for the view that unlawful act culpable homicide can be made out except where, as in assault or analogous cases, the conduct is directed in some way against the victim".[239] This would also appear to provide an answer to the issue raised by the decision in *Lourie* v *HM Advocate*[240] where a charge of unlawful act culpable homicide, apparently arising from theft, was put to the jury. The accused were acquitted but the case raised the issue of whether death arising in the course of the commission of *any* other crime could still constitute the unlawful act form of culpable homicide. Lord Hamilton's statement in *MacAngus* seems to indicate that it could not.

9.19   INVOLUNTARY CULPABLE HOMICIDE IN THE COURSE OF A LAWFUL ACT[241]

In cases of the other form of culpable homicide known as the "lawful **9.19.1** act" type, the accused will have caused death while engaged in an activity which is otherwise legal. Here, the accused has caused a death unintentionally, we might even say "accidentally", but there will have been a high degree of negligence involved. This was defined by *Paton* v *HM Advocate*[242] as "gross, or wicked, or criminal negligence, something amounting, or at any rate analogous, to a criminal indifference to consequences".[243] This definition is subject to the caveats arising from the case of *Transco plc* v *HM Advocate (No 1)*,[244] which will be discussed later.[245] For instance, suppose a farmer were to carry a loaded shotgun in a dangerous fashion, and the gun were to fire and kill a passer-by. Now, in some sense, this was an accident since the discharge of the gun was not intentional. The accused had, however, been grossly negligent in carrying the gun in such a way that it could go off.[246] It is this gross negligence which renders an accused blameworthy. This is clear from the case of *Tomney* v *HM Advocate*[247] where the accused killed his friend

---

[238] 2009 SLT 137.
[239] *Ibid* at 145, para 29.
[240] 1988 SCCR 634.
[241] This is also referred to as "unintentional lawful act culpable homicide".
[242] 1936 JC 19.
[243] *Ibid* at 22, per LJ-C Aitchison.
[244] 2004 JC 29.
[245] At section 18.5.7 below.
[246] See *David Buchanan* (1817); Hume, i, 192.
[247] [2012] HCJAC 138.

by the discharge of a pistol. The accused, the deceased and a third party were present in the living room of the accused's home with the gun and some ammunition on the floor. Having ingested both alcohol and cannabis, the accused picked up the gun and, in some way, exerted pressure on the trigger. The pistol was pointing towards the deceased, though the accused was not aiming at him. This was held to be culpable homicide because the discharge of the gun was culpable and reckless, rather than accidental. The judgment in *Transco* had clarified that a state of mind is required, rather than an objective assessment of whether the accused's *behaviour* falls below the standard expected. The question is not whether the accused acted recklessly, but rather whether she possessed the necessary state of mind alongside the action causing death.

9.19.2   This category of culpable homicide is perhaps the most confusing. It clearly arises where the accused's initial activity is lawful.[248] It is also used, however, where the accused is engaged in an *un*lawful activity but a charge of "unlawful act culpable homicide" is not deemed appropriate because the accused did not intend any physical harm, nor were her actions inappropriately directed against the deceased. This can be seen from the case of *Sutherland* v *HM Advocate*[249] in which an individual was killed as he set fire to the accused's house. The deceased had been employed by Mr Sutherland to do so for the purpose of making a fraudulent insurance claim. The Crown argued that this should be treated as being within the *un*lawful act category but the trial judge would not allow this. He held that, although fire-raising to defraud insurers was a crime, it was not a relevant crime for these purposes; it did not involve behaviour directed against the deceased nor an intention to do him physical harm. Accordingly, the Crown had to prove that the accused acted with the requisite degree of recklessness and that his reckless actions actually caused the death.

9.20 EUTHANASIA

9.20.1   Euthanasia translates from the Greek as a "good death", but is more commonly used nowadays to describe the situation in which one person accelerates the death of another, generally with the latter's consent. We noted at the outset that suicide was no longer

---

[248] See *McDowall* v *HM Advocate* 1998 SCCR 343, where the trial judge instructed the jury that the charge of killing three people by reckless driving was an example of lawful act culpable homicide since "[i]f it is your own car and it's properly taxed and insured and so on, then you are performing a perfectly lawful act in driving it" (*ibid* at 345).
[249] 1994 JC 62.

a crime in Scots law.[250] Unlike in England, where intentionally doing an act capable of encouraging or assisting the suicide of another person is a statutory offence,[251] the position of a person in Scotland who assists someone else to commit suicide is not clear cut.[252] The current debate on euthanasia, and on assisted suicide in particular, focuses on the extent to which the right to life, safeguarded by Art 2 of the ECHR, should be read as requiring recognition of a "right to die".[253] Viewing the issue from the perspective of a feminist ethic of care[254] would shift the focus away from rights and concentrate more on how we can best care for people who have reached the final stage of their lives. It may be that the best method of caring is in fact to hasten death to avoid a painful dying, but we should ensure that other avenues to a pain-free and comfortable death are first explored. An "ethic of care" approach would also note that the individual whose life is coming to an end is not the sole protagonist here. The patient's family and healthcare professionals also have a need for care. It is less a question of whether the law ought to recognise that a patient's "right" to die ought to trump the rights and interests of others, and more a question of how to ensure an outcome in which no party feels that her interests have been forsaken. The aim should be for a dying which is "good" from the perspective of all those who are intimately involved.[255]

Where a doctor has caused death in order to alleviate a patient's suffering, the *actus reus* of murder or culpable homicide is seldom in doubt.[256] Whether it is murder or culpable homicide depends, at least in theory, on the accused's *mens rea*, but those who hasten death in this way can generally be said to have intended to kill, hence

9.20.2

---

[250] See section 9.3.2 above.

[251] Suicide Act 1961, s 2(1), as amended by the Coroners and Justice Act 2009, s 59(1) and (2): "A person ("D") commits an offence if – (a) D does an act capable of encouraging or assisting the suicide or attempted suicide of another person, and (b) D's act was intended to encourage or assist suicide or an attempt at suicide."

[252] See P R Ferguson, "Killing 'without getting into trouble'? Assisted suicide and Scots criminal law" (1998) 2 *Edin LR* 288.

[253] The courts in England have refused to recognise such a right – see *R (on the application of Pretty)* v *DPP* [2002] 1 AC 800; also *R (on the application of Nicklinson)* v *Ministry of Justice* [2013] HRLR 36 – and it seems likely that the Scottish courts would do likewise were a similar case to come before them.

[254] See from section 1.14 above.

[255] See now the Assisted Suicide (Scotland) Bill, proposed by Margo MacDonald MSP.

[256] See, however, *R* v *Cox*, prosecuted at Winchester Crown Court in 1992, in which the patient's body had been cremated before suspicion fell on her doctor, hence the prosecution was unable to establish that he had caused her death. He was convicted of attempted murder.

could be charged with murder. In practice, doctors (and relatives) are rarely prosecuted. The 2nd edition of Gordon's *Criminal Law* suggested that criminal liability would not result

> "for the case of the doctor who prescribes pain-killing drugs in the knowledge that they will shorten life, provided they are given *with the intention of easing pain* and not as a measure of euthanasia. This exception has no legal basis but is an example of the law turning a blind eye for sympathetic reasons. It does not extend to acts intended to accelerate death".[257]

This meant that a doctor whose primary intention was to alleviate pain would not be liable for murdering a patient in circumstances where it is accepted that a consequence of relieving pain was that death was hastened. Ordinarily, accused persons are taken to have intended the "inevitable" or "reasonably foreseeable" consequences of their acts: if A blows up a plane which is in mid-flight, intending to claim on an insurance policy for the cargo, the law would treat A as having intended to kill those on board, since the deaths of the crew and passengers were an inevitable result of blowing up the plane. Likewise, a doctor who knows that administering high doses of morphine to a patient will accelerate that patient's death could be said to intend to alleviate pain, and also to accelerate death. To prevent this conclusion, the "doctrine of double effect" is employed. This provides that doctors who act with the primary purpose of relieving pain are not to be regarded as causing the death of their patients merely because death is certain, or almost certain, to occur earlier than otherwise.[258]

9.20.3   The doctrine of double effect does not seem to be discussed in the latest edition of *Gordon*. It may be that, following the case of *Drury* v *HM Advocate*,[259] there is no longer any need for recourse to this doctrine, since one who intends to alleviate suffering or pain can hardly be said to have the requisite "wicked intent to kill" which is now required for murder.[260] Where the person hastening death is a relative, a plea of diminished responsibility may be a potential mechanism for avoiding a conviction for murder. In practice, the Crown will often accept a plea of guilty to culpable homicide in such cases, without requiring the accused to establish diminished responsibility. An example of this is the case of *HM Advocate* v *Brady*,[261] discussed in section 9.16.5 above.

---

[257] G H Gordon, *Criminal Law* (1978), p 728, n 14 (emphasis added).
[258] See also the *Draft Criminal Code*, s 37(2). This provides that the patient must consent, or the doctor have lawful authority.
[259] 2001 SLT 1013.
[260] *Drury*'s case was discussed in detail from section 9.11.1 above.
[261] 1997 GWD 1–18.

Finally, a brief word is required about attempts to commit 9.20.4
common law forms of culpable homicide. We have seen that
attempted murder is a competent charge, and that the *mens rea*
is the same as for murder.[262] Attempted murder simply means an
unsuccessful murder. Can we have a charge of attempted culpable
homicide? In fact, there is no such charge.[263] The charge would be
assault to severe injury.

9.21 CRITIQUE OF THE COMMON LAW ON HOMICIDE AND PROPOSALS FOR REFORM

The extent to which murder and culpable homicide really constitute 9.21.1
separate offences is an interesting question. At one level, it is clear
that they do, in that each has its own *mens rea* and the Crown must
exercise a conscious decision as to which to prosecute. On the other
hand, it is difficult to perceive them as other than degrees of the
same behaviour – acts or omissions causing the death of another
person. It would be impossible to be convicted of both offences
arising from the same set of circumstances. The (English) Law
Commission has acknowledged, overtly, that all homicide can be
placed on a scale or "ladder" which moves upwards in terms of
seriousness from manslaughter through second-degree murder to
first-degree murder.[264] The image of the ladder, however, suggests
distinct "rungs". In other words, although the three offences move
upwards in terms of seriousness, they are clearly demarcated so that
an accused person would have to meet the exact terms of the offence
for the rung at which she arrives, to be convicted of that offence. It
is not a continuum, therefore, but three discrete offences, each more
serious than the last.

Prior to the "clarification" of the *mens rea* for murder in 9.21.2
the case of *Drury* v *HM Advocate*,[265] the notion of a scale or
continuum was more easily applied in Scotland, certainly to cases
of voluntary culpable homicide. If provocation "reduced" the crime
to culpable homicide, this could be perceived as a downgrading
of the seriousness of the offence. Now, however, the appeal court
has stated that intentional killing under provocation simply does
not meet the criteria for murder. It is, specifically *not* the crime
of murder. It is, instead, that of culpable homicide.[266] It would

---

[262] At section 6.9.4 above.
[263] See *HM Advocate* v C 2007 SLT 963. For an argument that there should be, see
T H Jones, "Attempted culpable homicide" (1990) *JLSS* 408.
[264] Law Commission (2006), para 1.64.
[265] 2001 SLT 1013. This case is discussed in detail from section 9.11.1 above.
[266] Christie (2002) at 281.

be possible to have only one offence of homicide.[267] This would obviate, at a stroke, the mandatory life sentence and would allow gradations between individual acts of killing to be manifested only in the sentence. If a separate offence of murder is to be retained, then, it must serve a purpose, even if that purpose is largely the symbolic one of delineating the sphere of the most blameworthy crime. Indeed, in most legal systems murder *is* regarded as the ultimate criminal offence, carrying with it particular connotations of seriousness. In the UK, when capital punishment was abolished, life imprisonment became the mandatory sentence for murder.[268] In a society where calls for the reinstatement of the death penalty are commonplace, certainly from the families of murder victims,[269] the life sentence has an important symbolic function, setting murder apart from culpable homicide where life imprisonment (and, indeed, any form of imprisonment) is discretionary. Even if the convicted murderer does not remain in prison for life,[270] release will be on life licence, subjecting the individual to a heightened level of state surveillance, with the possibility of instant recall to prison if the terms of the licence are not met.[271] While limited recognition of the circumstances of the killing itself can be given in terms of the

---

[267] See, for example, Law Commission (2006), paras 2.18–2.22. Its rejection of a single offence is welcomed by Barry Mitchell in "Distinguishing between murder and manslaughter in practice" (2007) 71 *J Crim L* 318 at 341.

[268] Murder (Abolition of Death Penalty) Act 1965. The relevant Scottish provision in this respect is now found in the Criminal Procedure (Scotland) Act 1995, s 205.

[269] See, for example, "Mother of all crusades", *The Sun*, 20 March 2008, reporting that the mothers of three women, each murdered by a different person, had met with senior politicians to ask, *inter alia*, for the return of the death penalty.

[270] Some prisoners do remain in prison "for life". Myra Hindley (convicted in 1966 of several murders of children) died in prison and Steve Wright (convicted in 2008 of the murder of five sex workers in Suffolk) was given a whole-life tariff. In Scotland, tariffs must be specified in years and months but it is specifically provided that any such period may be specified "notwithstanding the likelihood that such a period will exceed the remainder of the prisoner's natural life": see the Prisoners and Criminal Proceedings (Scotland) Act 1993, s 2(3A) (a) and (b). The English Court of Appeal held in *Attorney General's Reference (No 69) of 2013* ([2014] HRLR 7) that whole life tariffs were not precluded in England and Wales so long as there was a prospect of release despite the ruling of the Grand Chamber of the European Court of Human Rights in *Vintner* v *United Kingdom* (66069/09) (unreported, 9 July 2013) that such tariffs were incompatible with Art 3.

[271] In *Campbell, Petitioner* 2008 SLT 231, for example, the police had, allegedly and among other allegations, seen Mr Campbell using a mobile phone while driving (thereby committing an offence contrary to the Road Vehicles (Construction and Use) Regulations 1986 (SI 1986/1078), reg 110(1), and the Road Traffic Act 1988, s 42(a)), and his life licence was revoked as a result.

tariff, or punishment element, of the life sentence,[272] the fact that it is mandatory leaves very little scope for mitigation.

Over the years, several commentators have made a cogent case that the absence of any flexibility in the life sentence leads to injustice in individual cases, and that the life sentence should no longer be mandatory.[273] Even apart from this practical consequence, the principle of fair labelling requires that only the most egregious of cases should be termed "murder". Fair labelling requires crimes to be named and defined "to reflect their degree of moral wrongfulness and relative gravity".[274] It should go without saying that those acts categorised as murder are recognisably graver, with a higher degree of blameworthiness, than those defined as culpable homicide.

9.21.3

9.22 STATUTORY HOMICIDES

There is now an offence of "corporate homicide" under the Corporate Manslaughter and Corporate Homicide Act 2007.[275] This offence is discussed later, at section 18.5.14, in the context of corporate criminal liability, more generally. It is also an offence under the Road Traffic Act 1988 to cause death by dangerous driving, or by careless or inconsiderate driving. These road traffic offences will now be considered.

9.22.1

9.23 ROAD TRAFFIC HOMICIDES

It is clear that death can be caused in a wide variety of circumstances, from the purely accidental to the pre-meditated and vicious. The common law is able to take account of this in its distinction between murder and culpable homicide, and in the breadth of sentencing options available on conviction for the lesser crime. Nonetheless, the law still deems it necessary to make special provision for deaths caused by driving, specifically by driving "dangerously",[276] or

9.23.1

---

[272] See, currently, Prisoners and Criminal Proceedings (Scotland) Act 1993, s 2, though this will be repealed and substituted by the Custodial Sentences and Weapons (Scotland) Act 2007, s 20, if this is brought into force.

[273] See, for example, T Morris and L Blom-Cooper, "The penalty for murder: a myth exploded" [1996] *Crim LR* 707; and Lord Windlesham, "Life sentences: the paradox of indeterminacy" [1989] *Crim LR* 244. See also House of Commons, Home Affairs Committee, First Report, *Murder: The Mandatory Life Sentence*, Session 1995–1996, HC 111 (1995).

[274] B Mitchell, "Multiple wrongdoing and offence structure: a plea for consistency and fair labelling" (2001) 64 *MLR* 393 at 398. The principle of fair labelling was described from section 4.6 above.

[275] Section 1(5)(b).

[276] Road Traffic Act 1988, s 1, as substituted by the Road Traffic Act 1991, s 1.

"without due care and attention or without reasonable consideration for other[s] ... using the road".[277]

9.24 CAUSING DEATH BY DANGEROUS DRIVING

9.24.1 Causing death in the first of these ways was initially criminalised in its own right by the Road Traffic Act 1960, apparently because of a marked unwillingness on the part of juries to convict of culpable homicide in these circumstances.[278] This may reflect the lack of seriousness attached to road traffic crime in that period. It is perhaps indicative of how far this pendulum has swung the other way that the most recent high-profile road traffic homicide in Scotland (*HM Advocate* v *Purcell*[279]) was an attempt by the Crown to secure a murder conviction. In that case, the defence argued that the convention was to prosecute road traffic homicides either under the Road Traffic Act 1988, or as culpable homicide, but never as murder. It was held, even in this case, where the risks incurred by the standard of driving were very great, that the *mens rea* for murder could not be satisfied. Of course, if A has deliberately driven her car at B with intent to kill B, the appropriate charge will be murder.[280] Leaving that aside, it is possible to draw at least implicit support from the judgment in *Purcell* for the view that, if death caused by driving is to be prosecuted as a common law crime, it should always be culpable homicide. Even this will only be possible in the most serious cases. Generally the statutory charge should be used. This is apparent from *Brodie* v *HM Advocate*,[281] where the fact that the accused was under the influence of alcohol when his car ploughed into a group of four cyclists, killing one of them outright, was deemed sufficient to "elevate" the crime to the category of culpable homicide. If alcohol had not been a factor, a conviction under the Road Traffic Act would have been returned. It

---

[277] Road Traffic Act 1988, s 2B. See also s 3ZB of that Act, which makes it an offence to cause the death of another person when driving without a licence, while disqualified, or while uninsured. All of these offences were inserted into the 1988 Act by the Road Safety Act 2006, ss 20 and 21. Section 3A of the 1988 Act (as inserted by the Road Traffic Act 1991, s 3) criminalises causing death by careless driving when under influence of drink or drugs.

[278] A Brown, *Wheatley's Road Traffic Law in Scotland* (4th edn, 2007), p 35.

[279] 2008 JC 131. The case was discussed at section 9.12.7 above. See also M Hirst, "Causing death by driving and other offences: a question of balance" [2008] *Crim LR* 339.

[280] This happened in an English case in 2009: see "Life for driver who mowed down Aston Villa fan at Birmingham derby", available at http://www.thetimes.co.uk/tto/news/uk/crime/article1876260.ece.

[281] 1992 SCCR 487.

can also be seen in *McDowall* v *HM Advocate*,[282] where the risks
taken by the accused were high and resulted in the deaths of three
people and the serious injury of a fourth. The accused was convicted
of culpable homicide.[283]

As previously noted,[284] killings by organisations have been   **9.24.2**
criminalised in their own right under the Corporate Manslaughter
and Corporate Homicide Act 2007. Apart from this, road traffic is
the only area in which specific provisions are made for a particular
way of bringing about the death of the victim. Is it desirable to
have the overlap with the common law which is indicated in both
Brodie[285] and *Purcell*?[286] In each case the death was, patently, caused
by "dangerous driving" – the exact behaviour proscribed by the
statute – yet a conviction for culpable homicide was returned. The
purpose of the original road traffic legislation was to ensure that
traffic homicides were treated appropriately to their seriousness.
As public opinion has viewed these offences more gravely over the
years, so have their maximum sentences increased.[287] Accordingly,
the statutory offences have demonstrated an ability to keep step with
developments in society. The availability of culpable homicide allows
an extra level of opprobrium to be heaped on the most egregious
examples. While we are generally critical when there are several
offences, each of which criminalises the same basic behaviour, it
appears to work well in this area. This may also be because the
behavioural element is always constituted by driving, an activity with
which jurors are usually familiar – whether as drivers themselves or
as passengers. This may be less true, however, in relation to the more
recently enacted offences of "causing death by driving", discussed
from section 9.25 below.

The leading case on the characterisation of the standard of driving   **9.24.3**
for the purposes of the statutory offence is still *Allan* v *Patterson*,[288]
despite the fact that it related to "reckless" driving and the offence
now consists of "dangerous" driving. Lord Justice-General Emslie
stated:

> "Judges and juries will readily understand, and juries might well be reminded,
> that before they can apply the adverb 'recklessly' to the driving in question

---

[282] 1998 JC 194.
[283] For further discussion of this case, see sections 6.15.3 and 14.8.1.
[284] Section 9.22.1 above. The offence is discussed in more detail from section
18.5.12 below.
[285] 1992 SCCR 487.
[286] 2008 JC 131.
[287] The maximum sentence has increased from 5 years' imprisonment to 14 years:
Road Traffic Offenders Act 1988, Sch 2, Pt I, as amended by Criminal Justice Act
2003, s 285(3). See also Hirst (2008) at 339, n 1 and accompanying text.
[288] 1980 JC 57.

they must find that it fell far below the standard of driving expected of the competent and careful driver and that it occurred either in the face of obvious and material dangers which were or should have been observed, appreciated and guarded against, or in circumstances which showed a complete disregard for any potential dangers which might result from the way in which the vehicle was being driven."[289]

He also stated that what the statute was seeking to define was "a manner of *driving*".[290] The utility of Lord Emslie's words as a generalisable definition of "recklessness" have been doubted in the context of a common law crime, but their value in relation to defining a standard of driving has not.[291]

9.25   UNLICENSED, DISQUALIFIED OR UNINSURED DRIVERS WHO CAUSE DEATH

9.25.1   Causing death by dangerous driving is a well-established crime, albeit that it has taken a number of statutory forms over the years. A newer form of road traffic homicide – causing death by driving while unlicensed, disqualified or uninsured in terms of s 3ZB of the Road Traffic Act 1988 – is, however, worthy of further scrutiny. It provides:

> "A person is guilty of an offence under this section *if he causes the death of another person by driving a motor vehicle* on a road *and, at the time when he is driving, the circumstances are such that he is committing an offence* under –
> (a) section 87(1) of this Act (driving otherwise than in accordance with a licence),
> (b) section 103(1)(b) of this Act (driving while disqualified), or
> (c) section 143 of this Act (using motor vehicle while uninsured or unsecured against third party risks)."[292]

The section appears, at first sight, to be clear in terms of its drafting, but it raises an issue, in terms of fair labelling and the attribution of blameworthiness, which is of importance in the context of both causation and homicide. In cases brought under this section, the accused is, indeed, culpable, for having driven at all in that she falls into a category of persons who are prohibited from doing so because of not having a driving licence, being barred by court order from driving or not having insurance for the driving being undertaken. Driving in each of these circumstances is an offence in

---

[289] 1980 JC 57 at 60.
[290] *Ibid* at 61 (emphasis added).
[291] See, for example, *Transco plc v HM Advocate (No 1)* 2004 JC 29 per Lord Hamilton at 49, para 39.
[292] Emphases added.

its own right. Until recently, however, where the accused, through no further fault on her part, caused death while driving, it seemed that she was automatically, by virtue of s 3ZB, guilty of an offence of homicide. She incurred criminal responsibility for a death in relation to the causation of which, in reality, she may not even have been negligent. This was the approach taken by both the Scottish and English courts[293] prior to the decision of the Supreme Court in *R v Hughes*.[294] The accused was involved in a collision with a car being driven by a Mr Dickinson, as a result of which the latter was fatally injured. On the day of the collision Mr Dickinson had driven 200 miles following eight consecutive 12-hour night-shifts. He had methadone and benzodiazepine in his system and had taken heroin shortly before the accident. According to a toxicologist, such drugs cause "drowsiness, inability to concentrate and a lack of co-ordination".[295] A witness testified that Mr Dickinson had been driving erratically "weaving from side to the road, crossing the white lines at the nearside ... , and crossing the central white lines by about 1 foot ... for 2 miles immediately prior to the collision".[296] Hughes was convicted at first instance and this was upheld by the English Court of Appeal. Although the latter had found the wording of s 3ZB to be perfectly clear, and admitting of only one interpretation, the Supreme Court took the view that the provision was ambiguous. Their Lordships noted

> "if unequivocal language ... had been used, it would have been beyond doubt that the new offence was committed simply as a result of the defendant being in a situation, viz a fatal accident, whether caused by his driving or not, when committing one of the three specified offences. If such had been the intention of Parliament, it was very easy of achievement. Parliament did not, however, adopt language of this kind".[297]

The Court emphasised the serious nature of the offence, referring to it as a penal provision "of very considerable severity":[298]

---

[293] *Rai v HM Advocate* 2012 SCL 283, which followed the English case of *R v Williams* [2011] 1 WLR 588. For criticisms of the legislation, see P W Ferguson, "Road traffic law reform" (2007) SLT 27; M Hirst, "Causing death by driving and other offences: a question of balance" [2008] *Crim LR* 339; A P Simester and G R Sullivan, "Being there" (2012) *CLJ* 29; G R Sullivan and A P Simester, "Causation without limits: causing death while driving without a licence, while disqualified or without insurance" [2012] *Crim LR* 753.

[294] [2013] 1 WLR 2461. See P R Ferguson and C McDiarmid, "A victory for fairness and common sense: *R v Hughes*" (2014) 18 *Edin LR* 84; C J Newman and A Lowerson, "Causing death by unlicensed, disqualified or uninsured driving: blameless driving and the scope of legal causation" (2014) 78 *J Crim L* 16.

[295] [2011] EWCA Crim 1508, at para 15, per Hooper LJ.

[296] *Ibid*, para 16.

[297] [2013] 1 WLR 2461 at 2470, paras 19–20.

[298] *Ibid* at 2472, para 26.

"The offence created is a form of homicide. To label a person a criminal killer of another is of the greatest gravity. The defendant is at risk of imprisonment for a substantial term. Even if, at least in a case of inadvertent lack of insurance or venial lack of licence, a sentence of imprisonment were not to follow, the defendant would be left with a lifelong conviction for homicide ... to carry the stigma of criminal conviction for killing someone else, perhaps a close relative, perhaps ... an innocent child, is no small thing."[299]

The offence required to be interpreted in a manner favourable to the accused, since it had to be assumed that Parliament did not intend to create a harsh offence unless there was no other way of interpreting a provision. The principle of legality meant that fundamental rights could not be overridden by "general or ambiguous words".[300] Given the section's ambiguity, juries ought to be directed that an accused could only be convicted if there was "something open to proper criticism",[301] "some act or omission ... some element of fault"[302] in the driving, and this had to be something other than the mere presence of his vehicle on the road at the time of the fatality.[303]

9.26 CRITIQUE OF ROAD TRAFFIC HOMICIDE AND PROPOSALS FOR REFORM

9.26.1 Driving is a common activity which may have fatal consequences because of either a momentary loss of concentration, or a total and deliberate failure to pay heed to other road users. Few other everyday pastimes are quite so inherently dangerous. Its very familiarity means that juries are generally well able to make judgements concerning its quality.[304] In addition, as we have noted, public opinion on death caused by driving has changed quite radically. Legislation has made it possible to keep step with the public mood through changing the penalties as shifts in the public perception of the seriousness of the behaviour become apparent. This may also explain the criminalisation of new forms of driver-induced fatality, as causing death by driving in all its forms becomes increasingly condemned by society.[305] The interplay between the statutory offences and the common law allows a final layer of opprobrium to

---

[299] [2013] 1 WLR 2461, at 2472–2473, para 26.
[300] *Ibid* at 2473, para 27, quoting Lord Hoffmann in *R v Secretary of State for the Home Department, Ex p Simms* [2000] 2 AC 115 at 131E.
[301] *Ibid* at 2475, para 33.
[302] *Ibid* at 2476, para 36.
[303] See now *R v Uthayakumar*; *R v Clayton* [2014] EWCA Crim 123.
[304] See, for example, J Chalmers, "Just an expert group that can't say no: reforming corporate homicide law" (2006) 10 *Edin LR* 290 at 294.
[305] For examples of new offences introduced by the Road Safety Act 2006, for instance, see section 9.23.1 above.

be reserved for truly appalling driving. As we will see, death arising through a company's activities may similarly inflame the public[306] but the need for a bespoke offence in this context is based primarily on the difficulty of holding an artificial "person" to account. In both areas, however, the specificities of the subject-matter render customised legislation appropriate.

In respect of the offences of causing death by driving while unlicensed, disqualified or uninsured, it is, of course, open to the Westminster Parliament to amend s 3ZB in a manner which leaves no doubt that it is indeed intended to hold an uninsured (etc) driver criminally liable for causing death, without proof of fault in the manner of the driving. It is to be hoped that Parliament stays its hand. The level of fault required remains rather unclear, since it may be less than that necessary for the offence of careless or inconsiderate driving. Repeal of s 3ZB may therefore be the better option, given that driving while uninsured, unlicensed or disqualified is already criminalised in its own right.

9.26.2

---

[306] For example, the Piper Alpha disaster in 1988 and the Stockline explosion in 2004. See from section 18.5 below.

CHAPTER 10

NON-FATAL OFFENCES AGAINST THE PERSON

10.1 INTRODUCTION

Freedom from unwanted or intrusive physical contact is an important **10.1.1** aspect of liberalism, and it is a truism that the criminal law ought to safeguard the physical integrity of individuals. Non-fatal offences include those which are of a sexual character – these are considered in Chapter 11. This chapter focuses on non-sexual offences.

10.2 ASSAULT

The *Scottish Crime and Justice Survey 2012/13* estimated, on the **10.2.1** basis of interviews conducted between April 2012 and March 2013, that 28 per cent of crime was assault, of which 2 per cent were "serious" assaults.[1] The Survey defines "serious assault" as involving fractures (that is, the breaking or cracking of a bone), internal injuries, severe concussion, loss of consciousness, lacerations requiring sutures which may lead to impairment or disfigurement, and any other injury which may lead to impairment or disfigurement, or which requires treatment in hospital as an in-patient.[2] In 2012–13, 12 per cent of non-sexual violent crime took place in pubs, bars or clubs; 12 per cent in or around a shop, supermarket, shopping centre or precinct; 32 per cent occurred in or near the victim's workplace (a large increase from the previous year, which was 19 per cent); and 20 per cent in or immediately outside the victim's home.[3]

As William Wilson suggests: **10.2.2**

"Because hurting people is presumptively wrong it makes particular sense to signal this core value by singling out those who deliberately flout it for special

---

[1] *Scottish Crime and Justice Survey 2012/13*, p iii.
[2] *Ibid*, p 123.
[3] *Ibid*, Table 3.2, para 3.4.1. Compare: *Scottish Crime and Justice Survey 2010/11*, para 3.5.1.

condemnation while leaving other cases of causing harm inexcusably to be addressed in lesser offences."[4]

This is reflected in Scots criminal law; assault requires a deliberate attack[5] which means that it must be done with intent to cause personal injury, or intent to place the victim in a state of fear of harm. One cannot be guilty of assault by acting negligently, or even recklessly. This is apparent from the case of *John Roy*,[6] in which the accused deliberately broke a window. A girl was injured when some of the broken glass struck her eye, but Roy was acquitted of assaulting the girl since he had not intended to injure her.

10.2.3   The appeal court often refers to the *mens rea* of assault as "evil intent". This ties in with the idea of moral blameworthiness in common law crimes. However, the notion of evil intent is also used to explain why surgical operations do not result in an assault charge. *Prima facie*, what separates the incision by a surgeon's scalpel from the slash of the thug's Stanley knife is that the former acts for the good of the patient – which is more a question of motive than intent. It might be imagined that the surgeon does not commit an assault on the patient because the latter consents to the infliction of the injury, but the case of *Smart v HM Advocate*[7] makes clear that the consent of the victim is no defence to a criminal charge of assault. In the *Smart* case the accused and the ultimate victim agreed to have a "square go" (that is, a fight without weapons) during which Smart got the upper hand and inflicted a number of injuries on his opponent. Smart argued that he could not be convicted of assault since the other party had consented to fight. In rejecting this, the appeal court stated:

> "If there is an *attack* on the other person *and it is done with evil intent*, that is, intent to injure and do bodily harm, then … the fact that the person attacked was willing to undergo the risk of that attack does not prevent it from being the crime of assault."[8]

10.2.4   Joel Feinberg proposed an alternative way of looking at cases such as that of *Smart*.[9] In relation to "settling a quarrel by a test of fisticuffs" he suggested:

> "If the two adversaries then settle their grievances in a quiet unobserved place, they cannot be charged with an affray or public disturbance. Each of them can be understood, at least in some clear cases, voluntarily to assume the risk of personal injury to himself, and also to promise tacitly not to

---

[4] W Wilson, *Central Issues in Criminal Theory* (2002), p 140.
[5] See J H A Macdonald, *A Practical Treatise on the Criminal Law of Scotland* (5th edn, 1948), p 115.
[6] (1839) Bell's Notes 88.
[7] 1975 JC 30.
[8] *Ibid* at 33 per LJ-C Wheatley (emphases in original).
[9] 1975 JC 30.

inflict a beating on the other beyond what is required to establish a clear victory. ... To make such conduct criminal would be to tell grown men that they are not permitted to engage privately in primarily self-regarding conduct to which they have both consented. If criminal prohibition of their conduct is to be justified by the harm principle, it must be on the ground that it is necessary to prevent harm to public interests."[10]

Scots criminal law does indeed have resort to the "public interest" in such cases. The courts use the idea of "evil intent" to separate assaults from injuries which are permitted on public policy grounds, such as those occurring in the course of surgical operations. Similarly, it could be argued that a boxer would not generally be guilty of assaulting an opponent, not because the latter consents but because the former is said to lack evil intent. This aspect was addressed by the court in *Smart*:

"if persons engage in sporting activities governed by rules, then, although some form of violence may be involved within the rules, there is no assault because the intention is to engage in the sporting activity and not evilly to do harm to the opponent. But where the whole purpose of the exercise is to inflict physical damage on the opponent in pursuance of a quarrel, then the evil intent is present, and consent is elided".[11]

Subsequent to *Smart*, the appeal court stated that physical violence in sport would be criminal where it could "be shown to be outwith the normal scope of the sport",[12] thus moving away from overt reliance on the absence of *mens rea*. Clearly, then, players cannot inflict any injuries on their opponents with impunity. Players must obviously stay within the rules of the game. Excessive violence may constitute an assault and there have been cases in which sports people have been so charged.[13] This doctrine of "evil intent" really means that people are generally not permitted to inflict intentional injuries on others, but public policy allows for certain exceptions to this rule, which the law itself may characterise in different ways.

In the English law case of *R v Brown*[14] the House of Lords **10.2.5** determined that the consent of participants to homosexual sado-masochistic activities was no defence, since it was not in the "public interest" for one person to wound or cause actual bodily harm to another unless there was a good reason for this, and the court

---

[10] J Feinberg, *The Moral Limits of the Criminal Law: Harm to Others* (1984), p 222.
[11] 1975 JC 30 at 33, per LJ-C Wheatley.
[12] *Lord Advocate's Reference (No 2 of 1992)* 1993 JC 43 at 48, per LJ-C Ross.
[13] See, for example, *Ferguson v Normand* 1995 SCCR 770, in which a footballer head-butted a member of the opposing team during a match, and was successfully convicted of assault.
[14] [1994] 1 AC 212.

was not prepared to hold that satisfying sado-masochistic desires amounted to a good reason.[15] Given the liberal emphasis on there being a private sphere which should remain uncontrolled by the criminal law, it might have been thought that the accused's appeal to the European Court of Human Rights, based on an alleged breach of Art 8, would have been successful. Since many men were involved in *Brown*, and indeed they had made and distributed video tapes of their activities, the court was not persuaded by the argument that these were essentially private acts.[16] Furthermore, it stated:

> "... one of the roles which the State is unquestionably entitled to undertake is to seek to regulate, through the operation of the criminal law, activities which involve the infliction of physical harm. This is so whether the activities in question occur in the course of sexual conduct or otherwise".[17]

The *Brown* case was heavily criticised by many academic commentators.[18] As Chrisje Brants has put it, at issue is such cases is not "that actual bodily harm occurs, that blood flows, that scarring results" but rather "whether this is relevant to anyone but the participants".[19]

10.2.6   In the later case of *R v Wilson*,[20] the accused was acquitted of assault occasioning actual bodily harm, despite having branded his initials on his wife's buttocks, at her request. The English Court of Appeal distinguished *Brown*[21] on the basis that there was no aggressive intent on Mr Wilson's part. Brants has suggested that the difference between the decisions in *Brown* and *Wilson* is that in the former "these men were homosexuals, that there were more than two of them, and that this conduct was therefore regarded as degrading, immoral, not in the public interest and the legitimate subject of prosecution".[22]

Whether consent ought to be a defence to a charge of assault in Scots law, and whether this should apply to relatively trivial injuries only, or more widely, is discussed from section 19.9 below.

---

[15] "I am not prepared to invent a defence of consent for sado-masochistic encounters which breed and glorify cruelty ..." *ibid* per Lord Templeman at 236.

[16] *Laskey, Jaggard and Brown* v *UK* (1997) 24 EHRR 39.

[17] *Ibid* at 58.

[18] See, for example, P Alldridge, *Relocating Criminal Law* (2000) at p 124 on; N Bamforth, "Sado-masochism and consent" [1994] *Crim LR* 661.

[19] C Brants, "The state and the nation's bedrooms: the fundamental right of sexual autonomy" in P Alldridge and C Brants (eds), *Personal Autonomy, the Private Sphere and Criminal Law* (2001) 115 at p 132.

[20] [1996] 3 WLR 125.

[21] [1994] 1 AC 212.

[22] Brants (2001) at p 134.

An attack can range from trivial to something very serious.[23]   **10.2.7**
Threatening gestures may constitute an assault.[24] There need not
be any physical contact – it is an assault for A to try to punch B,
even if A misses. It follows from this that there can be no crime
of "attempted assault" since to attempt to assault someone *is* to
assault that person. But what if the blow misses its intended victim,
but hits someone else – if A aims a blow at B but hits C instead? As
we have previously noted in discussing transferred intent,[25] A is said
to have assaulted both B *and* C (though in practice the Crown will
generally opt to prosecute the assault on C only). At a theoretical
level, there is unfairness in seeking to prosecute both offences using
the single state of mind which can be identified. The accused had
the *mens rea* for only one crime: the assault of B. We have already
criticised the notion that intention, as a concept, can be transferred
from B to C at all. If the criminal law seeks to hold individuals to
account on the basis of their blameworthiness, which is in certain
respects represented by *mens rea*, then A should be blameworthy
for a single assault only. As Anthony Dillof has argued in relation
to murder, transferred intent is

> "a doctrine with a strong proportionality requirement. The notion of intent
> being 'transferred' is usually derided as fiction. Yet this fiction is a useful
> device for ensuring that punishment is proportional to moral culpability. If
> A's intent to kill B is transferred to C, it is no longer available to support A's
> liability for the attempted murder of B. In contrast, if [transferred intent]
> rendered A liable for murdering C, but did not negate his liability for the
> attempted murder of B, A's total punishment for murder and attempted
> murder would be disproportionate to his culpability".[26]

In Scotland, this disproportion is avoided only by Crown Office
practice. In principle, since the *actus reus* and *mens rea* of each
crime can be proved (albeit only by using the *mens rea* twice),
convictions for both crimes could be obtained. Nonetheless, if
the view which we expressed in Chapter 6 is correct and intent is,
effectively, not transferable, then perhaps the accused could be more
fairly charged with the assault of B (towards whom the intention

---

[23] In relation to the former, in *Hynd* v *McGlennan* 2000 SCCR 231 the accused
was found guilty of an assault by spitting.
[24] *Atkinson* v *HM Advocate* 1987 SCCR 534. See also the case of *David Keay*
(1837) 1 Swin 543, where the accused whipped a pony as he passed it in his
carriage. The pony threw its rider, causing serious injuries to one of his legs:
Keay was convicted of assault. See also the more recent case of *Quinn* v *Lees*
1994 SCCR 159, in which the accused assaulted some boys by ordering his dog
to attack them.
[25] See from section 6.13 above.
[26] A M Dillof, "Transferred intent: an inquiry into the nature of criminal
culpability" (1997–98) 1 *Buff Crim L Rev* 501 at 506.

was directed) and with recklessly injuring C. It seems reasonably plausible, existentially, that an individual could simultaneously both intend to injure B while disregarding a risk to C where, clearly, she does not hold two separate intentions. This position better reflects the accused's actual blameworthiness.

10.3   AGGRAVATED ASSAULT

10.3.1   An assault may be aggravated in several ways.[27] One obvious way relates to the extent of injury suffered by the victim, for example, assaulting someone to their disfigurement, or to severe injury. In the past, complaints libelled assaults "to the effusion of blood",[28] but this is not used nowadays. An assault is also aggravated by the use of a weapon, such as a knife, gun, or broken bottle, or by the fact that the accused intended great harm such as "assault with intent to rape"; "assault with intent to rob"; and "assault with intent to kill".[29] An assault may be libelled as being "to the danger of life" and this aggravation may be charged even when no injury is actually sustained: it is sufficient that there was a high risk of danger. For example, a child who is pushed from a moving car has been put in great danger even if not injured, hence the person doing the pushing would have committed an assault "to the danger of life". The *mens rea* required to prove an aggravation is determined on an objective basis; there is no need for the Crown to prove that the accused actually intended to endanger life nor is there any need for corroboration of the aggravation.[30] The type of place in which the assault is committed (referred to as the "locus") may also be an aggravation. The crime of hamesucken involves attacking a person in the victim's own home, having entered the house for that purpose.[31] As a *nomen juris* (legal label),[32] "hamesucken" is rarely used,[33] but such attacks are still seen as a serious aggravation.

---

[27] Criminal Procedure (Scotland) Act 1995, Sch 3, para 9(3) provides that the prosecution may be able to obtain a conviction for simple assault where it has been unable to prove any aggravation libelled.

[28] See, for example, *O'Neill* v *HM Advocate* 1934 JC 98, discussed at section 12.21.2 below.

[29] Sexual assaults are further described in Chapter 11 below.

[30] *Murray* v *HM Advocate* 2012 SCCR 173.

[31] It has been suggested that "hamsocna" was a crime in Anglo-Saxon law, dating from the 11th century; see K Laird, "Conceptualising the interpretation of 'dwelling' in section 9 of the Theft Act 1968" [2013] *Crim LR* 656 at 663–664.

[32] See section 5.13.1 above.

[33] But see *Gemmell* v *HM Advocate* 2012 JC 223, in which this seems to have been charged, and *Jakovlev and Podgornoi* v *HM Advocate* 2012 JC 120, in which Lord Hardie stated (at 131 para [12]): "Although hamesucken is no longer charged as a specific crime, it is nevertheless still regarded as an aggravated form of assault."

Assaults on certain categories of victim are seen as more serious 10.3.2
than others. There are no fixed categories of aggravated assault
at common law, based on the nature of the victim, but an assault
is likely to be regarded as more serious if the victim is a judge,
young child or elderly person. Assaulting a member of the police
force is a statutory offence, by s 90 of the Police and Fire Reform
(Scotland) Act 2012.[34] This is but one of a range of aggravated
assaults where the complainer belongs to a particular occupation
or profession. The Scottish Parliament has created several such
provisions; for example, the Emergency Workers (Scotland) Act
2005 makes it an offence to assault, obstruct or hinder certain
providers of emergency services while they are acting in their
professional capacities.[35] This applies to constables, members of
the Scottish Fire and Rescue Service or Scottish Ambulance Service
Board, medical practitioners, nurses and midwives.[36] It is a separate
offence to assault, obstruct or hinder certain people who are
responding to emergency circumstances.[37] This category includes
prison officers, coastguards, the crews of the Royal National
Lifeboat Institution and social workers, as well as anyone who is
assisting such persons.[38] In relation to these offences, the accused
must know, or ought to know, that the person she is assaulting or
impeding is acting in the relevant capacity.[39]

10.4 DOMESTIC ABUSE

"Domestic violence" and "domestic abuse" are not the names of 10.4.1
particular crimes, but rather are classifications given to a range of
crimes. The terms are not synonymous; "domestic violence" tends
to be used to cover cases in which the victim has been physically
assaulted, whereas "domestic abuse" encapsulates cases of verbal
or psychological abuse, as well as physical assaults. It is difficult
to provide a precise definition as to whether a particular crime
is within the category of "domestic abuse" or "domestic violence".
The definition used in statistics of domestic abuse recorded by the
police is:

---

[34] This repealed the Police (Scotland) Act 1967, s 41(1).
[35] Emergency Workers (Scotland) Act 2005, s 1(1).
[36] *Ibid*, s 1(3), as amended by the Fire (Scotland) Act 2005, s 38(2), the Emergency
Workers (Scotland) Act 2005 (Modification) Order 2008 (SSI 2008/37), art 2(b),
and the Police and Fire Reform (Scotland) Act 2012, Sch 7(2), para 67.
[37] Emergency Workers (Scotland) Act 2005, s 2(1).
[38] *Ibid*, ss 2(3) and 3(1).
[39] *Ibid*, ss 1(2), 2(2) and 3(3).

"any form of physical, sexual or mental and emotional abuse [that] might amount to criminal conduct and which takes place within the context of a relationship. The relationship will be between partners (married, cohabiting, civil partnership or otherwise) or ex-partners. The abuse can be committed in the home or elsewhere".[40]

10.4.2 Fifty years ago, domestic abuse was not treated as seriously by the police or the courts as it ought to have been, and was frequently regarded as a "private" matter which was not the concern of the criminal law.[41] In *M'Arthur* v *Grosset*[42] in 1952, the accused was charged with a breach of the peace which libelled that he had put his wife in a state of fear and alarm by bawling and shouting at her. Despite the fact that the charge also libelled that he had "thrown articles of furniture" around the living room, Lord Justice-General Cooper referred to this as being "of an apparently trivial character".[43] Attitudes to domestic abuse have changed considerably since then; as Sandra Marshall and Antony Duff recognise:

"The wrong committed by a husband who beats up his wife might be 'private' in the sense that it occurs within the home, and has no material impact on the wider social world; but it is ... a public wrong in the sense that it is one that should concern us all, and that should not be left to the couple to sort out for themselves as a merely domestic affair."[44]

10.4.3 Dedicated domestic abuse courts have been established in Glasgow (since October 2004) and more recently in Edinburgh (since February 2012).[45] Incidents of domestic abuse – or at least the reporting of such incidents to the police – seem to be increasing year on year; Scottish police forces recorded 60,080 incidents in 2012–13, a slight increase from the previous year and more than a 7 per cent increase from 2010–11.[46] Of these, 42 per cent were assaults, and 19 per cent involved "threatening or abusive behaviour".[47] There seems to be a correlation between sporting

---

[40] Scottish Government, *Domestic Abuse Analytical Paper* (2013), p 4, para 1.1.
[41] See section 1.18 above for further discussion of the "public" and "private" spheres in relation to domestic abuse.
[42] 1952 JC 12.
[43] *Ibid* at 13.
[44] R A Duff and S E Marshall, "Public and private wrongs" in J Chalmers, F Leverick and L Farmer (eds), *Essays in Criminal Law in Honour of Sir Gerald Gordon* (2010) 70 at p 72.
[45] See Scottish Government News Release, 16 February 2012: "Stamping out domestic violence", available at http://www.scotland.gov.uk/News/Releases/2012/02/domesticviolencecourt.
[46] See *Domestic Abuse Recorded by the Police in Scotland, 2012–13*, p 1, para 1.2. The report is available at: http://www.scotland.gov.uk/Resource/0043/00435586.pdf.
[47] *Ibid*, p 5. The latter is an offence by virtue of the Criminal Justice and Licensing (Scotland) Act 2010, s 38. This is discussed further in section 15.5.1 below.

events and domestic violence. To give but one example, researchers at St Andrews University have reported a statistically significant increase in domestic abuse incidents following all 21 Old Firm matches from 2008 to 2011.[48]

Victims of domestic abuse can be of either gender, but in 80 per cent of incidents the perpetrator is male and the victim is female. This percentage has decreased gradually since 2003–04; at that time 89 per cent of victims were female.[49] Similar statistics in the USA have led one American academic to comment that "sex-neutral" terms such as "domestic violence" "obscure the gendered nature of intimate violence".[50]   **10.4.4**

10.5   CONSENT[51]

In England the victim's consent can be a defence to some forms of assault (though not to the offence of assault occasioning actual bodily harm). While the position is not free from doubt, the approach taken by the Scottish courts to anything other than a "minor injury" of the nature of a tattoo or a body piercing is likely to be similar to that of the House of Lords in *R v Brown*;[52] consent by a victim will not, *per se*, prevent an accused from being found guilty of assault. This does not apply, however, to sexual assaults (unless there is serious injury) since these types of behaviour are regarded as harmful by virtue of the lack of consent of the complainer, rather than being intrinsically harmful. In the case of *McDonald v HM Advocate*[53] the accused inserted the handle of a whip into his wife's rectum, allegedly with her consent. This proved to be fatal, hence his conviction was for culpable homicide. Had she survived, a charge of assault could have been brought, despite her consent to the penetration. The appeal court reserved its opinion as to whether an intention to cause pain could justify a conviction for assault in the absence of an intention to cause actual physical injury, notwithstanding the fact that the victim may have consented to the infliction of pain in a sexual context.[54]   **10.5.1**

---

[48] See "Researchers call time on old firm-related domestic violence": http://www.st-andrews.ac.uk/news/archive/2013/title,227665,en.php.

[49] *Domestic Abuse Recorded by the Police in Scotland, 2012–13*, para 3.3. This is said to be the result of an increase in the proportion of incidents with a male victim and a female perpetrator: 17% of cases in 2012–13 (*ibid*).

[50] A Scales, *Legal Feminism: Activism, Lawyering, and Legal Theory* (2006), p 99. For a critique of the focus on female victims of male violence, see B Dempsey, "Gender-neutral laws and heterocentric policies: 'domestic–abuse as gender–based abuse' and same-sex couples" (2011) 15 *Edin LR* 381.

[51] This is also discussed from section 19.9 below.

[52] [1994] 1 AC 212 (HL), discussed in section 10.2.5 above.

[53] 2004 SCCR 161.

[54] *Ibid* at 170, para 23, per Lord Kirkwood.

10.5.2   What if an accused mistakenly believed that a complainer was consenting to the contact or touching which formed the basis of an assault charge? In *Stewart* v *Nisbet*[55] the appellant was a police officer who was convicted of assault by having wrapped Sellotape around a woman's head, causing her breathing to be restricted. The appeal court rejected the proposition that a mistaken belief in consent was a defence:

> "[T]here is no defence of 'reasonable' or 'honest' belief on the part of an attacker about his victim's state of mind in the context of assault. Indeed, as the law stands at present, even if the complainer had in fact consented, it is doubtful whether that would have amounted to a defence ... Be that as it may, whether the appellant thought he was engaging in 'banter' or 'horseplay' with the complainer, and no matter how he thought the complainer would react to his actions, what he did was deliberately attack the physical person of the complainer. That constitutes the crime of assault."[56]

10.6   CRITIQUE OF THE LAW ON ASSAULT AND PROPOSALS FOR REFORM

10.6.1   In English law, an assault can be committed by either the intentional *or reckless* application of force.[57] It is submitted that the Scottish approach is preferable; fair labelling requirements suggest that recklessly caused injury ought to be distinguished from the deliberate infliction of injury. There is, however, room for improvement in Scots law in relation to consent and assault, if only to clarify the position, since it is unclear whether consent is capable of rendering legitimate what would otherwise be an assault. The case of *Stewart* v *Nisbet*[58] seems to suggest that consent is of little relevance. As noted above, the accused wrapped Sellotape around the complainer's head in such a way that her breathing was restricted, and it may be that it was the high risk of death or at least collapse associated with restricting someone's airways which was a key factor in this decision. In general, however, a reasonable and honest belief that one's "victim" is consenting ought to be a defence. Even quite radical plastic surgery, for purely cosmetic reasons, seems not to attract criminal liability. It may be that this is because the surgeon is said to lack "evil intent". Body dysmorphia (or body dysmorphic disorder) is a psychiatric illness involving a preoccupation with the appearance of a particular part of one's body. In extreme cases, patients may come to believe that they

---

[55] 2013 SCL 209.
[56] *Ibid* at 221, para [38], per LJ-C Carloway.
[57] See *R* v *Venna* [1975] 3 All ER 788.
[58] 2013 SCL 209. See section 10.5.2. above.

will be unable to live a "normal" life unless the offending body part is removed. On two occasions, Mr Robert Smith, a surgeon at Falkirk Royal Infirmary, has carried out single-leg amputations on patients who were suffering from this condition. The legality of these operations is unclear, yet there was no prosecution.[59] It may be that the Crown chose not to prosecute on the basis that it would not be "in the public interest" to do so: the operations may have been justified on psychiatric grounds, since there is evidence that such amputations provide therapeutic benefit.[60]

As we have seen from our earlier discussions,[61] liberalism would allow consent to be a defence to a charge of assault, or would redefine the crime to restrict the prohibition to non-consensual attacks. The English sado–masochism case of *R* v *Brown*[62] would have been decided quite differently under a liberal philosophy, while a communitarian approach emphasises the impact on the wider society of decriminalising such behaviours. It may be argued that allowing A to inflict harm on B with B's consent, or even at B's instigation, is likely to lead to a society in which there is greater tolerance of violence, in general. A feminist ethic of care might suggest that it is neither possible nor desirable to compartmentalise the behaviour of sadists when acting in these situations from how such people behave in other relationships – the line between enjoying hurting people who themselves enjoy being hurt, and enjoying hurting people who do not, may well be a thin one.

10.6.2

A communitarian approach is also evident in the approach the law takes to female circumcision; this is proscribed even where the "victim" is a consenting adult.[63] This is because it is widely accepted that the practice constitutes genital "mutilation", yet ritual male circumcision for religious purposes commands relatively wide acceptance. In *Brown*,[64] Lord Templeman noted in passing, and therefore only *obiter*, that ritual male circumcision was a lawful activity.[65] Nonetheless, that procedure involves the "amputation

10.6.3

---

[59] See *BBC News*: "Surgeon lodges new limb amputation bid", 21 August 2000, available at: http://news.bbc.co.uk/1/hi/scotland/889749.stm.

[60] For discussion of the issues, see: C J Ryan, "Out on a limb: the ethical management of body integrity identity disorder" (2009) 2 *Neuroethics* 21.

[61] See from section 1.2 above for a discussion on liberalism.

[62] [1994] 1 AC 212.

[63] See the Prohibition of Female Genital Mutilation (Scotland) Act 2005. For a comparative approach, see L Bibbings, "Human rights and the criminalisation of tradition: the practices formerly known as 'female circumcision'" in Alldridge and Brants (2001) at pp 139–159.

[64] [1994] 1 AC 212.

[65] *Ibid* at 231.

of healthy, nerve-rich skin" in a way which is "irreversible and permanent".[66] It could therefore be argued that it too constitutes mutilation.

10.6.4   The Scottish *Draft Criminal Code* provides that certain behaviours which would otherwise amount to an assault may be lawful if the other party consents,[67] but this does not apply where the activity in question is a socially unacceptable one which is likely to cause serious injury, or risk serious injury.[68] Whether one favours consent operating as a defence in all, some or no circumstances, it can surely be agreed that the extent to which consent is a defence ought to be clarified.

10.6.5   In relation to domestic abuse, Susan Moller Okin has suggested that:

> "People are far more tolerant of physical abuse of a woman by a man when they believe she is his wife or girlfriend than otherwise. This is probably due in part to the fact that violence used to be a legally sanctioned part of male dominance in the patriarchal family."[69]

It is to be hoped that such attitudes are changing. It has been suggested that we ought to have a distinct offence of "domestic abuse", to reflect its often repetitive and systematic nature, and the breach of trust involved in such cases.[70] Rather than create a new crime, it is submitted that a statutory provision be enacted, similar to that provided by the *Draft Criminal Code*. This specifies that offences may be aggravated "by the intent or motivation with which it is committed, by the manner or circumstances in which it is committed, by the serious nature of the effects produced, by the special vulnerability of the victim; or *by the abuse of a special relationship between the perpetrator and the victim*".[71] While recognising the serious nature of domestic violence, it avoids the creation of a new offence or offences, which would overlap with existing crimes.

10.7   JUSTIFIABLE FORCE

10.7.1 Some physical attacks may be justified or permitted by common law or statute. Identifying certain individuals who may be entitled

---

[66] H Gilbert, "Time to reconsider the lawfulness of ritual male circumcision" [2007] *EHRLR* 279 at 287.

[67] *Draft Criminal Code*, s 111 provides general rules on consent.

[68] *Ibid*, s 111(2).

[69] S M Okin, *Justice, Gender, and the Family* (1989), p 129.

[70] This point is made in V Tadros, "The distinctiveness of domestic abuse: a freedom based account" (2005) 65 *Louisiana Law Review* 989.

[71] *Draft Criminal Code*, s 7(1) (emphasis added).

to use some violence in their professional capacity, Lord Sands stated:[72]

> "It happens from time to time that charges of assault are made against officials and others who are entitled in virtue of their office to exercise in certain circumstances physical force. I may cite as examples police officers, prison warders, asylum attendants, railway servants, and ships' officers."[73]

Thus, the police have the defence of justifiable force at common law when they use reasonable force against a person whom they are trying to arrest.[74] Another example of justifiable force is self-defence, which we will consider later.[75] In *HM Advocate* v *Harris*[76] the accused was a bouncer in a night-club, and the majority of the judges assumed that he was entitled to manhandle people in order to eject them from the premises.[77] This aspect of the decision is interesting, in that the appeal court has not generally shown much enthusiasm for extending defences or exceptions to allow those who would otherwise be guilty to escape liability.[78] It is submitted that the view taken by Lord McCluskey in that case – that there "is not one law for bouncers and another law for the rest"[79] – is the correct one.

It may be that a teacher has a common law right to use moderate **10.7.2** and reasonable force to control a child, particularly where this is necessary to maintain general discipline in the classroom. This was argued by the defence, and conceded to be so by the Crown, in *Barile* v *Griffiths*.[80] While the appeal court proceeded on the basis that this concession was rightly made, it stressed that the limits and extent of any such power of control had not been fully explored before it, and therefore did not attempt to formulate any such precise limits.

A citizen's arrest may be a form of justifiable force, but anyone **10.7.3** attempting to make such an arrest must use no more than reasonable force, and must generally have personally observed the commission

---

[72] *Brown* v *Hilson* 1924 SLT 35.
[73] *Ibid* at 41.
[74] See *McLean* v *Jessop* 1989 SCCR 13, in which a police officer struck someone over the head with his baton when trying to arrest a suspected housebreaker. In fact, the recipient of the blow was the innocent householder.
[75] This is discussed from section 21.8 below.
[76] 1993 JC 150.
[77] Lord McCluskey alludes to this in his judgment: *ibid* at 161.
[78] An example of this is its treatment of the defence of non-insane automatism – see from section 20.16 below.
[79] *HM Advocate* v *Harris* 1993 JC 150 at 161.
[80] 2010 SLT 164.

of a crime by the person being arrested.[81] If such direct knowledge is lacking, there must be circumstances which are so incriminating that there is a moral certainty that the person being arrested has committed the crime.[82]

10.8   CHILD ABUSE

10.8.1 The Children and Young Persons (Scotland) Act 1937 provides that it is an offence for a person aged 16 or older who has parental responsibilities for a child or young person, or has charge or care of such a person, to ill-treat, neglect, abandon or expose the child in a manner likely to cause unnecessary suffering or injury to health.[83] A "child" is defined as someone under the age of 14 for the purposes of this provision, and a "young person" as aged 14 to 16.[84] "Neglect" is assessed objectively; it involves failing to provide the care and attention which a reasonable parent would provide.[85] It has been held that this does not require an awareness of the consequences of such neglect.[86]

10.9   CRITIQUE OF THE LAW ON CHILD ABUSE AND PROPOSALS FOR REFORM

10.9.1 The word "neglect" in s 12 of the 1937 Act has proved problematic. The meaning to be ascribed to it was discussed in *H* v *Lees; D* v *Orr*[87] which concerned two unconnected cases which were conjoined because they dealt with the same issue. In the former, a 9-month-old baby had been found asleep and warmly wrapped in his cot. The conviction for neglect at first instance arose because the only person present in the house at the time was his mother, and she was heavily intoxicated. In the latter, a 13-year-old girl was left at home on her own by her father for a 6-hour period on a February evening after she had refused to go out with him. Both convictions were quashed on appeal. Neither child had been "neglected". In his judgment Lord Justice-General Hope noted that "the conduct must be more than transient or trivial" and that "the element of cruelty which is indicated by the headnote [to the section of the Act] is to be found in the

---

[81] *Codona* v *Cardle* 1989 JC 99.
[82] See *Wightman* v *Lees* 2000 SLT 111.
[83] Children and Young Persons (Scotland) Act 1937, s 12(1).
[84] *Ibid*, s 110(1).
[85] *HM Advocate* v *Clark* 1968 JC 53; *H* v *Lees* 1993 JC 238.
[86] *HM Advocate* v *Clark* 1968 JC 53; *Dunn* v *McDonald* 2013 SLT (Sh Ct) 34.
[87] 1993 JC 238.

manner, or the likely effect, of the conduct, which must of course be wilful" (ie deliberate).[88] He continued: "the appropriate standard is what a reasonable parent, in all the circumstances, would regard as necessary to provide proper care and attention to the child".[89] This is, of course, very vague and Lord Hope accepted that parents would hold "widely varying views".[90] It is submitted that, generally, the term "neglect" requires some ongoing component, something which is implicit in Lord Hope's rejection of "transient" conduct and in the fact that some importance was attached to the fact that the 13-year-old had been left alone "on a single occasion" only.[91]

Section 51 of the *Draft Criminal Code* provides that an offence is   **10.9.2** committed when a person who has parental responsibilities towards a child, or who otherwise has charge or care of a child, intentionally or recklessly –

"(a) subjects the child to violence, maltreatment or abuse;
(b) causes the child physical or mental injury;
(c) abandons or neglects the child in a manner likely to cause the child suffering or injury to health; or
(d) allows the child to be used or exploited for sexual or pornographic purposes".[92]

This is a tighter provision than the current legislation and enactment of a statutory provision along these lines would serve to clarify the responsibilities of carers.

10.10   THE PHYSICAL PUNISHMENT OF CHILDREN

When a court is determining whether a person has committed   **10.10.1** justifiable chastisement, that is, a physical punishment carried out in exercise of a parental right, or of a right derived from having charge or care of a child, s 51(1) of the Criminal Justice (Scotland) Act 2003 provides that it must take into account several factors. These include what was done, the reason for it and the circumstances in which it took place. Consideration must also be given to the duration and frequency of the chastisement; any effect (whether physical or mental) which it has been shown to have had on the child, and the child's age and personal characteristics (including sex and state of health) at the time the

---

[88] 1993 JC 238 at 244.
[89] *Ibid* at 245.
[90] *Ibid*.
[91] *Ibid* at 247.
[92] *Draft Criminal Code*, s 51(1).

punishment was administered. The court may also consider "such other factors as it considers appropriate in the circumstances of the case".[93] However, the legislation explicitly provides that justifiable assaults do not include a blow to the head, shaking, or the use of an implement.[94]

10.11 CRITIQUE OF THE LAW ON PHYSICAL PUNISHMENT OF CHILDREN AND PROPOSALS FOR REFORM

10.11.1 The physical punishment of children is an issue which tends to polarise views. Some people consider that smacking a child is no different from striking a stranger and ought always to be treated as an assault by the criminal law.[95] Others stress that parents who smack their children are generally acting in what they perceive as the best interests of their children, and thus the law should treat this in the same way as boxing or medical operations, namely as justified on public policy grounds. It can certainly be argued that the criminal law's failure to proscribe smacking reflects a liberal philosophy in which parental chastisement of children is seen as being within the "private" rather than the "public" sphere.[96] As Okin reminds us: "The privacy of the home can be a dangerous place, especially for women and children."[97] The United Nations Committee on the Rights of the Child has stated that limiting, rather than removing, the defence of reasonable chastisement is not in keeping with the provisions of the UN Convention on the Rights of the Child, and that all forms of corporal punishment in the family should cease to be regarded as lawful.[98] Scots law ought, therefore, to proscribe violence against children irrespective of the relationship between the perpetrator and the child, and the motivation behind the violence.

---

[93] Criminal Justice (Scotland) Act 2003, s 51(2). A "child" is defined in s 51(4) as someone who is aged 15 years or younger.

[94] *Ibid*, s 51(3). Historically, wooden spoons and belts were commonly used implements of punishment.

[95] For an example of a parent prosecuted for assaulting his child, see *G v Templeton* 1998 SCLR 180.

[96] "It is a standard liberal view that intervention by the state in family life is to be avoided if at all possible": K O'Donovan, *Sexual Divisions in Law* (1985), p 14.

[97] Okin (1989), p 29. See also S S M Edwards, "All in the name of privacy – domestic violence" in *Sex and Gender in the Legal Process* (1996).

[98] *UN Committee on the Rights of the Child* (2002, CRC/C/15/Add.188), paras 35–36.

10.12   RECKLESSLY CAUSING INJURY

We have already noted that an assault requires a deliberate   **10.12.1**
attack.[99] In *HM Advocate v Harris*[100] a Bench of Five Judges
made clear that recklessly causing injury is a separate crime from
assault, namely "reckless injury". The Crown has, however, used
a variety of different labels in prosecuting such behaviour; as well
as "causing real injury", the terms "reckless injury", "reckless
endangerment", "culpable and reckless injury" and "reckless
conduct" have been used in indictments and complaints.[101] We
have already considered a number of these cases. In *MacPhail v
Clark*[102] a farmer set fire to a field, for a legitimate purpose, but
was convicted of reckless endangerment for omitting to act when
the smoke from the fire blew onto a road, causing danger to several
vehicles. In *W v HM Advocate*[103] the accused injured a passer-
by by throwing or dropping a bottle from a fifteenth-floor flat.
He had been warned, previously, of the dangers in doing so. A
conviction for culpable and reckless injury was upheld on appeal.
We have also considered the case of *Khaliq v HM Advocate*[104] in
which the accused were charged with risking causing real injury
by "culpably, wilfully and recklessly" supplying glue-sniffing kits.
In *Mallin v Clark*[105] the accused was charged that he "did culpably
and recklessly conceal a used syringe on [his] person and fail to
disclose said fact to police officers when being searched whereby
... an officer of the Fife Constabulary was injured". The charge in
the case of *Normand v Robinson*[106] was of "culpable and reckless
conduct" for having organised a "rave" in a derelict warehouse.
The complaint narrated that there was no mains electricity and
lighting was provided by candles. There were no fire alarms or
fire escapes and there were large holes in the floor. The sheriff had
dismissed the complaint on a plea to the relevancy. It was held on
an appeal by the Crown that this was a relevant charge. According
to Lord Murray it was culpably reckless to organise this type of
gathering in derelict premises with the attendant dangers. It has
been held that it is not necessary for the Crown to lead evidence of

---

[99] In section 10.2.2 above.
[100] 1993 JC 150.
[101] See *HM Advocate v McArthur* [2010] HCJ 10: culpable and reckless conduct
involving an omission.
[102] 1983 SLT (Sh Ct) 37. See section 6.7.7 above.
[103] 1982 SLT 420. See section 6.15.5 above.
[104] 1984 JC 23. See section 7.3.7 above.
[105] 2002 SLT 1202. See also *Kimmins v Normand* 1993 SLT 1260; *Normand v
Morrison* 1993 SCCR 207; and *Donaldson v Normand* 1997 SCCR 351.
[106] 1994 SLT 558.

actual danger in order to found a charge of culpable and reckless conduct.[107]

10.13 CRITIQUE OF THE LAW ON RECKLESSLY CAUSING INJURY AND PROPOSALS FOR REFORM

10.13.1 As we can see from the preceding section, Scots criminal law has a plethora of similar offences involving culpable and reckless endangerment, conduct, or injury, some of which are ill defined. It is not always clear why the Crown has libelled one, as opposed to the others. In *Donaldson* v *Normand*[108] the word "endangerment" did not even appear in the complaint; rather, the accused was charged that he "did culpably and recklessly deny being in possession [of a needle] ... and did thus expose [a turnkey] to the risk of injury and infection". The law would be simplified, and clarified, if these multiple offences were replaced by one offence of "recklessly causing injury", and one of "causing an unlawful risk of injury".[109]

Assault and recklessly causing injury are the two most commonly encountered non-fatal, non-sexual offences against the person, but there are several others. We now consider these.

10.14 THREATS

10.14.1 The common law proscribes the making of certain types of threat, but it seems that these must be threats to kill or seriously injure the victim, or to cause serious damage to property. Lesser threats may amount to robbery, extortion or attempting to pervert the course of justice, depending on the circumstances, but are not criminal unless the ulterior purpose of depriving the victim of property or perverting justice is present. In *MacKellar* v *Dickson*,[110] the charge stated that the accused "did ... wickedly and feloniously write and send, or cause to be sent ... [two] threatening letter[s]". Both letters contained clear death threats. It was held that this was a competent charge. Section 38 of the Criminal Justice and Licensing (Scotland) Act 2010 creates the offence of "behaving in a threatening or abusive manner". To constitute an offence, the behaviour must be such as would be likely to cause a reasonable person to suffer fear

---

[107] *Robertson* v *Klos* 2006 SCCR 52.
[108] 1997 SCCR 351.
[109] For an indication of how this might be done, see the *Draft Criminal Code*, ss 42 and 43.
[110] (1898) 2 Adam 504.

or alarm, and the accused must intend to cause fear or alarm or be reckless as to this.[111] This is discussed further in Chapter 15, as an offence against public order.[112]

10.15   DRUGGING

This is a form of causing real injury. Administering drugs to someone cannot ordinarily be prosecuted as an assault, since the physical attack required for an assault will usually be absent. Both English and Irish law refer to "poisoning" rather than "drugging".[113] Gordon's *Criminal Law* suggests that for Scots law there must be shown to be some intent to injure the victim, or recklessness as to injury,[114] although a footnote reference states that: "it is probably always criminal to give a child a quantity of whisky which injures its health".[115] This may be based on the view that such behaviour is always objectively reckless. In *Borwick* v *Urquhart*[116] the accused was convicted of having wilfully (ie deliberately) supplied alcohol (a half-bottle of vodka) to a 13-year-old girl, knowing that its consumption could be dangerous to her life and health, and causing and procuring its consumption by the girl. The appellant had not actually administered the vodka to the complainer, but the appeal court held that "the case is very much the same as if he had done so".[117] It is a statutory offence to administer a substance "for sexual purposes".[118] This offence is considered in Chapter 11.[119]

10.15.1

10.16   CRITIQUE OF THE LAW ON DRUGGING AND PROPOSALS FOR REFORM

The *Draft Criminal Code* provides:

10.16.1

"A person who administers any drug or other substance to another person –
   (a) with intent to stupefy that person or being reckless as to whether that person is stupefied;
   (b) with intent to facilitate the commission of an offence against that person or being reckless as to whether such an offence is committed; or

---

[111] Section 38(2) provides a defence if the behaviour was "reasonable" in the circumstances. A person being attacked who responds with verbal abuse could presumably rely on this defence.
[112] See from section 15.5 below.
[113] In Ireland the offence is now contained in the Non-Fatal Offences Against the Person Act 1997, s 12.
[114] Gordon (2001), para 29.48.
[115] *Ibid*, fn 92.
[116] 2003 SCCR 243.
[117] *Ibid* at 247, para 7, per Lord Coulsfield.
[118] Sexual Offences (Scotland) Act 2009, s 11.
[119] At section 11.11.1 below.

(c) with intent that that person commits an offence, or being reckless as to whether that person commits an offence,

is guilty of the offence of drugging."[120]

"Administration" is defined to include causing the substance to be taken,[121] and the section excludes substances administered in the course of lawful medical or dental treatment, or where the other person consented to being drugged, knowing the drug's likely effects.[122] While the statutory offence of administering a substance for sexual purpose[123] mirrors some of the *Code*'s provisions, the former is a much more narrowly defined offence; the *Code* offence applies where the person administering the substance intends to commit *any* offence against the other person (for example, to injure, kill or steal from them).

10.16.2   The *Code* also provides an offence of "exposing a child to harm", the first part of which would cover the common law offence of drugging. This is committed by any person who

"supplies or administers an article or substance to a child under the age of sixteen when that person knows or ought to know that the article or substance is likely to pose a serious risk of harm to the child".[124]

That section of the *Code* also provides that an offence is committed by a person who

"causes or permits a child under the age of sixteen to engage in an activity when that person knows or ought to know that engaging in the activity is likely to pose a serious risk of harm to the child".[125]

There are exceptions for bona fide medical or dental treatment,[126] and for educational, sporting or recreational activities which do not pose exceptional or unacceptable risks.[127] It is a defence that the accused has exercised all due diligence to avoid committing an offence under this provision.[128] As well as covering the situation in *Borwick* v *Urquhart*,[129] this protects children from a wider range of harmful things and behaviours, as the *Commentary to the Code* makes clear:

---

[120] *Draft Criminal Code*, s 47(1).
[121] *Ibid*, s 47(3).
[122] *Ibid*, s 47(2).
[123] See sections 10.15.1 above, and 11.11.1 below.
[124] *Draft Criminal Code*, s 52(1)(a).
[125] *Ibid*, s 52(1)(b).
[126] *Ibid*, s 52(2)(a).
[127] *Ibid*, s 52(2)(b).
[128] *Ibid*, s 52(3).
[129] 2003 SCCR 243. See section 10.15.1 above.

"The section would cover such conduct as using children as chimney sweeps; using children in dangerous or unhealthy work in factories or shops or on farms; supplying glue-sniffing kits to children; supplying children with explosive materials or dangerous weapons which they are unlikely to be able to control properly; giving young children alcohol or drugs likely to cause them harm; allowing children to take part in dangerous performances such as knife throwing or lion taming; allowing children to engage in severe athletic or gymnastic training before their bodies are ready for it, or encouraging them to participate in sporting or other recreational activities which present abnormal risks."[130]

While there are several statutory provisions, designed to protect children from specific dangers such as cigarettes,[131] fireworks[132] and alcohol,[133] the current law provides no general offence of exposing children to harm. Enactment of a provision such as the one contained in the *Code* would fill a *lacuna* in the law.

10.17   ABDUCTION/DEPRIVATION OF LIBERTY

In *Brouillard* v *HM Advocate*[134] the appeal court approved Lord **10.17.1** Kincraig's direction to the jury in *M* v *HM Advocate*[135] that "it is a crime to carry off or confine any person forcibly against their will without lawful authority". The court in *Brouillard* also confirmed that the exercise of lawful authority may excuse what would otherwise be the crime of abduction; this point arose in *Elliott* v *Tudhope*,[136] in which a police constable was charged with abducting a man by unlawfully arresting him. There are also statutory offences of abduction.[137] Where the person being carried off is a child, the common law crime of plagium may be charged. According to Hume, plagium involved "the away-taking of an infant child. For in this instance the creature taken, which has no will of its own, is a *thing*, under the care and in the possession of others, from whom it is taken".[138] It seems that the child must be under the age of puberty (that is, 14 for a boy and 12 for a girl).

---

[130] *Commentary* to s 52.
[131] The Tobacco and Primary Medical Services (Scotland) Act 2010, s 4(1) makes it an offence to sell tobacco products or cigarette papers to a person under the age of 18. For defences, see s 4(2). It is also an offence for a person aged under 18 to buy or attempt to buy such items: s 5(1).
[132] Fireworks Act 2003, s 3, and the Fireworks Regulations 2004 (SI 2004/1836), reg 4(1).
[133] Licensing (Scotland) Act 2005, s 102.
[134] 2004 JC 176.
[135] (1980) SCCR Supp 250.
[136] 1987 SCCR 85.
[137] See the Child Abduction Act 1984, s 6, as amended.
[138] Hume, i, 84 (emphasis in original).

10.18 CRITIQUE OF THE LAW ON ABDUCTION/ DEPRIVATION OF LIBERTY AND PROPOSALS FOR REFORM

10.18.1 Although *M v HM Advocate*[139] makes clear that abduction can be charged when there has been both a "carrying off" and an "unlawful detention", it seems preferable to separate these two elements into distinct offences, since one's liberty can be deprived without any carrying off; if A locks B in a room, even in the latter's own home, this would amount to a deprivation of liberty. The *Draft Criminal Code* defines this as occurring where the accused intends to deprive the other person of her liberty, or is reckless as to whether liberty is deprived.[140] Where the person being abducted is a child, it is unclear whether it is sufficient under the current law for the Crown to aver that the child was induced or enticed to go away with the accused, or whether it is an essential element of abduction that the accused acted against the child's will. This point was raised in the case of *Oates*[141] in 1861 but was not decided in that case, and remains undecided today. *M v HM Advocate* concerned a 6-year-old child. Lord Kincraig directed the jury that it would be sufficient to constitute abduction if the child was led away by, or induced to follow, the accused, since either would be sufficient to prove that the child was taken away against her will. This is not necessarily so, since a child may willingly follow someone. The Scottish Law Commission recommended 27 years ago that the law be clarified, but this has not been implemented.[142] The *Code* contains an offence of abduction where a person is carried off or taken away without her consent, and a separate offence of "child abduction" when the person being taken is under the age of 16 and is removed from the control of a person who has lawful control of the child.[143] To alleviate the difficulties noted in *Brouillard v HM Advocate*,[144] the *Code* defines child abduction as taking, enticing or detaining a child. This offence differs from plagium in applying to older children, as well as those under the age of puberty.

---

[139] (1980) SCCR Supp 250.

[140] *Draft Criminal Code*, s 46. It is a defence (under s 22) that the accused acted with lawful authority (see from section 21.14.4 below). This would allow a police officer lawfully to detain or arrest a suspect, a prison warden to incarcerate a convict, and parents to prevent their child from leaving the house.

[141] (1861) 4 Irv 74.

[142] Scottish Law Commission, *Report on Child Abduction* (Cm 64, 1987), para 2.4.

[143] *Draft Criminal Code*, ss 45 and 54 respectively.

[144] 2004 JC 176.

10.19   SLAVERY

Slavery is proscribed by several international treaties and in domestic   **10.19.1**
law by the Slave Trade Act 1824. Fair labelling requirements come
into play here;[145] while the conduct of the accused in enslaving
another person could often fall within the ambit of the crimes of
abduction or deprivation of liberty,[146] slavery is generally regarded
as a distinct, and more serious, crime. Section 47 of the Criminal
Justice and Licensing (Scotland) Act 2010 makes it an offence to
hold another person in slavery or servitude.[147] This offence was
introduced following a French case in which the European Court of
Human Rights held that there had been a violation of Art 4 of the
European Convention on Human Rights (ECHR).[148]

10.20   TORTURE

As previously noted,[149] the ECHR prohibits torture,[150] as do several   **10.20.1**
other international treaties.[151] Torture is also an offence under s 134
of the Criminal Justice Act 1988, but this is restricted to acts by public
officials, or those acting at the behest of such officials. Furthermore,
legislation provides defences of "lawful authority, justification or
excuse" which is to be defined "under the law of the place where
[the torture] was inflicted" unless it was carried out overseas under
UK law, when the relevant law of the UK will apply.[152]

10.21   CRITIQUE OF THE LAW ON TORTURE AND PROPOSALS FOR REFORM

The *Draft Criminal Code* defines "torture" as inflicting severe   **10.21.1**
physical or mental pain or suffering on another person, solely or
primarily

"(a) to derive pleasure from the victim's pain or suffering;

(b) because of the victim's membership or supposed membership of a group
of persons defined by reference to race, colour, religion, gender, sexual
orientation, nationality, citizenship or ethnic or national origins;

---

[145] The principle of fair labelling is discussed from section 4.6 above.
[146] See from section 10.17 above.
[147] "Holding a person in slavery or servitude" and "forced or compulsory labour"
are to be construed in accordance with Art 4 of the ECHR: Criminal Justice and
Licensing (Scotland) Act 2010, s 47(2).
[148] *Siliadin* v *France* (2006) 43 EHRR 16.
[149] See section 1.4.1 above.
[150] Art 3.
[151] See the UN Convention against Tortute and other Cruel, Inhuman or Degrading
Treatment or Punishment, Art 4(1).
[152] Criminal Justice Act 1988, s 134(4) and (5).

(c) to obtain information or a confession from the victim or another person;

(d) to intimidate or coerce the victim or another person; or

(e) to punish the victim or another person".[153]

Unlike the common law, it does not restrict the application of the offence to those acting in an official capacity.[154] It could, of course, be suggested that offences such as aggravated assault already exist to deal with the accused who was not acting as a state official, but where the motivation of someone who commits such assaults is one of those listed above, it seems to us that the label of "torture" is merited.

10.21.2   The *Code* also includes a specific offence of inhuman or degrading treatment.[155] A person may complain to the European Court of Human Rights if her right not to be subject to such treatment has been breached. That court has set a high threshold for this; if there is no physical injury there must at least be intense physical and mental suffering which led to acute psychiatric disturbance.[156] The victim's age, gender and general health are all factors to be taken into account in assessing the effects of the accused's conduct.[157] The definition of "lawful authority" provided by the *Code* excludes the infliction of torture, inhuman or degrading treatment, or corporal punishment.[158] There is currently no specific crime in Scots law of treating someone in an inhuman or degrading way, and not all such instances could be subsumed into other offences, such as assault. For instance, if a nurse deliberately left a patient in a state of undress on a hospital trolley, or an employee in an old folks' home decided that a resident should remain in soiled bedding, perhaps as a punishment, this would not be an assault, but could constitute degrading treatment. Fair labelling requirements suggest that this form of behaviour merits being treated as a distinct crime. The Scottish Parliament should give consideration to enacting a provision similar to that suggested by the *Code*.

---

[153] *Draft Criminal Code*, s 39(1). For the avoidance of doubt, it is provided that paragraph (e) does not apply "to the infliction of normal and reasonable punishment on convicted persons in a way which is compatible with their human rights" (s 39(3)).

[154] *Ibid*, s 22(4)(b), discussed in section 21.14.4 below.

[155] *Ibid*, s 40(1). As with torture, it is provided that this does not apply "to the infliction of normal and reasonable punishment on convicted persons in a way which is compatible with their human rights" (s 40(2)).

[156] See *Ireland* v *UK* (1979–80) 2 EHRR 25.

[157] See *Tyrer* v *UK* (1978) 2 EHRR 1; *Costello-Roberts* v *UK* (1995) 19 EHRR 112; and *A* v *UK* (1999) 27 EHRR 611, each of which involved corporal punishment of children. The current Scots law on the reasonable chastisement of children is considered from section 10.10 above.

[158] *Draft Criminal Code*, s 22(4)(b).

CHAPTER 11

SEXUAL OFFENCES

11.1   INTRODUCTION

Though they are clearly a form of crime "against the person", Bruce **11.1.1**
MacFarlane, a Canadian author, has pointed out that sexual assaults
differ from other crimes:

> "Almost all perpetrators are male. Unlike other violent crimes, most incidents
> go unreported despite evidence suggesting that the rate of sexual assault is on
> the increase. While many forms of sexual activity are not in themselves illegal,
> the circumstances prevailing at the time – such as an absence of consent or the
> youthfulness of a participant – can make the activity illegal and expose one of
> the participants to a lengthy term of imprisonment. And despite the physical
> nature of the act constituting the crime, much of the harm is psychological or
> emotional in nature, not bodily."[1]

The term "sexual offences" covers a wide range of conduct, and
the crimes within its purview are not all directed at the same sorts
of harms; the criminalisation of bestiality, for example, is based
on different grounds from the criminalisation of rape or other
sexual assaults.[2] In some jurisdictions, the laws on sexual offences
reflect a belief that certain conduct is "against the rights of God".
Hence Iranian criminal law proscribes "zina" (extra-marital sexual
intercourse), sodomy and lesbianism,[3] none of which is criminalised
in Scottish law, so long as both parties are consenting adults. Sanford
Kadish has noted that "The use of the criminal law to prohibit moral

---

[1] B A MacFarlane, "Historical development of the offence of rape", in
J Wood and R Peck, *100 Years of the Criminal Code in Canada* (1993),
p 1, available at: http://www.canadiancriminallaw.com/articles/articles%20pdf/
Historical_Development_of_the_Offence_of_Rape.pdf.
[2] We have treated bestiality as primarily a crime which involves "offensive
behaviour". See section 16.4.1 below.
[3] See F Mahmoudi, "On criminalization in Iran (sources and features)" (2002) 10
Eur J Crime Crim L & Crim Just 45 at 47.

deviancy among consenting adults has been a recurring subject of jurisprudential debate".[4] Our law has to some extent moved away from the proscription of what was once perceived as "deviancy", with sexual offences now reflecting a philosophy which emphasises the liberty of consenting adults to engage in a range of sexual practices without interference from the criminal law. That this liberal ideal is not fully realised in practice, however, was illustrated by the prosecution of a man for attempting to have sexual intercourse with a bicycle.[5]

11.1.2 The corollary of the liberal maxim that the law ought to protect sexual freedom is that engaging in sexual activity with someone who is not consenting to this is a serious violation of the latter's sexual autonomy, and ought to be condemned by the criminal law. At the same time, the law attempts to protect vulnerable groups, such as children and the mentally handicapped, from exploitation. These various justifications for criminalisation were reflected in the approach taken by the Scottish Law Commission,[6] whose proposals for reform led to the enactment of the Sexual Offences (Scotland) Act 2009.[7] This Act created many new offences and redefined (and will ultimately replace) common law crimes such as rape. According to one commentator:

> "Scotland, some would say, has thereby been jet-propelled from the 'pre-2009 Act', Neolithic period, where serious sexual offences were determined and characterised by the presence or absence of force or violence, into the new modern era where the sexual autonomy of the individual and the presence or absence of consent is fully and clearly recognised and stated in primary legislation to be central to the sexual offences regime."[8]

Most of the offences in the Act came into force on 1 December 2010, but since some rapes and other sexual assaults may not be reported until many years after their commission, the common law will continue to be used for such offences.[9]

11.1.3 The Act uses the word "sexual" in relation to many of its provisions; offences include "sexual assault"; "sexual assault by penetration";

---

[4] S H Kadish, *Blame and Punishment: Essays in the Criminal Law* (1987), p 22.
[5] See section 1.1.1 above.
[6] Scottish Law Commission, *Report on Rape and Other Sexual Offences* (No 209, 2007). The "protective principle" the Commission espouses is discussed at para 1.28 of its report. See also C Brants, "The state and the nation's bedrooms: the fundamental right of sexual autonomy" in P Alldridge and C Brants (eds), *Personal Autonomy, the Private Sphere and Criminal Law* (2001) 117 at p 119.
[7] Henceforth "the Act" or "the 2009 Act".
[8] Commentary on *Dempster* v *HM Advocate* [2012] HCJAC 140 in 2013 SCL 40 at 44–45.
[9] For a description of the common law of rape, see Gordon (2001), Ch 33.

"sexual coercion"; "sexual exposure"; and "administering a substance for sexual purposes". The offence of "communicating indecently" involves written or verbal communications which are of a "sexual" nature; and several offences, such as voyeurism, require the Crown to prove one of several motives, including "sexual" gratification. The Act provides that in interpreting its provisions, an activity, a communication, a manner of exposure or a relationship is "sexual" if "a reasonable person would, in all the circumstances of the case, consider it to be sexual".[10]

11.2 RAPE

That rape involves the infliction of the types of physical and profound **11.2.1** psychological harm that a society would wish to proscribe seems axiomatic. It should, however, be borne in mind that until recently rape was defined in Scots law to require penile penetration of the vagina. Indeed, the laws of many jurisdictions historically viewed the harm as having been done to the complainer's father or husband, rather than to the girl or woman who was raped:

> "According to patriarchal ideology, rape is wrong because it violates a woman's 'honor'. Her honor is defined either as her virginity or as her sexual fidelity to her husband. ... Rape laws are justified by patriarchy as being necessary in part to defend a woman's power to bargain her virginity. Under patriarchy, however, a woman's virginity is intrinsically valuable not to the woman herself, but only to her future husband."[11]

In Hume's era, rape was regarded as most serious if the victim had **11.2.2** been a virgin prior to the attack, reflecting the view that the "wrong" of rape lay primarily in it being a violation of a man's property rights in his daughter's virginity.[12] Many of the reported cases of rape which Hume described involved young girls, whose virginity was frequently mentioned in the indictments: the "deflouring" [sic] of Janet Boussie, a "young virgine, not past ten yearis of adge"; of Janet Falconer, a "young maid of twelf yeris"; of Janet Craig, an "honest manis bairne, and ane young virgine nocht past the age of elivin yeiris"; and finally of Agnes Stewart, a "young virgine, and infant bairne of [six] yeir auld". Commenting on ancient Hebrew and Babylonian laws, Susan Brownmiller graphically put it thus:

> "virgin maidens were bought and sold in marriage for fifty pieces of silver. To use plain language, what a father sold to a prospective bridegroom or his family was title to his daughter's unruptured hymen, a piece of property he

[10] Sexual Offences (Scotland) Act 2009, s 60(2).
[11] A M Jaggar, *Feminist Politics and Human Nature* (1983), p 261.
[12] Hume, i, 301–302.

wholly owned and controlled. With a clearly marked price tag attached to her hymen, a daughter of Israel was kept under watch to make sure she remained in a pristine state, for a piece of damaged goods could hardly command an advantageous match and might have to be sold as a concubine".[13]

Where the victim of rape was a married woman, rape was regarded as infringing a husband's right to exclusive sexual access to his wife, and this remained the position in Scots law until 1989.[14] Furthermore, it was not until 2001 that rape became defined as intercourse without consent;[15] prior to that date, the Crown required to establish that the accused had engaged in sexual intercourse with the complainer by "overcoming her will". This history must be borne in mind in understanding and assessing the current law.[16]

The *actus reus* and *mens rea* of rape

11.2.3   The common law offence of rape is abolished by the Act,[17] and a broader definition provided in s 1: a person who intentionally or recklessly penetrates the vagina,[18] anus or mouth of another person with his penis[19] commits rape if that other person does not consent to the penetration.[20] The accused must have no reasonable belief that the complainer was consenting. Now that rape has been defined to include non-consensual anal penetration, this definition recognises what had been colloquially referred to as "male rape". The common law offence of "sodomy" has been abolished by s 52 of the Act.[21] Any degree of penetration is sufficient.[22] If the complainer initially agreed to penetration, but later changed her (or his) mind, then a person commits rape if the penetration continues to take place, thereafter.[23]

---

[13] S Brownmiller, *Against Our Will* (1975), pp 19–20.
[14] See section 11.2.6 below.
[15] See *Lord Advocate's Reference (No 1 of 2001)* 2002 SLT 466.
[16] Attitudes to rape are discussed further in section 11.2.5 below.
[17] Sexual Offences (Scotland) Act 2009, s 52(a)(i) (for crimes committed after 1 December 2010).
[18] "Vagina" is defined to include the vulva, and a surgically constructed vagina (together with any surgically constructed vulva), if it forms part of the complainer and had been created in the course of surgical treatment: Sexual Offences (Scotland) Act 2009, s 1(4).
[19] "Penis" is defined (*ibid*) to include a surgically constructed penis if it forms part of the accused and has been created in the course of surgical treatment. The definitions of "penis" and "vagina" apply throughout the Act, by virtue of s 60(1).
[20] For a case involving oral penetration, prosecuted under s 1, see *Lukstins v HM Advocate* 2013 SLT 11.
[21] Sexual Offences (Scotland) Act 2009, s 52(a)(iv).
[22] *Ibid*, s 1(1).
[23] *Ibid*, s 1(3).

The *mens rea* requirement is that the accused intentionally or **11.2.4** recklessly penetrated with his penis the vagina, anus or mouth of the complainer and that he acted without any reasonable belief that the complainer was consenting to the intercourse. The Act also provides a definition of "consent" in terms of "free agreement"[24] and specifies that when considering whether the accused's belief as to consent was reasonable, the court is to have regard to whether the accused took any steps to establish whether there was consent, and what those steps were.[25] It also stipulates a number of circumstances in which free agreement will not be present.[26] Thus there is no free agreement where the complainer is incapable of consenting because of the effects of alcohol or any other substance.[27] The original wording of the Bill included cases in which the complainer was unconscious or asleep, and had not given consent prior to this to the conduct taking place while she was in that condition. This was a controversial provision, with several of those who gave evidence to the Justice Committee suggesting that allowing an accused to claim prior consent in such circumstances would be open to abuse. As against this, Gerry Maher, the Commissioner with primary responsibility for the Scottish Law Commission's Report on sexual offences, responded that removal of the provision would merely shift the focus onto the general consent requirement.[28] The Act now provides that a person who is asleep or unconscious is incapable of consenting to the sexual behaviours described in the legislation.[29] There is, in addition, no free agreement according to s 13 where the complainer has agreed or submitted to intercourse (or other sexual activity proscribed in ss 1–9 of the Act) because of violence used or threatened against her, or against a third party,[30] or because she was unlawfully detained by the accused,[31]

---

[24] Sexual Offences (Scotland) Act 2009, s 12.

[25] *Ibid*, s 16. This removes the defence of unreasonable error as to consent. For a discussion of the common law position, see P R Ferguson and C McDiarmid, *Scots Criminal Law: A Critical Analysis* (1st edn, 2009) at section 11.3.5.

[26] 2009 Act, s 13. These are "without prejudice to the generality" of s 12 – that is, there may well be other examples of circumstances in which it would be appropriate for a court to hold that the circumstances in themselves establish a lack of free agreement.

[27] *Ibid*, s 13(2)(a). Unlike at common law, the substances need not have been supplied by the accused. For an argument in favour of the approach taken in the Act, see S Cowan, "The trouble with drink: intoxication, (in)capacity, and the evaporation of consent to sex" (2008) 41 *Akron L Rev* 899.

[28] Scottish Parliament Justice Committee, *Official Report*, 18 November 2008, cols 1364–1365.

[29] Sexual Offences (Scotland) Act 2009, s 14(2). This applies to offences in ss 1–9. For a criticism of this provision, see J Chalmers, "Two problems in the Sexual Offences (Scotland) Bill" (2009) *Scottish Criminal Law* 553.

[30] 2009 Act, s 13(2)(b).

[31] *Ibid*, s 13(2)(c).

or mistaken as to the nature or purpose of the conduct because of deception by the accused.[32] Free agreement is also absent where the complainer's consent is achieved because of the accused having impersonated someone known personally to the complainer,[33] or where the only expression or indication of agreement comes from a person other than the complainer.[34] These provisions have greatly improved the current law. They make clear that it is unacceptable to engage in sexual intercourse, or other sexual behaviours, in certain circumstances in which doing so fails to treat the other party as an autonomous human being, with the right to control her sexual encounters.

11.2.5   The Scottish police recorded 1,462 allegations of rape or attempted rape in Scotland in 2012–13.[35] Attitudes towards rape and rape victims have changed, and rape may now be viewed as a sex crime, a crime of violence, and an invasion of privacy. It is increasingly being understood as primarily a crime of violence, having to do with power, control and degradation. Studies of offender profiles have shown that those who rape strangers frequently have convictions for other crimes, and often these are crimes involving violence.[36] Four-month-old babies and 84-year-old adults are raped – there is little "sexual" in this. In the first edition of this book, we criticised Scottish official statistics for persisting in classifying rape and attempted rape as "crimes of indecency". This term has now been replaced by "sexual offences".[37] The classic picture many people have of rape is of a man who jumps out of the bushes, grabs a passing woman and attacks her. Such assaults do happen, but the vast majority of sexual attacks are committed by people who the victim knows – friends, relatives, husbands, boyfriends. A report by the Crown Office and Procurator Fiscal Service found that the accused was known to the victim in 81 per cent of cases, and in 28 per cent of attacks the accused was her partner. Only 6 per cent involved a stranger.[38]

---

[32] 2009 Act, s 13(2)(d).

[33] *Ibid*, s 13(2)(e). See the case of *William Fraser* (1847) Ark 280, discussed in section 12.16.3 below.

[34] 2009 Act, s 13(2)(f).

[35] Scottish Government Statistical Bulletin, *Recorded Crime in Scotland, 2012–13*, Table 1, p 17 (available at: http://www.scotland.gov.uk/Resource/0042/00425429. pdf).

[36] As the American organisation RAINN (Rape, Abuse and Incest National Network) states: "Rapists are more likely to be a serial criminal than a serial rapist" (available at: http://www.rainn.org/get-information/statistics/sexual-assault-offenders).

[37] Scottish Government Statistical Bulletin, *Recorded Crime in Scotland 2011–12*, para 7.15: "[Those] offences, previously called Crimes of indecency, are now referred to as Sexual offences."

[38] *Review of the Investigation and Prosecution of Sexual Offences in Scotland* (2006), para 2.30.

Marital rape

As previously noted,[39] until 1989 Scots law allowed the fact that the **11.2.6** accused was married to the complainer to be a defence to a charge of rape. Alison Jaggar has argued that marital rape exemptions were a clear demonstration of the fact that

> "rape laws exist to protect the rights of men over women's bodies rather than the rights of women over their own bodies ... Under patriarchy, her body is assumed to belong to him".[40]

The exemption had been narrowed prior to this in cases where the husband and wife were judicially separated,[41] and then narrowed further to include cases in which they were merely living apart,[42] but it was not until the case of *S v HM Advocate*[43] that the appeal court recognised that the fact that a man was married to his victim at the time of the forced intercourse should not prevent a charge of rape. Catharine MacKinnon has commented that similar reforms in the United States mean that "some of the most common rapes in life become rapes in law".[44] Hume's reference to the marital rape exception[45] copied a similar provision in Sir Matthew Hale's *History of the Pleas of the Crown*,[46] a highly influential English textbook, but neither Hale nor Hume cited any case law or statutory authority in support of the proposition. As MacFarlane has put it, the demise of the marital defence in Scotland and England was:

> "laudable, but tragically overdue. A community is not well served by laws that permit the abuse of one spouse by the other. How for three centuries that could have been sanctioned by common law courts on the basis of a paragraph in a textbook is almost beyond comprehension".[47]

11.3 CRITIQUE OF THE LAW ON RAPE AND PROPOSALS FOR REFORM

The redefinition of rape provided by the 2009 Act was long overdue, **11.3.1** but is to be welcomed. The inclusion of non-consensual anal penetration makes rape a gender-neutral crime, so far as the victim is concerned. However, the continuing focus on penile penetration

---

[39] At section 11.2.2 above.
[40] Jaggar (1983) at p 262.
[41] *HM Advocate v Duffy* 1983 SLT 7.
[42] *HM Advocate v Paxton* 1984 JC 105.
[43] 1989 SLT 469.
[44] C A MacKinnon, *Women's Lives, Men's Laws* (2007), p 125.
[45] Hume, i, 306.
[46] At 629. Hale's book was published in 1736, but had been written more than 65 years earlier.
[47] MacFarlane (1993) at pp 39–40.

in most jurisdictions' definitions of rape has been criticised as approaching the crime from "a very male point of view on what it means to be sexually violated".[48] The centrality of consent in the crime of rape is also regarded as highly problematic.[49] Thus MacKinnon argues:

> "when force is a normalized part of sex, when no is taken to mean yes, when fear and despair produce acquiescence and acquiescence is taken to mean consent, consent is not a meaningful concept".[50]

Noting that "consent to sex is not the same as wanting it",[51] she postulates the concept of "welcome sex": "An equality standard ... requires that sex be welcome. For the criminal law to change to this standard would require that sex be wanted for it not to be assaultive."[52]

11.3.2   John Gardner and Stephen Shute have pointed out that: "Many other acts which would be wrong in the absence of consent are perfectly innocent in the presence of consent – handshaking for example, or stripping someone's wallpaper while they are out at work."[53] But they suggest that the "wrongness" of rape does not merely lie in the fact that something has been done to the complainer without consent.[54] They offer a hypothetical scenario in which the victim is unconscious at the time of the intercourse, and so is "forever oblivious"[55] to the rape. Furthermore, in their scenario the rapist wore a condom (thus eliminating the risk of disease or pregnancy). The rape is never discovered by anyone, thus it does no harm. Yet surely all would agree that it was nonetheless a wrongful act. Concluding that "the wrongfulness of rape cannot, therefore, lie in the harmfulness of rape",[56] they argue that the wrong lies in the fact that rape is the "sheer use of a person", and is thus "a denial of [the victim's] personhood".[57]

---

[48] C A MacKinnon, *Feminism Unmodified* (1987), p 87.

[49] E Frazer and N Lacey, *The Politics of Community: A Feminist Critique of the Liberal-Communitarian Debate* (1993), p 92. See also S Cowan, "'Freedom and capacity to make a choice': a feminist analysis of consent in the criminal law of rape" in V E Munro and C F Stychin (eds), *Sexuality and the Law* (2007), p 51; V Tadros, "Rape without consent" (2006) 26 *OJLS* 515.

[50] MacKinnon (2007) at p 260.

[51] *Ibid* at p 244.

[52] *Ibid*.

[53] J Gardner and S Shute, "The wrongness of rape" in J Horder (ed), *Oxford Essays in Jurisprudence* (2000) 193 at p 194.

[54] *Ibid*.

[55] *Ibid*, p 196.

[56] *Ibid*, p 199.

[57] *Ibid*, p 205. For a critique of this approach, see: V Tadros, "Harm, sovereignty, and prohibition" (2011) 17 *Legal Theory* 35 at 50.

Criticism has also been levied against the *mens rea* requirement; **11.3.3**
MacKinnon suggests that the law bases its determination of what
amounts to rape "on the perspective of the accused rapist as opposed
to that of the victim".[58] One's initial reaction to this might be to ask:
how could the law do otherwise? *Mens rea* is, by definition, focused
on the mental state of the accused – in a rape case its focus is on what
the accused intended or foresaw: what was in his mind at the time of
the sexual intercourse. Did he intend to have intercourse without the
complainer's consent? Did he realise that the other party was not,
in fact, consenting, but decide to continue, regardless? Indeed, one
criticism which has been levelled at the law is that rape trials seem to
focus too much on the *complainer's* mental state – was s/he consenting
to intercourse? If not, did s/he communicate this mental state to
the accused? MacKinnon's approach does, however, merit further
consideration. Rape is a commonly occurring event, but one with an
unacceptably low conviction rate. If the purposes of the criminal law
include the prevention of certain wrongfully caused harms to others
(of which rape is a prime example), denouncing conduct which causes
such harm, and punishing the perpetrators of that harm, then the law
relating to rape is failing. If we are serious about these aims then we
must take a hard look at the law of rape – not only at its substantive
definition, but also at the rules of evidence and procedure.

The amendments made by the Act to the substantive law are **11.3.4**
unlikely to be sufficient, in themselves, to rectify the appalling low
conviction rate. Those who allege that they have been raped ought
to be treated with respect and dignity at all stages of the proceedings
– from being interviewed by the police, to cross-examination by
defence counsel. While there have been improvements in police
practices in recent years, the experience of many rape complainers
in the court room remains a harrowing one. The courts must also
ensure that the sentences meted out to those convicted of rape and
attempted rape reflect the gravity of the harm and potential harm.[59]
As Sharon Cowan makes clear:

> "Many feminists have recognized that law reform by itself will never solve
> the problem of rape. Social change regarding gendered expectations of
> appropriate sexual activity and beliefs about responsibility for sexual assault
> is also crucial."[60]

---

[58] MacKinnon (2007), p 34.
[59] See the case of *HM Advocate* v *Currie* 2009 SCCR 48 in which the accused was
given a non-custodial sentence for attempted rape, and this was upheld on appeal.
[60] Cowan (2008) at 901. See also S Cowan, "All change or business as usual?
Reforming the law of rape in Scotland" in C McGlynn and V E Munro (eds),
Rethinking Rape Law: International and Comparative Perspectives (2010) at
p 154, and W Larcombe, "Falling rape conviction rates: (some) feminist aims and
measures for rape law" (2011) 19 *Fem L Stud* 27.

11.4   SEXUAL ASSAULT BY PENETRATION

11.4.1   Section 2 of the Act makes it an offence for a person intentionally or recklessly to penetrate, with any part of the body or with "anything else", the complainer's vagina or anus where the complainer does not consent to this, and the accused had no reasonable belief that the complainer was consenting.[61] It is specifically provided[62] that the reference to penetration being with "any part" of the accused's body includes penile penetration – hence there is an overlap between ss 1 and 2. This is intended to cover the situation in which the complainer knows that penetration occurred, but does not know whether this was by the accused's penis, finger or some other object. The explanatory notes to the Act suggest that a blindfolded complainer may be an example of someone who may lack such knowledge. The same may be said for very young children, or complainers who are intoxicated or otherwise disorientated. If there is evidence that the penetration was by the penis, then the Crown will generally charge s 1 instead.[63]

11.5   SEXUAL ASSAULT

11.5.1   As well as sexual assault by penetration, the Act provides an offence of sexual assault, in s 3. As with ss 1 and 2, the accused must have acted without the complainer's consent, and without any reasonable belief in consent.[64] The section lists five different behaviours which, if done intentionally or recklessly, constitute sexual assault. These are: sexual penetration of the complainer's vagina, anus or mouth;[65] sexual touching;[66] ejaculating semen on to the complainer;[67] urinating or emitting saliva on to the complainer "sexually";[68] and engaging in any other form of sexual activity in which the accused has physical contact with the complainer.[69] Lest this list does not

---

[61] Sexual Offences (Scotland) Act 2009, s 2(1). "Penetration" is defined as a continuing act in s 2(2), similarly to the definition for rape in s 1(2). For a case involving digital penetration, see *Murray* v *HM Advocate* [2013] HCJAC 3.

[62] 2009 Act, s 2(4).

[63] See Scottish Law Commission (2007), para 3.45.

[64] Sexual Offences (Scotland) Act 2009, s 3(1)(a) and (b).

[65] *Ibid*, s 3(2)(a). As with s 2, this is specified to include penetration by the accused's penis: s 3(5). "Penetration" is defined as a continuing act (s 3(3)), as per ss 1 and 2.

[66] 2009 Act, s 3(2)(b). For a case involving sexual touching, see *Murray* v *HM Advocate* [2013] HCJAC 3.

[67] 2009 Act, s 3(2)(d).

[68] *Ibid*, s 3(2)(e).

[69] *Ibid*, s 3(2)(c). This is specified to include bodily contact or contact by means of an implement, and whether or not through clothing.

cover all possible forms of sexual assault, the common law crime of indecent assault is not repealed by the Act.

11.6   SEXUAL COERCION

Sections 4–6 of the Act create offences involving coercion. Thus **11.6.1** the offence of "sexual coercion" is committed where one person intentionally causes another to participate in a sexual activity, without the latter's consent and without any reasonable belief in consent.[70] It is also an offence to coerce someone into being present during a sexual activity,[71] or to look at a sexual image.[72] The former could occur where the accused intentionally engages in sexual activity in the presence of the complainer, or causes the complainer to be present while a third party is engaging in such activity. An activity is defined as taking place "in the presence of" the complainer where the complainer is observing the behaviour other than "by looking at an image", for example via a webcam. The complainer need not have actually observed the activity; it is enough that the activity was capable of being so observed.[73] A "sexual image" is defined for the purposes of the latter offence (in s 6) as an image of a person engaging in a sexual activity, or an image of human genitals. In either case, the image can be of a real or an imaginary person.[74] As with previous offences in the Act, for both ss 5 and 6 the complainer must not have consented, and the accused must have had no reasonable belief that there was such consent.[75] Motive is an essential ingredient in both offences; it must be shown that the accused acted for the purposes of obtaining sexual gratification, or in order to humiliate, distress or alarm the particular complainer.[76] Thus in relation to the offence in s 6 of coercing someone into looking at a sexual image, it seems that no offence is committed if the accused sent the image to the wrong person and the complainer received it in error.[77] In the (unreported) case of *Christopher Walker* (2009), the accused pled guilty to breach of the peace by sending a phone video message

---

[70] Sexual Offences (Scotland) Act 2009, s 4.

[71] *Ibid*, s 5(1).

[72] *Ibid*, s 6(1).

[73] *Ibid*, s 5(3).

[74] *Ibid*, s 6(3).

[75] *Ibid*, ss 5(1)(a) and (b), and 6(1)(a) and (b), respectively.

[76] *Ibid*, ss 5(2) and 6(2). See also s 49(1), which provides that the accused's purpose will be held to have been sexual gratification, or to humiliate, distress or alarm a complainer "if in all the circumstances of the case it may reasonably be inferred" that this was the accused's purpose. It is also stated to be irrelevant whether or not the complainer actually experienced humiliation, distress or alarm (s 49(2)). These provisions apply to ss 5–9, 22–26 and 32–36 (by virtue of s 49(1)).

[77] *Ibid*, s 6(2).

containing footage of his genitals to a stranger, having incorrectly dialled his girlfriend's phone number.[78] The requirements of s 6 may not be fulfilled by the facts of this case; the accused's intention was not to humiliate, distress or alarm the recipient, nor was the video sent for his own sexual gratification. Rather, it seems that it was sent for the gratification of the recipient.

11.7 COMMUNICATING INDECENTLY

11.7.1 The sending or giving of a sexual written or verbal communication to someone, without that other person's consent, and with no reasonable belief in consent, is an offence under s 7 of the Act. The communication must be intentional,[79] and be for the purpose of obtaining sexual gratification or in order to humiliate, distress or alarm the complainer.[80] In the case of *Kidd* v *McGowan*[81] the accused pled guilty to a breach of this section, the "sexual verbal communication" being that he had threatened to rape the two complainers.

11.8 SEXUAL EXPOSURE

11.8.1 One form of the common law crime of public indecency (involving "indecent exposure") has been codified by s 8 of the Act, such that a person who intentionally exposes his or her genitals to another in a sexual manner commits an offence.[82] This must be done without the complainer's consent, and without any reasonable belief in consent,[83] and in order to obtain sexual gratification or to humiliate, distress or alarm the complainer.[84]

11.9 VOYEURISM

11.9.1 Where one person observes another engaging in a "private act", the latter does not consent to being observed, and there is no reasonable belief in consent, then the former commits the offence of "voyeurism" under s 9 of the Act. A person is defined as doing

---

[78] See "Genital video caller avoids jail", *BBC News*, 4 March 2009, available at: http://news.bbc.co.uk/1/hi/scotland/tayside_and_central/7924271.stm. The common law crime of breach of the peace is described further from section 15.2 below.

[79] Sexual Offences (Scotland) Act 2009, s 7(1).

[80] *Ibid*, s 7(3). See s 7(4) for definitions of "written communication" and "verbal communication".

[81] [2012] HCJAC 163.

[82] The offence of "public indecency" is considered further at section 11.20 below.

[83] Sexual Offences (Scotland) Act 2009, s 8(1)(a) and (b).

[84] *Ibid*, s 8(2)(a) and (b).

a "private act" for the purposes of this section if in a place "which in the circumstances would reasonably be expected to provide privacy",[85] and the complainer's genitals, buttocks or breasts are exposed or covered only with underwear, or the complainer is using a lavatory, or is doing a sexual act "that is not of a kind ordinarily done in public".[86] It has been held in a case involving similarly worded English legislation that "breasts" means the female, but not the male, chest.[87] This is a regrettable interpretation, since it means that making a covert video recording of a 10-year-old boy, naked from the waist up, in a swimming pool shower, is not within the terms of s 9.[88]

In the unreported case of *James Jardine* (2009) the accused squatted   **11.9.2** in the aisles of a supermarket and took photographs up women's skirts using a mini camera.[89] He was charged with a breach of the peace. Since his victims were not "doing a private act", the statutory offence would not have applied.[90] However, the 2009 Act has since been amended so that voyeurism includes operating equipment or recording an image beneath the victim's clothing in order to observe the victim's genitals or buttocks or the underwear covering these parts of the body, in circumstances where the genitals, buttocks or underwear would not otherwise be visible.[91] This could now be prosecuted in cases such as *Jardine*. Breach of the peace has been charged where the accused has not gone beyond preparation to the actual perpetration of one of these statutory offences. An example of this is the case of *J* v *HM Advocate*[92] in which the accused had hidden a mobile phone in the complainer's bathroom "with the intention of taking indecent photographs of her". The Act could now be used in similar cases, since it is an offence to install equipment

---

[85] Sexual Offences (Scotland) Act 2009, s 10(1).

[86] *Ibid*, s 10(1)(a), (b) and (c).

[87] *R* v *Bassett* [2009] 1 WLR 1032, interpreting the Sexual Offences Act 2003, ss 67 and 68. See also to the same effect the Canadian case of *Chase* (1984) 40 CR (3d) 282 (NBCA), discussed at section 1.12.1 above. This was subsequently reversed: (1987) 59 CR (3d) (SCC).

[88] See D Selfe, "Case Comment: R v Bassett (Kevin): voyeurism – the meaning of 'privacy' and 'breasts'" (2009) 193 *Criminal Lawyer* 2; and also Chalmers (2009).

[89] See "Probation over skirt photographs", *BBC News*, 15 October 2009, available at: http://news.bbc.co.uk/1/hi/scotland/glasgow_and_west/8308945.stm. See also *Elphick* v *HM Advocate* (unreported, 7 August 2002) (HCJ Appeal), discussed by K Phillips in (2002) 60 (Dec) *Criminal Law Bulletin* 5.

[90] See A A Gillespie, "'Up-skirts' and 'down blouses': voyeurism and the law" [2008] *Crim LR* 370.

[91] Sexual Offences (Scotland) Act 2009, s 9(4A) and (4B), added by the Criminal Justice and Licensing (Scotland) Act 2010, s 43(2)(a).

[92] [2012] HCJAC 65. At the conclusion of the evidence the Advocate Depute withdrew the libel in respect of several charges, including this one.

with the intention of committing any of the offences in the section.[93] The accused must act to obtain sexual gratification or to humiliate, distress or alarm the complainer.[94]

11.10   CRITIQUE OF THE LAW ON VOYEURISM AND PROPOSALS FOR REFORM

11.10.1 In the case of *MacDougall* v *Dochree*[95] the accused spied on women who were using sun-beds in a leisure centre, and was charged with a breach of the peace. It might be thought that the Crown could use s 9 for similar case in the future, but although the women in *MacDougall* v *Dochree* were engaging in a private act, the offence would be committed only if they were in fact naked; if they were wearing swim-wear, the section may not apply.[96] As David Selfe has pointed out in relation to the similarly worded English law,[97] someone who

> "is wearing neither 'underwear' nor an item that could be regarded as serving the purpose of underwear, is not afforded protection. Thus, assume a woman (whether in a changing room facility or even in her own bathroom or bedroom) has covered herself with a small towel. She is observed by a defendant. Whilst that [complainer] clearly has a reasonable expectation of privacy, she is neither 'exposed' nor 'covered only with underwear' as required by [the legislation]".[98]

We agree with his conclusion that this is an "unacceptable lacuna" in the legislation.[99]

11.11   ADMINISTERING A SUBSTANCE FOR SEXUAL PURPOSES

11.11.1 The media attention given to so-called "date rape" drugs has caused public concern.[100] Section 11 of the Act makes it an offence

---

[93] Sexual Offences (Scotland) Act 2009, s 9(5)(a), as amended by the Criminal Justice and Licensing (Scotland) Act 2010, s 43(2)(b)(i) and (ii).

[94] 2009 Act, s 9(6) and (7).

[95] 1992 JC 154.

[96] See *Police Service for Northern Ireland* v *MacRitchie* [2008] NICA 26 (CA (NI)): "We do not consider that the meaning of underwear can be extended to cover swimwear worn on any occasion ... [W]e consider that if it is worn as underwear and for that purpose, it will qualify as underwear within the terms of the Act. Otherwise it does not." (*ibid*, para [16] per Kerr LCJ).

[97] Sexual Offences Act 2003, ss 67 and 68.

[98] D Selfe, "'Privacy' and 'underwear' – further developments in voyeurism" (2010) 199 *Criminal Lawyer* 3 at 4.

[99] *Ibid*.

[100] See A Tighe, "'Date rape drugs' are on the rise, UN warns", *BBC News*, 24 February 2010, available at: http://news.bbc.co.uk/1/hi/world/europe/8533736.stm.

to administer a substance for a sexual purpose. This is committed where the accused gives the complainer an intoxicant (alcoholic drink or other drugs) to stupefy or overpower her so that the accused or a third party can engage in a sexual activity with her. The complainer must not know that such a substance is being given to her[101] or, if she does know this, she must be induced by the accused to believe that the substance is weaker than in fact it is, or that she is taking a smaller quantity than is the case.[102]

11.12 SEXUAL OFFENCES INVOLVING CHILDREN

Several of the offences mentioned in the above sections have **11.12.1** similarly worded provisions which apply specifically to children. There are different provisions which apply to the "younger child" from those applying to the "older child". The former is defined as a child under the age of 13, while the latter encompasses children aged from 13 to 15, inclusive. Thus there is a specific offence of "rape of a young child",[103] which is defined in the same manner as rape in s 1, but without any reference to consent, since a child who is less than 13 years of age is incapable in law of consenting to sexual intercourse. There are also the offences of sexual assault on a young child by penetration;[104] sexual assault on a young child;[105] causing a young child to participate in a sexual activity;[106] causing a young child to be present during a sexual activity;[107] causing a young child to look at a sexual image;[108] communicating indecently with a young child;[109] sexual exposure to a young child;[110] and voyeurism towards a young child.[111] It is no defence to any of these offences that the accused believed that the child was aged 13 or older.[112] Sections 28–36 provide a similar list of offences where the complainer is an older child. It should, however, be noted that the *nomen juris* given to the offence of having intercourse (ie penile penetration of the anus, mouth or vagina) with an older child is not "rape of an older child" but "having intercourse with an

---

[101] Sexual Offences (Scotland) Act 2009, s 11(1).
[102] *Ibid*, s 11(2).
[103] *Ibid*, s 18.
[104] *Ibid*, s 19.
[105] *Ibid*, s 20.
[106] *Ibid*, s 21.
[107] *Ibid*, s 22.
[108] *Ibid*, s 23.
[109] *Ibid*, s 24.
[110] *Ibid*, s 25.
[111] *Ibid*, s 26.
[112] *Ibid*, s 27.

older child".[113] Likewise, penetration of an older child and other sexual activity with such a child are not labelled as sexual assaults as such but as "engaging in penetrative sexual activity with or towards an older child" and "engaging in sexual activity with or towards an older child".[114] Where the older child does not agree to this intercourse or activity, s 1 ("rape"), s 2 ("sexual assault by penetration") or s 3 ("sexual assault") is likely to be charged instead, and ss 28–30 reserved for cases in which the complainer is a willing participant.[115]

11.12.2   The criminal law struggles to find a balance between protecting children from abuse and exploitation, on the one hand, and respecting the rights of older children to some measure of sexual autonomy, on the other. Until the passing of the 2009 Act, if two children, both over the age of 13 but under the age of 16, had consensual heterosexual intercourse, then only the male committed an offence.[116] This has been changed somewhat by s 37 of the Act, which provides that an "older child" who penetrates the vagina, anus or mouth of another "older child" with his penis, or touches the latter's vagina or anus with his/her mouth, with the other child's consent,[117] commits an offence.[118] Where the other party (the older child to whom the penetration or orogenital touching is done) "engages by consent in the conduct in question"[119] s/he commits an offence – that of "engaging while an older child in consensual sexual conduct with another older child". As James Chalmers has noted, young people aged 13, 14 and 15 are therefore legally permitted to engage in forms of heterosexual or homosexual activity which fall "short of penile penetration or orogenital contact".[120]

11.12.3   In relation to offences involving older children, it is a defence that the accused reasonably believed that the complainer was

---

[113] Sexual Offences (Scotland) Act 2009, s 28.

[114] *Ibid*, ss 29 and 30 respectively.

[115] See also J Chalmers, *The New Law of Sexual Offences in Scotland: Supplement to Volume II of Gordon's Criminal Law* (2010), para 1.15.

[116] Criminal Law (Consolidation) (Scotland) Act 1995, s 5(3).

[117] "Consent" is also defined, specifically for these offences, as "free agreement" (2009 Act, s 38(3)) and there is no free agreement (for the purposes of the s 37 offences) in the circumstances described in s 13(2) of the Act (s 38(4)). (These circumstances are discussed at section 11.2.4 above.)

[118] The penetration or touching can be intentional or reckless: 2009 Act, s 37(1) and (3)(a) and (b). The reference to the "mouth" is to be construed as including a reference to the accused's tongue or teeth: *ibid*, s 37(5).

[119] *Ibid*, s 37(4).

[120] J Chalmers, "Regulating adolescent sexuality: English and Scottish approaches compared" (2011) 23 *CFLQ* 450 at 460.

aged 16 or older.[121] However, this defence does not apply if the accused had been charged on a previous occasion with a relevant sexual offence;[122] has a previous conviction for a relevant offence committed against a person aged under 16 in a foreign country;[123] or there is a risk of sexual harm order in force in relation to the accused.[124] A further defence is available to certain, but by no means all, of these offences where the difference between the accused's age and that of the complainer when the conduct took place did not exceed 2 years.[125]

11.13   CRITIQUE OF THE LAW ON SEXUAL OFFENCES INVOLVING CHILDREN AND PROPOSALS FOR REFORM

As the above sections have made clear, the Act proscribes a variety of *consensual* sexual behaviours between young people aged 13, 14 or 15, some of which criminalises girls for the first time. Having a statutory provision which does not discriminate between males and females may fail to protect young women from abuse. As Michele Oberman has commented: **11.13.1**

> "Although it is conceivable that a teenage girl might 'consent' to sexual intercourse in some circumstances, the seemingly facile conclusion that so long as she consents, any act of intercourse with her is freely chosen and, therefore, legally permissible is troubling. While girls may dress and act like sexy women, they are still girls. And the fact that some girls might consent to sex which is inherently exploitative ... is not evidence of their competence to consent, nor of their 'womanliness,' but rather, of their immaturity and vulnerability to exploitation."[126]

If we leave to one side arguments about undue pressure and "consent" being given only because of power imbalances in the relationship, another key question is whether truly consensual sexual intercourse between two 15-year-olds is sufficiently harmful or wrongful, such that the criminal sanction ought to attach to it. If not, then it should not be criminalised. It is not an issue, like driving on the wrong side of the road, where the criminalisation of a morally neutral act achieves valuable regulatory results. The

---

[121] 2009 Act, s 39(1).

[122] *Ibid*, s 39(2)(a)(i).

[123] *Ibid*, s 39(2)(a)(ia), inserted by the Criminal Justice and Licensing (Scotland) Act 2010, s 71(1) and Sch 4, Pt 2, para 13(2)(a)(ii).

[124] 2009 Act, s 39(2)(a)(ii).

[125] *Ibid*, s 39(3). For the list of offences to which this defence applies, see s 39(4).

[126] See M Oberman, "Turning girls into women: re-evaluating modern statutory rape law" (1994) 85 *J Crim L and Criminol* 15 at 18 (footnote omitted).

criminal law may be too blunt an instrument to be used where the real issue – discouragement of early penetrative sex – may be better achieved through education and dialogue.[127]

11.14   SEXUAL OFFENCES INVOLVING ABUSE OF TRUST

11.14.1   The Act contains two offences involving abuse of trust. The first is committed when a person who is aged 18 or older is in a position of trust in relation to a person aged under 18, and intentionally engages in a sexual activity with the younger person.[128] Those in a position of trust towards younger people are defined to include, *inter alia*, teachers and lecturers; coaches; those with parental rights or responsibilities towards the child; and those looking after children in a hospital, care home, or residential home.[129] It is also an offence for those providing care services to someone who is suffering from a mental disorder to engage in sexual activity with such a person.[130] Maher has summarised the rationale for this offence and explained how it differs from rape and other offences which involve a lack of free agreement:

> "Abuse of trust offences do not involve lack of consent on the part of the mentally disordered person, and so do not occupy the space where offences such as rape, in which lack of consent is the key element, should be. The wrong in the breach of trust offence is not that the complainer did not consent to sexual activity. It is instead that although the complainer did consent, the sexual conduct occurred between parties in a relationship where even consenting activity is not appropriate."[131]

There is no offence where the accused and complainer are spouses or civil partners, or if the accused was unaware that the complainer was suffering from a mental disorder.[132]

11.15   PORNOGRAPHY

11.15.1   "Pornography codes how to look at women, so you know what you can do with one when you see one."[133]

---

[127] See the earlier discussion (in section 2.4.2 above) on the desirability of employing non-criminal measures to discourage some forms of unwanted or unacceptable behaviours.

[128] Sexual Offences (Scotland) Act 2009, s 42. Defences are provided in s 45. A similar offence had been provided by the Criminal Law (Consolidation) (Scotland) Act 1995, s 3, but this was repealed by the 2009 Act.

[129] 2009 Act, s 43.

[130] *Ibid*, s 46.

[131] G Maher, "Rape and other things: sexual offences and people with mental disorder" (2010) 14 *Edin LR* 129 at 133.

[132] 2009 Act, s 47.

[133] C A MacKinnon, "Pornography, civil rights, and speech" (1985) 20 *Harv Civil Rights – Civil Liberties L Rev* 1 at 19.

Historically, the Crown had attempted to use the crime of "shameless indecency"[134] to prosecute those showing pornographic films[135] and selling pornographic magazines,[136] but with mixed success.[137] Such behaviours may now be prosecuted under s 51 of the Civic Government (Scotland) Act 1982, which proscribes displaying "obscene" material[138] in a public place, as well as selling or distributing such material, or having it with a view to its eventual sale or distribution.[139] It is not, however, an offence to possess pornography *per se*, unless the material constitutes "child pornography", or what has now been defined to constitute "extreme pornography".[140] In relation to the former, s 52(1) of the 1982 Act[141] makes it an offence to take or make an indecent photograph of a child; to distribute or show such a photograph; to possess such a photograph with a view to its being distributed or shown; or to publish an advertisement likely to be understood as conveying that the advertiser distributes or shows such a photograph.[142] A "child" is defined for the purposes of these offences as a person under the age of 18.[143] It was held in *Smart* v *HM Advocate*[144] that the *mens rea* of the offence of making such a photograph requires this to be an intentional act, with knowledge that the image made is, or is likely to be, an indecent photograph/pseudo-photograph of a child. However, where it was accepted that there was downloading of child pornography, and the only question in issue was whether it was the appellant who had downloaded the images, the Crown need not prove that the accused understood the nature of the

---

[134] This crime has since been redefined and renamed as a form of "public indecency". See section 11.20 below.
[135] *Watt* v *Annan* 1978 SLT 198.
[136] *Dean* v *John Menzies (Holdings) Ltd* 1981 JC 23. See section 18.5.4 below.
[137] *Ibid.*
[138] "Material" is defined to include "any book, magazine, bill, paper, print, film, tape, disc or other kind of recording (whether of sound or visual images or both), photograph, drawing, painting, representation, model or figure" (s 51(8)). No attempt is made to define "obscene", but this is generally taken to mean "corrupting" – see Gordon (2000), para 1.31.
[139] Civic Government (Scotland) Act 1982, s 51(1) and (2).
[140] See section 11.15.2 below.
[141] As amended by the Criminal Justice and Public Order Act 1994, s 84(6)(a) and (b).
[142] "Photograph" is defined to include data stored on a computer disk or by other electronic means which is capable of conversion into a photograph (Civic Government (Scotland) Act 1982, s 52(8)(c)(ii)). The offences apply equally to "indecent pseudo-photographs", defined as images which appear to be photographs (s 52(2A).
[143] *Ibid*, s 52(2), as amended by the Protection of Children and Prevention of Sexual Offences (Scotland) Act 2005, s 16(2).
[144] 2006 JC 119.

images.[145] In *HM Advocate* v *Graham*[146] the Lord Justice-Clerk, Lord Gill, stated:

> "Viewing, downloading and distributing indecent images of children is part of the process of child sexual abuse. Each photograph represents the serious abuse of the child depicted. Those who access this material through the internet bear responsibility for the abuse by creating a demand for the material ... Such offences can properly be said to contribute to the pain, discomfort and fear suffered by children who are physically abused, and to the psychological harm that the children concerned would suffer from knowing that others would get perverted pleasure from looking at the material."[147]

11.15.2　Section 51A of the 1982 Act makes it an offence to be in possession of an extreme pornographic image.[148] An image is "pornographic" if it is "of such a nature that it must reasonably be assumed to have been made solely or principally for the purpose of sexual arousal".[149] An "extreme pornographic image" is defined as one which is "obscene", "pornographic" and "extreme"[150] and depicts, in an explicit and realistic way, any of the following:

> "(a) an act which takes or threatens a person's life,
> (b) an act which results, or is likely to result, in a person's severe injury,
> (c) rape or other non-consensual penetrative sexual activity,
> (d) sexual activity involving (directly or indirectly) a human corpse,
> (e) an act which involves sexual activity between a person and an animal (or the carcase of an animal)."[151]

These provisions are more extensive than the equivalent English legislation; while the Scottish offence defines an explicit and realistic portrayal of "a person's severe injury" as extreme pornography, English law requires that the image portray an act which results, or is likely to result, in serious injury "to a person's anus, breasts or genitals".[152] The latter has been criticised – according to Clare McGlynn and Erika Rackley:

> "The specificity of body parts can only lead to potentially ludicrous results with some images being proscribed, but others not, simply because of the

---

[145] *MacLennan* v *HM Advocate* [2012] HCJAC 94.

[146] 2011 JC 1.

[147] *Ibid* at 11, para [28].

[148] Inserted by the Criminal Justice and Licensing (Scotland) Act 2010, s 42(2). For commentary, see R S Shiels, "The new law of extreme pornography" (2011) 111 (June) *Crim Law Bulletin* 4.

[149] Civic Government (Scotland) Act 1982, s 51A(3).

[150] *Ibid*, s 51A(2).

[151] *Ibid*, s 51A(6). Section 51B defines "excluded images" and s 51C provides defences.

[152] Criminal Justice and Immigration Act 2008, s 63(7)(b).

possible injury to specific body parts, rather than due to the nature of the images as a whole, their harm and impact."[153]

Rather than defining extreme pornography to include portrayals of "sexual activity" involving a human corpse, the English offence is restricted to "sexual interference" with a corpse.[154] Similarly, there is no equivalent to the Scottish Act's reference to "rape or other non-consensual penetrative sexual activity". As McGlynn and Rackley point out, this means that the English legislation will not cover pornographic pro-rape websites.[155]

11.16   CRITIQUE OF THE LAW ON PORNOGRAPHY AND PROPOSALS FOR REFORM

The liberal approach to pornography is to claim that it is a private matter, and simultaneously that it is an aspect of free speech – a public right. It follows from either approach that it ought to be beyond the reach of the criminal law: **11.16.1**

> "[P]ornography in liberal society has largely been constructed as a matter of private consumption, and hence as outside the ambit of political critique or action. Absent proof of the contribution of pornography to overt acts of violence, violence or coercion in its production, or indecency thought to impinge on public order, pornography has been taken to be either an instance of expression or a form of sexual practice and hence within the sphere of individuals' privacy."[156]

Some anti-censorship feminists have argued that women ought to create "female-oriented pornography" to give a female perspective on sexuality.[157] In relation to the criminalisation of "extreme pornography", it has been argued that the law has targeted the wrong harm; as Feona Attwood and Clarissa Smith point out, "if concern over violence against women is what drives the impulse to legislate, ... legislation should be targeting the actual practices of violence rather than representational media".[158]

In 1979, the Williams Committee on Obscenity and Film Censor-   **11.16.2** ship reviewed the laws in England concerning obscenity, indecency

---

[153] C McGlynn and E Rackley, "Criminalising extreme pornography: a lost opportunity" (2009) *Crim LR* 245 at 249.
[154] Criminal Justice and Immigration Act 2008, s 63(7)(c).
[155] McGlynn and Rackley (2009) at 249.
[156] N Lacey, *Unspeakable Subjects: Feminist Essays in Legal and Social Theory* (1998), p 88.
[157] See C W Daum, "Feminism and pornography in the twenty-first century: the Internet's impact on the feminist pornography debate" (2008–09) 30 *Women's Rights Law Reporter* 543 at 564.
[158] F Attwood and C Smith, "Extreme concern: regulating 'dangerous pictures' in the United Kingdom" (2010) 37 *J Law & Soc* 171 at 180.

and violence in publications, displays and entertainments. The Committee accepted the harm principle (though it referred to it as the "harm condition"). It described the argument for this condition as being

> "simply that there is a presumption in favour of individual freedom: that the incursions of government into that freedom have to be justified; that the proper sphere of government is the protection of the interests of citizens; and so what is justifiably curbed by government is only what harms the interests of some citizens".[159]

It concluded that there was little evidence of a link between pornography and violence or sexual crime. This finding is controversial, and it can be argued that possession of "extreme" forms of pornography as described in section 11.15.2 above is justifiably criminalised based on the harm such pornography does to women – those involved in the production of such pornography, as well as women generally. As previously noted,[160] many commentators believe that this type of legislation is an example of legal moralism, with the motivation for criminalisation being the legislators' disapproval of those who view such pornography.[161] Thus, Antony Duff has suggested that it is plausible to regard this as a public wrong, warranting criminalisation, "even when ... perpetrated in the 'privacy' of the person's home", since these types of crime constitute "serious violations of the respect that we owe each other, and thus denials (at least implicitly) of the moral status of those who are their objects".[162]

11.17   INCEST

11.17.1   Many societies criminalise sexual intercourse between people who are related, though the definition of a relation for these purposes is drawn differently in different jurisdictions. Both Scotland and England permit intercourse, and indeed marriage, between first cousins, and have done so since 1567. This was unusual in European terms.[163] As previously noted,[164] several criminal law commentators categorise incest between consenting adults as a "victimless" or

[159] Home Office Departmental Committee on Obscenity and Film Censorship (1979), p 51.
[160] See section 2.7.5 above.
[161] Legal moralism is discussed further from section 2.6 above.
[162] R A Duff, "Towards a modest legal moralism" (2014) 8 *Criminal Law and Philosophy* 217 at 232.
[163] Scots law dates from the Incest Act 1567, passed on the same day as the Marriage Act 1567, both of which copied English legislation enacted 27 years earlier. The English legislation was enacted to allow King Henry VIII to marry his deceased wife's cousin. See W D H Sellar, "Scots Law: mixed from the very beginning? A tale of two receptions" (2000) 4 *Edin LR* 3 at 8.
[164] See section 2.2.3 above.

"private" act which ought not to be criminalised.[165] According to Nigel Walker:

"Virtually all the prosecuted cases of incest involve fathers who have had intercourse with daughters who are under the age of consent, and could thus be prosecuted as unlawful sexual intercourse. It is incest between consenting adults which is hardly ever prosecuted and which could without loss be excluded from the criminal code ... There are even countries – France and Belgium being examples – where incest of any kind is not a crime, but abuse of authority for sexual purposes is." [166]

However, as Herbert Packer noted, his "community regards incest with such intense hostility that failure to condemn it will result in loss of respect for the criminal law generally".[167]

Incest is now proscribed by s 1 of the Criminal Law (Consolidation) (Scotland) Act 1995[168] and is defined as sexual intercourse between a male person and certain of his blood relations, namely his mother, daughter, grandmother, granddaughter, sister, aunt, niece, great-grandmother, great-granddaughter. It also covers a female and the equivalent blood relationships, that is: father, son, grandfather, great-grandfather, grandson, great-grandson, brother, uncle, nephew. It applies to adoptive parents and children, whether illegitimate or legitimate, and half-blood relatives too (for example, one's half-sibling). "Sexual intercourse" is not defined in the legislation, but at common law is defined as for the common law of rape, hence oral or anal intercourse is not incest.[169] It is a defence if the accused: **11.17.2**

"(a) did not know and had no reason to suspect that the person with whom he or she had sexual intercourse was related in a degree so specified; or

(b) did not consent to have sexual intercourse, or to have sexual intercourse with that person; or

---

[165] See also Lord Devlin's argument that proponents of the harm principle may find it impossible to justify a prohibition on incest involving consenting adults: P Devlin, *The Enforcement of Morals* (1965), p 139.

[166] N Walker, *Punishment, Danger and Stigma: The Morality of Criminal Justice* (1980), p 19, n 3. For a case of incest involving a father and his adult daughter, see *P v HM Advocate* 2011 SCCR 36. The daughter's sentence of 16 months' imprisonment was reduced on appeal to 2 years' probation.

[167] H L Packer, *The Limits of the Criminal Sanction* (1969), p 315. Although Packer was referring to American society in the 1960s, there seems little doubt that his observation holds true with equal force in Scottish society, today. For an argument in favour of decriminalisation, in the Scottish context, see K McK Norrie, "Incest and the forbidden degrees of marriage in Scots law" (1992) 37 *JLSS* 216.

[168] As amended by the Human Fertilisation and Embryology Act 2008, Sch 6.

[169] See section 11.18.1 below for a critique of this.

(c) was married to that person, at the time when the sexual intercourse took place, by a marriage entered into outside Scotland and recognised as valid by Scots law".[170]

In the case of *Stubing* v *Germany*[171] the applicant had been prosecuted for incest, having had consensual sexual intercourse with his adult sister, and argued that his conviction was a breach of his right to family life, under Art 8 of the ECHR. The Strasbourg Court noted that in 16 out of 31 Council of Europe Member States, a consensual sexual act between adult siblings is a criminal offence, and found that this breach of the applicant's rights was justified by a pressing social need.[172]

11.18   CRITIQUE OF THE LAW ON INCEST AND PROPOSALS FOR REFORM

11.18.1   The definition of "incestuous conduct" under the *Draft Criminal Code* is broader than the current law, since it is defined to include "sexual activity" between related people, as well as sexual intercourse.[173] It is therefore incest under the *Code* for there to be any form of sexual penetration, not solely penile penetration of the vagina, and other forms of sexual stimulation by contact.[174] The provision would make homosexual activity between, for example, a man and his son, father, or brother, "incestuous",[175] as would sexual behaviour between a woman and her (equivalent) relatives, whether male or female. Similarly, in English law s 64(1) of the Sexual Offences Act 2003 provides that it is an offence for a person intentionally to penetrate "another person's vagina or anus with a part of his body or anything else, or ... another person's mouth with his penis" where the parties are closely related.[176] A person who consents to such penetration also commits an offence.[177] If incest is regarded as a harm due to the

---

[170] Criminal Law (Consolidation) (Scotland) Act 1995, s 1(1).

[171] [2013] 1 FCR 107; (2013) 55 EHRR 24.

[172] For a criticism of the case, see J R Spencer, "Incest and article 8 of the European Convention on Human Rights" (2013) 72 *CLJ* 5.

[173] *Draft Criminal Code*, s 67. "Sexual activity" is defined in s 60(1)(c) of the *Code* to mean "sexual intercourse, sexual penetration and sexual contact", each of which is defined in s 60(1)(e), (f) and (d).

[174] English law has now criminalised sexual touchings involving a "child" (defined as a person aged under 18) where the parties are related in the forbidden degrees: see the Sexual Offences Act 2003, ss 25–29.

[175] As would similar behaviour with his grandson, grandfather, uncle, or nephew. See s 67(2) of the *Draft Criminal Code*.

[176] This is defined by s 64(2) of the Sexual Offences Act 2003 as a parent, grand-parent, child, grandchild, brother, sister, half-brother, half-sister, uncle, aunt, nephew or niece.

[177] *Ibid*, s 65(1).

exploitation of the family relationship involved, then it would seem to make sense to proscribe a broader range of sexual contact than that prohibited by the current law in Scotland.[178] The Scottish Law Commission ultimately made no recommendation in relation to the crime of incest,[179] and no provision was made for it in the Sexual Offences (Scotland) Act 2009. This seems a lost opportunity; even if it was felt that no change to the current law was necessary, the law of sexual offences would be more accessible if contained in one statute.

11.19   SEX TOURISM

Peter Alldridge has suggested that   11.19.1

> "whenever there is a serious human rights abuse anywhere in the world, the British Parliament should enact legislation to bring the British courts into play. This is a principle which has not been applied consistently, but which nonetheless is difficult to gainsay".[180]

The principle has been applied to sex tourism; where incitement has taken place in Scotland with a view to committing a sexual offence outside the United Kingdom, this is criminalised by s 54 of the Sexual Offences (Scotland) Act 2009.

11.20   PUBLIC INDECENCY

In *Webster* v *Dominick*[181] the accused was charged with conducting   11.20.1
himself in a "shamelessly indecent" manner by discarding material "showing naked female and male persons in a place and in a manner to which ... children could not help but view same and [did] induce them to view said material". There were several charges in similar terms. The accused raised a devolution issue, arguing that the crime of shameless indecency was unspecific, unclear and not properly defined, and therefore too vague to comply with Art 7 of the ECHR.[182] Having described in detail the history of the crime, Lord Justice-Clerk Gill stated that earlier decisions of the court[183]

> "have created a crime that rests on an unsound theory, has an uncertain ambit of liability and lays open to prosecution some forms of private conduct

---

[178] A similar argument is made in J A Roffee, "Incest: the exception to a principled Scottish sex law" (2012) *Jur Rev* 91 at 95 and 99. It can, however, be argued that incestuous relationships between adults are frequently continuations of child abuse: see J Tempkin, "Do we need the crime of incest?" (1991) 44 *Current Legal Problems* 185.

[179] Scottish Law Commission (2007), para 5.3.

[180] P Alldridge, *Relocating Criminal Law* (2000), p 144.

[181] 2005 1 JC 65. See also *Bott* v *MacLean* 2005 1 JC 83.

[182] See section 4.2.1 above which describes the requirements of Art 7.

[183] That is, *McLaughlan* v *Boyd* 1934 JC 19 and *Watt* v *Annan* 1978 JC 84.

the legality of which should be a question for the legislature. ... It is time that this court put the matter right".[184]

An examination of the case law led him to conclude that there were two separate crimes: "lewd, indecent and libidinous practices", and "public indecency". The former involved conduct directed against a specific victim who was within a class of persons whom the law wished to protect (for example, children). The Sexual Offences (Scotland) Act 2009 contains many specific provisions designed to protect children from sexual abuse, and the crime of "lewd and lib" (as it was known) has been abolished by that Act.[185]

11.20.2   In *Webster* v *Dominick*[186] it was held that where an act of indecency involved no individual victim, it should be criminal only where it offended public sensibility. This was to be referred to in future as "public indecency". The court left open the question whether that crime should extend to conduct that is *not* of a sexual nature. If it does not include such types of conduct, then it is difficult to know what this common law crime now encompasses. The behaviour of the accused in *Webster* v *Dominick* itself is now a statutory offence, namely that of "causing a young child to look at a sexual image";[187] and the "paradigm case" of public indecency[188] – namely indecent exposure – is also governed by the 2009 Act.[189] In *DF* v *Griffiths*[190] the charge of "public indecency" narrated that the (female) accused had performed oral sex on a man in a cemetery. According to Lord Bonomy,

> "before an accused can be guilty of committing an offence of public indecency, the circumstances must demonstrate that he acted in a certain mental state in regard to the risk of being seen so acting by members of the public".[191]

The court applied the test determined in *Usai* v *Russell*:[192]

> "proof of actual knowledge that some other person is in fact witnessing the [behaviour] is not an essential ingredient in a charge of this kind, ... the *mens rea* necessary ... can be properly inferred in circumstances where the accused

---

[184] *Webster* v *Dominick* 2005 1 JC 65 at 78, para 43.

[185] Sexual Offences (Scotland) Act 2009, s 52(a)(iii). Recent cases of "lewd and lib" include *PMG* v *HM Advocate* 2012 SLT 999; and *JM* v *HM Advocate* [2012] HCJAC 52.

[186] 2005 1 JC 65.

[187] 2009 Act, s 23.

[188] This expression was used by LJ-C Gill in *Webster* v *Dominick* 2005 1 JC 65 at 80, para [53].

[189] 2009 Act, s 8, discussed at section 11.8 above. See, however, *Barrie* v *Nisbet* [2012] HCJAC 160 in which masturbation was charged as public indecency.

[190] 2011 JC 158.

[191] *Ibid* at 162, para [12] per Lord Bonomy.

[192] 2000 JC 144.

person was in fact observed behaving as the appellant did behave, where the likelihood was that there would be persons who would observe what was being done, and when the appellant was recklessly indifferent as to whether or not he was observed".[193]

The appeal court did, however, quash the conviction:

"It is plainly unnecessary and indeed undesirable to criminalise conduct as public indecency when, as a matter of fact, the public are neither offended nor at any realistic risk of being offended. Whether or not conduct in public places, or indeed in private places where it is visible to members of the public, falls within the ambit of the crime of public indecency must depend upon the circumstances in which the conduct occurs."[194]

11.21 CRITIQUE OF THE LAW ON PUBLIC INDECENCY AND PROPOSALS FOR REFORM

Webster v *Dominick*[195] was a further example of the appeal court **11.21.1** effecting change to the law which was so far reaching that it could be said to amount to judicial law-making. Under the separation of powers doctrine, only the legislature is permitted to do this.[196] The case effectively decided that shameless indecency was no longer, and never should have been, a crime. Instead, the crime of "public indecency" would criminalise some of the behaviour which it had caught. Public indecency was not, however, included in the list of offences in Sch 3 to the Sexual Offences Act 2003 in relation to which convicted persons can be made subject to notification requirements (or, colloquially, placed on the Sex Offenders Register). Instead, "shameless indecency" appeared. We criticised this discrepancy in the first edition of this book, and are pleased to note that this has been rectified, such that those convicted of public indecency are now within the notification requirements, albeit only in cases in which the complainer is under 18, and the court determines that there was a significant sexual aspect to the offence.[197]

---

[193] 2000 JC 144 at 147 G–H per Lord McCluskey, cited in 2011 JC 158 at 163, para [12].
[194] 2011 JC 158 at 161, para [6].
[195] 2005 1 JC 65.
[196] The doctrine of the separation of powers specifies that it is the job of the parliament(s) to make the law; the courts merely apply it.
[197] Sexual Offences Act 2003, Sch 3, para 41A, inserted by the Sexual Offences (Scotland) Act 2009, s 61(1) and Sch 5, para 5(b).

PART IV

OFFENCES WHICH THREATEN OR HARM
INTERESTS IN PROPERTY

Since the publication of John Locke's *Second Treatise of Civil Government* in 1690, liberalism has regarded the ownership of private property as one of an individual's fundamental rights. Indeed, F A Hayek insisted that the right to own private property is essential for ensuring liberty.[1] It is unsurprising, therefore, that Joel Feinberg approved of various serious "crimes against property", which he defined to include "burglary, grand larceny, and various offenses involving fraud and misrepresentation".[2] As with offences against the person, these crimes involve "the direct production of serious harm to individual persons and groups".[3] Unless one takes the view that "all property is theft",[4] it seems clear that a legal system which failed to demarcate rules of ownership, and proscribe breaches of those rules, would face anarchy.[5]

Paul Robinson, an experienced drafter of criminal codes in the United States, has suggested that legislatures prepare two codes; one for the lay public and a separate one for criminal justice professionals.[6] Robinson favours the consolidation of what he

---

[1] F A Hayek, *New Studies in Philosophy, Politics, Economics and the History of Ideas* (1978), p 149: "There can be no freedom of the press if the instruments of printing are under the control of government, no freedom of assembly if the needed rooms are so controlled, no freedom of movement if the means of transport are a government monopoly."

[2] J Feinberg, *The Moral Limits of the Criminal Law: Harm to Others* (1984), pp 10–11.

[3] *Ibid*, p 11.

[4] P Proudhon, *What is Property? An inquiry into the Principle of Right and of Government* (1840).

[5] Alan Norrie has suggested that, in the 18th century, "[t]he lower classes on the land and in the cities, the peasants and the emerging working class, had to be made to understand that property rights were exclusive" (A Norrie, *Crime, Reason and History: A Critical Introduction to Criminal Law* (2nd edn, 2001), p 20).

[6] P H Robinson, *Structure and Function in Criminal Law* (1997), p 184.

describes as overlapping offences, and suggests a provision entitled "Damage to or Theft of Property" which would provide:

> "you may not damage, take, use, dispose of, or transfer another's property without the other's consent. Property is anything of value, including services offered for payment and access to recorded information".[7]

This seems to breach the principle against fair labelling; the taking of someone else's property is generally regarded, even by the lay public, as a wrong which is distinct from the damaging or destroying of that property. Scots criminal law provides separate offences depending on whether the property has been dishonestly appropriated, or damaged. We discuss the former types of offence in Chapter 12, and the latter in Chapter 13. While this is a convenient way to categorise these crimes, it must be borne in mind that some offences of dishonesty, such as fraud, do not always involve the appropriation of *property*.

---

[7] Robinson (1997), p 188.

CHAPTER 12

CRIMES OF DISHONESTY

12.1 INTRODUCTION

According to Jeremy Horder: **12.1.1**

> "Dishonest conduct may in itself cause no harm, even if it involves reprehensible
> wrongdoing. However, in many contexts (if not in all), if left unpunishable
> such conduct may lead to harm being – perhaps systematically – widely done.
> That is why dishonest or underhand conduct may in such contexts be made a
> criminal offence, as when providing important information or advice to the
> public at large or to public officials."[1]

Scots law recognises a number of crimes of dishonesty, of varying
degrees of seriousness, each of which arises in specific, defined
circumstances although, inevitably, there is some overlap. It is now
sometimes difficult to distinguish between theft and embezzlement,
for example. Charges of fraud[2] and uttering[3] could often arise from
the same set of facts. Historically, particular importance attached
to the distinctions between theft and fraud, and between theft and
breach of trust (which is now usually called embezzlement) because
conviction for theft could incur the death penalty.[4] This meant that
criminal behaviour which might now be regarded as relatively minor,
such as pocket-picking, could incur a capital sentence because of its
status as a form of theft.[5] Accordingly, this ultimate sanction could
be avoided if behaviour could be cast by the courts as a different –
and non-capital – crime of dishonesty.

---

[1] J Horder, "Bribery as a form of criminal wrongdoing" (2011) 127 *LQR* 37 at 52
(fn omitted).
[2] See from section 12.16 below.
[3] That is, issuing a false document as if it were genuine. See from section 12.19
below.
[4] Hume, i, 59. See, for example, *HM Advocate* v *James MacPherson* (1743)
Maclaurin No 48, 88, where the accused was condemned to death for stealing two
horses.
[5] For example, *Walter Ross* (1786) (Hume, i, 32).

12.2 THEFT

12.2.1 Theft can be said to be a harm "because it intrudes upon material resources of the person, over which he has a claim of ownership".[6] According to the most recent *Scottish Crime and Justice Survey*, theft or attempted theft comprised 44 per cent of all crimes.[7] These included personal theft, theft of, and from, a motor vehicle, theft from households, and bicycle thefts.[8] The purpose of the crime of theft is to protect rights of property in moveable items. In Hume's time, its essence lay in the taking – the actual, physical removal of the property from the person who held it.[9] To avoid imposing the death penalty, the courts devised an elaborate system of distinctions between different forms of appropriating property, so that certain categories of professionals would generally be found guilty of a lesser, non-capital offence, such as breach of trust. Hume drew a distinction between "possessors"[10] – those to whom the property was entrusted as a quasi-owner by virtue of which they could only be guilty of breach of trust – and "custodiers" – those into whose care the property was put for a particular purpose, without any right of "disposal or administration"[11] passing, for whom theft was the appropriate charge in the event of misappropriation. At one level, this scheme of liability seems to be related to social class. Estate factors, for example, who managed all of their employers' property, committed "fraud …, or breach of trust, and not an act of theft"[12] if they ran off with their employers' rents. Shepherds, on the other hand, acquired no right of quasi-ownership in their employers' sheep and, as custodiers, were guilty of theft if they appropriated the animals to their own purposes.[13] While couching the issue in class terms might provide a tidy explanation of a logically difficult issue, it is not sufficient, in that Hume confers a similar protection to that of the estate factor on a footman who runs off with his uniform.[14] However, if the historical reasoning is not always easy to follow, the distinction between theft and embezzlement in the modern law is clear. What is less clear is whether such a distinction still requires to be made, given the changes to the crime of theft

---

[6] A von Hirsch, "The offence principle in criminal law: affront to sensibility or wrongdoing?" (2000) 11 *King's College Law Journal* 78 at 79.

[7] *Scottish Crime and Justice Survey 2012/13* (available at: http://www.scotland. gov.uk/Resource/0044/00447271.pdf), para 2.1.

[8] *Ibid*, para 2.1.

[9] Hume, i, 57.

[10] *Ibid*, 58–64.

[11] *Ibid*, 64.

[12] *Ibid*, 60.

[13] *Ibid*, 64.

[14] *Ibid*, 60 – though not if he took, instead, his master's plate.

which have taken place since Hume's time. It is, therefore, necessary to consider the crime's modern incarnation.

12.3 PRINCIPLES IN THE MODERN LAW

Currently, theft is constituted by the appropriation of any item of **12.3.1** corporeal moveable property which is in the ownership of another person, without the owner's consent and with the intention to deprive the owner of that property permanently, temporarily or indefinitely. It is apparent from this that there are limits to the type of item which can be the object of the crime of theft. Accordingly, it is important to consider what can be stolen. In essence, the property must be: (1) moveable; (2) corporeal; and (3) in the ownership of someone other than the accused. There is no requirement for the thief to profit from the theft.

Moveable

"Moveable property" has a particular meaning in property law, in **12.3.2** which a distinction is made between "moveable" and "heritable" property (with the latter comprising land, buildings and rights to minerals and mining rights)[15] but, for the purposes of the criminal law, "moveable" simply means capable of being taken, in the sense of being lifted or moved physically. It is theft, therefore, to take fruit from a tree or to pull up plants, though property law might treat such property as "heritable" rather than moveable.[16]

Corporeal

"Corporeal" means things which can be touched. One exception **12.3.3** here is electricity which can be appropriated and is therefore capable of being stolen.[17] Intangible property – for example, shares in a company or rights of ownership in heritable property – cannot be stolen. Any misappropriation of such rights is likely to constitute the crime of fraud.[18]

A difficulty arises in relation to information held on memory sticks, **12.3.4** computer disks or CDs. The items which hold the information are

---

[15] For the purposes of property law, the category of heritable property also includes things which "adhere" to that property, such as growing trees. Once such items are detached from the land, they become moveable in property law terms.

[16] As Gordon notes, it is theft to take "fruit from a tree, potatoes from a field, grass from a lawn, lead from a roof, or a sash from a window frame" (Gordon (2001), para 14.20 (footnotes omitted)).

[17] See *Semple* v *Hingston* 1992 SCCR 605. In practice, the Crown generally prosecutes a contravention of the Electricity Act 1989, s 31 and Sch 7, para 11, in relation to interference with an electricity meter.

[18] See from section 12.16 below.

themselves corporeal, yet it is the information which they contain which is important. That information is, however, *in*corporeal and therefore not capable of being stolen. In considering whether the legal principles in this area are appropriate and sufficiently robust for use in the 21st century, it is interesting to note that one of the leading cases was decided in 1777. In *Dewar*,[19] an apprentice broke into his employer's office, removed a book containing trade secrets, copied them and then returned the book. He was charged with theft by housebreaking but convicted of an innominate offence,[20] thereby escaping the death penalty. According to Alison, the court in *Dewar*

> "did not consider this as a case of proper theft, the paper having been fraudulently abstracted, with a view merely to copy and return it; but they held it an irregular and punishable act".[21]

12.3.5 Dewar, then, seems to have been saved from the gallows by the fact that he returned the book. In 1777, the *mens rea* of theft required an intention to *keep* – or permanently to deprive the owner of – the misappropriated item. Similarly, in the more recent but still pre-information-society case of *HM Advocate* v *MacKenzies*,[22] there were two charges – one of theft of a book of secret trade recipes, and the other of making copies of the recipes with the intention of selling them. The second charge was dismissed as irrelevant. This indicates that the taking of information is not, in itself, criminal. Neither of these cases supports the proposition that incorporeal property can be stolen.

12.3.6   The modern case of *Grant* v *Allan*[23] has held that it is not a crime dishonestly to exploit confidential information. The accused had taken confidential computer print-outs containing lists of his employers' business customers and had offered to sell these to someone else. The appeal court held that this was not a crime known to the law of Scotland, nor was such behaviour so obviously of a criminal nature that they should declare it to be a crime. The employer should have sued in the civil courts. One of the authors was in the appeal court during the hearing of this case, assisting the Advocate-Depute (Alan Rodger) and remembers that there was much discussion in Crown Office as to whether the accused's behaviour amounted to theft. The Crown could, of course, have charged theft of the computer print-

---

[19] (1777), cited in Hume, i, 75.
[20] An innominate offence is one which lacks a recognised legal name (*nomen juris*) – see from section 5.13 above.
[21] Alison (1832), p 279.
[22] (1913) 7 Adam 189.
[23] 1987 JC 71.

outs themselves, but their value was negligible. It was the customer details that were valuable, and these were permanently appropriated, albeit not exclusively, in that the employer could still access them.[24] That removal of information without consent should not be made criminal was also the view which was taken by the Scottish Law Commission,[25] since this would involve treating "information" differently in civil and criminal law – as a form of "property" in the latter but not the former. The Commission also took into account that labour law would provide a remedy in the employer/employee situation.

In an age of technology, we must consider whether the dishonest appropriation of information *ought* to come under the aegis of the crime of theft. Hitherto, it has not done so because the wrong of theft is perceived to be that the owner is deprived of the stolen item. The nature of information is such that any number of people may possess it simultaneously. If an individual discovers the recipe for Coca-Cola, for example, it does not mean that the Coca-Cola Corporation is deprived of that information. It still holds it. But, clearly, this analysis ignores the value which is attached to holding information exclusively. If the recipe is published on the internet, it becomes considerably less valuable to its original owners. In other words: **12.3.7**

> "The theft of property is capable of doing economic harm to the owner in the sense that it deprives him not of the use (the information itself may remain intact) but of his monopoly value in it."[26]

The current legal position, fully endorsed by *Grant* v *Allan*,[27] is that this type of appropriation is a civil wrong and that the injured party will be able to seek recompense through civil remedies. In *Grant* v *Allan*, the nature of the employer/employee relationship would have provided a right of action against the taking of the client lists, quite apart from any separate term in his contract of employment. Likewise, the Coca-Cola Corporation would have rights in (civil) intellectual property law against anyone who discovered and used its trade secrets. Where the relevant information was stored on a computer, its appropriation may constitute a statutory criminal offence.[28] But **12.3.8**

---

[24] This is similar to the hypothetical situation discussed in section 12.3.7 below.
[25] Scottish Law Commission, *Computer Crime: Consultative Memorandum No 68* (1986), paras 4.12–4.16.
[26] J Hull, "Stealing secrets: a review of the Law Commission's consultation paper on the misuse of trade secrets" [1998] *Crim LR* 246 at 247.
[27] 1987 JC 71.
[28] Under the Computer Misuse Act 1990, s 1, or the Data Protection Act 1998, s 55(1).

this still brings the matter back to the question of whether, applying the criminalisation principles outlined in Chapters 1–4, theft of information *ought* to be a criminal offence. There seems to be no doubt that it satisfies the harm principle. The value of information usually is its exclusivity. The harm caused to a business by the loss of this exclusivity through dishonest appropriation is, arguably, greater than, for example, the theft of the machinery required to manufacture the product. It remains true, therefore, that "we live in a country where ... the theft of the board room table is punished far more severely than the theft of the board room secrets".[29] It is not unreasonable to suggest that the criminal law should protect against "pure economic loss". Indeed, the courts have themselves recognised this.[30] For Hume, some of the wrong of theft seems to have been in the invasion of the person yet, as will be discussed below, developments in the *actus reus* of the crime have moved it beyond this requirement of a physical taking.

12.3.9   In *Black* v *Carmichael*[31] the appeal court endorsed the notion that the bundle of rights of ownership could be split such that it could constitute theft even if the owner was deprived of only some of these. In this case the accused had wheel-clamped someone else's car, depriving him of its use. Although unable to drive the car, the owner could still, for example, sit in it, sell it, store items in the boot and, generally, exercise all rights of ownership consistent with a stationary vehicle. As noted previously, in Hume's day a central requirement of theft was that there had been a physical taking of the item from its owner.[32] *Black* v *Carmichael* represents a further dilution of this notion. It may not be the same as the dilution in value which arises from the loss of exclusivity in an unauthorised taking of information, but it does demonstrate a willingness to think about the items which form the subject-matter of the crime of theft in a less concrete fashion than had previously been the case.

12.3.10   Equally, the way in which both the concept of appropriation as the *actus reus* of theft and the temporal dimension of *mens rea* have developed[33] is indicative of a fluidity or adaptability in the theoretical basis of the crime which might allow it to incorporate

---

[29] Sir Edward Boyle in the House of Commons, 13 December 1968, during the second reading of the Industrial Information Bill (see HC *Hansard* for that date, col 806). He was quoting Alan Campbell, QC, who had used the phrase in an article in *The Times* in December 1967. See J Lang, "The protection of commercial trade secrets" (2003) 25 *European Intellectual Property Review* 462 at 465.

[30] See *HM Advocate* v *Wilson* 1984 SLT 117, discussed at section 13.2.2 below, in respect of the crime of malicious mischief.

[31] 1992 SLT 897.

[32] See section 12.2.1 above.

[33] See from sections 12.4.1 and 12.5.1 below.

information. If such a major change is to be effected, this should be by way of bespoke legislation, rather than by judicial development of the common law.

In the ownership of another

The third component of the definition of items which can be stolen is that they must belong to someone other than the thief. If the owner of a thing freely agrees to transfer the right of property, this is not theft. The thing must be taken without the owner's consent. Since the property must be owned by someone, a wild animal (which has no owner) cannot be stolen but it would obviously be theft to steal a pet dog, or fish from a garden pond. Gordon's *Criminal Law* states that "live human beings can be stolen if they are under the age of puberty, since over that age they cannot be 'owned'".[34] Hume recognised that

12.3.11

> "to carry off ... a person ... is a quite different sort of crime from theft or robbery; and in nowise a patrimonial, but a proper personal injury, and one of the highest sort. ... And even to call it a robbery, seems to be a perversion, and a figurative, rather than a judicial use of that term; since the injury here consists principally in the distress and suffering of the person himself who is taken, and not in any patrimonial damage sustained by others on that occasion".[35]

Although Hume confined this description to persons "of grown years and mature discretion",[36] in the modern era it should be recognised that children are not owned by their parents, and so a more appropriate charge would be abduction.[37]

It is theft to find someone else's property and decide to keep it.[38] Note that the finder does not need to know who owns the property; so long as she is aware that it is not her property, that is

12.3.12

---

[34] Gordon (2001), para 14.18, fn 10.

[35] Hume, i, 83.

[36] *Ibid*. He later states that an infant child can be the subject of a theft charge, since such a child "is as a *thing*, under the care and in the possession of others" (*ibid*, 84 (emphasis in original)).

[37] See Gordon (2001), para 29.52, and the *Draft Criminal Code*, s 45. The crimes of abduction and plagium are discussed from section 10.17 above.

[38] *MacMillan v Lowe* 1991 JC 13. The Civic Government (Scotland) Act 1982, s 67 specifies that the finder of lost or abandoned goods must deliver the goods, or at least report the fact that she has taken possession of the goods, to the police without unreasonable delay. Failure to do so is an offence. This provision has been commended for drawing an appropriate distinction between theft by means of an act, and theft by omission/failure to return found property: see S P Green, "Theft by omission", in J Chalmers, F Leverick and L Farmer (eds), *Essays in Criminal Law in Honour of Sir Gerald Gordon* (2010) 158 at p 161.

all that is required. So-called "abandoned property" may have an owner, since it generally reverts to the Crown, but it seems that the prosecution needs to prove that the accused must have appreciated that it was "property which someone intended to retain".[39] In *Butler* v *Richardson*,[40] the appeal court quashed the conviction for theft by finding (of copper wire) on the basis that it was quite possible that the property had been abandoned as unwanted or fly-tipped.

12.4   *ACTUS REUS*

12.4.1   When we think of theft, we picture the thief taking something away. However it is more accurate to say that theft involves an "appropriation" of property, which occurs when the thief assumes the rights of the owner of the property. This may not require a physical taking: if B lends A her bicycle and after a week A decides not to return it, but to keep it permanently, then at that later time A commits theft, even if the bicycle remains at all times in A's shed. The crime is committed at the moment when the thief decides to keep the thing. This is something which happens entirely in the mind of the thief, hence the problem is one of proof. Sometimes this dishonest intention can be inferred. For example, selling the item would create the necessary inference. Thus appropriation

> "involves conduct which without authorisation deprives the owner of one or more of those rights, for example possessory rights, which his ownership of the property in question would in the circumstances entail".[41]

12.4.2   It is conceptually simpler if "appropriation" is used to refer to all forms of taking. Nonetheless, Gordon's *Criminal Law* considers the concept of "*amotio*", referring to it as a "peculiarity"[42] of the law in Hume's time but which still constitutes a form of the *actus reus* of theft in its own right. *Amotio* arises if an object is physically removed from its place in a way which shows an intention to steal it. The amount of movement required varies, depending on the circumstances. The "slightest removal" is generally sufficient, but if the thing is in a container, such as a pocket or a drawer, it must be physically removed from that container before there is *amotio*.[43] If the property is in a room, *amotio* occurs if the property is taken out of the room, or even if moved elsewhere in the room in such a way as to indicate an intent to steal. Where the property is in the open, it is

---

[39] *Kane* v *Friel* 1997 JC 69, per LJ-G Rodger at 72.
[40] [2013] HCJAC 78.
[41] Gordon (2001) at para 14.10.
[42] *Ibid* at para 14.11.
[43] *Ibid*.

probable that any movement of the property will amount to theft. In fact, *amotio* requires so little in the way of movement that, where the *mens rea* can be inferred, the crime will be complete. For example, it is theft to take something from a shelf in a self-service shop, with the intention of not paying for it. In *Barr v O'Brien*[44] the accused took two computer tapes from a shelf in a Woolworths store and placed them in his pocket. He appears to have done this in the knowledge that he was being watched by the store detective, who eventually went out of the shop so that she could scrutinise the accused more closely if he tried to leave without paying. He walked past all but the last check-out before turning round and walking back to the middle of the shop where he was confronted by the store manager and the detective. The appeal court held that sufficient had been alleged here to make theft a relevant charge.

The Crown needs something more than simply the evidence of an **12.4.3** item being moved in order to establish that the accused's intention was to deprive the owner. Accordingly, while *amotio* can be established where the thief has done nothing more than, for example, move the goods nearer the door for ease of removal later, the crime itself will not be made out unless the court is convinced that that this was indeed with the purpose of theft.

In *Dewar v HM Advocate*[45] a crematorium manager retained two **12.4.4** children's coffins and the lids of over 1,000 other coffins. These seem, in the main, to have been used for firewood, or for other projects for which wood was required. Dewar made no profit from the retention of these items. They were taken on the accused's mistaken view that he had acquired an "unlimited right of property"[46] in them. In fact, they belonged to the families of the deceased, who had purchased the coffins. The court held that his intention to deprive the owners of them was made manifest when he detached the lids from the coffins. This constituted appropriation despite the fact that Dewar had clearly come into possession of the coffin lids lawfully, in his position as crematorium manager.

Reference has already been made to the case of *Black* v **12.4.5** *Carmichael*,[47] which concerned the wheel-clamping of cars which had been parked on private property.[48] The accused were charged with extortion and attempted extortion, or alternatively theft, and objected to the relevancy of the charges. The sheriff repelled the objections to the charges of extortion, but sustained those relating

---

[44] 1991 SCCR 67.
[45] 1945 JC 5.
[46] *Ibid* at 11, per LJ-G Normand.
[47] 1992 SLT 897.
[48] See section 12.3.9 above. The case is also discussed at section 12.24.2 below, in relation to extortion.

to the theft charges, and dismissed them. Both the Crown and the accused appealed against the sheriff's decision. The appeal court upheld the relevancy of all charges. The wheel-clamping of the cars could amount to theft by appropriation because the owners of the cars had been deliberately deprived of the possession and control of their vehicles. The intention to deprive the owners of the use of their vehicles became apparent when the clamps were applied. The only rights of ownership of which the cars' owners were deprived were possession and use.[49] Deprivation of *any* of the rights of ownership, then, appears to be sufficient to constitute theft.

12.4.6   The thief does not have to take the property away:

> "To deprive another of the possession and use of his property can only be described as theft if there is appropriation – whether by taking it away or doing something else to it to this effect".[50]

It is unclear whether "taking"[51] and "finding",[52] which have historically been regarded as forms of the *actus reus* in their own right, are now subsumed within the category of appropriation, as this *dictum* would suggest. This is certainly the view taken in Gordon.[53] However, in *Black* v *Carmichael*[54] Lord Allanbridge stated:

> "I agree with [Gordon's *Criminal Law*] ..., where it is stated that this intention [to deprive the owner of her goods] may be manifested in three different modes, namely, by taking, by conduct following on finding and by appropriating goods which have been neither taken from the owner without his consent nor found."[55]

An individual who finds property and retains it may be said to have demonstrated the intention of keeping it – or, more technically, of depriving the owner of it – and thus to have committed theft. In *MacMillan* v *Lowe*[56] the accused claimed that he had found several cheque books and cheque cards in a telephone kiosk. He had

---

[49] See section 12.3.9 above, for a discussion of the rights which the owner retained.

[50] *Black* v *Carmichael* 1992 SLT 897 per LJ-G Hope at 902.

[51] Hume, i, 57.

[52] Although Hume was of the view that retention of found items did *not* constitute theft (Hume, i, 62), the High Court found that it did as early as 1838 in the case of *John Smith* (1838) 2 Swin 28. In this case the accused had found items, including a pocket-book clearly marked with the owner's name, on a public road. He was convicted of theft for retaining them, though the judgment does use the term "appropriation" on occasion. All of the judges acknowledge expressly their departure from the principle set down by Hume – see, for example, Lord Mackenzie at 53 and Lord Cockburn at 59–60.

[53] Gordon (2001), para 14.11.

[54] 1992 SLT 897.

[55] *Ibid* at 903.

[56] 1991 SCCR 113.

attempted to conceal them from the police. The appeal court took the view that, even though a relatively short time had passed since the finding (4 hours) there was sufficient evidence from which to infer that the accused had appropriated the items.

Without the owner's consent

Lack of consent is central to the law of theft in Scotland, in contrast to the position in England. In *Lawrence v Metropolitan Police Commissioner*[57] the accused was a taxi driver who charged a foreign passenger six times the correct fare for the journey. The House of Lords dismissed the argument that since the passenger had consented to the taking of the money, the driver was guilty of "obtaining property by deception" rather than theft.[58] A Scottish taxi driver engaged in a similar scam would be more likely to be charged with fraud.   **12.4.7**

12.5   MENS REA

This can best be defined as the intention to deprive the owner of her property, an intention which may be inferred from the facts. Until the 1980s it was necessary to demonstrate that the accused intended to deprive the owner on a *permanent* basis. Judgments since then have, however, broadened the scope of the *mens rea*. The first of these was one of the most significant in the law of theft – the case of *Milne v Tudhope*[59] in 1981. The owner of a cottage was dissatisfied with building works and asked the builders to carry out remedial work free of charge. They refused to do so without payment. They removed various items from the premises without the owner's consent, including radiators, a boiler and a number of doors, intending to "hold them to ransom" until payment was given for the requested remedial work. They were convicted of theft and appealed. The main issue in the appeal was whether the *mens rea* of theft was sufficiently made out where the intention was only to deprive the owner of his property temporarily. The appeal court agreed with a statement made by the sheriff at first instance that "in certain exceptional cases an intention to deprive temporarily will suffice".[60] It also appeared to accept the sheriff's view that where the intention to deprive is only temporary, the taking must be clandestine, in the   **12.5.1**

---

[57] [1972] AC 626.
[58] For a detailed discussion of "appropriation" in the English law of theft, see E Melissaris, "The concept of appropriation and the offence of theft" (2007) 70 *MLR* 581.
[59] 1981 JC 53.
[60] *Ibid* at 57 per LJ-C Wheatley.

sense of being kept secret from the owner of the property, and the accused's purpose must be nefarious.

12.5.2   Unfortunately, subsequent cases have not provided much guidance as to what is necessary to make deprivation "clandestine", "nefarious" and "in exceptional circumstances". In *Kidston* v *Annan*[61] the owner of a broken television set answered an advertisement in a newspaper offering free estimates prior to repairs being carried out. The accused, who had placed the advert, did not provide an estimate but instead refused to return the set unless its owner paid him for repairs which he claimed to have completed. On appeal, the court held that he had been holding the television to ransom similarly to the circumstances of *Milne* v *Tudhope*.[62] The court took the view that the accused's actions were "nefarious" because he had lied to the sheriff about having authority to carry out the repairs. Beyond this, however, the case does not discuss when an intention to deprive only temporarily will be enough to constitute the *mens rea* of theft.

12.5.3   There was an intention to appropriate for a temporary period only, in *Black* v *Carmichael*[63] (the wheel-clamping case); the intention would have been to return the possessory rights to the owner once he paid the clamping fee. The court appears to have accepted that the intention to deprive temporarily was sufficient but there was no discussion of the three additional conditions which *Milne* v *Tudhope*[64] attached. The fact that the accused was also convicted of extortion may be sufficient to imply nefariousness. The law has continued to develop with the case of *Fowler* v *O'Brien*[65] in which the accused asked the owner if he could borrow a bicycle, and the owner refused. The accused then simply took the bicycle but did not say whether, or when, he would return it. The appeal court found this to be a relevant charge of theft, describing the *mens rea* as the intention to deprive the owner of his property indefinitely. Despite the fact that this case was determined subsequent to *Black* v *Carmichael*, both the district court at first instance and the appeal court seem to have taken the view that there would be a need for a clandestine taking, a nefarious purpose and exceptional circumstances if an intention to deprive temporarily were to be made out. This case, then, seems to have identified a "third way", in relation to the *mens rea* for theft. It leaves unanswered the question of whether the qualifications on the *mens rea*, where the intention is to deprive temporarily, still apply.

---

[61] 1984 SCCR 20.
[62] 1981 JC 53.
[63] 1992 SLT 897.
[64] 1981 JC 53.
[65] 1994 SCCR 112.

If these qualifications do still apply, it is submitted that they are less than helpful, and that the law is in need of reform.

12.6 TAKING AND USING

Fowler v *O'Brien*[66] bears all the hallmarks of borrowing something **12.6.1** without the owner's consent. The case of *Strathern* v *Seaforth*[67] in 1926 had, in fact, declared the existence of a similar crime, specifically to deal with joy-riding. This was known as "taking and using the property of another clandestinely". The crime would be charged where someone took an object without the owner's permission but did intend to return it to the owner at some point. There is now a clear overlap with the law of theft, as extended by *Milne* v *Tudhope*[68] and by *Fowler* v *O'Brien*, and also with s 178 of the Road Traffic Act 1988 which makes it an offence, *inter alia*, to take a motor vehicle without authority.

12.7 CRITIQUE OF THE *MENS REA* OF THEFT AND PROPOSALS FOR REFORM

As we have seen, the courts have engaged in an incremental expansion **12.7.1** of the *mens rea* of theft. This has left the law unclear, such that Gordon notes that

> "it is now very difficult to find any principle to which the *mens rea* of theft conforms. It is also very difficult even to describe the various types (for there are clearly several types) of *mens rea* which the courts have identified".[69]

This is not a satisfactory position, and is in danger of breaching the rule of law: criminal prohibitions ought to be knowable.[70] If academics find it difficult to describe the *mens rea* of theft, what hope has the lay-person of conforming to its requirements? The best advice may be that one should not act "dishonestly" but, as English law shows, this is not a concept which is free from ambiguity.[71] The

---

[66] 1994 SCCR 112.
[67] 1926 JC 100.
[68] 1981 JC 53.
[69] Gordon (2001), para 14.50.
[70] See section 4.2.1 above.
[71] In England the Theft Act 1968, s 1(1) provides that theft is committed where a person "dishonestly appropriates property belonging to another". Dishonesty has been described as an unacceptable "morally driven incursion into property rights" (A P Simester and G R Sullivan, "On the nature and rationale of property offences" in R A Duff and S P Green (eds), *Defining Crimes: Essays on the Special Part of the Criminal Law* (2005) 168 at p 177). "Dishonesty" is a term which has been rarely used in Scottish theft cases, but see *Kane* v *Friel* 1997 SLT 1274: in quashing the

Draft Criminal Code defines theft as appropriation of property, without the owner's consent, with the intention of depriving the owner permanently, or being reckless as to whether the owner is thus deprived.[72] This is designed to restore the definition to what the lay public would be likely to regard as theft. Other forms of interference with property are dealt with by different sections of the *Code*.[73]

12.7.2   In discussing the situation where a person makes a mistake as to consent, Gordon states that it is not theft "if A wrongly, but (probably) reasonably, believes that B has consented to his having the goods".[74] The fact that "probably" requires to be included in this description is a serious indictment of Scots law. Let us imagine that B has received a plastic bag from her local charity shop, with a request to fill up the bag with unwanted books. The charity will collect the bag if B leaves it outside her front gate. B fills the bag with books and takes it to her gate. A, who is B's neighbour, asks B what she is doing, and B explains the situation, saying "It's a great opportunity for me to get rid of these books. I've been meaning to dump them for ages. The charity will sell these books and the money will go to people in developing countries. It's good to know that I'm helping other people". Later that day, A decides that he can provide a good home for the books, so he takes them into his house and puts them in his bookcase. It seems clear in this scenario that A has fulfilled both the *mens rea* and *actus reus* of theft: he has appropriated property belonging to another person, and has done so without consent, and he clearly intends to deprive the owner of the property.

12.7.3   But what if A protests that he honestly thought that B would not mind if he took the books? A may stress the fact that B said she wanted to "get rid of" the books, and spoke about dumping them. Arguably, this is not a reasonable belief in consent, in the circumstances. The reasonable person would surely appreciate that part of B's motivation was to help other people, and that these other people did not include her neighbour. Before taking the books, A ought to have asked B whether she was indifferent about where they would end up. But irrespective of whether or not we think that A's actions were reasonable, it may well be the case that A was genuine in his beliefs. Is it theft if A really thought that B would be happy for

---

conviction LJ-G Rodger referred to the fact that there had been no sufficient basis on which the trial judge could have inferred the "necessary dishonest intention" on the part of the appellant. See also, now, *Butler v Richardson* 2013 SCL 734 where the appeal court quashed the appellants' convictions for theft because there was insufficient evidence of *dishonest* intent.

[72] *Draft Criminal Code*, s 77.
[73] For example, s 81 (criminal damage to property), s 82 (causing an unlawful risk of damage to property), and s 83 (criminal interference with property).
[74] Gordon (2001), para 14.54.

him to have the books? Scots law ought to provide a clear answer
to this question, and the fact that we can say only that an accused
"probably" needs to have a reasonable belief in consent (or, more
accurately here, a reasonable belief that the owner would have
consented, had she been asked) is far from satisfactory.

Error as to a key fact which negates the accused's *mens rea* can **12.7.4**
operate as a defence in relation to many crimes.[75] The issue of error
in theft more generally was discussed in *Dewar*,[76] the case in which
the crematorium manager removed and kept coffin lids. The accused
claimed that he thought the coffins belonged to no one and were
therefore at his disposal. The trial judge instructed the jury that
the accused's error could only provide a defence if it constituted an
"honest and reasonable belief, based on colourable [ie, plausible]
grounds".[77] It is not entirely clear whether the appeal court endorsed
this statement[78] or whether it would have taken the view that the *actus
reus* and *mens rea* of theft were satisfied, regardless of Dewar's actual
belief.[79] In any event, Dewar was convicted of theft. The Crown had
established the *actus reus* and *mens rea* of the crime. Dewar's error
was made unreasonably and therefore could not negate his *mens rea*.
Nonetheless, the later case of *Sandlan v HM Advocate*[80] seems to
suggest that an "honest, even if mistaken, belief"[81] that the accused
owned the property would suffice. Further areas of uncertainty in
the Scots law of theft are illustrated by the statement in Gordon's
Criminal Law that:

> "The person who takes someone else's umbrella knowing not that it is but
> that it might be someone else's, and being unmoved by that knowledge, is
> probably guilty of theft."[82]

Now there may be sound arguments for restricting theft to intentional
takings, and perhaps equally persuasive arguments that the reckless
taker merits the opprobrium associated with the label "thief".[83] But
it is not satisfactory that we are unable to be sure whether or not our
reckless umbrella remover commits the offence of theft.

---

[75] See from section 19.8 below.
[76] 1945 JC 5, discussed previously in section 12.4.4 above.
[77] *Ibid* at 8 per LJ-C Cooper.
[78] Lord Justice-General Normand sets out the trial judge's view on the need
for reasonableness mainly in order to emphasise that the charge to the jury was
particularly favourable. His own view seems to have been that the elements of theft
were made out, regardless of the appellant's personal beliefs (*ibid* at 11–12).
[79] Lord Moncrieff appears to take this more restrictive view: *ibid* at 14–16.
[80] 1983 JC 22.
[81] *Ibid* at 26 per Lord Hunter.
[82] Gordon (2000), para 9.03.
[83] *The Draft Criminal Code* adopts the latter approach – see s 77(2) and section
12.7.1 above.

12.8   THEFT BY HOUSEBREAKING

12.8.1   Although the basis of theft is appropriation of someone else's property, some "takings" are more serious than others. "Theft by housebreaking" is the major aggravation here. According to the Statistical Bulletin Crime and Justice Series: *Recorded Crime in Scotland*, there were 24,222 cases of theft by housebreaking, and housebreaking with intent to steal (the name given to the attempted crime) in 2011–12.[84] The housebreaking element must be committed before the theft, and be the means by which the theft takes place. Scots law has avoided the difficulties faced in English law where the similar crime of "burglary" distinguishes between theft from a "dwelling" and from a "non-dwelling"; in Scotland, "housebreaking" may be committed against any roofed building provided that it is "shut and fast" against intruders.[85] It has been held to be theft by housebreaking to break into a henhouse[86] or a church.[87] The crime requires either that the security of the premises has been breached (for instance, by smashing the door down, breaking a padlock, smashing a window, etc) or that entry has been achieved by an unusual means (such as climbing in an upstairs window, or a chimney). The thief who opens an unlocked door or turns a key which has been left in the lock does not commit housebreaking. There must be evidence that the building was secure. In *Lafferty* v *Wilson*,[88] the last time it could be established with certainty that the building had been properly secured was 3 months before the alleged housebreaking. It was held that there was insufficient evidence from which to infer that it had been secure when the accused effected entry. It is not housebreaking to break into individual rooms within a building.[89]

12.8.2   Is it theft by housebreaking when the mode of entry was via an open window? Once again, we find that the law is less clear than it ought to be. Gordon notes that this is "not free from doubt" and concludes:

> "Probably the position is that it is housebreaking to enter by a window through which entry was not to be expected, which means in effect that entry

---

[84] *Recorded Crime in Scotland, 2011–12*, table A4. It should be noted that the figures in this Bulletin represent crimes and offences which have been recorded and cleared up by the (then) eight Scottish police forces. The number of thefts by housebreaking has decreased dramatically in the past decade or so. In 1998–99 there were more than double the number: 55,784 cases.

[85] For a critique of English law, see K Laird, "Conceptualising the interpretation of 'dwelling' in Section 9 of the Theft Act 1968" [2013] *Crim LR* 656.

[86] *John Fraser* (1831) Bell's Notes 41.

[87] *Lees* v *HM Advocate* [2012] HCJAC 143.

[88] 1990 SCCR 30.

[89] This would be charged as "theft by opening a lockfast place"– see from section 12.10 below.

by a window is housebreaking, except where the window is a french [*sic*] window and so equivalent to a door, or where it is so near to the ground that one can easily step through it."[90]

Since theft by housebreaking commonly involves damage to property in order to steal, it is fitting that it should be an aggravation. Furthermore, where the housebreaking involves a domicile, the harm caused to the owner of the property is generally greater than that of simple theft, by virtue of the fact that it involves an intrusion into someone's home.

12.9 HOUSEBREAKING WITH INTENT TO STEAL

Housebreaking is not a criminal offence in itself; it is the stealing which makes it so. If nothing has actually been stolen, however, it may still be possible to charge the accused with "housebreaking with intent to steal". There would need to be facts from which this intent could be inferred. In *Burns* v *Allan*[91] the accused was caught running away from a building (the Royal Antediluvian Order of Buffalos) carrying housebreakers' tools. The burglar alarm had been activated, apparently because the accused had been trying to disconnect it. He was convicted. On appeal, the court affirmed the sheriff's view that a burglar alarm is integral to the security of any building and that trying to disconnect it amounted to an attempt to overcome that security. The accused's intent to steal could be inferred because it was unlikely that he would be found in those circumstances if he had a lawful purpose.

    It is only the intent to *steal* which makes housebreaking a criminal offence. Housebreaking with the intent to commit any other crime is not recognised as criminal in itself. In *HM Advocate* v *Forbes*,[92] the indictment charged that the accused had broken into a first-floor flat "with intent to assault and rape" a 14-year-old girl. A plea was taken to the relevancy of a charge in this form, and this was upheld by the appeal court since there is no crime in Scots law of "housebreaking with intent to rape".[93] In *Cochrane* v *HM Advocate*[94] the appeal court accepted that conspiracy merely to break into a house was not a crime known to the law of Scotland. There must be an allegation that the purpose of the housebreaking was to facilitate theft.[95]

12.9.1

12.9.2

---

[90] Gordon (2001), para 15.11.
[91] 1987 SCCR 449.
[92] 1994 SCCR 163.
[93] For a critique of this case, see section 12.11.2 below.
[94] 2006 JC 135.
[95] See also section 8.6.3 above.

12.10   THEFT BY OPENING LOCKFAST PLACES

12.10.1   The aggravation "theft by opening a lockfast place" consists in breaking into anything which is secured by a lock, other than a building, and stealing therefrom. Examples include a locked cash register, drawer, box or room. It is commonly charged for stealing from a locked vehicle. It is not theft by opening a lockfast place to steal a locked container and force it open thereafter. The opening of the lockfast place must precede and be for the purposes of theft.

12.11   CRITIQUE OF THE LAW ON AGGRAVATIONS OF THEFT AND PROPOSALS FOR REFORM

12.11.1   In relation to the aggravated crime of theft by housebreaking, we have seen that there is uncertainty as to whether this applies where the thief enters by an unlocked window. It might be said to be of little importance that the law is not clear cut in this area. After all, the only practical distinction between a charge of "theft" and one of "theft by housebreaking" is that the latter cannot be prosecuted in the justice of the peace court.[96] Nevertheless, a conviction for "theft by housebreaking" is generally regarded as more serious than one for merely theft, even though the value of the items stolen in the case of the simple theft may be greater than that acquired from the housebreaking. The law ought to provide a clearer description of the two offences.

12.11.2   We also noted that in *HM Advocate* v *Forbes*[97] the appeal court held that there is no crime in Scots law of "housebreaking with intent to rape". This is in contrast to the situation in England, where the crime of "burglary" involves entering a building as a trespasser (rather than requiring the breaking into a building) and encompasses not only an intent to steal, but alternatively an intent to inflict grievous bodily harm on any person in the building, or unlawfully to damage the building or anything in the building.[98] There is also a separate offence of trespass with intent to commit a sexual offence.[99] In *Forbes*, the Crown had to revert to a charge of breach of the peace. This does not adequately capture the nature of the wrong which is alleged to have been committed in the circumstances of that case. Jeremy Horder's plea for fair labelling bears repeating:

> "[W]hat matters is not just that one has been convicted, but *of what* one has been convicted. If the offence in question gives too anaemic a conception of

---

[96] Criminal Procedure (Scotland) Act 1995, s 7(8)(b)(ii).
[97] 1994 SCCR 163. See section 12.9.2 above.
[98] Theft Act 1968, s 9(1) and (2).
[99] Sexual Offences Act 2003, s 63.

what that might be, it is fair neither to the [accused], nor to the victim. For the wrongdoing of the former, and the wrong suffered by the latter, will not have been properly *represented* to the public at large."[100]

Scots law needs a more appropriate offence to cover the behaviour **12.11.3** alleged in the *Forbes*[101] case. The *Draft Criminal Code* renames and redefines "theft by housebreaking"; the offence in the *Code* is "breaking into a building" and is committed when the accused breaks in without the consent of a lawful occupier.[102] The prosecution is not required to prove any ulterior intention, whether to steal or rape etc, on the part of the accused, but where such an intention is established, this will be treated as an aggravated offence.[103] Enactment of the *Code* provisions would provide a more appropriate *nomen juris* for the crime of theft by housebreaking[104] and, more importantly, close the *lacuna* highlighted in *Forbes*.

As we have seen, theft involves the appropriation of corporeal **12.11.4** moveables, only; hence obtaining a service without the consent of the provider of that service is not theft. Gordon gives the example of someone who re-connects a phone line in order to make free calls, and suggests that the making of such calls could be charged as theft only of the (miniscule) amount of electricity involved, and that the receiving of incoming calls is not theft at all.[105] This type of behaviour ought to be proscribed by the criminal law. While some cases might be within the definition of fraud (for example, where the accused has made representations that she will pay for services, then deliberately fails to do so) not all will fall within the definition of that crime.[106] Where, for example, the accused has driven into a self-service car wash, washed her car and driven off without paying, it might be difficult to establish that she had made even an implied representation that she would pay, hence impossible to prove the false pretence necessary for fraud.[107] Section 83 of the *Draft Criminal Code* creates the offence of "criminal interference with property" to

---

[100] J Horder, "Rethinking non-fatal offences against the person" (1994) 14 *OJLS* 335 at 351 (emphases in original).
[101] 1994 SCCR 163.
[102] "Building" is defined to include a caravan, motor-caravan, tent or houseboat. See the *Draft Criminal Code*, s 78(3)(a)(i).
[103] *Ibid*, s 7(2)(a) provides that an offence may be aggravated if committed with intent to commit another offence.
[104] The *Code* also changes "theft by opening a lockfast place" to "breaking open a locked place" (*ibid*, s 79). This is more broadly defined, to include breaking into locked rooms (etc) with intention to commit a different crime from theft, or indeed with no further intention.
[105] Gordon (2001), para 14.17.
[106] "Fraud" is defined from section 12.16 below.
[107] See section 12.16.2 below.

cover situations which do not amount to theft or malicious mischief/vandalism, but which nonetheless do involve loss, harm or serious inconvenience to the owner:

> "(1) A person who interferes with another person's property or lawful possession or use of property, without that person's consent, so as to cause loss, harm or serious inconvenience to that person or to any other person is guilty of the offence of criminal interference with property.
>
> (2) A person is guilty of an offence under this section only if the person intended to cause such loss, harm or serious inconvenience, or was reckless as to whether any such result would follow."

Reform of the law to incorporate a provision such as this would close another gap in the current law.

12.12   RESET

12.12.1   Reset can be defined as possessing, or being "privy to the retention" of, property which has been dishonestly obtained by someone else. Although it is common to refer to reset of theft, it is equally reset to receive goods obtained in other criminally dishonest ways, for example, to retain goods taken in a robbery, or goods which have been embezzled. The accused must know, or be wilfully blind to, the provenance of the property. Wilful blindness involves deliberately turning a blind eye. A person cannot be convicted of both theft and reset of the same goods. Someone who has been charged with theft may instead be convicted of reset, but not the other way round.[108] This suggests that reset is regarded as a less serious crime than theft. The *actus reus* of reset can be constituted simply by the accused being "privy to the retention" of the goods. This means that there is an intention to deprive the owner of the property, as opposed to retaining the goods with a view to returning them. Minimal possession will be sufficient to satisfy this *actus reus*, so long as the necessary *mens rea* can be inferred. In *Robert Finlay and Others*,[109] the goods were thrown onto a bed in a room in the house of one of the accused. The accused then threw a cover over them and jumped out the window. This was sufficient to constitute the retention necessary for reset. His concealment of the goods allowed the court to infer his guilty knowledge of their origin.

12.12.2   In *Finlay*[110] the accused did have possession of the goods, even if only for a very brief period. Macdonald, however, stated that: "It is reset for a person to connive at a third party possessing or

---

[108]   Criminal Procedure (Scotland) Act 1995, Sch 3, para 8(2).
[109]   (1826), cited in Alison (1832), p 333.
[110]   *Ibid.*

retaining stolen goods even if the person charged never laid a finger on the property stolen."[111] This way of constituting the *actus reus* – simply by conniving in someone else's possession of the goods – can be criticised for unreasonably widening the scope of the offence. It has been used in relation to people who have allowed themselves to be driven in cars which they know to be stolen, or where stolen items have been placed in cars. In *McCawley* v *HM Advocate*[112] the accused was convicted of reset in respect of his having been a passenger in a stolen car. He had fled when police stopped the car, thereby inferring the guilty knowledge that he was privy to the car's retention.

The resetter must receive the goods, but not have stolen them herself; if a thief retains the goods she herself has stolen, this is not reset. The resetter need not, however, have obtained the goods directly from the thief. If A steals something and gives or sells it to B and B does likewise to C, then C is still liable for resetting the goods, so long as C knows that the goods are stolen, or is wilfully blind to their origins. Although a resetter may acquire the goods from a person other than the thief, the goods must be obtained by that third party with consent – hence if A steals a car, and B steals the car from A, then B is guilty of theft, rather than reset. **12.12.3**

As noted above,[113] the *mens rea* of reset has two requirements. First, there must be knowledge that the goods are stolen or have otherwise been dishonestly obtained. It is a definite requirement, set down by Hume,[114] that there should be actual knowledge that the goods are stolen, rather than mere suspicion that that is the case. This has, however, been modified by the courts' development of the doctrine of "wilful blindness", which is discussed below. This allows conviction where the accused did not know, but almost certainly should have known, that the goods were stolen. Second, there must be an intention to deprive the owner of the goods. Proof of this knowledge will usually come from the incriminating circumstances surrounding the discovery of the goods. **12.12.4**

In *Forbes* v *HM Advocate*[115] the goods consisted of a valuable painting which was in a parcel, measuring about a metre squared, found in the accused's car. The accused stated that he did not know that the cardboard packaging contained a painting nor how it could have got there. He also gave an "awkward story"[116] about the circumstances in which he came to be driving his car at **12.12.5**

---

[111] Macdonald (1948), p 67.
[112] (1959) SCCR (Supp) 3.
[113] See section 12.12.1 above.
[114] Hume, i, 114.
[115] 1994 SCCR 471.
[116] *Ibid* at 474 per LJ-C Ross.

all that day. He was convicted of reset. By contrast, in *Shannon* v
HM Advocate[117] the accused was found in possession of a sawn-
off shotgun. His conviction for reset was overturned because he
might have been attempting to conceal the gun simply because he
knew that to have it constituted a breach of the firearms legislation.
The doctrine of recent possession applies to both theft and reset;
if goods are found in the accused's possession soon after they have
been stolen, either theft or reset may be inferred. The difficulty is
in defining "recent". In the case of *MacLennan* v *MacKenzie*,[118]
2½ months was insufficiently recent for theft and in *L* v *Wilson*,[119]
7 days was too long for robbery. Both periods were short enough
for reset.

12.12.6   As noted above,[120] the courts have accepted a form of wilful
blindness to be equivalent to knowledge, on the basis that those
who are deliberately ignorant are not worthy of acquittal. This is
an extreme form of blinding oneself to the obvious, where the court
assumes that the only reason that the accused did not specifically
ask if the goods were stolen was that she had already reached the
conclusion that they were. The leading case is *Latta* v *Herron*[121] in
which a solicitor who collected weapons as a hobby was charged
with reset. He had bought two guns from one of his clients, paying
about half of their true value. The guns were collectors' items and
the solicitor received them from his client when they met in a close
or alleyway late at night. The appeal court held that the solicitor
had wilfully blinded himself to the obvious. If he did not know that
the guns were stolen when he bought them, this must have become
obvious to him shortly afterwards.

12.12.7   Until recently, one peculiarity of the law relating to reset was
that a wife was not guilty of the reset of stolen goods if she received
and retained them for her husband, in order to protect him from
detection or punishment. According to Alison, the rule did not
apply to husbands; a man who received goods which had been
stolen by his wife had no such immunity.[122] It has been suggested
that the rule dated from the time when the law considered that a
wife would submit as a matter of course to her husband, and hence
was not capable of going against his wishes, even in such matters.
In the first edition of this book, we suggested that it was unlikely
that the courts could limit the exemption to women only, should a

---

[117] 1985 SCCR 14.
[118] 1987 SCCR 473.
[119] 1995 SCCR 71.
[120] See section 12.12.1 above.
[121] (1967) SCCR (Supp) 18.
[122] Alison (1832), p 339.

suitable case come before them. It also discriminated against couples who were not married, including civil partners. Section 7(1) of the Marriage and Civil Partnership (Scotland) Act 2014 now provides:

"Any rule of law under which a wife who receives or concals goods stolen by her husband does not commit the offence of reset ceases to apply."[123]

The change in the law relating to reset is to be commended.

12.13 CRITIQUE OF THE LAW ON RESET AND PROPOSALS FOR REFORM

Hume considered whether reset was a lesser crime than theft, and noted that in some cases the courts seemed to have assumed that this was so.[124] He concluded that this view was a reasonable one: **12.13.1**

"For though the one course of life may be little less pernicious than the other, which it so much forwards and encourages; yet is there a substantial difference, in respect of boldness and profligacy, between him who carries off, and him who only receives the booty."[125]

Hume was right to point out that the "wrong" or "harm" perpetrated by a thief, especially if the theft has involved housebreaking, is likely to be regarded as worse, and therefore as deserving more punishment. On the other hand, it might be suggested that if fewer people were willing to turn a blind eye to the provenance of cheap goods, bought in market stalls and car boot sales, there would be fewer incentives for thieves.[126] This suggests that reset could be punished more severely than theft, to act as a deterrent. In England, the similar offence of "handling stolen goods"[127] is more serious than theft, with a greater maximum sentence.

12.14 EMBEZZLEMENT

It can be very difficult to distinguish between theft and embezzle- **12.14.1** ment. It is possible to be convicted of embezzlement on a charge of theft and vice versa.[128] The essence of embezzlement is that the

---

[123] This came into force on 21 May 2014. It is not retrospective: see s 7(2) of the 2014 Act.
[124] Hume, i, 119.
[125] *Ibid.*
[126] This argument is explored in S P Green, "Thieving and receiving: over-criminalizing the possession of stolen property" (2011) 14 *New Crim LR* 35.
[127] Theft Act 1968, s 22.
[128] Criminal Procedure (Scotland) Act 1995, Sch 3, para 8(3) and (4). The same applies to embezzlement and fraud: *ibid*, para 8(3A) and (3B).

accused appropriates to her own purposes property which was previously entrusted to her on the understanding that she would deal with this property on the victim's behalf. The accused must start dealing with the property as authorised but then form a dishonest intention to appropriate it and apply it in an unauthorised fashion, so that she is ultimately unable to account for it to the victim. There are several strands to the *actus reus* of embezzlement. The accused must:

(1) hold the property with the victim's consent;

(2) have the power to administer the property and a corresponding duty to account for those dealings;

(3) have commenced dealing with the property as authorised; and

(4) have failed to account to the victim for the property.

In relation to the fourth point, in *Guild* v *Lees*[129] the secretary of the World Curling Federation drew a cheque on an account which he was authorised to use when travelling abroad. He used the proceeds to pay his domestic electricity bill. The appeal court said that this *did* constitute embezzlement because he was using the money for an unauthorised purpose, ie the fact that the money came from that particular account was not key. What was essential was that he drew the money in the course of generally administering the club's account.

12.14.2   The *mens rea* of embezzlement is a dishonest intention to appropriate the victim's property to the accused's own use. The accused's intention to pay the money back is irrelevant. In *Allenby* v *HM Advocate*[130] the accused was an agent for fishermen. He advanced money from a bank account to fishermen who were *not* entitled to it, but he did this openly. It was not clear that his intention was dishonest since he had not tried to conceal his actions, nor had the jury been told that it needed to be. He was accordingly acquitted, on appeal. The *mens rea* of embezzlement was discussed more recently in *Moore* v *HM Advocate*,[131] where it was affirmed that there was a need for dishonesty. The accused in this case had been the director of a company in which he and his wife were the sole, 50/50 shareholders. The marriage got into difficulties and, in what seems to have been an overt attempt to strip out the company's assets so that there would be nothing for his wife on divorce, Moore withdrew from it large sums of money which he used to make highly speculative investments, and for gambling. It was held that the

---

[129] 1994 SCCR 745.
[130] 1938 JC 55.
[131] 2010 SCCR 451.

presence of bad faith, or the absence of good faith, in making these withdrawals, did amount to the dishonesty necessary to constitute the *mens rea*.

12.15 CRITIQUE OF THE LAW ON EMBEZZLEMENT AND PROPOSALS FOR REFORM

One might ask whether a crime of embezzlement remains necessary now that theft is no longer a capital offence, and where the *actus reus* of theft is specifically constituted by appropriation, rather than by a physical taking.[132] The fact that a conviction for theft can be returned on an embezzlement charge, and vice versa, suggests that the two crimes are regarded as equally serious in the modern law. Moreover, in Hume's time, the breach of trust element which is central to modern embezzlement must have been regarded as less blameworthy than the deprivation effected by a thief, in that conviction for theft incurred the death penalty but conviction for breach of trust did not. It is certainly arguable today that this breach of trust – this veneer of dealing appropriately in the initial stages with the victim's property – actually aggravates behaviour which would otherwise be likely to constitute theft.   **12.15.1**

It is a prerequisite of embezzlement that the accused's intention should have been dishonest. While theft is clearly a crime of dishonesty, it does not necessarily involve this element of deception.[133] For example, in *Fowler* v *O'Brien*,[134] the accused openly rode off on the victim's bicycle and in *Black* v *Carmichael*[135] there was, similarly, no attempt to conceal the fact that vehicles would be clamped until payment was made. The outstanding question, then, is whether theft could do all of the work of embezzlement, or whether there is some obviously blameworthy behaviour which would cease to be criminal altogether if the crime of embezzlement did not exist.   **12.15.2**

Honesty in accounting is fatal to a charge of embezzlement, even if the relevant funds have been applied to an enterprise in which the accused has an interest, so that they are not available for accounting to the actual owner.[136] It would be theft if the accused said to the   **12.15.3**

---

[132] "Appropriation" is described in more detail from section 12.4.1 above.

[133] See, however, the recent case of *Butler* v *Richardson* [2013] HCJAC 78, in which the appellants' convictions for theft were quashed partly on the basis of "[in]sufficient evidence of dishonest intent" (at para [5] per Lady Paton). See section 12.3.12 above. The case turned primarily on whether or not the accused were entitled to take the view that the property was abandoned. In essence, they were held to lack the *mens rea* for theft.

[134] 1994 SCCR 112.

[135] 1992 SLT 897.

[136] As in *Allenby* v *HM Advocate* 1938 JC 55.

victim: "I have taken your money, spent it and I am unable to give it back." It may no longer be necessary to have the crime of embezzlement if it is simply "high-class" theft,[137] although it is accepted that particular complexity may arise, if the funds with which the accused is dealing are not turned into cash, in relation to the requirement that the property must be corporeal to ground a charge of theft.

12.16 FRAUD

12.16.1 In principle, fraud can arise in the very widest imaginable circumstances, yet unlike breach of the peace[138] or the now departed, largely unlamented, crime of shameless indecency,[139] its definition is clear and certain. It appears to be regarded as broadly equivalent to theft in terms of seriousness, given that the accused can be convicted of fraud on a charge of theft and vice versa.[140] Macdonald defines "fraud" as "the bringing about of any practical result by false pretences"[141] but this is only a statement of the *actus reus*. The *mens rea* of fraud requires the accused to be aware of the falseness of the representation and to intend to bring about the practical result. There are three elements to the *actus reus*: (1) the false pretence; (2) the practical result; and (3) the causal link between the two.

The false pretence

12.16.2 This may be express or implied. In *James Paton*[142] bulls entered in a competition were made to look better by having air pumped under their skin and their horns falsely lengthened. This was held to amount to an implied representation that the bulls really were bigger. An omission can be sufficient if the accused is under a duty to make a representation.

The practical result

12.16.3 It is not fraud if A, a law student, meets someone at a party and tells that person that she is a solicitor. Telling a lie is not sufficient for fraud. If, however, A tells the same lie at a job interview and gains employment as a result, then this *is* fraud. Here, a practical result was intended, and has been achieved. The recipient of the false pretence

---

[137] For a discussion of "white collar" crime, see from section 18.4 below.
[138] This is considered from section 15.2 below.
[139] See from section 11.15.1 above.
[140] Criminal Procedure (Scotland) Act 1995, Sch 3, para 8(3) and (4).
[141] Macdonald (1948), p 52.
[142] (1858) 3 Irv 208.

(or, in other words, "the dupe") must actually be deceived by it. Almost any practical result of this deception will do to constitute fraud. For example, in *William Fraser*,[143] persuading a woman to have sexual intercourse by pretending to be her husband was held to be a type of fraud.

In *Adcock v Archibald*[144] a miner attached a tag which identified **12.16.4** a fellow worker's pile of coal as his, with a view to claiming a bonus for mining more coal than he had. In fact, the other miner's coal was not eligible for a bonus, either. The only practical result was that his employers recorded him as having dug more coal than he actually had. He did not receive any more money as a result. The practical result here is almost imperceptible and the case is often cited to demonstrate how little is required in this respect. It is an essential element of fraud that the deception should be successful. Without a practical result, it is not. Fraud differs from uttering in requiring this. In accepting so little, *Adcock v Archibald* comes close to criminalising the telling of lies, a point which will be considered further once we have discussed the crime of "uttering as genuine".[145]

Although the practical result will often be that the accused **12.16.5** gains money or an item of value from the false pretence, this is not essential. During employment in the COPFS, one of the authors drafted a complaint against two journalists, averring attempted fraud. They were alleged to have duped a nurse into letting them visit a hospital patient. The patient was recovering from an accident and the journalists wanted to interview him about the circumstances in which he had sustained his injuries. They asked to see him and were denied access. Armed with a large floral bouquet, they pretended to be the patient's niece and nephew and gained access to his hospital room. The newspaper's lawyers took a plea to the relevancy of the charge, arguing that there was no monetary gain accruing from the false pretence, but this contention was rejected by the sheriff; the averment that they had gained access to the patient which would otherwise have been denied was a sufficient practical result.

The causal link

The practical result must be caused by the false pretence. If the dupe's **12.16.6** actions would have been the same, even if there had been no false pretence then the crime of fraud has not been committed. In *Mather v HM Advocate*[146] the accused obtained delivery of some cattle, then

---

[143] (1847) Ark 280.
[144] 1925 JC 58.
[145] See section 12.20.1 below.
[146] 1914 SC (J) 184.

wrote a cheque in payment. He did not have sufficient funds in his account to cover the cheque but a charge of fraud was held to be irrelevant since the false representation (that he had money in his account) was not made until after the contract was completed – it did not cause this result.

12.17   IDENTITY THEFT AND IDENTITY FRAUD

12.17.1   Identity theft has been referred to as the "quintessential crime of the information age".[147] Marron has defined this as involving

> "the fraudulent use of *your* personal information in the following ways: appropriation of your credit card, the opening of a new credit card in your name, the opening of a bank account in your name and the running-up of an overdraft or the taking-out of [car] or other loans with your details".[148]

Apart from the initial appropriation of the credit card, each of these activities would be prosecuted in Scots law as fraud, rather than theft. According to the *Scottish Crime and Justice Survey 2012/13*, around 4 per cent of adults in Scotland had experienced "plastic card fraud", and a further 1 per cent had been a victim of identity theft, "where someone had pretended to be them or used their personal details fraudulently".[149] Invasion of privacy was traditionally viewed as a civil law (that is, non-criminal law) matter, a breach of "an individual right, remedied at the initiative of the individual".[150] It has been argued that identity theft needs to be viewed as a problem concerning how our personal information is handled, rather than simply as "a series of discrete instances of crime".[151] While identity fraud is in essence a variation of an existing crime, its impact on victims – psychologically as well as financially – can be great, hence it is likely to be treated as an aggravated form of fraud.

12.18   CRITIQUE OF THE LAW ON FRAUD AND PROPOSALS FOR REFORM

12.18.1   As we have seen,[152] any false pretence made with a view to gaining a practical result can constitute fraud. There is no need for the Crown to establish that someone's interests were prejudiced as a

---

[147] C Kahn and W Roberds, "Credit and identity theft" (Working Paper 2005–19), cited in D Marron, "'Alter reality': governing the risk of identity theft" (2008) 48 *British Journal of Criminology* 20 at 20.

[148] *Ibid* at 23 (emphasis in original).

[149] *Scottish Crime and Justice Survey 2012/13*, para 2.5.4, p 24.

[150] D J Solove, "Identity theft, privacy and the architecture of vulnerability" (2002–2003) 54 *Hastings LJ* 1227 at 1228.

[151] *Ibid* at 1251.

[152] See from section 12.16 above.

result of this deception. Hence, as the *Commentary* to the *Draft Criminal Code* points out, "to induce a person to attend a surprise birthday party would, technically, be a criminal offence at common law".[153] While in practice it is most unlikely that anyone would be prosecuted for perpetrating such a "fraud", it would be preferable for the crime to be defined in such a way that it was unnecessary to depend on prosecutorial discretion and common sense. Such a result is avoided by the definition of fraud provided by s 86 of the *Code* which requires the deception to have caused someone to act to her prejudice, or the prejudice of a third party.

12.19 UTTERING

In Scots criminal law it is not generally enough simply to forge a document; no crime is committed until the document is actually "uttered as genuine", in the sense of being issued or otherwise put beyond the control of the accused.[154] In *Barr v HM Advocate*[155] the appeal court was specifically asked by the Crown to declare that forgery itself was a crime in Scots criminal law. It declined to do so. Lord Justice-Clerk Alness stated: **12.19.1**

> "forgery is not, apart from uttering, in my judgment, a substantive and independent crime. The appellant in this case might have amused himself indefinitely by fabricating signatures, but, so long as he did not put them to any use, or attempt to do so, he was innocent of any crime known to the law of Scotland. The Crown may competently libel uttering only, but it may not competently libel forgery only. Forgery is merely the prelude of or preparation for the commission of a crime, viz. uttering. It is not in itself a crime".[156]

Uttering consists in the promulgation of a forged document in the knowledge of its falsity and with intent to deceive. There are two aspects to the *actus reus*: first, that the accused has a forged document, and second that she has deliberately exposed it to another person as if it were genuine. It is not necessary for the accused to have made the forgery herself; exposing it is sufficient. There is no need to establish a practical result. In the case of *Simon Fraser*,[157] it was held that a document is only a forgery where it is "intended to represent and pass for the genuine writing of another person". Where, as here, the accused, with the help of a colleague, created and **12.19.2**

---

[153] *Commentary* to s 86 of the *Draft Criminal Code*.
[154] But note that it an offence to make or possess a counterfeit of a currency note or protected coin without lawful authority or excuse. See the Forgery and Counterfeiting Act 1981, ss 14(2) and 16(2).
[155] 1927 SLT 412.
[156] *Ibid* at 415.
[157] (1859) Irv 467.

signed a document which contained completely false information, this was not uttering. The accused and his colleague still represented themselves as themselves. The second strand to the *actus reus* is that the accused has "uttered" the document as genuine. She may do this by giving it to an individual, presenting it to the public at large or simply by putting it beyond her control in some way, perhaps by posting it. The *mens rea* of uttering requires the Crown to prove that the accused *knew* that the document was false *and* that she intended the other party to be deceived by it.

12.20   CRITIQUE OF THE LAW'S RESPONSE TO LYING AND PROPOSALS FOR REFORM

12.20.1   Both fraud and uttering respond to the immorality inherent in telling lies, but neither seeks to criminalise this as a practice. Fraud requires some form of practical result; uttering that the accused should "utter" (ie present) the untruth as genuine. The question is whether this is appropriate – whether telling lies *per se* meets any of the various criteria for criminalisation described in Chapters 1–4. Neil MacCormick, the renowned legal philosopher, argued that telling lies, as a practice, is always and intrinsically wrong, because of the effect it has on the pre-existing relationship of trust between the parties. He nevertheless concluded that it "is sound legal policy" that

> "the law while acknowledging lies as in themselves always wrongful … goes further and treats deceit and lying as outside its scope unless further harmful consequences are aimed at by the deceiver, or result to the victim from reliance on false or even carelessly made misrepresentations, or from reliance on continuing intentions of the speaker".[158]

Most people would accept that telling lies is, in the abstract, morally wrong yet the breadth of behaviour which it encompasses is extremely broad. Criminalisation of the so-called "white lie" (for example, "Your new hairstyle is lovely") would obviously serve no purpose.

12.20.2   In fact, statutory offences have been created, criminalising specific forms of deception whereby the accused "impersonate[s] a [police] constable with an intent to deceive"[159] or "do[es] anything calculated to suggest that the person is a constable".[160] Similarly, it is an offence

---

[158] N MacCormick, "What is wrong with deceit?" (1983–1985) 10 *Sydney Law Review* 5 at 18. The question of whether lying is, in itself, sufficiently unacceptable to justify the imposition of criminal sanctions is also considered by David Ormerod in his discussion of the (English) Fraud Act 2006, s 2: "The Fraud Act 2006 – criminalising lying?" [2007] *Crim LR* 193 at 196.

[159] Police and Fire Reform (Scotland) Act 2012, s 92(1)(a).

[160] *Ibid*, s 92(1)(b).

to provide information "for the purpose of enabling or assisting any other person to be certified as a police custody or security officer if the person knows that, or is reckless as to whether, the information is false or misleading in a material respect".[161] If the dupe believed and acted upon the false representation, the behaviour itself would clearly be caught by the common law crime of fraud. However, this is not necessary to these offences. At the basic level, all that is required is that the accused has told a lie – albeit a highly specific lie involving deception as to status as a police officer. Indeed, in that it may be committed recklessly, the third offence does not even require a lie as such, if this is defined as deliberately making an untrue statement. It may be that the integrity of these (police) offices is sufficiently important to warrant this form of protection. In general, however, the telling of lies *per se*, while morally questionable, should not be within the scope of the criminal law.

12.21 ROBBERY

Although the *Scottish Crime and Justice Survey 2012/13* classifies robbery as a crime of violence[162] (which it undoubtedly is), it is often treated also as a crime of dishonesty.[163] One per cent of the crimes recorded by the 2012–13 survey were robberies[164] and 0.2 per cent of Scots were the victims of robbery during the survey period,[165] but this small percentage translates into more than 11,000 robberies per year.[166] Robbery and, by extension, piracy,[167] consists in theft accomplished by means of personal violence or the threat of such violence. It is not necessary that the victim should actually own the property – merely that it is in her care. The violence must be applied either immediately before, or at the same time as, the taking of the property, and be the means by which the item is acquired. Assaulting someone *after* taking their property is not robbery. The Crown must establish that the possessor's will was completely overcome. It appears that this can be achieved by intimidation alone, without any physical contact. In *Harrison* v *Jessop*[168] two employees were told that they would not be allowed to leave their employer's premises unless the contents of the till were handed over to an agent of an

12.21.1

---

[161] Police and Fire Reform (Scotland) Act 2012, s 30(1).
[162] *Scottish Crime and Justice Survey 2012/13* at p 11, para 2.1.
[163] Robbery is discussed within Gordon's *Criminal Law* as an offence of dishonesty: (2001), Chap 16.
[164] *Scottish Crime and Justice Survey 2012/13* at p 11, para 2.1.
[165] *Ibid* at p 23 and Figure 2.7.
[166] *Ibid* at p 16, Table 2.2.
[167] See from section 12.23 below.
[168] 1992 SLT 465.

alleged creditor of the employers. It was established that the money had been handed over against the employees' will, and a conviction for robbery was upheld on appeal.

12.21.2   Where physical violence is used towards the victim, it does not have to amount to an assault in law. In *O'Neill* v *HM Advocate*[169] the accused was originally charged with assault *and* robbery. He was convicted of the robbery but acquitted of the assault. He appealed on the basis that if he was not guilty of the assault the Crown should be regarded as having failed to prove the level of violence necessary for robbery, and he should only have been convicted of theft. The accused had forcibly snatched a woman's handbag, in the course of which she had banged her head against the wall of a close "to the effusion of her blood" and had suffered from concussion. Despite the jury's acquittal on the assault charge, the court was prepared to infer that the injuries had resulted from the degree of force with which the bag was snatched. This was sufficient to allow the robbery conviction to stand. The court took the view that there was ample evidence from which the jury could conclude that the taking of the handbag had been achieved through the use of physical violence. The separate assault charge was merely an aggravation of the basic charge of robbery. Lord Justice-Clerk Aitchison stated:

> "It is well settled that in robbery there must be violence. On the other hand, it is not necessary to robbery that there should be actual physical assault. It is enough if the degree of force used can reasonably be described as violence."[170]

If the Crown could not prove the aggravation, it was still entirely appropriate for the jury to return a verdict of guilty of the basic offence. The point was affirmed in the case of *Morrison* v *HM Advocate*,[171] where the accused was charged with assault and robbery but the jury deleted all references to the assault, convicting him only of robbery. The victim was intoxicated at the time of the attack and his evidence was, consequently, rather vague. It was held that violence had still been used in effecting the theft and this was all that was necessary.

12.22   CRITIQUE OF THE LAW ON ROBBERY AND PROPOSALS FOR REFORM

12.22.1   Andrew Ashworth has criticised the English crime of robbery, on the basis that one offence is applied:

---

[169] 1934 JC 98.
[170] *Ibid* at 101.
[171] 2010 SCCR 328.

"to all forms of violence used (from a push to serious bodily injury), all forms of taking (from a few dollars to millions), and all forms of threat (from no threat to the use of a knife or gun)".[172]

A similar criticism could be made of Scots law. Gordon states: "There is no dispute that a threat of immediate personal violence constitutes robbery. Whether threats of any other kind are sufficient is unsettled."[173] The case of *Harrison* v *Jessop*[174] is cited in support of this, though it is noted that this case raised but did not determine the issue. It should be noted that the charge in this case specifically stated that the accused placed the complainers "in a state of fear and alarm for their safety".[175] In the circumstances of the case, where the accused's threat was to prevent employees leaving a restaurant unless they handed over the contents of the till, it is submitted that this points to some degree of fear of immediate violence. Nonetheless, Gordon suggests that:

"if A picks up B's telephone and threatens that he will inform the police or even the press of something detrimental to B unless B hands over a sum of money, and B hands over the money because his will to refuse has been overcome by the threat, A is guilty of robbing B of the money".[176]

Our view is that, in fact, robbery does require at least a perceived threat of physical violence. It is, however, unacceptable for there to be any dubiety on this point, such that the requirements for the crime of robbery in Scots law are described in this leading work as "unsettled". The *Draft Criminal Code* limits robbery to the taking of property by violence or the immediate threat of such violence,[177] hence in the example suggested by Gordon, a threat to contact the police or press would not be robbery. Uncertainty as to whether or not the common law crime is restricted to threats of immediate personal violence is unsatisfactory. As with other unclear aspects of the common law, we will not know the answer to this unless and until the appeal court has to consider a relevant case. It would be preferable if a statutory definition of robbery were to be enacted, to put the matter beyond doubt.

Suppose that B has borrowed A's radio, but then refuses to return it. Were A to use violence to take back the radio, this would not be robbery at common law since robbery involves theft – defined as taking the property of *another*. It would, however, be robbery under

12.22.2

---

[172] A Ashworth, "Conceptions of overcriminalization" (2008) 5 *Ohio St J Crim L* 407 at 411.
[173] Gordon (2001), para 16.13.
[174] 1991 SCCR 329. See section 12.21.1 above.
[175] *Ibid* at 329.
[176] Gordon (2001), para 16.13.
[177] *Draft Criminal Code*, s 76.

the *Code*. This is because the *Code* defines robbery in such a way as to protect a person's interest in the peaceful possession or control of property.

12.23 PIRACY

12.23.1 The common law crime of piracy was defined by the appeal court in the 1971 case of *Cameron* v *HM Advocate*[178] as the robbery of a ship.[179] International treaties may supplement the domestic law but they do not supplant it.[180] There appear to have been no cases of piracy under Scots law since *Cameron*, in which members of the crew took over a trawler, named the *Mary Craig*, eventually putting the captain and other crew members ashore. The indictment did not use the term "piracy" but the court appears to have been satisfied that this was the crime committed. The crew members had surrounded and menaced the captain, forcing him into his cabin, and then taken his keys. The lack of blood-thirstiness was specifically stated to be no bar to a successful charge of piracy.[181]

12.23.2 It is not only ships that are seized by violence: aircraft may be "hijacked". This is currently covered by s 1 of the Aviation Security Act 1982 and is committed where a person on board an aircraft unlawfully seizes control of it by the use of force or the threat of force. Acts of piracy on the international stage have come to the fore in recent years.[182] It appears, however, that the number of such attacks may be declining.[183] Nonetheless, ships at sea and flying aircraft are particularly vulnerable to acts of violence because of their physical situation.[184] Accordingly, attacking them is of a different order to any of the other crimes which might be charged such as assault, robbery or even murder. It is therefore appropriate that there is a distinct crime for this.

---

[178] 1971 JC 50.
[179] *Ibid* at 54 and 55 per Lord Cameron.
[180] *Ibid* at 61 per Lord Wheatley.
[181] 1971 JC 50 at 62 per Lord Milligan.
[182] For example, the Saudi Arabian-owned supertanker the *Sirius Star* was taken by Somali pirates in November 2008 (see http://www.guardian.co.uk/world/2008/nov/18/somalia-oil) and British yachtsman Malcolm Robertson was murdered by pirates off the coast of Thailand in March 2009 (see J Meikle, "Burmese attackers jailed for murdering British yachtsman", *Guardian Unlimited*, 29 November 2009, available at: http://www.theguardian.com/uk/2009/nov/29/burmese-attackers-jailed-murdering-yachtsman).
[183] There were "46 [Somali pirate] hijackings in 2009[;] 47 in 2010 [and] ... only 14 in 2012": J Legge, "Huge decline in hijackings by Somali pirates", *Independent*, 3 May 2013 (available at: http://www.independent.co.uk/news/world/africa/huge-decline-in-hijackings-by-somali-pirates-8602901.html).
[184] See section 8.23.1 above, n 176.

12.24 EXTORTION

"Extortion" is the term used in Scots law for what is colloquially **12.24.1**
termed "blackmail". As Horder notes:

> "Bribery is rightly made a criminal offence because it is wrongdoing that, if
> left unpunishable, would result in an unacceptably enhanced risk that a whole
> variety of grave harms would become more widespread around the globe. In
> that respect, it is no real argument against the criminalisation of bribery that,
> in itself, an act of bribery involves only harmless wrongdoing."[185]

Extortion involves obtaining money, property or some other
advantage by use of threats.[186] It differs from robbery in that the
threat made by a robber is immediate, whereas in extortion the threat
is postponed. Either the threat or the demand must be illegitimate
to amount to extortion. So if A is owed money and threatens to sue
her debtor this is not extortion. The demand is for money to which
A has a right. It is a legitimate claim and the threat to sue is a legal
remedy, therefore there is no illegitimate threat. If, however, A is
owed money and threatens to break the debtor's legs to obtain that
money, although the demand is legitimate since the money is owed,
the threat is not. If no money is owed, then both the demand and the
threat are illegitimate. It is not necessary that the advantage which
the accused seeks to obtain should be the payment of money. For
example, in *Rae* v *Donnelly*[187] the accused threatened to disclose
that two of his employees had been having an affair, unless one
of them dropped a claim for wrongful dismissal. This was held to
amount to attempted extortion. In *Hill* v *McGrogan*[188] the sheriff
dismissed as irrelevant a charge which libelled that the accused had
threatened to write to the complainer's employers, informing them
of various misdemeanours allegedly committed by the complainer
(including theft), unless she resigned from her job as a cleaner. The
sheriff seems to have been influenced by the fact that there was no
averment that the accused had acted maliciously, taking the view
that where no money was demanded, the accused's motive in making
threats must be for revenge or malice.

If illegitimate threats are employed, it does not matter whether the **12.24.2**
advantage which the accused seeks to obtain is actually due. As Lord
Justice-General Hope stated in *Black* v *Carmichael*:[189]

---

[185] Horder (2011) at 53.
[186] Extortion involves undue pressure to obtain the advantage. Under the Bribery
Act 2010, Scots law also criminalises the offering, promising or giving of a "financial
or other advantage" (s 1(2)(a)) to induce or reward another person for the improper
performance of certain functions, including those "of a public nature" (s 3(2)(a)).
[187] 1982 SCCR 148.
[188] 1945 SLT (Sh Ct) 18.
[189] 1992 SLT 897. The case is discussed further in section 12.3.9 above.

"it is extortion to seek to enforce a legitimate debt by means which the law regards as illegitimate, just as it is extortion to seek by such means to obtain money or some other advantage to which the accused has no right at all. Furthermore, the only means which the law regards as legitimate to force a debtor to make payment of his debt are those provided by due legal process. To use due legal process, such as an action in a court of law or a right of lien or retention available under contract, or to threaten to do so, is no doubt legitimate. It is not extortion if the debtor pays up as a result. But it is illegitimate to use other means, such as threats which are not related to the use of legal process, or the unauthorised detention of the debtor's person or his property, and it is extortion if the purpose in doing so is to obtain payment of the debt".[190]

In this case, wheel-clamping carried out by a private company was held to amount to extortion. The owner of the car was faced with the "threat" that it would not be released from the clamp unless he paid a sum of money to the wheel-clampers. Lord Hope stated that:

"The essential step in the argument, which makes the practice of wheel clamping illegal on the ground of extortion unless authorised by statute, is that it amounts to a demand for payment accompanied by the threat that until payment the vehicle will not be released".[191]

12.24.3   It has been suggested that extortion is "unique among major crimes" since "no one has yet figured out why it ought to be illegal".[192] This is because "two separate acts, each of which is a moral and legal right, can combine to make a moral and legal wrong".[193] We can see that this is so if we take as an example A threatening to inform the police that B has stolen something unless B gives a large sum of money to A. It is perfectly legitimate to inform the police about the commission of a crime – indeed, one has a moral obligation to do so – and it is generally legitimate to ask for money. But combining the two amounts to extortion. Not all threats are illegitimate, so far as the crime of extortion is concerned. If A threatens her son that she will not let him play his PS3 computer game unless he tidies his room, he may retort "That's blackmail!". The law would not recognise his claim – but why not? We may say that this is because A's threat is a legitimate one; A is entitled to withdraw the child's use of the game. It may, however, be difficult to distinguish the legitimate threat from the illegitimate one. James Lindgren has suggested that the crucial component in extortion is the fact that the blackmailer "interposes himself parasitically in an actual or

potential dispute in which he lacks a sufficiently direct interest".[194]
Hence a threat to expose someone's criminal misdeeds unless
payment is forthcoming is always extortion since the blackmailer
has no legitimate right to withhold this information from the
authorities. Given the harm which extortion can cause, it seems
appropriate for the criminal law to proscribe illegitimate demands
and threats.

---

[194] Lindgren (1984) at 702.

CHAPTER 13

OTHER PROPERTY-RELATED CRIMES

13.1 INTRODUCTION

As noted in the introduction to this part of the book, the taking **13.1.1**
of someone else's property is generally regarded as a wrong which
is distinct from the damaging or destroying of that property. This
chapter considers the latter type of crime.

13.2 MALICIOUS MISCHIEF

Malicious mischief requires that the accused disregard another **13.2.1**
person's property rights, but it is a crime which relates, broadly, to
property damage. It does not involve a "taking" of the property,
hence is not theft. Generally, the property is damaged or destroyed as
it stands, though of course it is possible for someone to steal property
and then destroy it. It is committed intentionally or recklessly but
not by negligence. It is misnamed, since there is no requirement
for the Crown to prove malice, that the act was committed out of
spite. In *Clark* v *Syme*[1] the accused warned his neighbour that the
latter's sheep were straying on to the accused's land, destroying his
vegetation. When the neighbour took no action to prevent this, the
accused shot one of the sheep. He did so in the belief that he was
entitled to take this action to protect his land. This was an error of
law, and he was convicted on appeal.[2] The presence of a civil dispute
will not justify wilful damage of someone else's property.

It was formerly thought that the crime required actual physical **13.2.2**
damage to property. In the case of *HM Advocate* v *Wilson*[3] the
accused was charged with malicious mischief for having activated an
emergency stop button. This halted the turbine of a power station,

---

[1] 1957 JC 1.
[2] For a description of the law's approach to errors of law, see section 19.6.1 below.
[3] 1983 SCCR 420.

and £147,000 worth of electricity was lost. It must be emphasised that there was no physical damage; the loss was purely economic. The appeal court held that this could amount to malicious mischief.[4] In *Bett* v *Hamilton*[5] the appellant was charged with malicious mischief by moving a bank security camera so that it recorded activity in an area different from that which it was meant to cover. The complaint libelled that "the running costs associated with said camera were wasted and said building was exposed to increased risk of housebreaking, theft and vandalism". The appellant took a plea to the relevancy of the charge on the ground that there was no averment of patrimonial (ie financial) loss. The sheriff repelled the plea on the ground that the bank had suffered the loss of the benefit of surveillance. In allowing the appeal, the High Court held that a charge of malicious mischief requires intent to cause either physical damage or patrimonial loss. Since the running costs of the camera would have been incurred in any event, the bank had suffered no financial loss.

13.3   VANDALISM

13.3.1   It is more common for the prosecution to charge vandalism, rather than malicious mischief. This is a creation of statute and is now contained in s 52 of the Criminal Law (Consolidation) (Scotland) Act 1995:

> "(1) Subject to subsection (2) below, any person who, without reasonable excuse, wilfully or recklessly destroys or damages any property belonging to another shall be guilty of the offence of vandalism.
>
> (2) It shall not be competent to charge acts which constitute the offence of wilful fire-raising as vandalism under this section."

As the section makes clear, the property must belong to someone other than the accused; it is not vandalism to destroy one's own property.

13.3.2   The test of recklessness in vandalism was specified in the case of *Black* v *Allan*.[6] Three youths had been fooling about outside a bank, and one of its windows was broken during horseplay. Their convictions were quashed on appeal. The youths had certainly caused the damage, but not wilfully (that is, deliberately) and the court felt that there was not sufficient evidence of recklessness since there was no "obvious and material risk" that damage would be caused. The

---

[4] This means of developing the law is critically assessed at section 5.11.2 above.
[5] 1998 JC 1.
[6] 1985 SCCR 11.

damage must also be caused "without reasonable excuse", and if the accused avers a reasonable excuse, it is for the Crown to negate this.[7] In *McGregor* v *Vannet*[8] the accused claimed that his hand had been trapped in the door of a taxi by the taxi's driver. It was accepted by the court that if this were so, it would amount to a reasonable excuse for the accused having damaged the taxi's windscreen.

The *Scottish Crime and Justice Survey* found that acts of **13.3.3** vandalism accounted for about a quarter (27 per cent) of all reported crimes in 2012–13, with motor vehicle vandalism being more common (128,639 reports) than vandalism of other property (90,370 reports).[9] It must, of course, be borne in mind that people are more inclined to report certain crimes than others.[10] Property crimes such as theft and vandalism are commonly reported to the police, since this is a pre-requisite of making an insurance claim. Even so, this is a high proportion.

13.4 CRITIQUE OF THE LAW ON VANDALISM AND MALICIOUS MISCHIEF AND PROPOSALS FOR REFORM

While much has been written about vandalism and malicious **13.4.1** mischief, and how one differs from the other,[11] there is no need for two such similarly defined crimes. The *Draft Criminal Code* provides an offence of "criminal damage to property", similar to vandalism,[12] designed to replace both vandalism and malicious mischief. It also proposes a new offence of "causing an unlawful risk of damage to property".[13] The *Commentary to the Code* gives as an example of the latter "cutting another person's boat loose from its moorings in stormy weather". It concludes: "Even if, by good fortune, no damage ensued there could still be an intentional or reckless causing of a risk of destruction or serious damage." Were the *Code* to be enacted, prosecution under this provision would seem preferable to

---

[7] An example of the Crown failing to do so is *MacDougall* v *Ho* 1985 SCCR 199.

[8] 1999 GWD 23–1092.

[9] *Scottish Crime and Justice Survey 2012/13*, para 2.1 and table A 1.2.

[10] The *2012–13 Survey* estimates that only 39 per cent of personal crimes are reported to the police (*ibid* at para 5.2). The "dark figures" in criminal statistics have been defined as "those criminal incidents *not* known to or recorded by the police": F H McClintock, "Facts and myths about the state of crime" in R Hood (ed), *Crime, Criminology and Public Policy: Essays in Honour of Sir Leon Radzinowicz* (1974) 33 at p 35 (emphasis in original).

[11] See, for example, A M Cubie, *Scots Criminal Law* (3rd edn, 2010), para 18.6. The High Court held that these are distinct offences in *Black* v *Allan* 1985 SCCR 11 at 12–13 per LJ-G Emslie.

[12] *Draft Criminal Code*, s 81.

[13] *Ibid*, s 82.

a charge of "attempted vandalism". Section 83 of the *Code* provides an offence of "criminal interference with property" which involves non-consensual interference which causes loss, harm or serious inconvenience. The accused must have intended such a result, or been reckless as to whether any such result would follow.

13.4.2   Mention has already been made of the requirement that criminal wrongdoing be "fairly labelled", to distinguish the actor who deliberately causes harm from one who is merely reckless.[14] Were the criminal law to be codified, or the crimes of vandalism and malicious mischief to be otherwise redefined by statute, perhaps two separate offences should be enacted, based on the differing degrees of *mens rea*. As previously noted,[15] many people may be able to conceive of circumstances in which their reckless behaviour might cause damage to others' property, but would recoil from the idea that they would do so intentionally. Yet the person who is merely reckless is stigmatised as a "vandal" in the same way as the person who deliberately causes damage.

13.5   FIRE-RAISING

13.5.1 Scottish crime statistics distinguish between "primary fires", "secondary fires" and "chimney fires".[16] Primary fires: "Include all fires in non-derelict buildings and outdoor structures".[17] This term also includes any fires involving casualties, rescues, or attended by five or more appliances regardless of location.[18] Secondary fires: "Are the majority of outdoor fires including grassland and refuse fires unless they involve casualties or rescues, property loss or if five or more appliances attend. They include fires in derelict buildings but not chimney fires".[19] Statistics from the Scottish Government record that 60 per cent of all primary and secondary fires are set deliberately. This amounted to 15,061 cases in 2012–13.[20] How, then, does Scots criminal law approach such cases?

13.5.2   Historically, there were two crimes, namely "wilful fire-raising" and "culpable and reckless fire-raising". Despite this nomenclature, whether the charge was the former or the latter depended on the

---

[14] See from section 4.6 above.

[15] *Draft Criminal Code*, s 82. See section 4.6.2 above.

[16] *Statistical Bulletin: Crime and Justice Series: Fire Statistics Scotland, 2012–13*, Table 1, available at http://www.scotland.gov.uk/Resource/0043/00435498.pdf.

[17] *Ibid* at para 6.9.1

[18] *Ibid* at para 4.1.

[19] *Ibid* at para 6.9.1. Chimney fires are defined as fires in occupied buildings which are confined within the chimney structure, do not involve casualties or rescues, and are attended by four or fewer appliances (*ibid* at para 6.9.2).

[20] *Ibid* at Tables 17 and 19.

type of property set on fire, not on the *mens rea* of the accused. Hume drew together much of the older law and indicated that it was only wilful fire-raising (originally a capital crime) if houses, corn (in stacks or barns), coal-heughs or woods were burnt.[21] Clearly, such a restrictive list of subjects did little to reflect the accused's culpability.

In the (appropriately named) case of *Byrne* v *HM Advocate*[22] in 2000, the accused was charged with the wilful fire-raising of a building by setting fire to paper, whereby the building caught fire. The court held that either crime (wilful fire-raising or culpable and reckless fire-raising) can be charged in relation to any type of property, but it is only wilful fire-raising in relation to the property that has been deliberately set on fire, since this is in accordance with the ordinary meaning of the word "wilful". Commenting on the case of *Byrne*, Gerald Gordon noted: **13.5.3**

> "One's immediate reaction is just to say, 'And about time too.' It should, of course, have happened over a century ago. But at least students will be able to enter the twenty-first century without having to wonder ... how 'culpable and reckless fire raising' can be committed wilfully."[23]

A fire has been raised when property starts to burn. The property must belong to someone else. Setting one's own property on fire might amount to a breach of the peace, or be evidence of an attempt to defraud an insurance company,[24] but it will not be wilful fire-raising or culpable and reckless fire-raising. The doctrine of "transferred intent", which applies to the crime of assault,[25] has no application to fire-raising; if the accused set fire to a table in a room, and her sole intention was to destroy the table, she is not guilty of wilful fire-raising in relation to the house, or even the room in which the table is situated, if they too catch fire. She may, however, be guilty of "culpable and reckless fire-raising" in relation to the room and house if she took an unreasonable risk that the fire would spread in that manner.[26] In *Carr* v *HM Advocate*[27] "recklessness" was defined in this context as requiring "a complete disregard for any dangers which might result from what [the accused] was doing".[28] **13.5.4**

---

[21] Hume, i, 125–126.

[22] 2000 JC 155.

[23] 2000 SCCR 77 at 92.

[24] This is a form of fraud: see *Sutherland* v *HM Advocate* 1994 SLT 634.

[25] See section 6.8.2 above.

[26] Where the accused has been charged with wilful fire-raising in respect of particular property, the Crown will only be able to secure a conviction for the lesser crime of culpable and reckless fire-raising if this has been libelled as a separate charge.

[27] 1994 JC 203.

[28] *Ibid* at 208 per LJ-G Hope.

13.5.5   In *McCue* v *Currie*[29] in 2004, the accused accidentally set fire to
some property, but then did nothing to stop the fire from spreading.
As previously noted,[30] the appeal court held that his omission could
not amount to culpable and reckless fire-raising. Wilful fire-raising
can be charged as malicious mischief, but not vandalism.[31]

13.6   CRITIQUE OF THE LAW ON FIRE-RAISING AND PROPOSALS FOR REFORM

13.6.1   Given the "fair labelling" point made about vandalism and malicious
mischief,[32] it is appropriate that Scots law recognises two separate
crimes of fire-raising, as reflecting the different degrees of blame
involved. Furthermore, the exclusion of acts of fire-raising from being
charged as vandalism, as noted above, emphasises its more serious
nature; unlike most acts of vandalism, setting property on fire is
highly dangerous since fire has a tendency to spread unpredictably,
leading not just to extensive property damage but also potentially to
loss of life.

13.6.2   The *mens rea* for culpable and reckless fire-raising deserves
further consideration. Recklessness generally is perhaps easier to
recognise in practice than to define in words and this may explain
Scots law's tendency to define it differently for different crimes
and to shift between objectivism and subjectivism. Some statutory
offences allow reckless *behaviour* to satisfy the relevant requirement.
Thus vandalism has been held to require that the relevant *conduct*
should create "an obvious and material risk of damage".[33] This
definition was itself based on that required for "reckless driving", set
down in the case of *Allan* v *Patterson*[34] for the purposes of the Road
Traffic Acts. For common law crimes *Transco plc* v *HM Advocate
(No 1)*[35] confirmed that recklessness requires a state of mind.[36] This
makes perfect sense given that what is sought is a *mens rea* element,
and even more sense in the context of a case which was concerned
with the ability of a company – an artificial person – to formulate
that *mens rea*. Nonetheless, it does seem to introduce a subjective
element into an area which had hitherto been characterised largely

---

[29] 2004 JC 73.
[30] This case was discussed in more detail from section 6.8.1 above.
[31] See the Criminal Law (Consolidation) (Scotland) Act 1995, s 52(2) and section 13.3.1 above.
[32] See section 13.4.2 above.
[33] *Black* v *Allan* 1985 SCCR 11 at 13 per LJ-G Emslie, discussed at section 13.3.2 above.
[34] 1980 JC 57, quoted at section 9.24.3 above.
[35] 2004 JC 29.
[36] *Ibid* at 34 per Lord Osborne.

objectively: almost by definition a state of mind requires that the accused thought about the risk.[37]

What, then, of the *mens rea* for culpable and reckless fire-raising **13.6.3** itself? The case of *Carr*[38] pre-dates all of the other common law cases mentioned above, yet none of them, not even *Transco*,[39] would seem to impact on its statement of the *mens rea* for the crime. Accordingly, culpable and reckless fire-raising has its own definition of "recklessness". The context of *Carr* suggests that this has a subjective component. The fire must not have been started accidentally;[40] the accused must have *mens rea* for the commission of a crime;[41] and "the question [is] whether the accused's actions showed a complete disregard for any dangers which might result from what he was doing and in particular of the fire taking effect on the premises".[42] Taken together, these points tend to suggest that the accused must have given some thought to the risk.[43] Perhaps it is impossible to set a fire without some regard to that risk, given that fires are so inherently risky.[44] A person could not but be aware that she was creating a serious risk by setting a fire, particularly if, as in *Carr*, she does this inside a building. Nonetheless, this comes closer to an objective standard: reasonable people recognise the risks of fire-setting, therefore the accused does or, at least, ought to do so. Overall, our view is that an objective standard is appropriate here. An accused who has set a fire should not escape liability because she personally did not appreciate that fire-raising was risky, unless, as in the English case of *Elliott* v *C (a minor)*,[45] she lacked the capacity to make this determination.

The other noteworthy aspect is that the Crown cannot obtain a **13.6.4** conviction for culpable and reckless fire-raising where it has charged wilful fire-raising unless it specifically libels this as an alternative charge. This gives the accused fair notice of the crimes for which she may be convicted, but is out of step with the practice in other crimes, such as murder, where a culpable homicide verdict can be returned even if this has not been libelled as an alternative. In a fire-raising

---

[37] See, for example, *Robson* v *Spiers* 1999 SLT 1141 which turns on the foreseeability of the risk created.

[38] 1994 JC 203. See section 13.5.4 above.

[39] 2004 JC 29.

[40] *Carr* v *HM Advocate* 1994 JC 203 at 207.

[41] *Ibid* at 208.

[42] *Ibid*.

[43] Though, at first instance, the jury had been advised that the test was objective, and the appeal court did not expressly contradict that (*ibid* at 206).

[44] Gordon says that, in fire-raising, there is a "very high duty to take care not to injure anyone" (Gordon (2001), para 26.27, n 53).

[45] [1983] 1 WLR 939, discussed in sections 6.15.2 and 6.18.1 above.

case, an accused would simply have to be acquitted altogether if the Crown charged only the "wilful" form but was then unable to prove the necessary intention.[46] In homicide, it is important to convict at the appropriate *level* of blameworthiness.[47] In fire-raising, apprising the accused of the exact criminality which the Crown is seeking to prove seems to be the predominant value.

---

[46] *Byrne* v *HM Advocate* 2000 JC 155 at 162 per Lord Coulsfield.
[47] See *Ferguson* v *HM Advocate* 2009 SLT 67.

PART V

OFFENCES WHICH PROTECT THE COURSE OF JUSTICE AND PUBLIC ORDER

Chapter 14 considers offences against the course of justice, Chapter 15 public order offences, and Chapter 16 offensive behaviours. Offences against the course of justice have a parasitic quality, in as much as their existence can only be justified by reference to other substantive crimes. In other words, once a society has decreed that certain forms of behaviour are not to be tolerated (whether to prevent harm to others, or otherwise)[1] and that those who engage in such behaviours will be censured and punished, it then needs some sort of criminal justice system to enforce these norms, and to determine whether a particular individual has breached them on a given occasion. It also becomes necessary to make sure that the criminal justice system is not thwarted from doing so, hence the need for offences against the administration of justice.

In relation to public order offences, as Tony Smith has remarked, the criminal law is usually employed to "prevent harm to certain social interests such as personal safety and physical integrity, and rights in property. The deliberate infliction of harm that the criminal sanction entails is justified as being designed to protect one or other of those interests".[2] In light of this, he asks: "What is the comparable value in public order that we seek to preserve through the laws of riot, affray, violent disorder and other offences?"[3] It is not easy to provide a satisfactory answer to this, other than to say that some such crimes are necessary in order to allow people to enjoy a degree of tranquillity. It may be argued that some public order offences generally breach the harm principle;[4] they target behaviours which are sometimes offensive, and frequently inconvenient, but which are

---

[1] See Chapters 1–4 above.
[2] A T H Smith, *The Offences Against Public Order* (1987), p 1.
[3] *Ibid.*
[4] See Chapter 3 above.

rarely harmful to our personal safety or property interests. These offences, at best, aim to prevent a risk of harm to persons or property from materialising, but this must be balanced against the rights of those who wish to exercise their freedom of speech, and of assembly, safeguarded by the European Convention on Human Rights.[5]

Offences involving prostitution, such as soliciting and brothel-keeping, cross classification boundaries. Some might argue that their basis of criminalisation rests in morality, despite the difficulty of identifying societal consensus around this rather slippery concept.[6] Gordon's *Criminal Law* treats crimes relating to prostitution, such as soliciting, as sexual offences[7] and other textbook writers have followed his lead,[8] though not without questioning the appropriateness of this categorisation.[9] Crimes which are grouped as "sexual" are often linked by the absence of consent to sexual practices. The "harm" is, therefore, the breach of the individual's autonomy, which draws directly on liberal principles of the sanctity of freewill. In relation to prostitution, on the other hand, the law takes no interest in whether sexual intercourse even takes place. Its concentration is on soliciting, whether by the sex worker (male or female) or by the purchaser. For this reason, we take the view that it is more appropriately considered as a crime against public order, hence its inclusion in Chapter 15. Its harm, such as it is, rests in the unacceptability of selling and buying sex in a public space.[10]

The offences described in Chapter 16 are rather a disparate collection, which do not readily fit elsewhere. We have included in that chapter offences such as bestiality, cruelty to animals, violation of sepulchres and blasphemy – quite a motley collection! Our justification for doing so is that each is generally perceived, rightly or wrongly, as "offensive". We will explore whether this is an adequate basis for their criminalisation, in Chapter 16.

---

[5] Articles 10 and 11, respectively. See from section 15.2.4 below.
[6] See from section 2.7 above.
[7] Gordon (2001), paras 36.38–36.47.
[8] For example, R A A McCall Smith and D Sheldon, *Scots Criminal Law* (1997), pp 208–209; and also the 3rd edition of that book by A M Cubie (2010), para 11.16; C H W Gane, C N Stoddart and J Chalmers, *A Casebook on Scottish Criminal Law* (4th edn, 2009), paras 9.36–9.44.
[9] Gane, Stoddart and Chalmers (2009), para 9.36.
[10] See, however, from section 15.13 below.

CHAPTER 14

OFFENCES AGAINST THE COURSE OF JUSTICE

14.1 INTRODUCTION

There is some uncertainty in Scots law as to whether there is, in **14.1.1** fact, a category of crimes against the course of justice or whether there is really only one such crime – attempting to pervert the course of justice – and all offences which would otherwise fall into this category are really just examples of this. A crime like perjury, for instance, is also an attempt to prevent the course of justice from running its proper course. Current practice seems to be that if there is a specific, named offence, and the accused satisfies the *actus reus* and *mens rea* for that (for example, perjury) then that is what will be charged. Anything else will be swept up as an "attempt to pervert the course of justice".

14.2 FALSE ACCUSATIONS OF CRIME/WASTING POLICE TIME

"False reporting to police", "wasting the time of the police", **14.2.1** "misleading the police" and "giving false information to the criminal authorities" are all basically the same crime, though the behaviour can be charged by any of these names. According to Caroline Pelser, the making of false accusation was criminalised by the Dutch Criminal Code in the 19th century because of the importance attached to honour which, she suggests, "was seen as the highest value".[1] Thus she claims that "[t]he intention to injure the honour or reputation of a particular person, not the wish to

---

[1] C M Pelser, "Criminal legislation in the nineteenth century: the historic roots of criminal law and non-intervention in the Netherlands" in P Alldridge and C Brants (eds), *Personal Autonomy, the Private Sphere and Criminal Law* (2001) 181 at p 197.

mislead the authorities, is the focus here".[2] This may also have been the historical position in Scots law; Hume recognised that it was a crime to make a false accusation that a particular, named individual had committed an offence.[3] The *mens rea* seems to be knowledge that the story is untrue. In one case, the accused falsely alleged that they had been injured by a police dog while being arrested. This resulted in the police investigating the matter and wasting their time over a false story.[4] In *Simpkins* v *HM Advocate*[5] a store detective concocted a shoplifting charge against two boys. The police were informed and the boys were under suspicion for a period. Simpkins was convicted of falsely accusing two persons in a shop of having committed the crime of theft and of fabricating evidence tending to support that false accusation which was reported to the police.

14.2.2   The other way in which this crime can be committed is simply by giving information to the police (or possibly to the procurator fiscal) which causes them to commence an investigation. There is no requirement that the accused implicate a specific individual, nor need there be an allegation that a crime has been committed. In *Kerr* v *Hill*[6] a bus driver simply told the police that he had seen a cyclist being hit by a bus, run by a rival company. This was the first time such a charge had been brought where no specific individual had been falsely accused of having committed an offence. Lord Morison's brief judgment in the appeal indicates that he was cautious about extending the crime in this way. His view was that "the suggested criminal or criminals could easily have been ascertained",[7] thereby potentially bringing the matter within the remit of the crime as recognised by Hume. Lord Justice-General Normand, on the other hand, had no hesitation in stating (though without reference to authority) that

> "the giving to the police of information known to be false, for the purpose of causing them to institute an investigation with a view to criminal proceedings, is in itself a crime".[8]

He stated that "the essence of the crime" consisted in the fact that "the criminal authorities were deliberately set in motion by a

---

[2] Pelser (2001), p 181.
[3] Hume, i, 341–343.
[4] *Robertson* v *Hamilton* 1987 JC 95.
[5] 1985 SCCR 30.
[6] 1936 JC 71.
[7] *Ibid* at 75.
[8] *Ibid.*

malicious person by means of an invented story".[9] *Kerr* v *Hill*, then, is yet another case in which the appeal court has, depending on one's perspective, either declared "an old crime to have been committed in a new way" or "created" new law.

The extended crime of telling lies to the police was further   **14.2.3** developed in the case of *Gray* v *Morrison*.[10] Here, the accused committed an offence, largely through excessive politeness. He had refused a lift from a friend by pretending that he planned to cycle home. When the friend discovered that there was no bicycle, Gray felt obliged to report its (non-existent) "theft" to the police. He pled guilty to a charge which can be summarised as falsely representing to a police sergeant that a bicycle belonging to him had been stolen, thereby causing officers of the local constabulary to waste their time in the investigation of this false story and "render[ing] the lieges liable to suspicion and to accusations of theft".[11] He was initially sentenced to 14 days' imprisonment, without the option of a fine. In delivering his judgment in an appeal against this sentence, Lord Justice-General Cooper expressed his concern that people might be deterred from giving information to the police if they feared that they could be charged with this offence should the information turn out to be incorrect. Accordingly, he stated that words like "knowing the same to be false" should always be included in the charge.[12] This, therefore, constitutes the *mens rea*. In terms of the *actus reus*, what is required is the making of a false statement to the police, as a result of which they set an investigation in motion. It is clear from *Gray* v *Morrison* that the crime is constituted whether or not the statement is made maliciously.[13]

14.3   CRITIQUE OF THE OFFENCE OF WASTING POLICE TIME AND PROPOSALS FOR REFORM

Since the accused in *Gray* v *Morrison*[14] pled guilty to the charge,   **14.3.1** there was no discussion by the court as to whether what he had done actually did amount to the developing crime of making false representations to the police, causing them to embark on an investigation. We are, however, concerned with whether such behaviour *ought* to be criminal. The issue comes down to whether

---

[9] 1936 JC 71 at 75.

[10] 1954 JC 31.

[11] *Ibid.*

[12] *Ibid* at 34. Gray's sentence of imprisonment was reduced to a £10 fine.

[13] The *Draft Criminal Code* extends this offence to include other emergency services (s 93), defined as including fire brigade and ambulance services, and any other service operated for the emergency protection of life.

"malice" ought to be required – but malice would constitute the accused's motive,[15] an issue which is generally irrelevant in criminal law. Mr Gray's moral blameworthiness seems low. Yet his behaviour – in advising the police that a crime had been committed when it had not – does seem sufficiently wrongful to satisfy the harm principle.[16] It is not inconceivable that an individual might have been arrested for the theft of Mr Gray's bicycle, even though no such crime had taken place; it is possible, after all, to be convicted of murder without a body being found.[17] It is therefore appropriate for the law to proscribe the making of a false statement that a crime has been committed, even when this has not involved any named individual being accused of being its perpetrator.

14.4 PERJURY

14.4.1 Witnesses in judicial proceedings swear an oath or affirm to tell the truth. If, having done so, they then give evidence which they know to be untrue, they can be charged with perjury. The requirements for this crime are: (1) The evidence must be given in judicial proceedings. This obviously applies to courts but it would also apply to proceedings before a tribunal which is empowered to take evidence on oath. (2) The statement must be definite and unequivocal. If it is ambiguous, and one interpretation would be true, the accused must get the benefit of this doubt. A witness may say that she does not remember the event about which she is being questioned. If this is true, clearly it will not constitute perjury. If, however, it can be proved that she *does* remember, the statement can be prosecuted as perjury. The converse is illustrated by the case of *Simpson* v *Tudhope*.[18] The accused was a serving police officer who was convicted of perjury on the basis of evidence which he gave that he had been accompanied, on a particular occasion, by a female police officer. In fact, he could not recollect whether he had been accompanied by her or by a male colleague. It was a lie, and hence perjury, to state that he recalled having been with A when the truth was that he did not know whether he had been with A or B. (3) The *mens rea* is that the accused must know that the evidence she is giving is false. (4) The false statement must be relevant to the point at issue in the case, or to the credibility of the speaker

---

[14] 1954 JC 31.
[15] See from section 6.10 above.
[16] See Chapter 3 above.
[17] *Fraser* v *HM Advocate* 2008 SCCR 407.
[18] 1988 SLT 297.

as a witness. In *Lord Advocate's Reference (No 1 of 1985)*,[19] the accused had previously been a Crown witness in a murder trial. While he was giving evidence on oath at that trial, it was put to him that he had said certain things to the police during an earlier interview. He denied making such a statement. On the basis of this denial he was charged with perjury, but subsequently acquitted. The Lord Advocate referred the matter to the High Court on a point of law.[20] It was held that perjury consists simply in making a false statement under oath. Here, the perjury was the denial that the accused had ever made such a statement to the police. The truth or falsity of the alleged statement itself, and any issue as to whether it had been lawfully obtained, were irrelevant in a perjury case. The court held that any evidence which is competent and relevant either in proof of the charge in the original case or in relation to the witness's credibility can ground a perjury charge.

Susan Edwards has identified two reasons for perjury being treated as a serious offence. First, its commission serves to undermine and destabilise the integrity of the criminal process. Second, a high incidence of perjury may lead to higher attrition rates, where prosecutions simply cannot succeed.[21] Edwards suggested that the effect of the perjury may also be relevant to the seriousness with which the court regards it. If it results in the wrongful conviction of an innocent person, the sentence is likely to be high.[22] If the perjurer has standing in the public eye, this may also aggravate the offence.[23]   **14.4.2**

14.5 SUBORNATION OF PERJURY

This consists in inducing someone to give perjured evidence. The form of the inducement is irrelevant. It can be done by threat, by bribe or simply by persuasion. The witness must actually give the perjured evidence for the crime to be complete. Where an accused tries to suborn perjury but the witness tells the truth in court or, for   **14.5.1**

---

[19] 1986 JC 137.
[20] See section 9.18.3 above n 229.
[21] S S M Edwards, "Perjury and perverting the course of justice considered" [2003] *Crim LR* 525 at 525.
[22] Edwards cites the sentence of 6 years' imprisonment imposed on a perjurer whose testimony helped wrongly to convict T C Campbell of the murders of six members of one Glasgow family in the so-called "ice-cream wars" case (*ibid* at 534). The Scottish Criminal Cases Review Commission reviewed the case and the convictions were finally quashed in 2004: *Campbell* v *HM Advocate* 2004 SLT 397.
[23] For example, the politicians Jonathan Aitken and Jeffrey Archer: Edwards (2003) at 534.

some other reason, the perjured evidence is not given, the charge is attempted subornation of perjury.

14.6 CRITIQUE OF THE LAW ON PERJURY AND PROPOSALS FOR REFORM

14.6.1 Prior to the case of *Lord Advocate's Reference (No 1 of 1985)*,[24] it had been thought that a perjury conviction could only be returned if the perjured evidence had been competently admitted, was relevant to the issue at the trial, and had a material bearing on the outcome.[25] The first criterion was required on the basis that "incompetent evidence [was] so prejudicial to the administration of justice that the Courts [would] not assign to it the character of perjury and [would] treat it as if it had not been given".[26] An example of a case in which the perjured evidence was held to have been competently admitted is *Angus v HM Advocate*;[27] the fact that Mr Angus (the accused in the trial for attempted subornation of perjury) had provided the name of a backstreet abortionist at that abortionist's trial was competent (and material) evidence. Mr Angus was, therefore, appropriately convicted of attempted subornation of perjury for having asked the principal witness to leave his name out of her evidence at the earlier abortion trial.

14.6.2 As noted above,[28] it was held in *Lord Advocate's Reference (No 1 of 1985)*[29] that so long as the evidence was competent and relevant it need not be particularly significant. While the evidence would have to be admissible, this could be merely for the purpose of testing the credibility of the witness. The decision in this case moves the law closer to a situation where simply lying under judicial oath would be sufficient to constitute the crime.[30] This is appropriate; a witness who lies under oath should not be able to escape liability because of the technicalities of the rules of evidence. Where the perjury has serious consequences, such as leading to the acquittal of someone who ought to have been convicted or, worse still, leading to the conviction of an innocent party, then this is an aggravation and can be reflected in the sentence.

---

[24] 1986 JC 137. See section 14.4.1 above.
[25] Hume, i, 369; *HM Advocate v Smith* 1934 SLT 485.
[26] *Ibid* at 487 per LJ-C Aitchison.
[27] 1935 JC 1.
[28] See section 14.4.1 above.
[29] 1986 JC 137.
[30] See the *Draft Criminal Code*, s 100, which would go further still and remove the requirement that the false evidence was competent and relevant when it was given.

14.7   ATTEMPTING TO PERVERT THE COURSE OF JUSTICE

As already noted,[31] each of the offences examined thus far could **14.7.1** be prosecuted as an attempt to pervert the course of justice. It is necessary now to look at the circumstances in which this crime is charged in its own right. This form of charge was first used in 1946 in the case of *Scott* v *HM Advocate*,[32] where the accused had tried to persuade two women to give false evidence that he had been in their house at a time when he had actually been involved in a car accident. Clearly this could have been charged as attempted subornation of perjury.[33] In *Dalton* v *HM Advocate*,[34] however, no other nominate crime had been committed. Here, the accused tried to induce a witness not to identify a robbery suspect in a police identity parade. The court held that attempting to pervert the course of justice in this way constituted a crime. Its provenance was discussed in the case of *HM Advocate* v *Harris*,[35] where the accused attempted to argue that the common law did not recognise such a crime and that there had been no purported exercise of the High Court's declaratory power to create it. Even if there had, such an exercise would breach Art 7 of the ECHR.[36] Accordingly, it was argued, "the common law had taken a 'wrong turn' and erroneously proceeded on the basis that such a crime existed".[37] The argument was rejected. Having reviewed the authorities, the High Court stated: "attempting to pervert the course of justice is, and has been since long prior to the advent of the [European] Convention into Scots law, a crime in this jurisdiction".[38]

The word "attempt" here is largely redundant and it is not being **14.7.2** used in the sense of a criminal attempt.[39] It is equally appropriate to charge exactly the same conduct as "perverting the course of justice" and this is sometimes done.[40] The crime consists of any act which interferes with the course of justice. Perhaps it is usually libelled as an "attempt" because the very fact that the accused is being prosecuted shows that the course of justice has prevailed. Regardless of the rationale for the use of the term, the *principles* of criminal

---

[31] See section 14.1.1 above.
[32] 1946 JC 90.
[33] See from section 14.5 above.
[34] 1951 JC 76.
[35] 2011 JC 125.
[36] See section 4.2.1 above for the terms of Art 7.
[37] 2011 JC 125 at 131, para [8].
[38] *Ibid* at 137, para [29] per LJ-G Hamilton. For further discussion of this case, see section 14.7.4 below.
[39] See from section 8.2 above.
[40] For example, *Lockhart* v *Massie* 1989 SCCR 421.

attempts – the *mens rea* of the completed crime and the *actus reus* of moving from preparation to perpetration – do not apply. The offences which are charged as "attempting to pervert the course of justice" are complete.

14.7.3 The *actus reus* of the crime requires behaviour which impedes the smooth progress of the course of justice. Words used to describe this in charges for attempting to pervert the course of justice include "hinder", "obstruct", "pervert" and "defeat". The proscribed behaviour can take many forms. It is common, for example, for actions taken to conceal a crime to be prosecuted in this way. In *Murphy* v *HM Advocate*,[41] the accused was convicted of murder, having mounted a serious assault on the victim using the stem of a broken wine glass, ornaments and other sharp instruments. She had also kicked and stamped on his body. He bled profusely. As well as the murder, the accused was convicted of attempting to defeat the ends of justice by washing blood from the deceased and changing her own clothes and footwear. Similarly, in *Crawford* v *HM Advocate*,[42] another murder case involving considerable bloodshed, there was a successful charge of attempting to defeat the ends of justice by, *inter alia*, contacting the emergency services using a disguised voice and also setting fire to clothing. In *Clark* v *Service*,[43] the allegation that police officers had submitted a false and misleading report on an incident formed the basis of a charge of perverting the course of justice.[44]

14.7.4 There must be a course of justice but this has been held to exist at a very early stage: in *Watson* v *HM Advocate*[45] it was held that the course of justice begins at the point when the police begin to investigate an incident, even before they know whether that incident constitutes a crime. Mention has already been made of the case of *HM Advocate* v *Harris*.[46] The accused had taken a car and driven it deliberately, in excess of the speed limit, past a speed camera. He had done this specifically so that the registered owner of the car would be (wrongly) identified as having committed an offence. It was argued on his behalf that "there was no course of justice running at the time the actions took place".[47] The High Court, however, took the view that: "If ... it is established that the [accused] deliberately set in train events designed falsely to

---

[41] 2013 JC 60.
[42] 2012 JC 360.
[43] 2011 SCL 809.
[44] Their conviction were quashed on appeal.
[45] 1993 SCCR 875.
[46] 2011 JC 125. See section 14.7.1 above.
[47] *Ibid* at 132, para [10].

incriminate the complainer, we see no reason why this should not constitute an attempt to prevent the course of justice".[48]

The *mens rea* is that the accused must intend to pervert the course   **14.7.5** of justice. As with the crime of assault,[49] the courts have tended to use the terminology of "evil intent". For instance, in *HM Advocate v Mannion*,[50] Lord Justice-Clerk Thomson stated that:

> "Evil intention, of course, is of the essence of the matter and must be established. This indictment clearly narrates the evil intention of the accused to avoid being called upon to give evidence".[51]

In this case, the accused deliberately left his home and went into hiding in order to avoid giving evidence at the trial of a third party for aggravated theft. The court held that this constituted an attempt to pervert the course of justice, even though Mannion had not actually been cited to appear as a witness at that point.

14.8   CRITIQUE OF THE LAW ON ATTEMPTING TO PERVERT THE COURSE OF JUSTICE AND PROPOSALS FOR REFORM

It is not uncommon for the Crown to charge a common law crime   **14.8.1** instead of a statutory one, even when the latter is arguably more appropriate. An example of this in relation to attempting to pervert the course of justice is the case of *McDowall v HM Advocate*.[52] The accused could have been charged with the statutory offence of failing to stop and report after a road traffic accident.[53] Instead, he was charged that

> "being the driver of a motor vehicle ... and an accident having then occurred ... you did fail to stop, fail to report the circumstances of the said accident to the police, fail to contact the emergency services, abandon your vehicle nearby and did flee from the scene, with utter disregard for the well-being of [those who were fatally injured in the accident] ... and all this you did with intent to prevent the police and criminal authorities from ascertaining the truth as to your involvement in the said crime and to avoid detection, arrest and prosecution in respect thereof, *all with intent to defeat the ends of justice and you did attempt to defeat the ends of justice*".[54]

---

[48] 2011 JC 125 at 137, para [31] per LJ-G Hamilton.
[49] See section 10.2.3 above.
[50] 1961 JC 79.
[51] *Ibid* at 80.
[52] 1998 SCCR 343. The case is discussed also in section 6.15.3 above in relation to the other charges on the indictment.
[53] Contrary to the Road Traffic Act 1988, s 170.
[54] 1998 SCCR 343 at 344 (emphasis added).

The appellant was sentenced to 2 years' imprisonment in respect of this charge, to run concurrently with the sentence of 8 years' imprisonment for the culpable homicide of those he had killed in the accident. The maximum penalty for a breach of the statutory provision was 6 months' imprisonment for failing to stop, and the same maximum for failing to report an accident. Interference with the course of justice in the form taken in this case is one obvious consequence of failing to report an acccident. It is arguable, therefore, that it is implied in the statutory offence. That being the case, consideration should be given to increasing its maximum penalty.

14.9   CRIMES COMMITTED AFTER CONVICTION

14.9.1   The course of justice continues until a convicted person's sentence has been completed. Sometimes, therefore, the course of justice is perverted by something which happens much later in the process, in relation to people who are being held in lawful custody.

14.10   PRISON-BREAKING AND ESCAPING FROM LAWFUL CUSTODY

14.10.1   It is clearly an offence – known as prison-breaking and recognised by Hume[55] – to escape from prison. It applies only to an escape from a prison itself, not to escape from police cells or any other similar place. Where the escape is from a place in which the accused is being lawfully detained, other than a prison, this is charged as "escaping from lawful custody". In *HM Advocate* v *Martin and Others*[56] one of the accused had been taken from Peterhead Prison to form part of a working party at the Admiralty Yard at Keith Inch, Peterhead. He escaped from there and was convicted of attempting to defeat the ends of justice by absconding from lawful custody. Similarly, in *McAllister* v *HM Advocate*[57] the accused had been escorted by two prison officers from Saughton Prison to Edinburgh Royal Infirmary so that he could have X-rays carried out. He escaped from the toilets at the hospital and was convicted of escaping from lawful custody and attempting to defeat the ends of justice.

14.10.2   Escape from custody (meaning, effectively, the custody of a police officer),[58] is now a statutory offence in terms of s 91(1) of the Police and Fire Reform (Scotland) Act 2012. It consists in either removing a person from custody or assisting the escape of a person in custody.

---

[55]   Hume, i, 401. Hume referred to the crime as "breaking prison".
[56]   1956 JC 1.
[57]   1986 SCCR 688.
[58]   See Police and Fire Reform (Scotland) Act 2012, s 91(2) and (3).

On summary conviction the offence carries a maximum sentence of 12 months' imprisonment or a fine not exceeding £10,000[59] or both. The relationship between this offence and the common law crimes outlined above is not specified. It would seem, therefore, that it remains possible to prosecute either the common law or the statutory offence in suitable circumstances. The implications of this practice have been discussed elsewhere in this book in relation to statutory versions of the common law crimes of attempting to pervert the course of justice[60] and breach of the peace.[61] As the commentary to *HM Advocate* v *Harris*[62] in the *Scottish Criminal Case Reports* states, "The question of the propriety of charging at common law behaviour which constitutes a statutory offence has never been properly discussed: it just appears to be accepted as competent".[63]

While it would be unfortunate if residence in a children's home **14.10.3** was regarded as in any way similar to penal incarceration, an attempt was made, in *Welsh* v *Richardson*,[64] to prosecute two co-accused for knowingly harbouring or concealing two children who had absconded from a children's home in circumstances which would have rendered the children liable to arrest under s 82(1) or (3) of the Children (Scotland) Act 1995. In the end, it was held that the children had not absconded, so that there was no case to answer.

14.11   CONTEMPT OF COURT

This has been described as "a sui generis offence committed **14.11.1** against the court itself which it is peculiarly within the province of the court to punish".[65] The fact that contempt can be punished by a fine or by imprisonment indicates that it could fall within the ECHR definition of a crime for the purposes of Art 6 (the right to a fair trial, by an independent and impartial tribunal).[66]

---

[59] That is, the "statutory maximum" in terms of the Criminal Procedure (Scotland) Act 1995, s 225(8).

[60] See section 14.8.1 above.

[61] See section 15.2.2 below. See also P R Ferguson, *Breach of the Peace* (2013), section 6.23.

[62] 2011 JC 125.

[63] *HM Advocate* v *Harris* 2010 SCCR 931 at 943.

[64] 2012 SLT 1153.

[65] *Robertson, Petitioner*; *Gough* v *McFadyen* 2008 SCCR 20 per LJ-C Gill at 30. ("*Sui generis*" means "of its own kind" or "unique" – in this context, that it is neither civil nor criminal.)

[66] In *Harman* v *UK* (1985) 7 EHRR CD146 a complaint that a conviction for contempt in English law was in breach of Art 7 of the ECHR (ie that crimes should be clearly defined) was declared admissible by the Commission, but the case subsequently settled.

In *Kyprianou* v *Cyprus*[67] a Cypriot advocate of 40 years' standing had been sentenced to 5 days' imprisonment imposed and served immediately following on the contempt. It arose from a heated exchange betwen the accused and the Bench, where, in response to a request from the judges that he apologise for his conduct and manner, Kyprianou said "You can try me".[68] He also accused the judges of passing between themselves "ravasakia", which translates as "love letters".[69] The ECtHR agreed with its Grand Chamber that "The applicability of Art. 6(1) of the Convention under its criminal head is not in dispute between the parties".[70] Though Scots law has developed as a result of this decision,[71] it remains the case that: "In Scotland contempt is not a crime (yet)".[72] The Crown does, on occasion, appear in such proceedings as if it were the prosecuting authority,[73] though this practice should be treated with some caution. According to Lord Justice-Clerk Gill:

> "Contempt of court is constituted by conduct that denotes wilful defiance of, or disrespect towards, the court or that wilfully challenges or affronts the authority of the court or the supremacy of the law itself, whether in civil or criminal proceedings."[74]

The *actus reus* consists in any behaviour which challenges the authority of the court. For example, in *Young* v *Lees*[75] the accused had previously been removed from Edinburgh Sheriff Court because of his behaviour during the trial of his cohabitee. When his partner

---

[67] (2007) 44 EHRR 27.

[68] *Ibid* at 571, para [17].

[69] *Ibid* at 572, para [18], and 580, para [41].

[70] *Ibid* at 584, para [64].

[71] See from section 14.11.3 below. Also Sheriff T Welsh, "The summary jurisdiction to punish for contempt of court in Scotland" in J Chalmers, F Leverick and L Farmer (eds), *Essays in Criminal Law in Honour of Sir Gerald Gordon* (2010) 326 at 337.

[72] *Ibid* at 336. For a detailed consideration of this point, see B Emmerson, A Ashworth and A Macdonald, *Human Rights and Criminal Justice* (3rd edn, 2012), paras 4.25–4.29.

[73] For example, in the appeal case of *Haney* v *HM Advocate* 2013 SCL 54, a senior Advocate Depute presented the case in favour of upholding the finding of contempt. This was presented as an appeal to the *nobile officium* rather than a straightforward appeal against "conviction". Nonetheless, as the commentary to *Haney* in *Scottish Criminal Law* (at 58–59) points out, in *Green* v *Smith* 1988 JC 29, LJ-C Ross made it clear that: "The [in that case] procurator fiscal is not the [in that case] sheriff's advocate. He is the public prosecutor taking his instruction not from the sheriff but from the Lord Advocate. In no sense is a procurator fiscal the advocate of the sheriff" (at 32). It is important, given that contempt of course is a "*sui generis* offence", that the roles played by the court and by the public prosecutor (if any) should be properly defined. *Haney* is discussed further in section 14.11.3 below.

[74] *Robertson, Petitioner*; *Gough* v *McFadyen* 2008 SCCR 20 per LJ-C Gill at 30.

[75] 1998 SCCR 558.

was remanded in custody, the accused opened the court door and shouted at the sheriff. He was found to be in contempt of court and sentenced to 60 days' imprisonment.

In relation to *mens rea*, the accused's conduct must be wilful (meaning, deliberate); contempt of court cannot be committed recklessly. In *McMillan* v *Carmichael*[76] the accused was held to be in contempt because he yawned noisily and unrestrainedly while sitting at the back of the court. The sheriff regarded his behaviour as extremely discourteous and reprehensible, and rejected the accused's explanation that he had been unaware of what he was doing. Quashing the conviction, the appeal court held that an intention to challenge or affront the authority of the court was a prerequisite of contempt of court and this was not made out here. Similarly, in *Caldwell* v *Normand*[77] the accused turned up half an hour late for his trial in the District Court in Glasgow because he had over-slept. The justice of the peace found him to be in contempt. This too was quashed on appeal because the justice had made no attempt to establish whether the accused was wilfully defying the order of the court or had intended disrespect to the court.

14.11.2

The contemptuous behaviour can be directed either against the administration of justice itself, or against a judge more personally. A good example of the former is where a witness prevaricates in giving evidence.[78] This is a clear example of contempt of court. Where the contempt is of this type, the presiding judge can deal with it there and then, but must apply the procedural safeguards set out in *Robertson, Petitioner*; *Gough* v *HM Advocate*.[79] In the case of *Haney* v *HM Advocate*,[80] the trial judge took account of the witness's failure to attend to give her evidence on the day on which she was cited and of the combative, argumentative style in which she later came to give certain aspects of it. The appeal court was clear in its judgment that it had to respect the trial judge's decision on the contempt because he "had the advantage of seeing and hearing the appellant as she gave her evidence in court. In particular he was best placed to gauge the manner in which the appellant responded

14.11.3

---

[76] 1993 SCCR 943.
[77] 1993 SCCR 624.
[78] In *Cowan* v *HM Advocate* 2009 SLT 434 an essential Crown witness was sentenced to 15 months' imprisonment for his refusal to testify.
[79] 2008 JC 146. These safeguards require the issue to be dealt with outwith the presence of the jury. The judge must make clear to the suspected contemnor the nature of the contempt that she may have committed and ensure that she has the opportunity to receive legal advice, to be represented in court and to be heard on the matter (see *ibid* at para 48).
[80] 2013 SCL 54.

to questioning from counsel".[81] Where the contemptuous behaviour is not directed against the judge personally, then her view of its severity would appear to be given particular weight in any appeal.

14.11.4   A judge who determines that *prima facie* a contempt has been committed should decide whether the contempt appears to have been directed at her personally. If it has been, or if the judge is in any doubt on the point, the case should be referred to a different judge or panel of judges.[82] This procedure was necessitated by the case of *Kyprianou* v *Cyprus*,[83] where specific reference was made to the Scottish procedure.[84] In *Robertson and Gough* it was stated expressly that the procedure followed in *Young* v *Lees*,[85] where the trial judge himself sentenced the contemnor to 60 days in prison, is no longer acceptable.

14.12   CRITIQUE OF THE LAW ON CONTEMPT OF COURT AND PROPOSALS FOR REFORM

14.12.1   The procedural safeguards identified above are set down in Sch 2, para 29B to the Act of Adjournal (Criminal Procedure Rules) 1996.[86] They have resonance with the Art 6 requirement for legal disputes to be determined by an "independent and impartial tribunal". Clearly, if the matter arises from personal criticism of the trial judge, permitting that same judge to decide whether the accused's behaviour amounts to contempt and, if so, the appropriate penalty, does not provide the degree of impartiality required by Art 6. Thus, in *Mayer* v *HM Advocate*,[87] it was held that the trial judge should have remitted the issue of contempt[88] to another forum, simply to preserve the appearance of impartiality, even though there was no suggestion that the case had been conducted other than objectively

---

[81] 2013 SCL 54 at 57, para [7] per LJ-C Carloway.
[82] See, for example, the case of *Anwar, Respondent* 2008 SCCR 709. Following his client's conviction, Mr Anwar was charged with contempt of court for, *inter alia*, criticising the trial judge. The case was remitted to the High Court to avoid it being heard by the judge who was the subject of the criticism (*ibid* at 713).
[83] (2007) 44 EHRR 565. (NB: The page number is given as 27 in some editions.) See section 14.11.1 above.
[84] *Ibid* at 582.
[85] 1998 SCCR 558. See section 14.11.1 above.
[86] SI 1996/513.
[87] 2005 1 JC 121.
[88] The alleged contemnor was an advocate. The question of contempt arose because he was not available to represent a client in the High Court in Edinburgh when he should have been, having accepted instructions in another case which was to call in Edinburgh Sheriff Court at the same time. He then recklessly made statements about this matter which were inaccurate, in response to questioning by the trial judge.

and fairly. Contempt of court fits oddly into the Scottish criminal justice system in that usually only the prosecution can bring charges. Where that power is, uniquely, conferred on the judiciary it must be seen to exercise it judiciously.[89] The procedure set out in the Act of Adjournal ensures that individual judges cannot act as prosecutor, decision-maker and sentencing authority all in the one case. This is to be welcomed.

---

[89] While not specifically referred to as "contempt of court", in January 2009, a judge in the High Court in Edinburgh ordered that the complainer in a rape case be detained overnight in the cells because of her difficulty, and consequent prevarication, in giving her evidence. The Lord Justice-General (Lord Hamilton) later upheld her complaint against the trial judge (see M Burman, "Evidencing sexual assault: women in the witness box" (2009) 56 *Probation Journal* 379 at 379).

CHAPTER 15

PUBLIC ORDER OFFENCES

15.1 INTRODUCTION

As noted in the introduction to this part of the book, public order **15.1.1** offences may breach the "harm principle"[1] of criminalisation since they frequently criminalise conduct which, while it may be offensive, annoying or inconvenient, is rarely harmful to persons or their property. Some of this conduct may pose a *risk* of harm but the courts must attempt to strike a balance between freedom of speech and of assembly (protected by Arts 10 and 11 of the European Convention on Human Rights (ECHR)),[2] on the one hand, and the rights of others not to be inconvenienced or offended by the exercise of such rights, on the other.

15.2 BREACH OF THE PEACE

Actus reus

Breach of the peace is a commonly charged, and widely defined, **15.2.1** crime.[3] Despite attempts by the appeal court to clarify its ambit,[4] the plethora of cases continuing to come before that court suggests that some uncertainty remains. This section engages particularly with the issue of certainty in the law and the effect of the ECHR on the development of the crime. It was regarded by Hume as a form of rioting, but he used the expression to refer to a class of public order offences, rather than to a distinct crime.[5] Its ambit is wider now and many cases turn on their own particular facts. As

---

[1] See Chapter 3 above.
[2] See section 15.2.4 below.
[3] For a detailed commentary, see P R Ferguson, *Breach of the Peace* (2013) and M G A Christie, *Breach of the Peace* (1990).
[4] See, for example, *Smith v Donnelly* 2002 JC 65 and *Harris v HM Advocate* 2010 JC 245; 2009 SLT 1078, discussed at sections 15.2.3 and 15.2.8 below, respectively.
[5] Hume, i, 439.

well as the archetypal conduct of persistent shouting and swearing in a public place,[6] other examples of the sorts of behaviour which have been held by the courts to constitute a breach of the peace include: fighting;[7] aggressively begging for money;[8] participation in a peaceful protest;[9] kerb-crawling;[10] kicking a ball in the street;[11] and glue-sniffing.[12] In our discussion of homicide, we noted that although it is no longer a crime to attempt to commit suicide, this can be charged as a breach of the peace.[13] One person can be charged with breach of the peace in order to prevent another person from causing disorder or disruption in response. To cite but one example, in *Duffield* v *Skeen*[14] the appeal court noted that the trial judge had found the accused's conduct to be inflammatory and likely to occasion a breach of the peace by *other people*.[15] What all charges have in common is that they involve the accused engaging in anti-social behaviour which has the potential to disturb others.

15.2.2   The Crown has prosecuted breaches of the peace in circumstances where an alternative, and arguably more appropriate, charge could have been used instead. Examples here include careless and inconsiderate driving;[16] making "hoax" calls to the emergency services;[17]

---

[6] *Craig* v *Normand* 1996 SCCR 823; *Boyle* v *Wilson* 1988 SCCR 485; *McGivern* v *Jessop* 1988 SCCR 511. This type of conduct was so commonly prosecuted in the 1980s that such cases were referred to by fiscals as "a two-cop breach" since frequently the only evidence led was the testimony of the two arresting officers.

[7] *Derrett* v *Lockhart* 1991 SCCR 109.

[8] *Wyness* v *Lockhart* 1992 SCCR 808. Note the requirement that this be done in an aggressive fashion; begging is not a breach of the peace, as such. See *Donaldson* v *Vannet* 1998 SLT 957.

[9] *Donaghy* v *Tudhope* 1985 SCCR 118; *Colhoun* v *Friel* 1996 SLT 1252; *Docherty* v *Thaw*, January 1962 (unreported, but see Gordon (2001), para 41.01).

[10] *Lauder* v *Heatly* 1962 (unreported, but see Christie (1990), p 98). This could now be charged as a contravention of the Prostitution (Public Places) (Scotland) Act 2007, s 1. See section 15.13.1 below.

[11] *Cameron* v *Normand* 1992 SCCR 866.

[12] *Taylor* v *Hamilton* 1984 SCCR 393. For further examples, see C H W Gane, C N Stoddart and J Chalmers, *A Casebook on Scottish Criminal Law* (4th edn, 2009), para 16.02.

[13] See section 9.3.3 above, and also *Baker* v *McLeod* 1998 GWD 11–540.

[14] 1981 SCCR 66.

[15] See also *Stewart* v *Lockhart* 1991 SLT 835. For a critique of this approach, see section 15.3.1 below.

[16] *Smillie* v *Wilson* 1990 SCCR 133; *Craig* v *Herron* (1976) SCCR (Supp) 152; *Austin* v *Fraser* 1998 SLT 106. See the Road Traffic Act 1988, s 3.

[17] Unreported, but see *The Scotsman*, 8 July 1997. If this related to a hoax fire, it could have been charged as a contravention of the Fire Services Act 1947, s 31(1). See now the Fire (Scotland) Act 2005, s 85, as amended by the Police and Fire Reform (Scotland) Act 2012, Sch 7, para 68(25).

playing loud music in one's flat;[18] making threatening telephone calls;[19] pretending to be a professional hairdresser and offering to cut women's hair;[20] exposing the penis and masturbating;[21] urinating in a public place;[22] painting a swastika on someone else's property;[23] firing a shotgun above the head of a policeman;[24] and kicking a fox to death.[25] While we do not favour the proliferation of offences, particularly where there is a high degree of overlap in the types of behaviour which they proscribe (for example malicious mischief and vandalism),[26] the range of behaviours being subsumed under the heading of breach of the peace does seem excessively wide, and the "harm" (such as it is) that the law is denouncing in, for example, criminalising urinating in a public place is arguably quite different from that involved in kicking a fox to death.

Academic commentators had predicted that breach of the peace **15.2.3** was a crime which was ripe for challenge under various provisions of the ECHR,[27] and the incorporation of the Convention into domestic law by the Human Rights Act 1998 led to a series of such challenges.

---

[18] *Hughes* v *Crowe* 1993 SCCR 320. This could have been charged as a breach of the Civic Government (Scotland) Act 1982, s 54(1), which makes it an offence, *inter alia*, to "operate any radio or television receiver, record player, tape-recorder or other sound producing device so as to give any other person reasonable cause for annoyance".

[19] *Robertson* v *Vannet* 1999 SLT 1081. This could have been charged as a breach of the Telecommunications Act 1984, s 43(1)(a), which made it an offence, *inter alia*, to make a phone call of a "menacing character". See now the Communications Act 2003, s 127(1)(a).

[20] Unreported, but see *The Scotsman*, 7 December 1999. This could have been charged as attempted fraud.

[21] *Hutchison* v *HM Advocate* 1998 SLT 679. This could have been charged as a form of public indecency, a common law crime. "Sexual exposure" is now a statutory offence: see Sexual Offences (Scotland) Act 2009, s 8, discussed at section 11.8 above.

[22] Unreported, but see *The Herald*, 6 December 1997. This is an offence under the Civic Government (Scotland) Act 1982, s 47.

[23] Unreported, but see *The Herald*, 7 January 1999. See also *Walsh* v *Heywood* 2000 GWD 15–591, in which the accused kicked a bus and broke its windscreen with a stone. These types of cases could be prosecuted as malicious mischief, or as vandalism under the Criminal Law (Consolidation) (Scotland) Act 1995, s 52. See from sections 13.2 and 13.3 above.

[24] *Buttercase* v *Russell* 1999 GWD 21–992. This is an assault, even though the gun was loaded with blanks.

[25] *Dempster* v *Ruxton* 1999 GWD 1–24. This could be charged under the Wild Mammals (Protection) Act 1996, s 1.

[26] See from sections 13.2 and 13.3 above, respectively.

[27] See the 3rd edition of Gane, Stoddart and Chalmers (2001), para 16.10; and P R Ferguson, "Breach of the peace and the European Convention on Human Rights" (2001) 5 *Edin LR* 145.

In *Smith* v *Donnelly*[28] the accused was convicted of a breach of the peace for lying on a roadway, disrupting the traffic. She appealed on the basis that the crime of breach of the peace had been defined by the Scottish courts in such a broad fashion that it violated Art 7;[29] citizens could not know with reasonable certainty what actions would infringe the law:

> "breach of the peace is an all-encompassing charge which has been used to cover any type of behaviour deemed inappropriate in various circumstances and is therefore too vague to be aligned with the [Convention]".[30]

This was rejected by the appeal court, but it nonetheless accepted that in some cases breach of the peace had been held to be established "on grounds which might charitably be described as tenuous".[31] Lord Coulsfield offered a narrower definition of the crime than that which had been employed hitherto, namely that it comprises conduct "*severe* enough to cause alarm to ordinary people and threaten *serious* disturbance to the community".[32] In *Lucas* v *United Kingdom*[33] this modified definition was held by the European Court of Human Rights to be compliant with the Convention:

> "The court considers ... that the definition of the offence of breach of the peace as stipulated in *Smith (P)* v *Donnelly* is sufficiently precise to provide reasonable foreseeability of the actions which may fall within the remit of the offence. The concept of breach of the peace has been clarified by the Scottish courts recently and in *Smith (P)* v *Donnelly*, the High Court, in formulating its definition, had regard to the requirement of certainty in the Convention. The Court notes that ... the test set down in Scottish law has the objective standard of the reasonable person. In *Larissis* v *Greece* ... (1998 ...) the Court stated that considering the need to avoid excessive rigidity and to keep pace with changing circumstances, many laws are inevitably couched in terms which, to a greater or lesser extent, are vague and considered that this in itself does not disclose a violation of the certainty required by the Convention (in relation to Article 7). With this in mind, the Court finds that the current definition is formulated with the degree of precision required by the Convention and it provides sufficient guidance to individuals as to the consequences of their actions."[34]

---

[28] 2002 JC 65.

[29] This provides: "No one shall be held guilty of any criminal offence on account of any act or omission which did not constitute a criminal offence under national or international law at the time when it was committed." See from section 1.4 above for a discussion of Convention rights.

[30] *Smith* v *Donnelly* 2002 JC 65 at 66.

[31] *Ibid* at 72, per Lord Coulsfield.

[32] *Ibid* at 71 (emphases added).

[33] Application no 39013/02 – see also *Jones* v *Carnegie* 2004 SCCR 361 in which the *Lucas* case is described in Gordon's commentary at 377 onwards.

[34] *Ibid* at 381.

In *Smith* v *Donnelly*[35] itself, Lord Coulsfield was critical of some 15.2.4
"recurrent themes" which emerged from a consideration of the case
law:

> "there have been repeated instances in which refusal to co-operate with
> police or other officials has led to a charge of breach of the peace; but such
> a refusal, even if forcefully or even truculently stated, is not likely to be
> sufficient in itself to justify a conviction. ... there have been cases in which
> actions done or words spoken in private have been held to amount to breach
> of the peace, or conduct likely to provoke such a breach, more because of
> some perceived unpleasant or disgusting character than because of any real
> risk of disturbance. In such cases, it is perhaps particularly necessary to bear
> in mind what the essential character of the crime is".[36]

He also stressed that some breach of the peace cases raise issues
relating to Art 10(1) of the ECHR, which specifies:

> "Everyone has the right to freedom of expression. This right shall include
> freedom to hold opinions and to receive and impart information and ideas
> without interference by public authority and regardless of frontiers."

Consideration must also be given to Art 11(1) which provides that:

> "Everyone has the right to freedom of peaceful assembly and to freedom of
> association with others."

The compatibility of breach of the peace with these Convention 15.2.5
rights arose in *Jones* v *Carnegie*; *Tallents* v *Gallacher*.[37] Several
accused had been convicted of breach of the peace while engaging
in various forms of civil disobedience; for instance, one accused,
Barrett, had been convicted of behaving in a disorderly manner by
sitting on a roadway; another, Tallents, had engaged in a protest in
the Scottish Parliament. They appealed against their convictions on
the basis that their rights under Arts 10 and 11 had been breached.
The appeal court accepted that the actions taken against the accused
were an interference with these rights but held that the prosecutions
were based on the provisos in Arts 10(2) and 11(2) that these rights
can be subject to restrictions, so long as these are prescribed by law
and necessary in a democratic society *inter alia* for the prevention of
disorder.[38] These convictions were accordingly upheld. Nonetheless,

---

[35] 2002 JC 65.
[36] *Ibid* at 72.
[37] 2004 JC 136.
[38] Both Arts 10(2) and 11(2) provide that restrictions may be imposed in the interests
of national security or public safety, for the prevention of disorder or crime, for the
protection of health or morals, or for the protection of the rights of others. Article
10(2) also allows restrictions to be imposed for safeguarding territorial integrity,
protecting the reputation of other people, or for maintaining the authority and

were the circumstances of some earlier reported cases to occur again today, it seems less likely that a conviction for breach of the peace would result: could it really now be argued, other than in exceptional circumstances, that playing football in the street at night[39] or urinating in a public place[40] threatens "serious disturbance" to the community? The European Court of Human Rights has emphasised that restrictions on a right must be "proportionate to the legitimate aim pursued".[41] It has been suggested that:

> "This means that even if a policy which interferes with a Convention right might be aimed at securing a legitimate aim of social policy, for example the prevention of crime, this will not in itself justify the violation if the means adopted to secure the aim are excessive in the circumstances."[42]

In *Dyer* v *Brady*[43] the accused were charged with breach of the peace by chaining themselves together during a peaceful protest. The sheriff had sustained a submission that there was no case to answer, and this was upheld by the appeal court since the demonstration was "entirely peaceful" and there was "no evidence of anyone being alarmed or distressed"[44] by the accused's conduct.

15.2.6 A case in which a prosecution was unsuccessful is *Thompson* v *MacPhail*.[45] The accused had locked himself into a toilet cubicle in a "fast food" restaurant. The manager of the premises became suspicious and called the police. They managed to unlock the door from the outside and caught the accused withdrawing a syringe from his arm. It is not known what the accused had been injecting; it may have been a controlled drug such as heroin – or it may have been insulin. The appeal court held that this was not a breach of the peace; it was essentially a private act and the accused had done all he could to keep it private. Of course, each case must be determined on its own facts and *Thompson* v *MacPhail* is not authority for the proposition that "shooting up" in the toilet of a restaurant will never amount to a breach of the peace. Nevertheless, the case does illustrate an important limitation upon the crime: there is doubtless a range of conduct which could cause alarm to the reasonable person but which, if committed in private, ought not to be criminal. If, however,

---

impartiality of the judiciary. In addition, Art 11(2) provides that the right does not prevent the imposition of lawful restrictions on the exercise of these rights by members of the armed forces, the police or the administration of the State.

[39] *Cameron* v *Normand* 1992 SCCR 866.
[40] Unreported, but see *The Herald*, 6 December 1997.
[41] *Handyside* v *United Kingdom* (1979–80) 1 EHRR 737 at 754.
[42] J Wadham, H Mountfield *et al*, *Blackstone's Guide to the Human Rights Act 1998* (6th edn, 2011), para 2.110.
[43] 2006 SLT 965.
[44] *Ibid* at 969.
[45] 1989 SLT 637.

the accused's behaviour is likely to be discovered by a third party, and once discovered could reasonably be expected to cause alarm, then the conduct will be a breach of the peace.

This point is also illustrated by the (unreported) case of *Robert* **15.2.7** *Stewart*, who was charged with breach of the peace for attempting to have sex with a bicycle.[46] It may have been determinative that his behaviour occurred in a hostel in which cleaners were permitted to open residents' rooms. It should, however, be borne in mind that Stewart was homeless. If we consider the public/private spheres identified in Chapter 1, it is hard to characterise his room in the hostel as, for him, anything other than his home – the embodiment of the private sphere. If he had not been homeless, but in his own "home", to which he had exclusive access, it is unlikely that his behaviour would have been discovered, far less prosecuted. As is apparent from our earlier discussions, we are generally sceptical of the public/private dichotomy; the mere fact that behaviour is committed "in private" does not, without more, determine that it should be free from the reaches of the criminal law. It is, however, difficult to find a justification for criminalising Mr Stewart's conduct, other than resorting to legal moralism.[47]

As the cases of *Robert Stewart* and *Thompson* v *MacPhail*[48] **15.2.8** demonstrate, until recently no distinction was made between conduct which occurred in public and that which occurred in private locations, so long as there was potential for alarm or disturbance. Lord Coulsfield's definition in *Smith* v *Donnelly*[49] has since been interpreted as offering a conjunctive test;[50] the Crown must show not only that the accused's conduct caused (or was likely to cause) alarm to ordinary people, but also that it threatened serious disturbance *to the community*. In *Harris* v *HM Advocate*[51] a Full Bench of the appeal court emphasised that there must be potential for public disturbance. That the behaviour in question alarmed or distressed an individual complainer was no longer sufficient. In *Harris*, the accused had made veiled threats to two police officers, but in each case only one officer and the accused were party to the conversation. In holding the charges to be irrelevant, the court stated that it was unnecessary for it to "give definitive guidance as to what *public*

---

[46] See section 1.1.1 above.
[47] See from section 2.6 above.
[48] 1989 SLT 637.
[49] 2002 JC 65 at 71.
[50] *Paterson* v *HM Advocate* 2008 JC 327.
[51] 2010 JC 245. For commentaries on the case, see F Stark, "Breach of the peace revisited (again)" (2010) 14 *Edin LR* 134; C Stephen, "Recapturing the essence of breach of the peace: *Harris v HM Advocate*" (2010) *JR* 15; and C Shead, "Breach of the peace: 'a reconsideration'" (2009) *Scottish Criminal Law* 560.

element would be sufficient" for breach of the peace.[52] This lack of guidance has resulted in several further appeals.[53]

15.2.9   That the law lacked clarity was apparent from the case of *Hatcher v Harrower*,[54] in which the appellant had been convicted of breach of the peace by shouting and swearing at his wife in the family home, placing her in a state of fear and alarm. As Lord Bonomy noted:

> "It was inevitable that the debate would soon move to the question whether severe oral abuse of, and unruly behaviour towards, one domestic partner by another over an extended period within the confines of the family home can amount to a breach of the peace, and more particularly whether in a given case that conduct did constitute a breach of the peace".[55]

In quashing the conviction, the appeal court found that the appellant's behaviour had not threatened serious disturbance to the community. The presence of two of the couple's children throughout the incident could not constitute the required "public" element.[56] That the redefinition of breach of the peace in the *Harris* case had created a gap in the law was noted by Lord Bonomy:

> "[I]f there is a lacuna in the law and domestic partners are not protected by the criminal law where one abuses the other in a way that would cause serious upset and distress to a reasonable person, but does so in private, then it is for Parliament and not the court to decide whether the law should be changed to criminalise such conduct."[57]

As we shall see below,[58] the Scottish Parliament has enacted s 38 of the Criminal Justice and Licensing (Scotland) Act 2010 to close this *lacuna*.

Mens rea

15.2.10   Noting that the *mens rea* of breach of the peace "has never been determined in any reported case",[59] Tim Jones and Michael Christie conclude that: "It is, therefore, uncertain what the *mens rea* might be. As breach of the peace is a common law crime, it must be assumed that strict liability ... is not applicable."[60] Other authors take the

---

[52] 2010 JC 245 at 254, para [25] (emphasis added).

[53] See, for example, *HM Advocate v Harris* 2011 JC 125; *Bowes v Frame* (*sub nom Bowes v McGowan*) 2010 JC 297; *Angus v Nisbet* 2011 JC 69; *Russell v Thomson* 2011 JC 164. For a discussion of these cases, see Ferguson (2013).

[54] 2011 JC 90.

[55] *Ibid*, para [1].

[56] *Ibid*. The case is discussed in (2010) *Crim LB* 5.

[57] 2011 JC 90 at para [5].

[58] See section 15.5 below, onwards.

[59] T H Jones and M G A Christie, *Criminal Law* (5th edn, 2012), para 12.17.

[60] *Ibid*.

view that "some degree of negligence" may suffice.[61] It seems that the accused must have intended to engage in the conduct in question, but there is no need for the Crown to show that she intended to cause a disturbance or to commit a breach of the peace. This comes close to saying that objective recklessness is sufficient; if a reasonable person would have realised that the behaviour was likely to result in a breach of the peace, then the accused ought to have foreseen this possibility.

It may be possible to draw some tentative conclusions from three cases which have touched upon the *mens rea* requirement. In *Ralston v HM Advocate*[62] the accused was convicted of breach of the peace in relation to a rooftop protest which he undertook during his incarceration in Barlinnie Prison. His protest was intended to draw attention to the poor conditions in which he was being held. He appealed against his conviction on the basis that his purpose in carrying out the protest had been entirely blameless and that the sheriff, through his directions, had effectively prevented any discussion by the jury of the *mens rea* for breach of the peace. Unsurprisingly, the appeal court held that his motives in carrying out the protest were irrelevant:

15.2.11

> "whatever his reason was for taking the action which he did, the question for the jury was whether his conduct amounted to disorderly conduct or conduct calculated to cause alarm or annoyance, and thus constituted a breach of the peace. There was no doubt that the appellant's behaviour was deliberate".[63]

In *Butcher* v *Jessop*,[64] the breach of the peace involved fighting between players during a Premier League football match. The court endorsed a view expressed in the second edition of Gordon's *Criminal Law*[65] that there was no need for the Crown to prove intention to cause a disturbance; all it needed to establish was that the conduct was "objectively calculated" to do so.[66] There was no doubt that the appellant's conduct was deliberate and he must also have been aware of the intense rivalry, sometimes turning to animosity, between the two groups of spectators at the match. His conduct "might reasonably be expected to lead to spectators being alarmed or upset or resorting to violent behaviour".[67]

---

[61] Gordon (2001), para 41.09. See also Gane, Stoddart and Chalmers (2009), para 16.10.

[62] 1989 SLT 474.

[63] *Ibid* at 476 per LJ-C Ross. For the law's approach to motive generally, see from section 6.10 above.

[64] 1989 SLT 593.

[65] G H Gordon, *Criminal Law* (2nd edn, 1978), para 41.09. The most recent edition of Gordon uses the expression "objectively likely", rather than "objectively calculated". See now Gordon (2001), para 41.09.

[66] *Butcher* v *Jessop* 1989 SLT 593 at 598 per LJ-C Ross.

[67] *Ibid.*

15.2.12   Our third and final case is *Hughes* v *Crowe*[68] in which the
accused played loud music and made loud banging noises in his flat
between 7.15 and 8.15 on a Saturday morning, causing considerable
disturbance to the occupants of the flat below. The court seems
to have taken the view that the accused must have been aware
that this type of behaviour at that time on a weekend day would
adversely affect other occupants. There was, however, no evidence
that the accused actually knew that the other flat was occupied.
Taken together, then, these cases seem to suggest that the *mens
rea* of breach of the peace is deliberate conduct with some degree
of awareness of the context in which it is taking place and, hence,
the likely effects.

15.3   CRITIQUE OF THE LAW ON BREACH OF THE PEACE AND PROPOSALS FOR REFORM

15.3.1   A serious criticism of breach of the peace is that, despite it being
a commonly prosecuted crime, its *mens rea* has not been clearly
stated by the courts. Furthermore, as our discussion has shown, one
person can be charged with breach of the peace in order to prevent
others from causing disorder or disruption in response.[69] The "harm
principle"[70] permits the criminalisation of conduct that creates a risk
of harm, as well as that which actually causes harm, but in practice
the courts seem content to brand conduct as a breach of the peace even
when the suggestion that the conduct could result in others causing
a disturbance is largely hypothetical. The law generally criminalises
individuals who are blameworthy on account of their own, freely
chosen, behaviour. Criminalisation on the basis that *others* might
respond alarmingly or violently is a departure from this principle. It
is possible to envisage circumstances where the accused's behaviour
is *so* likely to provoke immediate, serious and alarming action by
others that the test from *Smith* v *Donnelly*[71] of being *severe* enough
to cause alarm and threaten *serious* disturbance is met. An example
might be deliberately entering a "team" pub in the colours of a rival
football team, during a match, and shouting abusively at fans. If the
possibility of reprisals is much more remote, however, it is arguable
that it does not meet the test of harm.

15.3.2   In the first edition of this book, we criticised the overly broad
scope of breach of the peace.[72] Since then, several offences have

---

[68] 1993 SCCR 320.
[69] See section 15.2.1 above.
[70] See section 3.2.1 above.
[71] 2002 JC 65. See section 15.2.3 above.
[72] P R Ferguson and C McDiarmid, *Scots Criminal Law: A Critical Analysis* (2009), section 15.4 onwards.

been enacted which proscribe certain types of conduct which would hitherto have been prosecuted as the common law crime. Thus we now have statutory sexual offences of "coercing a person into looking at a sexual image";[73] "communicating indecently";[74] "sexual exposure";[75] and "voyeurism".[76] These statutory offences *must* now be prosecuted instead of breach of the peace.[77] Section 38 of the Criminal Justice and Licensing (Scotland) Act 2010 creates a "statutory form of breach of the peace",[78] where the accused has behaved in a "threatening or abusive manner". This provision is discussed in more detail below,[79] but it is notable that its enactment has led to a reduction in the number of cases being prosecuted as a breach of the peace.[80] Section 39 of the 2010 Act creates an offence of "stalking",[81] and the Offensive Behaviour at Football and Threatening Communications (Scotland) Act 2012 also contains several provisions which could be charged instead of common law breach of the peace.[82] As previously noted,[83] the principle of fair labelling requires a legal system to distinguish between differing types and degrees of wrongdoing, not only by imposing different sentences, but also by naming offences in a way which reflects these distinctions.[84] Having separate offences to cover different types of conduct is fairer, both to the accused and to the public, than having offence labels which are over-inclusive. The enactment of the offences in the 2010 and 2012 Acts reflects our argument that fair labelling requirements favour the use of more discrete and better defined offences than subsuming a wide range of conduct into "breach of the peace".[85] Despite these reforms, cases such as that of Robert Stewart[86] and of Stephen Gough, the so-called "Naked Rambler",[87] suggest

---

[73] Sexual Offences (Scotland) Act 2009, s 6, discussed at section 11.6 above.

[74] *Ibid*, s 7, discussed at section 11.7 above.

[75] *Ibid*, s 8, discussed at section 11.8 above.

[76] *Ibid*, s 9, discussed at section 11.9 above. For a breach of the peace involving voyeurism, see *Raffaelli* v *Heatly* 1949 JC 101.

[77] *Ibid*, s 52(b).

[78] Per Lord Carloway in: *Harvey* v *HM Advocate* [2012] HCJAC 80 at para [5]; *Reilly* v *Robertson* 2012 GWD 20–423, [2012] HCJAC 76 at para [5]; and *Young* v *McLintock* 2012 GWD 26–544, 2013 SLT 130 at 132, para [7].

[79] See section 15.5.1 below.

[80] See section 15.7.1 below.

[81] See from section 15.6 below.

[82] See from section 15.8 below.

[83] See from section 4.6 above.

[84] See also the seminal paper by J Chalmers and F Leverick, "Fair labelling in criminal law" (2008) 71 *MLR* 217 at 222.

[85] See Ferguson and McDiarmid (2009), sections 15.4.2–15.4.12.

[86] See section 15.2.7 above.

[87] See section 1.1.2 above.

that the common law crime of breach of the peace continues to fail the requirements of fair labelling. Informed that an accused person has a previous conviction for breach of the peace, a sentencing judge, a prospective employer, or indeed a member of the public, is unable to form an accurate picture of the nature of the conduct, beyond knowing that the accused's behaviour caused, risked causing, or made it reasonably likely that others might cause, *some sort* of a disturbance. This crime should be redefined by statute such that the accused must have intended to cause a disturbance, or have been reckless as to the causing of a disturbance.

15.4   STATUTORY DEVELOPMENTS

15.4.1   As noted above, several forms of behaviour which had previously been prosecuted as breach of the peace have now been further specified in legislative provisions. These include ss 38 and 39 of the Criminal Justice and Licensing (Scotland) Act 2010, and ss 1 and 6 of the Offensive Behaviour at Football and Threatening Communications (Scotland) Act 2012.

15.5   BEHAVING IN A THREATENING OR ABUSIVE MANNER

15.5.1   Section 38 of the 2010 Act represents a codification of some forms of common law breach of the peace. It makes it an offence to behave in a threatening or abusive manner which would be likely to cause a reasonable person to suffer fear or alarm.[88] The accused must intend to cause fear or alarm or be reckless as to this. There is a defence if the behaviour was "reasonable" in the circumstances.[89] A person being attacked who responds with verbal abuse could presumably rely on this defence. Section 38 is increasingly being used instead of breach of the peace. Since the behaviour need not involve, or be likely to cause, a public disturbance, this closes the gap in the law identified in *Hatcher* v *Harrower*,[90] resulting from the *Harris* case.[91] One commentator has suggested that this could also apply to situations such as that in *Bowes* v *Frame*,[92] in which the accused was a taxi driver who made "comments of a sexual nature" to his 14-year-old female passenger. Section 38 may be

---

[88] In *Reilly* v *Robertson* [2012] HCJAC 76, for example, the appellant called her ex-partner a rapist, a paedophile, a thief, and a liar, outside a court room.
[89] Criminal Justice and Licensing (Scotland) Act 2010, s 38(2).
[90] 2011 JC 90.
[91] *Harris* v *HM Advocate* 2010 JC 245. See section 15.2.8 above.
[92] 2010 JC 297.

charged in similar cases, in future, on the basis that "sexually explicit and inappropriate conversation, between an adult and a child, amounts to abuse".[93]

15.6 STALKING

Section 39 of the 2010 Act provides the offence of "stalking". This **15.6.1** requires that the conduct in question occur on more than one occasion, but is otherwise widely defined.[94] It includes following a person, contacting, or attempting to contact, them by any means; publishing any statement or other material about a person, or which purports incorrectly to be from that person; monitoring a person's use of the internet, e-mail or any other form of electronic communication; entering any premises; loitering in any place; interfering with any person's property; giving anything to anyone, or leaving anything where it may be found by, given to or brought to the attention of the person; watching or spying on someone; or acting in any other way that a reasonable person would expect would cause the other person to suffer fear or alarm.[95] The *mens rea* is defined such that the accused must intend to cause the complainer to suffer fear or alarm, or alternatively know, or ought in all the circumstances to know, that engaging in the course of conduct would be likely to cause fear or alarm.[96] It is a defence to a charge of stalking for the accused to show that the course of conduct was authorised by virtue of any enactment or rule of law, was engaged in for the purpose of preventing or detecting crime, or was reasonable in the particular circumstances.[97] Although the term "harassment" is not used in this legislation, it is apparent that repeatedly harassing someone falls within the definition of stalking. Several breach of the peace cases which involved repeated harassment would now be covered by this provision.[98]

---

[93] (2011) *Scottish Criminal Law* 54 at 69.
[94] Criminal Justice and Licensing (Scotland) Act 2010, s 39(6). For a critique of the law prior to this enactment, see S Middlemiss and L Sharp, "A critical analysis of the law of stalking in Scotland" (2009) 73 *J Crim L* 89; R Mays, "'Every breath you take ... every move you make': Scots law, the Protection from Harassment Act 1997 and the problem of stalking" (1997) *Jur Rev* 331.
[95] Criminal Justice and Licensing (Scotland) Act 2010, s 39(6).
[96] *Ibid*, s 39(3) and (4).
[97] *Ibid*, s 39(5)(a)–(c).
[98] See *McKenzie* v *Normand* 1992 SLT 130; *McAlpine* v *Friel* 1997 SCCR 453; *Egan* v *Normand* 1997 SCCR 211; *Shepherd* v *HM Advocate* 1999 GWD 31–1479; *Elliott* v *Vannet* 1999 GWD 22–1033; *Flanigan* v *Napier* 1999 GWD 14–637; *Morris* v *HM Advocate* 2000 GWD 29–1124; *Johnstone* v *HM Advocate* 2012 JC 79.

15.7 CRITIQUE OF SECTIONS 38 AND 39 AND PROPOSALS FOR REFORM

15.7.1 These provisions have the potential significantly to reduce the Crown's reliance on common law breach of the peace, and indeed it seems that they have already done so: there was a 34 per cent decrease in the number of breach of the peace offences being recorded by the police in the year following the coming into force of the 2010 Act.[99] Since these offences may be committed in any locus, they avoid the public/private difficulties which resulted from the *Harris* case.[100] The Crown is, however, free to charge breach of the peace instead of any of these statutory provisions, even if the latter are arguably more apposite. The requirement in s 39 for conduct on more than one occasion is potentially problematic. In *Hay v HM Advocate*[101] the accused pled guilty to an indictment which included several breaches of the peace involving repeatedly following girls in his car, and staring at them, to their fear and alarm. All the girls were aged between 14 and 16 and were not known to the accused. Only two of the girls were named, the rest being referred to as "unaccompanied females". The accused "stalked" different victims hence there was not a "course of conduct" in respect of each one.[102] It may be, then, that the Crown will have to continue to rely on breach of the peace in these types of situations – unless the legislation is amended to include a single event, or a course of conduct involving different complainers.

15.8 OFFENSIVE BEHAVIOUR AT FOOTBALL MATCHES

15.8.1 This offence is provided by s 1 of the Offensive Behaviour at Football and Threatening Communications (Scotland) Act 2012. It was designed primarily to criminalise the singing of sectarian songs at football matches but is worded more broadly than this. It is an offence to express hatred of, or stir up hatred against, a person or group

---

[99] In 2009–10 more than 85,000 breaches of the peace were recorded by the police. In 2010–11, this had fallen to fewer than 57,000: see *Statistical Bulletin: Recorded Crime in Scotland 2010-11*, Table 2, p 18, available at: http://www.scotland.gov. uk/Resource/Doc/933/0120682.pdf. At that time, "crimes such as threatening and abusive behaviour and stalking [under ss 38 and 39 were …] included in 'other miscellaneous offences' in the tables", rather than as breach of the peace (*ibid*, p 3). By contrast, in the 2012–13 *Bulletin*, they were reclassified as "Breach of the peace offences" so that they are counted *with* breach of the peace *per se*. See *Statistical Bulletin: Recorded Crime in Scotland, 2012–13*, p 9, para 4.10, available at: http://www.scotland.gov.uk/Resource/0042/00427834.pdf. The overall number of "Breach of the peace offences" was 70,075 (*ibid*, Table 2, p 19).
[100] See sections 15.2.8 and 15.2.9 above.
[101] 2012 SLT 569.
[102] Section 39(1) refers to it being an offence "where A stalks *another person* ('B')" (emphasis added).

of persons based on their membership (or presumed membership) of a religious group, a social or cultural group with a perceived religious affiliation, or a group defined by colour, race, nationality, ethnic or national origins, sexual orientation, transgender identity, or disability.[103] The behaviour must occur at a "regulated football match",[104] but this is given an extended definition such that it includes a place, other than domestic premises, where a match is being televised.[105] Behaviour is defined as occurring at such a match if it occurs in the ground where the regulated football match is being held on the day on which it is being held; while the accused is entering or leaving that ground; or during a journey to or from the regulated football match.[106] It also includes behaviour which is directed towards, or is engaged in together with, another person who is in the ground, entering or leaving the ground or travelling to or from the match.[107] It is an offence if the proscribed behaviour is motivated by hatred of such a group, or is threatening, or is such that a reasonable person would be likely to consider offensive.[108] The behaviour must be likely to incite public disorder, or would be likely to incite public disorder[109] but for the fact that measures are in place to prevent public disorder, or those likely to be incited to disorder are not present or are not present in sufficient numbers.[110] This is intended to prevent the accused from asserting that the fact that one team's supporters greatly outnumbered those of the other, or the police had a strong presence at the match, meant that disorder was in fact unlikely.[111]

---

[103] Offensive Behaviour at Football and Threatening Communications (Scotland) Act 2012, s 1(1), (2)(a), (2)(b) and (4). See "Ayr United fan faces Dumfries offensive singing charge", BBC News, 2 April 2012, available at http://www.bbc.co.uk/news/uk-scotland-south-scotland-17584972.

[104] Offensive Behaviour at Football and Threatening Communications (Scotland) Act 2012, s 2(1) defines "regulated football match" broadly in accordance with the Police, Public Order and Criminal Justice (Scotland) Act 2006, s 55(2).

[105] Offensive Behaviour at Football and Threatening Communications (Scotland) Act 2012, s 2(3).

[106] Ibid, s 2(2)(a). See Ferguson v McFadyen 1999 GWD 22–1051 (breach of the peace committed when accused travelling home from a match).

[107] Ibid, s 2(2)(b). The maximum penalty if prosecuted under summary procedure is 12 months' imprisonment, and on solemn procedure is 5 years' imprisonment: s 1(6).

[108] Ibid, s 1(2)(c)–(e).

[109] Ibid, s 1(1)(b).

[110] Ibid, s 1(5).

[111] See the Explanatory Notes accompanying the Offensive Behaviour at Football and Threatening Communications (Scotland) Bill, at para 10, available at: http://www.scottish.parliament.uk/S4_Bills/Offensive%20Behaviour%20at%20Football%20and%20Threatening%20Communications%20(Scotland)%20Bill/b1s4-introd-en.pdf.

15.9   THREATENING COMMUNICATIONS AND COMMUNICATING RELIGIOUS HATRED

15.9.1   Section 6 of the 2012 Act makes it an offence to communicate material to someone which consists of, contains or implies, a threat, or an incitement, to carry out a seriously violent act against a person or against persons of a particular description, and which would be likely to cause a reasonable person to suffer fear or alarm. The accused must intend to cause fear or alarm, or be reckless as to this.[112] It is also an offence under this section to communicate threatening material to someone which is intended to stir up hatred on religious grounds.[113] It is a defence to show that the communication of the material was reasonable, in the particular circumstances of the case.[114] It is specifically provided in s 7 that this offence does not apply to communications which are discussions or criticisms of religions or the beliefs or practices of adherents of religions, expressions of antipathy, dislike, ridicule, insult or abuse towards those matters, proselytising, or urging of adherents of religions to cease practising their religions.[115] The offence is defined broadly and encompasses communications made by post, internet websites, e-mail, blogs, podcasts etc.[116] It does not, however, extend to "unrecorded speech",[117] thus would not cover the situation in the first *Harris* case, in which the implied threats were spoken.[118] This exception is designed to protect individuals' freedom of speech, guaranteed by Art 10 of the ECHR.[119]

15.10   CRITIQUE OF THE 2012 ACT AND PROPOSALS FOR REFORM

15.10.1   The Offensive Behaviour at Football and Threatening Communications (Scotland) Bill was subject to much criticism during its

---

[112] Offensive Behaviour at Football and Threatening Communications (Scotland) Act 2012, s 6(1) and (2).

[113] *Ibid*, s 6(5). The penalties are the same as for s 1: see s 6(7).

[114] *Ibid*, s 6(6).

[115] "Religions" is broadly defined to include "religions generally", "particular religions", and "other belief systems" (*ibid*, s 7(2)). This last term could include all sorts of groups; one wonders whether "white supremacists", "creationists" and "Moonies" would be considered to be religions, based on their belief systems. The right to freedom of religion under Art 9 of the ECHR has been held to include Druidism, Scientology, the Moon Sect and Divine Light Zentrum: see J Murdoch, *Protecting the Right to Freedom of Thought, Conscience and Religion under the European Convention on Human Rights* (2012), p 17.

[116] See the Explanatory Notes (n 111 above) at p 6, para 32.

[117] Offensive Behaviour at Football and Threatening Communications (Scotland) Act 2012, s 8(2).

[118] Discussed further at section 15.2.8 above.

[119] See section 15.2.4 above.

passage through the Scottish Parliament,[120] and it was felt that its provisions relating to football matches could largely be dealt with using the crime of breach of the peace. Sarah Christie concluded

> "the fact that [s 1 of] the Bill covers situations where behaviour is likely to, rather than actually does incite public disorder, takes us no further than the current common law".[121]

By contrast, Kay Goodall welcomed the provisions in the Act which relate to incitement to religious hatred, on the basis that "it is an insult to victims to subsume this under religiously aggravated breach of the peace".[122] This reflects concerns that the behaviour of offenders should be accurately labelled.[123] It would not be overly cynical to suggest that the creation of s 1 of the 2012 Act represents ad hoc law reform, with the Scottish Parliament reacting to media outcries over sectarianism,[124] however, it does give a more specific label to certain forms of sectarian misconduct. The Convenor of the Justice Committee drew a distinction between having a conviction for s 1, which would make clear that this related to sectarian behaviour, and a conviction for a breach of the peace, which covers a wide variety of behaviours of varying seriousness:

> "If ... we are looking at the bill as a deterrent in some respects, a stigma would attach to a person who was convicted under it, because they would not be able to say, for example, that they were convicted of breach of the peace when they fell down, kicked over some buckets and woke folk up."[125]

---

[120] See S Christie, "The Offensive Behaviour at Football and Threatening Communications (Scotland) Bill – strong on rhetoric but weak on substance?" (2011) *SLT* 185; D McArdle, "Too much heat, not enough light" (2011) 56 *JLSS* 9. See also K Goodall, "Tackling sectarianism through the criminal law" (2011) 15 *Edin LR* 423.

[121] Christie (2011) at 187. Examples of breaches of the peace occurring at or in football stadia include: *Wilson v Brown* 1982 SLT 361; *McGivern v Jessop* 1988 SCCR 511; *Huston v Buchanan* 1994 SCCR 512; *Hannah v Vannet* 1999 GWD 29–1380; *Allison v Higson* 2004 SCCR 720; *Dyer v Hutchison* 2006 JC 212; and *Walls v Brown* 2009 JC 375.

[122] Goodall (2011) at 426.

[123] For the importance of "fair" or "accurate" labelling in criminal law, see section 4.6 above.

[124] The Scottish Parliament enacted more than 400 offences in its first decade. For a critique of this approach to "law reform/creation", see P R Ferguson, "Criminal law and criminal justice: an exercise in ad hocery" in E E Sutherland, K E Goodall, G F M Little and F P Davidson (eds), *Law Making and the Scottish Parliament: The Early Years* (2011) at p 208 on.

[125] *Justice Committee Official Report*: 22 June 2011, col 90, available at: http://www.scottish.parliament.uk/parliamentarybusiness/28862.aspx?r=6366&mode=pdf.

The willingness of the Scottish Parliament to enact new legislation – even where the overlap with common law breach of the peace is considerable – could be regarded as an indication of a growing acceptance of the need for fairer/more accurate offence labelling, and clearer definitions, in Scottish criminal law.

15.11 BIGAMY

15.11.1 A bigamist is someone who marries one person while still lawfully married to another. The bigamist must know that she is not free to marry, hence a mistaken belief that one's first spouse is dead, that the earlier marriage is invalid as a matter of fact (rather than law),[126] or that the marriage had been annulled or the subject of a valid divorce, will all exculpate, so long as the belief was based on reasonable grounds. It is not only the already-married party who commits bigamy; the second "spouse" may be guilty on an art and part basis if aware that the other is not free to marry, as may the celebrant and witnesses to the marriage ceremony.

15.12 CRITIQUE OF THE LAW ON BIGAMY AND PROPOSALS FOR REFORM

15.12.1 It is difficult to determine the primary wrong in the crime of bigamy, and we have debated at length whether this should be regarded as a "public order" offence, or one primarily involving "offensive behaviour".[127] Gordon's *Criminal Law* suggests that it "is perhaps best regarded as an offence against *public order and decency*",[128] hence its inclusion in this chapter. The *Draft Criminal Code* categorises bigamy under the heading of "offences relating to marriage", a sub-division of "non-sexual offences against life, bodily integrity, liberty and other personal interests". Historically, it was viewed as a sexual offence, since the unlawful marriage meant that the parties were guilty of adultery. Polygamy is acceptable in many countries, and some libertarians support its decriminalisation on the basis that people ought to be allowed to organise their family and living arrangements as they see fit. It should be noted, however, that in many cases of bigamy, the second "spouse" is unaware of the prior marriage and, in almost all cases, the first spouse will be being deceived. For this reason, bigamy may be viewed as akin to fraud, the main harm being the deception caused either to the innocent party to the "second marriage" (if

---

[126] See section 19.6.1 below for a discussion of error in law.
[127] See Chapter 16 below.
[128] Gordon (2001) at para 45.01 (emphasis added).

there is an innocent party) or to the spouse in the earlier marriage. The harm caused here is one of hurt feelings or perhaps outrage on the part of the innocent party – and these are not generally regarded as sufficient to justify criminalisation on the basis of the "harm principle".[129] However, the hurt caused by bigamy can be keenly felt, as is shown by the case of *Gray* v *Criminal Injuries Compensation Board*,[130] in which the second "wife" of a bigamist argued (unsuccessfully) that sexual intercourse between the couple should be treated as rape.

The *Draft Criminal Code* created two new offences, namely those of "entering into forced marriage" and "entering into unlawful marriage".[131] The former is now governed by s 122(1) of the Anti-social Behaviour, Crime and Policing Act 2014, which makes it an offence to use violence, threats or any other form of coercion for the purpose of causing another person to enter into a marriage, where the accused believes, or ought reasonably to believe, that the conduct may cause the other person to enter into the marriage without free and full consent.[132] Enactment of the *Draft Code* would also make it an offence for one party to marry another knowing that it is an invalid marriage for reasons other than bigamy, or the invalid consent of the other party.[133] That the other party was under the age of 16 or within the prohibited degrees of relationship to the accused are examples of the sorts of circumstances which would make the marriage unlawful. The *mens rea* here is again that the accused was aware of, or reckless as to, the existence of the impediment.

15.12.2

15.13 PROSTITUTION AND SOLICITING

As Sanford Kadish has noted, few institutions have proven as enduring as prostitution.[134] He suggested that "the driving force behind prostitution laws is principally the conviction that prostitution is immoral".[135] How widely this conviction is felt is put in doubt by his reference to data which suggests that, in the United States, "over two-thirds of white males alone will

15.13.1

---

[129] The "harm principle" is described in Chapter 3 above.
[130] 1999 SC 137.
[131] *Draft Criminal Code*, ss 58 and 59.
[132] At the time of writing, this provision had not been brought into force.
[133] *Draft Criminal Code*, s 59.
[134] S H Kadish, *Blame and Punishment: Essays in the Criminal Law* (1987) at p 24. For the role of the law in this, see J Scoular, "What's law got to do with it? How and why law matters in the regulation of sex work" (2010) 37 *J Law & Soc* 12.
[135] Kadish (1987) at p 25.

have experience with prostitutes during their lives".[136] It will be recalled from our discussion in Chapter 2 that the Wolfenden Committee was established, more than 50 years ago, to consider the appropriate stance which English criminal law should take towards prostitution.[137] It recommended that prostitution itself should not be punishable, but that the prohibition on soliciting in public places should remain.[138] Prostitution *per se* is not a crime in Scots law, but soliciting is proscribed by virtue of s 46 of the Civic Government (Scotland) Act 1982. This provides that a prostitute who, for the purposes of prostitution, (a) loiters in a public place, (b) solicits in a public place or in any other place so as to be seen from a public place, or (c) importunes any person who is in a public place, is guilty of an offence. While the section explicitly refers to a prostitute "whether male or female", in practice the vast majority of prostitutes are women. As was noted in a Policy Memorandum published by the then Scottish Executive in 2006, the law:

> "focused on those (predominately women) who sell sex on the street and not on those (predominately men) who purchase. There is a need to redress this balance in order to protect communities from the nuisance, alarm or offence arising from street prostitution-related activities in or near public places, whether caused by seller or purchaser".[139]

This led to the Prostitution (Public Places) (Scotland) Act 2007, s 1(1) of which provides that it is an offence to solicit in a public place "for the purpose of obtaining the services of a person engaged in prostitution". It is also an offence for a person to loiter in a public place "so that in all the circumstances it may reasonably be inferred" that this was for the purpose of obtaining the services of a person engaged in prostitution.[140] Provisions in the Bill which would have

---

[136] A C Kinsey, W B Pomeroy and C E Martin, *Sexual Behavior in the Human Male* (1948), p 597, cited in Kadish (1987) at p 24.

[137] Wolfenden Committee, *Report of the Departmental Committee on Homosexual Offences and Prostitution* (Cmnd 247, 1957).

[138] *Ibid*, paras 224, 285 and 318.

[139] Scottish Executive, *Prostitution (Public Places) (Scotland) Bill: Policy Memorandum* (2006), para 2 (available at: http://www.scottish.parliament.uk/S2_Bills/Prostitution%20(Public%20Places)%20(Scotland)%20Bill/b69-introd-pm.pdf).

[140] Prostitution (Public Places) (Scotland) Act 2007, s 1(3). The legislation refers to the locus as being a "relevant place" but this is largely defined as a public place, that is, a place where the public are permitted to have access (whether on payment or otherwise). A person convicted under either of these sections may now be disqualified from holding or obtaining a driving licence where "the court is satisfied that, at the time the offence was committed, the person was driving or was otherwise in charge of a motor vehicle": Prostitution (Public Places) (Scotland) Act 2007 (Disqualification from Driving) Order 2011 (SSI 2011/2490), art 3(1).

required the prosecution to show that someone was alarmed or offended by this behaviour were not included in the final version of the Act.

It is also an offence for a man to live on the earnings of prostitution,[141] or to solicit or importune in any public place for "immoral purposes".[142] Where the prosecution proves that a man is living with a prostitute, or even that he is habitually in her company, or is proved to have exercised control, direction or influence over her movements in such a manner as to show that he is aiding, abetting or compelling her prostitution, he is deemed to be knowingly living on the earnings of prostitution, unless he can satisfy the court to the contrary.[143] Section 22 of the Criminal Justice (Scotland) Act 2003 creates the offence of trafficking for the purposes of sexual exploitation, that is, for prostitution, or the making of "obscene or indecent material".[144]

15.13.2

15.14 CRITIQUE OF THE LAW ON PROSTITUTION AND SOLICITING AND PROPOSALS FOR REFORM

As previously noted, the fact that s 46 of the Civic Government (Scotland) Act 1982 is phrased in gender-neutral language belies the fact that in practice the vast majority of prostitutes are women. The discussion of prostitution in Gordon begins by defining a prostitute as "a person who commonly offers *her* body for lewdness in return for payment",[145] and continues:

15.14.1

"The lewdness is not limited to normal [*sic*] sexual intercourse but includes all forms of carnal connection and also other forms of sexual behaviour, such as active or passive participation in masturbation or in sadistic or masochistic practices, where *the woman* offers herself as a participant in physical acts of indecency for the sexual gratification of men."[146]

Chris Gane has explained the different stance the law has taken to soliciting (a criminal offence), as compared with prostitution (not an offence):

"The distinction can be justified on the ground that the sexual act involved in prostitution, though immoral, is essentially private, and therefore not

---

[141] Criminal Law (Consolidation) (Scotland) Act 1995, s 11(1)(a). Similar offences apply to those living on the earnings of male prostitution by the 1995 Act, s 13(9).
[142] *Ibid*, s 11(1)(b).
[143] *Ibid*, s 11(3). Offences in connection with brothel-keeping are provided by s 11(5).
[144] This was designed to implement the European Council *Framework Decision on Trafficking in Human Beings*, 2002/629/JHA of 19 July 2002.
[145] Gordon (2001), para 36.39 (emphasis added).
[146] *Ibid* (emphasis added).

the business of the criminal law. But when a prostitute solicits in public for clients, this is a fit subject for penal sanctions because it intrudes upon the public domain."[147]

He points out the implications of this approach:

"The vast majority of prostitutes are women, and the vast majority of their clients are men, with the result that the allocation of soliciting to the 'public' domain exposes women, rather than their male clients, to criminalisation."[148]

Catharine MacKinnon has pointed out the hypocrisy inherent in the

"biased enforcement of biased laws against prostitution so that prostitutes (most of them women) are harassed and violated while pimps and johns (men) are allowed to ensure that prostitution, something men made a crime, will continue to exist for their pleasure".[149]

15.14.2 As we noted in our introduction to this part of the book, the fact that soliciting, rather than prostitution *per se*, is the focus of the criminal law's proscription tends to suggest that its harm, such as it is, is based on the unacceptability of selling and buying sex in a public space. It should, however, be noted that research carried out in five areas across the United Kingdom for the Joseph Rowntree Foundation suggests that for many residents of areas frequented by sex workers, their overall quality of life was not impaired by the presence of prostitutes in the neighbourhood.[150] The Wolfenden Committee claimed that the

"great majority of prostitutes are women whose psychological makeup is such that they choose this life because they find in it a style of living which is to them easier, freer and more profitable than would be provided by any other occupation".[151]

The Committee concluded that: "In the main the association between prostitute and ponce [ie a pimp] is voluntary and operates to mutual advantage."[152] Similarly, Lord Devlin stated:

---

[147] C H W Gane, *Sexual Offences* (1992), p 13.
[148] Gane (1992), p 13.
[149] C A MacKinnon, *Women's Lives, Men's Laws* (2007), p 20.
[150] See J Pitcher, R Campbell, P Hubbard, M O'Neill and J Scoular, *Living and Working in Areas of Street Sex Work* (2006) (http://www.jrf.org.uk/publications/living-and-working-areas-street-sex-work). The research did, however, identify some specific concerns and greater intolerance among certain residents than among others.
[151] Wolfenden Committee (1957), para 223.
[152] *Ibid.*

> "There may be cases of exploitation in this trade, as there are or used to be in many others, but in general a ponce exploits a prostitute no more than an impresario exploits an actress."[153]

English law now provides that the user of the prostitute (often referred to as the "punter" or "john") commits an offence if the prostitute was being controlled for another person's gain.[154] The punter is responsible for verifying the position; ignorance is not a defence.[155] Attempts to introduce similar legislation in Scotland have failed, to date.

As we have noted above,[156] provisions in the Prostitution (Public **15.14.3** Places) (Scotland) Bill which would have required the prosecution to show that someone was alarmed or offended by this behaviour were not included in the final version of the Act, making it easier to criminalise the purchase of sex. The corollary of this is that it moves further away from a public order justification for criminalising such behaviour. Why is the behaviour of the *user* of prostitutes/ sex workers being criminalised at all? Is it considered sufficiently serious to constitute a criminal offence because of the harm which prostitution may cause to the prostitute, or on moral grounds, or simply to re-balance the equation so that both parties to the prostitution transaction may be subject to similar consequences? Any justification for punishing the client must be dependent on the rationale for continuing to criminalise soliciting itself. The debate here seems to have shifted from a "legal moralism" approach, which focused on the perceived immorality of prostitution, to the liberal perspective of Wolfenden, which saw prostitution as a "lifestyle choice", to increasing acceptance of the harm caused to women who engage in prostitution:[157] there is a wealth of evidence that many suffered sexual abuse as children,[158] and that prostitutes are "subject to more violence than any other group of women in the

---

[153] P Devlin, *The Enforcement of Morals* (1965), p 12.

[154] Sexual Offences Act 2003, s 53A, as inserted by the Policing and Crime Act 2009, s 14. For a critique of the Bill which led to this Act, see B Brooks-Gordon, "Bellwether citizens: the regulation of male clients of sex workers" (2010) 37 *J Law & Soc* 145.

[155] Sexual Offences Act 2003, s 53A(2)(b).

[156] See section 15.13.1 above.

[157] Note, however, that some liberals, including some liberal feminists, champion the prostitute's right to choose her own way of life and argue that this is a choice which the law ought to recognise as valid.

[158] See the studies cited by Catharine MacKinnon in "Trafficking, prostitution and inequality" (2011) 46 *Harv Civil Rights–Civil Liberties L Rev* 271 at 279, n 23. Belinda Cheney also notes the "alarming correlation between incest and assault on young girls and women and their later involvement in prostitution" (B M M Cheney, "Prostitution – a feminist jurisprudential perspective" (1988) 18 *Victoria U of Wellington L Rev* 239 at 243).

world".[159] If the rationale behind the continuing criminalisation of soliciting is paternalistic – to prevent harm to prostitutes – then this ought to be clearly articulated by the legislature.[160] One would then expect the users of prostitutes to be punished more severely than the prostitutes themselves.[161] A recent study by Melissa Farley et al explored the attitudes and social characteristics of 110 men who had used prostitutes in Scotland.[162] When asked what would deter them,

"[a] significant majority of interviewees (89%) stated that being placed on a registry of sex offenders would deter them from buying sex. Most of the men (78–86%) said that they would be deterred by public exposure such as having their photos or names posted on the Internet, in the local newspaper, or on a billboard. A majority of the study participants (69–79%) stated that they would be deterred by greater criminal penalties, such as a greater monetary fine, having a car impounded, or jail time. Some of the men suggested that a combination of criminal sanctions and public exposure would be most effective. Most of the men told us that any amount of jail time would deter them. 'An hour would be enough.'"[163]

If the Scottish Parliament is serious about eradicating prostitution, it seems that a first step to achieving this would be to embark on a campaign in which the punters were "named and shamed".

15.14.4   The European Parliament's Committee on Women's Rights and Gender Equality has concluded that the Netherlands has become a major destination for human trafficking since it decriminalised prostitution.[164] Pointing out that "economic problems and poverty are major causes of prostitution among young women", it calls for "Europe-wide campaigns specially targeted at socially excluded communities".[165]

---

[159] MacKinnon (2011) at 285.
[160] See from section 3.5 above.
[161] See MacKinnon (2007), p 1: prostitution should no longer be "misconceived as a crime which they [ie sex workers] commit".
[162] M Farley, J Macleod, L Anderson and J M Golding, "Attitudes and social characteristics of men who buy sex in Scotland" (2011) *Psychological Trauma: Theory, Research, Practice, and Policy* 1.
[163] *Ibid* at 8.
[164] *Report on Sexual Exploitation and Prostitution and its Impact on Gender Equality (2013/2103 (INI))* pp 16–17.
[165] *Ibid*, p 13.

CHAPTER 16

OFFENSIVE BEHAVIOURS

16.1 INTRODUCTION

As we noted in our introduction to this part of the book, this **16.1.1** chapter considers a variety of behaviours which have little in common, beyond the fact that they do not readily correspond to the requirements of the harm principle: it could be argued that violation of sepulchres, bestiality and blasphemy all involve the causing of harm, but this would require a broader definition of "harm" than liberalism would generally countenance. Incivility involves "acting rudely or discourteously without regard for others, in violation of norms of respect in social interactions",[1] but the behaviours we consider here go beyond mere breaches of etiquette or polite conduct. As well as violation of sepulchres, bestiality, and blasphemy, we consider cruelty to animals. Each is liable to provoke strong feelings of outrage in others, which is why we have grouped them together under the rubric of "offensive behaviour".

16.2 VIOLATION OF SEPULCHRES

It is a common law offence, known as "violation of sepulchres", to **16.2.1** disinter a human body once it has been buried.[2] Gordon's *Criminal Law* suggests that the essence of the crime is "irreverence".[3] There may well be no "harm", in a sense recognised by proponents of the harm principle, though digging up a recently buried body is likely to cause distress to the deceased's relatives, and such behaviour is likely to offend many people, whether or not they have any connection with the deceased. This seems, then, to be a rare example of behaviour being criminalised by virtue of the disrespect involved. The crime

---

[1] L M Andersson and C M Pearson, "Tit for tat? The spiralling effect of incivility in the workplace" (1999) 24 *Academy of Management Review* 452 at 455.
[2] Hume, i, 85.
[3] Gordon (2001), para 42.01.

arose from the practice of "bodysnatching", which developed in the mid-18th century because of a demand by anatomists and medical students for recently dead corpses on which to experiment and practise their skills of dissection. According to Sheila Livingstone, who has explored Scottish crimes from the 16th century, in 1815 an Aberdeen professor of anatomy was discovered with corpses in his coach, and two of his students were charged with what she calls *"crimen violati sepulcri"*.[4] She explains the public outrage caused by such behaviour as being based on a "superstitious reverence for the dead":

> "This was borne out in the customs which were attached to death and in the belief that the powers of evil would be unleashed if these were not adhered to. They also believed that the body would be resurrected in Heaven and worried that dissection would prevent this happening. This led to revulsion at the idea that the corpses of their relations could not rest safely in their graves for fear of violation."[5]

The activities of bodysnatchers, or "susie-lifters" as they were called, declined following the passing of the Anatomy Act 1832 which allowed the executors of a deceased to permit anatomical examination.

16.3   CRITIQUE OF THE LAW ON VIOLATION OF SEPULCHRES AND PROPOSALS FOR REFORM

16.3.1   Violation of sepulchres is a very narrowly defined crime, and it is suggested that there are other forms of interference with human bodies – including interference prior to interment – which ought to be criminalised.[6] Section 104 of the *Draft Criminal Code* creates the offence of interfering with human remains in ways which are likely to cause offence to a reasonable person. There is a defence of "reasonable excuse", to ensure that the legitimate activities of undertakers and pathologists are not criminalised. The term "human remains" is wide enough to include a part or an organ of the human body. This section could be employed to cover the situation in *R v Gibson and Sylveire*,[7] in which the first accused made a pair of earrings using two freeze-dried human foetuses of 3–4 months' gestation, and the second accused displayed the earrings in his art

---

[4] S Livingstone, *Confess and Be Hanged: Scottish Crime and Punishment Through the Ages* (2000), p 24.
[5] *Ibid*, p 23.
[6] Such behaviour is criminalised elsewhere – see, for example, the Canadian Criminal Code, s 182, which prohibits indecently interfering with a corpse. For a discussion of necrophilia – which is not a specific offence in Scotland nor in many states in the USA – see T T Ochoa and C N Jones, "Defiling the dead: necrophilia and the law" (1996–97) 18 *Whittier L Rev* 539.
[7] [1990] 3 WLR 595.

gallery. The *Code* offence would also strike at the retention, without parental consent, of organs from deceased children as occurred in Bristol Royal Infirmary, and elsewhere, for many years.[8]

16.4 BESTIALITY

It is a common law offence to have "unnatural carnal connection **16.4.1** with a beast".[9] Gordon notes that there is no reported case involving a female accused and suggests that the crime is restricted to behaviour involving a male person and an animal.[10] If there were to be a case involving sexual activity between a female human being and an animal, Gordon opines that "it is unlikely that any such charge would now be brought".[11] While bestiality might not be charged in cases involving a female human, such behaviour may well be prosecuted as public indecency.[12] Far from being a rare occurrence, Jonathan Schonsheck has suggested that about 17 per cent of boys who are raised on farms "experience orgasm as the product of animal contacts which occur sometime after the onset of adolescence".[13]

16.5 CRITIQUE OF THE LAW ON BESTIALITY AND PROPOSALS FOR REFORM

The prohibition on bestiality can be traced to the Bible, and is an **16.5.1** example of the enforcement of Judeo–Christian perceptions of sexual morality.[14] As we noted in our discussion of criminalisation principles, the fact that a form of behaviour such as bestiality is widely regarded as morally wrong is arguably an insufficient basis in itself on which to base a rationale for its criminalisation.[15] Bestiality is generally discussed under the heading of "sexual offences",[16] but

[8] For the civil actions resulting from these circumstances, see *A v Leeds Teaching Hospitals NHS Trust* [2005] 2 WLR 358.
[9] Hume, i, 469.
[10] Gordon (2001), para 34–04. Note that, in England, s 69 of the Sexual Offences Act 2003 defines the offence of intercourse with an animal to include female as well as male human beings.
[11] *Ibid.*
[12] See from section 11.20 above.
[13] J Schonsheck, *On Criminalization: An Essay in the Philosophy of the Criminal Law* (1994) at p 219, citing A C Kinsey, W B Pomeroy and C E Martin, *Sexual Behavior in the Human Male* (1948), p 667.
[14] Leviticus 18: 22. For a discussion of the enforcement of morality, see from section 2.6 above.
[15] See section 2.7.1 above.
[16] As noted above (n 10), in English law "intercourse with an animal" is an offence by virtue of the Sexual Offences Act 2003, s 69. For a critique, see I Jones, "A beastly provision: why the offence of 'intercourse with an animal' must be butchered" (2011) 75 *J Crim L* 528.

although it obviously has a sexual element, it is not analogous to crimes such as rape or indecent assault; if the purpose of sexual offence laws is to protect, and punish those who violate, others' sexual autonomy, then it may be more appropriate to regard bestiality as a "public order" type of offence. Indeed, the *Draft Criminal Code* offence of "sexual activity with an animal" – an offence which is defined in such a way that both women and men are capable of breaching its provisions[17] – is contained in Part 9 of the *Code*, which deals with "Offences Involving Animals", rather than in Part 3, "Sexual Offences". Yet, as Kent Greenawalt has pointed out, bestiality "is almost universally criminal, and the main reason is not animal protection".[18] Can its prohibition be justified without resorting to legal moralism, ie without arguing that the perceived immorality of bestiality is in itself sufficient justification for its criminalisation?

16.5.2   Both Schonsheck and Joel Feinberg argue that continued criminalisation is not justified, and the latter provides pragmatic reasons which support decriminalisation, including the vulnerability to blackmail faced by those who engage in such pursuits.[19] It could, however, be argued that decriminalisation of bestiality would not (and ought not to) decrease the revulsion most people would feel towards such behaviour, and the widely held perception that the practice is immoral would in itself render perpetrators vulnerable to blackmail. A threat publicly to expose someone as one who enjoys fornication with animals would surely be as powerful as a threat to report the behaviour to the police. Putting that argument aside, both Schonsheck and Feinberg are correct in saying that liberalism traditionally sanctioned criminalisation only where conduct harmed or risked harm to other *people*. This would mean that there ought not to be criminal laws protecting animals from harm, including sustained torture. Even if we extend the harm principle to include the prohibition of harm to other sentient beings, it is not necessarily the case that bestiality is harmful to the (non-human) animal.

16.6   CRUELTY TO ANIMALS

16.6.1   There are many statutory offences governing cruelty to animals but the rationale for such legislation is not always clear. Commenting on similar statutes in the USA, Luis Chiesa notes:

---

[17] *Draft Criminal Code*, s 109.
[18] K Greenawalt, "Legal enforcement of morality" (1995) 85 *J Crim L and Criminol* 710 at 723.
[19] Schonsheck (1994), p 222.

"Whereas some jurisdictions seem partially motivated to enact [legislation] because people who harm animals are more likely to inflict suffering on human beings, others seem to have been moved into action by a deeply felt conviction that inflicting harm on a sentient being is morally wrong. Moreover some ... laws are drafted in a manner that suggests that one of the preeminent reasons for adopting such legislation was the protection of property."[20]

In the UK, the Animal Health Act 1981 makes it an offence for a person knowingly to do anything which causes or is intended to cause, or recklessly causes, certain types of animals or birds to be infected with specified diseases.[21] Under the Animal Health and Welfare (Scotland) Act 2006, it is an offence to sell an animal (defined here as a non-human vertebrate)[22] to a child who is under 16 years of age,[23] or to offer or give such an animal as a prize.[24] The 2006 Act also contains offences which apply to "protected animals", defined as animals which are "commonly domesticated in the British Islands", and are either under the control "of man [sic] on a permanent or temporary basis", or "not living in a wild state".[25] It is an offence intentionally or recklessly to cause unnecessary suffering to a protected animal, whether by an act or omission.[26] Other offences in the 2006 Act include "mutilation";[27] "cruel operations";[28] "administration of poisons";[29] involvement in "animal fights";[30] and abandoning an animal.[31]

16.7 CRITIQUE OF THE LAW ON ANIMAL CRUELTY AND PROPOSALS FOR REFORM

The above paragraph provides a flavour of some of the many offences designed to protect animals from unnecessary suffering. These are fairly technical provisions, which differentiate between vertebrates and invertebrates for some offences, and between "protected animals" and other kinds of animals in others. It is   16.7.1

---

[20] L E Chiesa, "Why is it a crime to stomp on a goldfish? – harm, victimhood and the structure of anti-cruelty offenses" (2008) 78 *Miss LJ* 1 at 4–5.
[21] Animal Health Act 1981, s 28C, inserted by the Animal Health and Welfare (Scotland) Act 2006, s 10. The specified diseases are listed in Sch 2B to the 1981 Act.
[22] Animal Health and Welfare (Scotland) Act 2006, s 16(1).
[23] *Ibid*, s 30.
[24] *Ibid*, s 31.
[25] *Ibid*, s 17(1).
[26] *Ibid*, s 19.
[27] *Ibid*, s 20.
[28] *Ibid*, s 21.
[29] *Ibid*, s 22.
[30] *Ibid*, s 23.
[31] *Ibid*, s 29.

suggested that a preferable approach would be to enact one offence which would allow for the repeal of several (though not all) of these provisions.[32]

16.7.2   Unlike bestiality, it is clearer that the behaviours struck at by the offences described in section 16.6.1 cause, or have the potential to cause, harm to animals. As outlined above, there are difficulties in fitting such offences into a strict liberal conception of the function of the criminal law which has traditionally been to protect *humans* from harm. Nonetheless, some attempts have been made:

> "there are plausible ways for the standard conception of liberalism also to account for the intuition that liberals can endorse public spending on … [*inter alia* preventing cruelty to animals]. If cruelty to animals tends to result in cruelty to humans, then the standard conception can straightforwardly require punishing those who put cats in microwave ovens. If animals also have (negative) rights to live as they see fit, then the standard conception could be understood to make the state's proper work include the protection of such rights".[33]

Human beings have domesticated animals and have also trained them for work. This imposes upon them an obligation to prevent suffering. We believe that the harm principle should be defined to include harms or potential harms to non-human animals. If this broader version of the principle is not acceptable to liberals, then perhaps this is simply an area where application of the offence principle is entirely appropriate, since many people would be offended by the cruel treatment of animals.[34]

16.8   BLASPHEMY

16.8.1   Hume devoted a chapter of his *Commentaries* to "offences against religion".[35] He suggested that these were included within the criminal calendar since they tended "to loosen the foundations of morality, and undermine the fabric of the national strength and prosperity".[36] He listed blasphemy, profanity, heresy, nonconformity, popery, offences by episcopals, intrusion into churches, simony (the selling or buying of a church-office), and witchcraft, most of which were no longer prosecuted even in Hume's day. He defined blasphemy as "the uttering of impious and profane

---

[32] *Draft Criminal Code*, s 108(1) provides such an offence, where the accused causes suffering to an animal solely or primarily to derive pleasure from that suffering. An "animal" is defined in s 110(a) of the *Code* to exclude human beings.

[33] T Metz, "How to reconcile liberal politics with retributive punishment" (2007) 27 *OJLS* 683 at 694.

[34] See from section 3.10 above.

[35] Hume, i, Chapter 29.

[36] *Ibid*, 568.

things against God, or the authority of the Holy Scriptures".[37] Gordon notes that this was last prosecuted in 1843[38] and concludes that: "It is extremely unlikely that any prosecution will now be brought for blasphemy, and it may be said that blasphemy is no longer a crime".[39] He does, however, add that some blasphemous statements may be dealt with as a breach of the peace, and Angelo Falsone has pointed out that the Offensive Behaviour at Football and Threatening Communications (Scotland) Act 2012 may be used to prosecute some blasphemous pronouncements at football matches.[40]

16.9 CRITIQUE OF THE LAW ON BLASPHEMY AND PROPOSALS FOR REFORM

It could be argued that the reference to "Holy Scriptures" in Hume should be interpreted in the modern context to include non-Christian holy books, such as the Qur'an, the main religious text of Islam. This would allow for the prosecution of, for example, the *Jyllands-Posten* cartoons of Muhammad. Published in a Danish newspaper, these depicted the Islamic prophet in an unflattering way and were regarded as blasphemous by many Muslims. The Republic of Ireland has broadened its blasphemy laws in this way; the Defamation Act 2009, s 36(1) provides that "A person who publishes or utters blasphemous matter shall be guilty of an offence" and defines this as matter "that is grossly abusive or insulting in relation to matters held sacred by *any religion*, thereby causing outrage among a substantial number of the adherents of that religion".[41] We suggest that a preferable approach is for it to be made clear that in Scots law blasphemy is no longer a crime. While this is widely believed to be the case, the position is not entirely free from doubt. In January 2005, a complaint of blasphemy relating to the broadcasting of *Jerry Springer – The Opera* was investigated

16.9.1

---

[37] Hume, i, 568.

[38] Thomas Paterson was sentenced to 15 months' imprisonment for selling blasphemous books.

[39] Gordon (2001), para 41-28.

[40] See *ibid*; A Falsone, "Redundant crimes of blasphemy in Scotland" (2014) 16 *Ecc LJ* 190 at 191. The 2012 Act is discussed from section 15.8 above under the heading of "Public Order Offences".

[41] Defamation Act 2009, s 36(2)(a) (emphasis added). The accused must intend to cause such outrage: *ibid*, s 36(2)(b). It is a defence for the accused to prove that "a reasonable person would find genuine literary, artistic, political, scientific, or academic value in the matter to which the offence relates" (s 36(3)). "Religion" is defined to exclude any "organisation or cult" which, *inter alia*, employs oppressive psychological manipulation" (s 36(4)(b)).

by the Crown Office.[42] Although no prosecution was brought, it remains uncertain whether the courts would have recognised the validity of a complaint libelling blasphemy as such. The argument that the English crime of blasphemy was incompatible with the ECHR was rejected in the case of *Wingrove* v *UK*.[43] Nevertheless, that crime was abolished by statute in 2008.[44] It is suggested that Scots criminal law should do likewise.

16.10   OTHER FORMS OF OFFENSIVE BEHAVIOUR

16.10.1   The crimes which we have looked at so far in this chapter are disparate but clearly they do not exhaust the category of offensiveness. In German law, for example, some forms of offensive behaviour are criminalised by specific provisions; Art 189 of the German Criminal Code makes it an offence to insult the memory of a deceased person, and Art 130 criminalises those who incite hatred against certain sections of the population. Amendments have included within Art 130 expressions of denial of the Holocaust perpetrated by the Nazis against the Jews during the Second World War. This denial must be likely to disturb the public peace.[45] The question of whether Scots law ought to enact a specific offence of "Holocaust denial" has not received much attention, perhaps because it is less of a problem here than in Germany.[46] However, in Scotland (and England and Wales) s 18 of the Public Order Act 1986 makes it an offence to use threatening, abusive or insulting words or behaviour if the accused intended to stir up racial hatred, or even if no such intention is proved but the circumstances were such that racial hatred was likely to be stirred up as a result. Furthermore, any crime may be treated as aggravated if it is shown to have been motivated by, or to have evinced, religious or racial prejudice,[47] or prejudice based on a victim's actual or presumed disability, sexual orientation or transgender identity.

---

[42] See http://www.scotsman.com/news/uk/springer-tv-opera-faces-blasphemy-complaint-1-1401608. For an (unsuccessful) attempt to bring a private prosecution in England for blasphemous libel relating to this Opera, see *R (on the application of Green)* v *City of Westminster Magistrates' Court* [2008] HRLR 12.

[43] (1997) 24 EHRR 1.

[44] Criminal Justice and Immigration Act 2008, s 79(1).

[45] For a detailed discussion of these issues, see B Swart, "Denying Shoah" in P Alldridge and C Brants (eds), *Personal Autonomy, the Private Sphere and Criminal Law* (2001), p 161.

[46] For the argument that "individuals and societies suffer harm as a result of Holocaust denial", see L B Lidsky, "Where's the harm? Free speech and the regulation of lies" (2008) 65 *Wash & Lee L Rev* 1091 at 1093.

[47] These aggravations are discussed from section 7.9 above.

PART VI

STATUTORY OFFENCES AND BUSINESS CRIME

The topics which we consider in this part cut across the other boundaries we have drawn hitherto between, for instance, crimes against the person and crimes against property. Thus, for example, an offence is defined as "statutory" simply because it is set down in legislation; as with common law crimes, its purpose can obviously include direct prevention of harm to persons or to property, or a host of other aims, including regulation of road traffic, protection of the environment, raising of revenue etc. Accordingly, anything ranging from homicide to minor motoring offences can fall within this category. In fact, many, perhaps most, other legal systems would not need to discuss statutory crime as a distinct heading because legislation forms the mainstay of their criminal law.[1] The Scottish system is still so common law based that statutory offences do merit independent consideration. Chapter 17, then, considers mechanisms by which statutes hold "persons" – whether natural or artificial – to account, including the more specific topics of strict liability (where there is no *mens rea* element) and vicarious liability (where a party other than the actual perpetrator of the offence is held criminally liable for it).

Chapter 18 is more concerned with certain types of protagonist – with the criminal accountability of "white collar criminals" and corporate entities. Just as statutes cover a wide range of behaviours, corporations can commit a wide range of crimes. Of course, statutory offences can apply very narrowly to a particular industry[2]

---

[1] For example, some leading textbooks on English criminal law contain no "statutory crime" heading: see C M V Clarkson, H M Keating and S R Cunningham, *Clarkson and Keating, Criminal Law: Text and Materials* (7th edn, 2010); and A Ashworth and J Horder, *Principles of Criminal Law* (7th edn, 2013).
[2] For example, the Scottish fur farming industry: Fur Farming (Prohibition) (Scotland) Act 2002, s 1.

or universally to all individuals.[3] Human beings are the principal protagonists in offences against the Misuse of Drugs Act 1971 and the Road Traffic Acts. By contrast, the Corporate Manslaughter and Corporate Homicide Act 2007 applies only to organisations. Many regulatory offences are aimed primarily at employers – for example, the Factories Acts – and these tend to be directed primarily at non-human legal persons. While individual human beings are similarly disadvantaged by the concept of strict liability, it is also a useful device for facilitating the conviction of corporations because it obviates the need to ascribe a "mental element" to a non-human entity.

In summary, then, Chapter 17 looks at principles of statutory offences which apply across the board, whether the accused is a human person or only a legal person. These principles sometimes have particular resonance in the business crime context, because of the peculiar difficulties created by a corporate accused, but this should not allow us to lose sight of their generality. By contrast, Chapter 18 is concerned exclusively with some of the ways in which the criminal law interacts with business.

---

[3] For example, carrying an article with a blade or sharp point in a public place: Criminal Law (Consolidation) (Scotland) Act 1995, s 49(1).

CHAPTER 17

GENERAL PRINCIPLES OF STATUTORY OFFENCES

17.1 INTRODUCTION

As taught in Scottish universities, the canon of the criminal law **17.1.1** is still based around the common law. Murder, theft, assault and fire-raising have all developed, more or less exclusively, through judgments of the appeal court. Every year, however, increasing numbers of statutory offences are created. Examples include the offence, committed in the main by a shop's occupier, for any large shop to open on Christmas Day for the purpose of making retail sales.[1] Under different legislation, it is an offence for directors of diagnostic laboratories to fail to provide certain information to their local health board, where their laboratory has identified a "notifiable organism".[2] Neither of these offences is likely to be widely known. Their moral content is certainly less than in relation to murder or theft, yet the legislature has deemed both behaviours sufficiently blameworthy to criminalise them. This chapter is concerned with statutory offences in general and with strict liability in particular.

Technically, statutory offences are easier to conjugate into their **17.1.2** constituent elements than their common law counterparts. In order fully to understand and identify the principles of the (common law) defence of provocation, for example, it might be necessary to read and consider five separate cases.[3] This can be compared with the relatively straightforward statutory offence of vandalism which is stated in the following three lines:

---

[1] Christmas Day and New Year's Day Trading (Scotland) Act 2007, ss 1 and 4.
[2] Public Health etc (Scotland) Act 2008, ss 16 and 17.
[3] That is, *Drury* v *HM Advocate* 2001 SLT 1013; *Gillon* v *HM Advocate* 2007 JC 24; *Low* v *HM Advocate* 1994 SLT 277; *Thomson* v *HM Advocate* 1986 SLT 281; and *HM Advocate* v *Hill* 1941 JC 59.

"any person who, without reasonable excuse, wilfully or recklessly destroys or damages any property belonging to another shall be guilty of the offence of vandalism".[4]

- The *actus reus* is the destruction or damage of someone else's property.
- The *mens rea* is "wilfulness" or "recklessness".
- There is a defence of reasonable excuse. In this instance, if the defence leads evidence of an excuse, it is for the Crown to prove beyond reasonable doubt that this was not "reasonable".

It is relatively easy to extrapolate these core elements of the offence, and the defence, from the section. This is a good illustration of the convenience and certainty of legislation, which are two of the arguments sometimes deployed in favour of codification of the criminal law.[5]

17.2 STRICT LIABILITY

17.2.1 Some legislation, like the above section creating vandalism, states clearly and unequivocally the mental element of the crime. Where the statutory words do not *clearly* specify a *mens rea*, the offence may not require the Crown to prove any mental element. If this is the case, it is a crime of strict liability. Strict liability is a contradiction of the basic principle that people should only be found guilty of offences for which they are criminally responsible, in the sense of being blameworthy. As such, it has been criticised by academic commentators.[6] Their approach is epitomised by Lon Fuller, who has stated that:

> "the most serious infringement of the principle that the law should not command the impossible ... lies in laws creating a strict criminal liability – laws under which a man may be found guilty of a crime though he acted with due care and with an innocent intent".[7]

17.2.2 Where a statute specifies *mens rea* for an offence, as the vandalism section does, using unequivocal terminology such as "intentional",

---

[4] Criminal Law (Consolidation) (Scotland) Act 1995, s 52(1). This offence is considered further from section 13.3 above.
[5] For further arguments in favour of codification, see the Commentary to the *Draft Criminal Code*, and Chapter 22 below.
[6] See, for example, V Tadros, *Criminal Responsibility* (2005), pp 73–74; S P Green, "Six senses of strict liability: a plea for formalism" in A P Simester (ed), *Appraising Strict Liability* (2005) 1 at p 17.
[7] L L Fuller, *The Morality of Law* (1964), p 77.

"wilful", "reckless" or "knowingly", no question of strict liability arises. However, where the legislation does not include such clear words, there is always the possibility of strict liability. Where strict liability applies the prosecution satisfies the requirements for a conviction by establishing that the accused carried out the *actus reus*. In any case where it is unclear whether or not *mens rea* is required, it is for the Crown to satisfy the court that the offence is one of strict liability.

A legislature which wanted to try to prevent certain consequences, such as people being harmed, or even killed, from food poisoning, dangerous electrical equipment, or speeding motorists, could enact statutory provisions to the effect that it is an offence "to supply unsound meat", "to sell dangerous electrical goods", or "to drive in excess of the speed limit". That defines the *actus reus* of each offence but says nothing about *mens rea*. The legislature could decide to make these require intent: this would catch people who sell meat or electrical equipment, knowing that it is contaminated or unsafe, and would also catch those who deliberately exceed the speed limit. Statutes drafted in this way might state that it is an offence "to sell meat, knowing that it is unfit for human consumption", "intentionally to drive in excess of the speed limit" etc. Alternatively, recklessness could be sufficient for *mens rea*, so that the legislation could say "any person who does X wilfully or recklessly ... commits an offence". This is a formula with which we are familiar, from the definition of vandalism.[8] The statute could employ the lowest form of *mens rea*, such that a person who negligently sells unfit food commits an offence. This would catch yet more people. The problem is, however, that the legislature wants to make sure that unsound food and dangerous electrical goods will not be supplied. If it makes people liable only when they have knowingly done so, or where the Crown is able to prove that such people have been reckless, or even negligent, then many people will escape conviction, and others will be harmed as a result. A retailer could sell a mouldy pizza without being negligent; a seller may not be aware of the fact that its electric toasters are a fire hazard. Furthermore, it is very difficult for the prosecution to show that the seller or supplier has been negligent. The solution is to create an offence of strict liability. This means that the statute simply provides that it is an offence "to sell unsound meat" or "to exceed the speed limit", and the Crown needs to establish only the *actus reus* – that the accused sold the meat or exceeded the limit. It need not prove that this was done deliberately, recklessly, or through negligence.

17.2.3

---

[8] See from section 13.3 above.

17.2.4   To some extent, strict liability is a paradigm example of Herbert Packer's "crime control model" in operation.[9] This accepts that where an offence has been committed and the perpetrator identified, little more is necessary for a conviction. While it does not presume guilt – the prosecution must still prove beyond reasonable doubt that the accused carried out the *actus reus* – it effectively removes the fault element. This is demonstrated by the case of *Smith* v *HM Advocate*[10] in which the appellant had been convicted of possession of a firearm.[11] The weapon had been wrapped in a balaclava, and the trial judge directed the jury that:

> "The Crown does not require to prove that the accused knew he had a pistol or that he had a firearm. What the Crown does require to prove is that the accused knew he had some object, whatever it was, in his hand and that he had control over the object to the extent that he had a meaningful say in what was to be done with it."

This direction was approved by the appeal court, which stressed that there were important public policy reasons for interpreting the firearms legislation as imposing strict liability.[12]

17.2.5   The operation of strict liability is also illustrated by the case of *Gordon* v *Shaw*[13] in which the accused was charged with a statutory offence of having used certain fishing methods in the Moray Firth. The legislation was held to have imposed strict liability, hence the accused was convicted once the prosecution had established that the boat was using the illegal fishing methods while in the Moray Firth at the time. It did not have to establish that the accused knew of the boat's position, even though he was merely a crew member and not the master of the vessel.

17.2.6   Money laundering, described as "the most significant new serious crime to appear on statute books worldwide since publication of [Feinberg's] *Moral Limits [of the Criminal Law]*",[14] is generally regarded as a serious offence. However, in attempting to prevent criminals from benefiting from their ill-gotten gains, the legislature has enacted broadly defined strict liability offences. "Money laundering" itself has been defined as

---

[9] H L Packer, "Two models of the criminal process" (1964) 113 *University of Pennsylvania Law Review* 1 at 9–13. See also H L Packer, *The Limits of the Criminal Sanction* (1969), and from section 5.2 above.

[10] 1996 SLT 1338.

[11] This is a contravention of the Firearms Act 1968, s 1.

[12] A similar approach had been taken in England in *R* v *Waller* [1991] Crim LR 381 and *R* v *Hussain* [1981] 1 WLR 416.

[13] 1908 SC (J) 17.

[14] P Alldridge, "The moral limits of the crime of money laundering" (2001–02) 5 *Buff Crim L Rev* 279 at 282.

"the process by which criminal proceeds are sanitised to disguise their illicit origins. Acquisitive criminals will attempt to distance themselves from their crimes by finding safe havens for their profits where they can avoid confiscation orders, and where those proceeds can be made to appear legitimate".[15]

The Proceeds of Crime Act 2002 imposes obligations on professional people who work in the regulatory sector (including lawyers, accountants, bankers and financial advisers) to disclose that a client or customer is involved in money laundering. The obligation is such that it is a criminal offence to fail to disclose a suspicion of money laundering. Furthermore, it is an offence to fail to disclose if there are *reasonable grounds* for suspicion.[16] This is an objective test; a person may be found guilty of money laundering even though she personally did not suspect that anything was amiss. This is an unacceptable extension of criminal liability. Following a detailed critique of the criminalisation of money laundering, Peter Alldridge concluded:

"There are good grounds for the existence of some powers of confiscation of the proceeds of crime, but they do not imply that laundering should also be a crime. We should beware of criminalization of remote harms, overcriminalization, and the deployment of the criminal law in the economic sphere."[17]

17.3   DETERMINING WHETHER AN OFFENCE IMPOSES STRICT LIABILITY

Mens rea is the norm

In English law, there is a presumption in favour of *mens rea*. This was authoritatively stated by the House of Lords in the case of *Sweet v Parsley*.[18] The case concerned the sub-tenant of a farmhouse in Oxfordshire who rented certain rooms to persons "of the 'beatnik fraternity'".[19] The defendant did not live on the premises. It transpired that her tenants were smoking cannabis there, without her knowledge. She was charged with being "concerned in the management of premises used for [the purpose of smoking cannabis resin]", a statutory offence.[20] The prosecutor accepted that the defendant did not know that the premises were being used for this

17.3.1

---

[15] Crown Prosecution Service website: http://www.cps.gov.uk/legal/p_to_r/proceeds_of_crime_money_laundering/#Introduction_to_Money.
[16] See the Proceeds of Crime Act 2002, ss 327–329, and the Proceeds of Crime Act 2002 (Investigations: Code of Practice) (Scotland) Order 2009 (SSI 2009/245).
[17] Alldridge (2001–02) at 318 (footnotes omitted).
[18] [1970] AC 132.
[19] *Ibid* at 150 per Lord Reid.
[20] Dangerous Drugs Act 1965, s 5(b).

purpose, but she was convicted at first instance on the basis that the offence was one of strict liability. Her appeal succeeded in the House of Lords, their Lordships accepting that it would be most unfair to convict someone of a relatively serious offence without *mens rea* having to be established. Lord Pearce explained the rationale behind this, saying:

> "one must remember that normally mens rea is still an ingredient of any offence. Before the court will dispense with the necessity for mens rea it has to be satisfied that Parliament so intended. The mere absence of the word 'knowingly' is not enough".[21]

The current drugs legislation is now defined such that the accused must be the occupier or concerned in the management of premises and "knowingly" permit or suffer certain drug-related activities to take place on those premises.[22]

17.3.2   The presumption in favour of *mens rea* has subsequently been reiterated in England, in even more definite terms, in the cases of *B (A Child)* v *DPP*[23] and *R* v *K*.[24] In the Scottish case of *Duguid* v *Fraser*[25] Lord Justice-Clerk Cooper said:

> "it has, I think, been the practice to insist that the Crown should show that the language, scope and intendment of the statute require that an exception should be admitted to the normal and salutary rule of our law that *mens rea* is an indispensable ingredient of a criminal or quasi-criminal act; and I venture to think that it would be a misfortune if the stringency of this requirement were relaxed".[26]

In *H* v *Griffiths*[27] Lord Eassie stated that:

> "the starting point must be the presumption that *mens rea* is required for all the elements of a statutory offence, unless that requirement is excluded by express words in the legislative provision in question or by necessary implication".[28]

The courts therefore start out from the view that strict liability will not apply and require to be convinced by the Crown that it does. Certain principles are applied in making this determination. These include: whether the offence is regarded as "truly criminal",

---

[21] [1970] AC 132 at 156.
[22] Misuse of Drugs Act 1971, s 8, discussed at section 8.9 above.
[23] [2000] 2 Cr App R 65.
[24] [2002] 1 AC 462.
[25] 1942 JC 1.
[26] *Ibid* at 5.
[27] 2009 SLT 199.
[28] *Ibid* at 202. See also *Smart* v *HM Advocate* 2006 JC 119 and *King* v *Webster* 2012 SLT 342 (affirming the presumption in favour of *mens rea*).

or merely regulatory; the purpose of the statute; whether imposing strict liability will act as a deterrent; the seriousness of the potential penalty; and of course whether there are any terms importing *mens rea* in the wording of the offence itself.

Mala in se or mala prohibita?

Where the offence is "truly criminal" the likelihood is that there will be a *mens rea* requirement. This relates to the distinction often drawn in the criminal law between *"mala in se"* and *"mala prohibita"*. The former translates as "things which are wrong in themselves" and relates to behaviour with a strong moral content. It covers all of the traditional common law crimes such as murder, fire-raising and theft, which are pre-legally wrongful, and accepted by society as such. *Mala prohibita*, on the other hand, are acts or omissions which are only wrong because legislation has declared them to be wrong or, in other words, because there is a statute prohibiting them. They are less serious offences, usually regulatory in character, which attract little societal opprobrium. Examples include parking offences or driving without a seat belt.[29] Many theorists have, however, suggested that the criminal law is not the most appropriate mechanism for ensuring good order on the highways. Trevor Nyman has stressed their *mala prohibita* quality:

17.3.3

> "The gut feeling in the general public about motoring offences not being real crimes, is fortified by the fact that the errant motorist is not likely to be guilty of other 'real crimes'. He is not one of the criminal fraternity, his associates are not crooks and hoodlums, he is not at war with society; he does not expect to get his living other than by honest work. The general public's attitude towards traffic offences as a whole is that they are in quite a different category from other offences yet the criminal law persists in the fiction that they are the same."[30]

Referring to road traffic laws which proscribe failing to obey a stop sign or red traffic light, performing illegal U-turns etc, he argues that such offences "catch the stupid, the forgetful, the not-very clever but neither the defiant nor the wicked".[31] Most would agree that it is not the role of the criminal law to punish people merely for being stupid or forgetful.[32] Nyman concludes:

---

[29] Road Traffic Act 1988, s 14(3). See also the Motor Vehicles (Wearing of Seat Belts) Regulations 1993 (SI 1993/176), reg 5.
[30] T Nyman, "The dilution of crime" (1981) 55 *The Australian Law Journal* 506 at 508.
[31] *Ibid.*
[32] See, however, our discussion of *Crowe* v *Waugh* 1999 JC 292 at section 8.11.8 above.

"It is lazy and unsuccessful to try and enforce road safety with criminal sanctions. Our community should be prepared to invest large sums in research and education in this generation, to make better motorists and safer roads for the next generation."[33]

It is, however, questionable whether education alone is likely to be successful. It is widely known that using a phone while driving or exceeding the speed limit are dangerous activities, which risk harm not only to the user of the phone or the speeder, but also to other drivers and pedestrians. However, this knowledge does not always act as a sufficient deterrent, particularly for the driver who is running late. The deterrent effect of the criminal law has a more immediate impact – it is the presence of a speed camera, or the sight of a police car and the fear of being caught which is more likely to change behaviour.

17.3.4   Lon Fuller has suggested that road traffic laws "provide for our citizens a framework within which they can organize their relations with one another in such a manner as to make possible a peaceful and profitable coexistence".[34] He addresses the question of what should be done about the motorist who fails to comply with a "stop" sign in the early hours of the morning when no other traffic was about. This driver may have looked carefully to check that there was no possibility of causing harm. Should such a person avoid liability? Concluding that the motorist can rightfully be punished, Fuller states:

"One of the functions of fixed rules of interaction [such as road traffic legislation] ... is to relieve the actor of the burden, and the risks, involved in attempting to appraise the peculiar qualities of each separate situation in which he finds himself. What we call 'rules of thumb' set us free to use our more flexible fingers in the solution of the more subtle kinds of tasks."[35]

17.3.5   It should, however, be noted that not all road traffic offences are *mala prohibita*, and that the allocation of offences between the two categories is not fixed, but is contingent on the social norms prevailing at a particular time. In contrast to Nyman's view that the motoring offender is not likely to be guilty of other, "real" crimes, one study found that 79 per cent of disqualified drivers had a criminal record (even if only a single previous conviction) as did about 50 per cent of dangerous drivers.[36] At the more serious end of the driving scale, then, road traffic crime is not completely divorced from other

---

[33] Nyman (1981) at 508.
[34] L L Fuller, "Law as an instrument of social control and law as a facilitation of human interaction" (1975) *Brigham Young University Law Review* 89.
[35] *Ibid* at 91.
[36] G Rose, *The Criminal Histories of Serious Traffic Offenders: Home Office Research Study* 206 (2000) at p x.

forms of offending. Only a few decades ago, drunk driving was not particularly stigmatising. Today, the reverse is true.

The effect of the distinction between *mala in se* and *mala prohibita*   **17.3.6** is that strict liability is not generally regarded as appropriate where the offence is a statutory version of a traditional crime. For example, were wilful fire-raising – something which is clearly wrong in itself – to be proscribed by statute, but the parliamentary drafters omitted to include any mention of *mens rea*, it would be difficult to convince a court that this created a strict liability offence. Where the offence is *not* "truly criminal", it is more likely to be classified as strict liability. This is illustrated by *Duguid* v *Fraser*[37] itself. The case concerned the Prices of Goods Act 1939, a piece of wartime legislation passed to prevent profiteering on certain items which were in short supply. An item covered by the Act was sold for a price in excess of the maximum permitted. It was held that strict liability applied. Clearly the actual pricing – the item was sold for 7s and the price cap was set at 4s 9d – was unlikely to set the pulse racing. Since the usual principle of business is that goods may be sold for the maximum price achievable in the market, it was only considered "wrong" to charge 7 shillings in this case because the statute had declared it to be so.

The purpose of the statute

The courts will also consider whether the legislation is designed to   **17.3.7** regulate an issue of social concern. For example, the Food Safety Act 1990 imposes strict liability for selling food which has a label falsely describing the food.[38] The Prices of Goods Act 1939, the statute at issue in *Duguid* v *Fraser*,[39] served the social purpose of preventing profiteering in wartime. In our discussion of the statutory offence of "having an article with a blade or sharp point in a public place"[40] we looked at the case of *Crowe* v *Waugh*.[41] It will be recalled that the court emphasised that the purpose of the legislation was to ensure that people did not carry knives in public places and that the imputation of strict liability would assist in bringing about this aim. The prevention of knife crime was – and remains – an issue of social concern, hence strict liability was regarded by the court as appropriate.[42]

---

[37] 1942 JC 1. See section 17.3.2 above.
[38] Food Safety Act 1990, s 15(1)(a).
[39] 1942 JC 1.
[40] Criminal Law (Consolidation) (Scotland) Act 1995, s 49(1).
[41] 1999 JC 292. See section 8.11.8 above.
[42] For a criticism of this decision, see section 8.13.2 above.

17.3.8   The English courts have been particularly proactive in convicting without *mens rea* in relation to pollution. In *Alphacell* v *Woodward*,[43] a company was convicted of causing polluting matter to enter a river[44] despite the fact that it had not been negligent and had taken a number of precautions. Its operations involved waste water flowing into tanks on the side of a river. Overflow of this polluted water into the river was prevented by the operation of two pumps. On the day in question, the pumping equipment had been checked by an employee of the company on four separate occasions. The last check took place 45 minutes before a rivers inspector discovered that the pumps had failed and the waste water was polluting the river. Clearly, the prevention of pollution is an issue of social concern and this was an element in the court's decision that strict liability applied. The case also illustrates that the courts seem to regard strict liability as appropriate where the offence is concerned with the regulation of business.

The promotion of greater vigilance

17.3.9   If imposing strict liability would have no effect whatever in terms of encouraging compliance with the terms of the legislation, either by the accused or by others, then *mens rea* is likely to be required. In the case of *Lim Chin Aik*,[45] the accused was charged with remaining in Singapore illegally after an Order had been made prohibiting him from entering the colony. Although the Order identified Lim Chin Aik by name, nothing whatsoever had been done by the authorities to bring its existence to his attention. His appeal against conviction succeeded, the Privy Council ruling that finding him guilty would do nothing to encourage anyone else to adhere to the law. Accordingly, strict liability did not apply.

The penalty

17.3.10   As *Sweet* v *Parsley*[46] shows, the courts are very reluctant to impose strict liability, particularly where the sentence for the offence can be one of imprisonment. This is not, however, an invariable rule; the carrying of knives and certain types of offensive weapons can involve strict liability, yet imprisonment is an option.[47] This again

---

[43] [1972] AC 824.
[44] Contrary to the Rivers (Prevention of Pollution) Act 1951, s 2(1).
[45] [1963] AC 160.
[46] [1970] AC 132. See also section 17.3.1 above.
[47] The maximum penalty for carrying an offensive weapon, or for having an article with a blade or point, in a public place is 4 years' imprisonment: Criminal Law (Consolidation) (Scotland) Act 1995, s 47(1)(b) and s 49(1)(b), respectively.

moves further away from the notion that strict liability is tolerable because is applies, generally, in relation only to non-stigmatising regulatory offences. The fact of having been imprisoned may, in itself, cause stigma. Imprisonment "subjects the prisoner to the pains and deprivations of incarceration, often including overcrowding and fear for personal safety".[48] Andrew Ashworth has, therefore, argued that "imprisonment would be monstrously unfair in the absence of proof of fault".[49]

The particular words used in the section

The basic principle is that *mens rea* will only be dis-applied by express wording in the statute or necessary implication. It is, however, unusual for a statute to state explicitly that there is no requirement for the Crown to prove any mental element.[50] The door is left open for consideration of strict liability where the statute does not specify a mental element. Certain words have sometimes been interpreted so as to import one. These include "possessing" and "permitting". The courts have also considered the word "causing" in statutory offences but have generally interpreted it to import strict liability. The following sections consider the courts' interpretation of these words.   **17.3.11**

"Possessing"

The courts have taken the view that, where an offence consists in "possession", for example, of drugs under the Misuse of Drugs Act 1971,[51] or of firearms under the Firearms Act 1968, the accused would have to *know* that she had custody or control of something (which turns out to be the illegal article) in order to be convicted. Their interpretation has effectively "read in" the word "knowingly" to statutes proscribing possession. All that seems to be necessary, however, is that the accused should know that she has the relevant article with her and that she is able to exercise control over it. Her knowledge does not have to extend to the exact content or nature of the item.[52] In relation to possession of indecent images of children   **17.3.12**

---

[48] A Ashworth, "Should strict criminal liability be removed from all imprisonable offences?" (2010) 45 *Irish Jurist* 1 at 15.

[49] *Ibid* at 21.

[50] Though a few statutes may state specifically that the offence is one of strict liability. See, for example, Christmas Day and New Year's Day Trading (Scotland) Act 2007, s 6.

[51] See from section 8.9 above.

[52] See, for example, *Henvey v HM Advocate* 2005 SLT 384 and, in relation to firearms, section 17.2.4 above.

kept on the hard drive of a computer it was held in England and Wales that "'possession' ... refer[s] to images that are within the defendant's *control*".[53] Lady Paton endorsed this approach, in the Scottish context, in *MacLennan* v *HM Advocate*.[54]

"Permitting"

17.3.13   The courts have also interpreted the word "permitting" as requiring knowledge on the part of the accused. In *MacKay Brothers & Company* v *Gibb*,[55] the accused was a garage business which had hired out a car to a man named Sneddon. He had an accident while driving the car and it was found that one of its tyres did not have the legally required depth of tread. The relevant legislation provided, *inter alia*, that "no person shall ... cause or permit to be used on a road any motor vehicle ... a wheel of which is fitted with a pneumatic tyre, if ... the tread pattern ... does not have a depth of at least 1 mm".[56] Although the firm's garage controller had not specifically checked this before hiring out the car, it was held that he had "permitted" the car to be used with a defective tyre in breach of the legislation. His "knowledge" was imputed by his failure to check the tyre. He should have done this and, because he had not, he had wilfully blinded himself to the potentially dangerous state of the car.

17.3.14   Similarly, in *Anderson* v *Higson*,[57] the charge was a contravention of s 49(1) of the Civic Government (Scotland) Act 1982 which makes it an offence if any person "suffers or permits any creature in his charge to cause danger or injury to any other person". The court accepted that the phrase "suffers or permits" requires knowledge that the creature (in this case, a dog) is likely to cause alarm or annoyance to others if loose in a public place.

17.3.15   In *MacDonald* v *Howdle*[58] it was held that the accused did not "cause or permit" another person to use her motor car where there was no policy of insurance in force.[59] The accused had quizzed her friend, to whom she was lending her car, as to whether he had his own insurance. He stated, incorrectly, that he had. The court held that her permission to use the car had been conditional on him having the necessary insurance. Since that condition had not been

[53] *R* v *Porter* [2006] 1 WLR 2633 per Dyson LJ at 2640, para [23] (emphasis added).

[54] 2012 SCL 957 at 962, para [19].

[55] 1969 SLT 216.

[56] Motor Vehicles (Construction and Use) Regulations 1966 (SI 1966/1288), reg 82(1)(f), as amended by Motor Vehicles (Construction and Use) (Amendment) (No 4) Regulations 1967 (SI 1967/1753).

[57] 2001 SLT 1035.

[58] 1995 SLT 779.

[59] Contrary to the Road Traffic Act 1988, s 143(1) and (2).

satisfied, she had not "permitted" him to drive her car, in terms of the statute. This is a rather different approach from simply stating that she did not "knowingly" permit him to drive but it illustrates the courts' tendency to look behind the word "permit" for some form of mental attitude on the part of the accused.

"Causing"

The courts have tended to take a harsher line with the word   **17.3.16** "causing" – perhaps because its plain meaning is more indicative of action than thought. The case of *Mitchell* v *Morrison*[60] related to the record of hours worked which drivers of heavy-goods vehicles are required to keep. The driver in question had been in the habit of loading his lorry for the next day's delivery before leaving work for the night. He then drove the loaded lorry to his home and kept it there overnight, setting off on the delivery from there the following morning. However, his record of hours did not reflect this accurately. It gave the impression that his working day always started and ended at the depot. The driver, then, had clearly breached the statute requiring a proper record to be kept. The question was whether his employer, who had not known that the record was false, had also committed an offence. The statutory provision specified that the licence holder "shall keep or cause to be kept" current records, showing the times at which each driver started and stopped work.[61] The court held that this did import strict liability. The accused had failed to satisfy the exact terms of the statute even though he had no knowledge that the record kept was false.

Two English cases concerning the pollution of rivers also illustrate   **17.3.17** this approach. In *Attorney-General's Reference (No 1 of 1994)*,[62] the English Court of Appeal held that the term "causing", in relation to the offence of "causing polluting matter to enter controlled waters" (a river),[63] required some active participation on the part of the accused company, but not necessarily its knowledge that the pollution had taken place. Similarly, in *Environment Agency* v *Empress Car Co (Abertillery) Ltd*,[64] it was held that Empress did cause polluting matter to enter controlled waters, contrary to the legislation,[65] when an unknown third party opened the unlockable

---

[60] 1938 JC 64.
[61] Road and Rail Traffic Act 1933, s 16(1).
[62] [1995] 2 All ER 1007.
[63] Contrary to the Water Act 1989, s 107(1)(a).
[64] [1998] 1 All ER 481.
[65] Water Resources Act 1991, s 85(1).

tap on its diesel tank, causing the diesel to drain into a river. This
was the case even though the company was unaware at the time of
the polluting that it had occurred.

17.3.18   This is clearly a narrow approach to the concept of causation
itself, especially in the *Empress* case where the pollution was caused
by the act of a third party. In other circumstances, such behaviour
might have been held to constitute a *novus actus interveniens*
in the causal chain.[66] Julie Adshead notes that this demonstrates
that "[t]he purpose here is to make the polluter pay and not to
allocate blame".[67] This purpose is in keeping with the use of strict
liability both to encourage compliance and to respond strongly to
the regulation of matters of particular social concern. After all,
"[w]hereas initially environmental regulation was primarily
concerned with the threat to public health, the protection of the
environment is now recognised as important to the survival of
mankind".[68] It is not necessarily the case, however, that this situation,
which heightens the stigma attaching to such offences, is such as
to justify the separation of responsibility from blameworthiness
which strict liability entails.

17.4   DEFENCES TO STATUTORY OFFENCES

17.4.1   To mitigate the potential unfairness which the imposition of strict
liability may cause, many (though by no means all) statutes which
create such liability also include defences. Where a statute provides
a defence, the onus of proving this is often placed on the accused.
The standard of proof is on the balance of probabilities. This can
be seen in operation in relation to ss 47 and 49 of the Criminal Law
(Consolidation) (Scotland) Act 1995. As we have seen, s 47 (which
criminalises carrying an offensive weapon in a public place) provides
the defences of "lawful authority" or "reasonable excuse" while
providing specifically that the proof of these defences rests with the
accused.[69] Section 49 (proscribing the carrying of articles with a
blade or point in a public place) provides the same two defences as
well as those of having the article for "use at work", for "religious
reasons" or that the prohibited article was worn "as part of a
national costume".[70] It is for the accused to prove whichever defence
she seeks to use.

---

[66] See from section 7.3 above.
[67] J Adshead, "Doing justice to the environment" (2013) 77 *J Crim L* 215 at 219.
[68] *Ibid* at 215.
[69] See section 8.11.4 above.
[70] Criminal Law (Consolidation) (Scotland) Act 1995, s 49(4) and (5). See section 8.11.7 above.

Some statutes provide a defence without specifically shifting the onus of proof on to the accused. In these cases, the accused need only bring evidence to support the existence of the defence to the court's attention. It is then for the prosecution to establish, beyond reasonable doubt, that the defence is not established. An example of this is the defence of "reasonable excuse" in vandalism.[71] **17.4.2**

17.5 DUE DILIGENCE

One of the most common statutory defences is that of "due diligence" – that the accused exercised a high degree of care to prevent the commission of the offence. An example is the Consumer Protection Act 1987 which provides a strict liability offence of selling a dangerous product. Section 39(1) of that Act allows someone so charged to establish on the balance of probabilities that she (1) took all reasonable steps and (2) exercised all due diligence to avoid committing the offence. A similar defence is provided by s 21 of the Food Safety Act 1990.[72] The first strand is usually taken to require some evidence that the accused had a system in place to ensure that dangerous products are not sold. The second requires her to establish that she took steps to ensure that the system worked in relation to the particular product to which the charge relates. **17.5.1**

Some legislation may be more specific as to what exactly needs to be done to demonstrate that proper steps have been taken to prevent the commission of an offence. For example, under s 1 of the Crossbows Act 1987, "A person who sells ... a crossbow ... to a person under the age of eighteen is guilty of an offence". Section 1A(1)(a) and (b) provides a defence where the accused believed the purchaser to be aged 18 or over and had taken "reasonable steps" to establish the purchaser's age.[73] "Reasonable steps" are only deemed to have been taken where the purchaser provided documentary evidence of age in the form of a passport or European Union photocard driving licence[74] and "the document would have convinced a reasonable person".[75] This has the advantage of certainty and provides clear direction to crossbow sellers as to the nature of the system which they need to put in place. **17.5.2**

---

[71] See section 13.3.2 above.

[72] See also s 141A(4) of the Criminal Justice Act 1988, which provides this defence for someone charged with selling knives etc to those under the age of 18 (discussed in section 8.12.1 above).

[73] The defence is not specifically named as one of due diligence but it applies the same principles.

[74] Crossbows Act 1987, s 1A(2) and (3).

[75] *Ibid*, s 1A(2)(b). There is a further defence where "no reasonable person could have suspected from the purchaser['s] ... appearance that the purchaser ... was under the age of 18" (s 1A(1)(b)(ii)).

17.5.3   An important case which discussed the due diligence defence
is *Tesco Supermarkets Ltd* v *Nattrass*.[76] A Tesco store displayed
a poster advertising a special offer on washing powder at a time
when it had no special offer packs in stock. This constituted a strict
liability offence under the Trade Descriptions Act 1968, since Tesco
was making a false statement that a specific product could be bought
at a low price. The company was, however, able to establish that it
had an elaborate system in place for ensuring that such breaches did
not happen, hence it was able to make out the due diligence defence.
This system included sending the manager of the store in question
on a half-day training course specifically about trade descriptions
legislation, and providing him with circulars on a regular basis
about the Act's operation. Senior members of Tesco's management
also regularly visited the store and gave oral instructions about how
it should be managed.

17.5.4   Although the Trade Descriptions Act 1968 is now, largely,
repealed,[77] this case continues to be an important point of reference
in the law on the operation of due diligence defences.[78] *Croydon
London Borough Council* v *Pinch a Pound (UK) Ltd*,[79] which relied
on it, also reaffirmed that, where the offence is one of strict liability,
there is no place for a fault element. Here, the defendant retailer had
sold a knife to a test purchaser aged under 18, in contravention of s
141A of the Criminal Justice Act 1988. The facts that the sale had
taken place, and that the defendant had not taken all reasonable
precautions and exercised all due diligence to avoid its commission,
were sufficient for conviction. Signs in the shop advising about the
age limitations were handwritten on cardboard and the restricted
items themselves were "displayed in a piecemeal, confused and
cavalier way";[80] training was not extensive and the shop's register
of purchases which had been refused was not used systematically or
well. This, in itself, demonstrated an absence of due diligence and
it was incorrect to seek, in addition, negligence and a blameworthy
state of mind by the defendant retailer.

---

[76] [1972] AC 153.

[77] Most of the operational sections of the Trade Descriptions Act 1968 ceased to
have effect in terms of the Consumer Protection from Unfair Trading Regulations
2008 (SI 2008/1277), Sch 2, paras 7–12. Sections 2–4 continue to "have effect for
the interpretation of expressions used in this Act" (*ibid*, para 9).

[78] See, for example, *R (on the application of Thames Water Utilities Ltd)* v *Bromley
Magistrates' Court* [2013] Env LR 25 [NB: case starts at p 601] at 609 para [34] per
Gross LJ; *R (on the Application of Tesco Stores Ltd)* v *City of London Corporation*
[2010] EWHC 2920 (Admin) at para (4) per Ouseley J.

[79] [2011] 1 WLR 1189.

[80] Finding of the Crown Court, quoted *ibid* by Roderick Evans J at 1196, para
[33].

The due diligence defence operates similarly in Scotland, England **17.5.5** and Wales. This is illustrated by the Scottish case of *First Quench Retailing Ltd* v *McLeod*,[81] which concerned a breach of licensing laws by selling alcohol to a 15-year-old girl.[82] An employee of the company had asked the girl for identification, but had sold her the alcohol anyway when none was forthcoming. This seems to have been on the basis that he mistakenly thought that he had previously seen ID from her and also that he thought he had seen her in an over-18s' club. The company's conviction was upheld on appeal. It was established that a lackadaisical attitude of the manager of that particular store had led to company procedures on ID not being adhered to. It was, however, reasonable to assume that the company's training programme for managers would include elements to ensure that the appropriate systems were followed in practice. Accordingly, because this had not happened in this particular store, the company had not exercised all due diligence to prevent the commission of an offence.

17.6   COMMON LAW DEFENCES

As well as defences provided by the statute creating the offence, some **17.6.1** common law defences may be available. The rationale for this was described well in one American case, in which a statute proscribed public drunkenness, but provided no defences or exceptions for this. As the Supreme Court of Kansas put it:

> "[A]re idiots, insane persons, children ... babes, and persons who have been made drunk by force or fraud, and carried into a public place, to be punished under the statute? And if not, why not? And, if these are not to be punished, then no sufficient reason can be given for punishing those who have become drunk through unavoidable accident, or through honest mistake."[83]

It concluded:

> "We should not suppose, in the absence of specific words saying so, that the legislature intended to make accidents and mistakes crimes. Human actions can hardly be considered as culpable, either in law or in morals, unless an intelligent consent of the mind goes with the actions; and to punish where there is no culpability would be the most reprehensible tyranny."[84]

---

[81] 2001 SLT 372.

[82] The law on this point is now found in s 102 of the Licensing (Scotland) Act 2005. It includes a due diligence-type defence in terms similar to those found in s 1A of the Crossbows Act 1987 – see section 17.5.2 above. As proof of age, in addition to a passport or a driving licence, other acceptable documents are listed in the Sale of Alcohol to Children and Young Persons (Scotland) Regulations 2007 (SSI 2007/93), reg 2.

[83] *State* v *Brown* 38 Kan 390 (1888), 16 P 259 at 260.

[84] *Ibid.*

17.6.2 This does not appear to be a matter which has caused difficulty in Scots law. Indeed, *Moss v Howdle*,[85] the leading case on the (common law) defence of necessity, related to the statutory offence of driving on a motorway in excess of the speed limit.[86] In delivering the appeal court's judgment, Lord Justice-General Rodger twice indicated that the necessity defence could apply to offences under the Road Traffic Acts,[87] notwithstanding that a similar, but more narrowly drawn defence existed under the legislation itself.[88] In *MacLeod v Mathieson*,[89] it was accepted that the defence of automatism – that is, that the accused should not be held criminally liable since she was not fully conscious at the time of the offence – could be pled to a strict liability road traffic charge.[90]

17.6.3 Theoretically, problems may arise if the appeal court has held that the underlying rationale for a particular defence is that it operates to negate *mens rea*.[91] If the offence at issue has no *mens rea* (because it is of strict liability) then it is difficult to understand how such a defence can operate at all. In practice however, the Scottish courts seem to accept the moral argument made in the American judgment (above) and have had no difficulty in allowing common law defences to statutory crimes where these fit the circumstances.

17.7 CRITIQUE OF STRICT LIABILITY OFFENCES AND PROPOSALS FOR REFORM

17.7.1 An ever-increasing number of new offences created every year impose strict liability.[92] Arguments in favour of this stress that these types of offence lower the costs of the criminal process: the prosecution's job is greatly simplified if it does not have to prove *mens rea*. Any potential unfairness is limited since strict liability is restricted to regulatory offences, to which little, if any, stigma attaches. It may also have a deterrent effect; for example, if it is known that simply carrying a

---

[85] 1997 JC 123. See section 21.4.7 below.

[86] This is a contravention of the Motorways Traffic (Speed Limit) Regulations 1974 (SI 1974/502), reg 3.

[87] *Moss v Howdle* 1997 JC 123 at 125 and 129. The point was reiterated in *Ruxton v Lang* 1998 SCCR 1, though the defence itself was unsuccessful.

[88] Road Traffic Act 1988, s 34(4).

[89] 1993 SCCR 488.

[90] The defence of automatism is discussed from section 20.16 below.

[91] This has been a view taken by the court in relation to the defences of automatism (*Ross v HM Advocate* 1991 JC 210 at 222 per LJ-G Hope, and at 230 per Lord McCluskey) and coercion (*HM Advocate v Raiker* 1989 SCCR 149 at 154 per Lord McCluskey). In fact, we take the view that automatism is better understood as negating the *actus reus* element. See section 20.20.2 below.

knife in a public place is a criminal offence with serious sanctions, then fewer people will do so.[93] However, none of these justifications serves to dissipate completely the unease felt by many concerning the absence of proof of a fault element. Like reverse burdens of proof, strict liability seems to offend against basic principles of the criminal law and criminal procedure.[94] It seems unjust for the state to be allowed to impose sanctions where the accused is not, in general terms, blameworthy for the crime. There seems little doubt that the moral force of the law is weakened by the existence of so many "crimes" for which a person who may be morally blameless may receive a conviction.

As we have seen, attempts to justify the imposition of criminal **17.7.2** liability without proof of *mens rea* commonly assert that such offences are not really "criminal" but are merely breaches of regulations. The argument that there is little moral blame attached, hence no injustice is done in holding an accused person strictly liable, is dubious; while it is true that speeding or driving without a seat-belt are indeed regarded with only minor disapproval, the same cannot be said of many strict liability offences, even within the realm of road traffic legislation. Driving while under the influence of alcohol is a strict liability offence, in that there is no need for the prosecution to establish that the accused intended to drive with excess alcohol in her bloodstream, or even that she was reckless in so doing, yet it is an offence to which a great deal of moral blameworthiness is attached.

A more plausible justification for strict liability offences is a **17.7.3** pragmatic one: society wants to prevent certain activities from occurring, and the best way of ensuring this is to hold individuals strictly liable. We can readily see the benefits of a system of strict liability in safeguarding public health. As we have previously noted,[95] if it is felt desirable to deter drivers from speeding, or retailers from selling unfit food, a strict liability provision which proscribes speeding or selling such food will be a greater deterrent than one which requires the prosecution to show that the speeding was deliberate, or even reckless, or that the seller knew or ought to have suspected that the food sold was unfit. As a matter of fairness, however, it may be suggested that whenever the legislature creates a

---

[92] It has been suggested that, in England and Wales, strict liability offences "constitute at least half of the more serious offences (those triable in the Crown Court) and the large majority of all offences". See C Wells and O Quick, *Lacey, Wells and Quick, Reconstructing Criminal Law* (4th edn, 2010), p 116.

[93] For a fuller discussion, see J Stanton-Ife, "Strict liability: stigma and regret" (2007) 27 *OJLS* 151.

[94] See Green (2005) at p 17.

[95] See section 17.2.3 above.

strict liability offence, it ought also to consider whether to provide a defence for the accused who is able to show that she did not act recklessly, or even negligently. While this may be difficult for the accused to demonstrate, it would at least help prevent the most egregious injustices. Furthermore, where defences such as "due diligence", "reasonable excuse" or "lawful authority" are available, the courts should interpret them in a way which makes sure that only the blameworthy are convicted – unlike the approach taken in *Crowe* v *Waugh*.[96]

17.8 VICARIOUS LIABILITY

17.8.1 We have seen that, in general, the criminal law holds an accused person criminally liable only for her own acts or omissions.[97] Apart from the doctrine of art and part liability, the general rule is that one is not held liable for crimes committed by other people. Hence parents cannot be prosecuted for the crimes committed by their children. An exception to this general rule is "vicarious liability". This term is used where someone is convicted of an offence which has been committed by someone else. It is most commonly used to impose liability on an employer (often a company) for the acts or omissions of its employees.

17.8.2   The rationale for the imposition of vicarious liability was explained by Lord Justice-General Clyde in the case of *Bean* v *Sinclair*:[98]

> "If a trader is ... allowed to carry on his trade only under certain conditions, the trader is ... answerable for any breach of those conditions committed in the course of his trade. A breach is none the less committed in the course of *his* trade because the actual delinquent is a servant or other person acting within the authority committed to him by the trader."[99]

Similarly, in *Tesco Supermarkets Ltd* v *Nattrass*[100] it was stated in defence of vicarious liability that:

> "the most effective method of deterrence is to place upon the employer the responsibility of doing everything which lies within his power to prevent his employees from doing anything which will result in the commission of an offence".[101]

---

[96] 1999 JC 292. This is the case in which the appeal court held that forgetfulness could not amount to a "good reason" therefore the accused had no defence to having a knife in a public place. See section 8.11.8 above.
[97] See the discussion of art and part liability from section 7.5 above.
[98] 1930 JC 31.
[99] *Ibid* at 36 (emphasis in original).
[100] [1972] AC 153. See section 17.5.3 above.
[101] *Ibid* at 194 per Lord Diplock.

Vicarious liability can only be imposed where an employee is acting   **17.8.3**
within the scope of her employment – it generally does not operate if
she has disobeyed instructions. An example of vicarious liability is
to be found in s 2(1) of the Breastfeeding etc (Scotland) Act 2005,[102]
which provides that:

> "Anything done by a person in the course of that person's employment shall ...
> be treated for the purposes of this Act as done also by that person's employer,
> whether or not it was done with the employer's knowledge or approval."

This form of liability is applicable only to statutory offences, not
common law crimes. For example, if an employee commits a breach
of the peace or assaults a colleague in the workplace, the employer
will not be held vicariously liable for this.

---

[102] See section 5.16.1, n 184 above.

CHAPTER 18

BUSINESS CRIME, REGULATORY OFFENCES, "WHITE COLLAR" CRIME AND CORPORATE LIABILITY

18.1   INTRODUCTION

As is clear from the foregoing parts of this book, and particularly **18.1.1** the first four chapters, criminal law, criminal theory and criminal responsibility are largely predicated on an individual, autonomous subject who exercises free will in deciding to commit a criminal offence. The mental attitude accompanying this exercise of will constitutes the mental element or the *mens rea* and renders the individual blameworthy, such that it is appropriate for the state to impose sanctions. Thus far, we have paid little attention to the actual perpetrator. This is partly because it is one of the underlying assumptions of the criminal process that justice itself is blind and treats all who commit similar wrongs on an equal footing. In this chapter, we will examine four aspects which, in different respects, present a challenge to these assumptions: business crime, regulatory offences, "white collar" crime and corporate or organisational liability.

18.2   BUSINESS CRIME

In its various forms, this is an area which has been discussed fairly **18.2.1** extensively in sociology and criminology[1] but, apart from the difficult question of mechanisms for holding companies to account for their misdeeds, most texts on substantive criminal law have not particularly engaged with it. This is partly because some of the debate, especially in relation to "white collar" crime, concerns how to define "crime" for this purpose and whether it is appropriate

---

[1] See, for example, G Geis (ed), *White Collar Criminal: The Offender in Business and the Professions* (1968); M Clarke, *Business Crime: Its Nature and Control* (1990); D Nelken (ed), *White-Collar Crime* (1994); M Punch, *Dirty Business: Exploring Corporate Misconduct: Analysis and Cases* (1996).

or, indeed, necessary to go beyond the traditional boundaries. The thalidomide and Dalkon Shield scandals,[2] for example, attracted no criminal consequences, but nonetheless satisfy many of the criteria for "business crime" identified by criminologists, in that serious harm was caused to many people by corporations in the course of their businesses, to the end of increasing their profits.[3]

18.2.2   At various points, this book has engaged with the relative fluidity of Scots criminal law and the problems this presents in relation to the requirement that the law be certain, non-retrospective and knowable. Nonetheless, if pressed, we could probably fall back on the definition of the subject matter of criminal law provided in Gordon as behaviour "of which the state may take cognisance by prosecution in the criminal courts".[4] A book on substantive law has to draw a line between criminal activity and wrongdoing in a more general, moral sense. This enables us to sidestep some, though not all, of the highly significant debates concerning the appropriate contours of white collar crime.[5] Indeed, having canvassed many of the conflicting and overlapping definitions of the concept, Stuart Green concludes that:

> "The discipline of criminal law is defined by what is criminal. ... To replace
> the concept of white collar crime with the concept of deviant behavior is thus
> to blur a distinction that, at least in legal discourse, is foundational."[6]

At one level, then, the actual crimes committed in the course of business are not, and should not be, conceptualised differently from any other crime. Bernard Madoff, who pled guilty in the United States to a $65 billion fraud,[7] is, in an important sense, "a criminal" in the same way as Robert Fowler, who stole a bicycle.[8] Accordingly, it is the nature of the perpetrators, and the mechanisms for holding them to account which are of interest. However, to some extent, this constitutes a normative decision – that all "crime" *should* be treated the same. In fact, this is an area in which the distinction between real crime and regulatory crime – between *mala in se* and *mala prohibita*[9] – assumes particular importance.

---

[2] Discussed in section 3.3.4 above.

[3] H Croall, *Understanding White Collar Crime* (2001), pp 71–72.

[4] Gordon (2000), para 1.04.

[5] See, for example, E H Sutherland, *White Collar Crime* (1949) (1961 reprint), pp 29–55; also D Nelken, "White-collar and corporate crime" in M Maguire, R Morgan and R Reiner, *The Oxford Handbook of Criminology* (5th edn, 2012), pp 623–659.

[6] S P Green, "The concept of white collar crime in law and legal theory" (2004–05) 8 *Buff Crim LR* 1 at 7.

[7] See http://www.guardian.co.uk/business/bernard-madoff.

[8] *Fowler* v *O'Brien* 1994 SCCR 112, discussed at section 12.5.3 above.

[9] See section 17.3.3 above.

18.3   REGULATORY OFFENCES

"Regulation" has been (loosely) defined as   18.3.1

> "obligations imposed by public law designed to induce individuals and
> firms to outcomes which they would not voluntarily reach. Regulation is
> largely enforced by public officials and compliance is aided by the threat or
> imposition of some sanction. As such, regulation covers a vast array of state
> controls over industrial and commercial activities".[10]

Regulatory offences are often characterised as the paradigm
examples of *mala prohibita* – "victimless, serving the purposes of
social coordination or the promotion of a collective welfare".[11] Yet
their relative seriousness shifts as societal mores change. Issues which
start out as wrong only because a statute declares them so to be may
subsequently assume moral content – and vice versa. Causing death
by driving in various ways is an example: there was a time when it
was not regarded as excessively blameworthy, but this is no longer
the case.[12] Conversely, the prevention of profiteering on luxury goods
may be a social and moral imperative in wartime;[13] in peacetime,
making as much money as possible on a sale seems rather to be a basic
principle of capitalism. Regulation is not always connected to the
criminal law[14] but there is a particular crossover in relation to health
and safety in terms of the Health and Safety at Work etc Act 1974.
The Health and Safety Executive (HSE), which enforces the Act, is
empowered, in England and Wales, to bring its own prosecutions. In
Scotland, the decision is still one for the COPFS.[15] In May 2013, the
Crown Office officially launched a new Health and Safety Division
recognising the need for procurators fiscal involved in prosecuting
such cases to be specialists. In this book, we are concerned only with
regulation where the relevant sanction involves criminal liability.
While we adhere to the view that "a crime is a crime is a crime",
regulation, on which there is a vast literature in its own right,[16] brings
us up against the issue of differential *enforcement*.

---

[10] A Ogus, "Regulation revisited" (2009) *Public Law* 332 at 333.

[11] L Farmer, "Tony Martin and the nightbreakers: criminal law, victims and the
power to punish" in S Armstrong and L McAra, *Perspectives on Punishment: The
Contours of Control* (2006) 49 at p 60.

[12] See M Hirst, "Causing death by driving and other offences: a question of
balance" [2008] *Crim LR* 339 at 339.

[13] See *Duguid* v *Fraser* 1942 JC 1, discussed in section 17.3.6 above.

[14] For example, the regulatory regime set up to prevent market abuse under the
Financial Services and Markets Act 2000, Pt VIII, while bearing some of the
hallmarks of criminal offences, is not enforceable through the criminal courts.

[15] HSE, *Enforcement Policy Statement* (2009), at 7, para 38.

[16] For example, J Rowan-Robinson, P Watchman and C Barker, *Crime and
Regulation: A Study of the Enforcement of Regulatory Codes* (1990); K Hawkins
and J M Thomas (eds), *Enforcing Regulation* (1984); I Ayres and J Braithwaite,

18.3.2   In an assessment of 56 UK business regulators and 468 local authorities, Richard Macrory found that although regulators had a range of sanctions at their disposal, including advice, warning letters, and various types of statutory notices, breaches of the regulations often met with a criminal law response.[17] He noted that the criminal sanction could be a disproportionate response, particularly where there had not been deliberate non-compliance.[18] Furthermore, the frequency with which criminal law sanctions were imposed had led to many businesses viewing fines as just a cost of doing business, rather than as a stigmatic event which ought to be avoided. The Macrory Report recommended greater use of administrative penalties.[19]

18.3.3   It is a given of the academic commentary on regulation that two approaches – a compliance strategy and a deterrence strategy – co-exist.[20] The former involves persuading and encouraging businesses to do what is required of them – a "carrot" approach. The latter prosecutes and punishes for failure to comply – the "stick". In practice, these approaches are not dichotomised in this way and, indeed, the regulatee may be an important player in determining what form the regulation should take. This has been characterised as a shift from "command-and-control" regulation to "co-regulation".[21] Ian Ayres and John Braithwaite have characterised regulation as almost akin to a game, with continuous interaction between the various players; the goal, from the regulators' point of view, being to select those strategies which are most likely to ensure compliance, though within a cost–benefit framework.[22]

18.3.4   Despite this, and notwithstanding the findings of the Macrory Committee, it is widely accepted that prosecution generally remains a last resort.[23] There is some empirical evidence to suggest that, even where regulatory offences have no *mens rea* element, only the most flagrant rule-breakers will be prosecuted.[24] This is particularly

---

Responsive Regulation: Transcending the Deregulation Debate (1992); Ogus (2009); R Baldwin, M Cave and M Lodge, *Understanding Regulation: Theory, Strategy, and Practice* (2nd edn, 2012).

[17] R B Macrory, *Regulatory Justice: Making Sanctions Effective* (Macrory Report, 2006), para 1.14.

[18] *Ibid.*

[19] *Ibid* from para 3.17.

[20] Rowan-Robinson *et al* (1990) pp 8–9.

[21] Ogus (2009) p 336. See also T Eccles and J Pointing, "Smart regulation, shifting architectures and changes in governance" (2013) 5 *Int J of Law in the Built Environment* 71, especially at 75.

[22] Ayres and Braithwaite (1992). See also Ogus (2009) at pp 338–339.

[23] Rowan-Robinson *et al* (1990) at p 8.

[24] See D Nelken, "Criminal law and criminal justice: some notes on their irrelation" in I H Dennis (ed), *Criminal Law and Justice: Essays from the W G Hart Workshop 1986* (1987) 139 at pp 149–150.

important in England and Wales, where the HSE may itself decide to prosecute. In Scotland, that decision rests with the COPFS, though the HSE (which is one of around 50 "specialist reporting agencies") still has some power to recommend cases for prosecution. The fact that in Scotland overall control is vested in the body which makes decisions in relation to other forms of crime should help to ensure uniformity.

Regulation is, at base, concerned with ensuring compliance. **18.3.5** A regulatory regime would be regarded as successful if those it regulated consistently met the standards (whether of safety, honesty or accountability) which it required. It is important, therefore, to consider carefully the role of the criminal sanction within this. Where prosecution is deemed appropriate, the criminal courts, with their role to uphold the public interest, should signal the societal disapproval of the conduct which is inherent in the Crown's decision to bring criminal proceedings. The importance of recognising the seriousness of a criminal law intervention is apparent in the (English) Law Commission's Consultation Paper on *Criminal Liability in Regulatory Contexts*[25] which takes up the "unfinished business"[26] of the Macrory Report. It takes as one of its starting points that

> "few are likely to disagree with the proposition that, in general terms, the criminal law can and should be used for the most serious cases of non-compliance with the law. The question is whether it is possible to develop some guidelines about the principles to be followed when considering the creation of criminal offences to support the regulation of the activities of individuals and businesses".[27]

In Scotland, the appeal court has also recognised the need to signal **18.3.6** the gravity of the criminal sanction. In *HM Advocate* v *Doonin Plant Ltd*,[28] the accused company was charged with a breach of s 33(1)(c) of the Environmental Protection Act 1990. It had been disposing of waste products into a landfill site without a licence to do so and without having taken the necessary precautions (here, the use of an impermeable liner to avoid leakage) to prevent pollution. In upholding the Crown's appeal that the sentence (an £8,000 fine) was unduly lenient, the judgment stated:

> "it is a matter of considerable public concern that companies may fail to comply with their environmental responsibilities if it costs them less to pay the penalty for breaking the law than it would to install proper safeguards, or to desist from the conduct in question. Conduct of the sort revealed in the

---

[25] No 195 (2010).
[26] *Ibid*, para 1.3.
[27] *Ibid*, para 1.5.
[28] 2011 JC 81.

circumstances of this case, in our judgment, has to be regarded as serious having regard to the potential of serious harm that arises therefrom. A fine in a case such as the present, in our judgment, requires to be large enough to bring the message home to those who manage and are shareholders in companies like the present that the statutory provisions designed to protect our environment must be taken seriously by them".[29]

A fine of £90,000 was substituted.[30]

18.3.7　Overall, the use of the criminal law may be regarded, within regulation, as a last resort but it is important that its significance in its own right, as the embodiment of state censure of the proscribed activity, should also be recognised.

18.4 "WHITE COLLAR" CRIME

18.4.1　This aspect of crime was popularised by the sociologist Edwin H Sutherland, and his definition has been quoted extensively: "[w]hite collar crime may be defined approximately as a crime committed by a person of respectability and high social status in the course of his occupation".[31] Sutherland explains in a footnote that "[t]he term 'white collar' is used here to refer principally to the business managers and executives".[32] He also described "white collar" criminals as "persons of the upper socio–economic class".[33] A main issue identified by Sutherland was that such people offended more frequently than had previously been supposed and, in an apparent contradiction of the claim that "justice is blind", when they did so, they were treated differently – better or more leniently – by the criminal justice system than working class offenders.

18.4.2　Sutherland's definition of "white collar" criminality is problematic because it seeks to encompass both the perpetrators and the crimes which they commit.[34] Crime committed "in the course of [a person's] occupation" covers an extreme spectrum, from the employee who sends the odd personal letter out in an envelope belonging to her employer, writing on it at home with a pen taken from the employer's

[29] 2011 JC 81 at 88–89, para [22], per Lord Clarke.
[30] For a further example of the discrepancy between fines imposed at first instance and those imposed by the appeal court, see *HM Advocate* v *Munro & Sons (Highland) Ltd* 2009 SLT 233, in which the fine was increased from £3,750 to £30,000.
[31] Sutherland (1949) at p 9.
[32] *Ibid* at p 9, n 7.
[33] *Ibid* at p 9. Crime committed by an individual from a lower social class is often referred to as "blue collar" crime.
[34] For a full discussion of the definitional problems, see Nelken (2012). For an attempt to reconcile these strands, see Green (2004–05) at pp 8–10.

stationery cupboard, to Nick Leeson's actions in apparently single-handedly bringing down Barings Bank.[35] These examples involve crimes committed against the employer. They are often referred to as "occupational crime" but Sutherland's definition can apply equally – indeed was intended to apply – to businesses which are conducted illegally, whether by defrauding shareholders or by passing off counterfeit goods.[36]

If it is accepted that all of these behaviours – and many between – can be categorised as "white collar" crime, should we categorise those who perpetrate all such crimes as "white collar criminals"? This raises a difficulty because, if the criterion is, simply, committing a crime in the course of one's occupation, many who are patently not "of high social standing" will be implicated. Indeed, this distinction itself, and the apparent differential enforcement of the criminal law which Sutherland identified, is unacceptable. As Green notes: "Deeply rooted equal protection-type norms forbid us from distinguishing among offenders on the basis of wealth, occupation, race, gender, ethnicity, or other personal characteristics."[37] This does not necessarily mean that such discriminatory practices do not happen[38] but, if there is evidence that Sutherland's thesis on this point is correct, the practice should not be allowed to continue. Certainly, some high-profile, "white collar" criminals – Bernard Madoff,[39] key Enron personnel,[40] Nick Leeson[41] and Ernest

18.4.3

---

[35] Leeson was a broker who engaged in speculative trading on Singapore's International Monetary Exchange, leading to such huge losses (£208 million) that Barings Bank, the oldest investment bank in the UK, collapsed. He pled guilty to fraud and was sentenced to 6½ years' imprisonment. See also R Sarker, "Daiwa and Barings: a blueprint for disaster" (1996) 17 *Company Lawyer* 86.

[36] H Croall, "Who is the white collar criminal?" (1989) 29 *Br J of Criminology* 157.

[37] Green (2004–05), at 8.

[38] See, for example, D Cook, *Rich Law Poor Law: Differential Responses to Tax and Supplementary Benefit Fraud* (1989) which argues that tax fraud is treated more leniently than benefit fraud.

[39] Bernard Madoff defrauded thousands of investors of $65 billion. He did this by a so-called "Ponzi scheme", which means that those who gave him money to invest in the stock exchange were paid from funds given to him by subsequent investors, rather than from any actual investments. In June 2009, he received the maximum sentence of 150 years' imprisonment.

[40] Key personnel, including its former Chairman (Kenneth Lay) and Chief Executive Officer (Jeffrey Skilling), were charged with a large number of offences, including fraud, money laundering and insider dealing following the collapse of Enron, an energy company based in America. Skilling was sentenced to more than 24 years in prison. Lay faced up to 45 years in prison, but died prior to being sentenced.

[41] See n 35 above.

Saunders of the Guinness corporation[42] – do appear to have had substantial penalties imposed.[43]

18.4.4   In the context of traditional criminal law then, "white collar" crime, while a fixture of the legal and, indeed, societal, landscape, is not a particularly illuminating concept. It is vague and over-inclusive[44] and it is unclear whether certain categories of offender *are* treated more leniently. If they are, this indicates a failure on the part of the criminal justice system to live up to its own norms of equality. Sutherland's basic principle – that criminal behaviour is not the preserve of the poor or working classes – was a sound one, but in its elaboration it raises more questions than it resolves. Despite this, the notion of white collar criminals as a class to whom the criminal law is applied differently is an enduring one. We turn our attention now to a further category of particular offenders: corporations.

18.5   CORPORATE CRIMINAL LIABILITY

18.5.1   A number of high-profile disasters has brought to the fore the issue of the ability of the state to hold corporations to account for apparently criminal acts. In Scotland, a notable example is the explosion on the Piper Alpha offshore oil installation in 1988 in which 167 people died. The operating company, Occidental Petroleum, was never prosecuted, despite clear failings on its part.[45] More recently, the fatal gas explosion in Larkhall in 1999, caused by failures on the part of the gas company, Transco plc, provided an impetus for the issue to be addressed by the Scottish Government. Some of the legal points arising from this seminal case will be considered further, below.[46]

18.5.2   The central issue is the liability of a company for common law crimes or indeed any crime which is not of strict liability. Alan Norrie has contended that the criminal law's traditional focus was on property crimes and crimes involving inter-personal violence

---

[42] Saunders, then Chief Executive of Guinness plc, was convicted in 1990 of false accounting and theft arising from the company's takeover of United Distillers plc. He was sentenced to 5 years' imprisonment.

[43] It is, however, noteworthy that both Nick Leeson and Ernest Saunders served shorter prison sentences than those initially imposed. Leeson was released from prison in 1999, having served 4½ years, following a diagnosis of colon cancer. Saunders was released in 1991 after spending only 10 months in prison. He claimed to have Alzheimer's disease, but then made a remarkable recovery. At the time of writing, both men are still alive.

[44] Green (2004–05) p 18 indicates that, in at least one of the contexts in which it has been used in the United States, it could encompass the commission of incitement to murder "which could [not] even remotely be considered a white collar crime".

[45] The Hon Lord Cullen, *The Public Inquiry into the Piper Alpha Disaster, Volumes 1 and 2* (Cm 1310, 1990).

[46] See from section 18.5.7 below.

in order to "maintain the illusion that socially dangerous and unacceptable activity was predominantly the province of the lower orders".[47] He continued:

> "One result of this is that corporate criminality is usually seen either as not criminal at all, or as a lesser form of criminality properly regulated by a regime of minor offences on the edge of the criminal law proper. ... it is only in recent times and after a spate of major disasters, involving large-scale death and clear evidence of corporate wrongdoing, that the criminal law has been forced to consider how it should deal with this phenomenon – one for which, functionally, it was not primarily intended."[48]

The spate of disasters to which he refers includes the King's Cross underground railway fire and the Zeebrugge/*Herald of Free Enterprise* ferry disaster, both in 1987. Scottish examples now include the Transco case,[49] the ICL Plastics case (commonly referred to as "Stockline") in 2004,[50] and the 1996 e-coli food poisoning case in Wishaw, Lanarkshire, which was traced back to John Barr's butcher's shop.[51]

As has been discussed earlier,[52] the criminal law is largely **18.5.3** predicated on a liberal concept of responsibility which seeks to maximise individual freedom while also holding individuals to account on the basis of their personal blameworthiness. One of the purposes of *mens rea* is to attach this culpability. Clearly, individual human beings are capable of formulating the states of mind which constitute *mens rea* for various offences. Perhaps equally clearly, companies, which are fictional persons (though capable of holding legal rights) cannot "think" in the manner envisaged by the criminal law.[53] As Norrie has argued:

> "The standard *mens rea* doctrine of the criminal law is a singularly inappropriate form with which to organise the control of the corporation. Yet corporations are responsible amongst other things for acts of

---

[47] A Norrie, *Crime, Reason and History: A Critical Introduction to Criminal Law* (2001), p 82.

[48] *Ibid.*

[49] This is discussed further from section 18.5.6 below.

[50] Nine people were killed and 33 others injured following an explosion at this plastics factory in Glasgow. Two companies were each fined £200,000 for breaches of health and safety legislation. For further information on the circumstances leading to the explosion, see Universities of Strathclyde and Stirling, *The ICL/Stockline Disaster: An Independent Report on Working Conditions Prior to the Explosion* (2007) (available at http://www.hazards.org/icldisaster/icl_stockline_report.pdf).

[51] For a full discussion, see H Croall and J Ross, "Sentencing the corporate offender: legal and social issues" in C Tata and N Hutton (eds), *Sentencing and Society: International Perspectives* (2002), pp 523–547.

[52] At section 1.2 onwards.

[53] See Lord Osborne in *Transco plc v HM Advocate* 2004 JC 29 at 36, para 9.

violence that in their potential scope and impact far outweigh the effects of similar culpable acts performed by individuals. It is not unnatural in such a situation to wish to criminalise the malefactor, be it a natural or artificial person."[54]

18.5.4   Whether companies are capable of forming *mens rea* was first considered in Scots law in *Dean v John Menzies (Holdings) Ltd*[55] in 1981, but the case did little to clarify the position. The newsagent John Menzies was charged with the common law crime of "shameless indecency" for selling obscene articles (pornographic magazines). The appeal court held that a company could not be convicted of shameless indecency, since that crime required certain human characteristics.[56] The broader question – whether a company could commit *any* common law crime – was not fully answered. Lord Stott suggested, *obiter*:

> "there are certain crimes and offences which cannot be committed by a corporate body. Murder is such a crime, not only ... because a company cannot be imprisoned but because it is incapable of having that wicked intent or recklessness of mind necessary to constitute the crime of murder. Other examples which come to mind are reset and perjury".[57]

This approach has been criticised in Gordon's *Criminal Law* on the basis that there is no good reason why a company which has a policy of receiving stolen goods should not be convicted of reset, for example.[58] According to Lord Cameron:

> "The criminal law has long recognised that a corporate body may be guilty of breaches of statute and incur a penalty, and therefore be susceptible to prosecution as a person recognised in the eyes of the law. Further, the law has also recognised that an incorporation may be guilty of statutory offences the commission of which is the result of intended or deliberate action or inaction. ... the authorities cited by the Advocate-Depute illustrate the extent to which companies in Scotland can be and are rendered liable to criminal prosecution, even where commission of the offence libelled involves a conscious exercise of will or demonstration of intent. It would seem ... to follow that there should be no obstacle in principle to the same liability to prosecution where the offence is *malum in se* and not *malum prohibitum*."[59]

---

[54] Norrie (2001) at pp 104–105. Compare the judgment of Chief Judge Miles Lord in the litigation involving the Dalkon Shield intrauterine contraceptive, quoted in section 3.3.5 above.

[55] 1981 JC 23.

[56] As previously discussed, "shameless indecency" is no longer a recognised *nomen juris* in Scots law – see from section 11.21 above.

[57] *Dean v John Menzies (Holdings) Ltd* 1981 JC 23 at 35.

[58] Gordon (2000), para 8.107.

[59] *Dean v John Menzies (Holdings) Ltd* 1981 JC 23 at 28. For the distinction between crimes which are "*mala in se*" as opposed to "*mala prohibita*", see sections 5.4.6 and 17.3.3 above.

He continued:

> "If therefore a limited company has the capacity to form an intention, to decide on a course of action, to act in accordance with that deliberate intent … it is difficult to see on what general principle it should not be susceptible to prosecution where that action offends against the common law."[60]

The question arose again in the case of *Purcell Meats (Scotland) Ltd* **18.5.5** v *McLeod*[61] in 1986, in which the accused company was charged with attempted fraud. The company took a plea to the relevancy of the complaint, arguing that a limited company could not be charged with an offence at common law, since it was incapable of forming the necessary *mens rea*. The appeal court upheld the relevancy of the charge. Lord Justice-Clerk Ross cited the case of *Tesco Supermarkets Ltd* v *Nattrass*,[62] in which Lord Reid explained that:

> "A living person has a mind which can have knowledge or intention or be negligent and he has hands to carry out his intentions. A corporation has none of these: it must act through living persons, though not always one or the same person. Then the person who acts is not speaking or acting for the company. He is acting as the company and his mind which directs his acts is the mind of the company. There is no question of the company being vicariously liable. He is not acting as a servant, representative, agent or delegate. He is an embodiment of the company or, one could say, he hears and speaks through the persona of the company, … and his mind is the mind of the company. If it is a guilty mind then that guilt is the guilt of the company."[63]

Until 2004, then, the position seemed to be that Scots law recognised **18.5.6** that corporations could be – indeed should be – criminally liable, even for crimes of *mens rea* but was not particularly clear as to how the attribution of that liability should be achieved. Following Lord Ross's endorsement in *Purcell Meats*[64] of the "controlling mind" doctrine from *Tesco Supermarkets Ltd* v *Nattrass*,[65] it appeared likely that the Scottish courts would apply this, but the matter was not tested until *Transco plc* v *HM Advocate*.[66] It is interesting that one of the first questions Lord Osborne raised in that case was whether there existed in Scots law rules of attribution by which liability for the *mens rea*, and indeed the *actus reus,* of a common law crime could be brought home to a corporation.[67]

---

[60] 1981 JC 23 at 28–29.
[61] 1987 SLT 528.
[62] [1972] AC 153.
[63] *Ibid* at 170.
[64] 1987 SLT 528.
[65] [1972] AC 153.
[66] 2004 JC 29.
[67] *Ibid* at 38.

18.5.7   In the *Transco*[68] case the appellants were a company licensed to supply gas to houses. They were charged with culpable homicide following an explosion in which a family of four was killed.[69] The indictment narrated that the company had shown a "complete and utter disregard for the safety of the public". Transco lodged a plea to the competency of the culpable homicide charge. The plea to the competency was on the ground that a corporation was not able to carry out the *actus reus* or form the *mens rea* required for the crime. It was held to be competent to charge a company with culpable homicide. However, the mechanism by which the Crown had sought to establish *mens rea* on the part of the company, which was based on the principle of aggregation, was not accepted by the appeal court. Lord Osborne explained how the principle is intended to work:

> "the faults of a number of different individuals, none of whose faults would individually have amounted to the mental element of culpable homicide, are to be aggregated, so that, in their totality, they might have amounted to that element".[70]

18.5.8 The Crown's case was that the recklessness required as the *mens rea* for involuntary lawful act culpable homicide could be established through the actions and knowledge of certain committees and posts within the company. The court rejected this approach. At one level, aggregation offends against the basic principles of individual autonomy and responsibility on which the criminal law is based. If a number of individuals each do something insufficiently serious to constitute a criminal offence in its own right, then, in the absence of art and part liability, it seems unfair to add these together to hold another, completely separate "person", or entity – the corporation – liable for these acts. On the other hand, as Peter Glazebrook graphically illustrates,[71] corporations cannot actually *do* anything. They only act, as such, through human agents. From that perspective, aggregation seems less unfair.

18.5.9   The Scottish Executive's Expert Group on Corporate Homicide, set up in the aftermath of *Transco*,[72] took the view that aggregation

---

[68] 2004 JC 29.

[69] The indictment libelled, as an alternative charge, a breach of the Health and Safety at Work etc Act 1974, ss 3 and 33.

[70] 2004 JC 29 at 45, para 24. Corporate liability on the basis of aggregation had been attempted unsuccessfully in England in the prosecution of P&O Ferries for deaths arising from the sinking of the *Herald of Free Enterprise* in Zeebrugge Harbour in 1987. See *R v HM Coroner for East Kent, Ex p Spooner* (1989) 88 Cr App R 10.

[71] P R Glazebrook, "A better way of convicting businesses of avoidable deaths and injuries?" (2002) 61 *CLJ* 405 at 406–409.

[72] 2004 JC 29.

was not appropriate in relation to the *mens rea* element because of the difficulty of identifying those whose mental attitudes should be aggregated.[73] On the other hand, its view was that "[t]he *acts* of individuals should be capable of aggregation in order to establish the physical elements of the offence".[74] But companies can no more act than they can think without human intervention. If aggregation is appropriate in one context, it is not obvious why it should not also be in the other.

Returning to the *Transco*[75] judgment itself, while the court had little difficulty in accepting that corporations, even though they constitute legal fictions, *could* be criminally liable for culpable homicide, it still sought to attribute that liability through the medium of a human being. It took as the law of Scotland the "controlling mind" doctrine which had been expounded in English law in the leading case of *Tesco Supermarkets Ltd* v *Nattrass*.[76] As we have seen,[77] this requires the identification of an individual, sufficiently highly placed in the company, whose mental attitude can be taken as that of the company as a whole. If this person has the requisite *mens rea* in relation to the company's business, then that mental attitude can be imputed to the company itself. In *Transco,* this is referred to as the identification principle because the company is "identified" with one of its employees. As Jenifer Ross has pointed out, the judgments in the *Tesco* case itself, while in agreement that this was the governing principle, each pointed to a slightly different set of persons in which the "controlling mind" might be found.[78] Lord Reid located it in the board of directors and its delegates, the managing director and perhaps other superior officers.[79] Viscount Dilhorne looked instead, and more vaguely, for a person who is "in actual control of the operations of the company ... [and] who is not responsible to another person in the company for the manner in which he discharges his duties in the sense of being under his orders".[80] The identity of such persons will vary from company to company. Finally, Lord Diplock considered it necessary to identify

18.5.10

---

[73] Scottish Executive, *Corporate Homicide: Expert Group Report* (2005) at para 5.2.

[74] *Ibid* at para 6.1 (emphasis added). See J Chalmers, "Just an expert group that can't say no: reforming corporate homicide law" (2006) 10 *Edin LR* 290 for a critique of this Report.

[75] 2004 JC 29.

[76] [1972] AC 153.

[77] Section 18.5.5 above.

[78] J Ross, "Corporate criminal liability: one form or many forms?" (1999) *JR* 49 at 50.

[79] *Tesco Supermarkets Ltd* v *Nattrass* [1972] AC 153 at 171.

[80] *Ibid* at 187.

"those natural persons who by the memorandum and articles of association or as a result of action taken by the directors, or by the company in general meeting pursuant to the articles, are entrusted with the exercise of the powers of the company".[81] If the leading case is characterised by imprecision on this point, it is perhaps unsurprising that the difficulties of identifying the – or even *a* – controlling mind in large corporations like Transco have sometimes proved insurmountable.

18.5.11   The identification principle, then, while nominally a mechanism for attributing criminal liability to corporations, is flawed by its reliance on human agency and by the uncertainty as to who, within any given corporation, could qualify as the controlling mind. It discriminates against small companies in which one person performs most of the business's functions, because that individual *can* clearly be identified with the corporation for the purposes of the imputation of *mens rea*.[82] Large organisations might decide to structure their business so that decision-making authority is diffuse, making the operation of the identification principle more or less impossible.[83]

18.5.12   It was in recognition of the shortcomings of the existing liability principles, revealed by the *Transco* case,[84] that the then Scottish Executive set up the Expert Group on Corporate Homicide. James Chalmers has noted that, "[t]he most striking feature of the [Group's] *Report* [was its] disinclination to rule out any possible law reform proposal which it considered".[85] Certainly, it did not make clear recommendations, preferring instead to identify a possible "way forward".[86] Nonetheless, it is noteworthy that many of the points which it did make, such as aggregation of negligent acts in establishing the *actus reus*[87] and the inappropriateness of the concept of a "duty of care" in Scots criminal law,[88] were completely disregarded in the corporate homicide legislation which was subsequently passed by the United Kingdom Parliament: the Corporate Manslaughter and Corporate Homicide Act 2007.

18.5.13   In the end, it seems to have been accepted[89] that the issue was most appropriately characterised as a matter of health and safety

---

[81] [1972] AC 153 at 200.
[82] See R Craig, "Thou shall do no murder: a discussion paper on the Corporate Manslaughter and Corporate Homicide Act 2007" (2009) 30 *Company Lawyer* 17 at 18, which draws out this disparity between large and small companies, specifically in cases where manslaughter has been charged.
[83] Ross (1999) at 52.
[84] 2004 JC 29.
[85] Chalmers (2006) at 292.
[86] Scottish Executive (2005), from para 6.
[87] *Ibid*, para 6.2.
[88] *Ibid*, para 8.2.
[89] See A Anwar, "Killing in company" (2007) 52 *JLSS* 16.

law, an area which is reserved to the United Kingdom Parliament.[90] Accordingly, the Scottish Government had no authority to legislate. Prior to the Act, however, the issue was a matter for the Scottish common law of culpable homicide. In relation to a change to *homicide* law, the Scottish Government could have acted unilaterally. Indeed, the Health and Safety Executive website states that the Act is, quite specifically *"not* part of health and safety law".[91] Aisha Anwar notes that with the passage of the Act, "practitioners and organisations in Scotland breathed a sigh of relief – uniformity in health and safety law across the UK was seen by many as being an important overriding concern".[92] This is an important point, but it remains to be seen whether the application to Scotland of a homicide offence drafted primarily with English law in mind will work.

In Scotland (but not elsewhere in the UK) this crime is known **18.5.14** as corporate homicide.[93] The Act came into force on 6 April 2008. According to the official *Homicide in Scotland* statistics,[94] as yet, only four cases of (possible) corporate homicide have even been reported by the police in Scotland: one in 2008–09,[95] two in 2010–11 and one in 2012–13.[96] Research undertaken by the law firm Pinsent Masons indicates that the Crown Prosecution Service in England and Wales has taken on many more – 141 cases have been opened since 2009 – though with only three convictions to date.[97] It is interesting to compare these with the projected numbers. In 2006, Chalmers noted that only five cases per year were anticipated for England and Wales, and probably fewer in Scotland.[98]

The Act specifically abolishes the English common law crime **18.5.15** of gross negligence manslaughter as this applies to corporations[99] but there is no corresponding provision in relation to culpable

[90] Scotland Act 1998, Sch 5, Pt 2, para H2.
[91] http://www.hse.gov.uk/corpmanslaughter/about.htm (emphasis added).
[92] Anwar (2007) at 16.
[93] Corporate Manslaughter and Corporate Homicide Act 2007, s 1(5)(b).
[94] Available at http://www.scotland.gov.uk/Topics/Statistics/Browse/Crime-Justice/ PubHomicide for each year from 1997 to 2012–13.
[95] Scottish Government, *Statistical Release Crime and Justice Series: Homicide in Scotland, 2008–09* (2010), p 8, n 2.
[96] Scottish Government, *Statistical Release Crime and Justice Series: Homicide in Scotland, 2010–11* (2011), p 9, para 1.2 and Scottish Government, *Statistical Bulletin Crime and Justice Series: Homicide in Scotland, 2012–13* (2013), p 39, para 4.3.
[97] "New corporate manslaughter cases opened by CPS up 40% in 2012" (available at: http://www.pinsentmasons.com/en/media/press-releases/2013/new-corporate-manslaughter-cases-opened-by-cps-up-40-in-20121/).
[98] Chalmers (2006) at 296–297.
[99] Corporate Manslaughter and Corporate Homicide Act 2007, s 20.

homicide.[100] Thus it appears that the Scottish Government has hedged its bets so that the Crown could, if it wished, still bring a prosecution for culpable homicide, even with all its attendant difficulties. As its name suggests, the crime of "corporate homicide" only applies to situations where a company's activities have proved fatal. Where it is alleged that a company committed any other crime, the courts will apply the identification principle. What of the terms of the offence itself? It arises where "the way in which [the organisation's][101] activities are managed or organised (a) causes a person's death and (b) amounts to a gross breach of a relevant duty of care owed by the organisation to the deceased", but only if "the way in which its activities are managed or organised by its senior management is a substantial element of [that] breach".[102] Peter Ferguson has summarised the new offence as a "brief statement [which] conceals a considerable degree of complexity".[103] It is necessary, therefore, to unpack its terms to some extent. It is clear from the foregoing parts of this chapter that there are, currently, particular difficulties in rendering corporations criminally liable at all, let alone for homicide offences. This has led Ross to emphasise the need for a way of criminalising companies which corresponds appropriately to the way in which they operate.[104]

18.5.16   Some commentators have been attracted to the provisions in the Australian Criminal Code Act 1995[105] which draw the "corporate culture" into the equation. This means that proof that the company had written policies and procedures geared to achieve compliance with the law's requirements is insufficient to avoid criminal liability. It must also establish that its culture encouraged compliance with all relevant provisions.[106] Aurora Voiculescu has noted that this "represents a shift away from an individualist perspective as well as from a focus on the outcomes of corporate decision-making, towards the decision-making processes themselves".[107] Does the 2007 Act offer anything comparable?

---

[100] See P W Ferguson, "Corporate Manslaughter and Corporate Homicide Act 2007" (2007) SLT 251 at 259.

[101] The Act applies to other organisations also, including partnerships (discussed in more detail in section 18.6.4 below) and police forces (s 1(2)).

[102] Section 1(1)(a) and (b) and (3).

[103] Ferguson (2007) at 252.

[104] Ross (1999) at 64–65.

[105] Australian Criminal Code Act 1995, division 12.3(2)(c) and (d), (4) and (6).

[106] Scottish Executive (2005) at para 10.7.

[107] A Voiculescu, "Changing paradigms of corporate criminal responsibility: lessons for corporate social responsibility" in D McBarnet, A Voiculescu and T Campbell (eds), *The New Corporate Accountability: Corporate Social Responsibility and the Law* (2007) 399 at p 425.

Section 1, which creates the offence, makes slight inroads on   **18.5.17**
the individualisation inherent in the controlling mind doctrine
by using the broader concept of "senior management". However,
the Australian provisions impose criminal liability for matters
which have been authorised or permitted by the body corporate's
board of directors[108] or by "a high managerial agent of the body
corporate".[109] The sections on corporate culture are additional to
this. The 2007 Act offers no alternative to "senior management".
This may well leave the door open for large corporations to delegate
decision-making downwards, so that no one sufficiently senior can
be held liable.[110] Admittedly, s 8(3)(a) of the Act allows the jury, in
determining whether a gross breach of a relevant duty of care has
taken place, to

> "consider the extent to which the evidence shows that there were attitudes,
> policies, systems or accepted practices within the organisation that were
> likely to have encouraged any such failure as is mentioned in subsection (2),
> or to have produced tolerance of it".

This may be indicative of some attempt to introduce cultural elements
into the process.

The 2007 Act does address the *mens rea* issue in that the   **18.5.18**
need for an actual mental attitude – the problem with which the
identification principle is concerned – seems to be obviated. Section
1(4)(b) provides that "a breach of a duty of care by an organisation
is a 'gross' breach if the conduct alleged to amount to a breach of
that duty falls far below what can reasonably be expected of the
organisation in the circumstances". If this is judged objectively –
and Ferguson considers that it will be[111] – then it does not matter
what those involved in running the company thought or did: only
whether reasonable people would take the view that the company's
conduct fell far below the requisite standard. Glazebrook has
commented on earlier proposals for a corporate homicide offence
put forward by the English Law Commission.[112] Similarly to
the 2007 Act, these adopted the notion of conduct falling far
below what can reasonably be expected of the corporation in the
circumstances.[113] He concluded that requiring jurors to make such
a determination is problematic:

---

[108] Australian Criminal Code Act 1995, division 12.3(2)(a).
[109] *Ibid*, division 12.3(2)(b).
[110] See Ross (1999) at 52; Ferguson (2007) at 253.
[111] *Ibid* at 252.
[112] Law Commission *Legislating the Criminal Code: Involuntary Manslaughter* (Law Com No 237) (1996).
[113] *Ibid*, draft Involuntary Homicide Bill, cl 4(1)(b).

"[A]s everyone knows, commercial companies, let alone companies generally, do not form a homogeneous category. They range from the proverbial 'one-man' company to the multinational conglomerate. So comparisons may often not be easy to make, and in cases where the corporation is ... a monopoly undertaking, there may be no other corporation with whose management structures, internal organisation and working practices comparison can at all readily be made. How, then, in such a case are jurors to decide whether there was a gross management failure – i.e., whether the 'managers' had, individually or collectively, fallen far short of what could reasonably be expected of them in the circumstances? And of what value, other than an emotive one, would their decision, one way or the other, be?"[114]

Section 8 of the Act does provide some additional guidance to the jury in this respect but the determination which it has to make is still likely to require at least some of its members to enter uncharted waters. Chalmers takes the view that jurors probably can make this sort of determination about an issue like driving, with which they may well be familiar, but not about the practices of a multi-national corporation.[115]

18.5.19   Finally, it is worth noting that the fact that the offence is constituted by a gross breach of a *duty of care* introduces into Scots criminal law a doctrine which has previously belonged exclusively to the civil law:

"The [Expert] Group [felt] strongly that, as far as Scotland [was] concerned there [were] no particular advantages to importing the concept of 'duty of care' into a criminal offence of corporate homicide. [It] also [had] some general concerns about adopting wholly civil concepts into criminal law, which could have unintended consequences."[116]

Unfortunately, it did not specify what these concerns might be. In fact, the Act defines exactly what is meant by the term in this context[117] and this may obviate any need to refer to the common law of delict, thus diminishing the possibility of confusion.

18.6   CRITIQUE OF THE LAW ON CORPORATE LIABILITY AND PROPOSALS FOR REFORM

18.6.1   Companies did not exist as legal entities when the principles of criminal law, and particularly those of liability for homicide, were established.[118] It is therefore unsurprising that those principles did not fit particularly well with the activities of such organisations. It is more surprising that it has taken so long for a bespoke offence

---

[114] Glazebrook (2002) at 413 (footnote omitted).
[115] Chalmers (2006) at 294.
[116] Scottish Executive (2005) at para 8.2.
[117] Corporate Manslaughter and Corporate Homicide Act 2007, s 2.
[118] A point made in R v P&O European Ferries (Dover) Ltd (1991) 93 Cr App R 72 per Turner J at 73.

to be created to deal at least with the activities of corporations which have fatal consequences. In other areas, particularly where the common law applies, and in statutory offences with a mental element, the use of the identification principle will continue to allow large corporations to escape liability altogether.

As we have seen, the criminal law is not devoid of techniques which may assist in holding organisations to account. Both strict liability[119] and vicarious liability[120] allow for conviction without the need to prove that the company itself had *mens rea*. The limited circumstances in which these mechanisms apply, however, mean that effective and generalised principles are all the more necessary. **18.6.2**

The activities of companies continue to cause death yet, even with the advent of the 2007 Act, this is still most commonly prosecuted in terms of a breach of the Health and Safety at Work etc Act 1974.[121] It is not clear whether the failure to resort to the 2007 Act stems from a lack of familiarity with its terms (by comparison with the 1974 Act) or whether the level of wrongdoing is not such that corporate homicide is an appropriate charge. This is, however, partly due to the paucity of cases – thus creating something of a vicious circle: the fewer cases, the less law and the fewer principles for future application under the doctrine of precedent. With its reliance on the breach of a duty of care, the offence created by the Act may not easily fit the Scottish context but more prosecutions would allow for greater discussion of these issues. The crime of corporate homicide ought to ensure that companies whose severely negligent or dangerous activities lead to death are appropriately labelled, stigmatised and punished. If the offence is rarely charged, however, this desirable outcome will not be attained. **18.6.3**

Of course, companies are not the only form of organisation through which business may be conducted. Scots criminal law has struggled, to some extent, with the criminalisation of death arising through the activities of partnerships. Following a fire at a nursing home in Uddingston in 2004, causing the deaths of 14 residents, it became clear that there was no power at common law to impose criminal liability on a partnership which had dissolved – even where it would have been criminally responsible for the deaths if it had continued in existence.[122] This potential loophole has now been closed by s 1 of the Partnerships (Prosecution) (Scotland) Act 2013. **18.6.4**

---

[119] See from section 17.2 above.
[120] See from section 17.8 above.
[121] See, for example, *Scottish Sea Farms Ltd* v *HM Advocate* 2012 SLT 299; *HM Advocate* v *Munro & Sons (Highland) Ltd* 2009 SLT 233 (see n 30 above); and *LH Access Technology Ltd* v *HM Advocate* 2009 SCL 622.
[122] *Balmer* v *HM Advocate* 2008 SLT 799.

In addition, individual partners may now be criminally liable in similar circumstances to those in which directors of companies hold personal liability.[123]

18.6.5   Neither set of provisions – those on corporate homicide nor those allowing the criminalisation of dissolved partnerships and individual partners – answers the criticism that, in the business context, it is easier to bring to account small commercial entities, where the lines of command are clear, than larger, possibly multi-national organisations with diffuse management structures. However, it is clear that the law recognises that where an activity causes death and fault is apparent, criminal liability may well be appropriate.

---

[123] Criminal Justice and Licensing (Scotland) Act 2010, s. 53.

PART VII

DEFENCES

At the close of the prosecution case, an accused person has the option of leading evidence in exculpation, but is under no obligation to do so. Of course, the standard defence is generally "it wasn't me", which is equivalent to a denial of both *mens rea* and *actus reus* – a claim that the wrong person is in the dock. Sometimes, however, the accused is saying something more, or something different. An acquittal is in order if the accused manages to satisfy the court as to the truth of a defence, or even to raise a reasonable doubt about the prosecution's case. In relation to common law offences, the only time the onus of proving a defence is placed on the accused is in establishing "mental disorder" or "diminished responsibility". Here, the standard of proof is, rightly, the lower standard of "on the balance of probabilities"; it must be shown to have been "more likely than not" that the accused was mentally disordered or of diminished responsibility at the time of the offence.[1]

One might ask why the criminal law provides defences at all; if the *actus reus* and *mens rea* are both present (and any causal links between the accused's conduct and the resultant harm established, where required),[2] why should that not be an end of the matter? Antony Duff draws a distinction between "responsibility" and "liability" in the criminal law, such that "responsibility" is synonymous with "answerability":

> "If I am accused of wrongdoing, either formally in a criminal court or informally in moral discussion, I ... have two ways of averting conviction or blame. I can deny responsibility, claiming that I do not have to answer (in this forum) for that alleged wrong. In the simplest case, I deny responsibility by denying agency: I was not the person who broke your window. But ... there are many other ways in which, and grounds on which, I can deny responsibility – even for my actions and their anticipated effects. Alternatively, however, I can

---

[1] As discussed at section 20.3.1 below.
[2] See from section 7.2 above.

491

admit responsibility, but avert liability by offering a defence: I must, I admit, answer for what I have done, but I offer an answer that, I claim, exculpates me."[3]

This is an important distinction, offering as it does a profound insight into the structure of the criminal law.

A distinction must also be made between justifications, excuses, and capacity defences.[4] Justificatory defences are regarded as an indication that, not only was the accused's behaviour not culpable, it was in fact, in certain respects, acceptable. Self-defence is generally regarded as falling into this category. Excuse defences, on the other hand, still carry connotations of culpability in relation to the act in question. The law adopts the position that the accused ought to be excused all or some liability because of certain personal characteristics (such as the claim that the accused was not fully conscious, due to factors outwith her control) or exceptional circumstances (such as having been coerced, or having broken the law out of necessity). Capacity defences mean that the accused lacked the ability to understand the crime sufficiently to be held liable. Defences of mental disorder and non-age are usually so categorised, although the way in which the former defence operates in Scots law means that it could equally be classed as an excuse.[5]

In fact, several defences operate to frustrate the establishment of the *actus reus* or *mens rea*; although *prima facie* it looks as if both are present, further analysis shows that one (or both) is missing. Self-defence, mental disorder and coercion have sometimes been classified as involving a lack of *mens rea*.[6] In relation to English law, William Wilson postulates the hypothetical example of Eve, who pushes Adam off a cliff, killing him. If Eve is acquitted on the basis that she acted in self-defence, Wilson asks whether this is because of a lack of *actus reus, mens rea* or "because she has a separate defence superimposed onto the elements of the offence?".[7] He concludes, somewhat surprisingly:

"Readers should lose no sleep attempting to resolve this problem. What matters is that Eve is entitled to an acquittal on the grounds of self-defence

---

[3] R A Duff, *Answering for Crime: Responsibility and Liability in the Criminal Law* (2007), p 22.
[4] For a comprehensive description of defences in Scots law, see J Chalmers and F Leverick, *Criminal Defences and Pleas in Bar of Trial* (2006).
[5] See *ibid*, para 7.03.
[6] This is the view taken of the defence of mental disorder by T H Jones and M G A Christie, *Criminal Law* (5th edn, 2012) at para 8.11; and by Gordon (2000) at para 7.01. In *HM Advocate* v *Raiker* 1989 SCCR 149, Lord McCluskey directed the jury that one who is coerced lacks *mens rea*.
[7] W Wilson, *Criminal Law: Doctrine and Theory* (1998), p 67. The author does not repeat this conclusion in subsequent editions.

and not whether we categorize Eve's reason for killing as going to *actus reus, mens rea* or defence."[8]

Other authors suggest that in English law self-defence negates the *actus reus*.[9] The view taken in Gordon's *Criminal Law* is that in Scots law self-defence involves a lack of *mens rea*.[10] Whether self-defence is treated as negating *mens rea* or *actus reus*, or as being something separate, depends on whether assault is defined as the infliction of *unlawful* force. If it is, then even the deliberate act of punching someone will not be an assault if done in self-defence. Treating such defences as negating *mens rea* is really only feasible if we equate this with dole – with a "legally reprehensible state of mind" where "the test of reprehensibility is essentially a moral one, so that the ascription of *mens rea* is a moral judgment".[11] In our view, this only serves to muddy the waters. If we interpret *mens rea* to mean the specific mental element required for a particular offence, it may be suggested that many defences lead to an acquittal *despite* the presence of *mens rea*. Both the person who injures someone else while acting in self-defence and one who does so while suffering from a mental disorder may well intend to cause personal injury. Likewise, someone who participates in a robbery or theft due to having been coerced by the other robbers or thieves can hardly be said to lack an intention to deprive the owners of their property. If we say that the mentally ill or coerced person does not "really" intend to injure, to steal, or whatever, we come close to expanding the approach taken in *Drury*,[12] that is, we are interpreting "intent to cause personal injury", "intent to steal" etc as requiring "*wicked* intent" in all cases.

A better approach might be to focus on the principle that one should only be punished for having chosen to act in a way which breaches the criminal law, and that this choice must generally be a voluntary one. The accused must have had a fair opportunity to act otherwise.[13] This may be a preferable explanation for the law's recognition of the defences of coercion and necessity, which operate when the accused's choice is limited to obeying the criminal law and causing greater harm, or breaching the law. Similarly, it seems preferable to say that the law

---

[8] Wilson, *Criminal Law* (1998), p 67.
[9] "... a plea of justification such as self-defence goes to the 'actus reus' in the sense that it renders *the act itself* not wrongful – not within the scope of criminal law's prohibition": C Wells and O Quick, *Lacey, Wells and Quick: Reconstructing Criminal Law: Text and Materials* (4th edn, 2010), p 120 (emphasis in original).
[10] "If A mistakenly attacks B in self-defence, B is entitled to retaliate since, *although* A lacks mens rea, his attack on B is in fact unjustified" (Gordon (2000), para 3.04 (emphasis added)).
[11] *Ibid*, para 7.01.
[12] 2001 SLT 1013, discussed in section 21.6.2 below.
[13] See section 2.7.2 above.

acquits the accused person who was suffering from a profound mental disorder at the time of the offence *despite* the fact that she intended to injure or kill someone, or to steal property etc. There are, however, some defences in which it does seem appropriate to hold that they operate to prevent the formation of *mens rea*. The accused who acts while in a semi-conscious state – a state of automatism – can be said to lack *mens rea*, as can someone who makes a relevant error, such as believing that the umbrella she picks up when leaving a busy restaurant is really her own.

The issue of whether to employ a subjective or objective approach, discussed briefly in relation to defining the recklessness required as a *mens rea* for certain offences,[14] arises also in respect of defences. An entirely subjective approach risks the criminal law being unable to condemn anyone for doing anything, and comes close to a deterministic approach that holds that we do as we do, and the fact that we have done so proves we could not have done otherwise. On the other hand it may be that justice requires that people make every effort to resist breaking the law and can be punished when they succumb to the temptation to do so, even if the strength of that temptation is greater, or their ability to resist temptation is lower, than the "reasonable person", or even the average person. We consider this in relation to particular defences.

It is common for criminal law texts to discuss defences under "general principles",[15] and prior to consideration of offences.[16] Indeed, it has been suggested that "defences belong in the general part not only because they cut across various offences, but also because they articulate ... principles that are at the core of the criminal law enterprise – and which also belong in the general part of the criminal law".[17] We have chosen to reverse this order, on the basis that it is generally only once the Crown has established, at least *prima facie*, that an offence has been committed that the accused has to decide whether to exercise the option of leading evidence in exculpation or mitigation. While this is not the universal rule – pleas of "non-age" or "unfitness for trial" are taken prior to the

---

[14] See from section 6.15.1 above.

[15] For instance, Gordon's *Criminal Law* (2000) includes defences in vol I ("General Theory"), and in R A A McCall Smith and D Sheldon, *Scots Criminal Law* (1997, and also in the 3rd edn by A M Cubie (2010)), defences are listed under Part I ("General Principles"). W Wilson, *Criminal Law: Doctrine and Theory* (4th edn, 2011) and D Ormerod, *Smith and Hogan's Criminal Law* (13th edn, 2011)) both include defences as part of their discussion of "General Principles".

[16] See, for example, Jones and Christie (2012) and A Ashworth and J Horder, *Principles of Criminal Law* (7th edn, 2013).

[17] A P Simester and S Shute, "On the general part in criminal law" in S Shute and A P Simester (eds), *Criminal Law Theory: Doctrines of the General Part* (2002), 1 at p 4.

trial commencing – it is convenient to group these pleas in bar of trial with defences, and discuss them at this later stage.

In Chapter 19 we consider the defences of "alibi" and "incrimination" (both of which involve a claim by the accused that they neither had the *mens rea* nor committed the *actus reus* of the crime), as well as "non-age", "error" and "consent", each of which (arguably) involves a lack of *mens rea* on the part of the accused. Chapter 20 focuses on "mental disorder", "diminished responsibility", "intoxication" and "automatism". While only the last of these has been treated by the Scottish courts as being capable of negating *mens rea*, each involves the claim that the accused suffered from an altered mental state at the time of the crime. Finally, Chapter 21 addresses the issues raised by the pleas of "coercion", "necessity", "self-defence", "provocation", "superior orders" and "entrapment". Controversially, we suggest that each can be viewed as exculpating an accused person, *despite* the presence, at least *prima facie*, of both *actus reus* and *mens rea*.

As a procedural measure only, Scots law categorises several of these as "special defences", meaning that notice of the accused's intention to lead any of these defences in solemn proceedings[18] must be lodged in court prior to the commencement of the trial.[19] The notice requirement applies to alibi, incrimination, self-defence, mental disorder, diminished responsibility, automatism, coercion and consent.[20] This is part of the "equality of arms" requirement of the European Convention on Human Rights: the notion that the prosecution and the defence should each have the same ability to prepare their case and that the greater resources of the state, which are available to the Crown, should not be used oppressively against the accused. Just as the prosecution is required to disclose its case prior to the trial to allow the defence to prepare properly, the accused must advise the Crown in advance of any of these lines of argument.

---

[18] That is, proceedings on indictment in the High Court or sheriff courts. Such cases take place before a jury.

[19] By virtue of the Criminal Procedure (Scotland) Act 1995, s 78(1).

[20] The defence of necessity is absent from this list, though, like coercion, it is a species of duress. The status of the first three is discussed in *Lambie* v *HM Advocate* 1973 JC 53. In respect of mental disorder (previously termed "insanity"), see *Brennan* v *HM Advocate* 1977 JC 38. The case is discussed further at section 20.13.1 below. Diminished responsibility, automatism and coercion are to be treated as if they were special defences, by the Criminal Procedure (Scotland) Act 1995, s 78(2). Consent is to be similarly treated in respect of certain sexual offences in terms of the same subsection, as amended by the Sexual Offences (Procedure and Evidence) (Scotland) Act 2002, s 6.

CHAPTER 19

ALIBI, INCRIMINATION, NON-AGE, ERROR
AND CONSENT

19.1 ALIBI

This is the Latin word for "elsewhere" and is an assertion that the **19.1.1**
accused was not at the place libelled in the charge at the time of
the crime. It is equivalent to saying: "I was not there."[1] It may be
suggested that alibi is not a "defence" as such:

> "'In general, a defence comprises grounds excluding criminal responsibility
> although the accused has fulfilled the legal elements of a criminal offence.
> An alibi, however, is nothing more than the denial of the accused's presence
> during the commission of a criminal act. In that sense, an alibi differs
> from a defence in the above-mentioned sense in one crucial aspect. In
> the case of a defence, the criminal conduct has already been established
> and is not necessarily disputed by the accused who argues that due to
> specific circumstances he or she is not criminally responsible, e.g. due to a
> situation of duress or intoxication.' ... The plea of alibi ... typically leaves
> unperturbed the question whether the crime was committed at all, in terms
> of its conduct and mental elements. Its purpose is to insist that the wrong
> person is under prosecution."[2]

Thus the accused must specify that she was not present at the locus
of the crime at the time of its commission and must provide details
of where she was at that time, but need not prove the elements of her
alibi.

19.2 IMPEACHMENT/INCRIMINATION

If alibi is a plea of "I was not there" then incrimination is a plea **19.2.1**
of: "It was not me. It was her." In other words, the claim is that

---

[1] See *Balsillie v HM Advocate* 1993 JC 233 at 237 per LJ-C Ross.
[2] C Eboe-Osuji, "The plea of alibi in international criminal law as viewed through
the prism of the common law" (2011) 22 *Criminal Law Forum* 35 at 39–40
(footnote omitted) (initially citing *Prosecutor v Kamuhanda* (Appeal Chamber
Judgement) ICTR-95-54A-A (19 September 2005)).

the crime was committed not by the accused but by another named person.[3] Often a person's defence is that the crime was committed by someone else – by saying "It wasn't me" the accused is necessarily saying that it must have been someone else. Incrimination differs from this in requiring that the other person be specified. It has been held that failure by a trial judge to direct a jury specifically about a defence of incrimination is not necessarily a misdirection; it was sufficient that the jurors were told that if there was any evidence which they believed and which exculpated the accused, they should acquit, and that they should also acquit the accused even if they did not believe any such evidence, if it left them with a reasonable doubt about the prosecution case.[4] Both alibi and incrimination are more questions of procedure than of substantive law.

19.3   NON-AGE[5]

19.3.1 The principles represented by the defence of non-age are that no child aged 7 or younger can be guilty of a criminal offence,[6] no child under the age of 12 may be prosecuted for an offence,[7] and no child aged 12 or older may be prosecuted for an offence which was committed when under the age of 12.[8] The age of criminal responsibility does not operate simply as a rule of criminal procedure. It is also part of the substantive law.[9] This is evident from the case of *Merrin* v *S*[10] where an attempt was made to refer a child under 8 to a children's hearing on the ground that "he [had] committed an offence".[11] The majority in the appeal court[12] determined that, below the age of 8, children are deemed incapable of forming *mens rea*. They are, therefore, unable to commit an "offence" and thus cannot even be referred on that ground to a children's hearing, which would intervene only in a child's best interests.

---

[3] See *McQuade* v *HM Advocate* 1996 SLT 1129.
[4] See *Flanagan* v *HM Advocate* 2012 JC 98.
[5] For a detailed account, see C McDiarmid, *Childhood and Crime* (2007), especially pp 92–101.
[6] Criminal Procedure (Scotland) Act 1995, s 41.
[7] *Ibid*, s 41A(1), inserted by the Criminal Justice and Licensing (Scotland) Act 2010, s 52(2).
[8] Criminal Procedure (Scotland) Act 1995, s 41A(2).
[9] J Chalmers and F Leverick, *Criminal Defences and Pleas in Bar of Trial* (2006), para 9.01.
[10] 1987 SLT 193.
[11] Social Work (Scotland) Act 1968, s 32(2)(g). The relevant provision is now the Children's Hearings (Scotland) Act 2011, s 67(2)(j).
[12] LJ-C Ross and Lord Brand, with Lord Dunpark dissenting.

19.4   CRITIQUE OF THE LAW ON NON-AGE AND PROPOSALS FOR REFORM

The restriction on prosecuting children who are less than 12 years 19.4.1
of age is due to a recent amendment to the legislation. The age of
criminal responsibility, *per se*, however, has remained at 8 – one of
the lowest in the world.[13] In its current form, it represents the view
that very young children are incapable of committing crime[14] – that
they lack the necessary criminal capacity.[15] This provides a reason
for not criminalising them. Although the Scottish Government
spoke of raising the age of criminal responsibility itself to 12,[16] all
that is, in fact, conferred on children aged 8–11 is an immunity from
prosecution. Accordingly, the current law may still not comply with
international obligations which require a capacity-based approach
to the setting of the age.[17] In any event, as a spokesman for Children
1ST put it:

> "When we talk about the age of criminal responsibility we are really talking
> about the minimum age of criminal prosecution. The question is not whether
> children commit crimes but whether we should treat them like criminals
> when they do. Turning a child into a criminal at the age of eight steals their
> childhood and labels them for life. We question whether this is any less true
> for a 12 year old."[18]

---

[13] See D Cipriani, *Children's Rights and the Minimum Age of Criminal Responsibility* (2009), Annex 2.

[14] This is because the Criminal Procedure (Scotland) Act 1995, s 41, only applies its conclusive presumption of inability to be guilty of any offence up to the age of 8.

[15] See section 6.18 above. Obviously, this is not necessarily factually correct since children develop mentally, emotionally and psychologically as well as physically at different rates. Some younger children may have the necessary understandings. On the other hand, in *HM Advocate v S* (9 July 1999 and 15 October 1999) (unreported) the understanding of a 13-year-old was lacking in certain key respects. See http://www.scotcourts.gov.uk/opinions/845_99.html and http://www.scotcourts.gov.uk/opinions/ 845A_99.html.

[16] See, for example, Scottish Government news release: "Criminal age to be raised to 12", 1 March 2009 (available at http://www.scotland.gov.uk/News/Releases/2009/03/27140804).

[17] UN Convention on the Rights of the Child (1989), Art 40(3)(a). See E E Sutherland, "The age of reason or the reasons for an age? The age of criminal responsibility" (2002) SLT 1 at 3; C McDiarmid, "The age of criminal responsibility in Scots law" 2009 *SCOLAG* 116

[18] T Roberts, "Raising the age of criminal responsibility" (2009) *Scottish Criminal Law* 667 at 667. For a discussion of the operation of defences such as duress, provocation and diminished responsibility, as applied to children, see A Ashworth, "Child defendants and the doctrines of the criminal law" in J Chalmers, F Leverick and L Farmer (eds), *Essays in Criminal Law in Honour of Sir Gerald Gordon* (2010) at p 27.

19.5 ERROR

19.5.1 The criminal law distinguishes between errors of fact (which exculpate in certain circumstances) and errors of law (which generally do not). Don Stuart offers a description of these different types of error:

> "A mistake of fact is said to occur when the accused is mistaken in his belief that facts exist when they do not, or that they do not exist when they do. On the other hand, a mistake of law is said to occur when the mistake is not as to the actual facts but rather as to their legal relevance, consequence or significance."[19]

He does, however, point out that in practice it is not always easy to distinguish between the two: an error that one's spouse has been missing for 5 years and is therefore dead, and that one is accordingly free to marry again, is a mistake of both fact and of law, since a person must have been missing for at least 7 years before being presumed by the law to have died.[20]

19.6 ERROR OF LAW

19.6.1 Glanville Williams quipped that: "Almost the only knowledge of law possessed by many people is that ignorance of it is no excuse (*ignorantia juris non excusat*)."[21] This flows from the notion that everyone is presumed to know the law. The Latin maxim is illustrated by the case of *Clark* v *Syme*[22] in which the accused was charged with maliciously shooting and killing a sheep which belonged to his neighbour. He claimed that he had thought that he had a legal right to shoot the sheep, since he had previously warned his neighbour about the damage done to the accused's crops by the animal. The sheriff acquitted on the basis that the accused had acted in error. This was reversed on appeal by the Crown; the accused's error was one of law, and ignorance of the law is no defence. As Hume put it, an accused is "not excusable when he forgets that the courts of law are open to his complaint".[23]

19.6.2 The error made in *Clark* v *Syme*[24] concerned the nature of the criminal law; the accused erroneously believed that it was not a breach of criminal law to shoot a "trespassing" sheep. An error made by the accused relating to the non-criminal/civil law may exculpate,

---

[19] D Stuart, *Canadian Criminal Law: A Treatise* (6th edn, 2011), p 381.
[20] See the Presumption of Death (Scotland) Act 1977, s 1(1) which allows a court to grant a declarator of death in such circumstances.
[21] G Williams, *Textbook of Criminal Law* (2nd edn, 1983), p 451.
[22] 1957 JC 1, discussed at section 13.2.1 above.
[23] Hume, i, 124.
[24] 1957 JC 1.

hence the Latin maxim ought to be translated as "ignorance of the *criminal* law is no defence". Errors as to the civil law can provide a defence only if they affect the accused's *mens rea*. By way of example, suppose that A screws a mirror to the wall of the flat she is renting. Some time later, she moves out of the flat, taking the mirror with her. So far as the law of property is concerned, having been attached to the wall of the flat, the mirror has become the property of A's landlords, thus A had no right to remove it. If charged with theft of the mirror, however, A ought to be acquitted since her ignorance of the civil law position meant that she lacked the *mens rea* for theft – she had no intention to deprive the owners of their property. Whether or not the Scottish courts would accept this is a moot point, in light of the case of *Dewar* v *HM Advocate*,[25] in which the court was not sympathetic to the accused's claim that he believed that he had a legal right to recycle coffins, since he was the manager of the crematorium.[26]

19.7   CRITIQUE OF THE LAW ON ERROR OF LAW AND PROPOSALS FOR REFORM

The principle can sometimes operate harshly; while it may be reasonable to assume that people are aware of the requirements of the common law, in that they know that the law forbids intentional killing, taking other people's property without consent, and deliberately physically hurting someone or damaging their property, the intricate requirements of many statutory offences are less well known.[27] Nevertheless, to allow ignorance to operate as a defence would mean that there was little incentive for people to find out about the criminal law's prohibitions. Much of statute law is directed at individuals who are acting in a particular capacity – as employers,[28] retailers,[29] or drivers,[30] for example, and those who fall within such a description ought to find out what it is that the law requires of them. In the American case of *Long* v *State*[31] the Supreme Court of Delaware held that there could be a defence of error of law where

19.7.1

---

[25] 1945 JC 5.
[26] See section 12.4.4 above.
[27] For the argument that this is a "preposterous doctrine, resting on insecure foundations within the criminal law and on questionable propositions about the political obligations of individuals and of the State", see A Ashworth, "Ignorance of the criminal law, and duties to avoid it" (2011) 74 *MLR* 1 at 1.
[28] See, for example, the Health and Safety at Work etc Act 1974, s 33.
[29] See, for example, the Food Safety Act 1990, s 14.
[30] See generally the Road Traffic Act 1988.
[31] 65 A 489 (1949).

"before engaging in the conduct, the [accused] made a bona fide, diligent effort, adopting a course and resorting to resources and means at least as appropriate as any afforded under our legal system, to ascertain and abide by the law, and where he acted in good faith reliant upon the results of such effort".[32]

In contrast to this, in the Australian case of *Campbell*[33] a conviction was upheld despite the fact that the accused had relied on case law which was only later reversed on appeal. The appeal court stated that the principle that ignorance of the law is no defence "is not justified because it is fair" but "because it is necessary".[34] This seems an overly harsh approach. As Stuart has pointed out:

"This implies that the law exists in a body of discernible rules which the ordinary person remembers or is capable of discovering. If this proposition was ever valid, it is certainly laughable in our present complex society in which there is a vast proliferation of laws of every description, including complicated statutory provisions, obscure regulatory ones and intricate judge-made law."[35]

He suggests a test of "reasonableness";[36] an accused who has in *bona fides* relied on official information ought to be acquitted. Rather than having a rigid rule, it would be preferable if Scots law allowed a defence of error of law where the accused had taken reasonable steps to ascertain the correct legal position. The *Draft Criminal Code* provides that:

"A person who acts under a mistaken belief induced by reliance on official advice as to the lawfulness of the act is not guilty of an offence if ... it was reasonable ... for the person to rely on the official advice; and ... there would have been no criminal liability had the official advice been correct".[37]

Enactment of such a provision would ensure that people could not evade criminal liability merely by remaining ignorant, but would recognise that those who have made a reasonable attempt to find out what the law requires ought not to be penalised.

19.8 ERRORS OF FACT

19.8.1 It has been suggested that "it is incorrect to refer to [error] as a defence at all, as it is merely an application of the rule that the prosecution

---

[32] (1949) 65 A 489 at 497.
[33] (1972) 21 CRNS 273.
[34] *Ibid* at 280.
[35] Stuart (2011) at p 355.
[36] *Ibid* at p 360.
[37] *Draft Criminal Code*, s 28(2).

must prove all the relevant elements of the offence".[38] In practice, the only errors of fact which exculpate are those which have affected the accused's *mens rea*. In our initial discussion of *mens rea*, we noted the difference in liability between A, who steals a coat, and B, who takes someone else's coat in the mistaken belief that it is her own.[39] B acts in error – she thinks it is her coat and this mistake excludes the *mens rea* of intending to deprive the owner, which is necessary for theft. However C, who takes someone's coat thinking that it is real mink when it is only fake fur, has also made an error, but this has no bearing on *mens rea*, hence C is guilty of theft. Similarly, error as to the identity of one's victim is no defence. An example of this type of error is *Gallacher* v *HM Advocate*,[40] in which the accused mistakenly thought the person they were attacking was a member of the circus. This was not an error which affected their *mens rea* – they did intend to injure the person they were kicking and punching.

In addition, the courts have generally held that an error of fact **19.8.2** will only exculpate if it is both genuine and reasonable, that is, an error into which the hypothetical "reasonable person" could have fallen. The accused whose beliefs are both genuine and reasonable will be judged as if the facts were as she believed them to be. In the case of *Owens* v *HM Advocate*[41] the trial judge directed the jury that if the accused's belief (in this case, that his victim was threatening him with a knife) was completely wrong, then his plea of self-defence to a murder charge was to be rejected by them. It was held on appeal that this was a misdirection and Owens' conviction was quashed. The appeal court emphasised that self-defence was made out when the accused established that he believed himself to be in imminent danger and that he held such a belief on reasonable grounds. Such grounds may exist even if, in fact, the belief is erroneous, provided that it is genuinely held. Similarly, in *MacDougall* v *Ho*[42] the accused had damaged the windscreen of a taxi because he mistakenly believed that the taxi contained someone who had damaged his shop window. He was acquitted of vandalism since this mistaken belief was held to constitute a reasonable excuse. The position with regard to the crime of theft is comparable: mistakes must be made on reasonable grounds.[43] For some sexual offences, such as rape, statute provides

---

[38] P Charleton, P A McDermott and M Bolger, *Criminal Law* (1999), para 18.01. A similar point is made in P H Robinson, *Structure and Function in Criminal Law* (1997) at pp 68–69.

[39] See section 6.12.3 above.

[40] 1951 JC 38, discussed at section 7.5.7 above.

[41] 1946 JC 119.

[42] 1985 SCCR 199.

[43] Note, however, that, on Gordon's analysis, it may not be quite so clear cut. See section 12.7.2 above.

that in determining whether the accused's belief as to consent or knowledge was reasonable, regard is to be had to whether he took any steps to ascertain whether there was consent or, as the case may be, knowledge; and, if so, to what those steps were.[44]

19.9 CONSENT

19.9.1   In establishing the commission of some crimes, the prosecution requires to show a lack of consent on the part of the victim. This is the case in relation to theft, and various sexual assaults. An accused person who establishes that she had the owner's consent to damage property, or to set it on fire, cannot be convicted of vandalism, malicious mischief or fire-raising. Consent does not, however, exculpate all crimes. It is no defence that the victim to a (non-sexual) assault has consented (at least where that assault has caused injury),[45] nor can one consent to being killed. In *HM Advocate* v *Rutherford*[46] the accused killed the victim by strangling her with his tie. He claimed that he had put the tie round her neck and tightened it only to humour her, and thus the killing was an accident. According to the accused, the victim had asked him to strangle her to death, hence everything he had done had taken place with her consent. Lord Justice-Clerk Cooper directed the jury that consent was not a defence to murder – and this seems to have been accepted as a matter of law. This was affirmed by Lord Justice-Clerk Ross in *Lord Advocate's Reference (No 1 of 1994)*:[47]

> "Consent on the part of the victim – even instigation by the victim – is of no importance at all. Clear authority is to be found for that proposition in the cases of *HM Advocate* v *Rutherford* (murder); *Smart* v *HM Advocate* (assault) and *Finlayson* v *HM Advocate* (culpable homicide by injection of a controlled drug causing death)."[48]

19.9.2   The issue of consent is, however, important in relation to euthanasia. Mention has already been made of the case of *HM Advocate* v *Brady*[49] in 1997, in which the accused killed his terminally ill brother in order to bring his suffering to an end.[50] The Crown accepted a plea of guilty to culpable homicide. The current requirement that the intention to kill be "wicked" may, in itself, militate against a charge of murder in such circumstances.[51]

---

[44] Sexual Offences (Scotland) Act 2009, s 16.
[45] See *Smart* v *HM Advocate* 1975 JC 30, discussed in section 10.2.3 above.
[46] 1947 JC 1.
[47] 1996 JC 76.
[48] *Ibid* at 80.
[49] 1997 GWD 1–18.
[50] See sections 9.15.1 and 9.16.5 above.
[51] See from section 9.11.2 above.

19.10   CRITIQUE OF THE LAW ON CONSENT AND PROPOSALS FOR REFORM

As we have seen, consent is also an important issue in assault, particularly in relation to sexual sado–masochistic activities.[52] These practices are rarely prosecuted, due to the fact that they do not generally come to the attention of the police.[53] The Scottish Law Commission had recommended the decriminalisation of certain assaults to which the "victim" consents, and which are for the purposes of sexual gratification. This was to apply only to activities which were unlikely to result in serious injury, determined according to what the reasonable person would judge as being the likely outcome.[54] The Commission's approach did not find favour with the Scottish Government and the recommendation was not included in the Sexual Offences (Scotland) Act 2009. Clearly, the Commission's position endorsed a liberal perspective – that individuals should be free to exercise control over their bodies as they wish – though, in restricting the ability to consent to serious harm, the Commission stopped short of libertarianism.[55] A major issue here is the question of the possible power (im)balance between the parties. If this is heavily weighted in favour of the person inflicting the pain/injury then the quality of any "consent" by the other party may be adversely affected; she may be too afraid not to "consent".[56] It is for this reason that we do not favour a change in the law, believing that this would leave victims of assault vulnerable to suggestions that they consented. For example, if A bites B's breasts, hits her legs with a belt, or ties her wrists together, this is currently an assault, even though no serious injury is caused (or was likely to be caused). Decriminalisation on the lines suggested by the Scottish Law Commission would have allowed the accused to claim that the complainer consented, and that the biting, hitting etc was for the accused's (or even for the complainer's) sexual pleasure.[57] Others take the view that this should not prevent

19.10.1

---

[52] See section 10.2.5 above. For a detailed critique of the law, see S Cowan, "The pain of pleasure: consent and the criminalisation of sado–masochistic 'assaults'" in J Chalmers, F Leverick and L Farmer (eds), *Essays in Criminal Law in Honour of Sir Gerald Gordon* (2010) at p 126.

[53] See, however, the case of *McDonald* v *HM Advocate* 2004 SCCR 161, in which there were fatal consequences.

[54] See *Report on Rape and Other Sexual Offences* (Scot Law Com No 209, 2007), recommendation 57.

[55] See section 1.5.1 above.

[56] The issue of power imbalance is discussed in the restorative justice context in A McAlinden, "The use of 'shame' with sexual offenders" (2005) 45 *Brit J Criminol* 373, especially at 385.

[57] See P R Ferguson, "Reforming rape and other sexual offences" (2008) 12 *Edin LR* 302 at 307.

the law from recognising consent as a defence, arguing that the courts are routinely called upon to determine whether, in a scenario like the one described above, A's assertions as to the complainer's consent are plausible, and that the courts are well able to make such determinations.[58] In practice, however, the accused may assert when being interviewed by the police that the complainer consented and that the injuries were inflicted as part of rough foreplay, bondage or sado–masochistic practices. He may well decide not to testify at his trial, as is his right. The complainer, on the other hand, as the chief witness for the Crown, would require to give evidence, and may face the kind of unpleasant cross-examination that rape victims have complained about for many years.

19.10.2   We offered a general critique of the law on consent in the chapter on assault, in sections 10.6.1–10.6.5 in particular. As we noted there, some people believe that consent ought to operate as a defence to all charges, including what would otherwise be murder and serious assaults. Others favour consent being recognised as a defence to assaults which cause all but serious injury. Whatever view one takes, the extent to which the law recognises consent as a defence requires clarification.

---

[58] For the argument that the current law "demonstrates a neglect of the complex and nuanced specificities of people's sexual interactions", see S Cowan, "Criminalizing SM: disavowing the erotic, instantiating violence" in R A Duff, L Farmer *et al* (eds), *The Structures of the Criminal Law* (2011) 59 at p 80.

CHAPTER 20

MENTAL DISORDER, UNFITNESS FOR TRIAL, DIMINISHED RESPONSIBILITY, INTOXICATION AND AUTOMATISM

20.1 INTRODUCTION

Scots criminal law has a long history of engagement with lack **20.1.1** of criminal capacity[1] as removing, or diminishing, criminal responsibility. Hume discussed the defence of insanity, drawing on a number of previous cases;[2] Scotland was also in the forefront of the innovation of the partial defence of diminished responsibility.[3] Defences grounded in, or relating to, mental disorder have recently moved from their common law roots to become one of the few areas of substantive criminal law which are placed on a statutory footing. This was achieved by Pt 7 of the Criminal Justice and Licensing (Scotland) Act 2010 which introduced new ss 51A, 51B and 53F into the Criminal Procedure (Scotland) Act 1995. Gerry Maher has suggested that this is not the most obvious site for these provisions, given that two out of three are a part of the substantive law and not, in any sense, procedural.[4] This legislation was brought into force on 25 June 2012, from which date the special defence of insanity, the (common law) plea of diminished responsibility and any rule of law providing for insanity in bar of trial cease to have effect.[5]

The new provisions cover three issues: unfitness for trial as a **20.1.2** preliminary plea in bar of trial;[6] the special defence of lack of criminal

---

[1] For a discussion of this concept, see section 6.18 above.
[2] Hume, i, 37–45.
[3] *Dingwall, Alex* (1867) 5 Irv 466.
[4] G Maher, "The new mental disorder defences: some comments" 2013 SLT 1 at 1. The plea of unfitness for trial may be categorised as an aspect of criminal procedure but the special defence of mental disorder and the partial defence of diminished responsibility both belong to the substantive law.
[5] Criminal Justice and Licensing (Scotland) Act 2010, s 171. This was brought into force by the Criminal Justice and Licensing (Scotland) Act 2010 (Commencement No 10 and Saving Provisions) Order 2012 (SSI 2012/160).
[6] Criminal Procedure (Scotland) Act 1995, s 53F.

responsibility by reason of mental disorder;[7] and the mitigating factor, diminished responsibility.[8] Each of these will be examined in turn. This chapter will also consider the defences of intoxication and automatism. Like mental disorder, these also involve a claim that an accused person ought to be excused on the basis that her mental state was not that of a "normal person" at the time of the crime.[9] It is for this reason that they are included here. As we shall see, the courts' approach to such states is very much dependent on whether or not they are regarded as being self-induced.

20.2 MENTAL DISORDER, AND MENTAL AND PHYSICAL CONDITIONS AFFECTING FITNESS FOR TRIAL

20.2.1 Lack of criminal responsibility by reason of mental disorder is a special defence[10] which, if proved, results in acquittal, although the accused may nonetheless be subject to control mechanisms imposed by the court, because of her mental state. In addition, or as an alternative, an accused who is, by reason of a mental or physical condition, unable to participate effectively in a trial may plead unfitness for trial. Accordingly, the criminal law is concerned with the accused's ability to understand particular issues at two different stages: (1) at the time of commission of the offence and (2) at the time of the trial. Some of those who are suffering from severe and chronic mental illness may need to make use of *both* the plea in bar of trial (for their inability to participate effectively in the trial proceedings) *and* the special defence (for their lack of appreciation of the quality of their conduct at the time of committing the alleged offence). Others, for example those who recover their mental health between the time of the offence and the trial, may only require to make use of one or the other.

20.3 ONUS OF PROOF

20.3.1 Both the special defence of mental disorder and the plea of "diminished responsibility"[11] place the onus of proof on the accused,[12] though the standard of proof is on the "balance of probabilities". James Chalmers has expressed some misgivings about the absoluteness of the position, in terms of s 51A(4), that only the

---

[7] Criminal Procedure (Scotland) Act 1995, s 51A.

[8] *Ibid*, s 51B.

[9] Voluntary and involuntary intoxication are discussed further from section 20.12 below. The latter is commonly referred to as a form of "automatism".

[10] Criminal Procedure (Scotland) Act 1995, s 51A(3), and see the Introduction to Part VII above.

[11] The plea of diminished responsibility is described from section 20.10 below.

[12] Criminal Procedure (Scotland) Act 1995, ss 51A(4) and 51B(4) respectively.

accused may put in issue the special defence.[13] If an accused person
decides not to plead it but leads evidence that the offence was carried
out under a delusion arising from mental disorder, then it may be
that she lacks the *mens rea* for the crime committed. Chalmers gives
the example of an accused who kills under the impression that the
victim is an animal.[14] Such a person lacks the *mens rea* for murder.
Given that neither the Crown nor the court will now be able to raise
the issue of mental disorder, Chalmers fears that such an accused
would simply have to be acquitted, without recourse to any of the
disposals[15] which can operate to protect the public where a finding
of mental disorder is returned. Maher, on the other hand, takes
the view that this provision simply "removes some doubt [inherent]
in the common law ... in respect of who may raise the defence".[16]
If the accused is genuinely mentally disordered, we would suggest
that she would suffer no detriment if the defence could be raised
by the Crown, the court or her. This is the position in relation to
unfitness for trial.[17] The standard there is, again, on the balance of
probabilities.[18]

The reversal of the burden of proof, for the special defence and   **20.3.2**
for diminished responsibility, requires some discussion. Article 6(2)
of the European Convention on Human Rights enshrines, *inter alia*,
the presumption of innocence. There is much debate, in general,
as to whether reversing the burden of proof so that the accused
is required to prove her innocence, even in relation to only a very
minor aspect of the crime, is contrary to this presumption.[19] Is the
operation of the defence of mental disorder tantamount to assuming
the accused's guilt, if she can be acquitted only on the basis of
evidence which she herself requires to establish, albeit on the balance
of probabilities? While academic commentators are often sceptical
about the effect of reverse burdens on the presumption of innocence
generally, the courts have tended to permit them provided they can
be interpreted so as not to require the accused to prove the absence
of guilt. In fact, in relation to mental disorder, it is at least arguable

---

[13] J Chalmers, "Section 117 of the Criminal Justice and Licensing (Scotland) Bill: a dangerous loophole?" 2009 SCL 1240.
[14] *Ibid* at 1242.
[15] Criminal Procedure (Scotland) Act 1995, s 57.
[16] Maher (2013) at 3.
[17] Under the pre-existing (but similar) law, in *HM Advocate* v *Brown* (1907) 5 Adam 312 the Crown raised (the former plea of) insanity in bar of trial, and this was opposed by the defence. See also *HM Advocate* v *Alexander Robertson* (1891) 3 White 6, discussed in J Chalmers and F Leverick, *Criminal Defences and Pleas in Bar of Trial* (2006) at para 14.10.
[18] Criminal Procedure (Scotland) Act 1995, s 53F(1).
[19] See section 5.4.3 above.

that a reverse burden is not simply tolerable but appropriate;[20] this is an instance where the accused's ability to supply the appropriate evidence is demonstrably greater than that of the Crown.[21] The state of the accused's mental health is, quite simply, a matter about which she is better informed than the prosecution. On the other hand, David Hamer has noted the reluctance of the English courts to apply reverse burdens to serious crimes, and has pointed out that "insanity/mental disorder" can be used as a defence to murder – the most serious crime of them all.[22] Ultimately, Hamer's view is that "[t]he insanity issue goes less to the gravamen than to the appropriate way of dealing with the wrongdoer".[23] Accordingly, despite the seriousness of the crimes in relation to which it may be pled, the reverse burden is not objectionable.

20.3.3   The law sets down a different test for the special defence to that which it requires in relation to the plea in bar. One issue which straddles both concepts is the difficulty of striking a balance between fairness to the accused and the public interest in justice being seen to be done.[24] If the accused cannot understand either the crime or the court proceedings it is not fair either to prosecute[25] or to punish her. On the other hand, there may be compelling evidence that she was the perpetrator of what would otherwise be a crime. If she cannot be tried, convicted and punished (where merited), the public may feel cheated. The rules on mental disorder and on unfitness for trial need to negotiate this difficult interaction between two conflicting perspectives.

20.4 UNFITNESS FOR TRIAL

20.4.1   The law on unfitness for trial is contained in ss 53F–56 of the Criminal Procedure (Scotland) Act 1995. One of the purposes of the plea is to ascertain whether it would be fair for the trial to go ahead.[26] The test is whether or not the accused is "incapable, by

---

[20] See J Chalmers, "Reforming the pleas of insanity and diminished responsibility: some aspects of the Scottish Law Commission's Discussion Paper" (2003) 8 *SLPQ* 79.

[21] See *ibid* at 83–84.

[22] D Hamer, "The presumption of innocence and reverse burdens: a balancing act" (2007) 66 *CLJ* 142.

[23] *Ibid* at 152.

[24] See also R D Mackay, "Unfitness to plead – some observations of the Law Commission's consultation paper" [2011] *Crim LR* 433 at 442, who makes a similar point in respect of English law.

[25] See, for example, R A Duff, "Law, language and community: some preconditions of criminal liability" (1998) 18 *OJLS* 189.

[26] This was discussed in the old case of *Russell v HM Advocate* 1946 JC 37 at 47 per LJ-C Cooper.

reason of a mental or physical condition, of participating effectively in a trial".[27] This wording directly reflects the jurisprudence of the European Court of Human Rights in relation to the right to a fair trial under Art 6.[28] This is a different test to that for the special defence of mental disorder, and a wide range of mental health conditions, inabilities and disabilities might be brought under its aegis. It specifically applies to physical conditions as well as mental ones.[29] Section 53F(2) provides a list of factors to which the court should have regard in determining whether an accused is unfit for trial. These are:

> "(a) the ability of the [accused] to—
>> (i) understand the nature of the charge,
>> (ii) understand the requirement to tender a plea to the charge and the effect of such a plea,
>> (iii) understand the purpose of, and follow the course of, the trial,
>> (iv) understand the evidence that may be given against the [accused],
>> (v) instruct and otherwise communicate with the [accused]'s legal representative, and
> (b) any other factor which the court considers relevant."

In terms of s 53F(3), loss of memory as to the events constituting the crime does not on its own establish unfitness for trial. This again echoes the common law. In *Russell* v *HM Advocate*[30] it was determined that amnesia did not afford a plea in bar of trial and this was reiterated in *Hughes* v *HM Advocate*,[31] since an accused who cannot remember the events surrounding the alleged crime is not deprived of a fair trial, by virtue of that fact alone. There is also the concern that an accused might feign total memory loss to avoid a trial.

The old plea of insanity in bar of trial was used successfully in **20.4.2** *HM Advocate* v *S*,[32] in which the accused was 12 years old at the time of the offence and suffered from developmental delay.[33] The case highlights the breadth of the plea, which is retained under s 53F, which enables it to take account of grounds other than mental illness or disorder. Since children mature at different rates then it is a property of the status of being a child that development, for some,

---

[27] Criminal Procedure (Scotland) Act 1995, s 53F(1).
[28] *T* v *UK*; *V* v *UK* (2000) 30 EHRR 121 at 179 para 85.
[29] Under the pre-existing law, for example, in *HM Advocate* v *Wilson* 1942 JC 75, the accused was deaf and unable to speak, although the court ultimately determined that he could participate in the trial through an interpreter.
[30] 1946 JC 37.
[31] 2002 JC 23.
[32] (1999), unreported, but see http://www.scotcourts.gov.uk/opinions/845_99.html.
[33] The child's developmental delay affected some of his cognitive abilities, including his ability to understand certain key concepts and complex language.

will be slower than for others. In such circumstances, it is clearly preferable that inability to satisfy the statutory test should render the accused "unfit for trial" rather than "insane". This is a point which applies more generally; "insanity" is a term with potentially pejorative connotations which is not in current use in psychiatry.[34] The need to move away from it, as the new provision does, has been widely recognised.[35]

20.4.3   Where the evidence presented to the court satisfies it that the accused is "unfit for trial so that his [sic] trial cannot proceed"[36] it must go on to order an "examination of facts".[37] There is no longer a requirement of evidence from two medical practitioners which satisfies the court that the accused's mental state is such that the trial cannot proceed. This is in accordance with the Scottish Law Commission's recommendation.[38] Since the plea in bar specifically covers conditions other than those relating to mental health, the Commission noted that psychiatric evidence would not always be appropriate. Also, the type of information required to satisfy the test of unfitness for trial is concerned with the accused's ability to understand and function in those respects necessary to enable effective participation. Can she, for example, understand the concept of a crime and the meaning and implications of pleading "guilty" or "not guilty"? Can she process information in the form and quantity in which, and at the speed at which, it is presented at a criminal trial? Such information is more likely to be available from a psychological examination than a medical one.[39]

20.4.4   Until the Criminal Procedure (Scotland) Act 1995 came into force, a finding of "insanity" in bar of trial automatically led to incarceration in "a State hospital" – the secure psychiatric facility at Carstairs – or "such other hospital as for special reasons the court may specify".[40] The finding of insanity, on its own, triggered this outcome. No attempt was made to ascertain whether the "insane"

---

[34] See section 20.9.1 below and *HM Advocate v S*, reported at http://www.scot courts.gov.uk/opinions/845_99.html.

[35] Scottish Law Commission, *Report on Insanity and Diminished Responsibility* (No 195, 2004), paras 2.19 and 4.8; C Connelly, "Insanity and unfitness to plead" (1996) *JR* 206; Thomson Committee, *Criminal Procedure in Scotland (Second Report)* (Cmnd 6218, 1975) at para 52.13; *Draft Criminal Code*, s 27(1).

[36] Criminal Procedure (Scotland) Act 1995, s 54(1).

[37] *Ibid*, s 54(1)(b).

[38] Scottish Law Commission (2004), paras 5.60–5.63.

[39] See, for example, Connelly (1996) at 206. It should, nonetheless, be noted that the (English) Law Commission recently recommended that psychiatric evidence should be mandatory in any reformed provisions on the corresponding English plea of unfitness to plead: Law Commission, *Unfitness to Plead: A Consultation Paper* (No 197, 2010) at para 5.5.

[40] Criminal Procedure (Scotland) Act 1975, ss 174 and 375.

accused had actually committed the offence with which she was charged, nor was there any inquiry into whether detention in a psychiatric hospital was appropriate. In some cases this was clearly draconian. Mandatory detention may also have been incompatible with the requirement under Art 5 of the ECHR which provides a right to liberty. While Art 5(1)(e) permits the "lawful detention" of "persons of unsound mind", this would not describe the person who was "insane" at the time of the alleged crime but whose mental health had been restored by the time of the trial. This was remedied by the 1995 Act's requirement for the "examination of facts"[41] where a plea in bar of trial is successful. This takes the place of the trial and seeks to ascertain "beyond reasonable doubt" whether the accused "did the act or made the omission constituting the offence", and, if so, whether, "on the balance of probabilities", there are any grounds for acquittal.[42]

20.5 EFFECT OF ACQUITTAL OR FINDING OF GUILT IN A PLEA IN BAR OF TRIAL

Based on an analysis of the corresponding English case law, James **20.5.1** Chalmers and Fiona Leverick take the view that the examination of the facts determines only whether the accused committed the *actus reus* of the offence – as noted above, the provision refers to whether it has been proved that the accused "did the act or made the omission".[43] If a court holds that an accused did not carry out the criminal behaviour, she will be acquitted and that decision is determinative of the issue. She cannot later be subjected to a criminal trial. The examination of the facts takes place, as far as possible, exactly as if it were a trial.[44] If, in such proceedings, the Crown cannot prove beyond reasonable doubt that the accused committed the *actus reus*, it would be unfair to give it another bite at the identical cherry, were the accused to recover sufficiently to undergo a criminal trial. On the other hand, where the examination of the facts makes a finding that the accused "did the act or made the omission constituting the offence",[45] an accused who later regains "sanity" may then be subjected to prosecution. The value, and fairness, of this must depend on the view taken of the disposal imposed by the court in the interim period. If there is a level at which compulsory incarceration in the State hospital, for example, is punitive rather than solely therapeutic

---

[41] Criminal Procedure (Scotland) Act 1995, ss 54(1)(b) and 55.
[42] *Ibid*, s 55(1).
[43] Chalmers and Leverick (2006), paras 14.12 and 14.13.
[44] Criminal Procedure (Scotland) Act 1995, s 55(6).
[45] *Ibid*, s 55(1)(a).

and incapacitating then the prospect, raised by a new prosecution, of transfer from there to prison may seem oppressive. It appears to be the case that the question of whether or not to re-prosecute is a matter entirely for the discretion of the COPFS.[46]

20.6 CRITIQUE OF THE LAW ON UNFITNESS FOR TRIAL AND PROPOSALS FOR REFORM

20.6.1 The requirement for an examination of facts represents an improvement on the pre-1995 situation in that the court can impose restrictions on the accused only where there is a finding that she did commit the *actus reus* of the crime with which she is charged.[47] A major difficulty with this procedure is that the examination of facts is conducted as if it were a trial[48] – yet the reason for having it is that the court itself has just reached the conclusion that the accused in question is unfit to be tried.[49] As noted above,[50] in *T v UK; V v UK*[51] the European Court of Human Rights determined that an accused in a criminal trial must be able to "participate effectively".[52] If a similar approach is taken to the examination of facts, the requirement that the accused must be legally represented at such hearings[53] may not be enough to satisfy this, particularly since the court may dispense with the presence of the accused altogether where it is "not practical or appropriate" for her to attend.[54]

20.6.2   It is widely recognised, particularly following the work of Antony Duff, that subjecting to a trial those who lack the capacity to understand or to participate meaningfully is grossly unfair – indeed, in his terms, it would constitute a "travesty".[55] The plea of unfitness for trial, then, must operate to prevent those who are unfit in this sense from being subjected to the trial process. At the same time, it cannot be over-inclusive or it will keep from trial some people who could fairly and properly answer the charges. The test of "effective participation" in s 53F(1) overtly recognises that this is an issue

---

[46] D Chiswick, A P W Shubsachs and S Novosel, "Reprosecution of patients found unfit to plead: a report of anomalies in procedure in Scotland" (1990) 14 *Psychiatric Bulletin* 208 at 208.
[47] Criminal Procedure (Scotland) Act 1995, s 57(1)(a) – or where the ground of acquittal was a finding of mental disorder as a special defence.
[48] *Ibid*, s 55(6).
[49] Connelly (1996) at 208.
[50] See section 20.4.1, n 28 above.
[51] (2000) 30 EHRR 121.
[52] *Ibid* at 181, para 91.
[53] Criminal Procedure (Scotland) Act 1995, s 56(3).
[54] *Ibid*, s 55(5). The accused can object or have an objection made on her behalf.
[55] Duff (1998) at 194. See also R A Duff, *Answering for Crime: Responsibility and Liability in the Criminal Law* (2007), p 181.

of the accused's right to a fair trial.[56] The test is drawn broadly, including, as we have seen, the possibility of a physical condition preventing effective participation.[57] The specific points to which regard must be had in determining unfitness, found in subs (2)(a),[58] all point to cognitive understandings of various aspects of the trial process.[59] In relation to English law, Ronnie Mackay, adopting an argument made by Richard Bonnie, regards such an understanding or ability – the "competence to assist counsel" – as foundational.[60] An accused who lacks it is, on this view, automatically unfit for trial. In Scots law, however, s 53F(2)(b) then goes on to broaden the test exponentially so that it is constrained only by the court's discretion. Decision-makers must also have regard to "any other factor which the court considers relevant". The conjunctive "and" links subs (b) to the specific issues in subs (a). Accordingly, other relevant factors will have to be considered, even if only to determine that there is none, in every case.

Mackay has also argued that a test which relates only to cognitive ability may not be sufficiently broad to encompass all who are, factually, unfit to plead.[61] Some accused may possess such ability, in terms of understanding of the trial process, but for other reasons, perhaps the inability to control emotion in decision-making, find themselves, *de facto*, unfit for trial. He advocates a second limb to any fitness test, of what he calls "decisional competence",[62] which relates to the accused's ability to make rational decisions. This is quite a well-developed concept in the literature on mental health and is concerned only with the decision-making process – not with the quality of the actual decision made. Autonomy requires that rational people are permitted to make "stupid" decisions if they wish.[63] There is no doubt that the "any other factor" element leaves scope for consideration of this issue. If this "decisional competence"

20.6.3

---

[56] See section 20.4.1 above.

[57] Section 53F(1) and *ibid*.

[58] Listed in section 20.4.1 above.

[59] The final criterion – the ability to "communicate with [a] legal representative" (s 53F(2)(a)(v)) – may not always reflect cognitive functioning. It could, for example, relate to the absence of a translator.

[60] Mackay (2011) at 435, discussing an issue raised in R J Bonnie, "The competence of criminal defendants: a theoretical reformulation" (1992) 10 *Behavioral Sciences and the Law* 291.

[61] Mackay (2011) at 435.

[62] *Ibid*.

[63] See, for example, N F Banner, "Can procedural and substantive elements of decision-making be reconciled in assessments of mental capacity?" (2013) 9 *International Journal of Law in Context* 71; F Freyenhagen and T O'Shea, "Hidden substance: mental disorder as a challenge to normatively neutral accounts of autonomy" (2013) 9 *International Journal of Law in Context* 53.

is the only other factor of relevance, however, beyond the "effective participation" test itself, it would have been better to define it more exactly. Overall, the breadth of the s 53F test should ensure that all who are genuinely unfit for trial are able to be identified. It also leaves much room for more precise definition in future cases.

20.7   MENTAL DISORDER AS A SPECIAL DEFENCE

20.7.1   The old defence of insanity had been a rather underused plea because prior to 1995 its "success" led to automatic detention in the State hospital[64] – not an outcome sought by many. The new special defence of mental disorder applies where it is proven that the accused, when she committed what would otherwise be a crime, was not criminally responsible by reason of mental disorder. It is a complete defence, leading to acquittal, but the state does not surrender its power to exercise control over the accused. Although an accused who is found not to be criminally responsible by reason of mental disorder, by definition, lacks criminal responsibility, she may still be deprived of her liberty, though with a view to treatment rather than punishment.

20.7.2   The definition of the defence is now found in s 51A of the Criminal Procedure (Scotland) Act 1995: "A person is not criminally responsible for conduct constituting an offence ... if the person was at the time of the conduct unable by reason of mental disorder to appreciate the nature or wrongfulness of the conduct." We will use "mental disorder" as a shorthand referent for the defence but this is not entirely satisfactory[65] as, unlike "insanity", mental disorder is not a defined legal test but the reason for the absence of criminal responsibility. One of the few cases so far decided which touches upon the matter is careful, throughout, to use the longhand formulation of the section as a whole.[66] The definition of "mental disorder" used for a number of years in the civil law and contained in s 328(1) of the Mental Health (Care and Treatment) (Scotland) Act 2003 is adopted by the amended 1995 Act: "'Mental disorder' means any – (a) mental illness; (b) personality disorder; or (c) learning disability, however caused or manifested."[67]

20.7.3   In its Report, the Scottish Law Commission considered the quality of the inability to which a relevant mental disorder would have to give rise in order to remove criminal responsibility. The formulation in s 51A(1) – inability to "appreciate the nature or wrongfulness of

---

[64] Criminal Procedure (Scotland) Act 1975, ss 174 and 375.
[65] See, also, Chalmers (2009) at 1240; Maher (2013) at 1; and Scottish Law Commission (2004), paras 2.19–2.24.
[66] *Dunn* v *W* 2013 SLT (Sh Ct) 2.
[67] Criminal Procedure (Scotland) Act 1995, s 307(1).

the conduct" – is exactly as it proposed.[68] Its discussion is therefore of relevance. The root of the matter is taken to be cognitive failings on the part of the accused – or a severe inability to understand, in context, key aspects of the behaviour either generally or as wrongful.[69] The concept of "knowledge" of these issues is, however, too narrow.[70] It is perfectly possible to "know" that behaviour is unacceptable, or proscribed, yet still to engage in it because other aspects of the disordered mental state make it seem desirable or necessary. Thus, for example, the accused might recognise that killing is wrong and constitutes the crime of murder but proceed to attack, say, blue-eyed men, in the grip of a delusion that they are all alien assassins. The accused would still "know" both the nature and the wrongfulness of such acts, if asked. It is for this reason that the concept of "appreciation" is used. The Report states: "In our view the particular value of [that] concept ... is that it connotes something wider than simple knowledge and includes a level of (rational) understanding."[71] It should also be noted that it is sufficient for the defence to be established that the accused is unable to appreciate *either* the nature *or* the wrongfulness of the conduct by reason of the mental disorder.

The test in s 51A also places beyond doubt that the mental disorder must be the cause of the inability to appreciate the quality of the conduct. This relates to a debate in the academic and policy discussions surrounding mental disorder defences as to whether the fact of a diagnosis of severe mental illness persisting at the time of the criminal act should be sufficient to establish the defence.[72] The alternative, and more onerous, position is that a causal link between the two must be proved.[73] From a legal perspective, this latter view should be welcomed. Requiring that there be such a causal link is a "belt and braces" approach. It obviates any danger, however unlikely, of an accused killing in furtherance of a long-held, rational

20.7.4

---

[68] Scottish Law Commission (2004), para 2.51.

[69] *Ibid*, especially para 2.50.

[70] The Commission noted that, while the new test might appear to come close to the M'Naghten Rules which govern the defence of insanity in English law, it is, in fact, an improvement on those Rules because it does not rely only on the accused's "knowledge": *ibid*, paras 2.43-2.49. The M'Naghten Rules date from *M'Naghten's Case* (1843) 10 Cl & F 200. See R D Mackay, "Righting the wrong? – some observations on the second limb of the M'Naghten Rules" (2009) *Crim LR* 80.

[71] Scottish Law Commission (2004), para 2.47.

[72] This was the view of the Butler Committee *Report on Mentally Abnormal Offenders* (Cmnd 6244, 1975), para 18.17 in England and Wales. See H Howard, "Reform of the insanity defence: theoretical issues" (2003) 67 *J Crim L* 51.

[73] See, for example, D Prendergast, "The connection between mental disorder and the act of killing in the defence of diminished responsibility" (2013) 49 *Irish Jurist* 202.

grudge, perhaps during a transitory lucid period, with complete understanding of her actions.[74]

20.7.5 The other aspect of the mental disorder provision which requires some discussion is the position where the accused's inability to appreciate the nature or wrongfulness of the conduct rests on a claim of psychopathic personality disorder. Under the previous law, such a claim was excluded from grounding a plea of diminished responsibility[75] but not, at least specifically, from the special defence of insanity. That position is reversed under the new legislation.[76] As explained by the Scottish Law Commission, psychopathic personality disorder does not, on any definition, bring about the inability, which the new special defence requires, to appreciate the nature or wrongfulness of the behaviour. The accused will still know and understand that the conduct is wrong. At most, such a disorder makes it more difficult for an individual to conform their conduct to legal norms than this would be for an ordinary person.[77] Such an individual is simply not, therefore, "unable" to appreciate the quality of her conduct.[78]

20.7.6 While most, if not all, commentary relating to this provision speaks of "psychopathic personality disorder",[79] s 51A(2) itself refers to "a personality disorder which is characterised solely or principally by abnormally aggressive or seriously irresponsible conduct". The reason given by the Scottish Law Commission is that "in a legal context the expression is clearly understood to mean psychopathy".[80] This being the case, might it not have been better to use that term explicitly? In her discussion of this issue, Elizabeth Shaw considers the Law Commission's justification for its terminology, and suggests that it "could mean that this legislative phrasing is an accepted short-hand for a richer, more medically informed, concept. If this is the case", she continues "then the legislation should spell out precisely what this richer concept is, in order to make the law more transparent and in order to achieve consistency between cases".[81] Nonetheless, the

---

[74] Indeed, in England, a paranoid schizophrenic, Tennyson Obih, was found guilty of the murder (rather than manslaughter on the grounds of diminished responsibility) of a police officer, after the jury rejected the defence claim that he acted because of his illness. See http://www.bbc.co.uk/news/uk-england-beds-bucks-herts-11773392.

[75] *Carraher* v *HM Advocate* 1946 JC 108.

[76] Criminal Procedure (Scotland) Act 1995, s 51A(2).

[77] Scottish Law Commission (2004), paras 2.57–2.63.

[78] Maher (2013) at 2.

[79] *Ibid*; Scottish Government, *Explanatory Notes to the Criminal Justice and Licensing (Scotland) Act 2010*, para 707; E Shaw, "Psychopaths and criminal responsibility" (2009) 13 *Edin LR* 497.

[80] Scottish Law Commission (2004), para 2.62.

[81] See Shaw (2009) at 498.

Commission's *justification* for excluding psychopathy, however it is to be defined, from the special defence appears, at first sight, to be cogent: psychopaths are not cognitively impaired in the sense required to prevent them appreciating the quality of their behaviour. In fact, the definition, and characteristics of psychopathic personality disorder are contested and the condition does not necessarily manifest itself identically in all individuals who are diagnosed with it.[82] For this reason, there is certainly an argument that the general test in s 51A(1) would, on its own, have operated to ensure that all those who retain the ability to *choose* whether to offend were found to be criminally responsible. Shaw argues that at least some diagnosed psychopaths do "suffer cognitive deficiencies that ought to excuse them completely from responsibility".[83] Section 51A(2) will currently operate to prevent them successfully pleading this.

Victor Tadros has explored the relationship between an accused **20.7.7** person and criminal behaviour.[84] He identified two different concepts of responsibility, which he calls "attribution-responsibility" and "capacity-responsibility", and considered which of these underlay the former insanity defence. Lack of "attribution-responsibility" effectively means that the accused is unable to form, or at least lacks, *mens rea*, due to her mental disorder. Lack of "capacity-responsibility" means that regardless of whether or not she had the requisite *mens rea,* she lacked the ability to understand the crime sufficiently to be held criminally responsible for it. In its distinction between "knowledge" of the nature or wrongfulness of the criminal behaviour and "understanding", the Scottish Law Commission implicitly recognises that it is, of course, possible that even an accused who was severely mentally disordered might yet be able to formulate the required mental element.[85] A possible example may be found in the English law case of *James Hadfield*[86] in 1800. The defendant shot at the king, intending to kill him. Hadfield wanted to die, but in a way which avoided the sin of suicide. He believed that he had been commanded by God to achieve this and knew that he would be executed by the state for such an offence. Strictly, then, he had *mens rea* but, perhaps equally obviously, he was not able to exercise

---

[82] Shaw (2009) *passim.*

[83] *Ibid* at 502.

[84] V Tadros, "Insanity and the capacity for criminal responsibility" (2001) 5 *Edin LR* 325, especially at 326–327.

[85] It gives the example of a woman who kills her children by smothering them with a pillow in the belief that she is driving out demons from them. At one level, she clearly intends to kill them, satisfying the *mens rea* of murder: Scottish Law Commission (2004), para 2.45.

[86] (1800) 27 St Trials, 1281, discussed in Gordon (2000) at para 10.02.

rational control over his actions.[87] Thus, the second of Tadros's formulations (capacity-responsibility) seems closer to defining the function of both the old insanity defence and the new mental disorder one. Indeed, as Tadros noted, an accused who lacked *mens rea*, for whatever reason, ought to be acquitted in any event, whether or not she suffered from a mental disorder.[88] Mental disorder, then, like insanity before it, ought to be regarded as a determination that the accused lacked criminal capacity.[89]

20.7.8   The law on insanity made it clear that it was a purely legal concept.[90] While medical evidence might have been relevant, it was not the deciding factor. The jury was required to judge the issue as a question of fact taking into account *all* the evidence presented – medical and otherwise – and using their common sense. Similarly, the mental disorder defence carries no specific requirement of medical evidence. Although the Scottish Law Commission did state that the defence "reflects issues of legal policy and not simply the use of purely medical concepts"[91] it also noted that, in this field, while "the disciplines of law and medicine are not identical ... it is also the case that they are not in conflict with each other".[92] The use of the concept of "mental disorder" from the civil law[93] which "has been changed to reflect more up-to-date medical ideas"[94] may also reflect something of a rapprochement between the two fields.

20.8 DISPOSALS

20.8.1 As previously stated,[95] a successful defence of mental disorder leads to acquittal, but this is on the basis that the accused has in fact

---

[87] Gordon (2000) at paras 10.02, 10.08 and 10.10.
[88] Tadros (2001) at 339 cites Lord McCluskey in *Ross* v *HM Advocate* 1991 JC 210 at 228 where he states: "I know of no exceptions, other than statutory ones, to the rule that the Crown must prove *mens rea* beyond reasonable doubt. Even in a case where the defence lodge a special defence of insanity at the time of the offence the Crown has still to lead evidence from which *mens rea* can be inferred or by means of which *mens rea* can be proved directly. If there were to be no such evidence at all the proper verdict in such a case would be a simple verdict of 'not guilty'. It is only if there is evidence which would otherwise warrant a conclusion that *mens rea* had been proved beyond reasonable doubt that a jury would be entitled, if satisfied on the balance of probabilities that the special defence of insanity was made out, to acquit the accused on the ground of his insanity at the time of doing the (criminal) act."
[89] See from section 6.18 above.
[90] See *HM Advocate* v *Kidd* 1960 JC 61 at 70 per Lord Strachan; *HM Advocate* v *Brennan* 1977 JC 38 at 42–43 per LJ-G Emslie.
[91] Scottish Law Commission (2004), para 2.23.
[92] *Ibid*, para 2.10.
[93] See section 20.7.2 above.
[94] Scottish Law Commission (2004), para 2.10.
[95] Section 20.2.1 above.

performed an act which would otherwise constitute a criminal offence. It is on this basis that the law deems it appropriate to exercise continuing control over her. It is clear from the foregoing that the pre-1995 law on insanity, whether as a plea in bar of trial or as a special defence, left no space for discretion in disposal options. The 1995 Act allows for much greater flexibility, including the option of imposing no order whatsoever[96] – an option which might seem appropriate, for example, in the case of a diabetic or an epileptic who is forced, by the narrowness of the defence of automatism, to plead mental disorder.[97]

The 1995 Act sets down six possible disposals where the accused is found to satisfy the mental disorder defence.[98] These are to make: **20.8.2**

(1) a compulsion order, authorising the detention of the person in hospital;

(2) a restriction order, in addition to making a compulsion order;

(3) an interim compulsion order;

(4) a guardianship order;

(5) a supervision and treatment order; or

(6) no order.

The circumstances in which it is possible to make a "compulsion order" are circumscribed by detailed provisions in the legislation.[99] This is because Art 5(1) of the ECHR establishes a right to liberty and security of the person, and this can only be infringed in accordance with the exceptions set down in its sub-clauses. The relevant provision here is Art 5(1)(e) which permits "the *lawful* detention of persons ... of unsound mind".[100] To ensure compliance with the Convention the detention must accord with the principles set out in the jurisprudence of the European Court, and this requires evidence that the accused is suffering from a mental disorder such that public protection requires continued detention in hospital.[101]

It is conceivable that an accused might suffer from a transient lack of criminal responsibility because of mental disorder at the **20.8.3**

---

[96] Criminal Procedure (Scotland) Act 1995, s 57(2)(e).
[97] See section 20.19.3 below.
[98] Criminal Procedure (Scotland) Act 1995, s 57. This may arise either through directly pleading the defence set down in s 51A or where the examination of facts, following a successful plea of unfitness for trial, determines that the accused did carry out the criminal behaviour libelled but that the mental disorder defence would have applied (s 55).
[99] *Ibid*, s 57A.
[100] Emphasis added. See also *Reid v HM Advocate* 2013 SLT 65.
[101] *Anderson v Scottish Ministers* [2003] 2 AC 602 at 615, para 27, per Lord Hope.

time of the crime but, by the time of the trial, and subsequently, be restored to full mental health. While it may be difficult in those circumstances to *prove* the mental disorder at the time of the crime itself, an accused who is able to do so must be acquitted on this ground. The question then arises as to how the court is to deal with such a case. It is, of course, open to the judge to impose one of the disposal options listed in s 57 of the 1995 Act.[102] However, the circumstances in which, for example, a compulsion order could be made are strictly limited by s 57A and a person who is at the date of the disposal not suffering from any mental disorder simply would not satisfy them. It is likely, therefore, that the only appropriate outcome would be for the court to make no order.[103] This, then, raises the spectre of an individual who has committed a, possibly serious, crime being released without sanction. Legally, this would be an entirely correct outcome, since it has been established that the individual lacked criminal responsibility. Yet there may well be a sense that the public interest in justice being seen to be done has not been satisfied. A prominent example from the United States is the case of John Hinckley, who had attempted to assassinate President Ronald Reagan in 1981. Hinckley was allowed to plead insanity but this caused much public disquiet, to the extent that a number of states abolished the insanity defence.[104] The issue of the abolition of the defence is interesting. It is surely imperative that courts are permitted to recognise severe mental illness and the effect which this can have on the accused's ability to formulate *mens rea*.[105]

20.9   CRITIQUE OF THE SPECIAL DEFENCE OF MENTAL DISORDER AND PROPOSALS FOR REFORM

20.9.1   We have already noted that the term "insanity" may be stigmatising or pejorative.[106] For that reason, the shift to terminology of "mental disorder" is both welcome and long overdue. Accordingly, it is perhaps surprising that the only issue which seems to have arisen in case law following the coming into force of s 51A is its relationship to the pre-existing law. Frustratingly, the decision is only at sheriff court level and this key point was not directly in issue.[107] In his judgment, *obiter*, Sheriff Baird stated

---

[102] See section 20.8.2 above.
[103] Section 57(2)(e) of the 1995 Act.
[104] See R D Mackay, "Post-Hinckley insanity in the U.S.A." [1988] *Crim LR* 88.
[105] See also Scottish Law Commission (2004), paras 2.15–2.18.
[106] See section 20.4.2 above; see also Scottish Law Commission (2004), para 2.19.
[107] *Dunn* v *W* 2013 SLT (Sh Ct) 2.

"it is not completely clear if it was intended by Parliament to introduce a standard which is less than what might have been required under the old law or if all that was intended was a change in terminology, but not in the relevant test. That point may well have to be argued in an appropriate case".[108]

The definition of "insanity" in the "old law" was as follows:

"To serve the purpose of a defence in law, the disorder must ... amount to an absolute alienation of reason, ... such a disease as deprives the patient of the knowledge of the true aspect and position of things about him, – hinders him from distinguishing friend or foe, – and gives him up to the impulse of his own distempered fancy."[109]

This passage is somewhat hyperbolic but it is clear as to the extremeness of the level of mental disturbance from which the accused must have been suffering before insanity could be pled; she was required to have lost her grip on reality. The s 51A test is expressed in rather more prosaic language. It requires only that the accused is "unable ... to appreciate the nature or wrongfulness of the conduct". It eschews Hume's colourful terminology and does not require even that the accused's inability should be *absolute*. Nonetheless, in clarifying the distinction between "knowledge" and "appreciation"[110] the Scottish Law Commission stated: "the test we propose can be understood as making explicit, and in modern language, what is implicit in the classic definition to be found in Hume".[111] This suggests that no clear difference in standard was intended. The defence in s 51A exists to ensure that those who suffer from serious mental disorder are not held to be criminally responsible. Indeed, as the Law Commission has stated, it is "a fundamental principle of the criminal law ... that where a person suffers from a severe mental disorder it is unfair to hold that person criminally responsible".[112] As long as the test currently in use achieves the purpose of appropriately identifying those individuals who come into this category, it is a matter of purely academic interest whether it is now easier to make such a finding.

20.10 DIMINISHED RESPONSIBILITY

The law on diminished responsibility is now found in s 51B of the Criminal Procedure (Scotland) Act 1995. In some senses this is not a defence at all, since it neither excuses nor justifies, but as it is regarded as a lesser form of mental disorder it is convenient to

20.10.1

---

[108] 2013 SLT (Sh Ct) 2 at 4, para [16].
[109] Hume, i, 37.
[110] See section 20.7.3 above.
[111] Scottish Law Commission (2004), para 2.48.
[112] *Ibid*, para 2.17.

discuss it here. In terms of s 78(2) of the 1995 Act, it is subject to the same requirement to notify, in advance, the court and the Crown of the intention to plead it, as are special defences. Diminished responsibility arises "if the [accused]'s ability to determine or control conduct for which the [accused] would otherwise be convicted of murder was, at the time of the conduct, substantially impaired by reason of abnormality of mind".[113] Thus, it operates to mitigate murder to (voluntary) culpable homicide. Section 51B(1) relates only to conviction of culpable homicide where the charge is murder. Since any common law rule on diminished responsibility ceased to have effect from 25 June 2012[114] it seems clear that the plea is now only available in response to a murder charge.[115] Nonetheless, it is open to an accused charged with other crimes to suggest that her mental state was such that it ought to be taken into account in mitigation of sentence and, in practice, it is not uncommon for defence counsel to inform the court of their clients' mental health problems, prior to sentencing.[116]

20.10.2   As previously noted,[117] the onus of proving diminished responsibility is placed on the accused on the balance of probabilities.[118] The fact that this shifting of the onus is compliant with the presumption of innocence in Art 6(2) of the ECHR was affirmed in *Lilburn* v *HM Advocate*[119] where the court examined the relevant parts of the Scottish Law Commission Report[120] and authorities from other jurisdictions.[121] Unlike unfitness for trial and the special defence of mental disorder, the statutory definition of diminished responsibility largely codifies the pre-existing law. Accordingly, it is worth briefly tracing its common law evolution. A plea of diminished responsibility was introduced into England in the 1950s but had been available in Scotland for hundreds of years before that. It was defined in the case of *HM Advocate* v *Savage*[122] in 1923 as requiring:

---

[113] Criminal Procedure (Scotland) Act 1995, s 51B(1).

[114] Criminal Justice and Licensing (Scotland) Act 2010, s 171.

[115] Though, for an alternative view, see discussion in section 20.11.2 below.

[116] In *C* v *HM Advocate* 2009 SLT 707, the appeal court held that even where a plea of diminished responsibility has not been accepted by the jury, the sentencing judge could nonetheless take into account the accused's mental disorder in determining the punishment element of the life sentence.

[117] See section 20.3.1 above.

[118] Criminal Procedure (Scotland) Act 1995, s 51B(4).

[119] 2012 JC 150.

[120] Scottish Law Commission (2004), paras 5.21, 5.28, 5.47 and 5.48.

[121] *Lilburn* v *HM Advocate* 2012 JC 150 at 153–154 paras [6]-[9] per LJ-G Hamilton.

[122] 1923 JC 49.

"some form of mental unsoundness; ... there must be a state of mind which is bordering on, though not amounting to, insanity; ... there must be a mind so affected that responsibility is diminished from full responsibility to partial responsibility – in other words, the [accused] ... must be only partially accountable for his actions. And I think one can see running through the cases that there is implied ... that there must be some form of mental disease".[123]

The case of *Galbraith* v *HM Advocate (No 2)*,[124] on which s 51B is based, was an appeal relating to the interpretation of *Savage*. The the accused was charged with the murder of her husband, who was a police officer, after she shot him using one of his own rifles. She then took various steps to suggest that two intruders had broken in. Evidence was led from two psychologists that at the time of the killing she suffered from a form of post-traumatic stress disorder as the result of years of sexual abuse by her husband. This had overwhelmed her ability to think rationally and had led her to believe that the only possible way for her to escape from her husband was to kill him. A psychiatrist also gave evidence that the accused had been suffering from clinical depression. The trial judge directed the jury in terms of *Savage*,[125] that for the plea of diminished responsibility to succeed there must be (i) aberration or weakness of mind, (ii) some form of mental unsoundness, (iii) a state of mind bordering on though not amounting to insanity, (iv) a mind so affected that responsibility was diminished from full responsibility to partial responsibility, and also that there must be some form of mental disease. Galbraith's appeal against conviction for murder turned, effectively, on whether the trial judge's directions were correct.   20.10.3

The case was remitted to a Bench of Five Judges. The Crown conceded that the trial judge had misdirected the jury and accepted that all the elements in the *Savage*[126] test did not require to be satisfied. The appeal court held that there need not be evidence of some form of mental disease. Instead, the jury should be told that they must be satisfied that, by reason of the abnormality of mind in question, the ability of the accused to determine or control her actions was substantially impaired, as compared with a normal person. Accordingly, *Galbraith*[127] broadened the definition of diminished responsibility. The statutory test in s 51B echoes these principles though, in accordance with its approach to the special defence of mental disorder, it rightly concentrates on   20.10.4

---

[123] 1923 JC 49 at 51 per LJ-C Alness in his charge to the jury.
[124] 2002 JC 1.
[125] 1923 JC 49.
[126] *Ibid*.
[127] 2002 JC 1.

the effect of the abnormality of mind on the accused's ability to determine or control her conduct, rather than on any comparison with a "normal" person. The test itself is still a legal one: although evidence from medical witnesses and/or psychologists is likely to be pertinent, it is not a statutory requirement. Nonetheless, the Scottish Law Commission commented that, in relation to cases applying the *Galbraith* test: "various practitioners in the fields of psychiatry and clinical psychology have expressed general satisfaction ... and indicated that from their own perspective the new law is workable".[128] It is, initially, a question for the judge to decide whether, as a matter of law, the evidence discloses a sufficient basis on which the accused's responsibility for her actions could be regarded as diminished in terms of s 51B such that the matter can be put to the jury at all.

20.10.5   The five-judge court in *Galbraith*[129] gave general guidance as to the meaning of "mental abnormality". As examples, it suggested that (1) the accused might perceive physical acts and matters differently from a normal person; or (2) mental abnormality might affect her ability to form a rational judgement as to whether a particular act was right or wrong, or as to whether to perform that act.[130] Following previous decisions of the appeal court, *Galbraith* affirmed that neither self-induced impairment through the ingestion of alcohol or drugs[131] nor psychopathic personality disorder[132] could ground a plea of diminished responsibility. The new statutory test in s 51B departs from these restrictions.[133]

20.11   CRITIQUE OF THE LAW ON DIMINISHED RESPONSIBILITY AND PROPOSALS FOR REFORM

20.11.1   It should be noted that, at the time of making its recommendation that the test in *Galbraith* v *HM Advocate*[134] should, effectively, be retained but recast in statutory form, the Scottish Law Commission "had in mind a future project on the law of homicide [within which]

---

[128] Scottish Law Commission (2004), para 3.4.

[129] 2002 JC 1.

[130] *Galbraith* v *HM Advocate* 2002 JC 1 at 19, para [51] per LJ-G Rodger. The Scottish Goverment's *Explanatory Notes* to the Criminal Justice and Licensing (Scotland) Act 2010 state that "Comments by the Court in the *Galbraith* case on this part of the common law test will be of use in interpreting the statutory test" (note 711).

[131] *Brennan* v *HM Advocate* 1977 JC 38. This case is discussed further from section 20.13 below.

[132] *Carraher* v *HM Advocate* 1946 JC 108.

[133] See sections 20.11.4 and 20.11.5 below.

[134] 2002 JC 1.

... the whole issue of partial defences to murder ... could be fully considered".[135] While the Commission had included an examination of homicide in its *Eighth Programme of Law Reform*, at the time of writing, "Due to other priorities, work on this project is not progressing at present."[136] It is not clear whether the Commission would have made more radical proposals if this further opportunity to consider the issue had not been anticipated.

It is also interesting to look at the underlying rationale for the **20.11.2** diminished responsibility defence. Shortly before the new law came into force, in *HM Advocate* v *Kerr*,[137] the appeal court had stated that diminished responsibility could be pled in relation to a charge of attempted murder also, but to no other crime.[138] This was on the basis that the *mens rea* of attempted murder is the same as that of the completed crime.[139] If diminished responsibility were to be established, it would demonstrate that the necessary wicked intention or wicked recklessness[140] did not exist. Thus, lacking the *mens rea* for attempted murder, the accused could only be convicted of a crime for which the mental element could be proved, such as aggravated assault. This approach recognises diminished responsibility very much as a partial defence which operates directly to reduce the accused's criminal responsibility for the crime charged. The alternative view, propounded by the Crown in *Kerr*, was that diminished responsibility is a mitigating plea, required in relation to murder alone, where the mandatory life sentence is, in certain circumstances, accepted as too harsh.[141] The explicit reference to murder in s 51B(1) seems to suggest that it is this rationale which has been accepted by the legislature. Nonetheless, in *Kerr*, the court specifically reserved its position in relation to this matter under s 51B.[142] While it is widely understood that the rationale for diminished responsibility is as a "mitigating circumstance",[143] in a legal system which makes very little provision for lack of cognitive understanding, except in its extreme form, the "partial defence" approach is worthy of reconsideration.

In certain respects, s 51B has broadened and clarified the law on **20.11.3** diminished responsibility. First, it specifies that the basis of the plea

---

[135] Maher (2013) at 3.
[136] Scottish Law Commission website: homicide project page: http://www.scotlaw com.gov.uk/law-reform-projects/homicide/.
[137] 2011 SLT 430.
[138] *Ibid.*
[139] *Cawthorne* v *HM Advocate* 1968 JC 32.
[140] See from section 9.10.2 above.
[141] 2011 SLT 430, at [3]. See, also, Scottish Law Commission (2004), para 3.45.
[142] *Ibid* at 432, para [5] per Lord Hardie (referring, *inter alia*, to s 168 of the Criminal Justice and Licensing (Scotland) Act 2010 which inserted s 51B into the Criminal Procedure (Scotland) Act 1995).
[143] Scottish Law Commission (2004), para 3.16.

may be grounded in "mental disorder",[144] the same as the special defence. Cases decided under the pre-existing law had suggested that diminished responsibility would arise from a condition which bordered on but did not amount to (then) insanity.[145] Now, the pleas are separated primarily by the distinct tests. Diminished responsibility requires an abnormality of mind (which may be constituted by mental disorder but does not have to be) which substantially impairs the accused's ability to determine or control her conduct. The special defence requires mental disorder which renders her unable to appreciate the nature or wrongfulness of the conduct. The application of these self-standing tests will provide greater clarity than requiring the court, possibly without the benefit of medical evidence, to attempt to calibrate degrees of mental ill-health and/or disability.

20.11.4   Second, in making no provision at all in relation to accused who suffer from a psychopathic personality disorder, s 51B allows a plea of diminished responsibility where such a disorder is the cause of the alleged abnormality of mind.[146] We are critical[147] of the absolute exclusion of psychopathy as the basis of the special defence,[148] given the spectrum of conditions which it might encompass.[149] Accordingly, it is appropriate that it may be used as the basis of this broader category of "abnormality of mind".

20.11.5   Finally, s 51B(3) nuances the common law position that voluntary intoxication cannot constitute the basis of the plea.[150] As Maher explains, "although acute intoxication does not by itself constitute diminished responsibility, the fact that the accused was intoxicated at the time does not prevent diminished responsibility being established on the basis of some other mental condition".[151] While this principle may previously have been implied, it is useful to have it clearly specified.

20.11.6   With regard to mental disorder defences generally, but particularly to diminished responsibility, Hilary Allen has suggested that there is a gender dimension. She points out that in England and Wales women who are accused of crime are about twice as likely as men to be dealt with by a psychiatric disposal. Insanity and diminished

---

[144] Criminal Procedure (Scotland) Act 1995, s 51B(2).
[145] See, for example, *HM Advocate* v *Savage* 1923 JC 49 at 50 per LJ-C Alness; *Lindsay* v *HM Advocate* 1997 SLT 67 quoting the trial judge, Lord Hamilton, at 69.
[146] Scottish Law Commission (2004), paras 3.24–3.34.
[147] See section 20.7.6 above.
[148] Criminal Procedure (Scotland) Act 1995, s 51A(2).
[149] See Shaw (2009).
[150] *Brennan* v *HM Advocate* 1977 JC 38 at 47 per LJ-G Emslie.
[151] Maher (2013) at 4.

responsibility are also pled far more often by women. Allen's thesis is that this is in large measure due to stereotypical expectations on the part of judges, lawyers and psychiatrists as to how women and men ought to behave.[152]

As we have seen, the accused in *Galbraith*[153] alleged that her **20.11.7** husband had subjected her to physical and sexual violence over a number of years, and that this had caused her "mental abnormality". Although the term "battered woman's syndrome" was not used, it is arguable that the case opened the door to a defence based on this form of post-traumatic stress disorder. According to Lenore Walker:

> "Women who are repeatedly exposed to painful stimuli over which they have no control and from which there is no apparent escape, respond with the classic symptoms of learned helplessness. They become passive, lose their motivation to respond, and come to believe that nothing they do will alter or affect any outcome. ... they eventually cease trying to avoid pain and fail to recognise or take advantage of avenues of escape."[154]

Indeed, they may believe that their only means of escape – and survival – is to kill their abusive partner.[155]

Fiona Raitt and Suzanne Zeedyk have noted that the practice **20.11.8** in Scotland is for battered women who kill their abusive partners to plead guilty to culpable homicide, on the basis of diminished responsibility.[156] They point out that this is not as favourable to such women as it at first sight appears:

> "The woman has less opportunity to have her actions (ever) characterised as self-defence; they are immediately classified as disordered. The decision has already been taken that she killed [her partner] as a consequence of her disordered mental state. As it becomes known that an initial plea of diminished responsibility is likely to be 'successful', more and more women will have their experience forced into this mould. Less and less women will have a chance of asserting what it is that they believe and what it is that [battered woman's syndrome] was intended to help them communicate: that they acted reasonably, in self-defence."[157]

As we shall see when we consider the requirements of a successful plea of self-defence, one difficulty encountered by battered women

---

[152] H Allen, *Justice Unbalanced: Gender Psychiatry and Judicial Decisions* (1987). See also M S Zeedyk and F E Raitt, "Psychological theory in law: legitimating the male norm" (1997) 7 *Feminism & Psychology* 539.
[153] 2002 JC 1.
[154] L E Walker, *The Battered Woman* (1979), pp 49–50. Her theories are, however, controversial – see D L Faigman and A J Wright, "The battered woman syndrome in the age of science" (1997) 39 *Arizona Law Rev* 67.
[155] See also the discussion on "battered woman's syndrome", in relation to self-defence and provocation, from sections 21.9.7 and 21.11.8 respectively below.
[156] F E Raitt and M S Zeedyk, *The Implicit Relation of Psychology and Law* (2000), p 75.
[157] *Ibid.*

who kill their abusers is that in many cases the killings take place when the danger faced by the women is not an immediate one.[158]

20.12   INTOXICATION

20.12.1   The issues here have been well summarised by Rebecca Williams:

> "The problem of voluntary intoxication raises in a sharp form three of criminal law's most familiar dilemmas. How can we treat the [accused] subjectively and thus fairly while also protecting society at large? How can we respond to the various different impacts of intoxication without overcomplicating the law, and how can we achieve the level of specificity in criminal law that is compatible with fair labelling ... ?"[159]

Intoxication can be brought about by the consumption of alcohol or drugs, or a combination of both. It is important to bear in mind that it can be induced by drugs that can be acquired lawfully (on prescription, or even by being purchased from a pharmacy) as well as by proscribed drugs, such as heroin, cocaine, cannabis etc.[160] Celia Wells and Oliver Quick cite Home Office statistics which show that alcohol is associated with "football hooliganism, youth disorder and violence. It is estimated that 65 per cent of murders, 75 per cent of stabbings, and 50 per cent of fights or domestic assaults are committed while the offender is under the influence of alcohol or drugs".[161] According to the Justice Secretary, Kenny MacAskill, speaking in 2007, in Scotland seven out of ten of those accused of murder had been drinking or on drugs, and almost half of all prisoners report that they were drunk when they committed their offence.[162] The law distinguishes between culpable and non-culpable intoxication, though the terms "voluntary" and "involuntary" tend to be used.

20.13   VOLUNTARY INTOXICATION

20.13.1   Scots law does not accept voluntary intoxication as a defence to any charge. This follows from Hume's trenchant views on the subject:

---

[158] For a discussion of the immediacy requirement, see from section 21.10.12 below.

[159] R Williams, "Voluntary intoxication – a lost cause?" (2013) 129 *LQR* 264 at 288.

[160] For details of offences relating to the possession and supply of such drugs, see the Misuse of Drugs Act 1971, discussed from section 8.9 above.

[161] C Wells and O Quick, *Lacey, Wells and Quick, Reconstructing Criminal Law: Text and Materials* (4th edn, 2010), pp 268–269.

[162] The Justice Secretary was speaking at a World Health Organization conference on 17 July 2007. See http://www.scotland.gov.uk/News/Releases/2007/07/17091325.

"certain it is, that the law of Scotland views this wilful distemper with a quite different eye from the other, which is the visitation of Providence; and if it does not consider the man's intemperance as an aggravation, at least sees very good reasons why it should not be allowed as an excuse, to save him from the ordinary pains of his transgression".[163]

The current law on intoxication, which is still found in *Brennan v HM Advocate*,[164] restates this basic principle. The accused was found guilty of murdering his father by stabbing him repeatedly. This was despite the fact that he had voluntarily consumed between 20 and 25 pints of beer, a glass of sherry and a quantity of LSD before he did so. The approach Scots criminal law takes to extreme voluntary intoxication is to treat it as an act of recklessness, in itself. Accordingly, if the mental element of the particular crime libelled includes recklessness (or, by extension, "wicked recklessness") voluntary intoxication cannot be a defence.[165] Lord Justice-General Emslie stated:

"There is nothing unethical or unfair or contrary to the general principle of our law that self-induced intoxication is not by itself a defence to any criminal charge including in particular the charge of murder. Self-induced intoxication is itself a continuing element and therefore an integral part of any crime of violence, including murder, the other part being the evidence of the actings of the accused who uses force against his victim. Together they add up or may add up to that criminal recklessness which it is the purpose of the criminal law to restrain in the interests of all the citizens of this country."[166]

What if the *mens rea* for the crime requires an *intention* to do something? In reality, an accused may become incapable of forming any kind of intention through the ingestion of intoxicating substances. Despite this, as Lord Justice-General Hope made clear in the authoritative case of *Ross v HM Advocate*,[167] Scots law does not recognise any defence based upon the argument that self-induced intoxication has resulted in the absence of *mens rea*.This is the prevailing view because, in such cases, "the accused must be *assumed* to have intended the natural consequences of his act".[168] The Scottish Parliament has now passed legislation making clear

20.13.2

---

[163] Hume, i, 45.

[164] 1977 JC 38.

[165] In *Donaldson* v *Normand* 1997 JC 200 the court referred to *Brennan's* case in holding that it was irrelevant in a charge of culpable and reckless endangerment that the accused had forgotten that he had a needle in his sock, if this failure to remember was due to self-induced intoxication. See section 10.13.1 above.

[166] 1977 JC 38 at 51.

[167] 1991 JC 210. See also from section 20.17.1 below.

[168] *Ibid* at 214, per LJ-G Hope (emphasis added).

also that sentencing courts must not take voluntary intoxication into account by way of mitigation.[169]

20.14   CRITIQUE OF THE LAW ON VOLUNTARY INTOXICATION AND PROPOSALS FOR REFORM

20.14.1   The decision in *Brennan*'s case[170] is difficult to justify in strict legal theory. Murder requires an intent to kill or wicked recklessness;[171] the contemporaneity principle requires one or other of these mental states to be proven to have been present at the time of the killing.[172] The law holds Brennan to be morally blameworthy because of his prior fault in becoming extremely drunk, but that act did not, in itself, make it likely that he would cause harm to another person. Of course, it could be argued that those who deliberately become acutely intoxicated know, or ought to know, that they may well do things in that state that they would not otherwise do, and hence the criminal law is punishing them for their recklessness. It must, however, be borne in mind that the recklessness required for murder is "*wicked* recklessness". As previously noted,[173] this is an expression which is used only in relation to murder, and which has a particular meaning. A person is said to be wickedly reckless when she reaches a point of indifference as to the consequences of her attack on the victim; when she does not care whether the victim lives or dies. This can hardly be applied to the behaviour of Mr Brennan.

20.14.2   We have also noted hitherto that the case of *HM Advocate* v *Purcell*[174] had indicated that there had to be conduct which was intended to cause physical injury before the accused could be said to have had the wicked recklessness/indifference to the likelihood of causing death required for a conviction of murder.[175] This is not the case in English law where intoxication is sufficient for liability where the crime in question is one of "basic intent". If, however, a crime requires "specific intent" as, for example, murder does in its requirement that the accused intend *to kill or cause grievous bodily harm*, then it is accepted that voluntary intoxication may make

---

[169] Criminal Justice and Licensing (Scotland) Act 2010, s 26.
[170] 1977 JC 38.
[171] See section 9.11.1 above.
[172] See from section 6.19 above.
[173] See from section 9.12 above for a discussion of "wicked recklessness".
[174] 2008 JC 131, discussed at section 9.12.7 above.
[175] As James Chalmers has noted, it is difficult to reconcile *Brennan* and *Purcell* – see "The true meaning of 'wicked recklessness': *HM Advocate* v *Purcell*" (2008) 12 *Edin LR* 298 at 301.

it impossible for the accused to formulate the specific intent. The accused may therefore be convicted of manslaughter.[176]

20.14.3 The fact that the Scottish appeal court's stance on voluntary intoxication applies to all crimes, not just to murder, serves to compound its unfairness. If a crime can only be committed intentionally, and the accused does not, for example, intend to deprive the owner of her property (in theft) or to cause immediate bodily harm or fear of such harm (in assault) then the prosecution is unable to establish all the elements of its case. Logically, this is so even if the lack of intention results from self-induced intoxication. Nonetheless, Scots law allows the fact of voluntarily drinking (or taking drugs) to excess to supply a sufficient fault element in these crimes, also.[177] It certainly seems arguable that the specific *mens rea* for the crime in question may not be fulfilled. The emphasis appears to be more on the fact that the accused had the effrontery to become intoxicated than on the application of the principles of *mens rea*.

20.14.4 Clearly there are good public policy grounds for not allowing voluntary intoxication to constitute a defence. The appeal court has adopted a highly pragmatic approach: allowing a defence of voluntary intoxication would encourage people to drink themselves into a state of acquittal.[178] Furthermore, a person who is responsible for becoming drunk should be aware of the risks involved, so far as the law is concerned, at least. These do not, however, provide an adequate explanation for departing from the fundamental principle that the prosecution must prove the *actus reus* and *mens rea* of each common law crime, and must do so beyond reasonable doubt.

20.14.5 More than 30 years ago, the *Committee on Mentally Abnormal Offenders*[179] (the Butler Committee) recommended that English law be amended so that:

> "it should be an offence for a person while voluntarily intoxicated to do an act (or make an omission) that would amount to a dangerous offence if it were done or made with the requisite state of mind for such offence. The

---

[176] *DPP* v *Majewski* [1977] AC 443. See also A P Simester, "Intoxication is never a defence" [2009] *Crim LR* 3. The (English) Law Commisssion has re-examined the relationship between intoxication and criminal liability (*Intoxication and Criminal Liability* (Law Com No 314, Cm 7526, 2009)).

[177] In *Ebsworth* v *HM Advocate* 1992 SLT 1161 (a case in which the accused opted for the defence of automatism, rather than voluntary intoxication) Lord Hope stated: "The element of guilt or moral turpitude lies in the taking of drink or drugs voluntarily and reckless of their possible consequences" (at 1166).

[178] Hume emphasised the need for the law to provide protection against those "who might inflame themselves with liquor, on purpose to gain courage to indulge their malice" (Hume, i, 46).

[179] (1975).

prosecution would not charge this offence in the first instance, but would charge an offence under the ordinary law. If evidence of intoxication were given at the trial for the purpose of negativing the intent or other mental element required for the offence, the jury would be directed that they may return a verdict of not guilty of that offence but guilty of the offence of dangerous intoxication if they find that the defendant did the act (or made the omission) charged but by reason of the evidence of intoxication they are not sure that at the time he had the state of mind required for the offence, and they are sure that his intoxication was voluntary".[180]

The Butler Committee proposed maximum penalties of imprisonment of 1 year for a first offence, and 3 years for a subsequent offence.[181] These proposals may be regarded as excessively lenient; much depends on whether one believes that the law ought to be punishing the accused for the act of becoming so drunk, or for the harm caused once in that condition. In 1993, the English Law Commission considered that the penalties proposed by the Butler Committee were too low, and recommended that a statutory offence of causing harm while intoxicated be enacted, with a maximum sentence of two-thirds that of the underlying offence, or 10 years' imprisonment in homicide cases.[182] We suggest that similar proposals be considered for Scotland.

20.15   INVOLUNTARY INTOXICATION

20.15.1   The courts have held that where intoxication is *in*voluntary, the accused is entitled to an acquittal only if the effects of the intoxicant were to induce a semi-conscious state. "Automatism" is the term used to describe a person who is not fully conscious. One might imagine that the courts would simply find such people "not guilty"; someone who is in a semi-conscious state is, almost by definition, unable to form the *mens rea* which is necessary for a conviction. The difficulty with acquitting in cases of automatism is that the criminal courts can only impose controls over an accused person's future conduct if there is first a conviction.

20.16   AUTOMATISM

20.16.1   As we have seen,[183] historically a verdict of "not guilty by reason of insanity" resulted in compulsory incarceration without limit

---

[180] Butler Committee (1975), para 18.54.
[181] *Ibid*, para 18.58.
[182] Law Commission Consultation Paper: *Intoxication and Criminal Liability* (No 127, 1993). For the Law Commission's current thinking on this issue, see Law Commission (2009).
[183] See section 20.7.1 above.

of time in a hospital for the mentally ill. Because of these serious consequences, accused persons tried to argue that their condition was such as to negate *mens rea*, but that it fell short of insanity. The criminal law generally seeks to punish only voluntary actions, or actions which the accused would have been able to avoid committing. The defence of automatism is concerned with involuntary actions – actions where, although the accused was the agent who carried them out, it is recognised that it would have been impossible for her to have avoided doing so. Of crucial importance here is the absence of fault on the part of the accused in relation to the occurrence of the condition which made it impossible for her to avoid commission of the crime. In practice, the defence has most commonly been pled where an accused's alcoholic drink has been "spiked" with drugs.

In the modern law, automatism can be traced back to the 1925 **20.16.2** case of *HM Advocate* v *Ritchie*.[184] Ritchie was charged with driving culpably and recklessly as a result of which he knocked down and killed someone. He lodged a special defence which stated that he was not guilty because of "the incidence of temporary mental dissociation, due to toxic exhaustive factors".[185] At no time in the, admittedly brief, report of part of Lord Murray's charge to the jury is the term "automatism" used. Instead, Lord Murray explains that

> "where … a person … becomes – owing to a cause which he was not bound to foresee, and which was outwith his control – either gradually or suddenly not the master of his own action, a question as to his responsibility or irresponsibility for the consequences of his actions arises, and may form the ground of a good special defence".[186]

The relevant "cause" in this case was the "toxic exhaustive **20.16.3** factors";[187] the loss of mastery of action is characterised as "mental dissociation". The real issue here was the court's view that the accused could not control his actions. According to H L A Hart, the conditions in which it is appropriate to require an individual to take criminal responsibility are, broadly, that she has an understanding of the crime, and the ability to exercise her control and will either to act or not to act.[188] On this basis, it is debatable whether

---

[184] 1926 SLT 308.
[185] *Ibid* at 310.
[186] *Ibid*.
[187] For a discussion of the meaning of this phrase, see J M Ross, "A long motor run on a dark night: reconstructing *HM Advocate* v *Ritchie*" (2010) 14 *Edin LR* 193. See also section 20.18.1 below.
[188] H L A Hart, *Punishment and Responsibility: Essays in the Philosophy of Law* (1968), Chap 1. See also N Lacey, *State Punishment: Political Principles and Community Values* (1988), especially at pp 62–63.

someone who acts while in a state of automatism has sufficient understanding of the act in the first place. What is certain is that she does not have a fair opportunity to choose not to commit the criminal act.

20.17   THE CURRENT POSITION

20.17.1   The defence was occasionally pled between *Ritchie's* case in 1925 and the early 1990s,[189] but its parameters were not particularly clear. It was resurrected in the case of *Ross v HM Advocate*,[190] in which the accused had gone berserk with a knife. He had seriously injured various people, most of whom were complete strangers to him, and faced an indictment libelling, *inter alia*, seven charges of attempted murder. It was established that he had been drinking lager from a can but that, *unknown to him*, five or six tablets of temazepam and some LSD had been added to it. The appeal court recognised the inherent unfairness of convicting someone in these circumstances and quashed the accused's conviction, on the basis that he had been rendered unable to formulate *mens rea* due to no fault of his own. Since *mens rea* is an essential element of the Crown's case, the inability to establish it beyond reasonable doubt means that acquittal is the only possible outcome.[191]

20.17.2   Four conditions must be satisfied to establish the defence[192] (though only an evidential burden is placed on the accused):[193]

(1) The accused must have been suffering from "a total alienation of reason amounting to a complete absence of self-control".[194] (It was established that the drugs which Ross ingested had this effect on him.)

(2) Such alienation must have been caused by an external factor (the drugs in the lager).

(3) That factor must not have been self-induced (someone else put the drugs there).

---

[189] See, for example, *Stevenson v Beatson* 1965 SLT (Sh Ct) 11. The accused suffered a head injury when the vehicle he was driving collided with a wall. He tried, unsuccessfully, to plead automatism in relation to three further collisions which occurred thereafter when he continued driving while in a state of concussion.

[190] 1991 JC 210. See also section 20.13.2 above.

[191] *Ibid* at 217 per LJ-G Hope.

[192] *Ibid* at 218 and 222.

[193] *Ibid* at 221.

[194] *Ibid* at 218. Subsequently in his opinion, Lord Hope states this test as being constituted by "a total loss of control of ... actions in regard to the crime ... charged" (*ibid* at 222).

(4) The factor must also not be one which the accused was bound to foresee. (Ross had no idea that he was taking drugs therefore he could not foresee any consequences of this.)

All of these conditions were satisfied, thus it was held that Ross had no *mens rea* and his conviction was overturned.

Subsequent cases have demonstrated that the appeal court's **20.17.3** endorsement of the existence of this defence did not mean that it would be easy for an accused to make use of its terms. Instead, the court has made clear that an accused would require compelling direct evidence on all four of the points covered by the test. In *Sorley* v *HM Advocate*,[195] no expert medical evidence was led as to the effect which LSD added to a can of lager would have had on the accused. Accordingly, the court took the view that it had no evidence either that there was a causative link between the ingestion of LSD and the accused's mental state, or that the mental state amounted to a total alienation of reason. The defence of automatism therefore failed. In delivering the judgment of the court, Lord Justice-General Hope stated that the case "should be seen as an illustration of the warning which was given in Ross about the strict limits which must be applied to this defence".[196]

This point was again affirmed in *Cardle* v *Mulrainey*,[197] where **20.17.4** amphetamines were introduced into the accused's lager without his knowledge. This led him to commit a series of criminal acts in a very short space of time. He knew that these acts were wrong but he claimed that the effect of the amphetamine was to rob him of the ability to stop himself. The judgment was again delivered by Lord Hope who stated:

> "Where, as in the present case, the accused knew what he was doing and was aware of the nature and quality of his acts and that what he was doing was wrong, he cannot be said to be suffering from some [*sic*] total alienation of reason in regard to the crime with which he is charged which the defence requires."[198]

This brings into focus the first of the tests from *Ross* identified in **20.17.5** section 20.17.2 above: the need for "a total alienation of reason amounting to a complete absence of self-control".[199] This was, of course, also the test of insanity at common law as set down by

---

[195] 1992 JC 102.
[196] *Ibid* at 107.
[197] 1992 SLT 1152.
[198] *Ibid* at 1160.
[199] *Ross* v *HM Advocate* 1991 JC 210 at 218.

Hume[200] and refined in *Brennan* v *HM Advocate*.[201] The discussion in *Cardle* v *Mulrainey*[202] draws on the relevant passage in Hume as well as on the insanity cases of *HM Advocate* v *Kidd*[203] and *Brennan* in order to explain the test.[204] Given the changes to mental disorder defences outlined in the earlier parts of this chapter, then, two questions arise: (1) if automatism is defined to map the mental state required for the establishment of the insanity defence, ought the standard to change in line with the shift, in that area, to the special defence of mental disorder? (2) if not, considering the issue raised in the case of *Dunn* v *W*,[205] does automatism now require a higher standard to be met than its mental disorder counterpart? In the absence of either case law or legislation it is difficult to provide a definitive answer. Since a successful plea of automatism results in a straightforward acquittal, with no further control exercised over the accused by the state, there is some justification for the test to be rigorous. There is no doubt, in fact, that the "total alienation of reason" test as applied in automatism, is stringent. Indeed, *Sorley*[206] indicates that it is unlikely that the requirements as to whether the accused was suffering from a total alienation of reason, and whether this was caused by an external factor, will be satisfied without some independent (and, generally, expert) evidence. The relevant state of mind is given a little more definition in relation to automatism than was the case for insanity. The cases accept that the total alienation of reason must amount to a complete absence of self-control. In insanity, "total alienation of reason" generally stood without additional explanation.

20.17.6   The appeal court has had to consider the circumstances in which automatism may be used in relation to the (voluntary) ingestion of legal drugs – whether prescribed specifically for the accused or available over the counter in pharmacies. The matter arose in the case of *Ebsworth* v *HM Advocate*.[207] Here, the accused had sustained a broken leg and there was some difficulty in uniting the fracture. To deal with the pain, and without medical advice, he had taken 50 paracetamol and 10 diamorphine tablets. He claimed that he lacked the *mens rea* for the offence of assault to severe disfigurement. In

---

[200] Hume, i, 37.

[201] 1977 JC 38, where LJ-G Emslie defines it as "absolute alienation of reason in relation to the act charged" (at 43).

[202] 1992 SLT 1152.

[203] 1960 JC 61.

[204] *Cardle* v *Mulrainey* 1992 SLT 1152 at 1160–1161 per LJ-G Hope.

[205] 2013 SLT (Sh Ct) 2 at 4, para [16] per Sheriff Baird; and see section 20.9.1 above.

[206] *Sorley* v *HM Advocate* 1992 JC 102.

[207] 1992 SLT 1161.

echoes of *Brennan*,[208] the court held that taking such a large quantity of these drugs was reckless in itself and that therefore the defence of automatism was not open to the accused.

The court did, however, state that where drugs were taken for a **20.17.7** legitimate purpose this would not generally deprive an accused of the automatism defence, provided there was no recklessness, even though the cause of the alienation of reason in those circumstances would have been self-induced.[209] Thus an accused would be able to use the defence of automatism if the drugs were legal and the accused followed the dosage instructions.

20.18 EXTERNAL FACTORS

The judgment in *Ross* v *HM Advocate*[210] does not directly define **20.18.1** "external factor" but the term appears to mean something which the accused inhaled, consumed or ingested *involuntarily*. Other possibilities include an anaesthetic administered for a therapeutic purpose, or a blow to the head.[211] Jenifer Ross has argued that the requirement of an external factor may, in fact, be "artificial".[212] Her research on the case of *HM Advocate* v *Ritchie*[213] demonstrates the difficulty of categorising factors as external or internal. The accused in *Ritchie* was charged with culpable homicide after he knocked down and killed a pedestrian while driving in Stirling, late at night. As previously noted,[214] Ritchie was in a dissociative state at the time, caused by "toxic exhaustive factors". This phrase had been taken, in subsequent cases, to mean toxic exhaust fumes from the car – an external factor. In fact, the term connotes a condition arising from wounds received by the accused at the Battle of the Somme in 1916 for which he had been treated in hospital earlier the same year. Such a "condition" would be more appropriately categorised as an internal factor. Equally, the wounds had, in turn, been caused by shrapnel – a further external factor.[215] This dissection of the causal chain may not be particularly productive. Ross's conclusion is that the issue of whether the condition is liable to recur is likely to be a better one for the court to pursue. It is this

---

[208] 1977 JC 38.
[209] 1992 SLT 1161 at 1166.
[210] 1991 JC 210.
[211] The last two are mentioned by LJ-G Hope in *Ross* v *HM Advocate* 1991 JC 210, having been suggested by Lord Diplock in the English case of *R* v *Sullivan* [1984] AC 156 at 172.
[212] Ross (2010) at 204.
[213] 1926 JC 45.
[214] See section 20.16.3 above.
[215] Ross (2010) at 198–199.

matter, after all, which will have the greater possible impact on the safety of the public.[216]

20.19   INTERNAL FACTORS

20.19.1   It is also possible that a factor *internal* to an accused might cause her to act criminally in circumstances which she cannot really control but where her mental state falls short of mental disorder. Somnambulism is a form of automatism. The early case of *HM Advocate* v *Simon Fraser*[217] treated a crime committed while the accused was in a state of wakeful unconsciousness (ie sleepwalking, with his eyes open) in a particular way. In that case, Fraser killed his young child while sleepwalking. He was found guilty but released from the court on signing an undertaking that he would sleep on his own, in future.

20.19.2   In the more recent case of *Finegan* v *Heywood*,[218] the accused had been celebrating the birth of his baby and had consumed at least six pints of beer. He had then returned home and fallen asleep. Later, in a state of "parasomnia", he took his friend's car keys and drove the friend's car. He was convicted of various motoring offences.[219] On appeal, the court held that Finegan could not use the defence of non-insane automatism because he knew that drinking alcohol could cause him to sleepwalk, therefore he was responsible for the circumstances which caused him to commit the crime. However, the court saw no reason why parasomnia could not ground a plea of non-insane automatism in the future, so long as it was not self-induced.

20.19.3   Other internal forms of automatism are hypoglycæmic states arising from diabetes, and epileptic fits. The basic rule for such "internal" states is that:

> "Any mental or pathological condition short of insanity – any question of diminished responsibility owing to any cause, which does not involve insanity – is relevant only to the question of mitigating circumstances and sentence."[220]

In the case of *MacLeod* v *Mathieson*[221] the accused was charged with careless driving. He was a diabetic who had suffered a hypoglycæmic

---

[216] Ross at 204. See also section 20.20.1 below.

[217] (1878) 4 Coup 70.

[218] 2000 JC 444.

[219] Namely, drinking and driving; taking and driving away a car without the consent of its owner; and driving without insurance. These are contraventions of the Road Traffic Act 1988, ss 5(1)(a), 178(1)(a) and 143(1) and (2) respectively.

[220] *HM Advocate* v *Cunningham* 1963 JC 80 at 84.

[221] 1993 SCCR 488.

attack, which caused an accident in which another motorist had died. The sheriff applied the four tests set down in *Ross*.[222] He accepted *expressly* that hypoglycæmia could constitute an external factor, but decided that because the accused knew he was diabetic, and therefore knew that he was prone to such attacks, it could not be argued that *this* attack was unforeseeable. Accordingly, the accused failed the fourth of the *Ross* tests and was convicted. Thus, it seems that once the condition of diabetes has been diagnosed, hypoglycæmic attacks become foreseeable, and the accused cannot thereafter employ the defence of automatism for crimes committed during that state. While this was only a sheriff court decision, it was subsequent to the appeal court's decision in *Ross*.

In relation to England and Wales, where the law in this area is more developed, John Rumbold and Martin Wasik[223] have expressed concern about the (at least on their interpretation) almost negligible degree of fault on the part of a diabetic driver which, in the case of *R v Clarke*,[224] operated to negate the automatism defence. *MacLeod v Mathieson*[225] suggests that mere knowledge of the existence of the condition may have this effect in Scotland. **20.19.4**

20.20 CRITIQUE OF THE LAW ON AUTOMATISM AND PROPOSALS FOR REFORM

Given the approach taken in *MacLeod v Mathieson*,[226] the position into which the test for automatism puts diabetics is far from satisfactory. No one would regard diabetes as a type of "mental disorder", yet the mental disorder defence may be the sole mechanism by which an accused can have a complete defence to an act committed during a hypoglycæmic episode. We have seen that automatism requires a total alienation of reason. The cause of this alienation, and its effect, is cast in the case law as a distinction between internal factors (diabetes[227] and epilepsy, for example), and external factors (often, the addition of drugs to alcoholic drinks). The matter would be better conceptualised as a distinction between one-off events (which correspond to "external factors"), and those which are likely to recur (currently thought of as "internal **20.20.1**

---

[222] 1991 JC 210.
[223] J Rumbold and M Wasik, "Diabetic drivers, hypoglycaemic unawareness, and automatism" [2011] *Crim LR* 863.
[224] [2010] 1 Cr App R (S) 26.
[225] 1993 SCCR 488.
[226] *Ibid.*
[227] Interestingly, it is established in English law that the insulin used to control Type 1 diabetes may be treated as an external factor for the purposes of the defence of automatism. See Rumbold and Wasik (2011) at 866.

factors").[228] In the case of recurring conditions, the accused has been shown to present some danger to the community by virtue of having committed the offence in the first place. There is, therefore, at least an argument for triggering the mental disorder rules, in that these allow the state to exercise some control over the accused's future behaviour. However, this weights the scales heavily towards the public interest and away from the rights of the accused, and it must be asked what purpose is served by characterising such diabetics as lacking criminal responsibility by reason of being "mentally disordered" and exercising mental health controls over them. Nonetheless, it is a reasonable argument that limitation is required, in a way which is not necessary where the accused's actions were caused by the surreptitious addition of a drug, and which will, therefore, almost certainly not happen again. This would also avoid the need for strained distinctions of the kind made in *MacLeod* v *Mathieson*,[229] that diabetes can constitute an "external factor".

20.20.2   It can also be argued that "automatism" ought to be regarded as involving a lack of a voluntary act on the part of the accused – a matter going to *actus reus*, rather than *mens rea*.[230] This is the approach taken in Canada; in the case of *Stone*,[231] Bastarche J stated: "[V]oluntariness, rather than consciousness, is the key legal element of automatistic behaviour since a defence of automatism amounts to a denial of the voluntariness component of the *actus reus*."[232] Whether the defence is treated as affecting the "forbidden situation" or the "mental element" is important; if it negates the latter only, as the Scottish courts have ruled,[233] then an accused person can be convicted of a strict liability offence even where this occurs during a semi-conscious state. In the *Ross*[234] case, had the accused been charged with a road traffic offence such as speeding, he ought surely to have been able to plead automatism if he was driving too fast as a result of someone having tampered with his drink. But since speeding is a strict liability offence, the Crown needs to prove

---

[228] See J C Smith, "Individual incapacities and criminal liability" (1998) 6 *Med LR* 138, where the author notes that "the internal factor is a continuing condition" (at 139). See also section 20.19.1 above.

[229] 1993 SCCR 488.

[230] See P R Ferguson, "The limits of the automatism defence" (1991) 36 *JLSS* 446 and P R Ferguson, "Automatism – negation of *mens rea*: a rejoinder" (1992) 37 *JLSS* 57. For a contrary view, see I MacDougall, "Automatism – negation of *mens rea*" (1992) 37 *JLSS* 57. Chalmers and Leverick (2006) suggest that automatism could be viewed as a "freestanding excuse defence so far as offences of strict liability are concerned" (at para 7.06).

[231] (1999) 24 C R(5th) 1 (SCC); [1999] 2 SCR 290.

[232] *Ibid* at para 170.

[233] See also Ross (2010) at 194.

[234] 1991 JC 210.

only that his vehicle was travelling at a particular speed and that this was greater than the permitted limit. There is no need to prove intention, recklessness, or any other form of *mens rea*.[235] Under the approach taken by the court in *Ross*, a person speeding as a result of automatism requires to be convicted, since the lack of *mens rea* is irrelevant to liability. Surely, however, someone in an automatic/semi-conscious state may be said not to be "driving", at all?

In practice, the courts have adopted a more pragmatic approach and have permitted the defence to be put forward even where the crime charged is one of strict liability. For example, in *Cardle* v *Mulrainey*[236] the accused pled automatism to a number of road traffic offences including driving without insurance,[237] a strict liability offence. While the defence was unsuccessful on the particular facts of the case itself, the court seems to have accepted that it was appropriately pled in the circumstances. Accordingly, it appears that automatism *could* be used to negate *actus reus*. It would be helpful if the courts could set down a clearer rationale for this practice. **20.20.3**

---

[235] Strict liability is considered further from section 17.2 above.
[236] 1992 SLT 1152. See section 20.17.4 above.
[237] Contrary to the Road Traffic Act 1988, s 143(1) and (2).

CHAPTER 21

COERCION, NECESSITY, SELF-DEFENCE, PROVOCATION, SUPERIOR ORDERS AND ENTRAPMENT

21.1 INTRODUCTION

As noted in the introduction to this part, the defences described **21.1.1** in this chapter can each be viewed as exculpating an accused person, *despite* the presence, at least *prima facie*, of both *actus reus* and *mens rea*. In *Moss* v *Howdle*[1] the appeal court merged the defences of coercion and necessity into a defence of "duress of circumstances". Intellectually, however, since coercion involves threats by another person and necessity relates to circumstances, more generally, it seems preferable to consider these as separate defences.

21.2 COERCION[2]

To establish coercion, the accused must show that she broke the **21.2.1** law in order to avoid imminent death or serious injury to herself or someone else. The accused must have been compelled to act by another person, or persons. For example, if A holds a gun to B's head and threatens to shoot B if she does not drive to the bank so A can rob it, B may well comply with this request. Likewise if A compels B to punch C, threatening to stab B if B fails to comply, B acts as a result of coercion. In both scenarios, A will be criminally liable, but not B. Coercion is recognised by the law since it is felt that compliance with the other party's demands – that is, violation of the law – is less serious in its consequences than adhering to it. The accused who is coerced chooses the lesser of two evils, and the law recognises this. It is also felt that the conduct of one who is coerced is less blameworthy.

---

[1] 1997 JC 123. The case is discussed further at section 21.4.7 below.
[2] Scots law usually uses the term "coercion", while English law refers to "duress". See section 21.3.2 below.

21.2.2 In the case of *Thomson* v *HM Advocate*[3] the accused was convicted of armed robbery for having driven the "getaway" van. He claimed that he was forced to participate, since he was threatened with a gun and indeed injured on the hand. The trial judge left the issue of coercion to be determined by the jury, directing them in accordance with Hume's criteria, that there had to be an immediate danger of death or great bodily harm and an inability to resist the threats of violence.[4] The plea is easier to substantiate if the accused alleging coercion can show that she played a backward and inferior part in the perpetration of the crime, and notified the police and returned any stolen goods as soon as it was safe to do so. Thomson appealed on the basis that threats of future harm ought to count as coercion, and averred that the trial judge had misdirected the jury in allowing them to consider only immediate threats. However, the appeal court reaffirmed the requirement of the immediacy of the threats. According to Lord Wheatley, what constitutes "immediate danger" has to be construed in the circumstances in which it is threatened:

> "clearly, if there is the opportunity to run away or to seek the protection of the forces of law and order before the crime is committed, then the accused cannot claim to have been coerced".[5]

21.2.3 In *HM Advocate* v *Docherty and Others*[6] three accused were charged with armed robbery. Two of them alleged that they had been coerced by the third accused and that he had threatened them and their families. Lord Keith left the issue to be decided by the jury but instructed them that the pleas could succeed only if the two accused had reason to believe that the threats would be carried out. Clearly, the courts are fearful that allowing such a defence could open the way to abuse; in many cases it has been stated that coercion should be approached with caution,[7] since it could become an easy allegation to make.

21.2.4 The accused in *Cochrane* v *HM Advocate*[8] was a 17-year-old youth who was convicted of assaulting and robbing an elderly woman. He claimed that his co-accused, a man named Cannon, had threatened to beat him, and blow up his house. Cochrane therefore broke into the woman's house, assaulted her with a candlestick and

[3] 1983 JC 69.
[4] Hume, i, 53.
[5] *Thomson* v *HM Advocate* 1983 JC 69 at 77.
[6] 1976 SCCR Supp 146.
[7] See, for example, *Thomson* v *HM Advocate* 1983 JC 69 at 73–74 per Lord Hunter (opinion of the trial judge); *DPP for Northern Ireland* v *Lynch* [1975] AC 653 at 687–688 per Lord Simon.
[8] 2001 SCCR 655.

robbed her. It should be noted that the second threat was a future one and, as such, insufficient to ground the defence of coercion in Scots law. Evidence led by the defence from a psychologist was to the effect that Cochrane's IQ was 74, which placed him "in the range of borderline mentally handicapped persons".[9] He also was in the "top 10 per cent" in terms of "compliance",[10] which meant that he was very easily manipulated. The then Lord Justice-General, Lord Rodger, stated:

> "To judge at least by the law reports, in Scots law the defence of coercion ... lay virtually dormant until about thirty years ago. Since then, coercion and necessity have enjoyed something of a vogue, as have their counterparts in other jurisdictions. The result of so many years of neglect is that the contours of the defence of coercion or duress are not as sharply defined as those of many other aspects of our law. At this late date, to deal with cases like the present, the courts must sketch in some of the detail."[11]

The trial judge had directed the jury in accordance with Hume[12] as explained in the case of *Thomson*,[13] emphasising that the threats had to be such as would have overcome the resolution of an ordinarily constituted person of the same age and sex as the appellant. Cochrane's counsel argued that the jury ought to have been permitted to consider the level of resistance to threats which could reasonably have been expected by the appellant, as a highly compliant individual with a low IQ. The appeal court affirmed that an objective test should be applied to ensure consistency of approach in dealing with accused persons, and to keep the defence of coercion within fairly strict bounds. The standard was described as "an ordinary sober person of reasonable firmness, sharing the characteristics of the accused"[14] – by which was meant the accused's age, gender and any physical (as opposed to mental) handicap[15] – hence Cochrane could not rely on the defence.

In the case of *HM Advocate* v *Raiker*[16] Lord McCluskey charged   **21.2.5** the jury in a manner which suggested that coercion operates in Scots law to negate *mens rea*:

> "where a person has a real, a genuine, a justifiable fear that if he does not act in accordance with the orders of another person, that other person will use life-threatening violence against him or cause it to be used, and if as a

---

9 2001 SCCR 655 at 659, para [8] per LJ-G Rodger.
10 *Ibid* at para [7].
11 *Ibid* at 657, para [1].
12 Hume, i, 53.
13 1983 JC 69 at 75 per LJ-C Wheatley.
14 *Cochrane* v *HM Advocate* 2001 SCCR 655 at 670, para [29] per LJ-G Rodger.
15 *Ibid* at 667, para [21] per LJ-G Rodger.
16 1989 SCCR 149.

result of that fear and for no other reason he carries out acts which have all the typical external characteristics of criminal acts like assault or theft, then in that situation he cannot be said to have the evil intention which the law says is a necessary ingredient in the carrying out of a crime. In other words, he lacks the criminal state of mind that is a necessary ingredient of any crime".[17]

It might, however, be more accurate to treat coercion as affording a defence, as a concession to human infirmity, *despite* the presence of both *actus reus* and *mens rea*. If B drives the "getaway" car in a robbery, or punches C, due in each case to threats from A (our examples from section 21.2.1), it is surely fictitious to suggest that B lacks *mens rea*; clearly she acts intentionally (albeit with great reluctance) in both scenarios.

21.2.6   The limits of the defence of coercion remain to be determined in Scots law. It is sometimes said that Hume suggested that it could not be used for any "atrocious" crime, but in fact Hume stated that the plea "can hardly be serviceable in the case of a trial for any atrocious crime" *unless* it have the support of the qualifications mentioned above (that is, an immediate danger of death or great bodily injury; an inability to resist the violence; a backward and inferior part by the accused in the perpetration of the crime; and a disclosure of the fact, as well as restitution of any spoils, on the first safe and convenient opportunity).[18] In England, the House of Lords determined in the case of *R v Howe*[19] in 1987 that coercion (or "duress", to use English law terminology) could not provide a defence where the charge was murder. According to Lord Mackay, the fact that the law affords great value to the protection of life was a strong argument against the defence being available in such cases; the law should not permit an individual to choose that one innocent person should be killed rather than another. The House of Lords ruled that it did not matter whether the accused was the actual murderer or (to substitute Scots law terminology) "art and part" liable for the murder. Lord Mackay's argument was adopted by the trial judge in *Collins v HM Advocate*[20] in an *obiter* direction to the jury that coercion was not a defence to the charge of murder. Nonetheless, Scots law has now allowed the defence of necessity to ground an acquittal in a murder case.[21] It is simply not clear, therefore, what approach would be taken in the future to any attempt to plead coercion in such circumstances. In terms of certainty, this is not a satisfactory position.

---

[17] 1989 SCCR 149 at 154.
[18] Hume, i, 53. See also section 21.2.2 above.
[19] [1987] AC 417.
[20] 1991 JC 204.
[21] See section 21.4.6 below.

21.3 CRITIQUE OF THE LAW ON COERCION AND PROPOSALS FOR REFORM

While it is understandable that the courts are anxious to ensure that **21.3.1**
the defence of coercion is not abused, lest it becomes an easy way for
one gang member to blame another, it is submitted that the defence is
too narrowly defined. Hume's requirement that the threat be of death
or serious personal injury is appropriate where the accused is being
coerced into committing a serious crime. But lesser threats ought to
suffice for lesser crimes. For example, suppose A's boss were to say
to her "We'll be late for an important meeting if you do not drive
faster. Increase your speed, or you are fired!". In such circumstances,
A ought to be able to plead coercion to a speeding charge.[22]

The English defence of duress is similar to the Scots coercion, **21.3.2**
but with some notable differences. In *R v Hudson and Taylor*[23]
the accused were two young women who were witnesses for the
prosecution in a criminal trial. They gave false evidence at the trial,
resulting in an acquittal, and were then prosecuted for perjury. They
conceded that they had given false evidence but claimed the defence
of duress, on the basis of having been threatened with violence from
an associate of the accused, who then watched from the public
gallery during their testimony. Their convictions for perjury were
quashed on appeal, Lord Widgery LJ noting:

> "It is essential to the defence of duress that the threat shall be effective at the
> moment when the crime is committed. The threat must be a 'present' threat
> in the sense that it is effective to neutralise the will of the accused at that
> time ... a threat of future violence may be so remote as to be insufficient to
> overpower the will at that moment when the offence was committed, or the
> accused may have elected to commit the offence in order to rid himself of a
> threat hanging over him and not because he was driven to act by immediate
> and unavoidable pressure. In none of these cases is the defence of duress
> available because a person cannot justify the commission of a crime merely
> to secure his own peace of mind.
>
> When, however, there is no opportunity for delaying tactics, and the
> person threatened must make up his mind whether he is to commit the
> criminal act or not, the existence at that moment of threats sufficient
> to destroy his will ought to provide him with a defence even though the
> threatened injury may not follow instantly, but after an interval."[24]

In the Canadian case of *R v Ruzic*,[25] the accused imported large **21.3.3**
quantities of heroin into Canada from Serbia. She claimed that

---

[22] See J Chalmers and F Leverick, *Criminal Defences and Pleas in Bar of Trial*
(2006) at para 5.12.
[23] [1971] 2 QB 202.
[24] *Ibid* at 206–207. (The judgment was prepared by Lord Widgery LJ but read by
Lord Parker CJ.)
[25] [2001] 1 SCR 687.

a man in Belgrade had threatened to harm her mother if she did not transport the heroin, and that she had no faith that the police in Belgrade would have been able to prevent this. It was accepted by the Canadian Supreme Court that many Serbian citizens held similar views on the ineffectiveness of the police, at that time. The court held that a defence ought to be available to the accused, even though she was not faced with an immediate threat of bodily harm at the time of the offence. This was based on the principle of "moral involuntariness":

> "It is a principle of fundamental justice that only voluntary conduct – behaviour that is the product of a free will and controlled body, unhindered by external constraints – should attract the penalty and stigma of criminal liability. Depriving a person of liberty and branding her with the stigma of criminal liability would infringe the principles of fundamental justice if the accused did not have any realistic choice."[26]

21.3.4 That Scots criminal law adopts a different approach is illustrated by the case of *Trotter v HM Advocate*.[27] The appellant was caught trying to smuggle drugs to his father in prison, to enable his father to pay off prison drug debts. He had been warned that his father would be stabbed if he did not comply and was accompanied to the door of the prison by those threatening him. It was held that he had the chance to inform the authorities of the threats, and in these circumstances coercion could not be a complete defence. It may be suggested that it is asking too much to require an accused to advise the authorities in such circumstances. As Lord Griffiths stated in the English case of *R v Howe*:[28]

> "if duress is introduced as a merciful concession to human frailty it seems hard to deny it to a man who knows full well that any official protection he may seek will not be effective to save him".[29]

The (English) Law Commission's draft Criminal Code would permit the defence of duress even where the accused could have had recourse to official protection "as long as he believed, however unreasonably, that the protection would prove ineffective".[30] We suggest a different test: where the accused claims that she believed that official protection would not be possible, she should be required to show that this was not an unreasonable belief for her to have held in the circumstances. In a case such as that of *Trotter v HM*

---

[26] [2001] 1 SCR 687 at para 47 per Justice LeBel.
[27] 2001 SLT 296.
[28] [1987] AC 417.
[29] *Ibid* at 443.
[30] Clause 29.6 of the English *Draft Criminal Code*. For the provisions of the Scottish *Draft Criminal Code*, see below at section 21.3.6.

Advocate[31] it would not be sufficient for the accused to show that he genuinely believed that the prison wardens would be unable to protect his father, but neither would he have to show that such protection would, in fact, be ineffective. He would, however, have to establish that it was not unreasonable for him to fear that his father would be assaulted by some of his fellow prisoners, notwithstanding the best efforts of the prison staff.

As noted above, it is unclear whether the defence of coercion is available in a charge of murder. Given that the law ought to be knowable, this is not satisfactory. As previously noted, the appeal court has expressed the view, even if probably incorrectly, that coercion overcomes the will of the accused so completely that it negates *mens rea*. On that analysis, there is no reason why it should not provide a complete defence to a homicide charge. Indeed, it ought to do so. If, however, the accused does have *mens rea* – taking the example of homicide, she does intend to kill the victim – but she has made this choice only as a result of the fear generated by the coercer's threat, the matter becomes more complicated. At one level, the moral and factual judgement required of the coerced accused might be characterised as of the same order as that required of an accused acting in self-defence: a serious threat is presented and the accused acts out of fear to save herself. The moral complication in homicide is that the person who is being coerced *makes a choice* which effectively amounts to preferring one life to that of another. In self-defence, any such element of choice is less apparent and might be acceptable anyway because the person whom she kills is the aggressor. In coercion, the difficulty is that she may well have killed an innocent third party. To an accused who is staring down the barrel of a gun, the difference may be hard to appreciate. In terms of the moral value attached to the sanctity of life,[32] however, the situations are distinguishable.

21.3.5

This is not to say that coercion should *not* be available in a homicide case. The issue is whether it is fair that the person being coerced should incur a murder conviction where fear is the operating cause of the fatal attack, and there is no reasonable opportunity to seek help from the police. One solution might be to allow coercion as a partial defence, such that pleading it successfully would result in a culpable homicide conviction being returned on a murder charge. Nonetheless, we take the view that: (1) if the threat meets the high standard required already for the defence of coercion, (2) the accused was unable to resist it or to seek assistance from the authorities, and (3) the killing averted at least one other death

21.3.6

---

[31] 2001 SLT 296.
[32] See section 9.1.1 above.

(even if that is the death of the person being coerced), then coercion should operate as a complete defence, even to murder. Enactment of the *Draft Criminal Code* would result in coercion being available as a defence to all charges, including murder, but only if the taking of life was done in order to save life.[33] It would not, however, avail the accused who has voluntarily exposed herself to the risk of coercion by joining a criminal organisation.[34] The threat(s) must be such that the accused could not reasonably be expected to have avoided,[35] and must be of immediate fatal or serious injury to the accused or a third party.[36] We recommend that the law be clarified in the manner suggested by the *Code*.

21.4 NECESSITY

21.4.1 Several of the defences we consider in this chapter involve the claim by an accused person that it was necessary to break the law: in coercion, the accused is claiming that it was necessary to act as she did because of threats from a third party;[37] in self-defence, the accused claims that she used necessary force to repel an unlawful attack.[38] The defence of necessity proper is similar. Here the accused is forced to choose the lesser of two evils because of natural forces or circumstances, rather than by threats from a human agent. It can only be pled where the accused acts to save life, or to prevent serious bodily harm to herself or others. The appeal court has held that the standard is whether a sober person of reasonable firmness, sharing the characteristics of the accused, would have behaved as the accused had done.[39] Two different rationales have been suggested: it may be treated as justifying conduct if it results in the avoidance of a greater harm or causes a greater good, or as merely excusing conduct where the accused cannot be expected to have complied with the law, given the circumstances.

21.4.2   The accused must show that her only choice was between breaking the law, or obeying it at the cost of greater harm. As with coercion, therefore, if another feasible alternative is present then the defence

[33] *Draft Criminal Code*, s 29(3).

[34] *Ibid*, s 29(2)(b).

[35] *Ibid*, s 29(2)(c).

[36] *Ibid*, s 29(2)(a). This is in contrast to the English *Draft Criminal Code* which applies even if the threat is not an immediate one, so long as there is no opportunity to seek official protection – cl 42(3)(a)(ii).

[37] See section 21.2.1 above.

[38] See section 21.8.1 below.

[39] *Lord Advocate's Reference (No 1 of 2000)* 2001 JC 143 at 158, para [42] per Lord Prosser, discussed further at section 21.4.8 below.

fails. Furthermore, the appeal court has held that the accused must have been aware of the dilemma between saving life/preventing serious bodily harm on the one hand, and breaking the law, on the other: if the accused did not apply her mind to this dilemma then the defence is not available. This is illustrated by the case of *Dawson* v *Dickson*[40] in which the accused was a fire-fighter who drove a pump to the scene of an accident, despite having excess alcohol in his blood. In upholding the conviction, the appeal court emphasised that to be afforded the defence of necessity, the dilemma "must have dominated the mind of the accused at the time of the act and ... it was by reason of that domination that the act was committed".[41] Gerald Gordon concludes that this means that necessity is categorised in Scots law as a defence which relates to *mens rea,* rather than *actus reus.*[42] This has not, however, prevented the appeal court from holding that necessity can be pled in relation to statutory offences which impose strict liability.[43]

It is a defence which generates some interesting cases.[44] In the English law case of *R* v *Dudley and Stephens*[45] in 1884, the two accused and two others were sailing a 40-tonne yacht to Sydney. They were cast adrift in an open boat after the yacht sank in a storm. They lasted for 20 days, surviving only on two tins of turnip. The two accused then killed the 17-year-old cabin boy, who was very ill. They and the third crew member survived by eating the boy's flesh for a couple of days, then were spotted by another ship and rescued.[46] At issue was whether necessity could provide a defence for murder. According to Lord Coleridge:

21.4.3

> "it is admitted that the deliberate killing of this unoffending and unresisting boy was clearly murder, unless the killing can be justified by some well-recognised excuse admitted by the law. It is further admitted that there was in this case no such excuse, unless the killing was justified by what has been called 'necessity'".[47]

---

[40] 1999 JC 315.

[41] *Ibid* at 318 per Lord Sutherland.

[42] Commentary on *Dawson* v *Dickson* 1999 SCCR 698 at 704.

[43] That is, offences for which the Crown do not require to establish *mens rea* (as discussed from section 17.2 above). Examples include *Ruxton* v *Lang* 1998 SCCR 1, in relation to a charge of driving with excess alcohol in the blood, and *Moss* v *Howdle* 1997 JC 123, in respect of a speeding offence (discussed further at section 21.4.7 below). For a critique of the court's approach to necessity, see section 21.6.1 below.

[44] See L Katz, *Bad Acts and Guilty Minds: Conundrums of the Criminal Law* (1987), Chap 1.

[45] (1884) 14 QBD 273. See also *US* v *Holmes* 26 Fed Cas 360 (1842).

[46] Whether or not cannibalism was a crime seems not to have been considered.

[47] (1884) 14 QBD 273 at 286–287.

He held that "it is not correct … to say that there is any absolute or unqualified necessity to preserve one's life", hence the accused had no such defence.[48] In the event, although convicted of murder and sentenced to death, the two accused served only 6 months in prison.

21.4.4   An instance of necessity seems to have occurred during the Zeebrugge disaster. In 1987 the *Herald of Free Enterprise* ferry capsized, killing 193 passengers and crew. According to *Smith and Hogan's Criminal Law*, an inquest into the disaster heard that a man who was blocking an escape ladder, paralysed with fear, had been pushed into the water and not seen again. This allowed many trapped passengers to escape. The coroner opined that it was "not necessarily murder" to cause death in such circumstances, since this had been done for self-preservation or for the saving of others' lives.[49] More recently, in *Re A (Children) (Conjoined twins: medical treatment)*[50] the English Court of Appeal had to determine whether it would be lawful for surgeons to operate on conjoined twin girls, in order to separate them. Since they shared a common artery, the operation would inevitably lead to the death of the weaker child. The court concluded that the operation would be lawful. One of the three judges (Brooke LJ) took the view that this was justified by necessity.[51]

21.4.5   It is also interesting to note that there is now a specific, and extremely limited, statutory defence in Scots law that "in the circumstances there was an overriding public interest which justified the person's actions".[52] This applies only to a charge of introducing into,[53] or taking out from,[54] a prison a personal communication device (such as a mobile phone) or, effectively, using such a device to make[55] or receive[56] a communication within the prison.[57] The rationale relates specifically to emergency situations. The Scottish Government's *Explanatory Notes* give the example of "an individual from the emergency service [having] to access the prison with a communication device, in an emergency situation, and there [being]

---

[48] For a vivid description of the case, see Katz (1987).

[49] D Ormerod, *Smith and Hogan's Criminal Law* (13th edn, 2011), pp 370–371.

[50] [2001] 2 WLR 480.

[51] For a critique of this approach, see Chalmers and Leverick (2006) at paras 4.23–4.24. One of the other judges favoured employing self-defence, and the third did not make clear his basis for holding that the proposed operation would be lawful.

[52] Prisons (Scotland) Act 1989, s 41ZB(7)(b), added by the Criminal Justice and Licensing (Scotland) Act 2010, s 34(2).

[53] Prisons (Scotland) Act 1989, s 41(1)(a).

[54] *Ibid*, s 41(1)(b).

[55] *Ibid*, s 41ZA(2)(a).

[56] *Ibid*, s 41ZA(2)(b).

[57] It can also be used in relation to giving such a device to a prisoner within the prison (*ibid*, s 41ZA(1)) and being in possession, within the prison, of such a device (s 41ZA(3)).

insufficient time for the individual to receive written authorisation".[58] "Overriding public interest" is, clearly, a different test from the common law test for necessity – indeed, it is conceivable that the excusable situation might not even involve danger to any person, let alone "danger of death or great bodily harm". It is, nonetheless, a legislative acknowledgement that, on occasion, circumstances may militate against rigid adherence to the letter of the criminal law.

As with coercion,[59] it is not clear whether necessity can be pled **21.4.6** as a defence to a murder charge in Scots law, since the appeal court has not yet had to decide this issue.[60] In the (unreported) case of *HM Advocate* v *Anderson* (2006) the accused was charged, *inter alia*, with murder by having driven his car at, and over, the victim. The trial judge, Lord Carloway, directed the jury that necessity is "a complete defence to the charges of murder, culpable homicide and assault", and that a person is

> "entitled ... to use reasonable means to escape from a life-threatening or serious injury-threatening situation, even if he knows that what he has to do to escape might cause serious injury or even potentially death to ... someone."[61]

The Crown did not lodge an appeal on the point of law, so the approach the appeal court is likely to take to a plea of necessity on a charge of murder remains uncertain.[62]

The reported cases of necessity have dealt with less serious offences; **21.4.7** the leading case of *Moss* v *Howdle*,[63] involved a charge of speeding. The accused claimed that when he was driving on the motorway his passenger had given a cry of pain. Believing him to be seriously ill, Mr Moss had driven at speed to get to the nearest service station. It turned out, he said, that his friend had only been suffering from cramp. The court stated that for the defence of necessity there must be an immediate danger of death or great bodily injury, which could be to a third party. Presumably a mistake about this could exculpate, if it were a reasonable error in the circumstances.[64] Indeed, that was the position in *Moss* v *Howdle*. As Lord Justice-General Rodger

---

[58] Scottish Government, *Explanatory Notes* to the Criminal Justice and Licensing (Scotland) Bill, n 163.
[59] See section 21.2.6 above.
[60] The Law Reform Commission of Canada has recommended that the defence of necessity not be available to one who "purposely causes the death of, or seriously harms, another person". See *Recodifying Criminal Law* (1987) at pp 35–36.
[61] Correspondence between one of the authors and Mr George Gebbie, who represented Mr Anderson at trial. The accused was acquitted of all charges.
[62] The Crown may appeal by a Lord Advocate's Reference: Criminal Procedure (Scotland) Act 1995, s 123. See section 9.18.3, n 229 above.
[63] 1997 JC 123.
[64] See from section 19.8 above for the law's approach to factual errors.

explained, "the appellant exceeded the speed limit in order to try to save [his passenger] from the effects of what he *believed to be* a serious illness".[65] The court endorsed the defence of necessity in these types of circumstances. Here, however, there was an alternative course of action open to the accused; instead of speeding, he could have pulled off the road to find out what was wrong with his friend. Interestingly, the court made clear that the defence of necessity is available in respect of common law *and* statutory offences, even where the latter involve strict liability. This suggests that it does not, in fact, operate to negate *mens rea*.

21.4.8   The accused must show that she acted in response to immediate danger of death or serious injury, to herself or someone else. Once the danger has ceased, however, so must the accused's criminal behaviour.[66] The immediate nature of the danger is illustrated by *Lord Advocate's Reference (No 1 of 2000)*[67] in which three accused were prosecuted following events in the waters of Loch Goil, on board the vessel *Maytime*. This ship was involved with submarines carrying Trident missiles. The relevant charges were of malicious damage, or alternatively theft. The Crown evidence was not really disputed by the accused; it was clearly established that they had intentionally damaged other people's property. The defence put forward was a novel one, namely that their actions were not criminal because they were justified. The grounds for this justification were said to be that the Government was in breach of international law, and therefore of Scots criminal law, by having nuclear missiles in the UK. The accused were acquitted, and the Crown appealed by stated case.[68] The accused had argued at their trial that:

(1) customary international law meant that the UK Government's policy in respect of nuclear weapons was itself contrary to international law;

(2) it is a defence for an accused person to commit an offence to prevent or end the commission of an offence by another person.

21.4.9 The appeal court found that it was not a defence to claim that the damage was done to prevent the commission of some other offence. People are not permitted to take the law into their own hands, hence one person may not commit an offence in an attempt to stop someone else from offending. Committing a crime to avoid a greater danger may, however, afford a defence of necessity. The danger may

---

[65] *Moss* v *Howdle* 1997 JC 123 at 128 (emphasis added).

[66] See *Ruxton* v *Lang* 1998 SCCR 1.

[67] 2001 JC 143.

[68] See n 229 in section 9.18.3 above.

come from a criminal act on the part of someone else, but that is not crucial. What is important is that there must be immediate danger, affording no opportunity for the accused to take a non-criminal course of action. Another factor is the range of choice presented in the circumstances. The general deployment of Trident in pursuit of deterrence was not the type of "threat" on which the accused could rely, since this was not illegal as a matter of customary international law.[69]

21.5 PRIOR FAULT

One of the authors was the prosecutor in an early case in which **21.5.1** the accused attempted to plead necessity as a defence.[70] In *McNab v Guild*[71] the charge was reckless driving and the accused testified that he had no choice but to drive as he had done, since his car was being attacked and he was attempting to escape. The author argued that the defence of necessity could not be employed by the accused since he had been at fault in driving his car back to the scene of an earlier altercation. The court of appeal commented, albeit *obiter*, that the appellant's behaviour did not rule out the defence, but that it would have done so had the sheriff found that the accused had indeed returned to confront those who had previously attacked him. This suggests that prior fault on the part of the accused may preclude the defence of necessity in Scots law.

21.6 CRITIQUE OF THE LAW ON NECESSITY AND PROPOSALS FOR REFORM

As *Lord Advocate's Reference (No 1 of 2000)*[72] and *Moss v* **21.6.1** *Howdle*[73] show, the defence of necessity is restricted to cases in which the accused has acted to avoid an immediate danger, which must be of death or serious injury. Such an approach seems overly narrow and it is submitted that the defence ought to be expanded to include cases involving lesser perils;[74] arguably, breaking the law

---

[69] The court reserved its judgment on the question of whether the incorporation of Trident in the UK's defence strategy was a justiciable one.

[70] The defence was not formally recognised by the appeal court until 8 years later, in *Moss v Howdle* 1997 JC 123.

[71] 1989 JC 72.

[72] 2001 JC 143.

[73] 1997 JC 123.

[74] See P R Ferguson, "Codifying criminal law (1): a critique of Scots common law" [2004] *Crim LR* 49 at 56. See also V Tadros, "The structure of defences in Scots criminal law" (2003) 7 *Edin LR* 60 at 67–69.

is justified if the harm incurred in doing so is less than the harm that would otherwise have occurred.[75] For instance, if a car bursts into flames, A is surely justified in grabbing a fire extinguisher from a petrol station, without stopping to pay for it. Although A has technically "stolen" the fire extinguisher, the law has been broken to achieve a greater good. This should apply irrespective of whether A can establish that there was a risk of death or serious injury from the fire. Surely a risk that the fire could spread to a nearby school or art gallery – even if closed – ought to suffice?[76] The statutory offence of vandalism already recognises this in providing a defence where the accused has a reasonable excuse for damaging or destroying someone else's property.[77]

21.6.2   As we noted earlier,[78] the use of necessity as a defence to a charge of murder is controversial.[79] It may be that the redefinition of murder in the case of *Drury* v *HM Advocate*[80] makes it possible for an accused person who kills out of necessity to claim that she lacked the "wicked intent" to kill.[81] An example of this could be where the accused throws a bomb out of the window of a school, killing a small number of passers-by but saving the lives of hundreds of others. Unless and until the appeal court is confronted with a suitable case, the issue will remain unresolved.[82] It is submitted that it should be available in such circumstances, but the difficulty here relates to balancing the harm avoided against the harm perpetrated. If these are equal – a life for a life – then it may be argued that the defence ought not to operate as a justification because the evil chosen is not – or at least not obviously – the lesser one. Saving one's own life may not be a sufficiently good reason

---

[75] A generous necessity defence for Scottish law has been advocated by T H Jones, "The defence of necessity in Scots law" 1989 SLT (News) 253. In the Netherlands, necessity has been used as a defence to charges of euthanasia and assisted suicide – see C Kelk, "Consent in Dutch criminal law" in P Alldridge and C Brants (eds), *Personal Autonomy, the Private Sphere and Criminal Law* (2001) 205 at pp 214–220.

[76] See Chalmers and Leverick (2006) at para 4.08.

[77] Vandalism is discussed in more detail from section 13.3 above.

[78] See section 21.4.6 above.

[79] See T H Jones and M G A Christie, *Criminal Law* (5th edn, 2012), p 180, n 180; A M Cubie, *Scots Criminal Law* (3rd edn, 2010), para 8.31.

[80] 2001 SLT 1013, discussed in Chapter 9 above.

[81] However, the appeal court's judgment in *Elsherkisi* v *HM Advocate* 2012 SCL 181 may have limited the scope of a "lack of wickedness" defence to murder. See section 9.16.4 above.

[82] As noted, the decision at the trial in *HM Advocate* v *Anderson* (2006), mentioned at section 21.4.6 above, was not referred to the appeal court. Section 24(3) of the *Draft Criminal Code* allows necessity to be a defence to a charge of murder, but only if this is done to save life.

to take some else's.[83] Nevertheless, in *R v Dudley and Stephens*,[84] Lord Coleridge recognised the harshness of rejecting this defence in charges of murder:

> "It must not be supposed that in refusing to admit temptation to be an excuse for crime it is forgotten how terrible the temptation was; how awful the suffering; how hard in such trials to keep the judgment straight and the conduct pure. *We are often compelled to set up standards we cannot reach ourselves, and to lay down rules which we could not ourselves satisfy.*"[85]

It seems most unfair for the criminal law to expect other than reasonable behaviour from citizens. The accused in this case may have failed to comply with high *moral* standards, but this ought not to be determinative of their *criminal* liability. In *HM Advocate v Anderson* (discussed in section 21.4.6 above), Lord Carloway (as he then was) directed the jury that it could acquit the accused if it found that he had driven over the victim in order to save his own life.[86] The issue of whether it was justifiable to sacrifice one life to save (only) one other life does not seem to have been discussed. This is an area of law which requires clarification.

21.7 SELF-DEFENCE AND PROVOCATION: INTRODUCTION

21.7.1 It is common for an accused person to plead self-defence and provocation at the same time but the effect of the pleas is very different and it is important to keep the two concepts separate. Each proceeds on a different basis: self-defence relates specifically to the degree of violence used and the possibility of an alternative means of escape; provocation requires a loss of self-control by the accused, a requirement which is wholly absent from self-defence.

21.8 SELF-DEFENCE[87]

21.8.1 It is tempting to treat self-defence as a sub-set of "duress", in so far as one who acts in self-defence is choosing the lesser of two evils. However, it should be borne in mind that a person who acts in self-defence is retaliating against someone who is using unlawful force,

---

[83] Necessity may then become an excuse rather than a justification – see Tadros (2003) at 69–70 (where he discusses this balancing process in relation to coercion) – but even this may be in doubt when the relative harms are equal.

[84] (1884) 14 QBD 273. See section 21.4.3 above.

[85] *Ibid* at 288 (emphasis added).

[86] As noted previously, the opinion of the appeal court was not sought so the value of this case as a precedent is limited.

[87] For a detailed examination of the issues raised in homicide cases by this defence, see F Leverick, *Killing in Self-Defence* (2006).

whereas acts committed out of duress (whether necessity or coercion) may impact on innocent third parties. While most of our discussion relates to cases in which the charge was murder (reflecting the case law), self-defence can also be pled to charges of assault.[88] In either case, it operates as a complete defence. The underlying rationale is that the physical force used by the accused was justifiable to protect herself (or someone else)[89] from an attack by an aggressor. It is of the essence of self-defence that the accused accepts that she did use the violence alleged against the victim, and that this was intentional, rather than accidental.[90] Accordingly, if the plea is unsuccessful, the accused will be left to face the consequences of her admission in that respect. Although it is a special defence, such that in solemn proceedings the accused must give the court and prosecution advance written notice of the intention to plead it,[91] this does not alter the burden of proof: the Crown is still required to prove its case beyond reasonable doubt. There are three essential elements to the plea, namely: (1) an imminent danger to life[92] (or possibly, of rape);[93] (2) the violence used by the accused must have been employed as a last resort;[94] and (3) the force employed must have been reasonable.[95]

Imminent danger to life

21.8.2   In a murder case, self-defence can be pled only when the violence was necessary for the protection of life or (perhaps) the prevention of rape.[96] In the former, the danger to life must be imminent.[97] Similarly to the defences of coercion and necessity, self-defence is not available where there is merely a threat or danger of violence in the future. The accused must fear that someone (herself or a third party) will be killed unless she acts immediately. This was affirmed

---

[88] Or even to breach of the peace where the charge involves an assault – see *Derrett v Lockhart* 1991 SCCR 109. This seems fair; the Crown ought not to be able to prevent a plea of self-defence by charging breach of the peace instead of assault.
[89] *HM Advocate v Carson* 1964 SLT 21.
[90] See *Lucas v HM Advocate* [2009] HCJAC 77. One commentator has suggested that: "The presence of both defences [ie self-defence and accident] targeted at the same crime is a recipe for disaster and always gives rise to confusion whenever it occurs" (2010 SCL 153 at 164).
[91] Criminal Procedure (Scotland) Act 1995, s 78.
[92] See from section 21.8.2 below.
[93] See section 21.8.7 below.
[94] See from section 21.8.10 below.
[95] See from section 21.8.12 below.
[96] The latter is discussed in more detail in section 21.8.7 below.
[97] This is in contrast to the situation in England – see *Attorney General's Reference (No 2 of 1983)* [1984] QB 456.

in the case of *HM Advocate* v *Greig*[98] in which the accused killed her husband while he was dozing in a chair. The trial judge (Lord Dunpark) refused to allow the issue of self-defence to go to the jury; since the victim had been sleeping, Mrs Greig could not have been in imminent fear for her life.

In *Boyle* v *HM Advocate*[99] a fight between two groups of armed   **21.8.3** men resulted in one of them being fatally stabbed. Three issues were clarified in that case: first, even an accused who starts a fight may be entitled to plead self-defence; second, it is not an absolute bar to the plea that the accused enters the fight armed with a lethal weapon; and finally, the fact that the accused acted to protect a third party, rather than to protect herself, is no bar to the plea: the imminence of the danger to life is the key element. Following the subsequent case of *Burns* v *HM Advocate*,[100] the issue of self-defence in a fight initiated by the accused depends on whether the retaliation by the eventual victim was such that the accused was entitled to defend herself.

Error as to imminence of attack

So long as the accused acted in the belief that she was facing   **21.8.4** imminent, life-threatening violence, the plea of self-defence is available, even if the belief is mistaken. The erroneous belief must, however, be a reasonable one.[101] In *Jones* v *HM Advocate*[102] the accused alleged that the victim had come to his house carrying a knife, and had threatened him. The accused stated that he had, therefore, taken a knife with him when he went out later that evening. He met the victim on the street, pushed him, and walked away. Feeling the prick of a knife, he pulled out his own knife and stabbed the victim on the leg and, as the victim fell to the ground, the accused stabbed him again on the chest. It was held that the test for self-defence was whether the appellant believed, on reasonable grounds, that he was in danger of his life.[103] In this case, however, the appeal court held that no reasonable jury could have found that there were such grounds.

---

[98] Unreported, High Court, May 1979. See C H W Gane, C N Stoddart and J Chalmers, *A Casebook on Scottish Criminal Law* (4th edn, 2009), para 10.40, p 444. For a critique of this case, see section 21.9.7 below.

[99] 1993 SLT 577.

[100] 1995 JC 154.

[101] As confirmed in *Lieser* v *HM Advocate* 2008 SLT 866. See section 21.8.6 below.

[102] 1990 JC 160.

[103] It is now generally accepted in Scots law that, where the accused seeks to rely on an error, it must rest on reasonable grounds. See, for example, Sexual Offences (Scotland) Act 2009, s 1(1)(b) with regard to the accused's belief in the victim's consent in rape.

21.8.5   Prior to the judgment in *Lieser v HM Advocate*,[104] concerns had
been expressed that the change in the *mens rea* of murder to "wicked
intention" in *Drury*[105] could have unanticipated and undesirable
consequences in relation to this reasonableness requirement. The
contention was that an accused who believed in all honesty that
her life was in danger, however unreasonable the grounds on which
she held that belief, could not be said "wickedly" to intend to kill.
She may well have intended to kill but her purpose was not wicked;
it was to save her own life.[106] Before *Drury*, Scots law had always
required a reasonable basis for an error in relation to defences.
Fiona Leverick had argued that this criterion demonstrated respect
for the sanctity of life, a value enshrined in Art 2 of the ECHR. The
problem with allowing an *unreasonable* error to ground a defence
to murder was that this would have left unpunishable the death of
a wholly innocent person, who had not threatened the accused in
any way, and who had not even done anything which might have
caused a reasonable person to think, erroneously, that her life was
in danger. On this analysis, if an accused had convinced the jury of
the genuineness of her fear for her own life, however unlikely this
really was, she would be acquitted. Leverick's concern was that
this seemed morally dubious. Furthermore, it would mean that the
state was not properly protecting the right to life of its citizens – a
potential violation of Art 2.[107]

21.8.6   The matter was settled in the case of *Lieser v HM Advocate*[108]
where the accused claimed that he had fatally stabbed the victim in
the mistaken belief that the latter had presented a threat to his life. In
dismissing the appeal against conviction for murder, Lord Kingarth
stated:

> "It is for reasons essentially of policy that the law has chosen to require
> certain conditions to be present before an accused may be said to be wholly
> justified when acting in self defence, even in the case of an intentional
> homicide, or before a killing which would otherwise be murderous can be
> excused on the basis of provocation. ...
>   Given that deliberate and intentional attacks may be said to be wholly
> justified on the basis of self defence, while it is understandable that allowance
> should reasonably be made for genuine mistakes of fact, it is equally
> understandable that not every such mistake should be thought to be capable of
> leading to exculpation. If it were otherwise even an intentional killing would
> fall to be regarded as wholly justified in circumstances where the accused's
> actions could be said to have been prompted by gross recklessness. In other
> words, an accused who intentionally killed in the mistaken belief that he

---

[104] 2008 SLT 866.
[105] 2001 SLT 1013. See section 9.11.1 above.
[106] See F Leverick, "Mistake in self-defence after *Drury*" (2002) *Jur Rev* 35.
[107] *Ibid* at 45.
[108] 2008 SLT 866.

faced a grave attack on his person, would (assuming all other requirements for self defence were met) be entitled to acquittal notwithstanding that he had recklessly ignored matters which would have destroyed that belief, had he not thus recklessly cast them aside; and his gross recklessness would go without penalty."[109]

Accordingly, the court upheld the requirement of reasonableness, and its generally robust approach to those seeking to evade liability for actions which have led to fatal consequences. While this decision is welcome, Leverick[110] and James Chalmers[111] have both argued that it does not, in fact, *argue* the issue arising from *Drury v HM Advocate*.[112] It merely asserts the solution. We would agree, nonetheless, that "While the appeal court's logic in *Lieser* is open to criticism, the result it has arrived at is the preferable one".[113]

We have stressed that where the accused has taken life, this **21.8.7** must have been due to a threat to her life (or that of someone else). According to Hume, however, self-defence may also be pled where the accused alleges that the killing was done to prevent an imminent rape.[114] This was accepted as being the true position as recently as 1998. In the case of *Pollock v HM Advocate*,[115] A killed B and claimed in court that he did so in order to prevent B from raping A's girlfriend. The court accepted that self-defence could be pled in these circumstances, but the plea was withdrawn from the jury because the accused had acted with excessive savagery towards the victim.[116]

Historically, self-defence could not be pled in relation to the **21.8.8** prevention of non-consensual sodomy. This was established in the case of *McCluskey v HM Advocate*[117] in which the trial judge refused to put the plea to the jury in circumstances where the accused admitted that there had been no threat to his life, but claimed that there had been an attempt to sodomise him, without his consent. On appeal, Lord Justice-General Clyde stressed that danger *to life* not merely to virtue was a necessary precondition of the plea. The court did, however, accept that rape (which, *at that time though not currently*, required a female victim)[118] was an exception to this rule. The refusal to extend the exception to non-consensual sodomy was

---

[109] 2008 SLT 866 at 869, para 10. See also F Leverick, "Unreasonable mistake in self-defence: *Lieser* v *HM Advocate*" (2009) 13 *Edin LR* 100.
[110] Leverick (2009) at 103–104.
[111] J Chalmers, "*Lieser* and misconceptions" 2008 SCL 1115 at 1121.
[112] 2001 SLT 1013.
[113] Leverick (2009) at 103.
[114] Hume, i, 218.
[115] 1998 SLT 880.
[116] The case is discussed further at section 21.8.12 below.
[117] 1959 JC 39.
[118] Sexual Offences (Scotland) Act 2009, s 1(1). See section 11.2.3 above.

repeated in *Elliott v HM Advocate*.[119] The evidence there indicated
that the accused's fear was that he would be subjected to a homosexual
attack, not that he was likely to lose his life. Accordingly, a plea of
self-defence was not available. The law has now changed so that non-
consensual sodomy constitutes one form of rape.[120] Accordingly, it
is submitted that this situation cannot continue. Either self-defence
must be permitted where rape is committed against a male person
or it must cease to be available to women in the same circumstances.
Any other outcome is discriminatory.

21.8.9   Hume stated that even fatal force could be used to repel an
invasion of one's property, but qualified this by saying that such
an invasion must be made "in that forcible and felonious manner,
which naturally puts the owner in fear".[121] He made clear that
it was not self-defence, for example, for someone to stab a pick-
pocket.[122] Although the position is not free from doubt, it seems
unlikely that fatal force would now be regarded as reasonable
where the accused is defending property. It is possible that self-
defence may, however, be a defence to a charge of assault where the
accused used reasonable force to prevent someone from damaging
or stealing something. A recent attempt was made to invoke Art
8 of the ECHR (right to respect for private and family life) in the
formulation of an argument "that [it] gave protection to a person's
home; consequently ... [it] thus conferred a right to use force
[thought not lethal force] against a trespasser".[123] The issue was,
in the end, regarded as irrelevant by the appeal court but it seems,
in any event, not to have found the argument strong, noting that it
was backed neither by authority nor by examination of the terms
of the Article.[124]

21.8.10   The violence used by the accused must have been employed as
a last resort: this second test generally requires the accused who
claims to have acted in self-defence to show that there was no
reasonable opportunity to escape.[125] In the case of *HM Advocate
v Doherty*[126] the accused was attacked by a man with a hammer.
The accused was with a number of his friends and there was an
open door leading down a flight of stairs and into a yard, behind
him. One of the accused's friends handed him a bayonet and
he stabbed his attacker with it, killing him. The accused had

---

[119] 1987 JC 47.
[120] See n 118 above.
[121] Hume, i, 218–219.
[122] *Ibid*, 219.
[123] *Purves v HM Advocate* [2012] HCJAC 89 at para [5] per Lord Eassie.
[124] *Ibid* at para [8].
[125] But see section 21.8.11 below, in relation to the defence of others.
[126] 1954 JC 1.

force on his side and an escape route available had he chosen to use it. Accordingly, he was convicted, as charged, of culpable homicide. The case of *McBrearty* v *HM Advocate*[127] emphasised that it is only if it is reasonable to expect the accused to utilise a means of escape that failure to do so will jeopardise the use of the defence. Accordingly, a direction by the trial judge in that case that the accused had to have "*no* means of escape or retreat"[128] was regarded as imprecise.[129] The requirement that self-defence must be the only option available is in contrast to the position in English law, where it has been held that those who fear attack are not required to retreat, but may stand their ground and fight back.[130]

In *Dewar* v *HM Advocate*[131] the appeal court affirmed that the requirement for the accused to have taken any reasonable escape route does not apply where the accused acts in defence of another, as opposed to acting to defend herself. This point was reiterated in *McCloy* v *HM Advocate*.[132]   **21.8.11**

Reasonable force

While the defence is available only if the accused has retaliated using a proportionate degree of force, the courts do take account of the fact that the accused acts in the heat of the moment, and they therefore do not weigh this requirement in "too fine scales".[133] Nevertheless, the force used by the accused must not be greater than that which is reasonably necessary to repel the attack. Reference has already been made to the case of *Pollock* v *HM Advocate*,[134] in which A killed B to prevent B from raping A's girlfriend. When A arrived at the locus, B had his hand over the girl's mouth. When this was removed, she shouted that B had been trying to rape her. A responded to this by repeatedly stamping on B's head, causing more than 70 injuries. In evidence he alleged that he thought that B   **21.8.12**

---

[127] 1999 SLT 1333 at 1337 per Lord Coulsfield.
[128] *Ibid* at 1337. See Lord Philip's charge to the jury at 1334 (emphasis added).
[129] *Ibid* at 1336 per LJ-G Rodger. Note that this issue was not determinative of the outcome of the case.
[130] *R* v *Field* [1972] *Crim LR* 435. For a critique of the Scottish approach, see section 21.9.10 below.
[131] 2009 JC 260.
[132] 2011 SCL 282.
[133] *HM Advocate* v *Doherty* 1954 JC 1 at 4, per Lord Keith. This is similar to the Canadian case of *Baxter* (1975) 27 CCC (2d) 96 (Ont CA): "A person defending himself against an attack, reasonably apprehended, cannot be expected to weigh to a nicety, the exact measure of necessary defensive action" (at 111 per Mr Justice Martin).
[134] 1998 SLT 880. See section 21.8.7 above.

had had a knife. A's plea of self-defence was rejected on the ground that the force used was far in excess of any danger which he or his girlfriend faced.

21.8.13   Similarly, in *Fenning* v *HM Advocate*[135] the accused was charged with murdering a man by the name of Paterson by hitting him repeatedly with an air-rifle and striking his head against a stone. He pled self-defence, alleging that the deceased had threatened him with a knife. According to the statement Fenning gave the police, the two men had gone on a fishing trip, in the course of which Paterson had revealed that he suspected his wife of having an affair with Fenning, and that he was going to "do" (ie assault) him. Fenning told the police:

> "he was sitting waving the knife about me so I was kneeling down beside him sorting the stuff out of the bag and I picked up a big boulder, walloped him on top of the heid [head], I hit him a few times, not just the once".[136]

The trial judge had pointed out to the jury that in considering the defence they had to be satisfied that there had been no cruel excess of violence on the accused's part. The jury convicted Fenning of murder, presumably on the basis that his repeated blows constituted a "cruel excess". This means that the courts are employing both a subjective and an objective test: whether the accused believed that the force used was necessary is a subjective question, but whether the amount of force used was reasonable, rather than a cruel excess, is an objective inquiry.[137] An accused who used excessive force in defending herself will be found guilty of murder if that force proves fatal, even if she believed that the force employed was reasonably necessary.

21.9   CRITIQUE OF THE LAW ON SELF-DEFENCE AND PROPOSALS FOR REFORM

21.9.1   There is a view that the term "self-defence" is a misnomer because it also covers those who act to defend someone else and, possibly, those who act to defend property. On the other hand, it may be that it has come to have this broader meaning even in common usage. Semantics aside, a more substantive criticism is that it is not clear whether the current law *does* permit reasonable force to be used in defence of property.[138]

---

[135] 1985 SLT 540.
[136] *Ibid* at 541.
[137] See section 6.15.1 above for a discussion of subjective and objective approaches to liability.
[138] See section 21.8.9 above.

Lindsay Farmer has considered this issue from a historical and   **21.9.2**
philosophical perspective by reference to the English case of Tony
Martin in 1999.[139] In protecting his remote farmhouse, Martin
fatally shot a 16-year-old burglar in the back. Farmer notes that
one practical option, in the English law context, would be to
introduce a partial defence where excessive force was employed in
self-defence. This would have the effect of "reducing" murder to
manslaughter (or in Scotland, to culpable homicide).[140] Historically,
he traces the way in which a strong right to protect property, even
to the extent of physically harming those who attacked it, was
gradually diluted by the rise of the state and the provision of a
police force to provide general protection. He posits that this,
together with the overarching importance of the right to life,
or the duty to preserve life, as enshrined in Art 2 of the ECHR,
detracts from the legitimacy which might otherwise attach to
defending property. Nonetheless, Tony Martin's argument was
that his property, in its rural location, was not protected by the
police. Farmer states that one reading of this case (and, possibly,
by extension, its resonances in relation to self-defence of property
generally) is as a "working out or renegotiation of the boundaries
between private right and public responsibility".[141] The Martin
case illustrates the particular difficulties in balancing the relevant
rights which arise in this area. This is an aspect of the law which
requires to be certain and knowable. Property owners will act to
protect their rights. The extent to which the law permits them to
do this needs to be clear.

The *Draft Criminal Code* broadens the definition of "self-defence"   **21.9.3**
so that it can be used by someone whose acts are "immediately
necessary and reasonable" to prevent or end unlawful detention
by an aggressor; to protect property from being unlawfully taken,
damaged or destroyed; or to prevent or end an unlawful intrusion
or presence on property.[142] This would not, of course, permit fatal
force to be used in defence of property, since that would not fulfil
the requirement of reasonableness. We suggest that the law be
clarified in this way.

Chalmers and Leverick define "self-defence" as involving "an act   **21.9.4**
directed towards someone who poses a direct threat to the life or

---

[139] L Farmer, "Tony Martin and the nightbreakers: criminal law, victims, and the
power to punish" in S Armstrong and L McAra (eds), *Perspectives on Punishment:
The Contours of Control* (2006) at pp 49–67.
[140] *Ibid* at p 52.
[141] *Ibid* at p 57.
[142] *Draft Criminal Code*, s 23(2)(b)–(d). For the last of these (force used to prevent
or end intrusion on property) the accused must have been in lawful possession of
the property.

physical integrity of the accused, whether as an aggressor *or as a passive threat*".[143] In respect of the latter:

> "The case of the roped mountaineer (A) who falls from a cliff edge while attached to a companion (B) is often used as an example ... If B cuts the rope, causing A to fall to his death, this is surely a case of self-defence. A is a passive threat and poses a direct threat to the life of B. ..."[144]

It may, however, be preferable to restrict self-defence to responses to an aggressor, leaving the plea of necessity to cover B's circumstances.

21.9.5   We have also seen that there is some uncertainty as to whether Hume's statement that a woman may plead self-defence where she has killed to prevent rape would be followed by the appeal court, in all cases. Hume may have based his view on the belief that women ought always to fight to the utmost to try to prevent rape, from which it follows that a woman's life was always in peril during a rape. The definition of the crime has, however, been broadened since Hume's era, such that rape now includes non-consensual sexual intercourse within marriage.[145] Is a woman who kills her husband to prevent him from raping her entitled to an acquittal on the ground of self-defence? There could be circumstances in which a woman who is being raped by her husband knows that she is not likely to be killed – perhaps he regularly forces her to have intercourse. If acquittal of a woman is based on the fact that her life is at risk (as with self-defence, generally) then it may be that we can no longer say that women can, in all circumstances, take life to prevent being raped. It may be, however, that the principle Hume was espousing was that rape is such a horrendous violation that a woman ought to be able to repel such an attack with fatal force, *even if* her life is not in peril from the rapist. We would favour the latter interpretation, but the approach the appeal court would adopt here remains to be seen.

21.9.6   Furthermore, rape is now defined to include non-consensual sodomy,[146] and it is anticipated that the courts will have to consider how this change in the law affects self-defence. In a homicide case, self-defence is only pled by those who admit that their actions have resulted in the death of the ultimate victim. Accordingly, it might be appropriate simply to abolish completely this form so that no one – male or female – can plead self-defence unless the attack by the ultimate deceased was actually life threatening. On the other hand, the courts could interpret Hume's views on self-defence in rape to

---

[143] Chalmers and Leverick (2006), para 3.02 (emphasis added) (footnote omitted).

[144] *Ibid.* This example is not merely hypothetical: see J Simpson, *Touching the Void* (1988).

[145] See section 11.2.6 above.

[146] Sexual Offences (Scotland) Act 2009, s 1(1), discussed from section 11.2.3 above.

include the expanded definition of rape, on the grounds that those who perpetrate such serious sexual violence should be placed in the same category as those who offer life-threatening violence, hence one who repels such an attack with fatal violence is entitled to an acquittal.[147] Again, we would favour the latter interpretation, so long as the usual limitations on self-defence apply, such as it having to be the only option available to the accused, and that the force used was reasonably necessary in the circumstances.

As we have seen, the plea of error in combination with that of **21.9.7** self-defence means that an accused is entitled to be acquitted even though she has made a mistake about her life being in danger, so long as this error was a reasonable one.[148] In relation to battered women who ultimately kill their abusers, there might be scope to extend self-defence even though such women do not necessarily act in response to threats of imminent violence. As previously noted, this approach was not permitted in the case of *HM Advocate* v *Greig*,[149] despite the fact that the accused's husband had been violent towards her on previous occasions, and she testified that she had been afraid of what he would do when he awoke. Rejecting this, Lord Dunpark stated:

> "There are various expedients open to a woman submitted to rough treatment by her husband but a licence to kill [is] not one of them ... [H]undreds indeed thousands of wives in this country, unfortunately, suffer this fate. ... The remedy of divorce or judicial separation is available to end this torment."[150]

This fails to take account of the financial, and often emotional, dependency which many women have on their partners.[151]

Canadian criminal law has recognised that the traditional rules **21.9.8** of self-defence may require to be amended to afford such women a defence; they may strike the first blow, yet nonetheless be defending themselves from attack:

> "[An] aspect of the cyclical nature of the abuse [suffered by the battered woman] is that it begets a degree of predictability to the violence that is absent in an isolated violent encounter between two strangers. This also means that it may in fact be possible for a battered spouse to accurately predict the onset of violence before the first blow is struck, even if an outsider to the relationship cannot."[152]

---

[147] See Leverick (2006), Chap 8.

[148] See section 21.8.4 above.

[149] Unreported, High Court, May 1979. See Gane, Stoddart and Chalmers (2009), para 10.40, p 444.

[150] Cited in F E Raitt and M S Zeedyk, *The Implicit Relation of Psychology and Law: Women and Syndrome Evidence* (2000) at p 80.

[151] See, for example, R Jones, "Guardianship for coercively controlled battered women: breaking the control of the abuser" (1999–2000) 88 *Georgetown LJ* 605.

[152] *Lavallee* v *R* (1990) 76 CR (3d) 329 (SCC) per Madam Justice Wilson at 351.

The suggestion that the law ought to afford such women a defence on the basis of "battered woman's syndrome" has been criticised.[153] Nonetheless, we believe that such killings are more appropriately categorised as, at most, culpable homicide rather than as murder.

21.9.9   We have also seen that a person who is judged to have used more than reasonable force is afforded no defence.[154] This means that someone who wards off an attack with fatal force will be convicted of murder. It would be preferable if excessive force, employed in the mistaken belief that this was necessary, could be used to reduce the charge to culpable homicide. In Ireland, unreasonable force results in a conviction for manslaughter, rather than murder, so long as the accused believed the force to be reasonable,[155] and this approach has been recommended by the English Law Commission.[156] It is submitted that Scotland should follow the Irish and enact a similar provision,[157] provided that, as in relation to errors of fact in other areas of Scots criminal law, the accused's belief is held on reasonable grounds.[158]

21.9.10   Finally, if the accused does not retreat from the fight when she has the chance, this should not automatically rule out a successful defence of self-defence. Instead, this ought to be regarded as merely one factor to be considered in assessing the overall reasonableness of the response to the initial attack, rather than being determinative. As Mr Justice Holmes put it, in the American case of *Brown*:[159]

> "Detached reflection cannot be demanded in the presence of an uplifted knife. Therefore ... it is not a condition of immunity that one in that situation should pause to consider whether a reasonable man might not think it possible to fly with safety or to disable his assailant, rather than to kill him."[160]

21.10   PROVOCATION

21.10.1   What, then, of provocation? It is fair to say that, across all those jurisdictions which allow it as a defence to a charge of murder, it has attracted a particularly high level of academic interest and commentary which is perhaps disproportionate to its practical significance. Much

---

[153] This is discussed further in relation to provocation, at section 21.10.12 and from section 21.11.10 below.

[154] See from section 21.8.12 above.

[155] *The People (AG)* v *Dwyer* [1972] IR 416.

[156] Law Commission, *Partial Defences to Murder* (Law Com No 290, 2004), Parts 3 and 4.

[157] See also C McDiarmid, "Don't look back in anger: the partial defence of provocation in Scots criminal law" in J Chalmers, F Leverick and L Farmer (eds), *Essays in Criminal Law in Honour of Sir Gerald Gordon* (2010) 195 at p 215.

[158] See section 19.8.2 above.

[159] *Brown* v *USA* 256 US 335 (1921).

[160] *Ibid* at 343, cited in D Stuart, *Canadian Criminal Law: A Treatise* (6th edn, 2011), p 516.

of this has related to the essentially masculine model of reaction in anger which it is said to embody and which, accordingly, may render it discriminatory on gender grounds.[161] In its modern incarnation it is a partial excuse, not a complete defence. Where an accused has taken life, a successful plea of provocation will result in a conviction for (voluntary) culpable homicide instead of murder.[162] The accused's action is still criminal but the law accepts that "human frailty"[163] will sometimes cause people to lose control if provoked. The classic definition in Scots law is still that given by Macdonald:

> "The defence of provocation is of this sort – 'Being agitated and excited, and alarmed by violence, I lost control over myself, and took life, when my presence of mind had left me, and without thought of what I was doing'."[164]

Macdonald's reference to the taking of life makes it clear that he is discussing provocation in relation to a charge of homicide. It should, however, be borne in mind that the plea can operate to mitigate sentence in respect of lesser crimes, such as assault;[165] if A punches B on the nose because B said or did something that made A so angry that she lashed out with her fist, this is more excusable than if she committed the same act of violence in a cool and calm manner. Also, of course, because B provoked the attack, we are less sympathetic; the victim is partly to blame.

It had generally been accepted that there were three requirements **21.10.2** for a successful defence of provocation, namely:

(1) loss of self-control, in response to particular types of provoking acts;[166]

(2) an immediate response;[167] and

(3) a response which was appropriate, in the circumstances.[168]

---

[161] As Jeremy Horder has stated: "Whilst the man of honour was certainly meant to resent an affront, he was also meant to avenge it through some characteristic retaliatory action, such as a blow in response to insulting words, a more serious attack in response to a blow, and so on." (*Provocation and Responsibility* (1992) at p 46).

[162] See from section 9.15 above.

[163] See, for example, *Drury v HM Advocate* 2001 SLT 1013 at 1022, para 31, per LJ-G Rodger. In the Canadian case of *Campbell* (1977) 38 CCC (2d) 6 (Ont CA) the court similarly stated that provocation was "an allowance made for human frailty" (*ibid* at 15 per Mr Justice Martin).

[164] Macdonald (1948), p 94. Although Macdonald uses quotation marks, he is not quoting another commentator. The quotes appear to indicate the position which a provoked person would adopt, if asked to explain her actions.

[165] See, for example, *Yip v HM Advocate* 2000 GWD 8–280.

[166] See from section 21.10.3 below.

[167] See section 21.10.12 below.

[168] See from section 21.10.13 below.

Following *Drury* v *HM Advocate*[169] and the subsequent case of *Gillon* v *HM Advocate*,[170] the third requirement varies depending upon the nature of the provoking act itself. Because of this, some commentators suggest that it is more accurate to say that there are now two separate defences of provocation.[171] This will become more apparent when we discuss the third element, but we must first consider loss of self control, and the immediacy of the response.

(1) Loss of self-control

21.10.3 This requirement is common to both forms of the defence, and is of the essence of provocation. The case of *Low* v *HM Advocate*[172] established that there must be some evidence of this loss. If the trial judge takes the view that there is none, then the defence should not be put to the jury. In *Low* the victim suffered 49 stab wounds, at least 22 of which were inflicted before death. The accused had one stab wound to his hand which he said had been inflicted when the victim came at him with a knife. This was alleged to be the provoking act. The appeal court held that there was no evidence of any loss of control on the part of the accused. Even if his evidence had been fully accepted, he was alleging that the victim had been stabbed accidentally in the course of the fight – not that the accused had lost control of himself as a result of the original stab wound.

21.10.4 Provocation mitigates murder because the accused has lost self-control in circumstances which the law specifically recognises as provocative. However, this is not an "all or nothing" matter; if the accused had lost *all* self-control, "mental disorder" might be a more appropriate defence.[173] In *Drury*,[174] the accused sought to argue that loss of self-control should be enough to establish the defence. His argument was that if the provocation had been sufficient to cause him to lose his self-control in the first place then, by definition, he had no control and could not be expected to exercise any restraint.[175] Were that view to be

---

[169] 2001 SLT 1013.
[170] 2007 JC 24.
[171] The suggestion is floated as a possible interpretation of the outcome of *Drury* in J Chalmers and F Leverick, "Murder through the looking glass: *Gillon* v *HM Advocate*" (2007) 11 *Edin LR* 230 at 233.
[172] 1994 SLT 277.
[173] *Drury* v *HM Advocate* 2001 SLT 1013 at 1020, para 23, per LJ-G Rodger. This defence is considered in section 20.7 above.
[174] *Ibid*.
[175] *Ibid* at 1020, para 22, per LJ-G Rodger.

accepted, all that would require to be proved was that the accused had been subjected to a provoking act and had lost self-control in response. The five-judge court rejected this as it implied that "there [was] no intermediate stage between icy detachment and going berserk".[176] Even where there has been a provoking act, individuals still retain some degree of control over their actions.

Scots criminal law accepts loss of self-control arising from anger **21.10.5** in limited circumstances. It is of course possible, and perhaps less blameworthy, that individuals could lose self-control in response to other strong emotions such as fear or despair.[177] In the offence of robbery[178] and the defence of coercion,[179] it is recognised that fear may cause the will of an individual to be completely overborne. There is no reason why fear could not cause a loss of self-control. Furthermore, it might be argued that everyone *ought* to be able to control their anger at least to the extent of not killing another person, no matter the provocative conduct. The question may therefore be whether there are better reasons to mitigate the crime of murder than a loss of self-control based in anger at all.[180] An alternative approach would be to emphasise that the ultimate victim, exercising free will and autonomy, and in the knowledge of the effect which this might have on the accused, did or said something without which the accused would not have lost control. If so, then it may be that it is the nature of the accepted provoking acts which requires re-definition. Issues arising with the current law in this regard will be discussed in the next section.

Provoking acts

Scots law recognises only two types of provoking act: (a) an initial **21.10.6** assault by the victim; and (b) the discovery of sexual infidelity. Informing an individual verbally of such infidelity is the only circumstance in which words can constitute a provoking act for the purposes of the defence.

(a) Initial assault by the victim

This is the "classic" form of provocation. Its historical foundations **21.10.7** in English law have been thoroughly investigated by Horder[181] and his analysis has been applied in the Scottish context by Juliette

---

[176] 2001 SLT 1013 at paras 23 and 24, quoting Lord Diplock in *Phillips* v *The Queen* [1969] 2 AC 130 at 137.
[177] See H Power, "Provocation and culture" [2006] *Crim LR* 871 at 876.
[178] *Harrison* v *Jessop* 1992 SLT 465.
[179] *HM Advocate* v *Raiker* 1989 SCCR 149.
[180] For a fuller discussion of these issues, see McDiarmid (2010).
[181] Horder (1992).

Casey.[182] In origin, it is firmly based in the concept of "honour" which not only permitted "gentlemen" to retaliate physically to perceived slights, such as assault, but actively required it in certain circumstances.[183] Because of this, it appears that provocation was at one time a complete defence. The case of *Hillan* v *HM Advocate*[184] seems to indicate that a vestige of this view survived until the 1930s, at least in relation to a charge of assault. Nonetheless, it is less clear, given the absence from 21st-century society of medieval notions of honour and the very strict rules for behaviour to which it gave rise, that mitigation should continue to be afforded to one who uses fatal violence in circumstances which do not amount to self-defence. In *Cosgrove* v *HM Advocate*[185] Lord Cowie stated, albeit *obiter*:

> "It must be remembered that every case depends on its own circumstances and I suppose it is possible that in some situations a judge might leave the question of provocation to the jury even though the evidence does not fit the classic definition in Macdonald but we have no doubt that the classic definition is still the proper direction to give."[186]

This suggests a weakening of the absoluteness of the position that only assault or the discovery of sexual infidelity will suffice to ground a plea of provocation. In practice, however, the courts appear to be holding resolutely to these traditional requirements.

(b) Sexual infidelity

21.10.8   Hume noted that a husband catching his wife in the act of sexual intercourse with another man could use the defence of provocation.[187] He did, however, express some misgivings:

> "And though the provocation is high, yet is it in some respects not so favourable as that of some other injuries; because the homicide is here done on the principle of rage and revenge, unaccompanied with that fear of further violence, or that trepidation and alarm, which in the ordinary case of an assault on the body of the killer, concur with his resentment, and materially strengthen his defence."[188]

The appeal court has explained the rationale behind this form of the plea as being

---

[182] J Casey, "*Gillon* v *HM Advocate*: provocation, proportionality and the ordinary person" 2006 SLT 193 at 197–200.
[183] As Horder (1992), p 45 points out, historically anger was viewed as an appropriate reaction to certain situations: "If someone is confronted by the illegal torture of their loved ones, the experience of only a moderate amount of anger would be too mild a response."
[184] 1937 JC 53.
[185] 1990 JC 333.
[186] *Ibid* at 339.
[187] Hume, i, 245–246, citing the case of *James Christie* in 1731.
[188] *Ibid*, 246.

"grounded in the law's recognition that a person who is told of another's infidelity may be swept with sudden and overwhelming indignation which may cause him to lose control and to react violently".[189]

As previously noted, informing the accused of sexual infidelity is also the only circumstance in which Scots law permits mere words to ground the partial defence.[190]

Far from restricting the use of sexual infidelity as a form of provoking act, the modern law has expanded it, accepting that being informed of a partner's infidelity after the fact can constitute provocation. This is illustrated by the case of *HM Advocate* v *Hill*[191] in 1941, in which the accused was a corporal in the military police, stationed in England. He travelled to his home in Glasgow because he was suspicious that his wife might have been unfaithful to him. On arrival, he confronted his wife and the other man and they confirmed that they had been having a sexual relationship. Hill immediately got his service revolver and shot his wife and her lover, killing them both. The trial judge directed the jury that provocation could be a valid defence in these circumstances and the accused was convicted of the lesser charge of culpable homicide on that basis. At that time, those convicted of murder faced capital punishment, and Gerald Gordon has suggested that the approach taken by the court in *Hill* may have been "because of a disinclination even to envisage hanging a soldier who returned from the wars to discover that his wife had been unfaithful and responded by killing her".[192]

21.10.9

Nonetheless, *Hill*[193] seems to have precipitated an expansion in the definition of this form of provocation and the principle has now been extended from adultery to other forms of sexual infidelity. In *HM Advocate* v *Callander*[194] it was accepted that a husband's discovery of his wife's lesbian relationship could ground a plea of provocation, though here the charge was assault to severe injury rather than homicide. It has also been extended beyond the marital relationship to any relationship where the court concludes that it is

21.10.10

---

[189] *Rutherford* v *HM Advocate* 1998 JC 34 at 45 per LJ-G Rodger.
[190] See section 21.10.6 above. In *Anderson* v *HM Advocate* 2010 SCL 584, comments by the appeal court designed primarily to uphold the trial judge's decision to withdraw provocation from the jury might have suggested that verbal provocation was generally acceptable (*ibid* at 589, para [18] per Lord Mackay of Drumadoon). In *Elsherkisi* v *HM Advocate* 2012 SCL 181, however, it was made clear that the traditional view prevails: "verbal abuse, however extreme, cannot palliate killing" (*ibid* at 194, para [17] per Lord Hardie).
[191] 1941 JC 59.
[192] Commentary by Gerald Gordon on *Drury* v *HM Advocate* 2001 SCCR 583 at 618.
[193] 1941 JC 59.
[194] 1958 SLT 24.

appropriate for partners to expect sexual fidelity from one another. *McDermott* v *HM Advocate*[195] illustrates both forms of extension. The accused, who was co-habiting with his girlfriend, lost his self-control when he discovered that she was having an "illicit association"[196] – though apparently one which, at least at that time, had involved nothing more than kissing another man, and indicating that she would prefer to be with him, rather than with the accused. In *HM Advocate* v *McKean*[197] the trial judge ruled that infidelity in a lesbian (or, indeed, any homosexual) relationship could provide the basis for a plea of provocation. It is interesting that even in 1996, Lord McLean still felt it necessary to clarify in his charge to the jury that:

> "In these somewhat more enlightened days of sexual equality I can see no reason why the law should not extend uniformly to a man and a woman. In other words, a wife or female companion should have the benefit of the mitigating plea of provocation equally with the husband or male partner."[198]

This suggests that there might have been some doubt as to whether the benefit of this plea extended to female partners. If *McKean* was indeed the first case in which a female accused had sought to use provocation in such circumstances, this may be a further indication of its inherent gender bias.

21.10.11   The discovery of sexual infidelity was the main issue in *Drury* v *HM Advocate*.[199] The accused had been having an intermittent sexual relationship with the victim, Marilyn McKenna, and had at one time lived with her for a 16-month period. Drury arrived at Ms McKenna's house at about midnight on the night of the attack. He had some difficulty in getting anyone to answer the door. Finally, a man ran into the street, adjusting his clothes, and Ms McKenna ran out behind him. Drury asked her what the man was doing there and her answer led him to believe that they had been having sex. Drury then grabbed a claw hammer from a coal bunker at the side of the house and attacked her, inflicting head injuries which one medical witness described as the worst she had ever seen. The five-judge court affirmed that the plea of provocation was available to an accused in such circumstances, provided that the expectation of sexual fidelity could be established by the evidence. The Crown seems to have conceded that Drury did have a legitimate expectation

---

[195] 1973 JC 8.
[196] *Ibid* at 11 per LJ-G Emslie.
[197] 1997 JC 32.
[198] *Ibid* at 33.
[199] 2001 SLT 1013.

of sexual fidelity[200] but his response was not an appropriate one, as we shall discuss further below, hence his conviction for murder was upheld.

(2) Immediacy of response

The other aspect of provocation which remains common to both of its forms is that the loss of self-control must be an *immediate* response to the provoking act; in the words of Hume, it requires "the sudden impulse of resentment".[201] Any delay leaves the accused's act open to the accusation that it was cold-blooded revenge for the alleged provocation rather than a hot-blooded response. This aspect has come in for particular criticism in relation to battered women who kill their abusive partners since, very often, their response will lack this quality of immediacy.[202]

21.10.12

(3) Appropriateness of response

For the plea to be accepted, the accused must have responded to the provoking act within well-defined parameters. These parameters differ depending on whether the provocation consists of sexual infidelity or violence.

21.10.13

(a) *Responding to sexual infidelity*

In *Drury*,[203] the five-judge court expressly rejected an argument by the Crown that the violence offered in response to the discovery of infidelity had to be proportionate to the provocation. This, it said, could not be the case because there was no mechanism for measuring the two responses against each other in any meaningful way.[204] Instead, the court held that at issue was whether the accused had reacted to the provocation in the way in which an ordinary person would have done. If so, the law would recognise the accused as weak rather than wicked and the plea of provocation would succeed. If, however, the accused had overreacted in a way which was not ordinary, the jury would be entitled to conclude that the accused had acted with the necessary wickedness to justify a conviction for murder.[205]

21.10.14

---

[200] Although this is not discussed in the case report, it appears that Drury had in fact been stalking Ms McKenna after she ended their relationship, which had been characterised by his violence towards her. See S Morris, S Anderson and L Murray, *Stalking and Harassment in Scotland* (2002) at p 17, n 63 and accompanying text.

[201] Hume, i, 239.

[202] See from section 21.11.9 below for a critique of this.

[203] 2001 SLT 1013.

[204] *Ibid* at 1021, para 28, per LJ-G Rodger.

[205] *Ibid* at 1022, para 32, per LJ-G Rodger.

(b) Responding to violence

21.10.15   The court in *Drury*[206] left unanswered the question of whether the requirement of a proportionate response no longer applied in cases in which the provoking act was violence, rather than infidelity. The issue was resolved in *Gillon* v *HM Advocate*[207] in which a five-judge court specially convened for the purpose confirmed that the position in cases of provocation by violence remained unchanged.[208] Thus, there must be "some equivalence between the retaliation and the provocation so that the violence used by the accused is not grossly disproportionate to the evidence constituting the provocation".[209] This is illustrated by the case of *Thomson* v *HM Advocate*.[210] The accused and his business partner had disagreed sharply and were in the process of agreeing severance terms. They met at their business premises so that the accused could remove certain articles which he needed to carry on business as a plumber. The accused was armed with a kitchen knife and explained at his trial that this was to protect himself, and to threaten anyone who tried to prevent him removing his equipment. He claimed that at the meeting his partner had laughed at him, had reneged on their agreement and had refused to allow the removal of the equipment. In rejecting the argument that verbal provocation was capable of mitigating murder, the court founded on Hume: "no provocation of words, the most foul and abusive, or of signs or gestures, however contemptuous or derisive soever, is of sufficient weight ... to alleviate the guilt".[211] Lord Justice-Clerk Ross concluded that:

> "It takes a tremendous amount of provocation to palliate stabbing a man to death. Words, however abusive or insulting, are of no avail. A blow with the fist is no justification for the use of a lethal weapon. Provocation, in short, must bear a reasonable retaliation to the resentment which it excites."[212]

---

[206] 2001 SLT 1013.

[207] 2007 JC 24.

[208] There is no requirement for the mode of resentment to be proportionate to the degree of provocation in Canadian law – see *Squire* (1976) 26 CCC (2d) 219 (Ont CA).

[209] *Low* v *HM Advocate* 1994 SLT 277 at 286 per LJ-C Ross.

[210] 1986 SLT 281.

[211] Hume, i, 247. Reference was also made to Macdonald: "Words of insult, however strong, or any mere insulting or disgusting conduct, such as jostling, or tossing filth in the face, do not serve to reduce the crime from murder to culpable homicide" (Macdonald (1948), p 93). Both writers are quoted in *Thomson* 1986 SLT 281 at 284 by LJ-C Ross.

[212] *Ibid*. These words are those of LJ-G Cooper in *Smith* v *HM Advocate* 1952 (unreported, but see Gordon (2001), para 25.19). The passage is also quoted in full by LJ-G Rodger in *Drury* v *HM Advocate* 2001 SLT 1013 at 1023, para 33.

The court held that, far from establishing evidence of provocation,   **21.10.16**
the history of increasingly embittered relations between the parties
provided the accused with a motive for murder. More specifically,
any violence in response to the course of dealings would not satisfy
the test of immediate retaliation.[213] Thomson also claimed that his
partner had pulled him back into the office as he was attempting
to leave. While this could constitute a provoking act, the accused's
response – he stabbed his partner 11 times with the kitchen knife –
was grossly disproportionate to the provoking act, and the plea of
provocation therefore failed.

21.11   CRITIQUE OF THE LAW ON PROVOCATION AND PROPOSALS FOR REFORM

A fundamental criticism of the provocation defence is the intuition   **21.11.1**
that everyone should be expected to control their anger, at least to the
extent of not killing another person.[214] Indeed, in *Drury*[215] the view
was taken that "ordinary" was a better adjective than "reasonable"
in relation to the hypothetical paradigm of the provoked person
because "it requires a considerable effort of the imagination to
envisage a reasonable man actually killing someone in circumstances
where the law provides that he ought not to do so".[216] Some further
consideration of this issue is warranted.

In the first edition of this book, we looked in some detail at the   **21.11.2**
then English law of provocation in terms of s 3 of the Homicide
Act 1957. That section is now repealed, and provocation has been
replaced by a partial defence to murder named "loss of control".[217]
The particular interest of the old law was that it overtly applied a
"reasonable man [*sic*]" standard, which offered a rich comparative
seam to Scots law's much less developed "ordinary man or woman".[218]
Despite its repeal, it is worth examining this briefly, since this is an
area of law which the Scottish law Commission is due to consider
with a view to recommending reforms.[219]

---

[213] See section 21.10.12 above.

[214] See McDiarmid (2010), especially at pp 212–213.

[215] 2001 SLT 1013.

[216] *Ibid* at 1020, para 24, per LJ-G Rodger. In the English case of *R v Smith (Morgan)* [2001] 1 AC 146, Lord Hoffmann (at 172) also suggested that "The jury may have some difficulty with the notion that the 'reasonable man' will, even under severe provocation, kill someone else".

[217] Coroners and Justice Act 2009, ss 54–56.

[218] *Drury v HM Advocate* 2001 SLT 1013, especially at 1022, para [32] per LJ-G Rodger.

[219] See Scottish Law Commission website at: http://www.scotlawcom.gov.uk/law-reform-projects/homicide/.

21.11.3   The difficulty with "reasonable" or "ordinary" person tests
is whether they should be completely objective – so that personal
characteristics of the accused which affect how she perceives the
provocation are irrelevant – or whether they require some level
of subjectivity so that accused persons are not held to impossible
standards. American authors Paul Robinson and Michael Cahill
argue that "there remains little justification for continuing in the use
of purely objective standards that hold actors to standards that they
cannot fairly be expected to meet".[220] On the other hand, a purely
subjective standard may ask no more of the accused than what she
has actually done.

21.11.4   The matter has not been advanced in Scots law following *Drury*,
where it was not discussed because it was not raised on the facts.[221]
It has been noted that the Israeli Supreme Court developed a "bare"
reasonable person standard, devoid of personal characteristics,
which did not then operate to secure the return of a manslaughter
conviction on a murder charge in a single case.[222] The "reasonable
person" became a "heterosexual Jewish man of average education".[223]
It is notoriously difficult to develop clear and fair standards in this
area. In the end, if the victim has deliberately taunted the accused in
relation to a characteristic which he knows the accused to possess:
say, "she slept with me because of your impotence",[224] then it seems
artificial for the law to ignore this. On the other hand, there is little
point in setting an "ordinary person" standard, if that person takes
on so many of the accused's characteristics that the only standard
set is the one the accused herself was able to conform to – even if
one of her characteristics is, say, a fiery and murderous temper. The
matter may best be resolved by looking more closely at the role of the
victim in precipitating the attack. Deliberate taunting in relation to
a specific characteristic should render the accused commensurately
less blameworthy.

21.11.5   In England and Wales, currently, the "loss of control" partial
defence may be pled, in relation to a charge of murder only,[225] where

---

[220] P H Robinson and M T Cahill, *Law without Justice: Why Criminal Law
Doesn't Give People What They Deserve* (2006), p 49.
[221] 2001 SLT 1013 at 1030, para [21] per Lord Johnston.
[222] See O Kamir, "Responsibility determination as a smokescreen: provocation
and the reasonable person in the Israeli Supreme Court" (2004–05) 2 *Ohio State
Journal of Criminal Law* 547 at 551–552. For a fuller discussion in relation to Scots
law, see McDiarmid (2010) at pp 200–201.
[223] Kamir (2004–05) at 553, n 12.
[224] The English law case of *Bedder* v *DPP* [1954] 1 WLR 1119 nonetheless
determined that the taunting of the defendant for his physical impotence was *not* a
relevant characteristic to be taken into account.
[225] Coroners and Justice Act 2009, s 54(1).

the killing resulted from a loss of self-control on the defendant's part.[226] That loss must have had a "qualifying trigger".[227] Any reference to "reasonable" or "ordinary" men or women is avoided but direction is provided on relevant characteristics in assessing the excusatory nature of the accused's response to the provocative behaviour.[228] Section 54(1)(c) states, as a requirement, that: "a person of D's sex and age, with a normal degree of tolerance and selfrestraint [sic] and in the circumstances of D, might have reacted in the same or in a similar way to D." Section 55 then provides further definition of "qualifying trigger". Circumstances can only constitute such a trigger in three situations:

(1) "if D's loss of self-control was attributable to D's fear of serious violence from V against D or another identified person";[229]

(2) "if D's loss of self-control was attributable to ... things done or said (or both) which – (a) constituted circumstances of an extremely grave character, and (b) caused D to have a justifiable sense of being seriously wronged";[230] or

(3) "if D's loss of self-control was attributable to a combination of the matters mentioned [at (1) and (2) above]".[231]

There is no doubt that the entry point into the "loss of control" defence is significantly harder for a defendant to attain than was the position in relation to the previous law of provocation. On this point, Lord Judge CJ stated:

"There is no point in pretending that the practical application of this provision will not create considerable difficulties. Section 55(3) [and] (4) define the circumstances in which a qualifying trigger may be present. The statutory language is not bland. In section 55(3) it is not enough that the defendant is fearful of violence. He must fear *serious* violence. In subsection 4(a) the circumstances must not merely be grave, but *extremely* so. In subsection 4(b) it is not enough that the defendant has been caused by the circumstances to feel a sense of grievance. It must arise from a *justifiable* sense not merely that he has been wronged, but that he has been *seriously* wronged. By contrast with the former law of provocation, these provisions ... have raised the bar. We have been used to a much less prescriptive approach to the provocation defence."[232]

---

[226] Coroners and Justice Act 2009, s 54(1)(a).

[227] *Ibid*, s 54(1)(b).

[228] The legislation uses the initials "D" and "V" which correspond to "defendant" and "victim".

[229] Coroners and Justice Act 2009, s 55(3).

[230] *Ibid*, s 55(4).

[231] *Ibid*, s 55(5).

[232] *R v Clinton* [2013] QB 1 at 10, para [11] (emphases in original).

Sexual infidelity is to be entirely disregarded in determining whether a qualifying trigger exists.[233] A number of useful comparative points may be drawn.

21.11.6   Considering first the provoking acts in Scots law alongside the English qualifying trigger, it is clear that, while the *quality* of the behaviour required to constitute that trigger is closely defined, the only factual limit on its breadth is the exclusion of sexual infidelity. In Scotland, discovery of sexual infidelity has always been regarded as an exceptional form of the defence, yet it is not clear on what grounds, other than historical happenstance, it should continue to be privileged in contemporary society.[234] It rests on the rationale that it is more acceptable to kill in hot than in cold blood provided that the reason for the accused's anger is justifiable. It is not clear that an initial assault by the victim or the discovery of sexual infidelity justify murderous rage. If they do, other reasons might also operate here. For instance, an accused who discovers that someone had sexually abused her child[235] or had killed her spouse, might be even more justified in losing self-control and killing. She would not, however, be able to use the defence of provocation. The law ought to broaden the forms of behaviour which it recognises as being capable of forming the basis of a provocation plea.[236]

21.11.7   The initially appealing alternative is to reject the notion that sexual infidelity should operate to palliate murder. The argument was well made in a Canadian case in which one of the dissenting judges argued that sexual infidelity should not be recognised as a form of provocation:

> "it would be a dangerous precedent to characterize involvement in an extra-marital affair as conduct capable of grounding provocation ... At law, no one has either an emotional or proprietary right or interest in a spouse that would justify the loss of self-control that the [accused] exhibited".[237]

This is, of course, exactly the course taken in English law[238] but it has not been straightforward because, as was stated in *R v Clinton*:[239] "The exclusion created by section 55(6) cannot and does

---

[233] Coroners and Justice Act 2009, s 55(6)(c).

[234] The (English) Law Commission has stated: "The evidence which we have tends to suggest that juries are less prone than is sometimes thought to return verdicts of manslaughter on grounds of provocation where the provocation alleged is simple separation or infidelity, but in our view such cases ought not to be left to the jury." (Law Commission (2004), para 3.145).

[235] See Gane, Stoddart and Chalmers (2009), para 10.40, p 442.

[236] The *Draft Criminal Code*, s 38(4)(a) would achieve this by including "acts or words or both" which can emanate from the ultimate victim, or from a third party.

[237] *R v Thibert* [1996] 1 SCR 37, para [65] per Justice Major (dissenting).

[238] Coroners and Justice Act 2009, s 55(6)(c).

[239] [2013] QB 1.

not eradicate the fact that on occasions sexual infidelity and loss of control are linked, often with the one followed immediately by the other."[240] The discovery of sexual infidelity is a situation in which "ordinary" or "reasonable" people might be expected to lose self-control. The 2009 Act seeks to outlaw killing out of a sense of sexual ownership of the victim. In so doing, it may leave an individual who would legitimately satisfy the high standard of "qualifying trigger" set down in s 55 with no "loss of control" defence, because the "thing said of an extremely grave character which caused her to have a justifiable sense of being seriously wronged" was an admission that her partner had been unfaithful. The judgment in *Clinton* therefore allows sexual infidelity to be part of the evidence considered where it "is integral to and forms an essential part of the context in which to make a just evaluation whether a qualifying trigger properly falls within the ambit of subsections 55(3) and 55(4)".[241] It is excluded where it constitutes the only potential trigger,[242] as is perhaps most likely to be the case in killings arising from sexual possessiveness.[243] We therefore suggest that Scots law should make sexual infidelity insufficient, alone, for a plea of provocation[244] but should not exclude it altogether from a reformed version of the defence with a wider set of provoking acts.

The sexual infidelity exclusion was an attempt predominantly **21.11.8** to prevent jealous men from mitigation where it was that sense of possessiveness which drove the attack. The expansion of the plea of provocation in Scots law to include non-heterosexual relationships, and confessions of infidelity as well as their actual discovery, may seem to obviate any suggestion that the law discriminates on the basis of gender or sexuality. In respect of the former, however, a glance at the Scottish homicide statistics suggests otherwise:

> "For homicides recorded [from 2003–2004 to 2012–2013], 50% of the female victims aged between 16 and 70 years were killed by their partner or ex-partner ... For male victims aged 16 to 70 years, only 6% were killed by their partner or ex-partner."[245]

---

[240] [2013] QB 1 at 16, para [36], per Lord Judge CJ.

[241] *Ibid* at 17, para [39], per Lord Judge CJ.

[242] *Ibid* at 16, para [35].

[243] See A Clough, "Sexual infidelity: the exclusion that never was?" (2012) 76 J Crim L 382 at 388.

[244] This is because: "In most cases involving an admission of sexual infidelity, there is often much more to the situation than meets the eye": *ibid* at 382.

[245] Scottish Government, *Statistical Bulletin: Crime and Justice Series: Homicide in Scotland, 2012–13*, p 15, and see Chart 10 on p 15 (available at http://www.scotland.gov.uk/Resource/0043/00435280.pdf).

In 2012–13, 80 per cent of those accused of homicide were male.[246] Taken together, these figures suggest that the defence of provocation where the provoking act is sexual infidelity is employed by men far more often than by women. There have been substantial advances in many jurisdictions in recognising the plight of battered women who kill, to the extent that their predicament is often a major consideration in proposals to reform the plea.[247] This has largely been due to feminist critiques of the law.[248] Nonetheless, the foregoing statistics illustrate that, in Scotland at least, the plea of provocation still has a sexist dimension. As a mechanism for conviction of culpable homicide on a murder charge, it remains more suitable for the circumstances in which angry men find themselves, rather than abused women. As Horder has put it:

"From a feminist perspective the existence of such mitigation simply reinforces in the law that which public institutions ought in fact to be seeking to eradicate, namely, the acceptance that there is something natural, inevitable, and hence in some (legal) sense-to-be-recognized forgivable about men's violence against women, and their violence in general."[249]

21.11.9 The new English law defence distances itself from the requirement of immediacy between the qualifying triggger and the loss of control by stating that the loss does not have to be sudden.[250] As we have seen, the continuing requirement in Scots law for an immediate response[251] and a provoking act of violence or fear of imminent violence[252] makes it very difficult for battered women to benefit from the plea. They commonly experience a "slow burn" of anger which eventually

---

[246] *Homicide in Scotland*, p 11, para 3.3 and Table 6 (on p 25). For comparison purposes, in 2011–12 this figure was 93% (Scottish Goverment, *Statistical Release: Crime and Justice Series: Homicide in Scotland, 2011–12*, p 10, para 3.3 and Table 6 on p 21 (available at http://www.scotland.gov.uk/Resource/0040/00407659. pdf.). In 2006–07, 92% of those prosecuted for homicide were male and the report notes that this statistic is similar to that of previous years (Scottish Government, *Statistical Bulletin Criminal Justice Series: Homicide in Scotland, 2006–07*, para 5.1 and table 7) (available at: http://www.scotland.gov.uk/Resource/Doc/207004/0054998.pdf).
[247] See, for example, Law Commission, *Partial Defences to Murder Consultation Paper* (No 173, 2003), Part X; Victorian Law Reform Commission, *Defences to Homicide Final Report* (2004), p xxviii.
[248] See, for example, V Nourse, "Passion's progress: modern law reform and the provocation defense" (1996–97) 106 *Yale LJ* 1331; A Howe, "Provocation in crisis – law's passion at the crossroads? New directions for feminist strategists" (2004) 21 *Austl Feminist LJ* 53. Feminism is discussed more generally from section 1.11 above.
[249] Horder (1992), p 194.
[250] Coroners and Justice Act 2009, s 54(2).
[251] Section 21.10.12 above.
[252] Section 21.10.7 above.

causes them to lose self-control and to kill, but usually not in response to the type of provoking act which is recognised by the law.[253] In fact, such an attack may take place at a time when there is little risk of retaliation, such as when the victim is asleep.[254] In general, there is an acceptance in the academic literature that it is inappropriate to convict of murder in such circumstances.[255] Under the pre-existing English law, it was affirmed specifically in *R v Ahluwalia*[256] that delay, in itself, was not fatal to a plea of provocation:

> "We accept that the subjective element in the defence of provocation would not as a matter of law be negatived simply because of the delayed reaction in such cases, provided that there was at the time of the killing a 'sudden and temporary loss of self-control' caused by the alleged provocation. However, the longer the delay and the stronger the evidence of deliberation on the part of the defendant, the more likely it will be that the prosecution will negative provocation."[257]

Nonetheless, the Court of Appeal did not find that the defendant had been provoked. Rather, it overturned her conviction and ordered a retrial on the ground of diminished responsibility. The law therefore categorised her as having acted out of an abnormality of mind rather than in the way that a reasonable person would have done.[258] Since the immediacy requirement has not been relaxed in Scots law,[259] the position for battered women seeking to utilise a defence of provocation remains unsatisfactory.[260]

Mention has already been made[261] of the concept of "battered **21.11.10** woman's syndrome", developed by Lenore Walker, which suggests that those who experience domestic violence on a regular basis may eventually come to be in a state of "learned helplessness" which

---

[253] See, for example, J Horder, "Reshaping the subjective element in the provocation defence" (2005) 25 *OJLS* 123 at 128–130, in which he discusses *R v Ahluwalia* [1993] 96 Cr App R 133.

[254] See, for example, *HM Advocate v Greig* (High Court, May 1979, unreported), discussed in section 21.8.2 above.

[255] See, for example, R Sanghvi and D Nicolson, "Battered women and provocation: the implications of *R v Ahluwalia*" [1993] *Crim LR* 728; K O'Donovan, "Defences for battered women who kill" (1991) 18 *J Law & Soc* 219; B J Mitchell, R D Mackay and W J Brookbanks, "Pleading for provoked killers: in defence of Morgan Smith" (2008) 124 *LQR* 675.

[256] [1993] 96 Cr App R 133.

[257] *Ibid* at 139 per Lord Taylor CJ.

[258] See D Nicolson, "Telling tales: gender discrimination, gender construction and battered women who kill" (1995) 3 *Fem L S* 185 at 196.

[259] See *Thomson v HM Advocate* 1986 SLT 281, discussed further at section 21.10.15 above.

[260] There have been no *reported* cases in Scotland where the issue has been addressed specifically in relation to a killing by a battered partner.

[261] See section 20.11.7 above.

leads them to believe that the only way to escape the situation is to kill the abuser.[262] As a theory, battered woman's syndrome has been heavily criticised:[263]

> "A fundamental problem … is that we risk transforming the reality of this form of gender oppression into a psychiatric disorder. The victim of spousal violence becomes the abnormal actor, the one whose conduct must be explained by an expert. When a woman uses force to defend herself, it is evaluated with reference to a male standard of reasonableness or to an exceptional standard for certain women, i.e. those who are 'battered women'. The focus is on the irrationality of a woman's response and on the need for medical terminology to transform that irrational response into a reasonable one for a 'battered woman'. She must either be reasonable 'like a man' or reasonable 'like a battered woman'. Trapped in this dichotomy, the 'reasonable' woman may disappear."[264]

While it has allowed evidence of domestic abuse to enter the discussion in some cases, where previously it would have been completely irrelevant,[265] its status as a syndrome means that it is treated as psychiatric evidence, which is better fitted to a defence of "diminished responsibility" than one of provocation.[266]

21.11.11   Fiona Raitt and Suzanne Zeedyk have pointed out that both self-defence and provocation, as currently defined, are unsuitable pleas for the majority of such women:

> "Both of these defences emphasise the spontaneity of behaviour. That is, imminence is the key consideration for self-defence, as is sudden loss of control for provocation. An emphasis on spontaneity takes no account of

---

[262] L Walker, *The Battered Woman Syndrome* (1984), as cited in O'Donovan (1991) at 230–231, where the salient points are summarised.

[263] O'Donovan (1991) at 231–233; Sanghvi and Nicolson (1993) at 733–734; D L Faigman, "The battered woman syndrome and self-defense: a legal and empirical dissent" [1986] 72 *Va L Rev* 619; D L Faigman, "Discerning justice when battered women kill" (1987–88) 39 *Hastings LJ* 207.

[264] I Grant, "The 'syndromization' of women's experience" in D Martinson, M MacCrimmon, I Grant and C Boyle, "A forum on *Lavallee v R*: women and self-defence" (1991) 25 *U Brit Colum L Rev* 23 at 51–52.

[265] The Home Office's report, *Crime in England and Wales 2007/8: Findings from the British Crime Survey and Police Recorded Crime* (2008) stated that domestic violence "was the only category of violence for which the risk for women (0.6%) was significantly higher than for men (0.2%) … 33 per cent of violent incidents against women were domestic violence, compared with 4 per cent of incidents against men" (at para 3.8). This point is not made in their most recent report: *Crime in England and Wales, Year Ending December 2013*. A recent HMIC Report, *Everyone's Business: Improving the Police Response to Domestic Abuse* (2014) states: "The 2012–13 Crime Survey for England and Wales estimated there [were] 1.2 million female victims of domestic abuse and 700,000 male victims … While both men and women can be victims of domestic abuse, women are more likely to be victims than men. Women are also much more likely to be high risk victims" (at p 30, footnotes omitted).

[266] Diminished responsibility is considered from section 20.10 above.

the ways in which women's experience tends to differ from men's, especially when the violence emanates from an intimate partner.

Important differences include the size differential; women are generally smaller and physically weaker than men, thus less able to defend themselves. Women are likely to be economically and even emotionally dependent on their abusers. Abused women who kill are often the recipients of long-term violence, so it is unlikely they are responding to a singular event. Perhaps most critically, the circumstances surrounding women's killing of their abusive partners usually do not fulfil the requirement of spontaneity. Women tend to act when the man is relatively defenceless, such as when he is asleep or incapacitated by alcohol, and they may have earlier hidden a weapon to assist them. These actions stem from their belief that a life-threatening episode of violence is imminent and that if they act when the man is unaware, they will have a better chance of successfully defending themselves. However, because their actions then appear to be planned, the criteria of 'imminent danger' and 'sudden loss of control' appear not to be met. They are therefore typically disqualified from pleading either self-defence or provocation." [267]

Overall, the law should be seeking the most effective and the fairest ways to mitigate murder to culpable homicide. It is not clear that provocation, as currently formulated, meets this criterion. We have suggested earlier in this chapter that excessive self-defence should be considered in this regard.[268] Beyond this, there have been calls for a more general defence to murder such as the one set down in the American Model Penal Code:

21.11.12

> "Criminal homicide constitutes manslaughter when ... a homicide which would otherwise be murder is committed under the influence of extreme mental or emotional disturbance for which there is a reasonable explanation or excuse. The reasonableness of such explanation or excuse shall be determined from the viewpoint of a person in the actor's situation under the circumstances as he believes them to be."[269]

In principle, we would welcome this concept of extreme emotional disturbance to the extent that it would make it easier for accused persons who act in the grip of emotions other than anger (which is of the essence of provocation) to bring any reasonable explanation or excuse for this to the court's attention. It would not, in our view, be appropriate, however, as has been proposed by some, to seek to merge the pleas of diminished responsibility and provocation.[270] It should remain clear that the response of the provoked accused, while blameworthy, was directly induced by the circumstances in which she was placed. A further alternative would be to change the penalty of life imprisonment for murder to a maximum, rather than a mandatory, one – a shift for which strong arguments have been

---

[267] Raitt and Zeedyk (2000), p 69.
[268] See section 21.9.9 above.
[269] Model Penal Code, s 210.3(1)(b).
[270] See R D Mackay and B J Mitchell, "Provoking diminished responsibility: two pleas merging into one?" [2003] *Crim LR* 745.

made over the years.[271] There is also much to be said for Horder's approach, which is that society should say to one who has killed while provoked that:

> "Provocation ought no more to be regarded as inviting personal retaliation than a woman's style of dress invites rape. It is one thing to feel great anger at great provocation; but quite another (ethical) thing to experience and express that anger in retaliatory form. For you there can be no mitigation of the offence."[272]

21.12 SUPERIOR ORDERS

21.12.1 In superior orders, the accused claims that she committed the crime only because of an order to do so. It is similar to coercion, but here the orders are usually considered, at least *prima facie*, to be lawful. One example would be an order to a soldier from a more senior officer. The Rome Statute of the International Criminal Court permits the defence of superior orders.[273] The plea was used (unsuccessfully) in the Nuremberg trials, following the Second World War.[274] The German accused argued that they had shot and gassed Jewish people and committed other atrocities because they were ordered to do so, and that these orders were lawful. The refusal to accept this defence was based on the premise that some orders are so obviously immoral that one should disobey them, even if that means disobeying the law. It may even be argued that such immoral "laws" are not really "laws" at all.[275]

21.12.2 Shlomit Wallerstein has argued that the disjuncture between national and international law in this area may give rise to what he terms "the soldier's dilemma".[276] A soldier who disobeys orders is breaching one of the fundamental rules of the military and may risk court martial for so doing. If he does, however, obey an order which turns out to be illegal in international law, he may find himself prosecuted in the international criminal court, or one of the special international tribunals.[277] Wallerstein's solution is that national law – he is concerned with English law – should not allow the defence

---

[271] See, for example, T Cotton, "The mandatory life sentence for murder: is it time for discretion?" (2008) 72 *J Crim L* 288; *Draft Criminal Code*, Sch 1; Lord Windlesham, "Life sentences: the case for assimilation" [1996] *Crim LR* 250.

[272] Horder (1992), p 197.

[273] ICC Statute, Art 33. See L Harris, "The International Criminal Court and the superior orders defence" (2003) 22 *University of Tasmania Law Review* 200.

[274] See the Nuremburg Charter of 1945, Art 8.

[275] See L L Fuller, "Positivism and fidelity to law – a reply to Professor Hart" (1957) 71 *Harv L Rev* 630.

[276] S Wallerstein, "Why English law should not incorporate the defence of superior orders" [2010] *Crim LR* 109, especially Part II.

[277] *Ibid* at 115.

but should, in appropriate cases, take account of superior orders as a mitigating factor at sentencing.[278] This would recognise both that the soldier, even subject to orders, is still a reasoning agent with the ability to assess the lawfulness and morality of what he is instructed to do and also the nature of the dilemma. The Scottish courts have rarely engaged with the defence. Since it is in many respects a species of duress, its utility for homicide offences would be in question in the same way as for coercion and necessity.[279]

An old Scottish case which considered this defence was *HM*   **21.12.3**
Advocate v *Hawton and Parker*[280] in 1861. A boatswain was sent to intercept a trawler and ordered a marine to fire at the boat. The marine fired, intending to go wide, but in fact killed someone on board the trawler, and both sailors were charged with murder. The marine pled that he was acting under superior orders, the orders he received from the boatswain, and the boatswain in turn pled that he had orders from his superiors, and that what he had done was in accordance with normal naval practice. Lord Justice-General McNeill instructed the jury that it was the duty of subordinates to obey their superior officers, unless the orders given were so flagrantly wrongful that no one could be expected to obey them. He stressed, however, that the accused should be convicted if they had deviated from naval rules, or had been careless in executing the orders. The jury returned a verdict of not guilty. The approach taken in this case is similar to that adopted in the United States, such that a defence of superior orders is available so long as the orders were not "manifestly illegal". This "allows the subordinate to presume that his orders are legal, and obedience to those orders is a defense unless the illegality of the orders is obvious to any person of ordinary understanding".[281]

In *HM Advocate* v *Sheppard*[282] in 1941, a soldier was charged   **21.12.4**
with culpable homicide when he fired at, and killed, a deserter who was trying to escape. His superior officer had told him to "stand no nonsense and to shoot if necessary". Although the defence of superior orders was not mentioned, as such, Lord Robertson directed the jury that they should ask themselves whether the shooting was, in a proper sense, in the line of the accused's duty as reasonably understood by him. The accused was acquitted. It should be borne in mind that the case took place during wartime, when executing deserters was an accepted practice. The approach Scots law takes to superior orders

---

[278] Wallerstein (2010) at 125.
[279] See from sections 21.2 and 21.4 respectively, above.
[280] (1861) 4 Irv 58.
[281] J B Insco, "Defense of superior orders before military commissions" (2003) 13 *Duke Journal of Comparative and International Law* 389 at 393.
[282] 1941 JC 67.

reflects the reality of life in the armed forces, where disobedience of
orders, or even questioning one's superiors, is generally considered to
be contrary to military ethos.

21.13   ENTRAPMENT

21.13.1   The accused who pleads entrapment is arguing that she was tricked
into committing the crime by the police; in other words, that the
state has acted as *agent provocateur*. In *Brown* v *HM Advocate*[283] it
was stated that

> "the nature of the unfairness complained of in a case of entrapment is
> that an accused has been pressurised by the state into committing a
> criminal act which, *but for that pressure*, would never have seen the light of
> day".[284]

This case suggests that entrapment fundamentally affects the
legitimacy of the prosecution and is therefore akin to a plea in bar of
trial, rather than a defence.[285] It is a plea which is recognised in other
jurisdictions; the American Model Penal Code provides:

> "A public law enforcement official or a person acting in cooperation with
> such an official perpetrates an entrapment if for the purpose of obtaining
> evidence of the commission of an offense, he induces or encourages another
> person to engage in conduct constituting such offense by either:
>
> (a) making knowingly false representations designed to induce the belief that
> such conduct is not prohibited; or
>
> (b) employing methods of persuasion or inducement which create a substantial
> risk that such an offense will be committed by persons *other than those
> who are ready to commit it.*"[286]

In *Sherman* v *United States*[287] the American Supreme Court stated
that "a line must be drawn between the trap for the unwary innocent
and the trap for the unwary criminal".[288] The case of *Brown* v *HM
Advocate* shows that Scots law adopts a similar approach. In the case
of *Jones* v *HM Advocate*,[289] it was held that the appropriate remedy
where a plea of entrapment is successful is a stay of proceedings so
that the case cannot proceed. This is on the basis that "the moral
integrity of the criminal justice process would be compromised if

---

[283] 2002 SLT 809.
[284] *Ibid* at 812, para [11] per Lord Marnoch (emphasis added).
[285] *Ibid*. See also Lord Philip at 815.
[286] Model Penal Code, s 2.13(1) (emphasis added). The accused must prove the
defence "by a preponderance of evidence" – s 2.13(2).
[287] 356 US 369 (1958).
[288] *Ibid* at 372.
[289] 2010 JC 255.

the prosecution went ahead because the state effectively created the crime in order to prosecute it".[290]

21.14 OTHER DEFENCES?

By virtue of the fact that Scots criminal law is a common law system, defences have been developed by the courts over hundreds of years to deal with new circumstances. It may be, however, that there remain *lacunae* in the law. Perhaps other defences ought to be recognised? An example of a defence which is not necessarily recognised in Scots criminal law is that of "impossibility".[291] Lon Fuller noted:

> "On the face of it a law commanding the impossible seems such an absurdity that one is tempted to suppose no sane lawmaker, not even the most evil dictator, would have any reason to enact such a law. Unfortunately the facts of life run counter to this assumption."[292]

The defence seems to have been recognised in the case of *Middleton v Tough,* in 1908.[293] The case related to a bye-law, made under the Salmon Fisheries (Scotland) Act 1868, which required salmon nets in the River Conon in Ross and Cromarty to be removed completely from the water between 6 pm on Saturdays and 6 am on Mondays. The accused had left her nets in place over the weekend. The weather on Saturday night had been so bad that the nets could not have been lifted safely. This was no longer a problem on the Sunday but the issue was whether anyone in that area of Scotland, in that era, could be expected to perform any work on the Christian Sabbath day. Lord Dunedin, the then Lord Justice-General, seemed to have had little difficulty in stating that there existed an "answer" to a charge, "which has always been as an answer satisfactory to avoid conviction, namely that there was impossibility".[294] He took the view, however, that it was inapplicable in this case. The accused had taken no steps either to instruct her own employees to remove the nets or, if they were unwilling, to find others to perform this work. It seems not to have been doubted that impossibility prevented conviction in relation to the non-removal of the nets on the Saturday night.

The issue has received little discussion apart from this, though the case of *Macmillan v Wright*[295] seems to suggest that it would be

21.14.1

21.14.2

---

[290] F Leverick and F Stark, "How do you solve a problem like entrapment? *Jones & Doyle v HM Advocate*" (2010) 14 *Edin LR* 467 at 472.
[291] For the argument that the law ought *not* to recognise this defence, see Stuart (2011) at p 572.
[292] L L Fuller, *The Morality of Law* (1964), p 70 (footnote omitted).
[293] (1908) 5 Adam 485.
[294] *Ibid* at 490.
[295] 1944 SLT (Sh Ct) 5.

available in appropriate circumstances.[296] The *Draft Criminal Code* provides a defence of "impossibility".[297] This would apply where the accused has failed to do something which was, in the circumstances "and without fault on that person's part", impossible to do.[298] It is submitted that this is the only rational solution. If performance is impossible, yet the law requires it, this would make a mockery of the principles of autonomy and free will on which the criminal law is based.

21.14.4   The *Code* also provides a general defence of "lawful authority".[299] As we have seen, some statutes specifically include this as a defence – for example, vandalism is defined as the wilful (that is, intentional) or reckless damaging or destroying of someone else's property "without lawful authority or reasonable excuse",[300] and this phrase is also used in the offensive weapons legislation,[301] and in relation to the crime of being found in or on premises in circumstances in which intent to commit theft can reasonably be inferred.[302] It seems that some common law offences also have a lack of lawful authority as part of their definition – for example, abduction.[303] Under the *Code*, behaviour would be justified by lawful authority if an enactment or rule of law required it to be done, or conferred a right to do it.[304] Specific mention is made of those who are to be regarded as having lawful authority by virtue of their role or function, so long as they are exercising that role or function properly.[305] Such people include judges, police and prison officers, parents, teachers and those having the care of an adult with incapacity.[306] The *Code* also makes clear that lawful authority will not excuse someone who has used excessive force, in the circumstances,[307] or who has inflicted torture, inhuman or degrading treatment or corporal punishment.[308]

---

[296] Gordon (2000), para 8.30 discusses the issue in relation to statutory offences, taking the view that, where the statute requires that a specific thing should be done, and this is impossible, the defence could apply.

[297] *Draft Criminal Code*, s 26.

[298] *Ibid.*

[299] *Ibid*, s 22(1).

[300] See from section 13.3 above. See also Forgery and Counterfeiting Act 1981, ss 14(2) and 16(2), in relation to making and possessing counterfeit money.

[301] See from section 8.11 above.

[302] See from section 8.17 above.

[303] See from section 10.17 above.

[304] *Draft Criminal Code*, s 22(2)(c).

[305] *Ibid*, s 22(3).

[306] *Ibid*, s 22(3)(a)–(e).

[307] *Ibid*, s 22(4)(a).

[308] *Ibid*, s 22(4)(b). Nor can lawful authority justify violence, abuse or maltreatment by *inter alia* parents, guardians, teachers, or those having the care of an adult with incapacity – s 22(4)(c), (d) and (e).

CHAPTER 22

THE FUTURE DEVELOPMENT OF
SCOTS CRIMINAL LAW

22.1 INTRODUCTION

Throughout this book, we have sought to articulate some of the philosophical foundations of the criminal law of Scotland and to show how these principles underlie crimes, defences and principles of liability. We have seen that while liberalism is the dominant philosophy, elements of communitarianism and of some feminist philosophies can also be detected, with the last two offering a critique of and, to some extent, a limitation on, the operation of the first. As these philosophies sometimes contradict each other, it is perhaps not surprising that the law is not always internally consistent or, indeed, certain. No law can envisage every possible form of wrongdoing with which it might be called upon to deal. *Some* flexibility is, therefore, valuable.

22.1.1

22.2 FUTURE DIRECTIONS

Summarising a common approach to the criminal law, Lindsay Farmer referred to:

> "an unreflective separatism that assumes that being Scottish, and a subject of the Scottish legal system, confers certain benefits and that this should not be tampered with or criticised for fear of endangering a hard-won independence".[1]

22.2.1

This overtly nationalistic approach may have been understandable in an era in which Scots law felt threatened by its bigger and politically dominant southern neighbour, but the re-establishment of the Scottish Parliament meant that it was no

---

[1] L Farmer, *Criminal Law, Tradition and Legal Order: Crime and the Genius of Scots Law 1747 to the Present* (1997), p 22.

longer appropriate.[2] Indeed, as we write "independence" has taken
on political connotations as we approach the Referendum.[3] Scots
criminal law ought to be coherent, clear and certain. The political
context into which it fits is of lesser significance. Reflecting on law
reform generally, former Lord Justice-General Alan Rodger pointed
out that:

> "people affected by a statutory provision are not concerned with the purity of
> its legal antecedents or with the idea that it embodies some principle of their
> national law. Understandably enough, they are simply concerned with the
> way in which it affects their own position".[4]

Recent years have witnessed increasing use of legal resources from
other jurisdictions by the Scottish Law Commission, by counsel, and
by the courts, themselves.[5] We should reject an unreflective adoption
of other countries' laws, yet we can learn much from studying our
legal neighbours.

22.2.2   Whatever its primary sources – statutes, cases, or even institutional
writings – the criminal law is constantly evolving since no two sets
of circumstances in which it is implicated are ever identical. The
fact that law, as text, whether a statute or a case report, is always
open to the interpretation of the person seeking to make use of it
means that absolute certainty is unattainable. It is inconceivable that
anyone should not know that intentionally to kill someone, deprive
them of their property, or have sexual intercourse with them in the

---

[2] There are of course examples of English law being imported into Scots law,
with unfortunate consequences, but the most egregious of these in the criminal
law sphere were as a result of a decision of the Scottish High Court of Justiciary,
rather than the Westminster Parliament (eg *Meek* v *HM Advocate* 1983 SLT 280,
in relation to the *mens rea* of rape at common law). For an account of other English
law importations, see C Gane, "Civilian and English influences on Scots criminal
law" in E Reid and D L Carey Miller (eds), *A Mixed Legal System in Transition:
T B Smith and the Progress of Scots Law* (2005), pp 218–238.
[3] See the Scottish Independence Referendum Act 2013, which provides for "the
holding of a referendum on a question about the independence of Scotland" from
the rest of the UK.
[4] A Rodger, "Thinking about Scots law" (1996) 1 *Edin LR* 3 at 9.
[5] For example, in *Cochrane* v *HM Advocate* 2001 SCCR 655, Lord Rodger
referred to cases on coercion from England (at 663–665), Ireland (at 663), the
United States (at 662), South Africa (at 664–665), and Canada (at 665). Similarly,
in *Webster* v *Dominick* 2005 1 JC 65, Lord Gill referred to judgments in the area of
public indecency from South Africa (at para 51), England (at para 52), Canada and
Australia (both at para 58). More recent cases include *Gage* v *HM Advocate* [2011]
HCJAC 40 (Australian case cited at para 29); *Strachan* v *HM Advocate* 2011 SCL
796 (at 798–799, para 5); *Jenkins* v *HM Advocate* 2011 SCL 927 (at 937–938, paras
18–20; 941, para 27; 948–949, paras 44 and 45); *Gage* v *HM Advocate* [2012]
HCJAC 14 (at para 31) (reference made to Canadian cases); *Jones* v *HM Advocate*
[2009] HCJAC 86 (particularly at paras 11, 13, 16 and 32); and *Gemmell* v *HM
Advocate* [2011] HCJAC 129 (at para 59) (both Australian and Canadian cases).

knowledge that they do not consent, each constitutes a contravention of the criminal law. Whether there is the same awareness that it is an offence to open a large shop for retail trade on Christmas Day[6] or to keep an animal for slaughter for its fur[7] is less obvious. It does, however, seem likely that large retailers and fur farmers (legitimate and illegitimate) will be aware of these provisions, and that may well be sufficient. It seems that the vast majority of recently created offences apply only to those acting in some form of special capacity;[8] as well as traders and fur farmers, these include farmers of fish and shellfish,[9] directors of diagnostic laboratories,[10] and operators of sunbed premises.[11] There are, however, many offences which apply to the population more generally, and there may well be widespread ignorance about some of these. For instance, a quick survey of about 70 first-year law students revealed that, prior to embarking on their studies, about a third of them were unaware that it was a crime (reset) to buy goods which one suspects, but does not *know*, to have been stolen. This is a startling example of ignorance of the criminal law on the part of the lay-public. At least reset is a crime which is clearly defined and can readily be explained. The same cannot be said about some other crimes.

22.2.3   The rule of law[12] mandates that criminal law should be certain (as far as it can be), knowable, and indeed known.[13] The critique offered by this book suggests that Scots criminal law rests on solid foundations, but could nonetheless be improved. All legal systems need to be kept under constant review, for the systematic clarification of areas of uncertainty and ambiguity, and to ensure that their provisions remain relevant for the needs of modern society. Current mechanisms for achieving this include the Scottish Law Commission, the legal profession, the courts, and the Scottish Parliament.

22.3   THE SCOTTISH LAW COMMISSION

22.3.1   The Commission has done a superb job, but it would be naïve to believe that it can keep under review the whole of the substantive

---

[6] Christmas Day and New Year's Day Trading (Scotland) Act 2007, ss 1 and 4.
[7] Fur Farming (Prohibition) (Scotland) Act 2002, s 1(1).
[8] See J Chalmers and F Leverick, "Tracking the creation of criminal offences" [2013] *Crim LR* 543 at 557–558.
[9] Aquaculture and Fisheries (Scotland) Act 2007, ss 1 and 2.
[10] Public Health etc (Scotland) Act 2008, s 17(1).
[11] *Ibid*, ss 95(1) and 98(1).
[12] See section 4.2 above.
[13] Glanville Williams identified certainty as an aspect of the rule of law, along with accessibility, non-retroactivity and strict construction: G Williams, *Criminal Law: The General Part* (2nd edn, 1961), pp 578–591.

criminal law. It has limited resources and heavy demands on its time; its remit includes all of Scots law, not merely criminal law.[14] Even when the Commission does recommend law reform, the legislature does not always implement this. As previously noted,[15] the Scottish *Draft Criminal Code* was an unofficial exercise, its drafters being four law professors (including one of the authors of this book). The Commission generously published the *Code* in 2003, and invited comment. Several of those who responded urged the Commission to explore whether codification of Scots criminal law was desirable, in principle.[16] More than a decade later, it still has not acted on these suggestions. This may be because of lack of time and resources, rather than interest; a handful of commissioners is expected to keep under review the whole of Scots law, and there is generally only one commissioner who has an active interest in criminal law. Adoption of the *Code* would require acceptance of both the value and the efficacy of the principle of codifying the law, as well as discussion of the specific changes to the existing criminal law which it proposes. This would indeed be a considerable enterprise – but one which a mature legal system ought to be capable of undertaking.

22.4   THE LEGAL PROFESSION

22.4.1   Our suggestion that the criminal law would benefit from reform may come close to heresy for many lawyers. As Farmer has astutely observed:

> "Many Scots lawyers are uncomfortable with questions of change or reform. The attitude we have uncovered is the belief that to meddle with the law is to invite disaster for, after all, there have been no complaints about the way that it works."[17]

---

[14] This is not to say that the SLC has no interest in substantive criminal law. It has published consultation papers on "Mobbing and Rioting" and "Attempted Homicide" (1984), as well as reports on "Incest" (1981), "The Mental Element in Crime" (1983) and "Art and Part Guilt of Statutory Offences" (1985). More recently it has considered "Age of Criminal Responsibility" (2002), "Insanity and Diminished Responsibility" (2004), "Rape and other Sexual Offences" (2007) and the "Criminal Liability of Partnerships" (2011). Its eighth programme of law reform includes an examination of the law of homicide, but at the time of writing the Commission's website states: "Due to other priorities, work on this project is not progressing at present": http://www.scotlawcom.gov.uk/law-reform-projects/homicide/.

[15] See section 5.10.4 above.

[16] This was recommended by the Sheriffs' Association, the sheriffs principal, and SACRO. For a summary of responses received by the Scottish Law Commission to the *Draft Code*, see E Clive, "Codification of Scottish criminal law" (2008) SCL 747.

[17] Farmer (1997), p 185.

While they do contribute to law reform proposals, the Law Society of Scotland and the Faculty of Advocates have so far seemed unwilling to champion the cause of major criminal law reform.[18]

22.5 THE COURTS

Prior to devolution, Scotland had a separate and distinct criminal law, yet shared a legislature with its more dominant neighbour – a legislature whose approach to Scots criminal law can most charitably be described as one of benign neglect. This meant that the courts had to develop the common law to fill the vacuum. Since devolution, the High Court of Justiciary, sitting as a court of appeal, has been increasingly active in the criminal law field, and there have been numerous five-judge Bench decisions.[19] As we have seen, however, some of these have raised as many questions as they have answered. Moreover, the High Court's role in shaping the law is a relatively passive one, in as much as it is dependent on an appropriate case coming before it in order to reform the law, and there are limits to what it can achieve without breaching the rule of law. Even when it calls for legislation to reform the law (as it did in relation to provocation, generally; the appropriateness, or otherwise, of recognising sexual infidelity as a form of provocation;[20] and the *mens rea* of murder[21]), there is often a lengthy delay between a problem being recognised by the Court, and the Scottish Parliament acting on its recommendation.

22.5.1

---

[18] An example of the conservatism of the legal profession was the evidence of the Faculty of Advocates to the Justice Committee in its consideration of the Sexual Offences (Scotland) Bill. The Faculty representative stated: "although I accept that, if something is broken, it should be fixed, my experience suggests that the law of rape is not broken in such a fundamental way that it requires a change in the way that is proposed" (*Justice Committee Official Report*, 18 November 2008, col 1376). This is a somewhat surprising stance to take, given the widespread criticism of the then current law.

[19] These include *Byrne* v *HM Advocate* 2000 JC 155 (on the *mens rea* of wilful fire-raising); *Galbraith* v *HM Advocate (No 2)* 2002 JC 1 (diminished responsibility); *McKinnon* v *HM Advocate* 2003 JC 29 (art and part liability); *MacAngus and Kane* v *HM Advocate* 2009 SLT 137 (on the need for an indictment to libel recklessness in charges of culpable homicide by supplying a controlled drug); *Lilburn* v *HM Advocate* 2012 JC 150 (on the onus of proof of diminished responsibility); and *Petto* v *HM Advocate* 2012 JC 105 (on the *mens rea* of murder). In *HM Advocate* v *Purcell* 2008 JC 131 (on the meaning of "wicked recklessness") a three-judge Bench was convened at the trial stage. The *Lord Advocate's Reference (No 1 of 2001)* 2002 SLT 466 (on the definition of rape) was a seven-judge decision.

[20] See *Drury* v *HM Advocate* 2001 SLT 1013 at 1032 per Lord Nimmo Smith.

[21] See *Petto* v *HM Advocate* 2012 JC 105 at 112, para [22] per LJ-C Gill, cited in section 22.5.2 below.

22.5.2   There is also an issue of whether a court is the most appropriate forum in which to undertake criminal law reform, particularly in relation to sensitive areas. In the realm of sexual offences, for example, whether or not to criminalise consensual sexual intercourse between two 15-year-olds, and whether any such crime should apply to *both* parties, is a vexed question, with reasonable people taking different approaches.[22] Such finely balanced policy questions are better left to our elected representatives, who can spend many months assessing a range of views and can draw on a wealth of expert evidence which will influence their decision.[23] Some, at least, of the judiciary share this conviction; according to Lord Marnoch:

> "[I]t respectfully seems to me that the legislature – quite apart from having the only constitutional right to change the law – is, in fact, far and away the best 'judge' of when changing circumstances require laws to be altered."[24]

Similarly, Lord McCluskey argued:

> "Judges are entitled to express their opinion that the established law appears to be producing unacceptable results and that it appears to be in need of change; but, unless they can find the existing law to be wrong, as a result of a discernible mistake, they must leave the possible reform of the law to the legislature."[25]

Referring specifically to the reform of sexual offences, he cautioned:

> "If the time has come to review the law with a view to reforming it, let it be reviewed by the legislature, with such assistance (for example, from the Scottish Law Commission, and from the judiciary among others) as is thought appropriate; and let it be reformed on the basis of the kind of study that we cannot undertake. But let us not exceed our constitutional role by reforming the law simply because we think that it is out of date."[26]

In relation to the reform of the *mens rea* of murder, Lord Gill has stated that while a comprehensive re-examination of this was "long overdue", it was "not the sort of exercise that should be done by *ad hoc* decisions of this court in fact-specific appeals. It is pre-eminently an exercise to be carried out by the normal processes of law reform".[27]

---

[22] See section 11.12.2 above.

[23] For another perspective, see T H Jones and M G A Christie, *Criminal Law* (5th edn, 2012) at para 14.07.

[24] *Lord Advocate's Reference (No 1 of 2001)* 2002 SLT 466 at 479.

[25] *Ibid* at 484.

[26] *Ibid* at 490.

[27] *Petto v HM Advocate* 2012 JC 105 at 112, para [22].

22.6   THE LEGISLATURE

As the previous sections have suggested, there is a strong argument **22.6.1**
that in a mature legal system crimes and defences ought to be
defined by the legislature, rather than by the judiciary. This should
result in clarity, as required by the rule of law, and is also more in
keeping with democracy. The Scottish Parliament has been active in
enacting criminal legislation, but this has been mainly in the field
of procedure, rather than substantive law. Its most comprehensive
foray into the substantive law to date is the enactment of the Sexual
Offences (Scotland) Act 2009. It has also criminalised, *inter alia*, the
hunting of wild mammals; smoking in public places; and proprietors
who prevent women from breastfeeding their babies;[28] – issues which
are very much on the margins of the criminal law.

Transforming the common law into statutory form could be **22.6.2**
achieved by wholesale codification as proposed in section 22.3.1
above. The arguments have been well rehearsed;[29] those who favour
codification stress that citizens must be able to find out what it is that
the criminal law provides if they are to conform to its requirements.
The principle that ignorance of the law is no defence[30] is predicated
on the belief that individuals ought readily to be able to make
themselves aware of the law's core provisions. Even the most diligent
of citizens would find it impossible to familiarise themselves with
all the law's prohibitions. That is, perhaps, inevitable in a modern
society. But it is neither inevitable nor acceptable for core offences to
be inaccessible, such that someone looking for a primary source (as
opposed to a textbook) definition of theft or robbery has to wrestle
with Hume's *Commentaries*, then trawl through several reported
cases – and even then will be left in some doubt as to their precise
application.[31] Codification is unlikely to appeal to the Scottish
Parliament. As Paul Robinson has explained, in relation to failed
attempts to update the American Model Penal Code:

"the characteristics of an effective criminal code – meaningful organization,
internal consistency, rationality in formulation, and comprehensiveness

---

[28] The statute is expressed in wider terms than this, but this is the mischief at which
the provision is aimed. See section 5.16.1 at n 184 above.
[29] In the Scottish context, see: L Farmer, "Enigma: decoding the draft Criminal
Code" (2002) 7 *SLPQ* 68; T H Jones, "Towards a good and complete Criminal
Code for Scotland" (2005) 68 *MLR* 448, both of which are hostile to the idea. For
a response to the former, see E Clive and P R Ferguson, "Unravelling the enigma: a
reply to Professor Farmer" (2002) 7 *SLPQ* 81. See also P R Ferguson, "Codifying
criminal law (1): a critique of Scots common law" [2004] *Crim LR* 49.
[30] See from section 19.6.1 above.
[31] See sections 12.7.3 and 12.22.1 for discussion of the lack of clarity in the definitions
of theft and robbery, respectively. Glanville Williams identified accessibility as an
aspect of the rule of law: see n 13 in this chapter and section 5.10.3 above.

in coverage – apparently are not of sufficient political payoff to interest ...
legislators. These matters are of great practical importance to the day to day
operation of the system, however, and have a significant effect on who get
convicted of what and what gets appealed and reversed. Unfortunately, the
value of such reforms cannot be reduced to a sound bite that will generate
votes at the next election".[32]

22.6.3 As an alternative to wholesale codification, a legislature could effect
a gradual transformation of the common law by enacting selected
parts of it, as the Westminster Parliament has done with road
traffic offences[33] and misuse of drugs,[34] and the Scottish Parliament
achieved with the Sexual Offences (Scotland) Act 2009. The Act
comes close to codifying this area of the law, and the success of the
legislation in practice may well determine the extent to which MSPs
remain willing to reform distinct portions of the criminal common
law, in future. Each of these law reform bodies (Law Commission,
courts, legal profession and Parliament) is largely reactive – even
the legislature is no exception to this. Indeed, the sexual offences
legislation had its origins in the decision of a trial judge to uphold
a submission of "no case to answer" in a rape case, on the basis
that the Crown had failed to show that the accused had overcome
the complainer's will by force.[35] The judge's decision was correct,
given the then current definition of rape, but the realisation that this
was in fact the law caused such an outcry that Parliament asked the
Scottish Law Commission to report on reforming rape and other
sexual offences.

22.7   A CRIMINAL LAW REVIEW BOARD

22.7.1 Scotland needs a more systematic approach to keeping its criminal
law under review. If he is aware of nothing else about the law, the
"Naked Rambler" must be clear by now that it treats his conduct as
criminal,[36] but he may be having difficulty understanding the basis
of its proscription. Is the criminal law treating him fairly? Breach of
the peace, the crime with which he has consistently been charged,
should not have been used as a "catch-all" for behaviour which
was regarded as inappropriate. More importantly, there should be

---

[32] P H Robinson, "Reforming the Federal Criminal Code: a top ten list" (1997)
1 *Buffalo Crim L Rev* 225 at 225–226.
[33] These are largely contained in the Road Traffic Act 1988, and the Road Traffic
Regulation Act 1984.
[34] The Misuse of Drugs Act 1971 has been described as a statute "of a largely
codifying character" (K S Bovey, *Misuse of Drugs: A Handbook for Lawyers*
(1986) at p 1).
[35] The Crown's appeal against this decision is reported as *Lord Advocate's
Reference (No 1 of 2001)* 2002 SLT 466.
[36] See section 1.1.2 above.

scope for issues of this nature to be properly analysed and then criminalised only after informed debate – or, indeed, left unregulated by the criminal law. For this reason, the first edition of this book suggested that the Scottish Parliament establish a standing Criminal Law Review Board, with the remit of consulting on a wide range of issues, and producing proposals for reform. We now reiterate this proposal. Such a Board should comprise specialist criminal defence lawyers, procurators fiscal, academics and representatives from the judiciary and the police, seconded on a full-time basis. There should also be lay involvement.

Its remit would be to ensure that the criminal law:

(1) employs appropriate terminology;
(2) minimises overlapping offences;
(3) is clearly worded, such that, in general, the lay-person would be able to understand its provisions;
(4) accords with principles of fairness and justice, such that it is generally only those who have freely chosen to breach its requirements who are convicted and punished;
(5) is comprehensive, in the sense of having no obvious *lacunae*; and
(6) corresponds to the principle of fair labelling, so that it is clear what it is that someone convicted of a crime has done, and the nature of the harm or wrong risked or caused thereby.[37]

As this book has shown, the current law does not always correspond to these ideals. Some of these issues are summarised below. Mindful of Lord Rodger's comment in *Galbraith* v *HM Advocate* that it is easier to tear down an existing edifice than suggest what should go in its place,[38] we also make some tentative suggestions for reform. Many of our proposals are controversial; others may take a different view of how best to reform particular aspects of the law, or indeed of which aspects require reform. As we said at the outset of the book, our aim here is to further the dialogue on law reform, and we do not pretend to have the definitive answers. Nevertheless, we believe that whether or not others agree with our suggestions, the law should strive for greater clarity.

22.8 TERMINOLOGY

Terminology may be less important than clarity or consistency, yet **22.8.1** law surely requires the precise use of language. In the first edition of

---

[37] See from section 4.6 above.
[38] 2002 JC 1 at 10, para [21]. See section 20.10.3 above.

this book, we criticised the continued use of outmoded and rather offensive terms, such as "insanity" and "insanity in bar of trial".[39] As we have seen in Chapter 20, these have now been replaced by "mental disorder" and "unfitness for trial", nomenclature which is more appropriate to the 21st century and accords with modern understandings of mental illness.[40] Clarity would also be promoted if "theft by housebreaking" were to be replaced by "theft by breaking into a building". In relation to the *mens rea* of murder, in *Petto v HM Advocate*[41] Lord Justice-Clerk Gill noted:

> "In Scotland we have a definitional structure in which the mental element ... is defined with the use of terms such as wicked, evil, felonious, depraved and so on, which may impede rather than conduce to analytical accuracy."[42]

This terminology requires modernising.

22.9   OVERLAPPING OFFENCES, DUPLICATION AND CONSISTENCY

22.9.1   It should be possible to de-clutter the criminal calendar, at least to some extent, so that there are fewer overlapping offences, duplication is avoided, and consistency of terms is employed where possible. In the first edition of this book, we suggested that there seemed little rationale for providing that a "reasonable excuse" could be a defence for having an offensive weapon in a public place, but that an accused had to establish a "good reason" for having an article with a blade or sharp point.[43] As our earlier discussion of the law has shown, this suggestion has now been acted upon.[44] However, the sections which prohibit having such items in schools and prisons could usefully be amalgamated with those relating to possession in public places. Other examples of areas which would benefit from rationalisation include:

- "Culpable and reckless injury", "causing real injury", "culpable and reckless conduct", and "reckless endangerment".[45] These could be replaced by two offences, namely

---

[39] See also the criticism made by the Thomson Committee: *Criminal Procedure in Scotland (Second Report)* (Cmnd 6218, 1975), paras 52.13 and 53.10.

[40] See the Criminal Procedure (Scotland) Act 1995, ss 51A and 53F, as inserted by the Criminal Justice and Licensing (Scotland) Act 2010, ss 168 and 170, discussed at sections 20.7 and 20.4 respectively above.

[41] 2012 JC 105.

[42] *Ibid* at 111, para [21].

[43] See P R Ferguson and C McDiarmid, *Scots Criminal Law: A Critical Analysis* (1st edn, 2009), section 22.9.1; and P R Ferguson, "Criminal law and criminal justice: an exercise in ad hocery" in E E Sutherland *et al* (eds), *Law Making and the Scottish Parliament: The Early Years* (2011) at p 208.

[44] See from section 8.11.8 above.

[45] See from section 10.12 above.

"recklessly causing injury", and "causing an unlawful risk of injury".[46] This would also make clearer the parameters of these offences.

- *Statutory aggravations based on characteristics of the victim.*[47] Rather than have three separate statutory provisions creating aggravated offences where the accused's behaviour was motivated by prejudice based on a victim's race,[48] religion,[49] sexual orientation, transgender identity or disability,[50] enactment of a single provision would help to de-clutter the statute books.[51]

- *Statutory frauds.* As we have seen,[52] there has been an increase in the enactment of specific offences involving fraud and/or impersonation. Thus there are separate offences of falsely pretending to be a fire services enforcement officer,[53] a wildlife inspector,[54] a police constable,[55] a social service worker,[56] or social worker.[57] Other statutes provide offences of making false statements in particular documents.[58] Some of these provisions are more extensive than common law fraud, since they include a *mens rea* of recklessness.[59] Whether recklessness ought to be a sufficient *mens rea* is a moot point but, on the assumption that it should, a better means of achieving this would be to create a general, statutory offence of fraud, with intention or recklessness as alternative forms of *mens rea*. This would avoid the need for so many separate offences.

---

[46] See section 10.13.1 above.

[47] See section 7.9.1 above.

[48] Crime and Disorder Act 1998, s 96(2). See also the Criminal Law (Consolidation) (Scotland) Act 1995, s 50A ("racially aggravated harassment").

[49] Criminal Justice (Scotland) Act 2003, s 74(2).

[50] Offences (Aggravation by Prejudice) (Scotland) Act 2009, s 1 (disability); and s 2 (sexual orientation or transgender identity).

[51] See section 7.10.4 above. For an example of how this might be done, see the *Draft Criminal Code*, s 7(1) and (2).

[52] See section 12.20.2 above.

[53] Fire (Scotland) Act 2005, s 72(4)(b).

[54] Wildlife and Countryside Act 1981, s 19ZC(8), as inserted by the Nature Conservation (Scotland) Act 2004, Sch 6, para 17.

[55] Police and Fire Reform (Scotland) Act 2012, s 92(1)(a) and (b).

[56] Regulation of Care (Scotland) Act 2001, s 52(1)(b).

[57] *Ibid*, s 52(1)(a).

[58] For example, Mental Health (Care and Treatment) (Scotland) Act 2003, s 318(1); Building (Scotland) Act 2003, ss 11(4) and 16(1).

[59] Building (Scotland) Act 2003, s 16(1)(b). See also ss 19(4)(b), 20(1)(b), 34(2) and 37(4)(c) of that Act; Police and Fire Reform (Scotland) Act 2012, s 30(1).

- *Vandalism/malicious mischief.*[60] The courts have held that these are different crimes, yet in practice they are prosecuted for a very similar range of conduct. Surely only one offence of "criminal damage to property" is needed?[61]

22.10 IMPROVING CLARITY

22.10.1 Some of the criticisms made in the first edition of this book have since been rectified. In relation to "public indecency", for example, we argued that greater clarity was needed as to its *mens rea*, and this has now been achieved by the courts.[62] However, other aspects of the law which remain open to criticism on this basis include:

- *Blasphemy.*[63] It may be widely believed that this is no longer a crime, but the position is not entirely free from doubt. While Art 9 of the ECHR explicitly provides for "freedom of thought, conscience and religion", including the right to "manifest ... religion or belief, in worship, teaching, practice and observance", consideration must be given to the right to freedom of expression which is enshrined in Art 10. Allowing A to blaspheme against B's religion does not prevent B from exercising freedom of religion. The crime of blasphemy has been abolished in England by statute,[64] and we suggest that Scots law do likewise.

- *Breach of the peace.*[65] Despite the many cases of breach of the peace which the appeal court has considered in recent years, and the further narrowing of its definition in *Harris* v *HM Advocate*,[66] the *mens rea* of this commonly prosecuted crime has still not been clearly stated. We recommend that breach of the peace should be re-defined by statute such that

---

[60] See sections 13.3 and 13.2 above, respectively.
[61] See section 13.4.1 above and the *Draft Criminal Code*, s 81. The *Code* also contains a new offence of "causing an unlawful risk of damage to property": *ibid*, s 82.
[62] See *DF* v *Griffiths* 2011 JC 158, discussed at section 11.20.2 above. We also recommended that the list of offences in relation to which convicted persons can be placed on the Sex Offenders Register should be amended to include this crime. The relevant schedule has now been amended in this way: see the Sexual Offences Act 2003, Sch 3, para 41A, inserted by the Sexual Offences (Scotland) Act 2009, Sch 5, para 5(b). This applies where the complainer was under 18, and the court determines that there was a significant sexual aspect to the offence.
[63] See from section 16.8 above.
[64] See from section 16.9.1 above.
[65] See from section 15.2 above.
[66] 2010 JC 245, discussed in section 15.2.8 above.

the accused must have intentionally or recklessly caused a disturbance.[67]

- *Child abduction.*[68] Is it sufficient for the prosecution to libel that the child was induced or enticed to go away with the accused? Or is it an essential element of abduction that the accused acted against the child's will? This question was first raised more than 150 years ago. It remains unanswered. We have described in section 10.18.1 the provision suggested in the *Draft Criminal Code,* which defines this crime as taking, enticing or detaining a child. An offence of this nature ought to be implemented.

- *Child abuse.*[69] The responsibilities of those who care for children are in need of clarification, and the current legislation requires to be tightened up.

- *Murder.*[70] The reformulation of its *mens rea* in *Drury*[71] to require "wicked intent" led to increased uncertainty as to the application of defences in homicide cases. Mention has already been made of the *dicta* of Lord Gill in *Petto* v *HM Advocate.*[72] He stated:

  "In recent years, the authors of the draft Criminal Code for Scotland have greatly assisted our thinking on the matter; but we remain burdened by legal principles that were shaped largely in the days of the death penalty, that are inconsistent and confused and are not yet wholly free of doctrines of constructive malice."[73]

  We propose that the *mens rea* of murder be specified using neither "wicked intent" nor "wicked recklessness". Instead, "intent to kill" and "callous recklessness" or "with extreme disregard for human life" could be employed.[74]

- *Omissions to act.*[75] The decision in *McCue* v *Currie*[76] left it unclear whether a person who has created a dangerous

---

[67] See section 15.3.1 above and the *Draft Criminal Code*, s 92. Note that the *Code* also specifies that the crime is committed only if a disturbance has actually been caused. For further criticism of breach of the peace, see section 22.13.2 below and P R Ferguson, *Breach of the Peace* (2013).

[68] See critique at section 10.18 above.

[69] See from section 10.9 above.

[70] See from section 9.10 above.

[71] 2001 SLT 1013.

[72] 2012 JC 105. See section 22.8.1 above. The case is described more fully in section 9.12.11 above.

[73] *Ibid* at 111–112, para [21].

[74] See the *Draft Criminal Code*, s 37(1).

[75] See from section 6.5 above.

[76] 2004 JC 73.

situation is liable for failing to rectify, or at least limit, any harm thereby caused. Consideration should be given to the appeal court's suggestion that there may be a case for enacting a new crime which would apply to those who, having exposed another person, or the property of another person, to a risk of injury or damage, omit to take reasonable steps to avert that risk.[77]

- *Robbery.*[78] It is not clear whether threats other than those of immediate personal violence will suffice for this crime. We are inclined to favour restricting robbery to threats of immediate personal violence, leaving the crime of extortion to be employed for other forms of threat. Enactment of a statutory definition of robbery would put this beyond doubt. As with our suggestions for theft and housebreaking (below), others will no doubt hold a different view. The law requires to be clarified, one way or another.

- *Theft.*[79] As previously noted, the *mens rea* of theft has been expanded to include an intention to appropriate property on a permanent, or temporary, or indefinite basis, so long as in the "temporary" type of case the appropriation was "clandestine" and/or "nefarious" and/or "in exceptional circumstances".[80] This has left the law far from clear. We propose that theft be defined by statute. Consideration should be given to recognising "recklessness as to whether the owner is deprived" as an alternative form of *mens rea*.[81]

- *Theft by housebreaking.*[82] The parameters of its *actus reus* are unclear: does the thief who enters premises via an unlocked window commit simple theft, or the aggravated crime of theft by housebreaking? We favour the latter, on the basis that it reflects the serious nature of a stealing which violates the sanctity of premises, even if they were not secured against intruders.

22.11 FAIRNESS AND JUSTICE

22.11.1 As well as areas of the criminal law which lack clarity, there are also aspects which, though clear, are arguably not in keeping with the

---

[77] See the rules on causation provided by the *Draft Criminal Code*, s 14(c), and the discussion of this issue at section 6.8.4 above.
[78] See section 12.21 above.
[79] See from section 12.2 above.
[80] See sections 12.5.1–12.5.3 above.
[81] See the *Draft Criminal Code*, s 77(2) and (3)(d), and section 12.7.4 above.
[82] See from section 12.8, and the critique from section 12.11 above.

interests of justice. In the first edition of this book, we argued that the crime of rape should be redefined to include non-consensual anal and oral penetration by the penis, and that unreasonable errors as to a complainer's consent ought not to exculpate.[83] These problems have been rectified by the Sexual Offences (Scotland) Act 2009.[84] We also criticised the wording of certain homosexual offences involving adult males;[85] the legislation was expressed in a negative fashion: "a homosexual act in private shall *not be an offence* provided that the parties consent thereto and have attained the age of sixteen years".[86] This section has now been repealed;[87] homosexual activities which are non-consensual, not in private, or where one of the parties is under 16 remain criminal – as do similar heterosexual activities committed in such circumstances – but the repeal of this section reflects a gender-neutral approach towards consensual sexual activities, and is to be commended. We also suggested[88] that the defences of duress (coercion and necessity) were too narrowly defined, and ought to be a defence to all charges, including murder, where the taking of life was done in order to save life. As we have seen, there has now been a case in which a jury was permitted to treat necessity as a complete defence to a charge of murder.[89] It is regrettable that the Crown did not appeal this case in order to clarify the law. Other aspects which continue to require reform include:

- *Art and part liability.*[90] Following *McKinnon* v *HM Advocate*,[91] the formulation of art and part liability in homicide cases involving pre-concert means that there is little scope for some co-accused to be convicted of murder, and others of culpable homicide. The approach taken by the appeal court in *Brown* v *HM Advocate*,[92] in which a separate assessment was made as to the *mens rea* of each accused, has much to commend it. This seems a fairer way of allocating blame, and diminishes neither

[83] See *Jamieson* v *HM Advocate* 1994 JC 88.
[84] See s 1(1)(b) which defines the *mens rea* of rape such that it is committed by an accused who acts "without any reasonable belief" that the other party is consenting. This is discussed in section 11.2.4 above.
[85] Ferguson and McDiarmid (2009), section 11.13.1.
[86] Criminal Law (Consolidation) (Scotland) Act 1995, s 13(1) (emphasis added). A "homosexual act" was defined as "sodomy or an act of gross indecency or shameless indecency by one male person with another male person": s 13(4).
[87] Sexual Offences (Scotland) Act 2009, Sch 6, para 1.
[88] Ferguson and McDiarmid (2009), section 22.11. See also the *Draft Criminal Code*, s 29.
[89] See section 21.4.6 above.
[90] See from section 7.5 above.
[91] 2003 JC 29.
[92] 1993 SCCR 382.

public protection nor the denunciatory role of the criminal law, since a conviction for murder can still be returned in respect of the principal perpetrator. The case of *Hopkinson v HM Advocate*[93] focused greater scrutiny on the individual co-accused's understanding of the common plan, but did not change the law. We adhere to our original recommendation that this should be done.

- *Involuntary intoxication/automatism.*[94] The criminal law's approach to diabetics is far from satisfactory. The defence of mental disorder is the sole mechanism by which an accused can have a complete defence to an act committed during a hypoglycaemic episode. Once a person has behaved violently during such an episode, future incidents may have the requisite degree of blameworthiness to justify a conviction. But the diabetic who follows her treatment regime and who has never before experienced a hypoglycaemic state – and had no reason to anticipate such a state – ought not to be denied a defence. Furthermore, automatism ought to be regarded as involving a lack of a voluntary act on the part of the accused – a matter going to *actus reus*, rather than *mens rea*. Whether the defence is treated as affecting the "forbidden situation" or the "mental element" is important: if it negates the latter only, as the Scottish courts have ruled, then an accused person can be convicted of a strict liability offence even where this occurs during a semi-conscious state.[95] This seems contrary to justice.

- *Dissociation.*[96] Most commentators take the view that where one of the parties to a criminal enterprise takes active steps to prevent the successful completion of the crime, or notifies the police, this ought to be recognised as a defence in Scots law. Legislation should clearly specify that this is the case.

- *Error of law.*[97] The principle that ignorance of the law is no defence can sometimes operate harshly; an accused who has *bona fide* relied on official information deserves to be acquitted. Scots law should recognise a defence of error of law where the accused had taken reasonable steps to ascertain the correct legal position.[98]

---

[93] 2009 SLT 292.
[94] See sections 20.15 and 20.16 above.
[95] See section 20.20.2 above.
[96] See section 7.8.4 above.
[97] See from section 19.6 above.
[98] See section 19.7.1 above and the *Draft Criminal Code*, s 28(2).

- *Impossibility.*[99] The *Draft Criminal Code* provides such a defence where the accused has failed to do something which was, in the circumstances, and "without fault on that person's part", impossible to do.[100] Recognition of this defence is required by principles of fairness.

- *Interpretation of statutory defences.*[101] As previously noted, we commend the rationalisation of the defences available for those who are found in a public place with either offensive weapons or articles with a blade or sharp point. However, it is important that the potential unfairness of the strict liability which applies to these offences should be mitigated in appropriate cases by employing a broad interpretation of what it means to have a "reasonable excuse" for having such an item. Thus, as we argued earlier, it ought not to be the purpose of the criminal law to stigmatise and punish those who are merely careless or forgetful.[102] At least these offence provisions do include defences, unlike many other strict liability offences. We further recommend that whenever the legislature creates a strict liability offence, it ought also to consider whether to provide a defence for the accused who is able to show that she did not act recklessly, or even negligently.[103]

- *Omissions.*[104] The criminal law fails to recognise a general duty to rescue. We have argued that it ought to do so. Again, others will take a different view. This is not an issue which has been considered by any law reform body in Scotland, but it surely ought to be.

- *Physical punishment of children.*[105] The United Nations Committee on the Rights of the Child has recommended that a state which limits, but does not remove, the defence of reasonable chastisement is in breach of the UN Convention on the Rights of the Child.[106] Scots law ought therefore to proscribe violence against children, irrespective of the relationship between the perpetrator and the child, and the motivation behind the violence.

---

[99] See from section 21.14.1 above.
[100] *Draft Criminal Code*, s 26.
[101] See section 22.9.1 above.
[102] See section 8.13.2 above.
[103] See section 17.7.3 above. It would also be helpful if strict liability offences were labelled clearly as such on the face of the legislation. See n 50 in section 17.3.11 above for a rare example of this being done.
[104] See from section 6.5 above.
[105] See section 10.11.1 above.
[106] See from section 10.11.1 above.

- *Possession offences.*[107] As we discussed in Chapter 8, there is an increasing tendency for legislatures to proscribe the possession of certain items, even where these items are innocuous in themselves. We suggested that the harms which the prohibition of possession of a police uniform, for example, are intended to prevent are remote, and criminalise conduct far in advance of behaviour(s) which could actually cause harm. It is suggested that these statutory offences are not justifiable and ought to be repealed.

- *Provocation.*[108] There are at least two possible approaches to reform. There is an argument that the law should be broadened to recognise that other forms of behaviour are capable of forming the basis of a provocation plea. The *Draft Criminal Code* widens the range of behaviours which may amount to provocation to include "acts or words or both".[109] This can emanate from the ultimate victim, or from a third party. The *Code's* test is that "an ordinary person, thus provoked, would have been likely to react in the same way", but the ordinary person is assumed to have any personal characteristics of the accused that affect the provocative quality of the acts or words. Alternatively, the notion that sexual infidelity can be sufficient provocation on its own to palliate murder should be rejected, though it should remain relevant where it is merely one strand of a broader provocative situation.

- *Torture.*[110] This offence ought not to be limited to those who are acting in an official capacity.[111]

- *Voluntary intoxication.*[112] The decision in *Brennan*'s case[113] that self-induced acute intoxication is tantamount to "wicked recklessness" or, indeed, can be equated with the *mens rea* required for any crime, is difficult to justify. We recommend that consideration ought to be given to the creation of a statutory offence of causing harm to persons or property while intoxicated.[114]

---

[107] See sections 8.15 and 8.21.1 above.
[108] See from section 21.10 above.
[109] *Draft Criminal Code*, s 38(4).
[110] See from section 10.20 above.
[111] See the *Draft Criminal Code*, s 22(4)(b), and section 10.21.2 above.
[112] See from section 20.13 above.
[113] 1977 JC 38.
[114] See section 20.14.5 above.

22.12   COMPREHENSIVE

As noted above, where it is recognised that there are unacceptable   **22.12.1**
behaviours which are not currently criminalised, but which ought to
be prohibited, the legislature should enact new offences to fill these
gaps.

- *Cruelty to animals.*[115] There is a plethora of statutory offences,
designed to protect animals from unnecessary suffering.
Many of these highly technical provisions could be repealed if
a general offence of animal cruelty were to be enacted.[116]

- *Housebreaking with intent to commit crimes other than
theft.*[117] The decision in *HM Advocate* v *Forbes*[118] was correct,
but it is nonetheless regrettable that there is no such crime
as "housebreaking with intent to rape" in Scots law. The
English law crime of burglary is defined to include entering
a building with intent to commit a wider range of crimes,
including serious assault, damage to the building or anything
in the building. We propose that a similar crime be enacted
for Scots law.[119]

- *Incest.*[120] It is generally accepted that the harm being struck at
by the crime of incest – unacceptable sexual contact between
people who are closely related – involves an abuse of trust and a
distortion of appropriate family relationships, rather than being
based on eugenic arguments designed to prevent congenital
disabilities in the offspring of incestuous relationships. This
being so, consideration should be given to broadening the
offence to include "sexual activity" between related people,
not solely penile/vaginal penetration. Homosexual as well
as heterosexual relationships ought to be included; a man
having sexual contact with his son is surely as great a
harm as such contact with his daughter.[121] Accessibility
of the law would be improved if the provisions on incest
(currently in the Criminal Law (Consolidation) (Scotland)
Act 1995) were re-enacted in the Sexual Offences (Scotland)
Act 2009.[122]

---

[115] See from section 16.6 above.
[116] See the *Draft Criminal Code*, s 108(1).
[117] See section 12.11.2 above.
[118] 1994 JC 71.
[119] The *Draft Criminal Code*, s 78(1) creates the offence of breaking into a building,
and this is aggravated if committed with intent to commit another offence (s 7(2)(a)).
[120] See from section 11.17 above.
[121] See section 11.18.1 above and the *Draft Criminal Code*, s 67.
[122] *Ibid.*

- *Interference with a corpse.*[123] As we have seen, "violation of sepulchres" is very narrowly defined. Other forms of interference with human bodies, such as interference prior to internment, should be criminalised.[124]

- *Obtaining services.*[125] It is not theft for someone to obtain a service without the consent of the provider of that service. The *Draft Criminal Code* creates the offence of "criminal interference with property" to cover situations which do not amount to theft or malicious mischief/vandalism, but which nonetheless do involve loss, harm or serious inconvenience to the owner.[126] Enactment of such a provision would close this gap in the current law.

- *Voyeurism.*[127] As previously noted, this offence offers no protection to complainers who are engaging in a private act such as using a sunbed if they are wearing swim-wear, nor does it include someone covered only by a small towel. The legislation should be amended to include anyone who is dressed in a way which affords a reasonable expectation of privacy, in the circumstances.[128] Thus someone dressed in swim-wear would not expect privacy while in a swimming pool or poolside, but does have such an expectation while in a changing cubicle, and the legislation should be amended to reflect this. Furthermore, the term "breasts" should be defined by the relevant legislation so as to protect young boys and pre-pubescent girls from voyeurism.[129]

22.13   FAIR LABELLING[130]

22.13.1   The importance of having appropriately labelled offences has been emphasised throughout the book. This is not merely a matter of terminology. Rather, fair labelling is about drawing appropriate distinctions between different types of offences based on the degree of wrongdoing involved. As Andrew Ashworth and Jeremy Horder have put it, this requires offence definitions which "represent fairly the nature and magnitude of the law-

---

[123] See section 16.3.1 above.
[124] See the *Draft Criminal Code*, s 104.
[125] See section 12.11.4 above.
[126] *Draft Criminal Code*, s 83.
[127] See from section 11.9 above.
[128] See section 11.10.1 above.
[129] See D Selfe, "Case Comment: R v Bassett (Kevin): voyeurism – the meaning of 'privacy' and 'breasts'" (2009) 193 *Criminal Lawyer* 2.
[130] See from section 4.6 above.

breaking".[131] Scots criminal law fails to meet this ideal in a number of areas. We have suggested, for example, that it might be fairer to accused persons if vandalism were to be defined to encompass deliberate damage only, with those who recklessly damage property facing a different, and less serious charge;[132] the lay-person may well regard a "reckless vandal" as an oxymoron.

In the first edition of this book, we argued that breach of the peace was a prominent example of a crime which breaches principles of fair labelling.[133] Despite the narrowing of its definition in *Smith v Donnelly*[134] (and, more recently, in *Harris* v *HM Advocate*[135]) its ambit was unacceptably broad. Adherence to the fair labelling principle would suggest that there ought to be distinct offences to cover the range of behaviours which were subsumed into this one crime, and we recommend that distinct offences such as "making unlawful threats",[136] "violent and alarming behaviour"[137] and "intrusive and alarming behaviour"[138] be employed instead. The recent enactment of the offences of "behaving in a threatening or abusive manner",[139] "stalking",[140] making "threatening communications"[141] and "communicating religious hatred"[142] means that certain behaviours which would hitherto have been subsumed into breach of the peace are now more accurately, and fairly, labelled.

22.13.2

22.14   RETURNING TO PRINCIPLES OF CRIMINALISATION

As Michael Moore has suggested, a conscientious legislator should question "the principled limits of legislation; What ends are proper ends to seek via legislation?".[143] He acknowledges that the appropriate

22.14.1

---

[131] A Ashworth and J Horder, *Principles of Criminal Law* (7th edn, 2013), p 77. See also J Chalmers and F Leverick, "Fair labelling in criminal law" (2008) 71 *MLR* 217.

[132] See section 13.4.2 above.

[133] Ferguson and McDiarmid (2009), section 22.13.1.

[134] 2002 JC 65. See section 15.2.3 above.

[135] 2010 JC 245. This is discussed at section 15.2.8 above.

[136] *Draft Criminal Code*, s 48. These threats are either of death or injury (s 48(a)) or of substantial harm to property or patrimonial interests (s 48(b)).

[137] *Ibid*, s 49.

[138] *Ibid*, s 50. Breaches of ss 49 and 50 may be committed intentionally or recklessly.

[139] Criminal Justice and Licensing (Scotland) Act 2010, s 38. This is described in section 15.5.1 above.

[140] *Ibid*, s 39. See section 15.6.1 above.

[141] Offensive Behaviour at Football and Threatening Communications (Scotland) Act 2012, s 6(1) and (2). See section 15.9.1 above.

[142] *Ibid*, s 6(1) and (5). See section 15.9.1 above.

[143] M S Moore, "Sandelian antiliberalism" (1989) 77 *California L Rev* 539 at 540.

legislative role "is a question of political theory".[144] This leads us back to where we began, to principles of criminalisation.[145] It is apparent that Scots criminal law has moved from a highly moralistic system, in which some behaviours were criminalised mainly because of their perceived immorality, towards one in which the harm principle has become more prominent. That principle has, however, been interpreted broadly to include considerations of the "public interest", such that Scots criminal law fails to reflect liberal values, in many instances. This may be entirely appropriate – we argued in Part I that the "harm principle" alone was insufficient as a determining factor in deciding whether or not undesirable conduct should be criminalised, and we advocated a limited role for the "offence principle" and even occasionally for paternalistic legislation, where the infringement on liberty is small and the harm avoided great. Others will no doubt hold very different views. The key point, however, is that there has been little articulation by the courts or legislature of what it is that our criminal laws should be trying to achieve, far less of the limits of criminalisation.

22.14.2   Another principle which those contemplating law reform ought to consider is that the criminal sanction should be employed sparingly, due to the harm caused by punishment, and by the criminal process, itself.[146] The proliferation of offences, particularly those involving fraud/impersonation, and possession of items which are innocuous in themselves, suggests that legislatures have few qualms about increased criminalisation.[147] As John Scott has put it:

> "If the law has to be used as a preventative tool our courts should continue to be as demanding as possible because this is a dangerous path and the greatest of care is required. Otherwise we may end up punishing people for crimes which would never, in fact, have occurred."[148]

Legislatures ought also to confine strict liability to regulatory offences connected to public welfare, to which little censure applies. Whenever it creates a strict liability offence, a legislature should state this explicitly in the wording of the provision.[149] As a matter of fairness, it ought also to give careful consideration as to whether to provide a defence where an accused is able to show that she did not act

---

[144] Moore (1989) at 540.
[145] See Part I above.
[146] See from section 2.3.1 above.
[147] For our critique of these, see sections 22.9.1 and 22.11.1 above.
[148] J Scott, "*Siddique (Mohammed Atif) v HM Advocate*: what are you thinking?" (2010) SCL 315 at 317.
[149] A rare example of this is the Christmas Day and New Year's Day Trading (Scotland) Act 2007, s 6 of which states that the offence "is one of strict liability". See n 50 in section 17.3.11 above.

recklessly, or even negligently. This may be difficult for the accused to demonstrate, but would at least help prevent the most egregious injustices. Douglas Husak has suggested that the courts in the USA generally construe statutory offences in a manner which protects "blameless conduct".[150] We believe that the Scottish courts ought to do likewise. Where defences such as "due diligence", "reasonable excuse" or "good reason" are available, the courts should interpret them in a way which makes sure that only the blameworthy are convicted.[151]

Finally, those contemplating adding to the criminal calendar should bear in mind that the criminal law is but one of several mechanisms by which to influence behaviour. An example we used early in this book was that of the "Naked Rambler". We must ask ourselves whether it is appropriate to criminalise his conduct. It must be borne in mind that we can make emphatic our disapproval of conduct which we dislike without resorting to criminalising (and punishing) those who persist in that conduct. We could make clear that the "Naked Rambler" is free to walk from coast to coast in the nude – that is his right – but forcefully remind him that he has moral responsibilities to those who would prefer not to be exposed to his nudity. We could make clear that we disapprove of his failure to take into account his responsibilities to others, but if these entreaties fall on deaf ears, it may be that we should simply ignore his behaviour. Where no tangible harm results from behaviour, the law's stance should generally be one of tolerance. At present, however, this debate, if articulated at all, is couched in claims by accused persons of their rights under the ECHR, countered by the appeal court's tendency to interpret crimes such as breach of the peace in a broad fashion, in the name of the "public interest". **22.14.3**

We are mindful of the fact that this final chapter may seem somewhat negative, focusing as it does on what we perceive as the apparent shortcomings of the law. Voltaire's sentiment – that "if you want good laws, burn those you have and make yourselves new ones" – is not one we share.[152] In the course of writing this book we came to a deeper appreciation of the richness of the law, and its many strengths. Lady Cosgrove once compared criminal law to **22.14.4**

---

[150] D N Husak, "Limitations on criminalization and the general part of criminal law" in S Shute and A P Simester, *Criminal law Theory: Doctrines of the General Part* (2002) 13 at p 31.

[151] Unlike the approach taken in *Crowe v Waugh* 1999 JC 292. See section 8.11.8 above.

[152] *Dictionnaire Philosophique*, cited in F A von Hayek, *New Studies in Philosophy, Politics, Economics and the History of Ideas* (1978) at p 5.

a "living tree", which should be "not only growing but shedding dead wood as it does so".[153] If we may continue this metaphor, conscientious gardeners tend carefully to their trees, and undertake regular pruning. Ours is a call for a more systematic approach to the future development of Scots criminal law, so that it can continue to be a system in which we take pride.

---

[153] *Lord Advocate's Reference (No 1 of 2001)* 2002 SLT 466 at 481, para [15].

BIBLIOGRAPHY

A

Adshead J, "Doing justice to the environment" (2013) 77 *J Crim L* 215

Alison, A, *Principles of the Criminal Law of Scotland* (1832) (Butterworths, 1989 reprint)

——, *Practice of the Criminal Law of Scotland* (1833) (Butterworths, 1989 reprint)

Alldridge, P, "What's wrong with the traditional criminal law course?" (1990) *Legal Studies* 38

——, *Relocating Criminal Law* (Ashgate, 2000)

——, "The moral limits of the crime of money laundering" (2001–2) 5 *Buff Crim LR* 279

Alldridge, P and C Brants (eds), *Personal Autonomy, the Private Sphere and the Criminal Law: A Comparative Study* (Hart, 2001)

Allen H, *Justice Unbalanced: Gender Psychiatry and Judicial Decisions* (Oxford University Press, 1987)

Anwar A, "Killing in company" (2007) 52 *JLSS* 16

Arenson A, "*Thabo Meli* revisited: the pernicious effects of result-driven decisions" (2013) 77 *J Crim L* 41

Aristotle, *Nicomachean ethics / translation (with historical introduction) by Christopher Rowe; philosophical introduction and commentary by Sarah Broadie* Book V iii 112–116, translation by W Ross, 1925) (Oxford University Press, 2002)

Ashworth, A, "Case comment on *Andronicou and Constantinou* v *Cyprus* (1996) 22 EHRR CD18" [1998] *Crim LR* 823

——, "Is the criminal law a lost cause?" (2000) 116 *LQR* 225

——, "Conceptions of overcriminalization" (2008) 5 *Ohio St J Crim L* 407

——, "Criminal law, human rights and preventative justice" in B McSherry, A Norrie and S Bronitt (eds) *Regulating Deviance: The Redirection of Criminalisation and the Futures of Criminal Law* (Hart Publishing, 2009) 87

Ashworth, A, "Should strict liability be removed from all imprisonable offences?" (2010) 45 *Irish Jurist* 1

——, "Child defendants and the doctrines of the criminal law" in J Chalmers, F Leverick and L Farmer (eds), *Essays in Criminal Law in Honour of Sir Gerald Gordon* (Edinburgh University Press, 2010) 27

——, "Ignorance of the criminal law, and duties to avoid it" (2011) 74 *MLR* 1

Ashworth, A and L Zedner, "Prevention and criminalization: justifications and limits" (2012) 15 *New Crim L Rev* 542

Ashworth, A and J Horder, *Principles of Criminal Law* (Oxford University Press, 7th edn, 2013)

Attwood, F and C Smith, "Extreme concern: regulating 'dangerous pictures' in the United Kingdom" (2010) 37(1) *JLS* 171

Automobile Association, *'Clunk Click': The AA Seat Belt Report*, pp 5–6, available at http://www.theaa.com/public_affairs/reports/aa-seat-belt-report.pdf

Avineri, A and A de-Shalit, *Communitarianism and Individualism* (Oxford University Press, 1992)

Ayres, I and J Braithwaite, *Responsive Regulation: Transcending the Deregulation Debate* (Oxford University Press, 1992)

B

Baker, D J, *The Right Not to Be Criminalized* (Ashgate, 2011)

——, "Omissions liability for homicide offences: reconciling *R* v *Kennedy* with *R* v *Evans*" (2010) 74 *J Crim L* 310

——, *G Williams' Textbook of Criminal Law* (3rd edn, 2012)

Baldwin, R, M Cave and M Lodge, *Understanding Regulation: Theory, Strategy, and Practice* (2nd edn) (Oxford University Press, 2012)

Bamforth, N, "Sado-masochism and consent" [1994] *Crim LR* 661

Banner, N F, "Can procedural and substantive elements of decision-making by reconciled in assessments of mental capacity?" (2013) 9 *International Journal of Law in Context* 71

Barendt, E, "Religious hatred laws: protecting groups or belief?" (2011) 17 *Res Publica* 41

Barry, B, *Justice as Impartiality* (Clarendon Press, 1995)

Bartky, S L, *Femininity and Domination* (Routledge, 1990)

Barton, J, "Recklessness in Scots criminal law: subjective or objective?" (2011) *Jur Rev* 143

Beale, S S, "The many faces of overcriminalization: from morals and mattress tags to overfederalization" (2004–5) *Amer U L Rev* 747

Bell, D A, *Communitarianism and Its Critics* (Clarendon Press, 1993)

Bell, D A, "A communitarian critique of liberalism" (2005) *Analyse & Kritik* 215

Bender, L, "From gender differences to feminist solidarity: Using Carol Gilligan and an ethic of care in law" (1990–91) 15 *Vermont L Rev* 1

Benhabib, S, *Another Cosmopolitanism* (Oxford University Press, 2006)

Benhabib, S and D Cornell (eds), *Feminism as Critique: Essays on the Politics of Gender in Late-capitalist Societies* (Polity Press, 1987)

Bennion, F, "The Law Commission's Criminal Law Bill: no way to draft a code" (1994) 15 *Statute L Rev* 108

Bentham, J, *Collected Works*, IV, 483 (London Athlone Press, 1981)

Berliner, D, "Rethinking the reasonable belief defense to rape" (1990–91) 100 *Yale LJ* 2687

Bibbings, L and P Alldridge, "Sexual expression, body alteration, and the defence of consent" (1993) 20 *J of Law and Soc* 356

Bird, C, *Myth of Liberal Individualism* (Cambridge University Press, 1999)

Bonnie, R J, "The competence of criminal defendants: a theoretical reformulation" (1992) 10 *Behavioral Sciences and the Law* 291

Bovey, K S, *Misuse of Drugs: A Handbook for Lawyers* (Butterworths and Law Society of Scotland, 1986)

Boyle, K (ed), *Everyday Pornography* (Routledge, 2010)

Brooks-Gordon, B, "Bellwether citizens: The regultion of male clients of sex workers" (2010) 37(1) *J of Law and Soc* 145

Brown, A, *Wheatley's Road Traffic Law in Scotland* (Tottel Publishing, 4th edn, 2007)

Brown, M and K Bolling, *Scottish Crime and Victimisation Survey 2006* (Scottish Executive, 2007)

Brownmiller, S, *Against Our Will: Men, Women and Rape* (Penguin, 1976) originally published by Secker and Warburg, 1975

Burchell, J and C Gane, "Shamelessness scotched: the domain of decency after Dominick" (2004) 8 *Edin LR* 231

Burman, M, "Evidencing sexual assault: women in the witness box" (2009) 56 *Probation Journal* 1

Busby, N B, Clark *et al*, *Scots law: A Student Guide* (T&T Clark, 2000)

Butler Committee: *Report of the Committee on Mentally Abnormal Offenders* (Cmnd 6244, London, 1975)

C

Cabinet Office, *Identity Fraud: A Study* (2002)

Cairns, J W, "Institutional writings in Scotland reconsidered" (1983) 4 *J of Legal History* 76

Carloway Review: Report and Recommendations (17 November 2011) (available at: http://www.scotland.gov.uk/Resource/Doc/925/0122808.pdf)

Campbell, L, *Organised Crime and the Law: A Comparative Analysis* (Hart, Oxford, 2013)

Casey, J, "*Gillon* v *HM Advocate*: Provocation, proportionality and the ordinary person" (2006) 30 *SLT* 193

Chalmers, J, "Sexually transmitted diseases and the criminal law" (2001) 5 *Jur Rev* 259

——, "Collapsing the structure of criminal law" (2001) *SLT* 241

——, "Is underage intercourse shameless indecency?" (2003) *SLT* 123

——, "Reforming the pleas of insanity and diminished responsibility: some aspects of the Scottish Law Commission's Discussion Paper" (2003) 8 *SLPQ* 79

——, "Fire-raising by omission" (2004) *SLT* (News) 59

——, "Merging provocation and diminished responsibility: some reasons for scepticism" [2004] *Crim LR* 198

——, "Corporate culpable homicide: *Transco plc* v *HM Advocate*" (2004) 8 *Edin LR* 262

——, "Distress as corroboration of *mens rea*" (2004) *SLT* 141

——, "Just an expert group that can't say no: reforming corporate homicide law" (2006) 10 *Edin LR* 290

——, "Fraud, mistake and consent in rape: some preliminary observations" (2006) 6 *SLT* 29

——, "*Lieser* and misconceptions" (2008) SCL 1115

——, "The true meaning of 'wicked recklessness': *HM Advocate* v *Purcell*" (2008) 12 *Edin LR* 298

——, "Two problems with the Sexual Offences (Scotland) Bill" (2009) SCL 553

——, "Section 117 of the Criminal Justice and Licensing (Scotland) Bill: a dangerous loophole?" (2009) SCL 1240

Chalmers, J and C Gane, "The aftermath of shameless indecency" (2003) *SLPQ* 310

Chalmers, J and F Leverick, *Criminal Defences and Pleas in Bar of Trial* (SULI, 2006)

——, "Murder through the looking glass: *Gillon v HM Advocate*" (2007) 11 *Edin LR* 230

——, "Fair labelling in criminal law" (2008) 71 *MLR* 217

——, "'Substantial and radical change': a new dawn for Scottish criminal procedure" (2012) 75 *MLR* 837

——, "Tracking the creation of criminal offences" [2013] *Crim LR* 543

Chalmers, J, F Leverick and L Farmer (eds), *Essays in Criminal Law in Honour of Sir Gerald Gordon* (Edinburgh University Press, 2010)

Chalmers, J, P Duff and F Leverick, "Victim impact statements: can work, do work (for those who bother to make them)" [2007] *Crim LR* 360

Charleton, P, P A McDermott and M Bolger, *Criminal Law* (Butterworths, 1999)

Cheney, B M M, "Prostitution: a feminist jurisprudential perspective" (1988) 18(3) *Victoria University of Wellington L Rev* 239

Chiesa, L, "Why is it a crime to stomp on a goldfish: harm, victimhood and the structure of anti-cruelty offenses" (2008) 78(1) *Miss L J* 1

Chiswick, D, A P W Shubsachs and S Novosel, "Reprosecution of patients found unfit to plead: A report of anomalies in procedure in Scotland" (1990) 14 *Psychiatric Bulletin* 208

Christie, M G A, *Breach of the Peace* (Butterworths, 1990)

——, "The coherence of Scots criminal law: some aspects of *Drury v HM Advocate*" (2002) *Jur Rev* 273

Christie, S A, "The relevance of harm as the criterion for the punishment of impossible attempts" (2009) 73 *J Crim L* 153

——, "The Offensive Behaviour at Football and Threatening Communications (Scotland) Bill – strong on rhetoric but weak on substance?" (2011) 25 *SLT* 185

Cipriani, D, *Children's Rights and the Minimum Age of Criminal Responsibility: A Global Perspective* (Ashgate, 2009)

Clarke, M, *Business Crime: Its Nature and Control* (Palgrave Macmillan, 1990)

Clarkson, C M V, H M Keating and S R Cunningham, *Clarkson and Keating Criminal Law: Text and Materials* (Sweet & Maxwell, 2007)

Clive, E, "Submission of a Draft Criminal Code for Scotland to the Minister for Justice" (2003) 7 *Edin LR* 395

——, "Codification of Scottish criminal law" (2008) SCL 747

——, "Codification of the criminal law" in J Chalmers, F Leverick and L Farmer (eds), *Essays in Criminal Law in Honour of Sir Gerald Gordon* (Edinburgh University Press, 2010) 54.

Clive, E, P R Ferguson, C H W Gane and A A McCall Smith, *A Draft Criminal Code for Scotland with Commentary* (Stationery Office, 2003) (published under the auspices of the Scottish Law Commission)

Clive, E and P R Ferguson, "Unravelling the enigma: a reply to Professor Farmer" (2002) 7 *SLPQ* 81

Clough, A, "Sexual infidelity: the exclusion that never was?" 76 *J Crim L* 382

Connelly, C, "Insanity and unfitness to plead" (1996) *Jur Rev* 206

Connelly, C, "Women who kill violent men" (1996) *Jur Rev* 215

Cook, D, *Rich Law Poor Law: Differential Responses to Tax and Supplementary Benefit Fraud* (Oxford University Press, 1989)

Cotton, T, "The mandatory life sentence for murder: is it time for discretion?" (2008) 72 *J Crim L* 288

Cowan, S, "'Freedom and capacity to make a choice': a feminist analysis of consent in the criminal law of rape" in V E Munro and C Stychin, *Sexuality and the Law* (Routledge-Cavendish, 2007)

——, "The trouble with drink: intoxication, (in)capacity, and the evaporation of consent to sex" (2008) *Akron L Rev* 899

——, "All change or business as usual? Reforming the law of rape in Scotland" in C McGlynn and V Munro (eds), *Rethinking Rape Law: International and Comparative Perspectives* (Routledge, 2010)

——, "The pain of pleasure: consent and the criminalisation of sado-masochistic 'assaults'" in J Chalmers, F Leverick and L Farmer (eds), *Essays in Criminal Law in Honour of Sir Gerald Gordon* (Edinburgh University Press, 2010) 126

——, "Criminalizing SM: disavowing the erotic, instantiating violence" in R A Duff *et al* (eds) *The Structures of the Criminal Law* (Oxford University Press, 2012)

Craig, R, "Thou shall do no murder: a discussion paper on the Corporate Manslaughter and Corporate Homicide Act 2007" (2009) 30 *Company Lawyer* 17

Criminal Justice Series, *Homicide in Scotland*, 2006–7

Criminal Law Revision Committee, 14th Report on *Offences Against the Person* (1980) (Cmnd 7844)

Crittenden, J, *Beyond Individualism: Reconstituting the Liberal Self* (Oxford University Press, 1992)

Croall, H, "Who is the white collar criminal?" (1989) *British Journal of Criminology* 29(2), 157

——, *Understanding White Collar Crime* (Open University Press, 2001)

Cubie, A M, *Scots Criminal Law* (Bloomsbury Professional, 3rd edn, 2010)

Cullen, W D, *The Public Inquiry into the Piper Alpha Disaster, Volumes 1 and 2* (HMSO, 1990)

D

Daum, C W, "Feminism and pornography in the twenty-first century: The Internet's impact on the feminist pornography debate" (2008–9) 30 *Women's Rights Law Reporter* 543

Davidson, R and G Davis, "'A field for private members': the Wolfenden Committee and Scottish homosexual law reform, 1950–67" (2004) 15 *Twentieth Century British History* 174

Davidson, R and G Davis, "Sexuality and the state: the campaign for Scottish homosexual law reform, 1967–80" (2006) 20 *Contemporary British History* 533

Davies, A, K Wittebrood and J L Jackson, "Predicting the criminal antecedents of a stranger rapist from his offence behaviour" (1997) 37 *Science & Justice* 161

Dawkins, R, *The Selfish Gene* (Paladin, 2nd edn, 1989)

Dempsey, B, "Gender-neutral law and heterocentric policies: 'domestic-abuse as gender-based abuse;' and same-sex couples" (2011) 15 *Edin LR* 381.

Dennis, I H, *Criminal Law and Justice: Essays from the W G Hart Workshop 1986* (Sweet & Maxwell, 1987)

——, "RIP: The Criminal Code (1968–2008)" [2009] 1 *Crim LR* 1

Devlin, P, *The Enforcement of Morals* (Oxford University Press, 1965)

Dicey, A V, *An Introduction to the Study of the Law of the Constitution* (1885)

Dillof, A M, "Transferred intent: An inquiry into the nature of criminal culpability" (1997–98) 1 *Buffalo Crim LR* 501

Duff, P, "The not proven verdict: jury mythology and 'moral panics'" (1996) *Jur Rev* 1

——, "Intermediate diets and the agreement of evidence: a move towards inquisitorial culture?" (1998) *Jur Rev* 349

——, "Disclosure in Scottish criminal procedure: another step in an inquisitorial direction?" (2007) 11 *International Journal of Evidence & Proof* 153

Duff, P, J Chalmers and F Leverick, "The pilot victim statement scheme in Scotland" (2007) *SLT* 71

——, *An Evaluation of the Pilot Victim Statement Schemes in Scotland* (Scottish Executive, 2007)

Duff, R A, *Intention, Agency and Criminal Liability* (Blackwell, 1990)

——, *Criminal Attempts* (Oxford University Press, 1996)

——, "Law, language and community: some preconditions of criminal liability" (1998) 18 *OJLS* 189

——, *Punishment, Communication, and Community* (Oxford University Press, 2001)

——, "Harms and wrongs" (2001) 5 *Buffalo Crim LR* 13

——, "Theorizing criminal law: a 25th anniversary essay" (2005) 25 *OJLS* 353

——, *Answering for Crime: Responsibility and Liability in the Criminal Law* (Hart, 2007)

——, "Towards a modest legal moralism" (2013) 8 *Criminal Law and Philosophy*: Minnesota Legal Studies Research Paper No 12–28, 1

Duff, R A and S P Green (eds), *Defining Crimes: Essays on the Special Part of the Criminal Law* (Oxford University Press, 2005)

—— (eds), *Philosophical Foundations of Criminal Law* (Oxford University Press, 2011)

Duff R A, L Farmer, S E Mashall, M Renzo and V Tadros, *The Structures of the Criminal Law* (Oxford University Press, 2011)

DTZ Pieda Consulting and Heriot-Watt University, *Use of Anti-Social Behaviour Orders in Scotland* (2007)

Dworkin, A, *Intercourse* (Free Press, 1987)

Dworkin, R, "Lord Devlin and the enforcement of morals" (1966) 75 *Yale Law Journal* 986

——, *Taking Rights Seriously* (Duckworth, 1977)

E

Easton, S, "Criminalising the possession of extreme pornography: sword or shield?" (2011) 75 *J Crim L* 391

Eboe-Osuji, C, "The plea of alibi in international criminal law as viewed through the prism of the common law" (2011) 22 *Criminal Law Forum* 35

Eccles, T and J Pointing, "Smart regulation, shifting architectures and changes in governance" (2013) 5 *International Journal of Law in the Built Environment* 71

Edwards, S S M, "Perjury and perverting the course of justice considered" [2003] *Crim LR* 525

——, *Sex and Gender in the Legal Process* (Blackstone, 1996)

Emmerson, B, A Ashworth and A Macdonald, *Human Rights and Criminal Justice* (Sweet & Maxwell, 3rd edn, 2012)

Etzioni, A, *The Spirit of Community: Rights, Responsibilities and the Communitarian Agenda* (Fontana, 1995)

F

Faigman, D L, "The battered woman syndrome and self-defense: a legal and empirical dissent" [1986] *Virginia L Rev* 72

——, "Discerning justice when battered women kill" (1987–8) 39 *Hastings LJ* 207

Faigman, D L and A J Wright, "The battered woman syndrome in the age of science" (1997) 39 *Arizona L Rev* 67

Farley, M, J Macleod, L Anderson and J Golding, "Attitudes and social characteristics of men who buy sex in Scotland" (2011) *Psychological Trauma: Theory, Research, Practice, and Policy* 1

Farmer, L, "The boundaries of Scottish criminal law" (1989) 148 *SCOLAG* 9

Farmer, L, "The obsession with definition" (1996) 5 *Social & Legal Studies* 57

——, *Criminal Law, Tradition and Legal Order: Crime and the Genius of Scots Law, 1747 to the Present* (Cambridge University Press, 1997)

——, "Tony Martin and the nightbreakers: Criminal law, victims and the power to punish" in S Armstrong and L McAra (eds), *Perspectives on Punishment: The Contours of Control* (Oxford University Press, 2006)

——, "Enigma: decoding the draft criminal code" (2002) 7 *SLPQ* 68

Farmer, L and S Veitch (eds), *The State of Scots Law* (Butterworths, 2001)

Feeley, M M, *The Process is the Punishment: Handling Cases in a Lower Criminal Court* (Russell Sage Foundation, 1979)

Feinberg, J, *The Moral Limits of the Criminal Law: Harm to Others* (Oxford University Press, 1984)

——, *The Moral Limits of the Criminal Law: Offense to Others* (Oxford University Press, 1985)

——, *The Moral Limits of the Criminal Law: Harm to Self* (Oxford University Press, 1986)

——, *The Moral Limits of the Criminal Law: Harmless Wrongdoing* (Oxford University Press, 1988)

Ferguson, P R, "The limits of the automatism defence" (1991) *JLSS* 446

——, "Automatism – negation of *mens rea*: a rejoinder" (1992) *JLSS* 57

——, *Drug Injuries and the Pursuit of Compensation* (Sweet & Maxwell, 1996)

——, "Killing 'without getting into trouble'? Assisted suicide and Scots law" (1998) 2 *Edin LR* 288

——, "Breach of the peace and the European Convention on Human Rights" (2001) 5 *Edin LR* 145

——, "Codifying criminal law (1): a critique of Scots common law" [2004] *Crim LR* 49

——, "Reforming rape and other sexual offences" (2008) 12 *Edin LR* 302

——, "'Smoke gets in your eyes ...' the criminalisation of smoking in enclosed public places, the harm principle and the limits of the criminal sanction" (2011) 31 *Legal Studies* 259

——, "Repercussions of the Cadder case: the ECHR's fair trial procedures and Scottish criminal procedure" [2011] *Crim LR* 743

Ferguson, P R, "Criminal Law and Criminal Justice: An Exercise in Ad Hocery" in E E Sutherland, K E Goodall, G F M Little and

F P Davidson (eds), *Law Making and the Scottish Parliament: The Early Years* (Edinburgh University Press, 2011)

——, *Breach of the Peace* (Dundee University Press, 2013)

Ferguson, P R and F E Raitt, "Reforming the Scots law of rape: redefining the offence" (2006) 10 *Edin LR* 185

Ferguson, P W, "Corporate Manslaughter and Corporate Homicide Act 2007" (2007) 35 *SLT* 251

——, "Wicked Recklessness" (2008) *Jur Rev* 1

——, "Case comment: *Clark* v *HM Advocate; Smith* v *HM Advocate; Fagan* v *PF Airdrie* 2008 SLT 787" (2008) *SLT* 27, 185

——, "The mental element in modern criminal law" in J Chalmers, F Leverick and L Farmer (eds), *Essays in Criminal Law in Honour of Sir Gerald Gordon* (Edinburgh University Press, 2010) 141

Field, S and M Lynch, "The capacity for recklessness" (1992) *Legal Studies* 74

——, "Capacity, Recklessness and the House of Lords" [1993] *Crim LR* 127

Finlayson, A (ed), *Contemporary Political Thought: A Reader and Guide* (Edinburgh University Press, 2003)

Finley, L, "The nature of domination and the nature of women: Reflections on *Feminism Unmodified*" 82 (1988) *Nw U L Rev* 352

——, "Breaking women's silence in law: The dilemma of the gendered nature of legal reasoning" (1989) 64 *Notre Dame L Rev* 886

Fletcher, G, *Rethinking Criminal Law* (Little, Brown, 1978); (Oxford University Press, 2000)

Ford, R, "Scots lead rebellion against oath of allegiance" *The Times*, 12 March 2008

Franklin, B and J Petley, "Killing the age of innocence: newspaper reporting of the death of James Bulger" in J Pilcher and S Wagg (eds), *Thatcher's Children? Politics, Childhood and Society in the 1980s and 1990s* (Falmer Press, 1996)

Frazer, E and N Lacey, *The Politics of Community: A Feminist Critique of the Liberal – Communitarian Debate* (Harvester Wheatsheaf, 1993)

Freyenhagen, F and T O'Shea, "Hidden substance: mental disorder as a challenge to normatively neutral accounts of autonomy" (2013) 9 *International Journal of Law in Context* 53

Friedman, M, "Feminism and modern friendship: Dislocating the community" in S Avineri and A de-Shalit (eds), *Communitarianism and Individualism* (Oxford University Press, 1992)

Fuller, L L, "Positivism and fidelity to law – A reply to Professor Hart" (1957) 71 *Harvard Law Review* 630

Fuller, L L, *The Morality of Law* (Yale University Press, 1964, and revised edition, 1969)

——, "Law as an instrument of social control and law as a facilitation of human interaction" (1975) *BYU L Rev* 89

G

Gane, C H W, C N Stoddart and J Chalmers, *A Casebook on Scottish Criminal Law* (W Green, 3rd edn, 2001)

Gane, C H W, *Sexual Offences* (Butterworths, 1992)

Gardiner, S and M James, "Touchlines and guidelines: the Lord Advocate's response to sportsfield violence" [1997] *Crim LR* 41

Gardner, J and S Shute, "The wrongness of rape" in J Horder (ed), *Oxford Essays in Jurisprudence* (Oxford University Press, 2000)

Geis, G (ed), *White Collar Crime: The Offender in Business and the Professions* (Atherton Press, 1968)

George, R P, *Making Men Moral: Civil Liberties and Public Morality* (Clarendon Press, 1993)

Gilligan, C, *In a Different Voice: Psychological Theory and Women's Development* (Harvard University Press, 1982)

Glendon, M A, *Rights Talk: The Impoverishment of Political Discourse* (Maxwell Macmillan, 1991)

Glazebrook, P R, "A better way of convicting businesses of avoidable deaths and injuries?" (2002) 61 *CLJ* 405

Goff, R, "The mental element in the crime of murder" (1988) *LQR* 30

Goodall, K, "Tackling Sectarianism through the Criminal Law" (2011) 15(3) *Edin LR* 423

Gordon, G H, *The Criminal Law of Scotland* (3rd edn, edited by M G A Christie, Volume I: 2000, W Green & Son)

——, *The Criminal Law of Scotland* (3rd edn, edited by M G A Christie, Volume II: 2001, W Green & Son)

Grant, I, "The 'syndromization' of women's experience" in D Martinson, M MacCrimmon *et al*, "A forum on *Lavallee v R*: Women and self-defence" (1991) 25 *U of British Colum L Rev* 23

Gray, J, *Liberalism* (Oxford University Press, 2nd edn, 1995)

Green, S P, "The concept of white collar crime in law and legal theory" (2004–2005) 8 *Buffalo Crim LR* 1

——, *Lying, Cheating, and Stealing: A Moral Theory of White-Collar Crime* (Oxford University Press, 2006)

——, "Theft by omission", in J Chalmers, F Leverick and L Farmer (eds), *Essays in Criminal Law in Honour of Sir Gerald Gordon* (Edinburgh University Press, 2010) 158

——, "Thieving and receiving: overcriminalizing the possession of stolen property" (2011) 14 *New Crim LR* 35

Green, S P and M B Kugler, "When is it wrong to trade stocks on the basis of non-public information? Public views of the morality of insider trading" (2011) 39 *Fordham Urb L J* 445

Greenawalt, K, "Legal enforcement of morality" (1994–1995) 85 *J Crim L and Criminol* 710

Griffith, J, *The Politics of the Judiciary* (Fontana, 3rd edn, 1985)

Gross, H, "Rape, moralism, and human rights" [2007] *Crim LR* 220

Gutmann, A, "Communitarian critics of liberalism" in S Avineri and A de-Shalit (eds), *Communitarianism and Individualism* (Oxford University Press, 1992) 120

H

Hale, M, *History of the Pleas of the Crown* (Sollom Evelyn, 1736)

Hamer, D, "The presumption of innocence and reverse burdens: a balancing act?" (2007) 66 *CLJ* 142

Hampton, J, "Correcting harms versus righting wrongs: the goal of retribution" (1992) 39 *UCLA L Rev* 1659

Harcourt, B E, "The collapse of the harm principle" (1999) 90 *J Crim L and Criminol* 109

Harris, G C, "The communitarian function of the criminal jury trial and the rights of the accused" (1995) 74 *Neb L Rev* 804

Harris, L, "The International Criminal Court and the superior orders defence" (2003) 22 *U Tas L Rev* 200

Hart, H L A, *Law, Liberty and Morality* (Stanford University Press, 1966)

——, *Punishment and Responsibility: Essays in the Philosophy of Law* (Clarendon Press, 1968)

——, "The aims of the criminal law" (1958) 23 *Law & Contemporary Problems* 401

Hartley, L P, *The Go-Between* (Hamish Hamilton, 1953)

Hawkins, G and F E Zimring, *Pornography in a Free Society* (Cambridge University Press, 1988)

Hawkins, K and J Thomas (eds), *Enforcing Regulation* (Kluwer Nijhoff, 1984)

Hayek, F A, *New Studies in Philosophy, Politics, Economics and the History of Ideas* (Routledge & Kegan Paul, 1978)

Hillyard, P, C Pantazis, S Tombs and D Gordon (eds), *Beyond Criminology: Taking Harm Seriously* (Pluto Press, 2004)

Hirschmann, N J, *Freedom, Flathman and Feminism* in B Honig and D R Maple (eds), *Skepticism, Individuality, and Freedom* (University of Minnesota Press, 2002)

Hirst, M, "Causing death by driving and other offences: A question of balance" [2008] *Crim LR* 339

Holmes, O W, *The Common Law* (Macmillan, 1882)

Home Office, *Crime in England and Wales 2007/8: Findings from the British Crime Survey and Police Recorded Crime* (2008)

Hood, R (ed), *Crime, Criminology and Public Policy: Essays in Honour of Sir Leon Radzinowicz* (Heinemann, 1974)

Hope of Craighead (Lord), "What a second chamber can do for legislative scrutiny" (2003) 25 *Statute L Rev* 3

Horder, J, *Provocation and Responsibility* (Clarendon Press, 1992)

——, "Re-thinking non-fatal offences against the person" (1994) 14 *OJLS* 335

——, *Oxford Essays in Jurisprudence* (Oxford University Press, 4th series, 2000)

——, "Reshaping the subjective element in the provocation defence" (2005) 25 *OJLS* 123

——, "Bribery as a form of criminal wrongdoing" (2011) *LQR* 37

Horder, J and L McGowan, "Manslaughter by causing another's suicide" [2006] *Crim LR* 1035

House of Commons, Home Affairs Committee, First Report, *Murder: The Mandatory Life Sentence*, Session 1995–1996, H.C. 111 (1995)

House of Commons, *Report of the Official Account of the Bombings in London on 7th July 2005* (HC1087) (The Stationery Office, 2006)

Howe, A, "Provocation in crisis – Law's passion at the crossroads? New directions for feminist strategies" (2004) 21 *Austl Feminist LJ* 53

Howard, H, "Reform of the insanity defence: theoretical issues" (2003) 67 *J Crim L* 51

HMSO, *Review of Counter-Terrorism and Security Powers: Review Fndings and Recommendations* (CM 2004, 2011).

HSE, *Enforcement Policy Statement* (HSE, 2009)

Hull, J, "Stealing secrets: a review of the Law Commission's consultation paper on the misuse of trade secrets" [1998] *Crim LR* 246

Hume, D, *Commentaries on the Law of Scotland Respecting Crimes* Vol I and II (4th edn, 1844, edited by B R Bell)

Hunt, A, "Criminal prohibitions on direct and indirect encouragement of terrorism" [2007] *Crim LR* 441

Hunter, R F (ed), *Justice and Crime: Essays in Honour of the Right Honourable The Lord Emslie* (Butterworths, 1993)

Husak, D N, "Transferred intent" (1996) 10 *Notre Dame J L, Ethics & Pub Pol'y* 65

——, "The criminal law as last resort" (2004) 24 *OJLS* 207

——, *Overcriminalization: The Limits of the Criminal Law* (Oxford University Press, 2008)

I

Ichikawa, M, S Nakahara and S Wakai, "Mortality of front-seat occupants attributable to unbelted rear-seat passengers in car crashes" (2002) 359 *The Lancet* 9300, 43

Insco, J B, "Defense of superior orders before military commissions" (2003) 13 *Duke J Comp Int'l L* 389

J

Jacobs, L A, *Pursuing Equal Opportunities: The theory and Practice of Egalitarian Justice* (Cambridge University Press, 2004)

Jaggar, A M, *Feminist Politics and Human Nature* (Rowman & Littlefield, 1983)

Jareborg, N, "Criminalization as last resort (*ultima ratio*)" (2004) 2 *Ohio St J Crim L* 521

Jareborg, N and A von Hirsch, "Gauging criminal harm: a living-standards analysis" (1991) 11 *OJLS* 1

Johnston, D, *The Idea of a Liberal Theory: a Critique and Reconstruction* (Princeton University Press, 1994)

——, "*McInnes v HM Advocate*: time for a(nother) definitive decision on disclosure" (2009) 13 *Edin LR* 108

Jones, R, "Guardianship for coercively controlled battered women: breaking the control of the abuser" (1999–2000) 88 *Geo LJ* 605

Jones, T H, "The defence of necessity in Scots law" (1989) *SLT* (News) 253

——, "Attempted culpable homicide" (1990) *JLSS* 408

——, "Splendid isolation: Scottish criminal law, the Privy Council and the Supreme Court" [2004] *Crim LR* 96

——, "Towards a good and complete criminal code for Scotland" (2005) 68 *MLR* 448

——, and M G A Christie, *Criminal Law* (W Green, 5th edn, 2012)

Junker, J M, "Criminalization and criminogenesis" (1972) 19 *UCLA L Rev* 697

K

Kadish, S H, *Blame and Punishment: Essays in the Criminal Law* (Macmillan, 1987)

Kamit, O, "Responsibility determination as a smokescreen: provocation and the reasonable person in the Israeli Supreme Court" (2004–2005) 2 *Ohio J Crim L* 547

Kaveny, M C, "Inferring intention from foresight" (2004) *LQR* 81

Katz, L, *Bad Acts and Guilty Minds: Conundrums of the Criminal Law* (University of Chicago Press, 1987)

Keen, T H, L H Hamilton *et al*, *The 9/11 Commission Report: Final Report of the National Commission on the Terrorist Attacks upon the United States of America: Executive Summary* (National Commission on Terrorist Attacks upon the United States, 2004)

Kennedy, C, "Criminal law and religion in post-reformation Scotland" (2012) 16 *Edin LR* 178

Kiralfy, A K R and H L MacQueen (eds), *New Perspectives in Scottish Legal History* (Frank Cass, 1984)

Kleinig, J, *Paternalism* (Manchester University Press, 1983)

Kohlberg, L, *Essays on Moral Development: The Philosophy of Moral Development, Moral Stages and the Idea of Justice* (Harper & Row, vol 1, 1984)

Kowalski, R M, *Complaining, Teasing and Other Annoying Behaviors* (Yale University Press, 2003)

Kymlicka, W, *Multicultural Citizenship: A Liberal Theory of Minority Rights* (Clarendon Press, 1995)

L

Lacey, N, *State Punishment: Political Principles and Community Values* (Routledge, 1988)

——, *Unspeakable Subjects: Feminist Essays in Legal and Social Theory* (Hart, 1998)

——, "The resurgence of character: responsibility in the context of criminalization" in R A Duff and S P Green (eds), *Philosophical Foundations of Criminal Law* (Oxford University Press, 2011)

Lamond, G, "What is a crime?" (2007) *OJLS* 609

——, "Coercion, threats, and the puzzle of blackmail" in A P Simester and A T H Smith, *Harm and Culpability* (1996)

Lang, J, "The protection of commercial trade secrets" [2003] 25 *European Intellectual Property Review* 462

Larcombe, W, "Falling rape conviction rates: (some) feminist aims and measures for rape law (2011) 19 *Fem LS* 27

Law Commission, *Defences of General Application* (Law Com No 83, 1977)

——, *A Criminal Code for England and Wales* (Law Com No 177, 1989)

——, Consultation Paper No 127, *Intoxication and Criminal Liability* (The Stationery Office, 1993)

——, Consultation Paper 131, *Assisting and Encouraging Crime* (The Stationery Office, 1993)

——, *Legislating the Criminal Code: Involuntary Manslaughter* (Law Com No 237, 1996)

Law Commission, *Partial Defences to Murder Consultation Paper* (Law Com No 173, 2003)

——, *Final Report on Partial Defences to Murder* (Law Com No 290, 2004)

——, Consultation Paper No 177, *A New Homicide Act for England and Wales* (The Stationery Office, 2005)

——, *Murder, Manslaughter and Infanticide* (Law Com No 304) (2006)

——, *Intoxication and Criminal Liability* (Law Com No 314, 2009)

——, Consultation Paper No 195, *Criminal Law in Regulatory Contexts* (The Stationery Office, 2010)

Law Commission of Canada, *Recodifying Criminal Law* (Law Reform Commission of Canada, 1987)

——, *What is a Crime? Challenges and Alternatives: Discussion Paper* (Law Commission of Canada, 2003)

——, *What Is a Crime? Defining Criminal Conduct in Contemporary Society* (University of British Columbia Press, 2004)

Lea, J and J Young, *What is to be done about Law and Order? Crisis in the Nineties* (Pluto Press, 1984)

Leach, R, *British Political Ideas* (1991), cited in C Bird, *Myth of Liberal Individualism* (Cambridge University Press, 1999)

Leverick, F, "Is English self-defence law incompatible with Article 2 of the ECHR?" [2002] *Crim LR* 347

——, "Mistake in self-defence after *Drury*" (2002) *Jur Rev* 35

——, *Killing in Self-Defence* (Oxford University Press, 2006)

——, "Unreasonable mistake in self-defence: *Lieser* v *HM Advocate*" (2009) 13 *Edin LR* 100

——, "The Supreme Court strikes back" (2011) 15 *Edin LR* 287

——, "The right to legal assistance during detention" (2011) 15 *Edin LR* 353

——, "The (art and) parting of the ways: joint criminal liability for homicide" (2012) *SLT* 227

Leverick, F and F Stark, "How do you solve a problem like entrapment?" (2010) 14 *Edin LR* 467

Lidsky, L B, "Where's the harm?: Free speech and the regulation of lies" (2008) 65 *Wash & Lee L Rev* 1091

Lindgren, J, "Unraveling the paradox of blackmail" (1984) 84 *Colum L Rev* 670

Livingstone, S, *Confess and Be Hanged: Scottish Crime and Punishment Through the Ages* (Birlinn, 2000)

Lord, M, "The Dalkon Shield litigation: revised annotated reprimand by Chief Judge Miles W Lord" (1986) 9 *Hamline L Rev* 7

Lukes, S, *Individualism* (Blackwell, 1973)

M

MacCormick, N, "What is wrong with deceit?" (1983–1985) 10 *Sydney L Rev* 5

Macdonald, J H A, *A Practical Treatise on the Criminal Law of Scotland* (4th edn, 1929)

——, *A Practical Treatise on the Criminal Law of Scotland* (5th edn by J Walker and D J Stevenson, 1948)

MacDonald, S and M Telford, "The use of ASBOs against young people in England and Wales: Lessons from Scotland" (2007) 27 *Legal Studies* 604

MacDougall, I, "Automatism – negation of *mens rea*" (1992) 37 *JLSS* 57

MacFarlane, B A, "Historical development of the offence of rape", in J Wood and R Peck (eds), *100 Years of the Criminal Code in Canada* (Canadian Bar Association, 1993)

MacIntyre, A, *After Virtue: A Study in Moral Theory* (Duckworth, 1st edn, 1981)

MacKinnon, C A, "Pornography, Civil Rights, and Speech" (1985) *Harvard Civil Rights – Civil Liberties Law Review* 1

——, *Feminism Unmodified: Discourses on Life and Law* (Harvard University Press, 1987)

——, *Towards A Feminist Theory of the State* (Harvard University Press, 1989)

——, *Women's Lives, Men's Laws* (Harvard University Press, 2007)

——, "Trafficking, Prostitution, and Inequality" (2011) 46 *Harv C R – CL L Rev* 271

Macrory, R, *Regulatory Justice: Making Sanctions Effective* (Cabinet Office, 2006)

Madden Dempsey, M, "Rethinking Wolfenden: prostitute-use, criminal law, and remote harm" [2005] *Crim LR* 444

Madden Dempsey, M and J Herring, "Why sexual penetration requires justification" (2007) 27 *OJLS* 467

Maher, G, "Blasphemy in Scots Law" (1977) *SLT* 257

——, "The enforcement of morals continued" (1978) *SLT* (News) 281

——, "'The most heinous of all crimes': reflections on the structure of homicide in Scots law" in J Chalmers, F Leverick and L Farmer (eds), *Essays in Criminal Law in Honour of Sir Gerald Gordon* (Edinburgh University Press, 2010)

——, "The new mental disorder defences: some comments" (2013) *SLT* 1

Mahmoudi, F, "On criminalization in Iran (sources and features)" (2002) 10 *Eur Just Crime Crim L & Crim Jus* 45

Marron, D, "'Alter reality': governing the risk of identity theft" (2008) *Brit J Criminol* 20

Martin, D L, "Retribution revisited: a reconsideration of feminist criminal law reform strategies" (1998) *Osgoode Hall L J* 151

Marshall, S E and R A Duff, "Criminalization and sharing wrongs" (1998) 11 *Canadian J of L and Juris* 7

——, "Public and private wrongs" in J Chalmers, F Leverick and L Farmer (eds), *Essays in Criminal Law in Honour of Sir Gerald Gordon* (Edinburgh University Press, 2010) 70

Matthews, R, *Prostitution, Politics and Policy* (Cavendish, 2008)

McAlinden, A, "The use of 'shame' with sexual offenders" (2005) 45 *Brit J of Criminol* 373

McArdle, D, "Too much heat, not enough light" (2011) 56(7) *JLSS* 9

McBarnet, D, A Voiculescu and T Campbell (eds), *The New Corporate Accountability: Corporate Social Responsibility and the Law* (Cambridge University Press, 2007)

McCall Smith, R A A and M M Menlowe (eds), *Duty to Rescue: The Jurisprudence of Aid* (Ashgate, 1993)

McCall Smith, R A A and D Sheldon, *Scots Criminal Law* (Butterworths, 2nd edn, 1997)

McCluskey, J, "Supreme error" (2011) 15 *Edin LR* 276

McDiarmid, C, "A feminist perspective on children who kill" (1996) 2 *Res Publica* 3

——, *Childhood and Crime* (Dundee University Press, 2007)

——, "Withholding culpable homicide: *Ferguson* v *HM Advocate*" (2009) 13 *Edin LR* 316

——, "The age of criminal responsibility in Scots law" (2009) *SCOLAG* 116

——, "Don't look back in anger: the partial defence of provocation in Scots criminal law" in J Chalmers, F Leverick and L Farmer (eds), *Essays in Criminal Law in Honour of Sir Gerald Gordon* (2010)

——, *Criminal Law Essentials* (Dundee University Press, 2nd edn, 2010).

——, "'Something wicked this way comes': the *mens rea* of murder in Scots law" (2012) *Jur Rev* 283

McEwan, J, "From adversarialism to managerialism: criminal justice in transition" (2011) 31 *Legal Studies* 519

McGlynn, C and E Rackley, "Criminalising extreme pornography: a lost opportunity" [2009] *Crim LR* 245

McGlynn, C and V Munro (eds), *Rethinking Rape Law: International and Comparative Perspectives* (Routledge, 2010)

McGuinness, S, "Law, reproduction and disability: fatally 'handicapped'"? (2013) 21 *Med Law Rev* 213

Mackay, R D, "Post-Hinckley insanity in the U.S.A." [1988] *Crim LR* 88

——, "The consequences of killing very young children" [1993] *Crim LR* 21

——, "Righting the wrong? some observations on the second limb of the M'Naghten test" [2009] *Crim LR* 80

——, "Unfitness to plead – some observations on the Law Commission's consultation paper" [2011] *Crim LR* 433

—— and B J Mitchell, "Provoking diminished responsibility: two pleas merging into one?" [2003] *Crim LR* 745

Melissaris, E, "The concept of appropriation and the offence of theft" (2007) 70 *MLR* 4

Mill, J S, *On Liberty and other Essays, Edited with an Introduction by John Gray* (Oxford University Press, 1998)

Mintz, M, *At Any Cost: Corporate Greed, Women, and the Dalkon Shield* (Pantheon Books, 1985)

Mitchell, B, "Public perceptions of homicide and criminal justice" (1998) 38 *Brit J Criminol* 3, 453

——, "Multiple wrongdoing and offence structure: A plea for consistency and fair labelling" (2001) 64 *MLR* 393

——, "Distinguishing between murder and manslaughter in practice" (2007) 71 *JCL*4, 318

Mitchell, B J, R D Mackay and W J Brookbanks, "Pleading for provoked killers: in defence of Morgan Smith" (2008) *LQR* 675

Monaghan, K, "Constitutionalising equality: new horizons" (2008) *European Human Rights L Rev* 20

Moon, G and R Allen, "Dignity discourse in discrimination law: a better route to equality" (2006) *European Human Rights L Rev* 610

Moore, M S, "Sandelian antiliberalism" (1989) 77 *Calif L Rev* 539

——, *Act and Crime: The Philosophy of Action and its Implications for Criminal Law* (Clarendon Press, 1993)

Morris, N and G Hawkins, *The Honest Politician's Guide to Crime Control* (Phoenix Books, 1970)

Morris, S, S Anderson and L Murray, *Stalking and Harassment in Scotland* (Scottish Executive Social Research, 2002)

Morris, T and L Blom-Cooper, "The penalty for murder: A myth exploded" [1996] *Crim LR* 707

Mullálly, S, *Gender, Culture and Human Rights: Reclaiming Universalism* (Hart, 2006)

Mulhall, S and A Swift, *Liberals and Communitarians* (Blackwell Publishers, 1st edn, 1992)

Munro, V E and C F Stychin, *Sexuality and the Law: Feminist Engagements* (Routledge-Cavendish, 2007)

Murdoch, J, *Protecting the Right to Freedom of Thought, Conscience and Religion under the European Convention on Human Rights* (Council of Europe, 2012)

N

Naffine, N, *Feminism and Criminology* (Polity Press, 1997)

Nelken, D (ed), *White-Collar Crime* (Dartmouth, 1994)

——, "White collar and corporate crime" in M Maguire, R Morgan and R Reiner, *The Oxford Handbook of Criminology* (Oxford University Press, 4th edn, 2007)

Nicolson, D, "Telling tales: gender discrimination, gender construction and battered women who kill" (1995) 3 *Fem L S* 185

Noddings, N, *Caring: A Feminine Approach to Ethics and Moral Education* (University of California Press, 1984)

——, *Starting at Home: Caring and Social Policy* (University of California Press, 2002)

Norrie, A, *Punishment, Responsibility and Justice – A Relational Critique* (Oxford University Press, 2000)

——, *Crime, Reason and History: A Critical Introduction to Criminal Law* (Butterworths, 2nd edn, 2001)

——, "Between orthodox subjectivism and moral contextualism: intention and the Consultation Paper" [2006] *Crim LR* 486

Norrie, K McK, "Incest and the forbidden degrees of marriage in Scots law" (1992) 37 *JLSS* 216

Nourse, V, "Passion's progress: modern law reform and the provocation defense" (1996–7) 106 *Yale L Rev* 1331

Nozick, R, *Anarchy, State, and Utopia* (Blackwell, 1974)

Nyman, T, "The dilution of crime" (1981) 55 *The Australian Law Journal* 506

O

Oberman, M, "Turning girls into women: Re-evaluating modern statutory rape law" (1994) 85 *J Crim L and Criminol* 15

Ochoa, T T and C N Jones, "Defiling the Dead: Necrophilia and the Law" (1996–1997) 18(3) *Whitttier L Rev* 539

O'Donovan, K, *Sexual Divisions in Law* (Weidenfeld & Nicolson, 1985)

O'Donovan, K, "Defence for battered woman who kill" (1991) 18 *Journal of Law & Society* 219

Ogus, A, "Regulation revisited" (2009) *Public Law* 332

Okin, S M, *Justice, Gender, and the Family* (Basic Books, 1989)

Ormerod, D, "The Fraud Act 2006 – criminalising lying?" [2007] *Crim LR* 193

——, *Smith and Hogan's Criminal Law* (Oxford University Press, 13th edn, 2011)

P

Packer, H L, "Two models of the criminal process" (1964) 113 *U Pa L Rev* 1

——, *The Limits of the Criminal Sanction* (Stanford University Press, 1969)

Padfield, N, "Case comment: The burden of proof unresolved" (2005) 64 *CLJ* 17

Pateman, C, *The Disorder of Women: Democracy, Feminism and Political Theory* (Stanford University Press, 1989)

Pedain, A "Intention and the terrorist example" [2004] *Crim LR* 579

Perésak, N, *Criminalising Harmful Conduct: The Harm Principle, Its Limits and Continental Counterparts* (Springer, 2007)

Phoenix, J, *Making Sense of Prostitution* (Palgrave, 1999)

Pickard, T, "Culpable mistakes and rape: relating *mens rea* to the crime" (1980) 30 *U Toronto L J* 75

Pitcher, J, R Campbell, P Hubbard, M O'Neill and J Scoular, *Living and Working in Areas of Street Sex Work* (2006) (http://www.jrf. org.uk/publications/living-and-working-areas-street-sex-work)

Plaxton, M, "Foreseeing the consequences of Purcell" (2008) *SLT* (News) 21

Prendergast D, "The connection between mental disorder and the act of killing in the defence of diminished responsibility" (2013) 49 *Irish Jurist* 202

Pound, R, "Common law and legislation" (1907–8) 21 *Harv L Rev* 383

Power, H, "Provocation and culture" [2006] *Crim LR* 871

Puka, B, "The liberation of caring: a different voice for Gilligan's *Different Voice*" (1990) 5 *Hypatia* 58

Punch, M, *Dirty Business: Exploring Corporate Misconduct: Analysis and Cases* (Sage Publications, 1996)

R

Raban, O, "Capitalism, liberalism, and the right to privacy" (2011–12) 86 *Tul L Rev* 1243

Rachels, J, *The Elements of Moral Philosophy* (McGraw-Hill, 3rd edn, 1999)

Rackley, E, and C McGlynn, "Prosecuting the possession of extreme pornography: a misunderstood and mis-used law" [2013] *Crim LR* 400

Raitt, F E and M S Zeedyk, *The Implicit Relation of Psychology and Law* (Routledge, 2000)

Rawls, J, *A Theory of Justice* (Belknap Press of Harvard University, 1971)

——, *Political Liberalism* (Columbia University Press, 1993)

——, *Justice as Fairness: A Restatement* (Harvard University Press, 2001)

Reid, E C and D L Carey Miller (eds), *A Mixed Legal System in Transition: T B Smith and the Progress of Scots Law* (Edinburgh University Press, 2005)

Reiman, J, *Justice and Modern Moral Philosophy* (Yale University Press, 1990)

Roach, K, "Four models of the criminal process" (1998–9) 89 *J Crim L and Criminol* 671

Roberts, P, "The presumption of innocence brought home: *Kebilene* deconstructed" (2002) 118 *LQR* 41

Robinson, P H, *Structure and Function in Criminal Law* (Clarendon Press, 1997)

——, "Reforming the Federal Criminal Code: a top ten list" (1997) 1 *Buffalo Crim L Rev* 225

Robinson, P H and J M Darley, "Objectivist versus subjectivist views of criminality: a study in the role of social science in criminal law theory" (1998) 18 *OJLS* 409

Robinson, P H and M T Cahill, "Can a Model Penal Code Second save the states from themselves?" (2003–4) *Ohio St J Crim L* 169

——, *Law without Justice: Why Criminal Law Doesn't Give People What They Deserve* (Oxford University Press, 2006)

Rodger, A, "Thinking about Scots law" (1996) 1 *Edin LR* 3

Rodogno, R, "Shame, guilt and punishment" (2009) 28 *Law & Phil* 429

Roffee, J A, "Incest: The exception to a principled Scottish sex law" (2012) *Jur Rev* 91

Rose, G, *The Criminal Histories of Serious Traffic Offenders: Home Office Research Study* (Home Office, 2000)

Ross, J M, "Corporate criminal liability: one form or many forms?" (1999) *Jur Rev* 49

——, "A long motor run on a dark night: reconstructing *HM Advocate v Ritchie*" (2010) 14 *Edin LR* 193

Rowan-Robinson, J, P Watchman and C Barker, *Crime and Regulation: A Study of the Enforcement of Regulatory Codes* (T&T Clark, 1990)

Rumbold, J and M Wasik, "Diabetic drivers, hypoglycaemic unawareness and automatism" [2011] *Crim LR* 863

Ryan, C J, "Out on a limb: the ethical management of body integrity identity disorder" (2009) 2 *Neuroethics* 21

S

Sandel, M, *Liberalism and the Limits of Justice* (Cambridge University Press, 1982)

Sanders, T, *Paying for Pleasure* (Willan Publishing, 2008)

Sanghvi, R and D Nicolson, "Battered women and provocation: the implications of *R v Ahluwalia*" [1993] *Crim LR* 728

Sarker, R, "Daiwa and Barings: a blueprint for disaster" (1996) 17 *Company Lawyer* 86

Scales, A, *Legal Feminism: Activism, Lawyering, and Legal Theory* (New York University Press, 2006)

Schonsheck, J, *On Criminalization: An Essay in the Philosophy of the Criminal Law* (Kluwer, 1994)

Schwartz, L B, "Moral offenses and the Model Penal Code" (1963) 63 *Colum L Rev* 669

Shaw, E, "Psychopaths and criminal responsibility" (2009) 13 *Edin LR* 497

Scott, J, "*Siddique (Mohammed Atif) v HM Advocate*: what are you thinking?" (2010) SCL 315

Scott, M E, "Redefined rape and the difficulties of proof" (2005) 11 *SLT* 65

Scottish Executive, *Seatbelt Wearing in Scotland: A Second Study of Compliance (Research Finding No. 157/2002)* (2002)

Scottish Executive, *Corporate Homicide: Expert Group Report* (Scottish Executive, 2005)

Scottish Government, *Promoting Positive Outcomes: Working together to Prevent Antisocial behaviour in Scotland* (2009)

——, *Proposals for Licensing Air Weapons in Scotland: Consultation Paper* (2012)

——, *Consultation on the Marriage and Civil Partnerships Bill* (2012)

——, *Reforming Scots Criminal Law and Practice: Additional Safeguards Following the Removal of the Requirement for Corroboration* (2012)

Scottish Government, *Domestic Abuse Recorded by the Police in Scotland, 2010–11 and 2011–12*

——, *Crime and Justice Survey 2010/11*

——, *Recorded Crime in Scotland 2012–13*

——, *Statistical Bulletin: Crime and Justice Series: Homicide in Scotland 2006–2007*

——, *Statistical Bulletin: Crime and Justice Series: Homicide in Scotland 2009–2010*

——, *Statistical Release: Crime and Justice Series: Homicide in Scotland, 2008–09* (2010)

——, *Statistical Release: Crime and Justice Series: Homicide in Scotland, 2010–11* (2011)

——, *Statistical Release: Crime and Justice Series: Homicide in Scotland 2011–12*

Scottish Law Commission, *Computer Crime: Consultative Memorandum No. 68* (1986)

——, *Responses to 1993 Review of Criminal Evidence and Criminal Procedure and Programming of Business in the Sheriff Courts* (1993)

——, *Report on Insanity and Diminished Responsibility* (SLC No 195, 2004)

——, *Report on Rape and Other Sexual Offences* (SLC No 209, 2007)

——, *The Criminal Liability of Partnerships* (SCL No 224, 2011)

Scottish Serious Organised Crime Group Mapping Project, *Preliminary Findings on the Scale and Extent of Serious Organised Crime in Scotland* (2010)

Scoular, J, "What's law got to do with It? How and why law matters in the regulation of sex work" (2010) 37(1) *J of L and S* 12

Szockyj, E and J G Fox (eds), *Corporate Victimization of Women* (Northeastern University Press, 1996)

Selfe, D, "Case comment: R v Bassett (Kevin): voyeurism – the meaning of 'privacy' and 'breasts'" (2009) 193 *Criminal Lawyer* 2

——, "'Privacy' and 'underwear' – further developments in voyeurism" (2010) 199 *Criminal Lawyer* 3

Sellar, D H, "Scots Law: mixed from the very beginning? A tale of two receptions" (2000) 4 *Edin LR* 3

Sevenhuijsen, S, *Citizenship and the Ethics of Care: Feminist Considerations on Justice, Morality and Politics* (Routledge, 1998)

Shead, C, "Breach of the peace: 'a reconsideration'" (2009) SCL 560

Shiels, R S, "Scots criminal law and liability for omissions" (2006) 70 *J Crim L* 413

——, "The unsettled relevance of dole" (2010) SCL 421

Shiels, R S, "The new law of extreme pornography" (2011) *Crim Law Bulletin* 4

Shute, S and A P Simester (eds), *Criminal Law Theory: Doctrines of the General Part* (Oxford University Press, 2002)

Simester, A P, *Appraising Strict Liability* (Oxford University Press, 2005)

——, "Intoxication is never a defence" [2009] *Crim LR* 3

Simester, A P and A T H Smith (eds), *Harm and Culpability* (Clarendon Press, 1996)

Simester, A P and A von Hirsch, "Rethinking the offense principle" (2002) 8 *Legal Theory* 269

Simester, A P and G R Sullivan, *Criminal Law: Theory and Doctrine* (Hart Publishing, 3rd edn, 2007)

Simpson, A W B, *Legal Theory and Legal History: Essays on the Common Law* (The Hambledon Press, 1987)

Simpson, J, *Touching the Void* (Jonathan Cape, 1988)

Skolnick, J H, "Criminalization and criminogenesis: a reply to Professor Junker" (1972) 19 *UCLA L Rev* 715

Smart, C, *Law, Crime and Sexuality: Essays in Feminism* (Sage, 1995)

Smith, J C, "The Law Commission's Criminal Law Bill: a good start for the criminal code" (1995) 16 *Statute L Rev* 105

——, "Individual incapacities and criminal liability" (1998) 6 *Med L Rev* 138

Smith, K J M, *Lawyers, Legislators and Theorists: Developments in English Criminal Jurisprudence* 1800–1957 (Clarendon Press, 1998)

Smith, A T H, *Offences Against Public Order* (Sweet & Maxwell, 1987)

Smith, T B, *A Short Commentary on the Law of Scotland* (W Green & Sons, 1962)

Solove, D J, "Identity theft, privacy and the architecture of vulnerability" (2002–2003) 54 *Hast LJ* 1227

Spencer, J R, "Case comment" (2004) *Archbold News* 9, 5

——, "Liability for reckless infection – part 1" (2004) 154 *NLJ* 7119, 384

——, "The drafting of criminal legislation: need it be so impenetrable?" (2008) *CLJ* 585

Stair Memorial Encyclopaedia, Criminal Law Reissue 1

Stanton-Ife, J, "Strict liability: stigma and regret" (2007) 27 *OJLS* 1

Stark, F, "Breach of the peace revisited (again)" (2010) 14 *Edin LR* 134

——, "The consequences of Cadder" [2011] *Crim LR* 293

——, "Rethinking recklessness" (2011) *Jur Rev* 163

——, "It's only words: on meaning and mens rea" (2013) *CLJ* 155

Stephen, C, "Recapturing the essence of breach of the peace: *Harris v HM Advocate*" (2010) *Jur Rev* 15

Stephen, J Fitzjames (1873) *Liberty, Equality, Fraternity, edited with an introduction and notes by R J White* (Cambridge University Press, 1967)

Stephens, M, "Pushing for glory" (2006) 156 *NLJ* 7217, 469

Stewart, H, "Harms, wrongs, and set-backs in Feinberg's *Moral Limits of the Criminal Law*" (2001) 5 *Buffalo Crim LR* 47

Stuart, D, *Canadian Criminal Law: A Treatise* (Thomson Carswell, 6th edn, 2011)

Sutherland, E E, K E Goodall, G F M Little and F P Davidson (eds), *Law Making and the Scottish Parliament: The Early Years* (Edinburgh University Press, 2011)

Styles, S C, "Something to declare: a defence of the declaratory power of the High Court of Justiciary" in R F Hunter (ed), *Justice and Crime: Essays in Honour of the Right Honourable The Lord Emslie* (T&T Clark, 1993)

Sutherland, E E, "The age of reason or the reason for an age: the age of criminal responsibility" (2001) 1 *SLT* 1

Sutherland, E H, *White Collar Crime* (1949) (Holt Rinehart and Winston, 1961 reprint)

Sypnowich, C, "Proceduralism and democracy" (1999) 19 *OJLS* 649

Szockyj, E and James G Fox (eds), *Corporate Victimization of Women* (Northeastern, 1996)

T

Tadros, V, "Insanity and the capacity for criminal responsibility" (2001) 5 *Edin LR* 325

——, "Recklessness, consent and the transmission of HIV" (2001) 5 *Edin LR* 371

——, "The structure of defences in Scots criminal law" (2003) 7 *Edin LR* 60

——, "The distinctiveness of domestic abuse: a freedom based account" (2004–5) 65 *La L Rev* 989, also published in R A Duff and S P Green (eds), *Defining Crimes: Essays on the Special Part of the Criminal Law* (Oxford University Press, 2005)

——, *Criminal Responsibility* (Oxford University Press, 2005)

——, "Rape without consent" (2006) 26 *OJLS* 515

——, "Justice and terrorism" (2007) 10 *New Crim L Rev* 658

——, "Harm, sovereignty and prohibition" (2011) *Legal Theory* 35

—— and S Tierney, "The presumption of innocence and the Human Rights Act" (2004) 67 *MLR* 402

Tapper, C, *Crime, Proof and Punishment: Essays in Memory of Sir Rupert Cross* (Butterworths, 1981)

Tata, C and N Hutton (eds), *Sentencing and Society: International Perspectives* (Ashgate, 2002) 523

Taylor, C, *Sources of the Self: The Making of Modern Identity* (Harvard University Press, 1989)

Teff, H and C R Munro, *Thalidomide – The Legal Aftermath* (Saxon House, 1976)

Thomson Committee, *Criminal Procedure in Scotland (Second Report)* (Cmnd 6218, 1975)

Thornton, M (ed), *Public and Private: Feminist Legal Debates* (Oxford University Press, 1995)

Throp, A, *"Age of consent" for Male Homosexual Acts,* House of Commons Research Paper 98/68, 19 June 1998 (House of Commons, 1998)

Tomkins, A, "Legislating against terror: the Anti-terrorism, Crime and Security Act 2001" (2002) *Public Law* 205

Tong, R P, *Feminist Thought: A More Comprehensive Introduction (Dimensions in Philosophy)* (Westview Press Inc, and revised edn, 1998)

U

Uglow, S, *Criminal Justice* (Sweet & Maxwell, 2nd edn, 2002)

UNAIDS, *Criminal Law, Public Health and HIV Transmission: A Policy Options Paper* (2002) available as a pdf from http://data. unaids.org/publications/IRC-pub02/JC733-CriminalLaw_en.pdf

Universities of Strathclyde and Stirling, *The ICL/Stockline Disaster: An Independent Report on the Working Conditions Prior to the Explosion* (2007) (available at http://www.hazards.org/icldisaster/ icl_stockline_report.pdf)

V

von Hirsch, A, "The offence principle in criminal law: affront to sensibility or wrongdoing?" (2000) 11 *King's College LJ* 78

von Hirsch, A, and A P Simester, *Incivilities: Regulating Offensive Behaviour* (Hart Publishing, 2006)

W

Wadham, J, H Mountfield *et al, Blackstone's Guide to the Human Rights Act 1998* (Oxford University Press, 4th edn, 2007)

Walker, C, "Case comment: terrorism: Terrorism Act 2000, ss 1 and 58 – possession of terrorist documents" [2008] 2 *Crim LR* 160

Walker, D, *The Scottish Legal System: An Introduction to the Study of Scots Law* (Sweet & Maxwell, 8th edn, 2001)

Walker, L E, *The Battered Woman* (Harper, 1979)

Walker, N, *Punishment, Danger and Stigma: The Morality of Criminal Justice* (Blackwell, 1980)

Wallerstein, S, "Why English law should not incorporate a defence of superior orders" [2010] *Crim LR* 109

Walzer, M, "The communitarian critique of liberalism" (1990) 18 *Political Theory* 6

Wells, C, "The death penalty for provocation" [1978] *Crim LR* 662

Wells, C, and O Quick, *Lacey, Wells and Quick: Reconstructing Criminal Law: Text and Materials* (Cambridge University Press, 4th edn, 2010)

Weisburd, D, *White-Collar Crime & Criminal Careers* (Cambridge University Press, 2001)

West, R, *Caring for Justice* (New York University Press, 1999)

White, R M, "Out of court and out of sight: how often are 'alternatives to prosecution' used?" (2008) 12 *Edin LR* 481

White, R M, "'Decriminalisation' – a pernicious heresy? (2009) 13 *Edin LR* 112

——, "Lay criminal courts in Scotland: the justifications for, and origins of, the new JP court" (2012) 16 *Edin LR* 358

Williams, G, "The definition of crime" (1955) *Current Legal Problems* 107

——, "Convictions and fair labelling" (1983) 42 *CLJ* 85

Williams, J C, "Deconstructing gender" (1988–89) *Michigan L Rev* 797

Williams, R, "Voluntary intoxication – a lost cause?" (2013) 129 *LQR* 264

Willock, I, "Scottish criminal law – does it exist?" (1981) 54 *SCOLAG* 225

Wilson, W, *Central Issues in Criminal Theory* (Hart, 2002)

——, "The structure of criminal defences" [2005] *Crim LR* 108

——, *Criminal Law: Doctrine and Theory* (Longmans, 4th edn, 2011)

Windlesham (Lord), "The paradox of indeterminacy" [1989] *Crim LR* 244

Windlesham (Lord), "Life sentences: the case for assimilation" [1996] *Crim LR* 250

Wolfenden, *Report of the Departmental Committee on Homosexual Offences and Prostitution* (1957) Cmnd 247

Y

Young, I M, *Justice and the Politics of Difference* (Princeton University Press, 1990)

Young, J and R Matthews (eds), *Rethinking Criminology: The Realist Debate* (Sage Publishing, 1992)

Z

Zeedyk, M S and F E Raitt, "Psychological theory in law: legitimating the male norm" (1997) 7 *Feminism & Psychology* 539

BIBLIOGRAPHY

INDEX

attempting to pervert the course of
   justice, definition/requirements
   (*cont.*)
mens rea, 14.7.5
preparation-perpetration stage,
   relevance, 8.2.6
principles of attempts, applicability,
   14.7.2
attempts
actus reus, 8.2.2
attempting to pervert the course of
   justice, applicability of principles to,
   14.7.2
conspiracy as alternative to, 8.6.3, 8.6.5
criminalisation of, 8.1.2
criminalisation of preparatory
   behaviour as alternative, 8.1.2
critical point, determination of, 8.1.2,
   8.2.3–8.2.9
   as fact for jury, 8.2.6, 8.2.7, 8.4.1
   irrevocability theory, 8.2.5
   last act, 8.2.5, 8.2.6
   preparation-perpetration stage, 8.2.6–
   8.2.9, 8.4.1, 8.6.5
   substantial step/proximity theory,
   8.4.1
critique and proposals for reform, 8.4
harm principle and, 8.1.2, 8.2.1
impossibility and, 8.3.1
mens rea, 8.2.2, 8.3.1, 8.4.2
   identity with completed crime, 8.4.2,
   9.12.1, 9.20.4
   intention, 9.12.1
voluntary abandonment, 8.4.3
Australia
codification of penal law, 5.14.2
corporate criminal liability, 18.5.16–
   18.5.17
duty to act as basis of liability, *Russell*,
   6.7.5
error of law, 19.7.1
authorised force: *see* lawful/justifiable force
automatism
actus reus and, 20.20.2, 22.11
awareness of condition, relevance,
   6.4.2, 20.19.2
   involuntary intoxication and,
   20.15.1, 20.16.1
balancing interests of accused and of
   needs of justice, 20.20.1
burden/standard of proof
   beyond reasonable doubt, 20.17.1
   compelling direct evidence, 20.17.3–
   20.17.5

automatism (*cont.*)
causes of, 6.4.2, 20.16.1–20.16.3
   diabetes, 20.9.1, 20.19.3, 20.20.1,
   22.11
   drugs misuse, 20.17.6–20.17.7
   epilepsy, 6.4.2, 20.8.1, 20.9.1,
   20.19.3, 22.11
   hypoglycæmia, 20.19.3
   "toxic exhaustive factors", 20.16.2–
   20.16.3
as common law defence available to
   statutory offences, 17.5.3
critique and proposals for reform,
   20.20, 22.11
definition/requirements
   external factor as cause of, 20.17.2,
   20.20.1
   inability to control actions, 20.16.1–
   20.16.3, 20.17.2
   involuntary cause, 20.17.2, 20.18.1
   somnambulism, 20.19.1–20.19.2
   temporary mental dissociation,
   20.16.2
   total alienation of reason, 20.17.2,
   20.17.5
   unforeseeability, 20.17.2
fairness and justice considerations,
   22.11
mens rea, as negation of, 9.11.3,
   17.6.3, Part VII (introduction),
   20.5.1–20.6.1
strict liability and, 20.20.3, 22.11
road traffic offences, 17.6.2
autonomy/individualism
see also communitarianism; victims'
   rights
abortion and, 1.18.1
art and part liability and, 7.8.1
communitarianism and, 1.6, 1.19.2
corporate criminal liability and,
   18.5.17–18.5.18
crime control model and, 5.2.2
criminal capacity and, 6.18.1
drugs abuse and, 7.4.1, 8.10.1
due process and, 5.2.1
feminism and, 1.13.1, 1.17.1–1.17.3,
   1.19.1–1.19.2, 3.9.1
harm principle and, 1.3.1, 1.19.4
legal paternalism and, 3.5.2
liberalism and, 1.2.2, 1.5.1
libertarianism and, 1.5.1
pre-assigned roles, 1.6.2
restrictions on, 2.8.3
self-interestedness and, 1.2.2, 1.4.2

intoxication

see also automatism

definition/cause of

culpable ("voluntary") and
non-culpable ("involuntary")
distinguished, 20.12.1

drugs/alcohol, 20.12.1

lawfully acquired drugs, 20.12.1

intoxication (involuntary) as a defence,
20.15

automatism and, 20.15.1, 20.16.1,
22.11

fairness and justice considerations,
22.11

mental disorder as special defence,
22.11

intoxication (voluntary/self-induced) as a
defence

see also drink driving; public
drunkenness/drunk and incapable
state

critique and proposals for reform,
20.14, 22.11

Butler Committee, 20.14.5

dangerous intoxication as alternative
charge, 20.14.5

diminished responsibility and, 20.10.5,
20.11.5

Hume on, 20.13.1

mens rea, 1.10.2, 20.14.1–20.14.3

intention and, 20.13.2, 20.14.2–
20.14.3

recklessness and, 1.10.2, 20.13.1,
20.14.1–20.14.3

wicked recklessness, 20.13.1,
20.14.1, 22.11

public interest/public policy and, 1.10.2,
20.14.4

involuntary culpable homicide in course
of lawful act, 9.11.4, 9.12.10,
9.16.3–9.16.4

mens rea of underlying crime

gross negligence, need for, 9.19.1

intention to cause physical harm,
9.19.2

reckless driving, 6.15.3, 9.19.2

state of mind and behaviour
distinguished, 9.19.1

involuntary culpable homicide in course
of unlawful act

actus reus, destruction of life, 9.18.1

definition/requirements, 9.18.1

mens rea of underlying crime, 9.18.1

assault, 9.18.2

involuntary culpable homicide in course
of unlawful act (*cont.*)

culpable and reckless fire-raising,
9.18.5

intention to cause physical harm,
9.18.5

recklessness, 9.18.3–9.18.4

wilful fire-raising, 9.18.5

"real injury" test, 9.18.3–9.18.4

"thin skull" rule, 7.2.6–7, 7.3.4–7.3.6,
7.3.10, 9.18.2

involuntary lawful act, as culpable
homicide: *see* involuntary culpable
homicide in course of lawful act

Iran, sexual offences, 11.1.1

Ireland

blasphemy, 16.9.1

codification of penal law, 5.14.2, 22.6.2

drugging, 10.15.1

infanticide, 9.7.3

offensive weapons in public, 8.11.3

self-defence/reduction of charge, 21.9.9

irrevocability theory, 8.2.5

Italy, codification of penal law, 5.14.2

J

joke, 6.10.3–6.10.4

Judicial Committee of the Privy Council

independence of Scottish legal system
and, 5.8.2

Scottish judges, participation in,
5.8.2

judicial law-making: *see* case law

judiciary

communitarianism and, 1.10

public interest/public policy and, 1.10

public opinion/common practice and,
5.16.2

as representatives of "community",
2.7.2, 5.16.2

junior ASBOs, 2.5.2

juries

communitarianism and, 1.9.2

as representatives of "community",
2.7.2

responsibility for determination of

blameworthiness, 8.2.6

coercion, 21.2.2–21.2.5

fact, 8.2.6, 8.2.7, 21.2.2–21.2.5

point of perpetration, 8.2.6, 8.2.7,
8.4.1

provocative act, 21.10.7

solemn procedure and, 1.9.2, 5.6.1

sexual coercion
generally, 11.6.1
sexual exposure, 11.8.1
indecent exposure and, 11.18.1, 11.20.2
mens rea, 11.20.2
intentional exposure, 11.20.2
"sexual image", 11.6.1
sexual infidelity as provocative act, 5.9.1,
21.10.6, 21.10.8–21.10.11
extension to
confession/report of, 21.10.6,
21.10.9, 21.11.8
intermittent sexual relationship,
21.10.11
lesbian relationship, 21.10.10
non-adulterous infidelity, 21.10.10–
21.10.11
non-heterosexual relationships,
21.10.10, 21.11.8
female partners, applicability to,
21.10.10
gender neutrality and, 21.11.8–
21.11.12
Hume on, 21.10.8
proportionality/appropriateness of
response, 21.10.14
proposals for reform, 5.9.1, 21.11.4
rationale, 21.10.8, 21.11.4
sexual offences
see also bestiality; bigamy; incest;
indecent assault; lewd, indecent and
libidinous practices; pornography;
public indecency; rape; sexual
coercion; sexual exposure; sexual
intercourse with young girls; sexually
aggravated breach of the peace;
shameless indecency; voyeurism
abuse of trust, 11.14.1
children, against, 11.12.1–11.12.3
codification, 5.9.1, 22.6.3–22.6.4
conspiracy to participate in sexual
offences against children, 5.15.1
as crime against the person, 11.1.1
definition/scope, 11.1.1
harm principle and, Part V
(introduction)
moral deviancy and, 11.1.1
morals/law, relationship, 11.1.1
prostitution, Part V (introduction)
stalking, 15.3.2, 21.10.11
statutory offences, 15.3.2
vulnerable groups, protection of, 11.1.2
sexual orientation, malice or ill-will based
on as aggravating factor, 7.9.1

sexual penetration as assault, 11.4.1
**sexual purposes, administering substance
for**, 10.15.1, 10.16.1, 11.11.1
sexually aggravated breach of the peace,
1.1.1
shameless indecency
corporate criminal liability and, 18.5.4
judicial endorsement, 4.3.1, 5.11.1
lewd, indecent and libidinous practice
distinguished, 11.20.1
Macdonald, J H A on, 4.3.1, 5.11.1
morals/law, relationship, 2.7.4, 4.3.1
reckless indifference and, 11.20.2
replacement by public indecency, 4.3.1,
5.11.1, 11.20.1, 11.21.1, 12.16.1
common law/statutory law, conflict of
terminology, 11.21.1
rule of law considerations, 4.3.1
scope of offence, 4.3.1
failure to stop children watching
pornographic film, 6.7.2
pornography, 4.3.1
sheriff courts
parallel criminal and civil jurisdiction,
2.3.3
solemn/summary procedure and, 5.6.1
sheriffs, independent and impartial
tribunal (ECHR 6(1)) and, 5.3.1
simultaneity principle: *see*
contemporaneity principle
skean-dhu
as article with blade or sharp point,
8.11.6
decriminalisation of, 5.15.1, 8.11.6
slavery
abduction/deprivation of liberty
distinguished, 10.19.1
fair labelling and, 10.19.1
international law, prohibition under,
10.19.1
ECHR 4, 1.4.1
as serious offence, 10.19.1
sexual slavery: *see* prostitution
statutory offence, as, 10.19.1
smoking, criminalisation, alternatives to,
2.4.2
**social background, enforcement of the
law and**
conviction, 4.5.1
inequalities, 4.5.1, 4.5.3
sentencing, 4.5.1
social harm, 3.3.2, 3.8.1–3.8.5
"social self", 1.13.1
society, changes in: *see* changing attitudes

theft, definition/requirements (*cont.*)
  taking of property
    12.2.1: *see also* confidential
      information/material, exploitation/
      theft of
    amotio, 12.4.1–12.4.2
    "appropriation", 12.4.1–12.4.5
    clandestine taking, 12.5.1–12.5.3,
      12.6.1
    confidential information, 5.12.1,
      12.3.4–12.3.8
    corporeal property, 12.3.1, 12.3.3,
      12.11.4
    damage or destruction of
      property distinguished, Part IV
      (introduction), 13.1.1, 13.2.1
    digitally stored information, 12.3.4–
      12.3.8
    divisibility of ownership, 12.3.9,
      12.4.5
    electricity, 12.3.3, 12.11.4
    intangible property, 12.3.1–12.3.8
    moveable property, 12.3.1–12.3.2
    retention of property lawfully
      obtained, 12.4.4
    "taking" and "finding", equivalence,
      12.4.6
    taking and using, 5.11.1, 12.6.1
    trade secrets, 12.3.4–12.3.8
    wheel-clamping, 12.4.5
    without consent, 12.3.1, 12.3.11,
      12.4.5, 12.4.7, 12.7.1–12.7.4
    fraud distinguished, 12.4.7
    honest belief/error and, 12.7.3–12.7.4
    obtaining by deception distinguished,
      12.4.7
"theftuous intention", evidence of, 8.18.1
"thin skull" rule, 7.2.6–7, 7.3.4–7.3.6,
  7.3.10
  emotional or psychological
    characteristics of victim, 7.3.5–7.3.6
  involuntary culpable homicide and,
    9.18.2
  public policy considerations, 7.3.6
  reduction of charge and, 7.3.6
threat of harm, 3.10.1, 3.11.1, 8.1.2, 8.2.1
threat as offence
  in association with other offence,
    10.14.1
  as independent offence, 10.14.1
  threat of serious damage to property,
    10.14.1
  threat to kill or seriously injure, 10.14.1
threatening communications, 15.9.1

threatening gesture, 10.2.7
threatening or abusive manner, behaving
  in
  statutory offence, as, 10.14.1, 15.3.2,
    15.5.1
torture, prohibition
  aggravated assault as alternative,
    10.21.1
  critique and proposals for reform,
    10.21.1–10.21.2, 22.11
  defences
    "lawful authority, justification or
      excuse", 10.20.1, 10.21.2,
      21.14.4
    lex loci actus as applicable law,
      10.20.1
    normal and reasonable punishment,
      10.21.1
  Draft Criminal Code, 10.21.1–10.20.2
  ECHR 3, 1.4.1, 10.20.1, 10.21.1
  inhuman or degrading treatment and,
    10.21.2
  public officials, limitation to acts of,
    10.20.1, 10.21.1
    fairness and justice considerations,
      22.11
  "torture", 10.21.1
"toxic exhaustive factors", 20.16.2–
  20.16.3
TPIMs *see* terrorism prevention and
  investigation measures
trade secrets, theft of, 12.3.4–12.3.8
traffic-signs, failure to obey, 2.6.1
trafficking in human beings, 15.13.2
transferred intent
  assault, 6.13.1–6.14.2, 10.2.7
  blameworthiness and, 10.2.7
  continuing offence principle and,
    6.19.2–6.19.3
  critique and proposals for reform, 6.14
  definition, 6.8.2, 6.13.1
  dole, relevance, 6.13.1
  fair labelling and, 6.14.2
  irrationality of doctrine, 6.14.2
  mens rea and, 6.13.1, 10.2.7
  proportionality and, 10.2.7
  recklessness and, 6.14.1
  sentencing and, 6.14.2
  state of mind and, 6.13.1, 6.14.1
  "wicked recklessness" and, 6.14.2
  wilful fire-raising, 6.8.2, 6.13.1,
    13.5.4
transgender identity, malice or ill-will
  based on as aggravating factor, 7.9.1